# BAHIA'S INDEPENDENCE

# BAHIA'S INDEPENDENCE

## Popular Politics and Patriotic Festival in Salvador, Brazil, 1824–1900

HENDRIK KRAAY

McGill-Queen's University Press

Montreal & Kingston | London | Chicago

© McGill-Queen's University Press 2019

ISBN 978-0-7735-5747-5 (cloth)
ISBN 978-0-7735-5748-2 (paper)
ISBN 978-0-7735-5797-0 (ePDF)
ISBN 978-0-7735-5798-7 (ePUB)

Legal deposit second quarter 2019
Bibliothèque nationale du Québec

Printed in Canada on acid-free paper that is 100% ancient forest free (100% post-consumer recycled), processed chlorine free

This book has been published with the help of a grant from the Canadian Federation for the Humanities and Social Sciences, through the Awards to Scholarly Publications Program, using funds provided by the Social Sciences and Humanities Research Council of Canada.

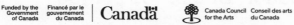

We acknowledge the support of the Canada Council for the Arts, which last year invested $153 million to bring the arts to Canadians throughout the country.

Nous remercions le Conseil des arts du Canada de son soutien. L'an dernier, le Conseil a investi 153 millions de dollars pour mettre de l'art dans la vie des Canadiennes et des Canadiens de tout le pays.

Library and Archives Canada Cataloguing in Publication

Title: Bahia's independence : popular politics and patriotic festival in Salvador, Brazil, 1824–1900 / Hendrik Kraay.
Names: Kraay, Hendrik, 1964– author.
Description: Includes bibliographical references and index.
Identifiers: Canadiana (print) 20190068760 | Canadiana (ebook) 20190068817 | ISBN 9780773557482 (softcover) | ISBN 9780773557475 (hardcover) | ISBN 9780773557970 (ePDF) | ISBN 9780773557987 (ePUB)
Subjects: LCSH: Dois de Julho (Independence of Bahia, Brazil)—Political aspects—History—19th century. | LCSH: Dois de Julho (Independence of Bahia, Brazil)—Social aspects—History—19th century. | LCSH: Brazilians—Brazil—Salvador—Ethnic identity—History—19th century. | LCSH: Salvador (Brazil)—Social life and customs—19th century. | LCSH: Bahia (Brazil : State)—History—19th century.
Classification: LCC F2551 .K73 2019 | DDC 394.263—dc23

Set in 11/14 Minion Pro with Berthold Bodoni
Book design & typesetting by Garet Markvoort, zijn digital

# CONTENTS

Map, Tables, and Figures
vii

Acknowledgments
ix

Author's Note on the Text
xiii

INTRODUCTION
"This Glorious Day for All of Brazil"
3

CHAPTER ONE
"Never Again Will Despotism Govern Our Actions":
The Invention of a Civic Ritual, 1824–47
43

CHAPTER TWO
The Volcano's "Most Magnificent and Sublime Spectacle":
From Political to Popular Festival, 1848–64
84

CHAPTER THREE
"Subdivided into a Thousand Festivals":
Late-Imperial Dois de Julho, 1865–89
127

CHAPTER FOUR
"On 2 July Nobody Fights":
The Multiple Meanings of a Festival
168

CHAPTER FIVE
Dramas "Appropriate for the Public Theatre":
Dois de Julho on Stage
200

CHAPTER SIX
"Cold as the Stone of Which It Must Be Made":
The Monument and Dois de Julho's Bifurcation
243

CONCLUSION
The "Greatest Symbol of the
Bahian *Povo*'s Struggle"
285

Notes
297

Bibliography
363

Index
401

# MAP, TABLES, AND FIGURES

## Map

I.1  Nineteenth-century Salvador | 20

## Tables

I.1  Salvador's population, 1872,
by race (*raça*) and legal status | 16

2.1  Dois de Julho Festival organizers'
social origins, 1845–64 | 100

3.1  Direção Geral dos Festejos members'
social origins, 1865–87 | 132

## Figures

I.1  Bento José Rufino Capinam's view of the
Exército Pacificador's entry into Salvador, 1830 | 7

I.2  Manoel Raimundo Querino | 29

1.1  The "original" Dois de Julho triumphal float | 55

1.2  Ladislau dos Santos Titara | 69

2.1  A *caboclo* on the masthead of a
radical liberal periodical, 1851 | 94

2.2  The *cabocla* on the Companhia do
Queimado Fountain, 1850s | 95

2.3  The Companhia do Queimado Fountain in its original location on Piedade Square, ca. 1860  |  96

2.4  The Caboclo, 2 July 2011  |  97

2.5  The Cabocla, 2 July 2011  |  97

2.6  Artillery preparing to fire salutes to welcome Pedro II, 6 October 1859  |  98

2.7  The Lapinha Pavilion, ca. 1900  |  102

2.8  Francisco Moniz Barreto  |  122

3.1  The stage on the Terreiro de Jesus, 1871  |  145

3.2  The triumphal arch on the Terreiro de Jesus, 1882  |  146

3.3  The statue of Emperor Pedro II displayed in 1872  |  148

4.1  The "Little Blacks' *Batuque*," 1867  |  175

4.2  Dois de Julho's dawn still finds Bahians in slavery, 1886  |  184

5.1  The Teatro São João, 6 October 1859  |  204

6.1  The Dois de Julho Monument, 1895  |  244

6.2  The Dois de Julho Monument on Campo Grande, 1897  |  245

6.3  The earliest known design for a Dois de Julho monument, 1877  |  260

6.4  The cart before the horse  |  263

6.5  The Dois de Julho stage, Santo Antônio Além do Carmo Parish, early twentieth century  |  276

6.6  A *caboclo* on the *Diário de Notícias'* front page, 2 July 1896  |  280

C.1  Antônio Carlos Magalhães in the procession, 2 July 1996  |  289

# ACKNOWLEDGMENTS

I first saw a Dois de Julho (2 July) parade in 1993, a few days before the end of my year of dissertation research in Salvador. It differed in striking ways from the Sete de Setembro (7 September) parade that I had seen in 1992, shortly after arriving in Bahia. A quarter century and two books later, I remain fascinated by Bahians' festive patriotism, whose early history I trace in this book, and its contrast to Brazilian patriotism as manifested on Sete de Setembro.

The generosity of Canada's Social Sciences and Humanities Research Council (SSHRC) is unmatched. I began my research on Dois de Julho with a postdoctoral fellowship from SSHRC in 1995–97 at the University of British Columbia. Two SSHRC Standard Research Grants (1999–2002 and 2011–14) supported research for this book, as did a Professor Visitante Estrangeiro fellowship from the Brazilian Ministério da Educação's Coordenação de Aperfeiçoamento de Pessoal de Nível Superior, held in the Programa de Pós-Graduação em História Social at the Universidade Federal do Rio de Janeiro (UFRJ) in 2004. The Izaak Walton Killam Foundation topped up my postdoctoral fellowship and provided me with a semester of leave in 2006. The University of Calgary's generous research and scholarship leave policy periodically gave me time to write; a 1997–99 starter grant from the University Research Grants Committee allowed me to purchase microfilm copies of Bahia's newspapers. A Calgary Institute for the Humanities resident fellowship during the final months of work on this book facilitated its completion.

During the decades of research on this project, I experienced the digital revolution, which has not yet run its course. The microfilmed newspapers that I acquired in the late 1990s now gather dust in boxes, for in 2012 the Biblioteca Nacional's Hemeroteca Digital Brasileira made them obsolete. Google Books, the Hathi Trust Library, and the many other commercial academic databases to which the University of Calgary Library subscribes now make library research a much rarer necessity. We no longer need to flip through crumbling bound volumes of the *Coleção das Leis do Brasil*, the *Anais da Câmara dos Deputados*, and the *Anais do Senado*, for they are available online from Brazil's congress. Handheld scanners and now digital cameras made the collection of documents and newspaper articles easier, although I still find that the only way to work effectively with manuscripts is to take notes in pencil on note cards (which, fortunately, are still manufactured). Brazilian journals' move to open-access format and the practice of Brazilian history departments to make their students' dissertations and theses available online means that *brasilianistas* can now be much more up-to-date with Brazilian scholarship (it also means that there is much more for us to read). While we may complain about the latest technologies' idiosyncrasies, we all owe a deep debt of gratitude to the anonymous techies who work behind the scenes to provide us with this digital cornucopia.

Numerous audiences in Brazil, North America, and Britain listened to earlier versions of what appears in the following pages, and I thank the commentators whose remarks on the nine papers that I presented at workshops and conferences helped me sharpen my arguments. Audiences at the Universidade Estadual do Sul da Bahia (Vitória da Conquista); the Universidade Federal do Recôncavao Baiano (Cachoeira); the Fundação Pedro Calmon (Salvador); the Universidade Federal da Bahia (Salvador); the University of California, Los Angeles; the Universidade Federal Fluminense (Niterói); and the Universidade Federal do Rio de Janeiro also provided helpful feedback.

Several colleagues contributed much to this book. The late Bert J. Barickman was a great friend with whom I shared many months of research in Rio de Janeiro; I am saddened that I could not benefit from his critical reading of the manuscript. As president of the Instituto Geográfico e Histórico da Bahia, the late Consuelo Pondé de Sena provided invaluable support to my work and, in 2011, inducted me into the Instituto as a corresponding member. The exemplary generosity of Lizir Arcanjo Alves, whom I only met in 2011, has left a deep imprint on this book. She pointed me to sources that I had missed, shared her many archival and literary discoveries about Dois de Julho, and spent hours with me discussing arcane details of the nineteenth-century festival. *Muito obrigado!*

Over the past two decades, I have had the privilege of working with several accomplished research assistants: Sonya Marie Scott (1999–2000), Lucineide Vieira dos Santos (1999–2001), Emelly Facundes (Mitacs Globalink Intern, 2013), David Barrios Giraldo (2015), Nina Olegovna Rojkovskaia (2017), and Isabel Fandino (2018). With his unmatched knowledge of the Arquivo Público do Estado da Bahia, Urano Andrade provided invaluable assistance in the 2010s.

Many other colleagues helped in innumerable ways, large and small. To all, a great big thank you: Dale T. Graden, Fabio Baldaia, João José Reis, Jocélio Teles dos Santos, John Collins, Luiz Mott, Maria Angela Leal, Martha Abreu, Mary Ann Mahony, Matthew Rarey, Marco Morel, Nadine Hoffman, Paulo Knauss, Richard Graham, Roderick J. Barman, Scott Ickes, Walter Fraga Filho, and Wlamyra R. de Albuquerque.

For as long as I have known her, my long-suffering supportive spouse, Judith Elaine Clark, has put up with my idiosyncratic interests in Dois de Julho and other aspects of nineteenth-century Brazilian history. Thank you for your understanding.

Unwisely, I began publishing about Dois de Julho before I had fully mastered the sources and come to grips with the festival's complexity. I discuss the problems with my 1999 article in the introduction to this book and rectify its errors in chapters 1 and 2 ("Between Brazil and Bahia: Celebrating Dois de Julho in Nineteenth-Century Salvador," *Journal of Latin American Studies* 32.2 [May 1999]: 255–86). Portions of chapter 6 appeared in "'Frio como a pedra de que se há de compor': caboclos e monumentos na comemoração da Independência na Bahia, 1870–1900," *Tempo* 7.14 (January–June 2003): 51–81. The last section of chapter 3 first appeared as "Política partidária e festa popular: o 'Incidente Frias Villar' e o Dois de Julho de 1875," *Revista do Instituto Geográfico e Histórico da Bahia* 109 (2014): 285–303. Portions of chapter 5 appeared in "A Independência no palco: o teatro histórico nacional na Bahia, 1857–1861," in *Seminário Internacional Independência nas Américas: 190 anos da Independência do Brasil na Bahia*, ed. Jacira Primo, Luís Sant'Ana, and Walter Silva (Salvador: Fundação Pedro Calmon, 2014), 221–43.

# AUTHOR'S NOTE ON THE TEXT

During the nineteenth century, the Brazilian currency was the mil-réis, 1,000 réis (singular, real), written 1$000; 1,000 mil-réis was known as a conto, and was written 1:000$000. The mil-réis fluctuated considerably in value from the 1820s to the 1890s, although for much of the period its value remained close to US$0.50. To make rough comparisons possible, I provide US dollar equivalents for the mil-réis figures mentioned in the text.[1] To avoid confusion with US dollars, I render currency amounts less than one mil-réis (1$000) as, for example, 800 réis, rather than $800.

Portuguese orthography has undergone a number of changes since the nineteenth century. Following convention, I have modernized the spelling of names and book and newspaper titles in the text, retaining the original spelling in the notes and bibliography except when, by convention, the archaic spelling is used. The most frequent instance of this is Rio de Janeiro's *Jornal do Commercio*, which maintained the nineteenth-century spelling of its name until it ceased publication in 2016.

No straightforward rules governed nineteenth-century Brazilian naming practices. Individuals were often known by a distinctive part of the first or last names. Thus, the poet and playwright discussed in chapter 5, Agrário de Souza Menezes, is commonly known as Agrário. I provide the full names on first mention of people in each chapter, after which I use the portion of the name by which they were most commonly known.

Many nineteenth-century newspaper articles appeared without title or byline. Where there was a title or a section heading, I provide it. In the interest of economy, all of the provincial correspondence is simply identified as Corr., rather than the lengthy titles that some newspapers gave to these letters from Bahia. Unless otherwise indicated, the newspapers and periodicals cited in the notes were published in Salvador, and correspondence was likewise written in that city.

# BAHIA'S INDEPENDENCE

# "This Glorious Day for All of Brazil"

On 2 July 1823, the "most splendid" scene that he would ever see in his long life greeted a fourteen-year-old boy looking out over the Bay of All Saints. He and his family had survived the year-long siege of Salvador by patriot forces, and he now watched the Portuguese naval squadron escort some fifty ships out of the "beautiful bay." On board were the troops that had occupied the city "and all those who did not support Brazil's independence."[1] A few hours later, the bedraggled patriots marched into Salvador, reaching the city centre by 1 p.m. Colonel José Joaquim de Lima e Silva, commander of the Exército Pacificador (Pacifying Army), who led the Division of the Right into the city from Pirajá, reported to the war minister in Emperor Pedro I's new government that it was impossible to describe the "joy of the city's inhabitants or to paint with perfection the patriotic scenes of this glorious day for all of Brazil." The nuns of the Soledade Convent, on Salvador's northern outskirts, had hastily prepared a triumphal arch and laurel wreaths to welcome Lima e Silva. Many more such arches greeted the troops as they made their way into the city amid cheers to the emperor, the constituent assembly, and the army, while "clouds of flowers" fluttered from upper-storey windows. Lima e Silva proudly reported that his men had maintained order during their entry, although he admitted that they and the hungry populace had helped themselves to foodstuffs and cattle abandoned on the docks by the Portuguese in their haste to embark.[2] The other contemporary account of 2 July 1823, published the next month in O Éco da Pátria, confirms the enthusiastic reception and emphasizes the privations that the soldiers had suffered: most lacked uniforms and shoes. The troops from the Division of the Left entered Salvador from Rio Vermelho; their battalions consisted of "generous citizens who left their homes and families for the salvation of their *pátria* [homeland]." All that they had to distinguish themselves as soldiers were their "reliable muskets, their skill at handling them, and their gallant marching." This account adds a detail not mentioned by Lima e Silva; after the reception at Soledade, the commander took a short detour to raise the Brazilian flag at nearby Barbalho Fort.[3]

"Decisive of Brazilian independence," as the British minister judged them a few weeks later,[4] these events marked the end of a year-long war that had mobilized tens of thousands of Bahians as well as troops from Rio de Janeiro, Pernambuco, and other neighbouring provinces. Led by members of the planter class in the sugar-growing Recôncavo (the region surrounding the Bay of All Saints) who had cast their lot with the future emperor, Pedro I, in mid-1822, the patriotic mobilization to expel Portuguese troops loyal to the constitutional government in Lisbon reached deep into Bahian society. Men from all classes had flocked to the colours over the previous year, and by July 1823 the patriot forces numbered close to 15,000 men. They included slaves; some were runaways while others – mostly belonging to owners who had remained loyal to the Portuguese government – had been enlisted in a special unit created by Pedro (Pierre) Labatut, the French mercenary whom Pedro I had named to command the patriot irregulars besieging Salvador as of July 1822.[5] The war included "little actual combat" and "much digging of trenches," as one historian puts it, for it mostly consisted of a siege of Salvador; the largest battle, the Battle of Pirajá (8 November 1822), involved only a few thousand combatants and resulted in only a few hundred casualties (the figures are contradictory).[6] Nevertheless, this was considerably more fighting than had taken place in any other province, and for that reason it would lay the foundation for a distinctively Bahian understanding of Brazilian independence. The naval blockade of Salvador, commanded by the British mercenary Lord Cochrane (Thomas Cochrane, the 10th Earl of Dundonald), contributed decisively to the patriot victory by cutting off resupply from Portugal, but because the naval forces had been mostly raised in Rio de

Janeiro (and abroad), this dimension of the war would have much less significance to Bahians than the land conflict.[7]

The peaceful occupation of Salvador masked numerous tensions in the Exército Pacificador and in Bahian society more generally. Lima e Silva, commander of the contingent from Rio de Janeiro, had taken command of the Exército Pacificador less than six weeks earlier, after officers closely linked to the planter-led Interim Council of Government (the civilian patriot authority) deposed Labatut and sent him under arrest to Rio de Janeiro. Since his arrival in October 1822, the French general had quarrelled with the council over the scope of his authority; his harsh discipline and his efforts to recruit slaves for the patriot forces had alienated many. The Exército Pacificador's very name hints at the concern for social order, as does Lima e Silva's praise for the unexpected discipline under which the troops entered Salvador.

Regardless of their role in the independence struggle, and whether or not their expectations of independence had been realized, Bahians of all classes soon came to see Dois de Julho (July Second) – often set in capital letters or otherwise emphasized in newspapers, pamphlets, and published poems – as a foundational moment for Bahia. Dois de Julho crystalized the events of the war against the Portuguese, and as a compound noun, it soon came to mean any sort of commemoration of the patriot victory. How Bahians invented and reinvented the celebrations of what many called "Bahia's independence" – technically incorrect, for Bahia did not gain its own independence as a result of the 1822–23 war – is the subject of this book, in which I analyze the annual Dois de Julho celebrations from 1824 to the end of the nineteenth century in the city of Salvador. Dois de Julho was (and still is) unlike any other civic ritual in Brazil, merging aspects of religious processions, military parades, and carnivals into a distinct patriotic festival that, over the course of the century, mobilized far more popular participation than the celebrations of other "days of national festivity," as civic holidays were formally known in the Brazilian empire. As so often happens in living rituals (Dois de Julho is still today Bahia's principal civic ritual and an important popular festival), there has been a tendency to smooth out or flatten its history. This process papered over many of the divisions among nineteenth-century Dois de Julho celebrants, emphasized some aspects of the historical celebrations over others, and stressed continuity over change in Dois de Julho's history.

## Civic Rituals and Politics

We might well wonder just how many arches Bahians would have had time to erect in the early hours of 2 July 1823, how many laurel wreaths the nuns would have been able to prepare, and how many baskets of flower petals people would have been able to gather to receive the Exército Pacificador. Bento José Rufino Capinam did not let such considerations trouble him. In 1830 this pioneering lithographer published the first image of the patriots' entry into Salvador (figure 1.1). Dapperly dressed troops, led by heroic commanders in full dress uniform, march underneath an elaborate triumphal arch festooned with garlands of flowers and flags. The road is strewn with fragrant leaves (or perhaps flower petals).[8] These elements in Lima e Silva's report, in *Éco da Pátria*'s article, and in Capinam's image signalled that this was a momentous event. They also reflected familiar practices in the repertoire of late-colonial civic ritual, the royal and religious festivals that brought Portuguese Americans together under the auspices of the two institutions that all had in common: Church and Crown. Like so many other artistic representations of historical events, Capinam's imagining of what the Exército Pacificador's entry should have looked like excluded many and placed others in subordinate positions. The visible faces (mostly of officers) seem to be mostly of white men, while an Indian auxiliary holding a bow and arrow crouches in the bottom right; there is no sign of the black men who constituted the majority of the patriots.[9]

Historians influenced by Eric Hobsbawm and Terence Ranger's concept of "invention of tradition" and Benedict Anderson's pithy characterization of nations as "imagined communities" have written extensively about civic rituals.[10] That all traditions are in some way products of human agency, and that nations – especially those in the Americas carved from European empires – had to be fashioned from the cultural raw materials available to statesmen and ideologues, have become commonplace assertions. Likewise, it has become a scholarly truism that however strongly they declare their inclusiveness, nations

Figure I.1 | Bento José Rufino Capinam's view of the Exército Pacificador's entry into Salvador, 1830

*Source*: AIGHBa, pasta 2, reg. 0105. Reproduced with permission.

define themselves in ways that necessarily exclude many, including the people of other nations and those *within* nations who are not allowed full membership. And the people in whose name the ideologues spoke often had their own ideas about the nation. These insights offer historians the tools to interrogate the nature of nation-states and their impact on contemporary identities. Civic rituals offer indications of how organizers envisaged the people's role in society and politics and how people engaged with the state and the nation.[11]

The Dois de Julho festival is distinct from the civic rituals on which most scholars have focused. It celebrates independence not in a nation-state but in one of its constituent parts. Dois de Julho is a civic ritual, yet the government played no direct role in organizing it during the nineteenth century, so we cannot speak of an "official" view of the nation-state as manifested in the festival. Indeed, in important ways, Dois de Julho celebrants' arguments about the Brazilian nation's origins directly contradict the empire's official history as celebrated on 7 September, which in the 1820s was constructed as Brazil's independence day. While Dois de Julho quickly came to serve as a symbol of Bahian identity and the war for independence in the province soon became an origin myth for Bahians, celebrants insisted that they were Brazilians and called for national recognition of Dois de Julho. Although these aspirations were frustrated, Dois de Julho gained an impressive level of popularity, unlike many – perhaps most – civic rituals.

Historian Kátia M. de Queirós Mattoso has observed that "everything was a pretext for celebration [*festas*]" in nineteenth-century Bahia, and invokes Dois de Julho as an example of this,[12] but the festival's political importance should not be so easily dismissed. In 1853 a writer in Bahia's diocesan newspaper lamented the recent reduction in the number of observed saints' days and explained that "political festivals produce healthy effects, for they serve to unite men among themselves, provide them with necessary rest [from regular work], temporarily make social inequalities disappear, and prevent the poor and the small from blocking the greed of the rich and the powerful." Some proof of this, he continued, could be found in Dois de Julho, "unfortunately the only public political festival among us."[13] This anonymous assessment of Dois de Julho's salutary effects is surprising given how controversial the celebrations had been since the 1820s. It predates structuralist or functionalist approaches to ritual that highlight its capacity to build what Victor Turner called *communitas* (social solidarity) and its function as a safety valve, one that temporarily obscures social distinctions but ultimately upholds hierarchies.[14] For much of the three quarters of a century covered by this book, Bahia's "rich and powerful" did not see Dois de Julho that way; rather, they were suspicious of a festival that brought so many of the *povo* (the common people) into the streets, albeit for reasons that changed over these years.

Civic rituals are best understood as inherently political. While accounts of ritual may, like early-modern European festival books or Capinam's image, portray what *ought* to have happened (at least in the author's or the artist's view) rather than what *actually* happened, nineteenth-century Brazilian sources fully bear out the post-structuralist insight that rituals mean different things to different people. Organizers, observers, and participants rarely shared a single understanding of Dois de Julho, and much of this book is devoted to mapping the festival's politics and the range of meanings attributed to it. Building on and appropriating portions of colonial Portuguese America's ritual heritage, radical liberals invented distinctive Dois de Julho celebrations in the late 1820s, an indication of politics' centrality to the festival. The authorities and conservative members of the provincial elite who tried to repress or to manipulate the radical liberal Dois de Julho failed to remake the festival to their liking in the late 1830s and 1840s, for elements of the celebrations increasingly appealed to broad swaths of the population. In the 1850s, Dois de Julho retained significant radical liberal elements, but it had also become a popular festival that involved most of the city's population and marked a Bahian identity, not distinct from Brazil but *integral* to it, at least in Bahians' understandings of their place in the nation.

This study of Dois de Julho thus joins other recent scholarship on the close and mutually constitutive relationship between region and nation, but it also complicates this approach, for Bahian patriots tenaciously sought recognition for Dois de Julho in the national narrative of independence. They would have denied that they were engaged in a regional identity project and would have insisted that they were true Brazilians. Others agreed. In an 1831 report on political unrest in Bahia, a São Paulo periodical described that province as "the centre of Brazilianism [*brasilismo*], the country [*país*] where the language, the customs, the manners, [indeed] everything has been for a long time eminently Brazilian."[15] Unlike the proponents of twentieth-century regionalisms, invented around notions of cultural and environmental particularity, and deeply imbued with hierarchies among regions,[16] nineteenth-century Dois de Julho patriots did not claim Bahian cultural distinctiveness; rather, they emphasized that they were worthy Brazilians, especially so because they (or their forefathers) had played what they judged a decisive role in winning the country's independence.

Through its analysis of a civic ritual that mobilized people by the thousands – often tens of thousands – this book contributes to the growing tendency of scholars to see nineteenth-century Brazilians as active and engaged citizens.[17] This runs counter to the long-standing dominant view, recently summarized by Marshall Eakin: "Despite the façade of electoral representation, the Empire was built on the politics of exclusion."[18] This assessment is not wrong, for those in power sought to construct an exclusionary state, but as he and others recognize, those excluded constantly struggled to make citizenship – here broadly understood as effective membership in the nation – meaningful for them. For much of the nineteenth century, Brazil shared in the Latin American pattern of large electorates, and careful studies of electoral participation have shown that Brazilian voters could not be simply herded to the polls.[19] Of course, politics encompasses much more than voting. Historians have begun to map Brazilians' often vibrant associational life. As well, the proliferation of newspapers and the press freedom that impressed so many foreigners (see below) suggests a lively public sphere, one that extended beyond the literate minority; indeed, we can envisage "a broader, more chaotic public sphere of the streets," as James Sanders has described it for Spanish America. The abolitionist movement that mobilized thousands of men and women in the 1880s indicates that, despite the 1881 reduction of the Brazilian electorate by some 90 percent, Brazilians were far from apathetic about great political issues; that movement linked the press and associational life as Brazilians formed hundreds of abolitionist societies and published countless anti-slavery articles in the press.[20] Likewise, participation in civic rituals constituted an important form of politics, for by its very nature, the commemoration of national holidays in honour of independence or major institutions such as the constitution or the monarchy invites political reflection.[21]

In these respects, nineteenth-century Brazilians were no different from the citizens of American republics (or from the many who had been marginalized or formally excluded from political citizenship by those regimes). Historians have traced the changes in political culture wrought by independence and the creation of new nations (usually republics) out of colonial empires and, more important, the ways in which people of all classes reshaped their political strategies and tactics to seize the opportunities offered by the new regimes.[22] Different social bases and distinct historical experiences gave rise to particular patterns of popular politics. Indigenous peasants appropriated and redefined the new republican notions of citizenship and nation to construct their own distinct understandings of their rightful place in the nation-state.[23] Peter Guardino has observed that "indigenous peasants are much better documented" than urban plebeians, who "do not show up in documents in particularly articulate ways."[24] Nevertheless, there is ample evidence that they were as savvy as their peasant counterparts, whose lengthy experience in defending their corporate communities through litigation in colonial courts could be employed against the challenges that liberal states posed. Often literate and usually concentrated in cities, artisans emerged as outspoken advocates of protectionism and vigorous defenders of their rights to citizenship.[25] Others have traced how the urban masses were often autonomous political actors.[26] The colonial corporate institutions of free people of African descent – militias and brotherhoods – generally proved insufficient to form the basis of political projects analogous to the indigenous peasantry's defence of community, and Afro-Spanish American political activism usually took liberal, republican forms.[27] Sometimes plebeian politics developed into vigorous defences of republicanism, but other times, especially in Brazil, it adopted forms of popular royalism.[28]

Because there was no indigenous peasantry in Brazil, the new empire lacked one of the dimensions of Spanish American popular politics, and it has proved difficult to insert indigenous peoples into Brazilian political history as active agents.[29] Slave resistance was, of course, political activity, and numerous historians have documented its many dimensions.[30] The increasingly diverse free poor – the *povo* – the not quite poor, and even the small middle classes are arguably still the frontier of imperial Brazilian political history. We know much about the rebellions in which they took part but far less about their day-to-day political engagement.[31] Many were voters, especially before the 1881 electoral reform; those who lived in the country's growing cities had extensive contact with the burgeoning nineteenth-century press; many were supplicants whose petitions for favour or justice directed at the emperor or his provincial representatives often amounted to political statements. By focusing on a civic festival that mobilized impressively large proportions of the populace in one of Brazil's largest cities, I show another dimension of Brazilian popular politics.

Struggles for fuller or more effective social and political citizenship inevitably threatened those in power, and what Sanders calls the elite's "primal fear ... of an engaged pueblo" (*povo* in Portuguese) in his study of Spanish American radical liberalism had numerous counterparts in

Brazil.[32] The reactions to popular politicization, which ranged from violent repression of revolts to the 1881 reduction of the franchise to the marginalization of radical abolitionism after slavery's end, all indicate the intensity of the struggle for fuller citizenship and subalterns' determination to claim membership in the nation. Sometimes those in power adopted more subtle strategies to deal with subalterns; there are, for example, hints that Bahia's Conservatives were building political connections to Candomblé houses (Afro-Brazilian religious centres) in the 1860s.[33] Some of the attempts to shape the Dois de Julho festival discussed in this book reveal similar dynamics as well as the elites' recognition that the urban lower classes could not simply be marginalized or ignored. For all their efforts to control the celebrations of Bahia's independence and their radical messages, those in power soon learned that neither repression nor cooptation nor manipulation could entirely do away with what they considered the festival's objectionable elements.

Over the course of the nineteenth century, Dois de Julho increasingly resembled a popular festival, although it always retained important civic components. The distinction between civic ritual and popular festival was never clear in the colonial period, for Church and state celebrations opened space for the popular classes to amuse themselves or to perform for the entertainment of their "betters."[34] Scholars of nineteenth- and early-twentieth-century popular festivals typically focus on authorities' concerns about proper comportment among members of the lower classes. Those who engaged in efforts to repress troubling aspects of popular culture left documents that today are often historians' only sources for these customs, as one scholar has observed for carnival.[35] In the archival and periodical records we can find traces of what those in power perceived as a threat to the new ("modern" or "civilized") nation, and this allows historical study.[36] Dois de Julho was no exception to this tendency. As the festival became an increasingly popular celebration in the second half of the nineteenth century, elites' criticisms shifted from its radical liberal elements to the popular cultural practices it embodied, which they now saw as old-fashioned, uncivilized, even backward and barbaric. Critics sought to mark independence with a monument and other more appropriate forms of commemoration that would do away with the popular festival. Late in the nineteenth century and more so in the next, nationalists and folklorists began searching for the national essence in popular culture, and later in the twentieth century, as numerous historians have shown, popular cultural practices were appropriated by states and incorporated into national discourses.[37] Dois de Julho went through this process in the first half of the twentieth century, but that is a subject for another book.

## Salvador: Society, Economy, and Culture

Located on a wide peninsula on the east side of the Bay of All Saints, Salvador was one of the Atlantic world's major ports. Founded in 1549 as the capital of Portuguese America, Salvador soon became the centre of thriving trades in sugar, tobacco, and slaves. While the city lost its pre-eminence as the viceroy's seat to Rio de Janeiro in 1763, through the end of the nineteenth century it remained Brazil's second-largest city and a major commercial centre. In 1824 a German observer of the newly independent empire judged that Bahia ranked with Cadiz, Bordeaux, Nantes, Marseille, and Hamburg in commercial importance.[38] The fertile lowlands surrounding the bay (the Recôncavo) were the sugar economy's centre, and the number of *engenhos* (plantations with a sugar mill) increased from 292 in 1818 to 635 in 1873; an 1875 count came up with 893 *engenhos* throughout the province, 282 of them with steam-powered mills.[39] Between 1821 and 1851, Bahians imported 175,908 slaves, with peaks of more than 15,000 per year in the late 1820s and more than 10,000 per year in the late 1840s.[40] After the opening of Brazil's ports to trade with friendly nations in 1808, Portuguese merchants quickly lost their dominant position in Bahia's trade; merchants from Europe and North America firmly embedded themselves in Salvador's commercial networks. Nevertheless, Portuguese nationals remained prominent in Salvador's commerce (especially in retail commerce), and the stream of migrants from the former mother country – many of them brought to work as clerks for established relatives – never seemed to slow, not even during periods of anti-Portuguese agitation in the 1820s and 1830s.[41]

The Recôncavo, as the late B.J. Barickman has convincingly shown, was far from a sugar plantation writ large. Throughout the region, and especially on the bay's south coast, small farmers produced the manioc that formed the staple of slaves' and the free poor's diet. A tobacco-growing district centred on Cachoeira originally supplied African markets, where tobacco was traded for slaves, and later found new markets in Europe. Distilleries attached to sugar plantations produced rum that was both consumed locally and exported to Africa. In the nineteenth century, coffee became an increasingly important export as well.[42] Dense commercial networks connected Salvador, the Recôncavo towns, and the food-producing districts. Thousands of small craft plied the bay and the Recôncavo's rivers, carrying food supplies to Salvador. Cattle trudged along the aptly named Estrada das Boiadas (Cattle-Drive Road) from ranches in the interior to the city's slaughterhouse.[43]

Since the 1500s, sugar had driven the Bahian economy. Thanks to the Haitian Revolution, Bahian sugar production boomed from the 1790s to the 1810s. Disruptions caused by the independence struggle and the unrest of the 1820s and 1830s depressed exports, but they recovered in the 1840s, and Barickman describes the years from 1845 to 1860 as a period during which sugar exports grew and secondary commodities like tobacco and coffee also did well; the diamond rush in Lençóis briefly added a new commodity to Bahia's export portfolio.[44] But this relatively favourable conjuncture soon ended, and early-twentieth-century economic historians perceived an extended crisis in the 1870s and 1880s as the volume and value of Bahia's exports declined steadily, falling to 1851 levels by 1889.[45] Efforts to modernize the sugar economy by constructing centralized mills won some investors titles of nobility, but those new mills did not ensure profitability, much less transform the sugar economy and make it possible for Bahia to compete effectively with Cuban cane and European beet sugar.[46] In 1879 the US consul blamed sugar planters for the industry's decline: "They lived extravagantly, neglected their estates, educated their sons for the professions, and left the charge of their plantations, in many cases their sole source of revenue, in the hands of their favourite blacks; the result has been gradually approaching decay and ruin."[47] The consul had underestimated the industry's structural difficulties, but he correctly perceived some of the family strategies that planters adopted in the face of decline. Sugar's decline caught contemporaries' attention, and this has led historians to miss Bahia's other exports such as tobacco and coffee; the value of the former sometimes exceeded that of sugar after 1871.[48] Along the province's south coast, cacao production was quietly expanding, although it would not boom until the early twentieth century.[49] In Salvador, a small manufacturing sector, mostly textile mills, heralded an industrial future, but these factories employed only a few thousand workers by the end of the 1890s.[50]

Limited sources make it difficult to determine Salvador's population, but at the time of independence, the city's inhabitants likely numbered around 50,000. No doubt the population's size fluctuated considerably as sailors came and went; as waves of slaves passed through the city en route to plantations, farms, and ranches in the interior; as people abandoned the city during periods of political and military conflict (1822–23, late 1824, 1831, and 1837–38); and as epidemic diseases such as yellow fever (1849) and cholera (1855–56) swept through the populace. An 1848 census recorded a population of 54,652, but this figure seems low, given that Brazil's first national census enumerated a population of 108,138 in 1872. The 1890 census (generally considered less reliable than its predecessor) counted 144,959 people in Salvador's urban parishes.[51] According to the 1900 census, the city's population stood at 205,813, but this figure included the rural parishes within its municipal boundaries; if the population of the eleven urban parishes grew at the same rate as the municipality's entire population, then we can estimate the urban centre's population at 171,057 in 1900.[52]

Brazil's census bureau did not publish detailed information from the 1890 or 1900 population counts, but the 1872 enumeration included data that can be compared with earlier population counts. João José Reis's estimate that 42 percent of Salvador's population of 65,500 consisted of slaves in 1835 has been generally accepted by scholars; fully 63 percent of these slaves were Africans, and they (and freed Africans) constituted fully one-third of the total population.[53] In 1855, slaves accounted for 27 percent of the population enumerated in the surviving schedules of an incomplete census begun just before the cholera epidemic.[54] Slaves' share of the city's population had declined to 11.6 percent by 1872 and continued to fall inexorably until abolition came on 13 May 1888. The proportion of Africans among the slaves fell even more rapidly until in 1872 it stood at 16.1 percent; by then, the majority

Table I.1 | Salvador's population, 1872, by race (raça) and legal status

| | Free and freed | Slave | Total | % |
|---|---|---|---|---|
| Branco (white) | 33,672 | – | 33,672 | 31.1 |
| Pardo (brown) | 42,332 | 4,589 | 46,921 | 43.4 |
| Preto (black) | 17,493 | 7,912 | 25,405 | 23.5 |
| Caboclo (Indian) | 2,140 | – | 2,140 | 2.0 |
| Total | 95,637 | 12,501 | 108,138 | 100.0 |

Source: Brazil, Directoria Geral de Estatísticas, Recenseamento, 3:2–34.

of Africans were freed people (3,202 out of 5,146, or 62.2 percent), and these foreigners accounted for only 4.8 percent of the city's population. The next-largest group of foreigners were the 2,499 Portuguese nationals, who accounted for 2.3 percent of the population; they were concentrated in the downtown commercial districts. The 1872 census also provided data on what it called "race [raça]" (see table I.1). How these data were gathered is not known, nor is it known how Bahians interpreted a question about race when "colour [cor]" or even "quality [qualidade]" were more familiar ways of speaking about what today is called race. The 1872 census makes it clear that Salvador was an over-whelmingly non-white city; that 31.1 percent of the population was classified as white is fully consistent with earlier counts and estimates that identified about three in ten Salvador residents as white.[55] While the 2,140 caboclos (usually understood to mean acculturated Indians) in table I.1 accounted for but one-fiftieth of the population, they serve as a useful reminder that indigenous people remained present in Salvador. Indeed, contingents from Indian villages had joined the patriot forces in 1822–23, and Capinam included an Indian man in his 1830 lithograph, albeit in a subordinate place (figure I.1).[56]

Nevertheless, these data confirm the many foreigners' observations that Salvador was an "African" and a "black" city, not just demograph-ically but also culturally.[57] Scholarship on nineteenth-century Bahia has focused strongly on Africans and their descendants and the ways in which their culture pervaded daily life.[58] The slave trade nurtured close commercial connections between Salvador and major African ports, especially in West Africa but also in West-Central Africa.[59]

While commerce with Africa declined dramatically after the slave trade's end in 1850, Africans and their descendants, especially those involved in the growing religion of Candomblé, regularly travelled back and forth across the Atlantic as they sought specialized religious knowledge and materials.[60]

The tens of thousands of slaves who laboured in Salvador included domestic servants, artisans, and food sellers, as well as agricultural labourers on suburban Salvador's many farms and the *escravos de ganho*, who worked on their own account, especially in the carrying trades (many were sedan-chair porters who carried people up the steep streets that connected the upper and lower cities). One historian has identified fully eighty-two occupations for male slaves and sixteen for female slaves.[61] Slaveownership was widespread in Salvador until mid-century; many of the poor, as well as freed people and even slaves themselves, owned slaves, and this ensured widespread support for slavery.[62] Recent scholarship on slavery has turned away from labour and resistance (notably the wave of rebellions that culminated in the African Muslim revolt of January 1835) to focus on the life histories of Africans and slaves.[63]

The slave trade's end set slavery on a steady decline. Urban slavery led the way, and the typical size of slaveholdings recorded in inventories shrank steadily along with the proportion of slaves in the population.[64] Contemporaries held that the 1855 cholera epidemic exacerbated a looming labour shortage, for slaves suffered especially high mortality in the Recôncavo plantation districts.[65] Nevertheless, as Barickman has shown, Bahia's sugar planters maintained their commitment to slavery, unlike their counterparts in Pernambuco, where a transition to free labour was well under way by 1888; until then, enslaved labourers remained Bahian planters' principal workforce. This meant that abolition, combined with declining sugar prices and followed by a devastating drought, was a major shock to the Bahian economy.[66] In 1887, Luiz Anselmo da Fonseca castigated his fellow Bahians for their lack of commitment to the abolitionist movement. To be sure, historians of Bahia have documented the abolitionist societies that existed in Bahia as of the 1870s, but it is difficult to argue that Bahia was anything other than a laggard in the movement to end slavery that seized Brazil in the 1880s.[67]

Slavery profoundly shaped Bahia's society and economy, and until the 1880s it pervaded daily life in Salvador; even so, its impact on Dois de Julho celebrations was relatively limited. Patriotic celebrants explicitly or implicitly argued that Bahians were not slaves – not in the metaphorical sense of slaves to illiberal despots, and not in the literal sense of human property. Moreover, slaves were not citizens in the Brazilian empire, and they could not be part of the nation as envisaged by Dois de Julho patriots. Nor could Africans, whether slave or freed. But Brazilian-born freed people could be contemplated as part of the nation, as demonstrated in the manumissions that regularly took place on Dois de Julho after 1850 (and occasionally in earlier years). Dois de Julho was primarily a festival of the free, with slaves and Africans serving as foils or others to the Bahian patriots. No slave revolts took place on Dois de Julho, and only twice were there rumours that slaves were plotting to rebel on that day, and this helped distance the festival from slavery. Thus, while slaves and slavery are not absent from this book, its focus is on political identity and festival culture among the free.

Other than freedom, however, the free shared little. There were enormous differences between the tiny merchant/planter elite whose members controlled most of Bahia's wealth, as Mattoso clearly demonstrates; the small middle class that included professionals, shopkeepers, a few successful artisans, and government employees (military officers, bureaucrats, clergy, and teachers); the lower classes of semi-skilled and unskilled labourers, domestic servants, sailors, and soldiers, and by the end of the nineteenth century also workers in the city's textile mills; and the unemployed or underemployed, who in the estimation of worried authorities appeared to be nothing more than vagrants. Descending the social hierarchy, the population was progressively less white and more Afro-Brazilian or African.[68] In these respects, of course, Salvador differed little from Brazil's other major cities. At the same time, as Mattoso and others show, dense webs of patronage and clientage connected people across class lines, and family networks straddled social divisions. Such ties bound Bahians in ways that secured the social order by mitigating tensions, benefited some clients, and gave Bahia an air of "apparent racial and, above all, social integration," as Mattoso puts it.[69] Likewise, as the writer in the diocesan newspaper suggested in 1853, the participation of people of all classes in Dois de Julho celebrations and other festivals reinforced social solidarities, albeit in unequal ways.

## Place

Dois de Julho celebrations were closely connected to the urban space in which they took place (see map 1.1). Nineteenth-century Salvador's centre stood on a high bluff overlooking the Bay of All Saints. The cathedral, the City Council building, and the Presidential Palace surrounded the relatively small Largo do Paço (Palace Square). To the north of this symbolic centre lay the Terreiro de Jesus, the largest downtown square, demarcated on the west by the old Jesuit church (now serving as cathedral, and from which the square derived its name). The attached buildings that extended around part of the square's north side housed the medical school. Other churches also faced this square, as did elite residences. After 1870, the Terreiro was officially known as the Praça Conde d'Eu (Count of Eu Square, after the heir apparent's consort and the last commander of Brazil's forces in the Paraguayan War of 1864–70); the republic erased this tribute to monarchy and dubbed it the Praça Quinze de Novembro (15 November Square, after the date on which the new regime was proclaimed in 1889). The new names did not take, and throughout this period, most continued to refer to this square by its old name. South of the Terreiro and east of the Palace Square stretched a grid of narrow streets where many of Salvador's wealthiest families resided. Other members of the elite lived north of the Terreiro on the streets that led down to what is today known as the Pelourinho (the square on which the public whipping post was located until its removal in 1835). Residential neighbourhoods stretched farther north, along the ridges defended by the Santo Antônio and Barbalho Forts, to Soledade and Lapinha, which marked the northern end of the upper city's mid-century built-up areas. The Dois de Julho parade, the principal part of the day's celebrations as of 1827, wound its way through Santo Antonio Parish's streets from Lapinha to the Terreiro, where most of the public celebrations normally took place.

South of the Palace Square loomed the Teatro São João (Saint John Theatre). Opened in 1812, this was Bahia's public theatre and an important gathering place for the city's elite; it hosted galas every 2 July.

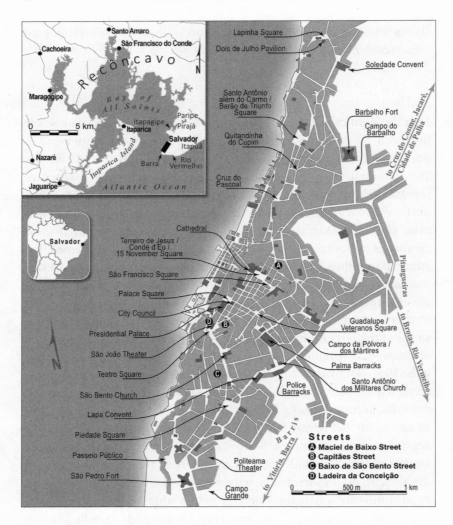

Map I.1 | Nineteenth-Century Salvador

*Source*: Cartography by R. Poitras, Department of Geography, University of Calgary, based on Adolfo Morales de los Rios, "Planta da cidade do Salvador, capital do Estado federado da Bahia," 1894, BN/Cartografia, ARC.009.05.011.

Past the square in front of the theatre, streets led towards Piedade Square, Campo Grande, and the São Pedro Fort, which marked the southern end of the city's old defensive perimeter. Along the ridge that led south from Campo Grande lay the district of Vitória, where over the course of the nineteenth century members of the city's elite built new, modern mansions that took advantage of the views over the bay. The narrow lower city was Salvador's commercial centre. The bustling port, tall warehouses, the customs house, the navy arsenal, small forts, and markets were located here. Farther north, the lower city widened into the Itapagipe Peninsula, where Bonfim Church was the centre of an important annual devotion. During the hot summer months, many of Salvador's downtown residents escaped to country houses on this peninsula.

In early-nineteenth-century Salvador there was little spatial segregation. Rich and poor alike could be found living on the same streets, and many of the multi-storey downtown *sobrados* reflected the social hierarchy, with the well-off living in the upper storeys, while people of more modest means lived on the lower floors and shops or workshops occupied the ground floors. Africans and slaves, especially those who had the freedom to work on their own account, could be found living in dank basements.[70] As elsewhere in the Atlantic world, public transportation dramatically changed how Salvador's residents distributed themselves across urban space. Animal-drawn omnibuses and, after the 1860s, mule-drawn streetcar lines enabled people to live farther from their places of work; two small steam trains, known as *maxambombas*, linked suburbs. Electrification of streetcar lines began in the 1890s.[71] Itapagipe's level ground was ideally suited to development and was soon the site of comfortable middle- and upper-class neighbourhoods; in 1889, Durval Vieira de Aguiar judged it the "most preferred" residential area because of its affordable housing and quick transit link to downtown.[72] Vitória's growth as an aristocratic neighbourhood likewise depended on transit, and by the end of the century, streetcar lines had reached Rio Vermelho and Barra; these formerly distant fishing villages became residential centres.[73] While the downtown was still the city's symbolic and administrative centre, by the early twentieth century only the lower classes resided there. A visitor marvelled in 1915 that so many of the old downtown buildings, even those in "splendid situations" overlooking the bay, were "taken up almost entirely by the descendants of slaves, with the accumulated uncleanliness of generations," and remarked that "the white minority of Bahia has been driven to the often less attractive suburbs."[74]

Salvador thus partook of the *melhoramentos* (improvements) that were rapidly transforming Atlantic World cities and that Brazilians eagerly sought.[75] In the late 1830s, coastal steamers first connected the city to the "Corte [Court]," as the national capital was known, and to other provincial capitals. By mid-century, Salvador was a regular port of call for transatlantic steamers en route to Rio de Janeiro and the River Plate ports. In the late 1830s the province began chartering and subsidizing steam navigation companies to link Salvador to Recôncavo towns and to the province's Atlantic coast.[76] Steam navigation had many implications; it facilitated the movement of troops and greatly aided the imperial government in its efforts to suppress revolts in remote provinces. It accelerated the flow of newspapers and news among provinces (in the 1860s, Bahian correspondents' reports often appeared in Rio de Janeiro newspapers as little as four or five days after they were written) and, as Anderson would argue, thereby facilitated the imagining of a national community.[77] Some port improvements came in the later 1860s, and a full modernization of the harbour began in the 1890s.[78] In 1889, Aguiar could describe Salvador as "a civilized city, directly connected to all of the world's capitals" by both steamships and the electric telegraph.[79] Inaugurated in 1874, the telegraph line between Rio de Janeiro and Salvador greatly accelerated the speed at which information and instructions flowed between the national and provincial governments. As we will see in chapter 3, this turned the 1875 Dois de Julho conflict between civilian patriots and an army battalion into a national political question in ways that would have been impossible two years earlier.[80] Improvements in overland communication came more slowly, but starting in 1858, the first railway inched its way into the Recôncavo and the *sertão* (the vast interior backlands); more lines were begun in the 1870s and 1880s.[81]

In addition to the public transportation that facilitated Salvador's growth, other urban infrastructure improvements after mid-century gave the city an air of progress and modernity, even if they did not benefit many of its neighbourhoods. The Companhia do Queimado was handed a thirty-year monopoly on the city's water supply in 1852 and in mid-decade began laying pipes and installing new fountains. The Bahia Gas Company won a contract for street lighting, and between 1862 and 1868 it installed more than two thousand gas jets to replace the old whale oil lamps. Projects initiated during the second presidential term of the Baron of São Lourenço (Francisco Gonçalves Martins) (August 1868–October 1871) sought to overcome the geographical obstacle of the ridge that demarcated the upper and lower cities. The Ladeira da Montanha (completed in 1878) and the Elevador Hidráulico da Conceição (opened in 1873, later known as the Elevador Lacerda) improved, respectively, cargo and passenger transportation between the lower and upper cities. Another elevator and two funicular railways were built in the 1880s and 1890s.[82] A small telephone exchange linked 298 subscribers, including 14 government departments, as of 1887; like streetcars, telephones enabled spatial segregation.[83]

Nevertheless, the assessment offered by an 1875 promotional volume still held true in the 1890s: when it came to *melhoramentos*, judged Manuel Jesuino Ferreira, "on first glance, it appears that much has been accomplished in Bahia's capital, but much remains to be done."[84] Such negative perceptions of Salvador's progress prompted interminable soul-searching among members of Bahia's elite, especially after 1889, when the proclamation of the republic cast into sharp relief how far Bahia lagged behind the country's rising economic centres of Rio de Janeiro and São Paulo.[85] But not until the 1910s would the state government undertake major efforts to reform Salvador.[86] Until then – and, indeed, long after – anthropologist-historian Antônio Risério's assessment of Salvador as "an essentially traditional urban centre, with the imposing character of a great monument and seemingly frozen in time," applied to the Bahian capital.[87]

## Politics and Polity

The independence struggle in Bahia and the turbulent 1820s and 1830s have drawn much scholarly attention. Historians have analyzed the class and racial tensions that wracked the province from independence to the Sabinada Rebellion's bloody defeat in March 1838 – tensions that manifested themselves in a series of conspiracies, revolts, and rebellions. These included the 1824 Periquitos' Rebellion, sparked by the murder of the governor of arms, which led to a month-long standoff between loyalist and rebel troops; the 1831 anti-Portuguese revolts connected to Emperor Pedro I's abdication; the 1832 and 1833 federalist revolts; and the Sabinada, which in November 1837 declared Bahia's temporary independence from Brazil. Each of these movements drew support from civilians and disaffected military personnel and expressed, in varying combinations, radical liberal ideals, anti-Portuguese nativism, support for federalism (the decentralization of power in the centralized Brazilian empire), discontent over military reforms, and class conflicts (particularly challenges to the dominance of society and government by planters and merchants). Historians have also highlighted the racial dynamics in these movements, for they drew strong support from free Afro-Brazilians.[88] Like slavery, this unrest provided both a background and a context for Dois de Julho celebrations, for none of these rebellions took place in early July. Unlike slavery, however, the ideals that underlay many of these rebellions were central to radical liberals' invention of Dois de Julho's distinct rituals (the procession into the city) and the creation of its symbols (notably the Indian allegories today known as the *caboclos*). These radical liberals or Exaltados had turned Dois de Julho into a unique festival by the 1830s.

Far less attention has been paid to Bahia's post-Sabinada pacification and the province's effective incorporation into the Brazilian empire. Dilton Oliveira de Araújo has recently analyzed the 1840s, but there is almost no scholarship on Bahia's politics during the last forty years of the imperial regime.[89] The province played, as many contemporaries pointed out, a disproportionate role in national politics, providing a large numbers of cabinet ministers and, after the position was established in 1846, presidents of the council of ministers (prime ministers) in the imperial government.[90] This political prominence, along with the conceit that they had a special vocation for arts and letters, underpinned the sobriquet "Brazilian Athens," eagerly embraced by the Bahian elite.[91] Nevertheless, little is known about how local and provincial politics interacted with national politics. National changes in government, particularly the transfers of power between Liberals and Conservatives in 1848, 1868, 1878, 1885, and 1889, deeply affected provincial politics, as did the more gradual transition from Conservative to Progressista rule in the late 1850s and early 1860s. These shifts brought wholesale turnovers in provincial administration, from the president (the province's chief executive) down to local police officials. Frequent elections for local offices, for deputies to provincial assemblies, and for national deputies and senators routinely mobilized thousands of voters across the province. Family feuds, exacerbated by partisan allegiances, regularly wracked the province's interior, and residents of Salvador were deeply embedded in the patron/client networks that shaped politics.[92] While we know much about how such networks functioned generally, the specific local context is often obscured in national studies.

This book does not purport to provide a political history of nineteenth-century Bahia; that said, analyzing the Dois de Julho festival requires careful consideration of the partisan politics that shaped the newspaper coverage of the annual celebrations. Moreover, to the very significant extent that early Dois de Julho celebrations belonged to radical liberals, the festival itself was part of the political repertoire. After mid-century, Dois de Julho gradually lost this partisan character, but it remained a space in which Bahians pursued their political disputes. Indeed, one of this book's key arguments is that Dois de Julho celebrations were politics by other means. In the following chapters I briefly survey political history insofar as it was relevant to Dois de Julho and to the press coverage of the festival.

Bahia's politics took place within an institutional framework established after 1823 and modified a number of times until the early 1840s (and again in the 1890s after the republic's proclamation). In 1823, Bahia became a province in the Brazilian empire, a centralized constitutional monarchy that lasted until 1889, when Emperor Pedro II was overthrown by a military coup that proclaimed a republic. Bahia then became a state in the decentralized Brazilian republic, and wrote its own constitution, proclaimed on 2 July 1891. All of the empire's provinces were governed in the same way, by presidents, chief executives appointed by the imperial government. Many of the sixty-seven men who served as Bahia's president were from outside the province, and especially after the 1850s, they tended to serve for only short periods. Until 1835, the provincial presidents were aided by an elected Conselho Geral da Província (General Council of the Province); the council member who received the most votes was known as the vice-president. Decentralizing reforms approved in 1834 replaced the council with an elected provincial assembly that, for a few years, had the authority to name vice-presidents. After 1841, vice-presidents were named by the

imperial government. Because many provincial presidents were senators or deputies to the general legislative assembly, they were often
absent from May to September (when the national parliament normally met in Rio de Janeiro), which meant that vice-presidents, all
Bahians, frequently administered the province for extended periods.[93]
Bahia's 1891 state constitution established an elected position of governor and a bicameral state legislature; by its terms, the president of the
state senate took over the governor's role in his absence.[94]

Other key government officials in the province included the army
garrison's commander, known as the governor of arms until 1830 and
the commander of arms after then; the chief of police, who after 1841
oversaw a hierarchy of delegates and subdelegates that eventually
reached every municipality; and the National Guard's superior commander. Who held these posts mattered. Journalists commented on
their activities and policies as well as on their character and foibles;
they were familiar figures on Salvador's streets and in the public theatre,
where the presidential box signalled the chief executive's authority. The
president's power extended far and wide, and every year, thousands of
men and women submitted petitions to him, seeking everything from
employment to charity, from protection from arbitrary officials to the
services of a military band for a street festival. Petitions directed to
the monarchy or to the imperial government also crossed the president's desk, and he spent many hours reviewing and assessing them.
Presidents, chiefs of police, National Guard commanders, and many
of their subordinates were political appointees, so changes in national
governments usually led to wholesale turnover of officeholders.

Military and police personnel were frequent and prominent participants in Dois de Julho celebrations until the 1870s. After the early 1830s,
the province maintained a military police force, usually several hundred strong, that was responsible for public policing. An army garrison
of one thousand or more soldiers was normally stationed in Salvador;
until the 1840s, its officers and men were mostly Bahians and had close
ties to local society and politics. After then, as part of the imperial government's efforts to build a national army, officers and units from other
provinces were more frequently stationed in the province.[95] Liberal
reformers in 1831 abolished the old colonial militias (segregated into
white, mulatto, and black battalions and reorganized in 1824). They

created the National Guard, a civilian citizens' militia whose members had the same income as was required for voting. For a few years in the 1830s, National Guardsmen elected their officers, but the Bahian provincial assembly put an end to this democratic experiment in 1838, after the Sabinada Rebellion, at which point officer posts in the Guard also became political appointments. Until 1873, the National Guard frequently provided detachments to aid in policing and to back up the army garrison when it was short of soldiers or when battalions were on campaign in Brazil's foreign wars or against internal rebellions. From 1873 to 1918, the Guard lingered on as a largely ceremonial institution that performed no police or military duties.[96]

Legislation passed in 1828 reformed the old colonial municipal councils (the *senados da câmara*); now known as *câmaras municipais*, their members were elected for two-year terms, extended after 1841 to three years and to four years in 1848. The 1828 law barred city councils from spending money on festivals and mandated that they focus their energies on local administration, which included everything from market regulations to public order offences.[97] Colonial municipalities had traditionally spent much of their revenue on Church and monarchical celebrations (between 1809 and 1812, for instance, Salvador spent more on festivals than on public works).[98] Salvador's city council enjoyed an important degree of legitimacy as the elected body closest to the population.[99] It also retained an important residual role in Dois de Julho, although it neither organized nor funded the festival. Besides voting for city councillors, Brazilian citizens elected justices of the peace, men who played an important role in local policing in the late 1820s and 1830s but whose role was considerably reduced after the creation of the police hierarchy of delegates and subdelegates in the early 1840s.[100] In the republic, state legislation passed in 1891 instituted elected municipal councils and the elected position of intendant, loosely equivalent to mayor; large municipalities like Salvador were divided into districts, each of which had an elected administrator and a three-member district junta.[101]

Elections in imperial Brazil were indirect, but given the low income requirement established by the 1824 constitution, large numbers of men could vote for electors, who in turn selected officeholders. While these typical nineteenth-century limits on the franchise may seem

restrictive in light of contemporary universal suffrage, they meant
that large numbers of Brazilian men – more than one million in the
1870s – could vote.[102] In 1872 there were 8,692 voters in Salvador, about
6.5 percent of the population, but in some rural Bahian municipalities, virtually the entire free adult male population was registered to
vote; close to three quarters of Salvador's voters were workers. These
voters, however, cast ballots for fewer than 300 electors in 1872.[103] The
1881 electoral reform instituted direct elections, but a literacy requirement and cumbersome registration procedures reduced the number of
voters by about 90 percent.[104] In the early 1890s, the republic roughly
doubled this number, and as Aldrin Castellucci has recently shown,
this opened up sufficient space for the election of a few working-class
candidates to municipal office in Salvador.[105] Thus, rather than further marginalizing the urban population, the republic, especially in its
early years, prompted significant popular engagement with the political opportunities that the new regime had opened.[106]

## Folklorists, Newspapers, and Other Sources

Much of this book dialogues with the folklorists, memoirists, and
novelists who, beginning in the 1860s, wrote about the Dois de Julho
festival. Their texts are essential sources for the festival's history, but
they often lack the historical detail necessary to trace the festival's evolution. Moreover, they often disagree on key elements of Dois de Julho's history. Some though certainly not all of what they wrote can be
confirmed in contemporary sources; sometimes these sources directly
contradict what folklorists assert. At other times, folklorists' accounts
of the festival are imprecise and generic, which makes it difficult to determine the period about which they were writing. Because their work
is mentioned so often in the following pages, it seems best to introduce
them as a group in this introduction, rather than present them and
their work over the course of the following chapters.

The most influential of these folklorists was Manoel Raimundo
Querino (1851–1923), a remarkable Afro-Brazilian political and cultural
activist whose writings about Dois de Julho laid the groundwork for
what today amounts to the festival's official history, the key elements
of which are considered in chapter 1 (see figure I.2). Orphaned by the

Figure I.2 | Manoel Raimundo Querino

*Source*: Querino, *Artistas*, frontispiece.

1855 cholera epidemic, Querino was placed in the care of a teacher; he learned to read and write and trained as a painter. After a brief stint in the army at the end of the Paraguayan War, he returned to Salvador and continued his studies at the Liceu de Artes e Ofícios, a trades school founded in 1872, at which he eventually became a teacher. In the mid-1870s, he was active in the Liga Operária, a workers' association founded under the auspices of the opposition Liberal Party. When the Liberals came to power in early 1878, they did little for Salvador's workers, and Querino joined Bahia's small group of republicans and campaigned against slavery. He wrote for a number of newspapers (and edited two periodicals himself); in the 1890s, he twice served on Salvador's city council. Appointed by the governor in 1891–92, he was elected as an alternate for the 1897–99 term and took office when the incumbent stepped down. From 1893 to his retirement in 1916, he worked as a state civil servant. Around 1900, he quit politics and devoted the rest of his life writing about, first, Bahia's artisans and, subsequently, Bahian culture and society, with a special interest in Afro-Bahia. His best-known book, *A Bahia de outrora* (Bahia in Former Times, 1916), collected articles on culture and customs previously published in newspapers and other periodicals. He drafted protests against police repression of Candomblé and documented the contributions of "men of colour" to Bahian history. His 1918 essay "O colono preto como fator da civilização brasileira" (*The African Contribution to Brazilian Civilization*) was a pioneering effort to include Afro-Brazilians in the country's history.[107]

Scholarship on Querino has either emphasized his work as a labour organizer and historian of Bahia's artisan classes, as do Maria das Graças Leal's recent biography and Jorge Calmon's short essay, or his role as pioneering black intellectual, which is how E. Bradford Burns presented him in the preface to the English translation of "Colono preto."[108] Elizabeth Cooper has recently suggested that such distinctions misrepresent Querino, for he fully understood "the interconnections of politics, labor, and culture, at all levels of the social hierarchy."[109] Querino was by no means a marginal figure in Salvador. In 1894, he was a founding member of the Instituto Geográfico e Histórico da Bahia, usually considered an institution in which the descendants of declining elite families gathered to celebrate their ancestors' achievements and to lament the changes taking place in Bahia – "an institution constituted by elites and for elites," as one historian has put it.[110] The Instituto's journal published much of Querino's work, including articles on Afro-Bahia, an indication of its openness to at least some critical voices.

Leal interprets *Bahia de outrora* as Querino's response to the urban reforms that in the mid-1910s were demolishing old neighbourhoods to make way for the new Avenida Sete de Setembro (7 September

Avenue). These reforms were part of a broader project that sought to do away with Afro-Bahian culture in favour of a Europeanized Bahia. Querino's book also contains critiques of the republic and praise for the gallant way in which "men of humble condition" upheld their political views under the empire.[111] For our purposes, the most important chapter in *Bahia de outrora* is the one on the Noite Primeira de Julho (First Night of July), in which Querino reconstructed the procession that took place on the night of 1–2 July (and was the most popular part of the festival from the late 1840s to 1861, as I discuss in chapter 2).[112] Before his death in February 1923, Querino was working on an "exhaustive study of the Dois de Julho celebrations since their origins," as his obituary noted, and the Instituto published an incomplete draft to commemorate Dois de Julho's centenary. Most of the text repeats material on the Noite Primeira from *Bahia de outrora*, but Querino had added seven pages, mostly on Dois de Julho after 1865. This new section is disjointed and contains errors that he might well have corrected had he been able to complete his work. It includes three unattributed quotations from Rozendo Moniz's 1886 biography of his father, the poet Francisco Moniz Barreto – an indication that Querino had been researching other accounts of the nineteenth-century festival.[113] The new section contains a brief account of the first Dois de Julho and the creation of the male and female Indian symbols, the *caboclo* and the *cabocla*, that have become part of Dois de Julho's official history. This story has been repeated by historians, anthropologists, and folklorists alike. He had first published this material in 1905 in an article on Bahian artisans, and he subsequently incorporated it into his biographical dictionary of Bahia's "artistas." At that time, his principal purpose was to identify the sculptors who had created the two images.[114]

Unfortunately, much of what Querino wrote about the nineteenth-century Dois de Julho celebrations is not confirmed by other surviving sources; in fact, those sources often contradict his assertions. Later twentieth-century scholars, notably Carlos Ott, dismissed Querino's work on artisans and lambasted him for his reliance on oral tradition and for his failure to undertake archival research.[115] It is clear that Querino consulted newspapers and other published documents for his work on Dois de Julho, although he did not examine these sources systematically. He likely also relied on his own recollections of the festival, in which he surely participated, although I have found no indication that he was ever an organizer. The greatest points of divergence among Querino and the others who wrote about Dois de Julho's origins concern the creation of the *caboclos* and the festival's invention in the 1820s, issues addressed in chapter 1.

Many other Bahians wrote accounts of Dois de Julho celebrations that they had witnessed in their youth or had heard about from elderly relatives and other informants. Unlike Querino's, these accounts have not directly shaped Dois de Julho's official history, but they often provide valuable information about the festival and its historical memory, even if it often cannot be accurately dated. Sometimes these authors published in periodicals that scarcely circulated in Bahia or in limited editions that were soon difficult to obtain. The earliest of them that I know of was Francisco Bernardino de Souza (1834–?), a Bahian priest and founding member of the short-lived Instituto Histórico da Bahia who settled in Rio de Janeiro around 1860 and, two years later, published a magazine article about Dois de Julho. This, the first of many memoirists' and folklorists' descriptions of the festival, appears to be unknown to all who have written about Dois de Julho.[116]

José Álvares do Amaral (1823–1882), the long-serving secretary of the Sociedade Dois de Julho (Second of July Society), left a detailed description of the 1871 festival in an ephemeral periodical, *O Reverbero*, and also provided a brief history of it in his *Resumo cronológico e noticioso da província da Bahia ...* (Chronological and Informative Summary of the Province of Bahia ...,* 1881), first published in an almanac in 1880.[117] Amaral admitted that he had written *Resumo* in just three months, and in 1919, historian Sílio Boccanera Júnior (1863–1928) lambasted it as full of "shocking historical heresies."[118] Querino knew Amaral's account of Dois de Julho's creation and vigorously criticized it; the disagreement turned on the identity of those who sculpted the *caboclos* and when they were created.[119]

Rozendo Moniz (1845–1897), a Bahian medical student who volunteered for the Paraguayan War (1864–70), completed his education in Rio de Janeiro and settled there after the conflict, eventually winning a post as philosophy teacher at the Colégio D. Pedro II.[120] His 1886 biography of his father, the poet Francisco Moniz Barreto (1804–1868), includes a chapter on the Dois de Julho festival.[121] Moniz Barreto regularly declaimed at Dois de Julho functions and was, in effect, mid-century Dois de Julho's poet laureate. Moniz's undated account of the festival focuses mainly on the period before his father's death and, presumably, on the festival that he had known as a youth.

One year after Rozendo Moniz, Alexandre José de Mello Moraes Filho (1843–1919) published an account of Dois de Julho in a Rio de Janeiro newspaper.[122] Born in Bahia, Mello Moraes Filho studied for the priesthood in the capital and returned to Salvador in 1867 to take orders. Soon after that, he abandoned this goal and studied medicine abroad. Eventually settling in Rio de Janeiro, he became a well-known defender of popular culture, whose traditions he documented in *Festas e tradições populares do Brasil* (Festivals and Popular Traditions of Brazil, 1895), a compilation of articles originally published in periodicals, which included an 1887 article on Dois de Julho.[123] Like Rozendo Moniz, whose work he knew, Mello Moraes Filho thus did not personally experience the changes in the festival that occurred in the last decades of the imperial regime.[124] Querino left no indication that he knew Mello Moraes Filho's book, although the chapter on Dois de Julho was published in a Bahian newspaper as early as 1896.[125]

Turn-of-the-century novelists incorporated Dois de Julho into their writings. In his 1897 novel, *O feiticeiro* (The Witchdoctor), issued in revised form in 1910, [Francisco] Xavier [Ferreira] Marques (1861–1942) includes several scenes set during a Dois de Julho in the early 1870s.[126] *Dois metros e cinco: aventuras de Marcos Parreira (costumes brasileiros)* (Two Meters and Five {Centimetres}: Adventures of Marcos Parreira [Brazilian Customs], 1905), by João Manuel Cardoso de Oliveira (1862–1965), contains scenes set during 1889's celebration, but the author appears to have drawn his information about the festival from Mello Moraes's book, and the chapter contains several anachronisms.[127] Ana Ribeiro de Góes Bittencourt's (1843–1919) unpublished 1900 novel, *Susana* (set in 1861) also contains scenes set during Dois de Julho celebrations of bygone years (her memoirs, with her recollections of 1857's Dois de Julho, were first published in 1992).[128]

A cohort of early-twentieth-century historian-folklorists engaged in a project to record disappearing customs wrote about Dois de Julho. In the first of three little-known books published between 1921 and

1936, João Varella (born ca. 1875) described nineteenth-century Dois de Julho in a chapter drawn from (or framed as) an elderly man's recollections.[129] João da Silva Campos (1880–1940), an engineer who wrote numerous descriptions of Bahian traditions, transcribed and published the sole surviving account of 1836's Dois de Julho celebration (from the *Diário da Bahia*), but he excised all of the radical-liberal rhetoric from the newspaper article, thereby profoundly altering the journalist's meaning.[130] Francisco Borges de Barros (1882–1935), director of the state archive (1915–35), published brief accounts of several Dois de Julho incidents.[131] Pedro Celestino da Silva (active 1920s–40s) wrote extensively about Bahia's monuments, Cachoeira's role in independence, and Dois de Julho.[132]

In 1950, their longer-lived contemporaries, Antônio Vianna (1884–1952) and Carlos Torres (1889–?), published books about Bahian traditions that included accounts of Dois de Julho; they appear to describe the early-twentieth-century festival.[133] Vianna's daughter, Hildegardes (1919–2005), twentieth-century Bahia's leading folklorist and a woman deeply involved in national efforts to consolidate the study of folklore as an academic discipline in the 1960s and 1970s, published some research on nineteenth-century Dois de Julho celebrations and commented extensively on the twentieth-century festival, whose evolution she condemned.[134] For forty-four years (1955 to 1999), she published a weekly column about Bahian traditions in *A Tarde*; she collected and published separately only a handful of these.[135] Cid [José] Teixeira [Cavalcante] (1924–) apparently wrote little directly about Dois de Julho, but he often commented on the festival and its history in the press.

There have been few studies of these folklorist-historians, but they clearly had much in common. Most combined their research with other professional activities, including journalism. Most were members of the Instituto Geográfico e Histórico da Bahia, which was not entirely exclusive in its membership and welcomed talented men of modest social origins like Querino who shared their members' interest in Bahia's past. José Teixeira de Barros (d. 1933), a post office employee, an associate of Querino, and the editor of the second edition of Amaral's *Resumo cronológico* (1922), is another example of the Instituto's openness to self-taught intellectuals from humble backgrounds.[136]

The following pages constitute a dialogue with these folklorists and the contemporary sources that I have collected during more than twenty years of research on the festival. The latter include the few accounts by travellers who witnessed Dois de Julho celebrations, scattered archival sources, and (primarily) newspaper articles. Like other major Brazilian cities, Salvador had a lively periodical press; by mid-century it was home to several dailies and a larger number of less frequently published newspapers, as well as numerous ephemeral periodicals. Students at the medical school published literary journals, while some of their teachers produced the *Gazeta Médica da Bahia* to publicize their innovative research on tropical diseases.[137] In 1888, Salvador supported six large-format dailies.[138] Newspapers regularly reported on Dois de Julho; they also published poetry, proclamations, and programs for the festival. Editorialists discoursed on the festival's meaning, while advertising provides indications of Dois de Julho's material culture. *Cronistas*, columnists who wrote about local society, also regularly commented on the festival. Beginning with the radical-liberal periodicals of the 1820s (and their conservative opponents), politics dominated Bahia's newspapers, and knowledgeable readers had no difficulty determining the party or factional affiliation of their morning and afternoon newspapers. These allegiances invariably coloured journalists' discussions of Dois de Julho and, indeed, all of the news.

Unfortunately, I can only very rarely map the full range of discussion about the festival, for few nineteenth-century Bahian newspapers have survived. The state library was largely destroyed in the 1912 federal bombardment of Salvador, while a 1913 fire in the Instituto Geográfico e Histórico da Bahia's library consumed some of its newspaper collection.[139] Brazil's Biblioteca Nacional microfilmed its small collection of Bahian newspapers in the 1970s, and since 2012, these have been available online in the Hemeroteca Digital Brasileira. By the early 2000s, the surviving collections of nineteenth-century Bahian newspapers in the Arquivo Público do Estado da Bahia, the Biblioteca Público do Estado da Bahia, and the Instituto Geográfico were mostly unavailable to researchers because of their deteriorated condition. As a result, I have been able to consult only a small and unrepresentative sample of Bahia's nineteenth-century press. Proposals to microfilm and, now, digitize the state's newspapers have come to naught, the important exception being the idiosyncratic *O Alabama* (1864–71), now available online from the Biblioteca Virtual Consuelo Pondé (formerly the Biblioteca Virtual Dois de Julho).[140]

To compensate for this lack of press sources, I turned to the Bahian provincial correspondence that, from the 1850s to the 1880s, regularly appeared in the major dailies of Rio de Janeiro and Recife. Always publicly anonymous, Bahia's correspondents wrote occasional but often lengthy letters about events in the province. They never failed to discuss Dois de Julho and, politicized like other journalists, they usually viewed it with partisan eyes. Rio de Janeiro's *Jornal do Commercio*, the capital's principal newspaper for most of the nineteenth century and the only one that took a politically neutral stance, often published letters from two Bahian correspondents, representing the major political parties. Because they were writing for audiences that included not only Bahian expatriates but also people who knew nothing about the province, correspondents often explained details about Dois de Julho that Bahian journalists writing for Bahian audiences did not need to mention.[141] On occasion, I have also found transcriptions of articles from Bahian periodicals in other cities' newspapers; sometimes these are the only surviving versions of these texts.[142]

After the late 1820s, Brazilian journalists enjoyed considerable freedom to publish. In 1888, Aguiar proudly wrote that Bahians had the "full right to freedom to speak in public or to write in newspapers, without fear of police detention, nor of the confiscation or suppression of newspapers."[143] This was an overly enthusiastic celebration of press freedom, for there is plenty of evidence that radical-liberal journalists suffered intimidation or worse during periods of conservative reaction, but it is true that governments found it difficult to win convictions on charges of abusing press freedom (juries usually refused to convict).[144] Instead, governments (and political parties) funded their own newspapers or provided subventions to ensure favourable coverage in other periodicals; authorities also resorted to extra-legal pressure.[145] Nevertheless, foreigners often remarked on what they saw as the surprising degree of press freedom in imperial Brazil; James Wetherell considered its "unlimited extent ... quite in excess."[146] What this means for this study of Dois de Julho is that I can only analyze the full debate about the festival for the few years in which accounts from periodicals from across the political spectrum have survived. These instances reveal that there was often intense debate about the festival's meaning and, not infrequently, deep disagreement about what actually happened. At several points in the following chapters, I pause the narrative to delve into the competing press coverage, for reports about the festival were often more important than the performance of its rituals.[147]

Numerous references to Dois de Julho celebrations are scattered through the thousands of bundles of nineteenth-century documents in the Arquivo Público. While researching Salvador's army garrison, I came across the festival in the form of conflicts involving army bands assigned to enliven Dois de Julho celebrations in the 1870s and 1880s (these incidents are discussed in chapter 3). Unfortunately, the police documentation is not organized chronologically so it is impossible to target research on the last weeks of June and the first weeks of July. However, sampling these bundles turned up a variety of key sources. Both the Arquivo Público and Arquivo Histórico Municipal de Salvador have compiled small collections of documentation on festivals, including Dois de Julho. The Instituto Geográfico e Histórico da Bahia's archive also contains much documentation on Dois de Julho, but most of it dates to the early twentieth century, which is unsurprising in light of the 1913 fire; founded in 1894, the Instituto won a role in managing the festival only in the 1910s. Institute members researched the festival's history while preparing to restore some of its old traditions in 1943; they summarized or transcribed materials from nineteenth-century newspapers that are no longer available to researchers.[148] The historian José Wanderley de Araújo Pinho (1890–1967), who apparently never published on Dois de Julho, collected some sources on the festival that are now among his papers in the Instituto Histórico e Geográfico Brasileiro.[149]

Historians have written little on nineteenth-century Dois de Julho. Wlamyra R. de Albuquerque's insightful analysis of the cultural conflicts surrounding Dois de Julho focuses mainly on the first decades of the twentieth century; she says little about the monument and the changes in the festival that took place in the 1890s, which I discuss in chapter 6.[150] Twenty years ago, I published my first article about Dois de Julho. Like Albuquerque and contemporary anthropologists who have written about the festival, I uncritically accepted Querino's history of the distinctive celebrations' origins, and this led me into a series of what I now consider major errors of fact about Dois de Julho's origins. Moreover, thanks to an inattentive reading of Bittencourt's memoirs and the key chapter in Querino's *Bahia de outrora*, I misrepresented the Noite Primeira de Julho procession.[151] More broadly, as Martha Abreu pointed out in a personal communication, I had absorbed too much of the rhetoric of continuity and antiquity of traditions that so often characterizes festivals. Chapters 1 and 2 correct these errors, while the rest of this book demonstrates how Dois de Julho changed over the rest of the century.[152]

In the following pages, I leave two terms untranslated, *pátria* and *povo*, for the English equivalents, *homeland* or *fatherland* and *people*, do not do justice to the full range of connotations that these terms encompassed in the nineteenth century. Before independence, *pátria's* meaning ranged from the local community, to one's place of birth (the contemporary dictionary definition), to the captaincy (later province). Over the course of the nineteenth century, some came to see Brazil as their *pátria*, which gave the term connotations close to that of nation (in both the sense of political community and the sense of a people who share a common heritage).[153] This semantic range of course allows considerable leeway for attributing meanings to the occurrences of *pátria* in Dois de Julho rhetoric. Likewise, *povo* had a range of meanings, from a general reference to all those from a province (the Bahian people) or a nation (the Brazilian people) to a narrower one that referred (often pejoratively) to the lower classes, the *povo miúdo* (petty people), often contrasted in late-nineteenth-century sources to *famílias* (families), those of the middle and upper classes who lived respectable lives. Sometimes this was underscored by the expression *pessoas do povo* (persons of the people) to highlight the lack of what the writer considered appropriate family life and connections.[154]

The six chapters that follow offer a chronological and analytical history of nineteenth-century Dois de Julho celebrations. In chapter 1, I trace how radical liberals invented Dois de Julho in the late 1820s by adding new elements to the traditional forms of colonial ritual. These included the 2 July civilian and military procession into Salvador from Lapinha – a re-enactment of the Exército Pacificador's 1823 entry – as well as the Indian symbols, today known as the *caboclos*, a term not used before mid-century (and only rarely thereafter). I depart most radically from Querino and Dois de Julho's official history by presenting evidence that the first *caboclo* was actually a *cabocla*, a female figure, something that Mello Moraes Filho recognized. Designated a day of national festivity in 1831, but only in the province of Bahia, Dois de Julho became a major festival by the middle of the 1830s, closely associated with radical liberals. After the Sabinada Rebellion, conservative authorities sought to repress the celebration. President José de Souza Soares de Andréa (1844–46) opened some space for the festival, which he apparently sought to shape. This led to public conflicts between him and radical liberals during 1846's celebrations, although there is no evidence for Querino's well-known assertion that Andrea sought to impose a passive female *cabocla* to replace an aggressive male *caboclo* as the festival's symbol.

Chapter 2 begins with radical liberals' use of Dois de Julho celebrations to campaign against the Conservative provincial administrations of Francisco Gonçalves Martins (1848–52) and João Maurício Wanderley (1852–55). Sometime during the early 1850s, male and female Indian statues became the Dois de Julho symbols, but there are insufficient surviving sources to document this development. By the late 1840s, it is possible to trace the festival's organization, shared by the Sociedade Dois de Julho, a relatively closed association that controlled the symbols, and the Direção Geral dos Festejos (loosely translated as the General Management Committee for the Celebrations), which consisted of leading citizens. The most important development of the late 1840s and early 1850s was the Noite Primeira de Julho, the nocturnal procession on the eve of 2 July during which patriotic battalions (civilian associations formed for parading on Dois de Julho) took the wagons that bore the symbols to Lapinha from downtown or from Piedade Square. By the mid-1850s, this had become a massive popular festival, full of radical liberal rhetoric, which increasingly preoccupied journalists and conservative critics, for tens of thousands of people took to the streets. In a surprising alliance, José Álvares do Amaral, secretary of the Sociedade Dois de Julho, cooperated with Gonçalves Martins and other Conservative figures to acquire a coach house at Lapinha where the *caboclos* would be stored as of 1861, thereby making redundant the Noite Primeira procession. This chapter also examines the official rituals of 2 July, the role of veterans of the independence war, and the emergence of Pedro Labatut as a Dois de Julho hero.

From the Paraguayan War to the late 1880s, the period analyzed in chapter 3, Dois de Julho changed relatively little even as it continued to mobilize thousands of men and women to celebrate independence in Bahia. In the 1870s, Dois de Julho became a more civilian festival; after 1873, National Guard battalions no longer participated in the procession into Salvador and, after a violent conflict between soldiers and a patriotic battalion in 1875, army battalions were excluded from the celebrations. Patriotic battalions proliferated during these years, and Dois de Julho celebrations spread throughout Salvador in the form of neighbourhood festivals – the so-called Dois de Julho de Bairro – that filled the winter months. Two years of especially well-documented Dois de Julho festivals offer an opportunity to examine how politics was conducted through and in the celebrations. In 1869, the Liberal opposition tried to use the festival to demonstrate against the Conservative government that had come to power in July 1868. Six years later, the conflict between soldiers and civilian patriots, which left two civilians dead, sparked an intense national press debate as Liberal and Conservative journalists sought to assign blame for the violence and critique government officials' and opposition leaders' conduct during the ensuing crisis.

Enthusiasm for Dois de Julho contrasted sharply with Bahians' limited interest in 7 September, which is Brazil's national independence day. Indeed, Dois de Julho was often the occasion for Bahians to reflect on their relationship to Brazil and to the empire's political arrangements, and on the nature of the Brazilian nation. These issues are the focus of chapter 4, in which I examine how Dois de Julho celebrants defined themselves through their celebrations. Unsurprisingly, they excluded Africans and slaves from those who could be defined as Bahians; yet as early as the 1850s, Dois de Julho patriots regularly freed slaves to commemorate the day. In the 1870s, abolitionists sought to associate Dois de Julho with their campaign against slavery, but the relative weakness of Bahia's anti-slavery movement limited Dois de Julho abolitionism. Anti-Portuguese nativism was surprisingly rare during most Dois de Julho celebrations, notwithstanding historians' and folklorists' assertions that lusophobia characterized the festival. A fourth section in this chapter examines the concepts of order and respectability threaded through many of the press discussions about the festival, as well as how men and women of the middle and upper classes celebrated. This chapter concludes with a discussion of the relationship between Brazil and Bahia. Bahian patriots celebrated the province's centrality to Brazilian independence as a way to win symbolic capital for a province that, by the end of the empire, was increasingly lagging behind Rio de Janeiro and São Paulo.

Chapter 5 examines the representations of Dois de Julho during the theatre galas that were held on the evening of 2 July. These gatherings of mostly middle- and upper-class Bahians, as well as much of official Salvador, were important public rituals during which audiences demonstrated their cultural sophistication and support for the imperial regime. Bahian playwrights in the 1850s and 1860s wrote many plays about independence in the province, but few of them were published. Five surviving plays written for Dois de Julho demonstrate how these Romantic playwrights sought to portray the struggle for independence in the province, Bahia's relationship with Brazil, and Dois de Julho's linkages with other events that were then being interpreted as precursors to independence. By giving prominent roles to popular characters, the playwrights highlighted the *povo*'s importance in the struggle. The playwrights were also the only Bahians to pay much attention to Maria Quitéria de Jesus, a woman who joined the patriot army in 1822, fought as a regular soldier, and briefly enjoyed minor celebrity; until the twentieth century, patriots usually ignored her. Closely associated with mid-century liberals, Bahia's playwrights were among the first to argue that independence had a long history and that the 1822–23 struggle in the province should be connected to the 1789 Inconfidência Mineira (a conspiracy in Minas Gerais) and the 1817 republican rebellion in Pernambuco. Republicans would eventually interpret these movements as precursors to a republican independence that Emperor Pedro I had blocked by seizing the leadership of the independence movement in Rio de Janeiro; the Bahian playwrights, for their part, saw these movements as precursors to their radical liberal ideals.

The 1895 inauguration of the long-planned monument to Dois de Julho on Campo Grande signalled major changes in the festival, which are analyzed in chapter 6. Given that it was closely associated with the empire, Dois de Julho was difficult for republican authorities to celebrate in the early 1890s. Moreover, in the 1870s and 1880s, more and more critics began to see Dois de Julho traditions as old-fashioned, backward, and inappropriate for Bahians who aspired to civilization. Critics scorned the Indianist symbols as evidence of Bahian barbarousness; others judged that the festival had fallen into an irredeemable decline. The proposals for a permanent monument sought to address both these concerns, and I examine the early proposals, the fundraising campaigns, the bitter debate about where to locate the monument, and its inauguration on 2 July 1895. The monument prompted a split in the Dois de Julho festival, with official ceremonies taking place in Campo Grande while the *caboclos* and the popular Dois de Julho festival moved to the main square of Santo Antônio Além do Carmo Parish. In the conclusion, I provide a brief overview of Dois de Julho's evolution in the twentieth and twenty-first centuries, consider some of the methodological issues raised in this work, and reflect on my role as a historian of the Dois de Julho festival.

# "Never Again Will Despotism Govern Our Actions": The Invention of a Civic Ritual, 1824–47

The bedraggled patriots who marched into Salvador on 2 July 1823 likely knew that they were participating in momentous events, although they could not have known that their actions would soon be symbolically re-enacted, year after year. How Bahian patriots invented the Dois de Julho festival is the subject of this chapter. When Eric Hobsbawm and Terrence Ranger coined the phrase "invention of tradition" in 1988, they implicitly distinguished between "real" traditions and those "invented" by the powerful or the wealthy for profit or to foster loyalty to new states.[1] Few today accept this distinction, for all traditions are in some way invented, the product of human action. What becomes important, then, is to determine who invented, in this case, the distinctive ways of celebrating Dois de Julho; whose interests the festival served; and for what purposes people took to Salvador's streets in late June and early July. These are not easy questions to answer, both because of the sources' limitations (historians' perennial lament) and because of an "official history" of the festival consolidated in the early twentieth century, drawing primarily on the work of folklorist Manoel Raimundo Querino (1851–1923). Little of the official history can be confirmed in the surviving sources, which include much that contradict it, so this chapter presents a new history of Dois de Julho's invention. At the same time, I recognize that Querino's account of the festival's origins (and the debates that it prompted) are themselves part of Dois de Julho's history and must be taken seriously.

Two contexts shaped the Dois de Julho festival's invention. Its initial forms derived from the larger Luso-Brazilian culture of royal and church festivals, and it eventually incorporated carnivalesque elements, which had also been important to early-modern civic celebrations. The Brazilian empire retained many elements of colonial royal and religious festivals as part of the official civic ritual that it mandated for its days of national festivity, which were formally instituted in 1826 (2 July would gain this status in 1831, but only in Bahia). The second context for Dois de Julho's rise as a distinct festival was the Exaltado (radical liberal) challenge to Emperor Pedro I, which gathered strength in the late 1820s and culminated in his abrupt abdication in 1831. Bahian radical liberals – or "patriots," as they were sometimes known – turned 1827's commemoration of the expulsion of the Portuguese troops into something quite different from the usual run of civic celebrations as they re-enacted the 2 July 1823 occupation of the city. This demonstration and their subsequent celebrations of Dois de Julho were integral to their campaign against those whom they considered tyrants and despots. Exaltados demanded that the emperor and other authorities abide by the constitution's terms as they understood them, called for racial equality among the free, and sometimes promoted anti-Portuguese nativism. This radical politics profoundly shaped early Dois de Julho celebrations.

The sources for this chapter are quite limited. The gradual freeing of the press in the late 1820s opened space for many new partisan periodicals (an indication of the lively political debate in the province). In late 1830, a Rio de Janeiro newspaper reported that six newspapers were being published in Bahia; fully thirty-two new periodicals were launched in Salvador in 1831–32, but most were ephemeral and few have survived. The radical liberal press recovered rapidly from the repression that followed the 1837–38 Sabinada Rebellion, and thirty-six new newspapers appeared in the ten years between 1838 and 1847.[2] Already in March 1840, long before the amnesty that pardoned most of the rebels, a Rio de Janeiro newspaper described Bahia as "inundated with periodicals, some defenders of the provincial administration, others oppositionists, and some of them extreme oppositionists"; it listed fully thirteen titles.[3] While one publisher of a radical liberal periodical complained during his 1842 trial for abuse of press freedom that the government was seeking to "mute the free press in all parts of the empire," such court cases almost always ended in acquittals for the journalists.[4] Unfortunately, lengthy but still incomplete runs of only two Bahian periodicals have survived for parts of the 1840s – the conservative *Correio Mercantil* and Domingos Guedes Cabral's radical liberal and even republican *O Guaicuru*. Other published sources, including sermons and poetry, offer clues to how Bahians commemorated the Portuguese troops' expulsion and provide evidence for how they discussed the festival's meaning.

This chapter sets Dois de Julho's invention in the twin contexts of colonial civic-ritual heritage and post-independence radical liberalism (and the reaction to it). While drawing on old-regime civic ritual forms, Exaltados or patriots invented new ways of celebrating independence in Bahia. Through their Dois de Julho festivities, they took politics into the streets. Conservative opponents of Dois de Julho radicalism took advantage of the post-Sabinada repression to restrict the festival and to tame its radical potential; but in the mid-1840s, a provincial president opened up space for Dois de Julho, likely intending to control the festival through more subtle means. Exaltados resisted these efforts, and by the end of the decade, Dois de Julho was again an unmistakably radical liberal festival. One further invention of radical liberals was the adoption of distinctive Indianist figures as Dois de Julho's principal symbol. Today known as the *caboclos* – a term rarely used in the nineteenth century – the two symbols' history remains obscure. In this chapter, I analyze the conflicting folklorists' accounts and juxtapose them with the surviving sources to construct a new history of their origins.

## The Civic Ritual Context, 1824–26

The events of 1822 that resulted in the independent empire of Brazil offered several dates that could be commemorated as the anniversary of Brazil's founding. In Rio de Janeiro, Pedro's Grito do Ipiranga (on 7 September) was rather quickly constructed as Brazil's independence day, although for a few years it remained subordinate to 12 October (the date of his acclamation as emperor and also his birthday). The date of Pedro's decision to stay in Brazil (9 January) – his first open defiance of the Portuguese parliament, which had ordered him to return to Lisbon – was also celebrated, as was the date of Pedro's coronation and consecration (1 December). In 1826, during its first session, Brazil's parliament designated five "days of national festivity": 9 January, 25 March (the date on which Pedro swore his oath to the constitution, which he granted in 1824), 3 May (the date on which parliament was to open each year), 7 September, and 12 October.[5] Four of these days were closely linked to the first emperor; all of them were celebrated throughout the empire with what were known as official festivities. These consisted of artillery salutes, a military parade, a reception at which people paid their respects to the emperor's portrait, and a theatre gala. The surviving sources from Bahia do not provide sufficient evidence to discuss these official rituals for most of the 1820s. However, a brief look at some of the first post-independence civic rituals reveals the context in which the Dois de Julho festival emerged.

Like the rest of Portuguese America, colonial Bahia had a vibrant ritual life through which Bahians demonstrated their allegiance to the Church and the monarchy, the two institutions that all had in common. While no historian has systematically examined Salvador's late-colonial ritual life, it is clear from a cursory perusal of the city's first gazette, the *Idade de Ouro do Brasil* (Golden Age of Brazil, 1811–23) that urban life was structured around a cycle of public rituals. Dozens of annual saints' festivals were the occasion for devotional processions, while royal birthdays, weddings, coronations, and other momentous events brought subjects together in demonstrations of loyalty to their rulers. These rituals represented the social hierarchy. Occasional conflicts over precedence among corporations and prominent individuals underscore that rituals were important to politics during the old regime. Colonial ritual reflected a corporate vision of society. Processions incorporated all social groups, even the lowest in the social hierarchy, so Africans and slaves performed their subordinate roles in the body politic. Moreover, the colonial regime ceded space for popular celebrations in tandem with official rituals.[6]

Because of the war against Portuguese forces in Salvador, civic rituals were far from Bahians' minds in 1822 and the first half of 1823 (although those besieged in the city did attempt to keep up with the cycle of religious festivals). Thus, the first major post-independence civic ritual in the province was Pedro I's acclamation, held on 12 October, a year after the acclamation in Rio de Janeiro (there is no evidence that Bahians took note of 7 September in 1823). Salvador's city council carefully described the acclamation in two letters to the emperor. In these classic festival-description texts, all aspects of the ritual come together in harmony; such works express the messages intended by festival organizers, whose efforts they also celebrate.[7] On 14 September, the council issued a proclamation calling on Bahians to celebrate the upcoming holiday. As had been the colonial custom, the proclamation (*bando*) was publicized by the councillors during a ceremony known as the *bando*, during which the council and its staff, "richly attired in gala dress," paraded from one end of the city to the other. Accompanied by musicians, they stopped from time to time to read the proclamation aloud. The city population did more than simply watch this parade: according to the councillors, "the most energetic cheers to the August Person of Your Imperial Majesty were heard." Residents had spontaneously decorated the façades of their houses and threw "clouds of flowers" on the passing parade; all of this formed "the most marvellous spectacle."[8]

The acclamation itself, held four weeks later, was impossible to describe fully, according to the council. It began with a Te Deum, complete with newly composed music and an "admirable sermon" on the "sublime object" in the "sumptuously adorned" cathedral. No one missed this opportunity to render tribute to the emperor, and the city's inhabitants "appeared to have been born for the purpose of celebrating Your Imperial Majesty's acclamation." After this religious festival, a "great parade of the troops" was held on the Terreiro de Jesus, during which civilian and military authorities led the population in cheers "for the things that are dearest to us," cheers that were repeated "with the greatest of enthusiasm by the entire concourse." The troops fired the customary number of volleys, and a levee was held in the palace, during which authorities and leading citizens paid their respects to the imperial portrait.[9]

Given that Pedro could not be personally present at Bahian civic rituals (and those elsewhere in his far-flung empire), his portrait stood in for his person, a common old-regime practice (indeed, in Rio de Janeiro, Pedro's portrait was also used in this way when he could not personally attend civic rituals).[10] Bahians paid their respects to this simulacrum of an emperor in a ceremony analogous to the *beija-mão* (hand-kissing) in the capital; in addition, the emperor's portrait was displayed publicly. A "brilliant illuminated monument" displayed the "August Effigy" in the "most sublime place." This temporary structure stood on one of Salvador's public squares (likely the Palace Square); there, the imperial portrait was unveiled by the provincial president and one of the council members, at which point bands broke into music, girandoles of fireworks were released, and the "most patriotic anthems" were sung. The president then led the crowds in cheers to "our Holy Cause, our love, respect, and gratitude for Your Imperial Majesty, and, finally, to our prosperity and unity."[11]

In the evening, a theatre gala was held, to which the council had contributed; during this ceremony, the cheers were repeated when the emperor's image was unveiled. For ten successive nights, the city was illuminated, and on the last night, the imperial portrait was conducted through the city, accompanied by citizens in a torch-lit procession.[12] Although the council did not mention it, the theatre gala included a "carefully considered drama" titled *Gratidão da Bahia* (Bahia's Gratitude), by Bernardino Ferreira Nóbrega; José Estanislau Vieira and João Gualberto Ferreira dos Santos Reis recited poetry.[13] An anonymous chronicler much taken by civic and religious festivals concluded that the entire ceremony was "such a magnificent and brilliant function that, if it were possible to describe it [all], it would take many days to write about all that happened, the great satisfaction and enthusiasm, and all the people's joy."[14]

The council concluded its letter by calling on Pedro to fulfill his promise to visit the province and reminding him that, "under the monarchical constitutional system directed by a most prudent and enlightened assembly, and executed by a most wise, active, and virtuous emperor, our cause will advance amid our prosperity, grandeur, unity, and loyalty, as is to be expected from a people that loves order and a perpetual emperor, defender of its rights, who will stand watch against those of less than good intentions."[15] Others shared the council's views. At a Te Deum sponsored by the Desterro convent, Friar Francisco Barauna preached on Pedro's qualities, which he described as analogous to those of Solomon – wisdom, daring, and wealth – but pointedly remarked that a sovereign's greatness lay in increasing the nation's wealth, not his own. Moreover, Barauna lashed out against those "who do not love our lord D. PEDRO. Damnation and death to him who attempts against our Independence, or in the madness of his ideas tries to change this beautiful order of things." His listeners would have readily identified these enemies with the recently expelled "vandals, who occupied our territory," the Portuguese.[16]

These pointed remarks – a mix of adulation and advice – underscored the delicate political context of 1823. Rumours of a republican revolt had run rife in the weeks leading up to 12 October.[17] Before the description of Bahia's acclamation arrived in Rio de Janeiro, the emperor had dissolved the constituent assembly. News of this arbitrary act set off several days of anti-Portuguese rioting in Salvador in mid-December, and in early 1824, Pedro's supporters narrowly succeeded in forcing the city council to accept the emperor's draft constitution against popular demands for revisions.[18] On 3 May 1824 – the anniversary of Brazil's discovery and, ironically, the date on which the constituent assembly had convened in 1823 – Salvador conducted its formal ceremony of swearing the oath to the new charter. It began with the usual artillery salutes and a military parade, after which the provincial president and city council walked from the Government Palace to the cathedral, carrying an open copy of the charter like a sacred relic. After the Te Deum, the entire constitution was read aloud; then, starting with the president, the cathedral chapter, and the city council, citizens swore their oath and signed the register. For three nights, the council building was illuminated and an imperial portrait prominently displayed. In his proclamation, the president hailed the "compatriots most distinguished by their enlightenment and love for national prosperity" who had "raised this indestructible monument to liberty." With the charter in place, he concluded, "the work of our emancipation is done."[19] At the theatre gala, Vieira likewise hailed Pedro's establishment of "the firm base on which, happily / Brazil will endure as long as the world endures."[20]

There are relatively few sources on Salvador's civic rituals in subsequent years. They suggest that, as in Rio de Janeiro, 12 October was still more important than 7 September.[21] In 1824 and 1825, the celebrations of Pedro's birthday and acclamation followed 1823's pattern, compressed into a single day, which began with artillery salutes, followed by a military parade from 10 a.m. until noon, a levy, and a theatre gala at night. "Many people" illuminated their houses.[22] A new portrait of the emperor proved to be a major attraction in 1824. Ordered by the provincial government for its main hall, it had arrived from Rio de Janeiro just before the celebrations. So many people wanted to see it that the president ordered the painting kept on public display for a week, watched over by an honour guard of twenty army cadets.[23] Official celebrations hailed Pedro as the grantor of the constitution and carefully ignored his dissolution of the 1823 assembly. In 1825, during the theatre gala, Alferes (infantry Second Lieutenant) Ladislau dos Santos Titara praised the emperor in verse: "Scarcely hadst thou broken the chains from our wrists / Constitution and Laws, sons of Astraia / That bring us happiness, thou proclaimest generously."[24] There are no indications that Bahians celebrated the coronation during these years, and the reports on 7 September in *O Independente Constitucional* suggest relatively perfunctory celebrations, along with continuing concern about order.[25] In 1824, the provincial president reported that he had led cheers in the theatre, which "had a great impact" and "spread tranquility" (at this time, the Confederação do Equador rebellion in Pernambuco had not yet been defeated).[26] The impact of the president's cheers did not last long; in late October a military rebellion, the Periquitos' Revolt, led to a month-long standoff between rebel soldiers and loyal troops.[27]

Given the almost complete lack of surviving newspapers from Salvador for the second half of the 1820s, it is impossible to trace the practice of civic rituals in Bahia's capital after the five days of national festivity were instituted in 1826. Titara later published laudations that he had recited at theatre galas on 7 September 1828 and 25 March 1829. On the former date, he hailed the Grito do Ipiranga as the origin of Brazil's constitutional regime:

> Thou art the sweet origin, from which came
> The Liberty and the Glory that today, happily,
> We enjoy alongside our good fortune
> To thee, sublime hymns we dedicate
> And to the *pátria*, to the Hero Pedro, whom we idolize.[28]

Political conflicts sometimes manifested themselves publicly during civic rituals. In 1829, the president, the Viscount of Camamu (José Egídio Gordilho de Barbuda), reported that he had been "insolently and atrociously insulted" on 12 October by João da Virgem Maria Kaxangá, a *pregador imperial* (imperial preacher) with radical leanings. Camamu did not indicate what Kaxangá had said but recommended that the priest be stripped of the honour (which probably would have made him ineligible to preach during civic ceremonies).[29] No doubt Camamu's involvement in the crushing of the 1824 revolt contributed to Kaxangá's outburst. In early 1830, Camamu was assassinated by unknown assailants.[30]

Official civic ritual in Salvador in the 1820s sought to tie Bahians to the monarchy. The intended meanings of these ceremonies are easy to identify: they highlighted the monarch's importance, visibly associated members of the provincial government and elite with the monarchy, and claimed divine sanction for the new regime's political institutions, notably the constitution. The first two Dois de Julho celebrations closely resembled these official civic rituals. The *Grito da Razão* reported in 1824 that the day had been "much celebrated, privately and publicly, by all." The celebrations included a Te Deum, a military parade, artillery salutes, the "customary cheers," illumination of the city, and a theatre gala, at which a drama titled *A guerra da Bahia ou A sedução frustrada* (The War of Bahia or The Frustrated Seduction) was performed. On the troops' faces, the *Grito da Razão*'s editor read "the most lively enthusiasm for the love for the *pátria* and Brazil's independence, and hatred for the colonial yoke."[31] Much the same ritual took place in 1825 and was effusively described in *O Independente Constitucional*. That same year, a new portrait of Pedro was unveiled at the mint. During the theatre gala, Francisco Moniz Barreto, a young artillery cadet with a knack for verse who would become Dois de Julho's leading poet by mid-century, hailed Pedro as the "Father of Brazil, a model monarch."[32] The imperial government also awarded a campaign medal to all those who had fought for independence in Bahia (news of this decree, issued on 2 July, only reached the province later).[33]

Largely official and monarchical rituals, these Dois de Julho celebrations were not quite consensual. The *Grito da Razão* complained in 1824 about Friar Barauna, who had furiously preached against the

Portuguese after the Te Deum. By contrast, *O Independente Consti-*
*tucional* judged his sermon "very judicious." Barauna had chosen as his
theme the Assyrian war against Jerusalem and compared it to the Portuguese war against Bahians. Despite the differences between the two
conflicts, the latter "among brothers, sons of the same Church, relatives
and friends, the results were the same." The *Grito* claimed that Barauna
concluded his sermon with a declaration that absolutely no Portuguese
was "a friend of Brazil, because all, without any exception, were sworn
enemies of Brazil, plotting its ruin." He called on the provincial president to dismiss all those born in Portugal who held government positions.[34] Such calls for the expulsion of Portuguese, especially those
who had opposed independence, appeared regularly in these years.[35]
In 1825, there were complaints in both newspapers about Portuguese
shopkeepers who remained open for business during the celebration,
even though they sold nothing.[36]

Uncertainty about administrative responsibility for organizing civic
rituals led to a much-reduced Dois de Julho celebration in 1826. The
city council, which had paid for the Te Deum in 1824 and 1825, discovered that it lacked authorization to spend this money and petitioned
Pedro I for retroactive permission.[37] Lingering doubts about whether
it could legally spend money on the festival apparently prompted the
city council to organize no commemorations in 1826, but the cathedral
chapter put on a Te Deum and the army garrison did the "customary
parade." Many citizens spontaneously decorated their façades, and at
the theatre, the night's performance began with the national anthem
and cheers to the emperor, the legislative assembly, and the "gallant
warriors, who, with their blood, freed the *pátria* and consolidated our
liberty."[38] The provincial government may have limited its involvement
as well, and the author of a letter to *O Independente Constitucional* lamented the lack of even "the slightest sign of public festivities" – no
artillery salutes, no flags on the fort in the harbour, "no forming up of
troops," and especially no city council–funded Te Deum.[39] Later critics
went further, describing 1826 as the year without a Dois de Julho celebration – an indication that municipal and provincial involvement in
the festivities was expected.[40]

The first Dois de Julho commemorations were thus standard official
civic rituals, very much like the primarily monarchical celebrations of

7 September and 12 October that presented Brazil's foundation as the product of Pedro I's actions. To be sure, many Bahians retained doubts about the connection to Rio de Janeiro and about the extent of Pedro's power, and Bahian civic ritual discourse contained explicitly radical overtones, notably the anti-Portuguese rhetoric that would periodically characterize Dois de Julho. Nonetheless, the first three Dois de Julhos did not depart significantly from the well-established old-regime forms of public celebration adopted (and adapted) by the new empire.

## The Exaltado Dois de Julho, 1827–37

Dois de Julho changed dramatically in 1827 when radical liberals invented a new way of celebrating the day – by re-enacting the victorious patriots' march into the city. Over the next few years, this turned into Salvador's premier civic ritual. Dois de Julho soon gained distinct symbols, including Indian allegories – eventually known as the *caboclos* – and its own anthem. These were major departures from (or, perhaps better, additions to) colonial ritual, and determining how and by whom they were invented is the key to understanding Dois de Julho's origins. What follows in this section departs significantly from what I have dubbed Dois de Julho's "official history," so I begin with a review of the folklorists' accounts that have shaped contemporary understandings of the festival's origins.

For close to a century, this official history of Dois de Julho's origins, originally assembled by Manoel Raimundo Querino, has been repeated by historians and folklorists alike; it is still reproduced annually in commemorative materials published by the festival's organizers. It goes as follows: "Patriots" first celebrated Dois de Julho in 1824 by decorating a wagon captured at the Battle of Pirajá with coffee, tobacco, sugar cane, and green-and-yellow croton leaves. An "old *mestiço* [man of mixed race]" served as a living allegory on the wagon, which they conducted from Lapinha (on the city's northern outskirts) to the downtown Terreiro de Jesus, accompanied by bands. They repeated this demonstration in 1825; the following year, they hired Manoel Inácio da Costa to design an allegorical float. He used the captured wagon's wheels and sculpted the so-called *caboclo*, the statue of a male Indian who "symbolizes free Brazil," trampling and stabbing the serpent of tyranny. The *caboclo* then became Dois de Julho's principal symbol, and in 1826, for the first time, patriots constructed a stage downtown to receive this allegory.[41] As we have seen, nothing in Querino's account of the first three anniversaries can be confirmed through the surviving newspapers or other contemporary sources. Querino was writing at a time when Dois de Julho's popular traditions – and particularly the Indianist *caboclos* – were under severe attack, and he perhaps was seeking to legitimize them by endowing them with a long history.[42] Since the beginning of the century he had been deeply engaged in a project to document Bahia's artists and artisans and to give them credit for their work. Indeed, his first remarks about the symbols' origins came in biographical sketches of these artists.[43]

In several key respects, Querino contradicted earlier histories of the festival's origins. José Álvares do Amaral (1823–1882), a provincial civil servant and long-serving secretary of the Sociedade Dois de Julho (from at least 1859 to 1871), claimed in 1871 that for four or five years after 1823, "true patriots" celebrated Dois de Julho by putting up triumphal arches and decorating the façades of their houses; as well, "all the troops" participated in the "triumphal entry." Then several citizens, including Francisco José Corte Imperial, Francisco Ribeiro Neves, and Canon Manoel Joaquim de Almeida, hired a sculptor, Bento Sabino, to make the "handsome statue that represents the Spirit of Brazil, majestic symbol of our independence." The image that accompanied this article showed a male Indian stabbing a serpent, but he is left-handed, rather than the right-handed contemporary *caboclo* (see figure 1.1).[44] Although published a half-century earlier than Querino's account, Amaral's history of early Dois de Julho celebrations also fails to correspond to the available contemporary sources, but it comes a bit closer than Querino's account. Querino did not acknowledge Amaral in his 1923 history of Dois de Julho, but he was well aware of his predecessor's work. A decade earlier, he had criticized Amaral's identification of Bento Sabino as the *caboclo*'s sculptor, for Costa's students had always attributed the statue to their mentor and one even recalled seeing sketches for the *caboclo* in Costa's workshop.[45] Leading Bahian cultural figures in the 1910s like Sílio Boccanera Júnior accepted Querino's account, condemned Amaral as hopelessly unreliable, and lambasted

Figure 1.1 | The "original" Dois de Julho triumphal float

*Source*: "Carro triumphal do Dous de Julho," *O Reverbero*, 6 August 1871.

those who accepted Amaral's version.[46] Contemporary anthropologists, folklorists, and historians, myself included (in my first article on Dois de Julho), have likewise taken Querino at his word.[47]

This debate, of course, says much more about later battles over historical memory and control over the festival than it does about the first Dois de Julho celebrations and the invention of its symbols. A careful examination of the scattered and incomplete contemporary sources reveals a very different history of Dois de Julho's origins, one that ties the festival directly to the tense post-independence political climate. A heady mix of radical liberal or Exaltado politics and identification with patriot victories won in Bahia, laced with lusophobia, drove Dois de Julho's rise as a distinct civic ritual. While official festivities continued to take place on Dois de Julho, it soon became primarily a popular festival, in the sense that its principal rituals were organized not by the government but rather by (for lack of a better term) civil society groups, and also in the sense that it attracted much more socially broad participation than other days of national festivity. In its celebration of Bahia's mobilization as the fount of independence, Dois de Julho challenged the official Brazilian history presented on days of national festivity, which celebrated the actions of a heroic prince (Pedro I) who founded a liberal, constitutional monarchy. Worries about Dois de Julho's popular elements and concern about its celebration of loyalty to the province shaped the festival's trajectory over the course of the nineteenth century. That said, in the decade after 1827, Dois de Julho was primarily an Exaltado festival.

Bahia's radical liberals were a diverse group of men who from independence to the Sabinada Rebellion of 1837–38 campaigned for change, sometimes radical change.[48] Their banners espoused nativism – that is, the expulsion of Portuguese who had opposed independence or who expressed illiberal ideas – as well as federalism (i.e., devolution of power to the provinces), liberal reforms to judicial and military institutions, and equality among citizens. Some of them noted specifically that such equality would end racial discrimination among the free.[49] For these men, independence and the institutions established in 1822–24 had not gone far enough and further reforms were needed. Exaltados adopted diverse strategies. They published newspapers and thereby contributed to the expansion of Brazil's public sphere; indeed, much of what we know about their ideology comes from newspapers published by men like Domingos Guedes Cabral.[50] They ran for office and enjoyed some electoral success, an indication that Brazil's political system was at least somewhat open to them. They elected Cipriano José Barata de Almeida to the 1823 constituent assembly, although he declined to take his seat. Several other men associated with radical liberals won election to parliament from Bahia, including José Lino Coutinho, Antônio Pereira Rebouças, and Antonio Ferreira França, who presented a motion to the chamber of deputies in 1835 that Brazil cease to be the "patrimony of a family" and become a republic.[51]

Exaltados enjoyed strong support among the armed forces, where they were able to capitalize on officers' and soldiers' discontent; each of the radical liberal revolts of the 1820s and 1830s had a core of military support.[52] Their ideals attracted many of Salvador's middling groups. Men with some education but with relatively few connections, often of mixed race, embraced an ideology that appeared to offer them greater opportunities in the new nation. Artisans and other members of the lower classes also embraced radical liberalism. Thanks to the constitution's relatively low income requirement for voting, many of this class could cast ballots for electors in the empire's two-tier elections. Only nine of the 203 men arrested in radical-liberal movements between 1824 and 1831 owned slaves, an indication of their relatively low class position.[53] Moreover, even men of means harboured doubts about the centralized and authoritarian empire that Pedro I seemed to be constructing in the aftermath of the constituent assembly's dissolution in November 1823. Having won independence from a Lisbon government that had failed to respect their local autonomy, they were in no mood to subject themselves to Rio de Janeiro, but fear of social unrest pushed many of them into accepting the new regime.

Pedro I's abdication in 1831 and liberal reforms in the late 1820s and early 1830s satisfied some radical liberals' demands, but others sought further change through direct action in 1831–33. Anti-Portuguese riots and more peaceful demonstrations in April and May 1831, associated with the abdication, forced the resignation of the provincial president and the commander of arms. Federalist revolts in October 1831 (Salvador), February 1832 (Cachoeira), and April 1833 (Salvador) drew strong support from disaffected soldiers and officers; the rebels articulated an increasingly clear ideology and perhaps were seeking to influence the debates taking place in the national parliament over amendments to the 1824 constitution. These debates resulted in the 1834 Ato Adicional, which devolved some powers to the provinces and instituted provincial assemblies, although critics contended that these nods towards federalism did not go far enough.[54] Even so, for a few years, radical-liberal and federalist agitation declined in Bahia. It would reappear, though, in the 1837–38 Sabinada Rebellion (see below).

Back in 1827, radical liberals had been central to the invention of new ways of commemorating Dois de Julho, as is clear in the two accounts of that year's festival that reached Rio de Janeiro. An anonymous writer accused "revolutionaries" of exploiting the "general discontent" at the appointment of certain Portuguese men to civil and military posts to stage "a church celebration, parade, dinners, illuminations, and speeches of the most violent nature."[55] More details about these demonstrations appear in Francisco Joaquim Álvares Branco Moniz Barreto's detailed report to Pedro I, in which he noted the political context of rumours about absolutist plots and the embarkation of regular troops to join the army in the increasingly unpopular (and ultimately unsuccessful) Cisplatine War (1826–28). The governor of arms, José Manoel de Almeida, had permitted militia battalions to gather at Lapinha on the eve of 2 July. On the day itself, they marched into the city, "covered in leaves," while the "rabble" proclaimed that the troops embarking that very day for the south represented the Portuguese and the militia the patriot army of 1823. As far as Moniz Barreto was concerned, the militia parade had turned a serious commemoration into a "farce" worthy only of the theatre, for troops' appropriate role on civic holidays was to line the streets and stand guard in squares. Worse yet, the parade was the occasion for numerous disorders, which began when some patriots tried to prevent a Portuguese-born militiaman from passing below a triumphal arch to join his company. He retorted something rude about entering "into the city with *cabras* [dark mulattoes] and mulattoes." After that, the battalions of blacks and mulattoes "only talked about *marotos* [a pejorative term for Portuguese]," which much offended the white militia; officers barely kept control of the situation.[56] This account makes no mention of allegorical floats, but both observers stressed the demonstration's Exaltado nature and the prominence of the black and mulatto militia, many of whose officers and men had played important roles in the independence war.[57] Official rituals also took place, as can be inferred from the requisition of 3,000 blank cartridges so that the regulars could fire the customary salutes.[58]

It is not clear whether such a parade was repeated in 1828, for the only contemporary description of that year's festival is Friar Joaquim das Mercês's allusion to "public celebrations that very much excite those who take part" in the sermon that he preached at the Te Deum. He railed against "odious despotism," declaring that it would soon feel the "merciless blows of the liberal constitution," and he called on Pedro I to "preserve our inalienable rights against despots' designs" – classic

Exaltado appeals.[59] The president acknowledged his invitation to the Te Deum and issued orders for the troops to fire salutes and to participate in "other demonstrations of public rejoicing." There was also a theatre gala, as can be inferred from Titara's later publication of the verses that he recited there.[60] Thus, while no surviving contemporary source confirms Amaral's account of an Indianist allegory's creation in 1827 or 1828, his identification of Francisco José Corte Imperial (a publisher with a long history of radical-liberal activism) and Francisco Ribeiro Neves (a notary who would later be involved in the Sabinada Rebellion) as responsible for hiring the artist who created the allegory is certainly consistent with these festivals' political leanings.[61] More generally, Amaral's comment that the festival arose four or five years after 1823 coincides with 1827's innovations.

The central place of an Indianist allegory in the procession can be confirmed for the first time in 1829. The *Abelha Pernambucana* transcribed a report from *O Bahiano*, a radical-liberal periodical founded by Rebouças and later edited by Nóbrega.[62] Full of Exaltado outbursts, the article described how Bahian troops (the militia) gathered before dawn at Lapinha while the regular troops took up positions downtown (at this time, these were battalions from outside of Bahia, recently stationed in the province after the end of the Cisplatine War, so their officers and men had no direct connection to the war for independence in Bahia).[63] The Bahian troops and large numbers of civilians conducted an "allegory of America trampling despotism underfoot" through streets covered with fragrant leaves, amid cheers to the constitution, the constitutional emperor, the assembly, and the Brazilian people. At the Te Deum, Francisco Gomes dos Santos e Almeida stressed that the constitution must be "religiously observed"; the service ended with a rousing cheer for the constitution, while the theatre gala included "very good patriotic anthems" as well as poetry.[64] In Rio de Janeiro, Evaristo Ferreira da Veiga's *Aurora Fluminense* added that the newly elected city council had contributed to the festival and observed with satisfaction that some authorities, such as the commander of arms, felt obliged to pay "tribute" to "the ideas of the times."[65]

In 1828, Bahian patriots had launched a campaign to turn Dois de Julho into a national holiday. President Gordilho de Barbuda was a foe of radical liberals, as we have already noted; nevertheless, he recommended that Pedro I decree such a holiday in the province.[66] When word of this reached Rio de Janeiro, Evaristo, the capital's leading moderate liberal journalist, lent his support, stressing that anything that strengthened "the greatest of civic virtues – love of the *pátria*" – deserved support, and adding that all provinces should have such a holiday.[67] In 1829, the Bahian liberal deputy, Lino Coutinho, presented to parliament a petition signed by more than one thousand "citizens of Bahia" requesting that 2 July be proclaimed a holiday, at least in the province.[68] There are few records of the debate over this proposal. Pernambucan deputies proposed that 27 January (the date on which the Dutch abandoned Recife in 1654) also be added to the roster of national holidays, to which Bernardo Pereira de Vasconcelos retorted that Pernambucans had merely thrown off "the yoke of one lord to subject themselves to another" whereas Bahians had broken "the irons of slavery to enter into independence and liberty." In response to this slight against Pernambucan patriotism – which made much of the 1654 restoration[69] – Pernambucan deputies insisted that their forebears had actually sought independence but had failed to win it for lack of aid from other provinces! Wisely, Lino Coutinho cautioned against mixing "business from the old testament with the new" and proposed an amendment that would allow provinces to proclaim their own holidays. The bill passed in the chamber; however, the senate rejected it in July 1830.[70] *O Brasileiro Imparcial*'s editor, Joaquim José da Silva Maia, who never missed a chance to provoke Bahian Exaltados, claimed that the senate's rejection was due to the fact that the patriots had obliged 12,000 people to abandon their homes and evacuate Salvador, "leaving thousands of families alone, without fathers, women without husbands, children without parents, and parents without children!"[71] Maia well knew about this from personal experience. As a journalist in Salvador between 1821 and 1823, he had vigorously defended the Portuguese cause; afterwards, he returned to his native Portugal and later found his way to Rio de Janeiro.[72] Only after Pedro I's abdication did parliament approve the establishment of 2 July as a "national festivity in the province of Bahia," equal in status to the other national holidays, a measure requested by eleven Bahian deputies on 2 July 1831.[73]

Contemporary sources for 1830's festival are thicker than for any year until 1836. Patriots convinced Bahia's archbishop to proclaim Dois de Julho a dispensed holy day, on which the faithful would be obliged to attend mass before going to work.[74] Many years later, he recalled just how controversial this decision was. Rumours spread that he had been reprimanded by the justice minister and that the government had considered overturning it: "It seems unbelievable that such irregularities could have taken place under the watch of the prince who, on the banks of the Ipiranga, had raised the cry for Independence, for which Dois de Julho in Bahia was nothing more than its echo and glorious complement."[75] Late in 1830's legislative session, Lino Coutinho requested that the justice minister present the chamber of deputies with a copy of the rumoured reprimand, but the minister reported that no such document had been issued.[76]

The 1830 festival itself was an elaborate affair, and Maia claimed that Bahian deputies had encouraged their constituents to spare no "efforts to celebrate that day with great pomp, to let it be known ... that this was a spontaneous action of all of the city of Bahia," as a message to the senate, which was still considering the holiday bill.[77] Rio de Janeiro's *Astréia* reprinted a description of the festival from Salvador's *O Escudo da Constituição* (published by Nóbrega, the periodical's title – *The Constitution's Shield* – indicates its political orientation). Fireworks saluted the sunrise at Lapinha, where the city's four militia battalions (white, mulatto, and black units alike), under the command of the governor of arms, had gathered the night before. Led by "two lavish triumphal floats," the troops, "adorned with coffee [leaves] and fragrant flowers," paraded into the city along a route marked with "many triumphal arches." As in 1829, the regulars formed an honour guard at the Presidential Palace but did not parade into the city.[78] However, the Fifth Battalion, raised in São Paulo, constructed an elaborate allegorical monument in front of its barracks that featured "a statue of America appropriately outfitted, holding in the right had the national coat of arms and in the left the arrow." Illuminated with six hundred candles, the structure also had allegorical figures representing Astraia (the goddess of justice) and Pallas (the titan whose shield proclaimed his intention to defend the free Brazilian nation).[79]

Authorities attended the Te Deum in the packed cathedral, after which the archbishop and the president led the assembled troops in the "customary cheers"; the soldiers saluted and marched by in review. At the theatre gala, the audience was presented with a new "dramatic laudation" and a newly written play about Dois de Julho; three new "patriotic anthems" were sung, and poets recited verses in honour of the day. The entire celebration took place in an orderly fashion, much to the satisfaction of "true constitutionalists."[80] The French consul added a few details. Three to four thousand men, "the majority of colour," joined the troops at Lapinha; bearing "coffee branches," they accompanied "two or three allegorical figures" that circulated through the city.[81] One Bahian newspaper promised to publish a special issue on 2 July that would include a "very attractive portrait" of Pedro I holding to his heart "the sacred social pact, the constitution," while *O Bahiano* warned foreigners (Portuguese) to avoid scandalizing the patriots by opening their shops or businesses on 2 July.[82]

Titara caught the spirit of the day with his "Elogio ao sempre memorável Dia Dois de Julho" (Laudation to the Always Memorable Day of 2 July), which highlighted Bahian patriots' valour and their leading role in winning Brazil's independence:

> ... this gilded Empire
> Can only be free men's *pátria*;
> And Bahia, the first to gallantly
> Tread on despotism's neck,
> Will be the first to firmly guard
> The constitution [and] independence.
> [...]
> On the majestic triumphal float
> See there how Victory enters
> Inside thy walls, already free! How she [is] followed
> By courageous lines of troops, and people
> How enthusiasm shines through in all.
> [...]
> Oh! Vandals tremble, growl in anger!
> Begrudge, if thou canst, the rejoicing
> With which today exult patriotic hearts!
> Hail, Bahians, free, triumphant!

He completed his image of the true patriots by contrasting them to the "cruel despots" and the "vile slaves, / Who cannot feel love for the *pátria*!"[83]

As copies of Bahia's newspapers trickled into Rio de Janeiro, the capital's press incorporated Dois de Julho into its debates. Maia's *O Brasileiro Imparcial* reported that the province's "Exaltados, who respect nothing," had coerced people into contributing to subscriptions for the celebration by insulting them with epithets of *"maroto, chumbeiro,* [and] recolonizer."[84] By contrast, Evaristo declared himself filled with "true jubilation" at Bahians' "patriotism."[85] In short, as Marco Morel has observed, 1830's Dois de Julho was a "majestic affirmation of patriotic identity."[86] At the time, "patriot" was a synonym for radical liberal; thus Bahian patriots had turned a civic ritual into a festive political demonstration that, if we accept the French consul's figures, brought close to one tenth of the city's population (and a much larger share of the free adult males) into the streets.

Unfortunately, much less is known about Dois de Julho celebrations until 1836. In 1831, the *Nova Sentinela da Liberdade* railed against the "Portuguese faction's treasonous plots" and praised Bahians' "refined patriotism" and appreciation for liberty, without however describing the many peaceful activities that took place.[87] The British consul heard rumours about a "rising of blacks" planned for 2 July, but he doubted their veracity.[88] The financial statement published by the organizers of 1832's celebration reveals that they raised 611$940 (US$434) through subscriptions in Salvador's parishes. Those funds paid for a mass in the Lapinha chapel, a triumphal arch on the Palace Square and its illumination, fireworks, and the repainting and decorating of the "triumphal float." The organizers even managed to leave 119$768 (US$85) for 1833's festival; the float and other leftover materials were stored at the Ordem Terceira do Carmo church.[89] That year, in a Moderado (moderate liberal) appeal for order, the *Gazeta da Bahia* called on Bahians to have confidence in the regency and the cabinet, all of whose members were Brazilians.[90] In 1834, the British consul marvelled that "this great day in Brazilian annals seems to be passing off tranquilly." To this he added, "A thing not altogether anticipated."[91] Year after year, Titara reliably produced new patriotic verse for the theatre gala, but he tended to avoid explicit political statements.[92]

By the middle of the decade, the celebrations were becoming institutionalized; a Sociedade Dois de Julho (Second of July Society) was founded on 5 July 1835 to look after the "patriotic symbols" and to

coordinate the annual celebrations. In keeping with the liberal orientation of most Dois de Julho celebrants, the society pressed the municipal government to remove the public whipping post, an "instrument
of despotism," which it did on 7 September of that year.[93] From 1834 to
1837, members of the "commission charged with [organizing] the celebration" (who never specifically identified themselves as part of the
Sociedade) issued annual invitations to the city council to attend the
Te Deum and sought authorization to raise triumphal arches at various locations (the 1828 law regulating municipal governments banned
spending on civic or religious festivals by city councils).[94] In 1836,
Inácio Acioli de Cerqueira e Silva described the annual parade into the
city as "a perfect representation" of the events of 1823, underscoring
its centrality in commemorating the Exército Pacificador's entry into
Salvador.[95] That same year, a Bahian absent from his home province lamented in verse that he could not "attend the festival of independence,"
a further indication that it was a regular and expected celebration.[96]

At about this time, Dois de Julho gained a new element, the so-called
*bando anunciador*, the colonial practice in which the city council announced the upcoming celebrations in a proclamation read throughout the city (as its members had done prior to 12 October 1823). From
1834 to 1837, invitations to the city council included requests that it
announce the upcoming festival, but there are no mentions of a *bando*
in the documentation for earlier years. According to folklorist João da
Silva Campos, who relied on the *Diário da Bahia*,[97] the 1836 *bando* was
a "carnivalesque parade" in which two hundred masked and costumed
revellers on horseback called on patriots to celebrate the day in appropriate fashion. The proclamation ended with cheers to constitutional
liberty and to Emperor Pedro II.[98]

The celebrations of 1836 began at midnight, with fireworks announcing the start of a parade in which "large numbers of patriots" conducted a "triumphal float" from the downtown São Francisco Square
to Lapinha. The following morning, the regular troops and the civilian
National Guard joined the patriots for the march into the city. This is
the first explicit indication of a two-stage parade, a nocturnal one to
Lapinha during the night of 1–2 July and the daytime entry into the
city, a pattern that became fully established in the late 1840s (see chapter 2). During the procession into Salvador, citizens dressed in leather
clothes or cotton homespun that recalled the garb of the Exército

Pacificador's irregular troops. The "triumphal float" was followed by *"cacumbis [sic = cucumbi] dances"* – a rare uncritical acknowledgment of the Afro-Brazilian cultural presence in the celebrations. The troops, and many more citizens, were all adorned with coffee leaves and flowers. The usual Te Deum, military review, cheers, and theatre gala followed.[99] In his sermon, João Pereira Ramos addressed the pressing political issues of the day, notably the outbreak of the Farroupilha Rebellion in Rio Grande do Sul, and called for a return to the patriotism that had brought Brazilians from many provinces to aid in the expulsion of the Portuguese from Bahia.[100]

An elaborate triumphal arch had been raised in front of the Presidential Palace; well-lit, it included an effigy of Pedro II, beside which stood "Brazil's first princess, Catarina Álvares," an allusion to the Indian woman, also known as Paraguaçu, whose marriage to a shipwrecked Portuguese man, Diogo Álvares (known by his Tupi name Caramuru) laid the foundation for the first Portuguese settlements in sixteenth-century Bahia.[101] An artificial garden and fountain surrounded this monument, and the triumphal float stood on display before it. On the Terreiro de Jesus, the First National Guard Battalion constructed an arch, topping it with a "symbol of America, having at her feet a monster, representing defeated despotism"; paintings of major battles in 1822 and 1823 covered the arch's sides. Similar ephemeral monuments stood in at least five other locations. For three nights, the city and the monuments were illuminated, and even the elements cooperated as the winter rains let up for the festival.[102]

Dois de Julho's importance for some of its participants is clear from a dispute regarding the participation of the National Guard's Third Battalion in the parade. Based in Salvador's commercial lower city, this unit enrolled large numbers of Portuguese-born shopkeepers and clerks. In 1836, well before 2 July, *O Democrata*, an Exaltado newspaper edited by Cabral, railed against the commander's assertion that he and his men would parade on the day: "The celebrations of Dois de Julho are not the government's; they belong especially to the Bahian people, who do not on that DAY want to line up with their oppressors, those rude vandals who did not respect virgins, widows, the elderly, [or] the sanctuaries of religion."[103] It is not clear whether this battalion paraded in 1836, but the following year, the president ensured that it would not by rearranging the National Guard duty roster. An impassioned appeal from its lieutenant colonel, in which he argued for the equality of all guard battalions and pointed out that there were many natives of Portugal in other units, did not move the authorities, who were pandering to nativism or perhaps simply seeking to forestall violence.[104]

Several elements of these early Dois de Julho celebrations raise important questions about the invention of this tradition and its meaning for Bahians. Its origins lie squarely in the heady mix of radical-liberal politics, Bahian identification with the *pátria* (the homeland or the province), and lusophobic nativism. The celebration of Bahia should not, however, lead us to reduce Dois de Julho to a regional festival or to argue that when Bahians spoke about the *pátria* on Dois de Julho, they meant only their province. Rather, Bahian patriots – like the archbishop in 1830 – saw Dois de Julho as central to Brazilian independence. As the *Diário da Bahia* concluded in 1836, it was "one of the Brazilian empire's most magnificent days," on which our "political independence was decided" – a theme to which Bahian patriots would repeatedly return.[105] Likewise, Rio de Janeiro's *Diário Fluminense* stressed in its report on 1826's Dois de Julho that "Bahians are Brazilians, and their patriotism does not die."[106]

Some looked to their past to endow Bahian patriotism with a long history. On 2 July 1837, Inácio Acioli de Cerqueira e Silva, then the São João Theatre's manager, produced Manuel Antonio da Silva's *A restauração da Bahia em 1625 ou A expulsão dos holandezes* (The Restoration of Bahia in 1625 or The Expulsion of the Dutch), a transparent allegory that drew explicit parallels between "the first Bahian triumph over oppression and despotism" and Dois de Julho two centuries later (unlike during the 1828 parliamentary debate, no one appears to have questioned the parallel between fighting for the restoration of Portuguese colonial rule and fighting for independence).[107] No doubt Inácio Acioli's research into Bahian history, which was then resulting in the first volumes of his *Memórias históricas e políticas da província da Bahia* (Historical and Political Memoirs of the Province of Bahia, 1835–37), informed Silva's play, given the friendship between the two men noted in the play's dedication.[108]

As in post-revolutionary France, Bahian patriots' mobile allegories – the *carros triunfais* – were considered more radical than fixed ephemeral monuments.[109] The nature of these floats, however, remains unclear. None of the contemporary accounts from this period refer to the figure on them as a *caboclo*, a term that would not come into use until after mid-century, and then only sporadically. Notwithstanding their differences regarding the dating and the sculptor to whom they attributed the emblem, Amaral and Querino concurred that the first allegory was a male figure. However, all of the explicit descriptions from these years refer to a female figure. Like *O Bahiano* in 1829, the *Diário da Bahia* referred in 1836 to the "symbol of America, trampling underfoot a monster representing Despotism," while João Pereira Ramos, who preached that year, identified it as "Catarina, first-born queen of Brazil and a spirited representation of the beautiful American continent."[110] Alexandre José de Mello Moraes Filho, the Bahian-born folklorist whose work Querino never acknowledged, referred in 1887 to the "triumphal float" that "in the early days [*em épocas primitivas*] ... carried a *cabocla* with her savage attire, stepping on a dragon, surrounded by little *caboclos* likewise dressed in feathers," which was understood as an allegory of "Paraguaçu crushing despotism at her feet."[111]

This evidence, in short, suggests that the first *caboclo* was actually a *cabocla*, that a female Indian allegory was the first symbol of Bahian independence. It likely drew on older European representations of America as an Indian woman, which Brazilian artists also deployed.[112] This female allegory had much in common with Spanish American patriots' use of Indian women as symbols for their new nations. As Rebecca Earle has shown, these female figures typically held bows and arrows but rarely assumed aggressive poses.[113] What makes the early Dois de Julho symbol distinct is thus her vigorous stance in the act of subduing the serpent or dragon representing (Portuguese) despotism. These aggressive qualities are today associated with the male *caboclo*, not the passive contemporary female *cabocla*. The association of this active woman with Catarina Paraguaçu marked another innovation – colonial portraits represented her as a demure and devout Catholic.[114]

Such use of Indian allegories began well before the rise of romantic literary *indigenismo*, usually dated to the late 1830s. Like the later literati, Bahian patriots identified with an indubitably American but safely distant past and traced their ancestry back to a non-Portuguese source; hence the allusions to Paraguaçu (much the same reasoning underlay Romantics' interest in finding an indigenous past to stand in for the medieval history that Brazil did not have).[115] Members of the late-colonial elite boasted of their (remote) Indian ancestry, and at the time of independence, hundreds of Bahians changed their names to identify with Bahian places, flora, and fauna; one in ten of them chose an indigenous name.[116] Tracy Devine Guzmán adds that Indians' relatively small numbers, their dispersion over Brazil's vast territory, and their division into small groups that "lacked any meaningful access to self-representation" made them easy to appropriate as symbols.[117] Needless to say, Bahians could hardly trace their origins back to Africa, given the presence of slavery and the numerous African slave revolts that were taking place at this time; Indians were in these respects a safe choice. As many have pointed out, the appropriation of Indians as a symbol for the nation flew in the face of the brutal and sometimes even genocidal frontier warfare being waged against independent indigenous people.[118]

Dois de Julho patriots sang enthusiastically, as indicated by the many new anthems reported in the press. What is today known as the Dois de Julho anthem is usually attributed to Ladislau dos Santos Titara, whose poetry has often been cited on these pages (see figure 1.2). It begins with the lines:

> The sun rises on Dois de Julho
> It shines more brightly than on the first [of July]
> It's a sign that on this day
> Even the sun is Brazilian.[119]

The illegitimate mixed-race son of a lawyer who fathered two other poet sons (Antônio Ferreira dos Santos Capirunga and João Gualberto Ferreira dos Santos Reis), Titara could not go to Portugal to continue his studies because of the independence war. Instead, he served in the Exército Pacificador as a scribe and archivist, and as Pedro Labatut's secretary. He combined an undistinguished military career on the army staff with his literary ambitions and would eventually publish eight volumes of poetry, including the massive *Paraguaçu* (1835–37), a history of the independence war in verse.[120] Titara published two anthems, composed for Dois de Julho celebrations in 1828 and 1829. A note in his collected verse explains that the music for the former was

Figure 1.2 | Ladislau dos Santos Titara

*Source:* AIGHBa, pasta 09, reg. 0710. Reproduced with permission.

by José dos Santos Barreto, to whom the anthem's music is today attributed.[121] However, neither anthem contains the modern lyrics. The earliest explicit reference to them that I have found is in Constantino do Amaral Tavares's 1857 *Elogio dramático* (Dramatic Laudation, 1857), which concludes with the "day's old anthem: *The sun rises on Dois de Julho*."[122]

The 1828 anthem's lyrics include a radical-liberal refrain that would eventually be incorporated into the current Dois de Julho anthem:

> Never again will despotism
> Govern our actions
> Brazilian hearts
> Do not tolerate despots.[123]

Alongside the radical-liberal refrain, Titara's 1828 anthem praised Pedro I as the defender of Brazil's liberty and called on Bahia's leading citizens to follow his example, to "respect the laws," and to "spurn vile [self]-interest."[124] These were not just shameless bits of adulation; they remind us that, until very near the end of his reign, many saw Pedro I as a liberal champion. This also likely meant that after 1831 it would have been difficult for radical liberals to sing anything but the refrain, which, as early as 1833, a French visitor recorded as one of Bahia's characteristic winter sounds.[125] In September 1829, the refrain turned up in a much more forcefully radical-liberal anthem sung by Pernambucan Exaltados during Recife's independence-day celebrations.[126]

Several accounts from this period indicate that on 2 July Bahian patriots wore coffee leaves, a symbol whose meaning remains obscure. One folklorist suggests that coffee sprigs, like olive branches, symbolized peace. While Bahia produced some coffee, it was then still very much a secondary crop; moreover, at that time coffee was not yet a major Brazilian export, although the Brazilian coat of arms and flag featured coffee and tobacco leaves. As in Rio de Janeiro, coffee leaves, as well as green and yellow croton foliage, were also partisan, Exaltado symbols, and the refusal of some officers to wear coffee leaves in 1830's Dois de Julho sparked critical comment from *O Escudo da Constituição*.[127]

Up to this point, I have often alluded to the nativist anti-Portuguese rhetoric that figured prominently in the early Dois de Julho celebrations, even though it was often criticized as dangerous and inappropriate. Citizens of the former mother country had an ambiguous status in newly independent Brazil. Under the terms of the 1824 constitution, all of those living in the empire at the time that independence was proclaimed in their province of residence automatically gained Brazilian citizenship (provided that they had not opposed independence).[128] This generosity did not sit well with Bahian patriots, who repeatedly called for the dismissal of Portuguese natives from government posts or for their expulsion from the country (especially if they had expressed only lukewarm support for independence). As the Portuguese-born Pedro I increasingly demonstrated what Exaltados saw as authoritarian tendencies and displayed (in their view) excessive interest in Portuguese affairs, an association between Portuguese and absolutist emerged in political rhetoric as well. That many Portuguese were petty shopkeepers lent an economic edge to this hostility, especially among the poor, who targeted them for violence during the revolts of 1824, 1831, and 1837–38.[129] Dois de Julho patriots regularly declaimed against Portuguese and refused to associate with them during the celebrations; however, I have found no sources indicating that anti-Portuguese violence took place during the celebrations.[130]

The archconservative Viscount of Pirajá (Joaquim Pires de Carvalho e Albuquerque), whom patriots had suspected of plotting to proclaim Pedro I an absolute ruler in the mid-1820s, saw nothing redeeming in the festival. He complained that in 1837, patriots had obliged a Portuguese man to free a slave, and he worried that scenes of "blacks killing whites" would surely lead to "some trouble."[131] Given the social composition of the contending forces in 1822–23, any reasonably accurate representation of a battle could be interpreted in the way as was done by Pirajá. In all likelihood, obliging a Portuguese man to free a slave did not represent an incipient anti-slavery sentiment among patriots; rather, the slave in question probably had a claim to patriotic service during the independence war. Some slaves who had served in the Exército Pacificador received freedom after the war; others did not.[132]

Dois de Julho, which began as a radical-liberal demonstration in 1827, had turned into a popular civic ritual that, to judge by Campos's transcription of the *Diário da Bahia*'s coverage of 1836's festival, united Bahians in commemoration of the mobilization that had been necessary to win independence. Campos, however, carefully omitted all of the radical-liberal outbursts that punctuated the *Diário*'s accounts, an indication of this folklorist's effort to suppress the early Dois de Julho festival's political context and to portray it as a consensual, patriotic celebration. The full texts of the *Diário*'s articles, as transcribed by Lizir

Arcanjo Alves, make it clear that their authors saw the festival as a radical-liberal political demonstration.[133] To be sure, not all shared this view, but there is no way to know whether any Bahian periodicals criticized the celebrations the same way that Maia's *O Imparcial Brasileiro* questioned 1830's Dois de Julho or the same way that Pirajá rejected the festival's radical elements. The founding of the Sociedade Dois de Julho had the effect of institutionalizing the celebrations; it likely also imposed greater coherence and order on them. As in so many other realms of Bahian society, however, the Sabinada marked a turning point. For a few years, it appeared that the festival had been largely destroyed, along with Bahia's radical-liberal movement.

## Repression and Restoration, 1838–47

Military discontent and radical liberalism fused in the November 1837 Sabinada Rebellion, which drove the provincial government from Salvador, proclaimed a republic (albeit a temporary one, to last only until the majority of Pedro II), and held off planter-led forces until its bloody repression in mid-March 1838. The Sabinada's outbreak is usually understood as a reaction to the September 1837 Regresso, a change of government in Rio de Janeiro that brought to power the Saquaremas (conservatives closely tied to the interests of planters and slave traders in Rio de Janeiro). However, Juliana Serzedello Crespim Lopes has recently suggested that it was also driven by the frustrations of Exaltados, who had expected that the institutions created by the Ato Adicional would open up more space for them in Bahian politics, an important recognition of provincial political dynamics.[134] An alliance among some former Moderados and former restorationists (advocates of Pedro I's return to the throne), the Saquaremas stood for a stronger and more centralized state. They were reacting to the liberal reforms of the late 1820s and early 1830s, and once in power, they facilitated the illegal slave trade. They identified themselves as the Party of Order in reaction to what they perceived to be growing disorder in the country.[135]

The Sabinada's bloody defeat cast a long shadow over the next decades. Two and a half years of intense repression, overseen by President Tomás Xavier Garcia de Almeida (April 1838 to August 1840), only ended with the August 1840 amnesty, issued by Pedro II shortly after the proclamation of his premature majority. Purges, military and civilian trials of rebels, a complete reorganization of the National Guard, the transfer of Bahian army battalions to other provinces, and efforts to root out radical-liberal elements dominated his administration.[136] Loyalty to the monarchy was the order of the day, and, like the national government, Bahian governments invested heavily in monarchical symbolism and ritual, all of which culminated in the July 1841 coronation, commemorated in Salvador on 7 September of that year.[137]

The "Majority," as it is known in Brazilian history, amounted to a parliamentary coup against Conservatives. However, members of the Party of Order or Saquaremas soon returned to power. They presided over the coronation and then completed the work of strengthening the state by reinterpreting the decentralizing Additional Act, instituting a national police hierarchy of delegates and subdelegates, and modifying other liberal reforms of the 1830s. When Pedro dissolved the chamber of deputies, which had been scheduled to meet in 1842 (elected in 1840, this legislature would have had a Liberal majority), Liberals in São Paulo and Minas Gerais took up arms in rebellions, which were quickly defeated. The Liberals' enemies dubbed them the Luzias, after the site of their defeat, Santa Luzia. This rebellion had relatively little impact in Bahia, likely because of the post-Sabinada repression and because of the still limited development of political parties in the province. Pedro pardoned the rebels in 1844 and called moderate Liberals back to power; a series of relatively weak Liberal cabinets held office until 1848, when Pedro recalled the conservative Saquaremas to power, a period analyzed in the next chapter.[138]

Needless to say, back in 1838, Garcia's administration saw little of merit in Dois de Julho. In 1846, the *Diário de Pernambuco*'s correspondent explained that after the Sabinada, "the program of the celebrations customarily held on this day was much changed, and the festivities limited to a simple parade, and almost nothing else." He credited Garcia with this and claimed that his successor was maintaining this policy.[139] Yet the new president could not entirely ignore Dois de Julho. In late June 1838, the city council issued its *bando* inviting citizens to attend the Te Deum, to illuminate their windows, and to engage in "licit entertainment." Loyal elements of the National Guard mustered for a parade downtown (not a procession into the city), and the *Correio*

*Mercantil* reported that "various demonstrations of public rejoicing" – official celebrations – had taken place.[140] The Viscount of Pirajá, who had been named director of the festival, claimed that there had been no time to prepare the floats and happily reported that he would limit Dois de Julho to a Te Deum and a "lavish illuminated monument" with an image of the emperor, which would "put an end to the fun and games [*divertimentos*]." Pirajá himself published a laudation (perhaps for distribution at the theatre gala) in which he hailed the victory of "Unity, Law, Throne, [and] Empire" and praised the patriotism of a long list of planter families.[141] Patriots attempted to raise funds for the festival in 1838 and 1839, but the provincial assembly refused to vote them any.[142] The celebrations of 1839 were little different and "on the Terreiro there was a sumptuous stage, on which could be seen the effigy of the August Brazilian Monarch." It would be illuminated for several days.[143] At the theatre gala, Titara steered a careful course, warning against "identical disasters":

> Vile, atrocious, and uncontrolled despotism,
> And liberty, when unrestrained and cruel
> Both are dragons that, desiring blood
> Devour, like Saturn, their own sons.

His brother, Capirunga, took the easy way out and recited some shameless adulation of Garcia.[144] In a poem produced for that year's *bando*, Titara alluded to the custom of parading into the city from Lapinha, but I have found no indication that this actually took place.[145]

Dilton Oliveira de Araújo suggests that the conservative *Correio Mercantil* – the only newspaper available for these years – deliberately ignored the popular or radical-liberal festivities as part of its effort to impose order on Bahia.[146] However, the fact that the *Correio* reported extensively on these celebrations in 1840 suggests that Garcia and Pirajá generally had their way in 1838 and 1839. The celebrations of 1840 began during the evening of 1 July at Lapinha, where a "large gathering of people" celebrated all night with "singing, music, fireworks," and other licit entertainment. The usual artillery salutes hailed the dawn, and all morning, "a numerous concourse of people from all classes" filled Lapinha and its environs. "Lavish triumphal arches adorned the streets" through which the "allegorical float" passed en route to downtown. This procession involved no military personnel, and the National Guard merely formed up on the Terreiro de Jesus for its parade after the Te Deum, an indication that Garcia's administration was maintaining its distance from the festival. An elaborate theatre gala took place that evening, while the city's main streets were crowded with "copious groups of ladies and men enjoying the beautiful spectacle" of the temporary monuments and the streets illuminated by lights that citizens had placed in their windows.[147]

The *Correio Mercantil's* report offered no indication of who organized these celebrations. Unsurprisingly, its coverage focused on Pedro II; it lovingly described his image on the monument on the Terreiro de Jesus and published poetry that hailed him as the hope for Brazil's future. It also devoted several paragraphs to the unanimous cheers to Garcia at the theatre gala, a pro-government demonstration also reported in the *Diário de Pernambuco*.[148] Three weeks after this Dois de Julho, Pedro was proclaimed of age. Garcia immediately tendered his resignation, and his successor was named two days before the 22 August amnesty.[149]

Before 1841's Dois de Julho, the liberal cabinet that had resulted from the majority collapsed and was replaced by another conservative administration, so provincial government policy towards the festival remained unchanged. The new cabinet's appointee as president, José Joaquim Pinheiro de Vasconcelos (June 1841 to August 1844), took office just before 1841's festival and would preside over three more Dois de Julhos. Very little is known about the festivities during these years, but nothing suggests that Vasconcelos departed from Garcia's policies. The police ordered that 1841's celebrants not disguise themselves; nor were they to engage in "dances, or games that are not permitted."[150] By 1843, however, the late June *bando* had regained its pre-Sabinada form, including "masqueraders on foot or on horseback, all conspicuous, either by the perfection or by the grotesqueness or humour of their costumes." The invitation issued a few days before the *bando*, however, merely recommended that people come "uniformed in white jackets and pants, and black hats wrapped with green and yellow ribbons." *O Comércio* reported that "the triumphal float ... had been conducted amid shouts of joy to Lapinha Square" on the night of 1 July and described the next day's procession: no military units had been ordered to accompany it on 2 July, so the "symbolic float" entered the city "alone, accompanied only by a few enthusiasts."[151]

The same newspaper condemned "those who begrudged seeing the people, the rabble, as they call them, amuse themselves, celebrate, and circulate through the streets crowned with palms and flowers." It also castigated Vasconcelos for his refusal to send troops to accompany the procession on 2 July. Although this had been the government's policy since 1838, it now presented an inexplicable insult to Bahians' patriotism that could hardly be justified by fear of "disorder and uproar," which had in fact never broken out during the celebrations.[152] Indeed, festival organizers had for some years been calling for military units to parade; in 1841, they petitioned the provincial assembly to pass a law that "all available military troops" accompany the procession into the city, "as in the first years." The disposition of military personnel was entirely outside of the assembly's jurisdiction, so nothing came of this.[153] Also that year, the assembly voted a subvention of 300$000 (US$162) to the festival; however, deputies declined to increase this amount as organizers requested in early 1842.[154] O Comércio further criticized Vasconcelos for failing to lead cheers to Dois de Julho at 1843's theatre gala.[155] As the Diário de Pernambuco correspondent noted in 1846, Vasconcelos was continuing Garcia's policy of limiting official involvement in the festival. Unlike Garcia, however, Vasconcelos was a Bahian who had played a part in the struggle for independence, so his reticence towards the festival was particularly offensive to O Comércio.[156]

President Francisco José de Souza Soares de Andréa (November 1844 to August 1846) adopted a new policy towards Dois de Julho. The future Baron of Caçapava was a surprising appointment by the cabinet of 2 February 1844, which pardoned the 1842 Minas Gerais and São Paulo rebels and ushered in the so-called "Liberal Quinquennium," a half-decade of government by a series of short-lived Liberal cabinets. An army general who had gained his principal political experience in suppressing rebellions in Pará and Rio Grande do Sul, Andréa had last served as the previous Conservative cabinet's president of Minas Gerais (March 1843 to May 1844), during which he oversaw the persecution of those associated with the 1842 revolt. In Bahia, Andréa received a simultaneous appointment as commander of arms, a concentration of civil and military authority normally only seen in provinces facing revolt. The Luzias and their Exaltado predecessors had long castigated him for his failure to respect the law and constitutional precepts; moreover, his Portuguese birth made him an easy target for nativists.[157] Contemporary observers were puzzled by the appointment; one historian suggests that the cabinet was seeking links to non-Saquarema conservatives like Andréa.[158] As president, Andréa tried to reform the provincial administration. He quarrelled with the provincial legislature and faced what he described as a mutiny of Salvador's National Guard when he imposed an unpopular commander.[159]

When it came to Dois de Julho, however, Andréa demonstrated considerably more political subtlety than he is normally credited with. He explained in 1846 that the "celebrations" were "more brilliant than normal ... because, for my part, I have joined in and accepted many demands," presumably from those who sought to restore the festival to its mid-1830s glory.[160] The *Diário de Pernambuco* correspondent described Andréa as "the restorer of the old festival, as it had been created during the first anniversaries" – in other words, he authorized army troops and the National Guard to accompany the patriots into the city – and he "associated himself to all of the celebrations." In these respects, he "demonstrated himself [to be] more Bahian, more Brazilian, than his predecessors, all native-born Brazilians." Even though one of his daughters was seriously ill in 1846, he spent the entire day among the celebrants. According to the correspondent, he "went everywhere to give cheers and to show a smiling face."[161]

To the radical-liberal opposition, led by Cabral's *O Guaicuru* and Inácio Acioli's *O Cabalista*, Andréa's actions must have looked like an attempt to take over their celebrations (and his smiling face like a cynical mask). In June 1845, *O Guaicuru* published two letters to the editor that condemned the prominent role that Andréa would play during the upcoming festivities; no self-respecting Brazilian would subject himself to a Portuguese man on Dois de Julho, declared one.[162] Apparently 1845's festival took place peacefully, but the conflict between Andréa and radical liberals came to a head during 1846's theatre gala, as the result of an incident that has entered Bahian folklore. Contemporary sources generally concur on the sequence of events. Manoel Pessoa da Silva, an amateur poet and former provincial civil servant whom

Andréa had reportedly tricked into resigning his post with the promise of a better position, recited an improvisation on the Dois de Julho anthem's refrain ("Never again will despotism / Govern our actions"), gesticulating towards the president as he declaimed against the "dregs [escória] of humanity / Who reneged their cradle," and making it clear that he was associating Andréa with tyranny.

While the audience roared approval or rejection of Pessoa's performance, Andréa's son, a major and his father's aide-de-camp, forced his way into the poet's box and struck him with a lash; a brief scuffle ensued during which, according to O Guaicuru, the poet's wife broke her ivory fan across the major's face (other newspapers denied this). The police delegate and theatre inspector, who had earlier warned Pessoa not to insult the president, intervened and arrested the major. Pessoa and the rest of the party in his box (including Inácio Acioli, the man whom Andréa blamed for the Guard "mutiny") left the gala, which resumed without incident. Four days later, after hearing a few witnesses, the police dropped charges against the major. On 4 July, the president received loud and enthusiastic cheers before the opera, which O Guaicuru attributed to people given tickets by the police to attend; another journalist doubted this, for the audience did not look like a paid one, but the Diário de Pernambuco correspondent admitted that "some friends of the president" had purchased about 100 tickets for a pro-government claque.[163] Inácio Acioli praised his friend, the "talented bard," for his "refined patriotic ideas" and hoped that Pedro II would soon dismiss Andréa.[164]

The incident quickly became a national one as opposition deputies brought it to parliament. José de Barros Pimentel attacked Andréa and declared the incident an insult directed against "all the enlightened men of Bahia," doubly so for it had taken place on 2 July.[165] Legislators took predictable positions. João Mauricio Wanderley (the future Baron of Cotegipe), who would soon emerge as a pillar of the Bahian Conservative Party, invoked the filial obligation to defend fathers and argued that the poet had deliberately set out to insult the first authority of the province.[166] Pimentel retorted that nothing justified such an action on Dois de Julho and worried that it would revive the "deplorable antagonism" against Portuguese.[167] Antônio Pereira Rebouças, himself an independence veteran, in an attempt to link Dois de Julho to Brazil, condemned this "unprecedented insult … against all of us Brazilians, on one of the most solemn days in the annals of our history and political independence."[168] On the last day that the issue was discussed, João José de Oliveira Junqueira, another Bahian deputy, made a striking comparison: had the president been insulted on 2 December (the emperor's birthday), "a day that we so greatly respect, Major Andréa would not have done what he did. But because it was the day of Bahia's glory, the day of triumph for Bahian arms, a day that appears not to have been understood by the Andréas," the major had felt no need to restrain himself.[169]

In light of Andréa's efforts to participate in Dois de Julho (and to manipulate it), Junqueira was mistaken about the general-president's ignorance of Bahian traditions. Nevertheless, by now it was clear that Andréa had lost the capacity to administer the province, and mere days after this debate, the government dismissed him, replacing him with Antônio Inácio de Azevedo (August 1846–September 1847). According to Dilton Araújo, this judge adopted a more conciliatory policy towards radical liberals. In August 1847, Pessoa returned to his post in the provincial treasury, but he remained tarred with the nickname "Manoel Chicotada [Whipped Manoel]." As late as 1877, a man offended at one of Pessoa's satires threatened to deal more harshly with him than had the Andréas.[170]

Querino made no mention of Andréa's role in restoring the Dois de Julho celebration. He did, however, write about the general-president's reservations about the indigenist symbol, particularly its aggressive posture. Before the 1846 festival, Andréa reportedly questioned the appropriateness of the male Indian stabbing a serpent or dragon; he considered it offensive to Portuguese, for it amounted to "one nation crushing another." He insisted that patriots adopt a more neutral symbol, Catarina Alvares Paraguaçu. Angry patriots refused to abandon their cherished symbol, but on Andréa's insistence, they accepted that the passive female figure would join the male one on 2 July.[171] In his 1910 biography of Manoel Pessoa da Silva, Querino claimed that the poet had been spurred to insult Andréa by patriots upset at the general-president's efforts to suppress the *caboclo*.[172] Elsewhere, Querino attributed the *cabocla*'s design to the sculptor Domingos Ferreira Baião, a student of Bento Sabino dos Reis (the artist to whom Amaral attributed the original *caboclo*).[173] As with the creation of the *caboclo*, Amaral told a very different story. In 1871, he referred vaguely to some "citizens" who "a few years ago" had another "wagon of modern style" constructed to carry "a beautiful *cabocla*, symbol of liberty." Some years later, he dated this to 1840.[174] João Varela's inform-ant told still another story about the *cabocla*, whom he described as having been created "on the initiative of students," years after the ori-ginal *caboclo*.[175]

Querino's account of the modern *cabocla*'s origins has been widely repeated and is now part of Dois de Julho's official history.[176] It seems consistent with Andréa's intervention in the festival, and many no doubt saw an Indian stabbing a serpent as an allegory of one nation crushing another; yet a careful reading of the available primary sources reveals no evidence to support Querino's account. Cabral's *O Guaicuru*, de-spite its frequent attacks on the president under the provocative head-line of "Andréa's Charlatanry and Stupidity," does not mention a *cabo-cla*'s creation.[177] Moreover, there is no contemporary evidence that by the mid-1840s the two allegories were parading together. In fact, all of the sources from this decade refer to a single "triumphal float," and as Socorro Targino Martinez observes, accounts of the festival only start to refer consistently to two allegorical figures in the parade as of the early 1850s.[178]

Descriptions of the symbol are far fewer than references to a single "triumphal float" in the late 1840s, and they rarely indicate the symbol's gender. Two explicitly refer to a male figure. In 1846, Cabral hailed "the republican Indian [índio]," while in 1847, the *Correio Mercantil* referred to the "triumphal float with the bust of the spirit of Brazil" (perhaps different from the statue of an Indian trampling and stabbing despot-ism), which it later characterized as a "caboclo," the first use of this term that I have found.[179] *Caboclo* today is a pejorative term for a rural hick or a person of mixed European and indigenous ancestry; in the nineteenth century, it was more commonly a synonym for Indian.[180] By contrast, a cluster of sources from 1849 referred to a single female allegory ("o carro da cabocla").[181] Likewise, the monk-poet Luís José Junqueira Freire celebrated an active, radical-liberal, female Indian in his 1848 poem "O hino da cabocla (canção nacional)" (The Cabocla's Hymn [National Song]).[182] The persistence of an active female figure

through the 1840s and the consistent references to a single allegorical float suggest that, of the nineteenth- and early twentieth-century
folklorists, Alexandre José de Mello Moraes Filho came closest to getting the *caboclos'* history straight. Unfortunately, he said little about
the *caboclo's* creation: "Later, this *cabocla* [the original active female
allegory] was replaced by the figure of an indigene [*por uma figura
de indígena*] [presumably a male one], without the same pomp or the
same following."[183]

But images of Indians were not necessarily radical in themselves.
Perhaps based on oral tradition or on his reading of newspapers that
have not survived, Querino described two "enormous" male Indians
sculpted in 1847 by Manoel Inácio da Costa (to whom the folklorist
attributed the original *caboclo*). They stood beside the bandshell in
front of the Presidential Palace; one of them "held a cornucopia [from
which] poured flowers, fruits, etc.," while the other "displayed the
national flag and held a heart." The *Correio Mercantil* described another Indian allegory on display that year as "the effigy of the spirit
of Brazil crushing the hydra of despotism."[184] These were, of course,
fixed allegories, and therefore less radical than mobile ones. The contradictions among the surviving sources make it impossible to provide
an exact description of the Dois de Julho symbol(s) as it (they) stood at
mid-century, but the allegorical figure(s) and its (their) wagon(s) were,
by then, well-established icon(s), carefully stored in a coach house on
Maciel de Baixo Street (rented by the Sociedade Dois de Julho) and
paraded each year through the city, much like the saints' images that
are so central to religious festivals.[185]

Dois de Julho's origins as a radical-liberal demonstration whose pro-
moters reworked parts of traditional colonial civic ritual and added
new elements make it a prime example of how a tradition is invented.
The radical-liberal patriots who invented Dois de Julho did not tailor
it out of whole cloth; rather, they adapted elements of colonial civic
and religious ritual and added their own innovations, such as the procession into the city and the Indianist allegory, which in turn drew on
older representations of America. Dois de Julho can also be seen as a
combination of the three forms of "ritualizing" in Brazilian culture described by Roberto DaMatta in the 1970s: carnivals, military parades,

and religious processions.[186] Bahian anthropologists have criticized DaMatta's model, and I have elsewhere suggested that his emphasis on military parades as Brazil's characteristic form of civic ritual flows from the practices of the military regime that then held power. Nevertheless, his model offers a means to disentangle Dois de Julho's elements.[187] Regardless of whether the symbol(s) was/were male or female, they resembled secular saints, conducted through the city like their Catholic counterparts. Authorities' efforts to ensure an orderly celebration, with disciplined military participation, reflected the state's concerns. The carnivalesque – often political and oppositional – flourished on Dois de Julho, just as it had existed alongside colonial civic and religious ritual.

A widespread contemporary view about Dois de Julho is that its early celebrations belonged to the *povo* (the people) and were appropriated over time by the authorities and the elite.[188] This tells the story backwards. Radical liberals, claiming to represent the *povo* (and certainly more representative of them than the more conservative provincial elite), seized elements of official civic ritual in 1827 and invented new forms of celebration. These remained controversial, and the authorities could never quite bring them under control, although Pirajá, Garcia, and their ilk came close to doing so in the aftermath of the Sabinada Rebellion. The first effort by authorities to intervene in the festival (as opposed to repressing or ignoring it) backfired. President Andréa opened space for radical-liberal patriots to restore key elements of the festival, and the 1850s would mark Dois de Julho's nineteenth-century apogee.

The recourse to Indian symbols to represent the nation was not unique to Bahia. Many new American nations sought legitimacy through embrace of their indigenous past. Patriots elsewhere in Brazil represented the nation as an Indian figure. In Pernambuco's 7 September 1829 celebrations, a painting of Pedro I receiving an Indian trampling the dragon of despotism was featured on a mobile pyramid towed through the streets by Indians.[189] Images of peaceful, reclining Indians appeared on the arch that welcomed the Baron (later Marquis and Duke) of Caxias into São João del Rei after the defeat of Minas Gerais's 1842 liberal revolt.[190] In a propaganda lithograph produced in the mid-1820s, Pedro I is portrayed as rescuing an attractive (and almost white) woman dressed in feathers from the clutches of a man with African features and a snake.[191] Later in the century, the illustrated press would develop the (usually unarmed) male Indian figure as the symbol of Brazil.

Much remains obscure about the first quarter century of Dois de Julho celebrations. It is clear that patriots adopted Indian allegories as their symbols; their actual form is less certain. All indications are that the original *caboclo* was a *cabocla* and that she was an active figure. This apparently bothered some – perhaps even Andréa – so it is worth noting that two of the three nineteenth- and early-twentieth-century folklorists or memoirists who described the earliest Dois de Julho celebrations wrote her out of their accounts. There are insufficient sources for us to reconstruct the patterns of commemoration, year by year, so we cannot ascertain today how key elements of the Dois de Julho celebrations were invented. Nor is there much information on how the festival was organized. Thus, this chapter's history of Dois de Julho's invention is necessarily suggestive rather than definitive.

# The Volcano's "Most Magnificent and Sublime Spectacle": From Political to Popular Festival, 1848–64

In 1861, a correspondent described Dois de Julho as "the political celebrations, the festivities of July, which Bahians remember wherever in the world they find themselves."[1] His observation is cryptic. On the one hand, he recognized Dois de Julho's political nature, which I emphasized in the previous chapter's discussion of the festival's radical-liberal origins. On the other, he implied that Dois de Julho belonged to all Bahians and served as a marker of Bahian identity. This claim signalled a major change from the festival's first decades, when it was primarily an Exaltado political demonstration. To be sure, Exaltados sought to speak for all Bahians (indeed, for all Brazilians), but this was merely a claim to representativeness, not an objective description. Building on the correspondent's observation, this chapter traces the changes in the festival that turned it into a civic ritual that all Bahians could claim for themselves.

Holding a festival for all Bahians implied drawing boundaries between those who were part of the community and those who were not, a task that is key to identity formation. I will examine this issue more fully in chapter 4. It also implied encouraging the broad participation of diverse sectors of society. In 1854, a writer in *O País* declared that the celebrants included "the young, the old, children, men, women, the poor, the rich, the happy or the unfortunate."[2] *O País* was then the mouthpiece of Bahia's radical liberals, so this may have been his attempt to claim broad support for their cause. That said, many others in the mid-1850s pointed out that Dois de Julho celebrations attracted participants from across the social spectrum. As was typical of nineteenth-century Brazilians, this writer said nothing about race and did not mention slaves; foreign observers, however, pointed to significant Afro-Bahian participation in the festival (also discussed in chapter 4). While Dois de Julho retained the forms and (more important) the rhetoric of the Exaltado years, by the second half of the 1850s it had become a celebration that mobilized *all* Bahians. The festival's scale – especially the massive 1 July nocturnal processions of the 1850s – preoccupied some authorities and observers, and in 1860–61 the Sociedade Dois de Julho and other festival organizers suppressed this element of the festival.

Bahian politics after mid-century have been barely studied; despite the prominence of Bahians in national politics, no narrative exists to guide us through the impact on the province of mid-century changes in national government. Bahia's Exaltados enjoyed a brief moment of glory during João Duarte Lisboa Serra's month-long presidency (11 September–12 October 1848). Appointed by the last and most partisan of the Liberal Quinquennium's cabinets, Serra hastily named sympathizers to government posts and, according to one conservative critic, threw open the Presidential Palace's doors to men who had not been allowed in since the Sabinada Rebellion.[3] On 29 September 1848, Pedro called the Party of Order to power, and the new cabinet quickly appointed Francisco Gonçalves Martins as provincial president. During his long tenure (October 1848–August 1852), this sugar planter and former chief of police imposed party discipline on the fractious Bahian conservatives.[4] Radical liberals in Pernambuco rebelled rather than relinquish office. Their so-called Praieira Rebellion of 1848–49 had many sympathizers in Bahia, but just as in 1817 and 1824, Bahia's radical liberals did not take up arms in support of their Pernambucan allies (or they were prevented from doing so). Nationally, the Saquarema cabinet achieved major successes by putting an end to the slave trade in response to British coercion and by removing Juan Manuel de Rosas from power in Buenos Aires (thus turning Brazil into the regional hegemonic power).[5] In Bahia, Gonçalves Martins, who as chief of police had presided over the Sabinada's repression, served as the lightning rod for radical-liberal criticisms during Dois de Julho celebrations.

The Saquarema cabinet gave way in 1852–53 to the so-called Conciliação, a ministry composed of moderates from both parties. Emperor Pedro II strongly supported this non-partisan cabinet, with its emphasis on *melhoramentos* (improvements or economic development). In the 1860 elections, radical liberals (now known as Históricos [Historicals]) returned to the political scene, scoring some electoral success in Rio de Janeiro. Pedro's distaste for what he saw as their excesses, and his reluctance to embrace the conservative Saquaremas (also known as Vermelhos [Reds] or Puritanos [Puritans]), led him to cobble together a series of moderate cabinets and eventually to sponsor the Liga Progressista (Progressive League), an unstable alliance of moderates from both parties that would dominate government until July 1868.[6] These shifts in national government, each of which brought new provincial presidents to Bahia and sometimes significant turnover among local officeholders in preparation for elections that the new government invariably won, were often reflected in the Dois de Julho festival as opposition groups used the celebrations to demonstrate their power and to make known their views. But this politicization of the festival differed from that of earlier years, in that by the 1860s, all parties were seeking to advance their interests through the celebration, which no longer belonged solely to radical liberals although it retained much of their rhetoric.

Despite its relative decline, Salvador remained Brazil's second city and an important commercial and cultural centre. Bahia could not keep up with the development of high culture such as opera in Rio de Janeiro, but Salvador could claim a lively intellectual life around the medical school and the Instituto Histórico da Bahia (Historical Institute of Bahia, 1856–77). Local playwrights developed a Bahian school of theatre (see chapter 5). The city boasted an active periodical press, and the 1912 catalogue of the state library's newspaper holdings lists fully 150 periodicals published between 1848 and 1864.[7] Only a handful of these newspapers, in partial runs, have survived in Rio de Janeiro's Biblioteca Nacional, and those still extant certainly give an incomplete view of the range of debate in the province's press. Like their

counterparts elsewhere in Brazil, Bahian journalists enjoyed considerable freedom to publish, although the government occasionally shut
down radical-liberal periodicals. Balduino José de Souza Magalhães,
publisher of *O País*, served two months in prison in early 1855 for abuse
of press freedom; before the end of his sentence, *O País* ceased publication, but another radical-liberal periodical, *O Protesto*, took its place.
One of the *Jornal do Commercio*'s correspondents judged that "there
was no greater anachronism" than *O Protesto*'s "radical and virulent
language" in the new era of Conciliação.[8]

This chapter begins by examining the highly politicized Dois de
Julho celebrations of the years after 1848. These marked the Exaltados' last hurrah as the festival's dominant group. The bitterly contested
celebrations of 1849, 1850, and 1852 are relatively well documented, and
that press coverage clearly indicates that the Exaltados remained the
loudest voices among Dois de Julho celebrants. However, parallel developments were turning Dois de Julho into a more broadly Bahian
festival. Some of these had been under way in the 1840s and then flourished in the 1850s. As patriots re-created the festival in the 1840s, they
founded the so-called patriotic battalions, civilian associations whose
members established a nocturnal procession on the night of 1–2 July
that, in the 1850s, grew larger that the 2 July parade into the city. Foreigners and Brazilians alike marvelled at this patriotic efflorescence;
some, though, had deep reservations about what they perceived as a
dangerous night-time gathering. It was abolished in 1861, and in later
years other nocturnal celebrations were eliminated. For radical liberals, the 1 July procession was the true popular Dois de Julho; the official
rituals of 2 July were merely empty state ceremonial.

## Exaltados and Saquaremas

The arrival of the Conservatives (Saquaremas) to power in September 1848 raised the stakes in Dois de Julho commemoration. The new
president, Francisco Gonçalves Martins, and his chief of police, João
Maurício Wanderley, faced determined opposition from radical liberals (Luzias) who claimed Dois de Julho for themselves and who excoriated Gonçalves Martins as the "Suit-Coat Napoleon," in other words,
a civilian despot.[9] Dois de Julho celebrations from 1849 to 1854 were

full of lively Luzia demonstrations laced with loud radical-liberal rhetoric. Exaltado periodicals portrayed Dois de Julho as a popular liberal
festival in opposition to the "despots" who governed Bahia and who
oppressed its long-suffering *povo*.

Well before 2 July 1849, Salvador's *Correio Mercantil* warned its readers not to listen to "certain perfidious individuals" and declared that
the holiday would be celebrated "with pomp, enthusiasm, and lively
patriotism, for Bahia loves her liberty, defends the constitution, and
adores the monarchy"; more important, Bahians were satisfied with
their political leadership, whose policy was one of "tolerance, justice,
and liberty."[10] The Luzia version appeared in a correspondent's letter
to Rio de Janeiro's *Correio Mercantil*: the Sociedade Dois de Julho did
not want to organize celebrations with which the Napoleon would be
associated, so Gonçalves Martins sought out "foreigners from a certain nation," in other words, Portuguese, for donations to fund the festival, an insult to Bahians' pride and dignity. Nevertheless, more than
six thousand people accompanied the "triumphal float" to Lapinha
during the night of 1–2 July "amid thunderous cheers to the Liberals, to the Luzia Party, to the memory of [Joaquim] Nunes Machado"
(the Praieira leader who died in the rebellion earlier that year), "to the
Pernambucan martyrs, and to *O Século*" (then Bahia's leading liberal
periodical). The "povo" did not join the daytime procession on 2 July
and "thereby signalled its disgust with the ways that the Napoleon conducted himself." Gonçalves Martins got a further comeuppance from
Friar Raimundo, whose sermon after the Te Deum was so "liberal" that
it left "the Napoleon and his people ... ashen-faced." On 4 July, some
Liberals sought to demonstrate outside of *O Século*'s offices, located
above the coach house where the allegorical float was stored on Maciel
de Baixo Street, but Gonçalves Martins "claimed that there would be
unrest that night" and put the police on alert, which prompted the
Luzias to disband their celebrations.[11]

Saquarema accounts of these events claimed that the cheers on
1 July included "Death to the Saquarema *marotos*" (a pejorative nickname for Portuguese) and "Death to the Miguelistas" (a nickname for
Saquaremas), but dismissed these as the work of a handful of medical
students, boys from "a liberal school run by Dr. Malaquias [Álavres
dos Santos]," and certain criminal elements. The celebration of 2 July
was "magnificent," and "waves of joyous people" joined the proces-

sion. Friar Raimundo only advocated support for the constitutional monarchy and "respect for and obedience to the legally constituted authorities." Reports that "the *liberalorum*" would disrupt the return of the floats on 4 July – in fact, "invitations for gatherings [of men] armed with clubs and knives" – prompted the police to double their patrols. When a group of thirty or forty demonstrators tried to raise Luzia cheers, Chief of Police Wanderley personally dispersed them by announcing that the festivities were over. Conservatives lamented this politicization of Dois de Julho and wished that people would just focus on "the commemoration of our emancipation."[12] Próspero Diniz's *A Marmota* tried to make light of the provocations between Saquaremas and Luzias, wished that all could have celebrated in peace, and condemned the "asinine cheers" during the nocturnal processions involving the triumphal float.[13] Of course, it was impossible to celebrate independence alone, without implicitly or explicitly commenting on the political arrangements that had resulted from the break with Portugal, so Diniz's hope remained, at best, a naïve wish.

In 1850, much the same squabbles about Dois de Julho took place. The Conservative *Correio da Tarde*'s correspondent reported that before the festival, "anarchists" had appealed to "men who had the misfortune of having been born slaves" to join "liberal patriots" in anti-government movements; it then praised Vice-President Álvaro Tibério Moncorvo Lima (Gonçalves Martins was then representing Bahia in the chamber of deputies) and Chief of Police Wanderley for their effective work to contain this imminent rebellion.[14] As far as the Liberal *O Século* was concerned, Dois de Julho had always been "odious to the *povo*'s enemies," and since the Saquaremas' rise to power, no one wanted to celebrate on that day. Its editors turned up their noses at the "pungent" official celebrations and claimed that there was no popular enthusiasm; only a few determined "members of the popular classes [*populares*]" had bothered to take the triumphal float to Lapinha. They offered an ironic compliment to Tibério when they praised him for not leading a cheer to the constitution at the theatre gala, for that was an accurate reflection of his government's policy.[15] Salvador's *Correio Mercantil*, strongly supportive of the government, highlighted the "enthusiastic *povo*" on 2 July, the "general satisfaction" during the great parade, the cheers "warmly repeated" before the imperial effigy, the massive crowd at the theatre gala (despite the rain), and the "numerous concourse of citizens" that returned the triumphal float to its depository on 3 July amid "acclamations."[16] Alexander Marjoribanks landed at Salvador on 1 July; knowing nothing of the political issues at stake, nor anything about Dois de Julho, he judged that Brazilians had a custom "of clubbing together a number of festival days" so as to celebrate them "with additional splendour." He saw "a review of the troops," the illuminated public buildings, and "a grand display of fireworks."[17]

It is impossible to determine which of these accounts of 1849 and 1850's Dois de Julho celebrations is more accurate. Each journalist saw the festival through the lens of his partisan leanings, and the traveller saw only the most visible aspects of the celebrations. *O Século* and the *Correio Mercantil* make clear that the celebrations had taken place according to the familiar forms, yet the festival's meaning was completely different for each. The radical liberals who cheered the defeated Praieira leadership sought to keep alive the struggle against the Saquaremas. With its extensive street festivities, Dois de Julho was particularly suited to such manifestations, during which Bahia's Luzias wrapped their message in patriotic celebration.

The bitterly disputed celebrations of 1849 and 1850 marked a high point in the public battles over Dois de Julho's meaning, although this assessment may be a reflection of the surviving press accounts (1850 is a rare mid-century year for which we have competing coverage from politically opposed Bahian periodicals). What *is* clear is that radical liberals were continuing their campaign with its anti-Portuguese rhetoric, calls to nationalize retail commerce, and demands for a constituent assembly, notably through the coordinated publication of the *Argos* newspapers in several provinces from 1850 to 1852–53.[18] In 1852, rumour had it that the "opposition [that wanted a] constituent assembly" planned to sully the festival "with disorders." Thus, "[t]he program for the liberal festivities included shouting *long live* and *death to*, throwing rocks at certain houses, and even demolishing the market building that Tomás de Aquino Gaspar [was] building."[19] Rio de Janeiro's *Correio da Tarde* also reported these rumours but dismissed them as "April fool's jokes, or *entrudo* [carnival] games."[20] Their source was apparently a 17 June article in the *Argos Baiano*, which proclaimed in its title that there would be "[a] Certain Revolution on the Glorious Day of Dois de Julho"; it called for a constituent assembly and the nationalization of retail commerce, while railing against Portuguese and tyrants. According to *O Grito Nacional*, which published the *Argos's* article in Rio de Janeiro, the hasty dispatch of two navy steamers to Salvador indicated that the government expected a revolution.[21] *O Século* reported that the provincial government had reinforced the police by calling up a National Guard battalion and issuing extra ammunition to the troops. It denied that a revolution was in the offing and reminded its readers that Dois de Julho had always been celebrated peacefully.[22] In the end, no revolt took place on 2 July 1852 and *O Grito Nacional* claimed that the celebrations had been more elaborate than in any previous year.[23]

Few sources are available for 1853's Dois de Julho. The following year, *O País* portrayed Dois de Julho as primarily a radical-liberal demonstration that focused on denunciations of despotic government, calls to nationalize retail commerce, and political poetry. All of the verses recited during the evenings "conformed to the liberal beliefs, censured the dark times in which we find ourselves, protested the oppressive politics that is crushing us: [all were] against the monsters in power, who have established an absolute and despotic government, through which they intend to enslave us entirely."[24] It seems that, unlike in previous years, the provincial and national governments did not view this rhetoric as threatening; apparently, they took no actions to forestall such demonstrations. The authorities did eventually force *O País's* closure by obtaining a rare conviction of its publisher for abuse of press freedom. On 2 July 1855, its successor, *O Protesto*, lamented the autocracy under which Bahians lived as well as the Conciliação, which merely served to silence Bahians' justified complaints.[25] Exaltados' efforts to retain control over Dois de Julho drove a major innovation in the festival that had been quietly gathering strength in the late 1840s – the 1 July nocturnal procession. Before examining this development, however, we must consider Dois de Julho's symbols and the festival's administration.

## The Festival's Symbols

In the last chapter, I presented evidence about the nature of Dois de Julho's Indianist symbols and concluded that, most likely, the original *caboclo* was a *cabocla* and, more important, an active female figure. This contradicts Dois de Julho's official history, which is based mostly on Manoel Raimundo Querino's accounts of the *caboclo*'s creation in 1826 and of President Francisco José de Souza Soares de Andréa's insistence that patriots adopt a passive *cabocla* in 1846. Almost all of the surviving evidence indicates that a single allegory was conducted into Salvador in the procession on 2 July until the early 1850s. As late as 1853, a correspondent described a single "wagon that carries the *cabocla*, a symbol of America crushing despotism underfoot" – in other words, an active female figure.[26]

The program for 1852, by contrast, announced that the procession would be led by "the old triumphal float, elegantly prepared, representing the struggle for independence, and the Spirit of Brazil crushing despotism." This allegory would be followed by "a lavishly prepared new triumphal float symbolizing the spirit of Brazil victorious."[27] Unfortunately, this program does not indicate the symbols' gender, but it suggests that one allegory was active and the other, perhaps, passive or resting contently. Was 1852 the year that the *cabocla* finally joined the *caboclo*, to summarize the point on which Querino and José Álvares do Amaral agreed (that the original symbol was male)? Or was it the year that the old *cabocla* began to give way to a *caboclo*, as Alexandre José de Mello Moraes Filho would have it? The evidence from subsequent years is too vague to answer this question with confidence.

Almost all of the references to the allegories in correspondents' reports from the rest of the 1850s and early 1860s are in the plural, but these writers offered no descriptions of them and rarely used the terms *caboclo* or *cabocla* (indeed, the terms scarcely appear in nineteenth-century press coverage of the festival).[28] The most important exception to this silence about the allegory's form comes from the pen of Francisco Bernardino de Souza, the first Bahian to describe the festival for the benefit of outsiders as so many folklorists later would. He referred only to a single image, which he described as "an indigenous [man], armed with bow and arrow, and vigorously trampling a serpent, arching up under the pressure, whose blood pours from a wound inflicted by the Indian's arrow."[29] He did not use the term *caboclo*, but his account describes an active male figure. If Padre Bernardino's account is, as it appears to be, a description of Dois de Julho in the mid-1850s, it is consistent with Mello Moraes Filho's version of the symbols' history, which held that a male figure predominated after the marginalization of the early active female one. However, it contradicts the large number of references to multiple allegories in this decade.

The earliest explicit contemporary source that contains all of the elements of the current *caboclos* – two Indian figures parading together, an active male figure and a passive female one – also dates to 1862, but comes from a literary source. The stage directions for the climactic scene in Constantino do Amaral Tavares's *Os tempos da Independência* (The Era of Independence; see chapter 5), first performed in 1861, called for "two old-fashioned elegant wagons, on the first of which stands a *caboclo*, stepping on a dragon, holding in his right hand an arrow, with which he injures the animal, and in the left the Brazilian flag; and on the other a *cabocla*, who holds in her right hand a flag and, in the left, a piece of paper on which 'Independence, Liberty, or Death' can be read." The lead character explains that the *cabocla* represents "a people's nationality [*nacionalidade de um povo*]" and the *caboclo*, "crushing the dragon ... Brazil winning its liberty."[30] In 1863, Francisco Moniz Barreto hailed "the beautiful Indian woman [*a indígena formosa*]" and "the triumphant Indian man [*o índio triunfante*]" as they passed on their return to Lapinha.[31]

According to Mello Moraes Filho, a "supply wagon [*carro da bagagem*]" followed the symbols in the procession into the city; laden with fruits and other produce, it apparently represented the Recôncavo's bounty brought into the starving city by the patriots. The surviving newspapers never mentioned this allegory, but in 1853, organizers borrowed agricultural implements and baskets from the Navy Yard for one of the wagons that would join the "triumphal retinue."[32] Much later, João Varella's informant recalled these heavy oxcarts, their noisy axles squealing, and the foodstuffs that were donated to a charity hospital after the parade.[33]

More important than the symbols' exact forms and their accompaniment were their multiple meanings. They might represent Brazil (or the "spirit of Brazil") or independence (sometimes described as "our Emancipation" or "our unparalleled victory") or America.[34] The dragon or the serpent might represent despotism or, as in Querino's account of Andréa's understanding of the symbol, the Portuguese

Figure 2.1 | A *caboclo* on the masthead of a radical liberal periodical, 1851

*Source*: *O Abatirá* (Santo Amaro), 2 July 1851.

nation (in radical-liberal rhetoric, the two were often synonymous). As political symbols, *caboclos* belonged mostly to radical liberals, and one of their newspapers featured a *caboclo* on its masthead: *O Abatirá* (Santo Amaro, 1850–51) (see figure 2.1).

The Queimado water company's fountain, erected in the mid-1850s on Piedade Square, shows a female Indian trampling and stabbing a serpent (see figures 2.2 and 2.3); as president, Wanderley approved the design in early 1853, but nothing else is known about how it was selected.[35] In 1859, Pedro II described it as "a statue of America treading on a dragon."[36] These active female figures apparently troubled some, and late-nineteenth-century and twentieth-century writers regularly called the figure on the Piedade fountain an "índio" or a "caboclo," both masculine terms, despite her naked breasts![37] The *cabocla* on this fountain, however, never figured in Dois de Julho celebrations, although it likely resembled the early active female allegories.

The discussions of the *caboclos'* origins in this and the previous chapter underscore the well-established insights that symbols have

Figure 2.2 | The *cabocla* on the Companhia do Queimado Fountain, 1850s

*Source*: Photo by Hendrik Kraay, 2001.

Figure 2.3 | The Companhia do Queimado Fountain in its original location on Piedade Square, ca. 1860

*Source*: Ribeyrolles, *Brasil*, vol. 3, plate 39.

multiple meanings and that they matter deeply. They are never merely symbolic, and changes to them are serious business. The changes in the symbols that made Tavares's stage directions accurate for a play set in the 1850s likely took place in the middle of that decade, perhaps as early as 1852 as suggested by the program for that year. A passive *cabocla* would, moreover, have been consistent with Conciliação-era values. All that can be said with certainty is that Indian figures meant many things when they appeared on Bahian streets and squares during Dois de Julho festivals. They ranged from the scourge of (Portuguese) tyranny or of despotism, to founding mother figures of an American nation in the form of Paraguaçu, to exemplars of American bounty, to symbols of the Brazilian nation or even republican champions. To many, they probably represented more than one of these at the same time. Regardless of their meaning, all knew that the symbols were important. As one poet put it in 1854, the allegory "means everything for the *povo* that surrounds it."[38] The continued prominence of these sym-

Figure 2.4 | The Caboclo, 2 July 2011

*Source*: Photo by Hendrik Kraay, 2 July 2011.

Figure 2.5 | The Cabocla, 2 July 2011

*Source*: Photo by Hendrik Kraay, 2 July 2011.

bols in twenty-first-century Dois de Julho commemorations (figures 2.4 and 2.5) underscores this mid-nineteenth-century assessment.

## Festival Administration

The newspaper coverage on which most of this book is based typically offers little direct information on how civic rituals were organized, but there are sufficient indications from mid-century to go behind the scenes to see Dois de Julho organizers at work. Some aspects of

Figure 2.6 | Artillery preparing to fire salutes to welcome Pedro II,
6 October 1859 (*Note*: This image is incorrectly identified as "Conflito
causado pela pintura do pano de boca do Teatro S. João, 1854," in Martins
et al., *Iconografia*, 109. It was, in fact, taken on the same day as figure 5.1.)

*Source*: BN/SI, n. 07047. Acervo da Fundação Biblioteca Nacional – Brasil.

the festival were routine matters. The president issued orders for the
National Guard and the army battalions to parade, which commanders relayed to their subordinates; commanders requisitioned blank
cartridges to fire salutes.[39] The artillery salutes that James Wetherell
described as "deafening" in 1855 were another regular part of the festival's official ritual.[40] In the early 1860s, field artillery stationed on the
Terreiro de Jesus joined in these salutes. One elderly homeowner on
this square worried that the reverberations would cause his house to
collapse and twice requested that the artillery be moved to the square
in front of the theatre, where such salutes had formerly taken place
(see figure 2.6).[41] The inevitable accidents also took place: in 1862,
two soldiers were injured when a cannon's breech was not properly
closed (one lost a hand and the other two fingers).[42] By this time, it
had become fully accepted that regular troops and the National Guard

would accompany the symbol(s) during their entry into the city, for orders to this effect regularly flowed through the command hierarchy. Theatre impresarios had the contractual obligation to stage galas on days of national festivity (see chapter 5). The city council issued a proclamation inviting citizens to engage in licit celebrations.

Most of what made Dois de Julho unique, however, fell within the purview of civil society. The Sociedade Dois de Julho, founded in 1835, eventually came to control the triumphal float(s) and organized some aspects of the parade and other street celebrations. Another committee – distinct from the Sociedade at mid-century – also administered parts of the celebration. In 1848, the temporary monument on the Palace Square was raised by the festival committee while the one on the Terreiro de Jesus was the Sociedade's handiwork.[43] In 1864, the Sociedade wrote to the president to propose the customary collaboration between its members and the "Diretoria Geral dos Festejos [General Directory of the Celebrations]"; similar distinctions appeared in the 1852 program and in an 1853 missive to the city council (it was more common in later years to refer to this body as the Direção Geral dos Festejos, so this is how I will refer to it in this and the next chapter).[44] Both the Sociedade and the Direção appointed subcommittees to coordinate aspects of the festival; in their correspondence, these bodies did not always indicate which organization had constituted them, so it is difficult to determine the division of labour between the two organizations. While the Sociedade functioned like other legally constituted associations and elected its officers, I have found no indication of who appointed the Direção, whose membership for the following year was announced at the end of the festival.

In 1852, the first year for which I have a full set of names for the Sociedade's executive and the Direção, they were completely different organizations, for no individual served on both, a pattern that persisted in subsequent years.[45] Of the 140 men whom I have identified as having served either on the Sociedade's board or on the Direção between 1845 and 1864, only 3 ever served in both organizations. The Sociedade was a relatively closed corporation, with considerable repetition of personnel on its board. Dr. José Pedreira França served as president in 1852 and 1859 and as vice-president in 1860, 1862, and 1863. Eustáquio Manuel de Figueiredo likewise served seven times on the

Table 2.1 | Dois de Julho Festival organizers' social origins, 1845–64

| | Sociedade Dois de Julho executive members | | Direção Geral dos Festejos members | |
| --- | --- | --- | --- | --- |
| | Number | % | Number | % |
| Doctor | 5 | 16.7 | 38 | 33.6 |
| Military rank | 1 | 3.3 | 16 | 14.2 |
| Merchant | | | 11 | 9.7 |
| Title of nobility | | | 7 | 6.2 |
| Judge (*desembargador*) | 1 | 3.3 | 5 | 4.4 |
| Priest | 1 | 3.3 | 4 | 3.5 |
| Engineer | | | 2 | 1.8 |
| Other honorific (*conselheiro, comendador*) | | | 4 | 3.5 |
| Civil servant | 1 | 3.3 | 1 | 0.9 |
| No information | 22 | 70.0 | 25 | 22.1 |
| Total | 30 | 99.9 | 113 | 99.9 |

*Note*: Three men served on both the Sociedade Dois de Julho executive and the Direção Geral dos Festejos.

*Sources*: Sociedade Dois de Julho executive members, 1845–64; Direção Geral dos Festejos members, 1852, 1853, 1856, 1858–64.

board between 1852 and 1863, and José Álvares do Amaral was secretary in 1859, 1860, 1862, 1863, and 1866. The 113 men who composed the nine Direções whose names I have found (1852, 1856, 1858–64) normally did not serve for a second term; only 25 (22.1 percent) did so, and a mere 2 (1.8 percent) served a third term.[46]

The limited information on these men's social origins suggests that the Direção was a more elite organization than the Sociedade Dois de Julho's executive, to judge by their titles (see table 2.1). Proportionally twice as many Direção members boasted the title of "Doctor" (which denoted the achievement of higher education) than did members of the Sociedade's board. The engineers and priests, as well as some of the merchants and nobles, also held advanced degrees. No merchants or men with titles of nobility participated in the Sociedade, and only one held a military rank, in contrast to the sixteen Direção members with commissions (but there is no indication whether they served in the army or the National Guard). Amaral had studied engineering but failed to complete his education and worked as a provincial civil servant for twenty-seven years, as he explained in 1881 when launching his unsuccessful candidacy for a seat in the national parliament.[47] There are some indications that the Sociedade retained ties to the more radical wing of the Liberal party, the Historical Liberals. In 1857, João José Barbosa de Oliveira (Rui Barbosa's father) was its president, while Agrário de Souza Menezes led cheers during one of its functions; both men were closely associated with the Historicals.[48]

The Sociedade Dois de Julho published its statutes in 1845, something that President Andréa may have encouraged and an indication that it was becoming more established.[49] Its stated aim was to "immortalize the memory of the victorious day – DOIS DE JULHO – of 1823 with an illuminated display or other public and licit entertainment" on the Terreiro de Jesus or another square. Most of the rest of the articles dealt with routine administration, and they made no mention of the Indianist symbols or other allegories. Membership was open to all Brazilians resident in Salvador who demonstrated "moral and respectable conduct" and "public support for the cause of Brazil's independence." Those who resided outside the city could become honorary members; apparently, the society had made the provincial president an honorary member, although in 1845 and 1846 Andréa declined to attend its annual meetings of 25 June, at which the following year's executive was elected.[50] Membership cost relatively little: an admission fee of 3$000 (US$1.56) and monthly dues of 300 réis (US$0.16). Nevertheless, it was not easy to collect this money, as can be inferred from an 1849 appeal that members pay up so that the directors could pay the bills for the upcoming festival.[51] In 1847, the Sociedade put up a "little palace to display the effigy of His Majesty the Emperor" on the Terreiro de Jesus, requested that the president assign army or National Guard bands to perform on the evenings of 2–4 July, and asked that he lead cheers from this stage after the Te Deum.[52] Two years later, perhaps because of the problems in collecting dues, the Sociedade was less well prepared and *A Marmota* castigated its directors for failing to get to work early enough.[53] In 1855, the provincial assembly licensed the Sociedade to hold twenty lotteries to raise funds; it also sought an exemption from the national taxes levied on lotteries.[54]

Figure 2.7: The Lapinha Pavilion, ca. 1900 (*Note*: The republican coat of arms indicates that this picture dates from after 1889; renovations in 1918 significantly changed the building's façade.)

*Source*: AIGHBa, pasta 6, reg. 0378. Reproduced with permission.

The Sociedade Dois de Julho's control of the triumphal floats and the Indian statues can also be inferred from its decision to purchase a building on Lapinha's small square to serve as a permanent depository for the wagons in lieu of the rented coach house on Maciel de Baixo

Street. The society borrowed 2:000$000 (US$1,020) to acquire the property; by 1871, it had paid off the loan, aided by a provincial law that exempted the building from property tax. Although renovations to the building were not complete, the floats were stored there at the end of the 1860 festival (see figure 2.7).[55] The reasons for the society's decision to move the floats are closely connected to the changes taking place in the festival in the late 1850s, to which I will return.

Limited means dogged the early Direções, but in 1848, the provincial government authorized twenty lotteries to support their work; if fully subscribed, each lottery would raise 500$000 (US$255). More cautiously, that year's Direção estimated that the total revenue would not exceed 8:000$000 (US$4,080), or 80 percent of the maximum.[56] This may have been a supplement to the provincial budget allocation of a 300$000 (US$162) to "the 2 July celebrations," first approved for fiscal year 1841–42; in 1854, *O País* praised legislators for raising this "paltry" amount to 1:000$000 (US$560) and castigated the nine deputies who voted against this expenditure. The following year, deputies doubled it to 2:000$000 (US$1,120), a figure that would not change until 1895, by which time it was equivalent to only US$400.[57] There are also indications that the directors solicited donations in cash or kind. In 1854, they ran a citywide fundraising campaign, as can be inferred from the appointment of parish agents to receive donations, and they regularly implored the city council to support these efforts.[58] In 1848, the opera company agreed to sing for free at the Te Deum; however, in 1845, the Banco Comercial refused to donate.[59] Directors were also expected to pay for part of the festival, but in 1860, six of the fifteen failed to do so.[60]

The limited information on the Sociedade Dois de Julho executive's social origins suggests that this organization was solidly rooted in Salvador's lower middle classes, whereas the Direção drew its membership from the city's economic and political elites. This points to the socially broad nature of Dois de Julho participation, which was expanding beyond the festival's original Exaltado or Luzia core. Neither association, it should be added, was ever accused of being a front for radical liberals, an indication of how the festival had evolved. These two institutions were joined by many other less formally organized groups that also contributed to the festival. This "civil society" engagement, to use a perhaps anachronistic term, indicates the extent to which Dois de Julho had become a Bahian popular festival.

## The *Bando* and the Noite Primeira

While the Sociedade Dois de Julho and the Direção Geral dos Festejos busied themselves with fundraising, building monuments, and sprucing up the symbols, thousands of Bahians prepared to celebrate, starting with the *bando* in late June. For many, the mid-century festival's high point came on the night of 1 July, the so-called Noite Primeira de Julho (First Night of July), when patriotic battalions took the empty wagons to Lapinha. Then followed the official festivities, the great parade into the city on 2 July, the Te Deum and public cheers, and the theatre gala. Additional festivities took place for a few more evenings until the allegorical floats were returned to their depository. The *bando* and the Noite Primeira flourished in the 1850s, despite authorities' concerns about them; the latter was repressed in 1860–61, an indication of the ongoing tensions between popular patriots (including radical liberals) and the authorities.

The *bando* retained the colonial form of a proclamation, read aloud by a crier on (usually) 29 June, inviting residents to participate in the celebrations and to decorate and illuminate the fronts of their houses. The crier was accompanied by a drummer and a police guard, as well as other celebrants, who by the 1850s followed a route that took them from Lapinha to Campo Grande and back to downtown.[61] In 1848, Francisco Fausto da Silva Castro, one of the "directors of the committee" charged with organizing the festival, announced that he would lend "appropriate apparel" to all who needed it to accompany the *bando*, but there is no indication of what sort of costume or uniform this impresario was offering; the following year, participants were encouraged to costume (*mascarar*) themselves.[62] Organizers divided the procession into sections for those on foot, those in carriages, and those on horseback; in her unpublished novel, *Susana* (1900), Anna Ribeiro de Góes Bittencourt (1843–1930) recounts how well-off young men purchased horses or tried to borrow them from relatives in the Recôncavo, and a June 1854 advertisement offered "a young and dapper horse, suitable for the day of the *bando*." Mello Moraes Filho likewise described the participants as "young men of very good name ... mounted on handsome horses," and Tupinambá, an anonymous 1896 *cronista*, recalled how horses, fattened in Recôncavo stables, were brought into the city especially for the celebrations.[63]

By the mid-1850s, this ritual had become "the July [*sic*] carnival."[64] In 1854, the archbishop condemned the sacrilegious satires of those who wore clerical garb and complained about those who used the parade to mock the recently arrived French Sisters of Charity. Worried, he had written to the vice-president to ask for police intervention. The chief of police admonished organizers to prevent these demonstrations and later claimed that his warnings had limited the number of inappropriate costumes. The following year, the diocesan newspaper praised the authorities and the festival committee for ensuring that such scandalous activities did not take place.[65] The *Diário da Bahia* thought the costumes "shabby and without taste" in 1861; however, one correspondent especially liked "a fellow who completely transformed himself into a grasshopper." He did not, though, care for the critics of the new public school regulations.[66] The *bando* remained a popular festival, and not even heavy rains could dampen the enthusiasm in 1862.[67]

The sources on the *bando* offer no indication of who the participants were, but they were likely the same young men who, in the late 1840s, had turned the night of 1–2 July into the main part of the Dois de Julho festival. As we have seen, patriot gatherings and vigils had been held at Lapinha on the eve of 2 July as early as the late 1820s, and in 1836, there had been an evening procession to take the wagon there. This aspect of the festival gained prominence in the late 1840s, when it turned into a massive nocturnal procession to this square on the city's northern outskirts. Querino described the Noite Primeira de Julho as the most important part of the festival, at least before 1864.[68] His account, however, mixes elements from the 1850s with those of later celebrations, and the rise and fall of this nocturnal celebration followed a trajectory quite different from the one sketched by the folklorist.

In 1845, the "conductor [*diretor*] of the triumphal float" invited citizens to join him at midnight to take the wagon from Maciel de Baixo Street to Lapinha Square and called on residents along the route to illuminate their windows and to decorate their façades.[69] This was the first such invitation that I know of, and its dating to 1845 – the first post-Sabinada year that army troops joined the procession of 2 July – may indicate that some organizers sought to distance themselves from

President Andréa's innovations and may also reflect Andréa's will-
ingness to let the festival return to the forms of the mid-1830s, but I
have found no direct evidence for these interpretations. In 1848, the
festival organizers arranged to take the wagon to Piedade Square in
advance, and that square soon became the customary starting point.
The procession started at 10 p.m.; led by a military band, it traversed
close to the full length of the upper city, from south to north.[70] The
following year, the youth of Santo Antônio Além do Carmo parish received an invitation to gather in front of the Carmo convent, dressed
in white jacket and pants, with a black tie and a cap, to take the wagon
to Lapinha from the Terreiro de Jesus.[71]

This nocturnal procession grew rapidly in size. In 1847, the *Correio
Mercantil* reported that it involved a "great number of people of both
sexes"; the following year, it estimated that six thousand people had
taken part. Estimates from 1849 ranged from "3,000–4,000 people" to
"more than 6,000." In 1853, Rio de Janeiro's *Correio Mercantil* estimated
ten thousand participants; the following year, *O País* claimed that eight
thousand men marched, accompanied by at least three times as many
people, including "a very considerable number of ladies." The British
consul claimed (improbably) in 1858 that fifty thousand people normally took to the streets for this "Saturnalia in commemoration of the
expulsion of the Portuguese army in 1823."[72] More important than the
actual numbers (which, by any reckoning, were enormous for a city of
perhaps seventy-five thousand inhabitants) was the gradual organization of this procession. In 1849, *A Marmota* referred to three separate
gatherings of "upper-class youth [*a melhor rapaziada*] uniformed as
civilians [*a paisana*] wearing caps" with "2 de Julho" stamped on them.
Under the leadership of the two festival directors and "officers named
from among themselves," they took the wagon to Lapinha. The *Correio
Mercantil* added that these "battalions" were from Santana, São Pedro,
and Santo Antônio Além do Carmo parishes.[73]

These are the first indications of what soon became known as patriotic battalions, a form of associational life that has received no scholarly attention. Sixteen of them marched in 1854, eighteen in 1855.[74] In
1859, the *Jornal do Commercio*'s correspondent distinguished among
four kinds of patriotic battalions. First, there were those organized by
occupational groups such as the Caixeiros Nacionais (National Shop
Clerks, the leading advocates for the nationalization of retail commerce,

that is, the banning of Portuguese nationals from employment in this sector), the Legião da Imprensa (the Press Legion, apparently typographers), and the students in the Batalhão Acadêmico (Academic Battalion, the great rivals of the Caixeiros). A second type – for example, União Brasileira (Brazilian Unity) – expressed patriotic ideals, while a third mobilized men from districts and parishes. Finally, the Veteranos da Independência (Independence Veterans), their ranks thinning year by year, enrolled those who had fought in 1822–23. "In any case," the correspondent concluded, "they are units of no fixed size, organized with flags, uniforms, and leaders with military ranks [*patentados*]."[75] Mello Moraes Filho added that a company of Germans, presumably merchants from the German states (and their employees), joined the patriotic battalions and stood out for their "lavish standard, embroidered with fine gold." This fifth kind of patriotic battalion is confirmed by correspondents who singled out the Germans for praise in 1853 and 1855; in the latter year, the procession's "foreign division" made Bahia look like "a true Crimea," an allusion to the multinational forces then seeking to prevent Russia's expansion at Ottoman Turkey's expense.[76]

Bittencourt, who saw this parade as a teenager in 1857, added that her cousins "took part in the battalions from the schools that they attended." She also described the straw hats that the members of these battalions wore. They were cheap, only 80 réis (US$0.04), and "other than on this day, only urchins [*moleques*] or poor people wore them." In honour of the day, the paraders decorated these hats with flowers and leaves, especially those of the "green-and-yellow croton"; Mello Moraes Filho reported that tobacco and coffee leaves were the preferred foliage for decorating "straw hats that cost a *vintém*" or 20 réis (US$0.01).[77] Pedro Celestino da Silva, a twentieth-century folklorist, later claimed that Mello Moraes Filho had erred in his assertion regarding the use of such cheap hats by respectable patriots, for only the "troublemakers" at the end of the parade wore such plebeian headgear. Respectable patriots wore imported Chilean and Manila hats, he stressed, in a retrospective effort to draw social distinctions among the patriots. Celestino added that it was acceptable to wear croton sprigs – "Dois de Julho leaves," as they were sometimes called.[78] While folklorists often described the custom of wearing these leaves, newspaper writers almost never mentioned it, perhaps an indication that the practice was so familiar that it did not merit comment.[79] Visitors to Bahia in the 1850s remarked on "the Brazilian independence tree" or the "Independence flower," recognizing the significance attributed to these plants.[80] Later, when the custom of wearing foliage had disappeared, folklorists thought it important to mention. The hats and leaves, of course, echoed the Exaltado symbols of the early 1830s, but by this time, they had lost most of their former political significance.[81]

In 1856 and in previous years, retired brigadier Luiz da França Pinto Garcez, an independence war veteran and "the most popular army officer in the province," was awarded the honorary command of the parade. The following year, he was ill and the Baron of São Francisco (José de Araújo Aragão Bulcão, "who loves this day with the dedication of a true citizen") did the honours. In 1858, *Brasil Comercial's* correspondent reported bitter conflicts among battalions over questions of command and precedence.[82] Over the course of the 1850s, patriotic battalions became increasingly organized. They acquired their own distinctive banners and had them dedicated in church.[83] Organizers invited members to dress in white jacket and pants and promised to supply them with "the battalion's insignia."[84] Battalion commanders met to organize the procession and to elect its commander-in-chief as well as the division and brigade commanders.[85]

Writing for Rio de Janeiro readers, one correspondent vividly described the 1 July 1859 parade: "On the night of 1 July, the sight of the city is most interesting. From one moment to another, distant noise approaching is heard, one distinguishes voices, catches glimpses of light that rapidly spreads, and then there appears an army of torches that moves in cadence to the sound of bands, to repeated and enthusiastic cheers, and almost always accompanied by fireworks and crackers: it is a patriotic squadron or battalion passing by, and sometimes two or three that cross paths."[86] Another wrote in 1855 that he enjoyed seeing "the leading men of my province with penny hats and jackets; the fun was priceless." He made it to Lapinha to watch the "battle of verse and cheers," then went home "overcome with fatigue" at 3 a.m.[87] Adolphe d'Assier, who saw the festival in 1859, did not perceive the marching groups' purpose, merely describing them as "troops of young people and blacks [*nègres*]" carrying flags and torches who circulated through the streets to the sound of music, "patriotic shouts, the noise of firecrackers, fifes, and drums." He added that, while he had seen "plenty of national festivals in old Europe, nowhere have I seen such overflowing joy and such uninhibited gaiety."[88] Brazilians too marvelled at Dois de Julho. In 1857, Rio de Janeiro's *Correio da Tarde* explained to its readers that "only those who have been in Bahia on the anniversary of 2 July can accurately judge what that festival is like and [appreciate] the enthusiasm that it excites in every heart: and, far from extinguishing themselves over time, these feelings gain new strength every year."[89]

Organizers struggled to maintain the procession in a respectable marching order. In 1858, they implored the patriotic battalions to keep within twenty paces of each other and begged poets to recite their work only before the wagons and not as individual battalions passed by, for this would break up the procession and therefore undermine "the march's good order and the celebration's splendour." The following year, some battalions stopped to listen to poetry, which prompted others to take a different route, leading to "a great gap, which discredited" the procession.[90] Indeed, the night was as much about the poetry as it was about the procession. In 1856, the "patriotic procession" had to stop at least once in "almost every street" so that bards could recite "poems about the object" of the celebrations. *O País* collected and published some fifteen poems recited along the parade route in 1854, and Querino recognized the poets' importance by devoting most of his account of the Noite Primeira to transcriptions of verse.[91] The frequent reports that nothing disturbed the orderly celebrations underscore that the nocturnal procession was a potentially dangerous event.[92] Rivalries between patriotic battalions sometimes led to blows, but according to Bittencourt, nobody ever suffered serious injury because the combatants used nothing more than torches in the fights (the man beaten with torches wielded by members of a rival battalion in 1858 would likely have disagreed with this assessment).[93] Nevertheless, one correspondent, writing in 1856, could overlook "a few blows ... over precedence between two battalions" and declared that "nothing happened," thanks to the Bahian populace's "spirit of order."[94]

Padre Bernardino attempted to explain the 1 July procession's political meaning: "Besides being the *povo*'s celebrations, it is also a celebration of liberty." He described the gathering of the patriotic battalions, the parade through the city under the command of an independence war veteran, the poetry readings, and the arrival of the "fatigued, tired

[and] hoarse" celebrants at Lapinha. In the wee hours of the morning, they would go home to prepare for "the festival of the 2nd or, better, for the official celebrations, for the *povo*'s festival is the one of the night of 1st." The celebrants, he concluded, were "a very living proof that the love of liberty has not died among us, and that Brazilians are worthy of this precious gift from the heavens."[95]

The priest's 1862 assessment is a moderate version of the radical-liberal interpretation presented by a writer in *O País* in 1854. "O Brasileiro [The Brazilian]" contrasted the "extraordinary pomp of the eve [of 2 July] with the nearly aristocratic indifference" of the official ceremonies, which true liberals had boycotted. He argued that the celebrations of 2 July had degenerated into "a mere distraction for the people, an entirely official ceremony for the Government." By contrast, the *povo* rendered "worship and adoration to Liberty" on 1 July.[96] On 2 July, those passing under the arches built by the *povo*'s sweat usually included "a stupid Lusitanian, a tormenter of Brazilians, a sworn enemy of our liberty, who, under the appearance of patriotism and happiness, commands the Bahian troops." The prominent display of Pedro II's portrait in the cathedral, in the theatre, and even on the Sociedade Dois de Julho's stage meant that a foreign visitor would judge the day a *"regal festival and not ... a popular festival, entirely liberal and patriotic."*[97]

Such radical rhetoric persisted long after Exaltados or Luzias had ceased to be a political force. Radical-liberal demonstrations regularly took place during the nocturnal procession and sometimes on 2 July itself, but after 1852 there were no more accusations that Luzias were plotting rebellion; instead, diehard radical-liberal patriots railed against the Conciliação in verse. They declaimed against tyranny, singing the praises of liberty and nationalized retail commerce.[98] In 1855, some "never stopped talking about the nationalization of [retail] trade," and in 1858, one hothead shouted "death to the Bahian aristocracy" in front of a sugar planter's city home.[99] The *caixeiros*' demand that retail trade be nationalized arose from the dominance of this sector by Portuguese shopkeepers, who tended to bring young relatives from Portugal to work in their shops, a pattern that persisted into the twentieth century.[100]

Authorities and observers disagreed on how best to deal with this radical rhetoric. In sharp contrast to the worried government in 1852, some took it all in stride. Already in 1846 President Andréa explained that, "on this day, which they call 'our day,' it is customary for these people to tolerate reciprocal petty insults" (he did not indicate whether he would have meekly tolerated the poet's insults at the theatre gala had his son not reacted violently).[101] In justifying his failure to prevent the 1854 anticlerical demonstration, the chief of police lamented the populace's lack of respect for the Church, but added that little could be done on "the occasion of such celebrations ... when all entertainment is permitted." "Repressive measures involve some risk," and he could only appeal to "the public's good sense and morality."[102] The *Diário de Pernambuco*'s correspondent judged in 1855 that most of this radical-liberal discourse was empty rhetoric and that Dois de Julho was a time when radicals could let off steam: "There is no shortage of speeches, poetry, etc.: the *povo* likes this stuff, and the so-called *liberals*, for lack of anything more substantial, spread it around, even though it does not have the desired effect. Even so, the clever ones benefit, for they present themselves as disinterested defenders of public liberty to win ephemeral fame. At the end of the commotion, which is a prominent part of the public rejoicing, everyone forgets what they did, and already the next day nobody remembers the heavy irons, despotisms, tyranny, slavery, etc., that the poets portrayed."[103] In short, according to these men, Dois de Julho served as a political safety valve during which radical liberals could speak their minds, without however threatening the established order in a meaningful way. This is a classic functionalist interpretation of rites of rebellion.

Radical liberals lamented these changes in Dois de Julho and, more important, that their hopes for true liberty had been dashed.[104] João Nepomuceno da Silva's sonnet captured their feelings of loss:

> Love of the *pátria* and healthy fraternity
> Unity, valour, glory, patriotism
> Many deaths to sad servility,
> Many *vivas* to sweet liberty.
> Nobility, compassion, and equality,
> Heroic acts of courage, acts of heroism,
> Many curses on sad despotism,
> Insults to perverse iniquities.

I see it all in Bahians' mouths
When wrapped in shades of pride,
[They] happily and proudly circulate through the streets.
But – just as quickly as this noise goes away
So end the sovereign
Rights enjoyed on Dois de Julho.[105]

In his 1857 report to the provincial assembly, whose session had been delayed until November, President João Lins Cansanção de Sinimbu (August 1856 to May 1858) held up that year's peaceful Dois de Julho as evidence of the Conciliação's success in mitigating party conflicts: "The moderation, with which the population of this great city applauded the anniversary of the memorable Dois de Julho, without diminishing the enthusiasm for remembering its glories," exemplified the new order.[106]

Not all agreed with Sinimbu's assessment of the Conciliação or shared the view that radical-liberal rhetoric on Dois de Julho was a harmless vestige. Late in the 1850s, an undertone of worry crept into the descriptions of the nocturnal festival. In 1858, the *Diário do Rio de Janeiro*'s correspondent emphasized that the "eminently popular" festival had, once again, been orderly. He criticized the government, however, for its untoward confidence in the populace's "good sense" and its failure to take precautionary measures. Like the city of Naples, Bahia's authorities rested indifferently "at the foot of this volcano that sometimes presents the most magnificent and sublime spectacle." The following year, the *Jornal do Commercio*'s correspondent invoked similar imagery when he recommended putting an end to the "nocturnal march ... because on this occasion the city has one foot on the volcano of anarchy." Reluctantly, he admitted that "this year, as always, for now, everything took place in perfect order."[107] Rumours about plans to restrict Dois de Julho celebrations were sufficiently common that Tavares's *Tempos*, set in the 1850s, contains a reference to those who reportedly wanted to "put an end to the festival."[108]

A more sympathetic correspondent wrote in 1858 that Dois de Julho "is the terrifying spectre for despots and, for this reason, many want to end the popular demonstrations."[109] That year, these included some familiar figures. Gonçalves Martins and Wanderley, both temporarily retired from politics and tending to their plantations, were in Salvador and watched the Noite Primeira procession from a relative's house near the São Bento church (located between Piedade and downtown). Gonçalves Martins reported their discussions to a fellow Bahian, Navy and War Minister José Antônio Saraiva. The "many thousands" of participants organized into battalions took fully two hours to pass and constituted an "army" larger than any force that Brazil had ever fielded. "It is definitely essential to disperse the entertainment [*diverti-mento*] and not concentrate it in organized fashion," he recommended, "this being the tactic of an able president, who prepares amusements to replace [the Noite Primeira] with illuminations, equestrian tour-naments [*cavalhadas*], costumed revelry [*máscaras*], fireworks, im-provised theatre, permanent monuments to decorate the city, etc." Instead, he lamented, recent presidents had tried to "win popularity among the masses" and had let patriotic battalions elect serving mil-itary personnel to command them. Other votes had resulted in "thugs [*capadócios*] and men of colour" commanding battalions. From this, it was but one step to "revolt." Two years earlier, Tibério (who held the presidency from August 1855 to July 1856 after filling in seven times as vice-president for absent presidents) had reportedly led "toasts to liberty, protesting that despotism would never win dominance over the heroic Bahian people." Despite being a "good man to entrust with power," Manuel Messias de Leão, the vice-president then governing the province for the fifth time, lacked the authority "to go against the strong and loudly expressed will of the popular masses." Nevertheless, Gonçalves Martins had to admit that "complete order reigned."[110] He sent the letter on 2 July and wrote nothing about the rest of the cele-brations, which reportedly included "thunderous cheers" to Messias at the theatre gala.[111]

In October 1859, José Álvares do Amaral, then beginning his long tenure as the Sociedade Dois de Julho's secretary, proposed that the "patriotic symbols" be transferred to a "dignified depository," pref-erably at Lapinha. He later recalled several reasons for moving them from their old depository: The nocturnal procession was "something that had no meaning nor explanation"; in other words, it did not have any historical precedent like the parade into the city, which re-enacted the Exército Pacificador's 1823 entry. Moreover, the Maciel de Baixo Street coach house was "not very decent." It was low, so the statues had to be taken down in the street before the wagons could be parked. He added that the "symbols" were not mounted on the floats until the patriotic battalions had taken the wagons to Lapinha. Instead, they went to Lapinha "on the heads of slaves for hire" (Varella's informant recalled that for some years, a *pardo* carpenter, Manoel da Rocha, took the symbol to Lapinha as an act of devotion). The patriotic battalions towed the empty wagons through the city, and they sometimes arrived at Lapinha damaged or stained by the smoke of the patriots' torches. Worse yet, the participants' excesses left many so exhausted or even sick that they could not do their duty the next day as members of the National Guard. In 1860, the Sociedade's new president, none other than Vice-President Tibério, named a committee to oversee the purchase of the building that to this day houses Dois de Julho's symbols (see figure 2.7).[112]

Gonçalves Martins, the Baron of São Lourenço after March 1860, arranged to serve as chair of 1860's Direção (he also donated 200$000 [US$104] to the festival).[113] With Tibério, a loyal Conservative party man (he would not embrace Progressismo), in charge of the Sociedade, it was clear that the festival's organization was in the hands of its critics (apparently Tibério's heart had never been in the populism for which Gonçalves Martins had criticized him in 1858).[114] Amaral's politics are more difficult to square with his support for ending the nocturnal procession, for he is usually identified as a Liberal; that he served as one of Salvador's police delegates during the Progressista years suggests his distance from Historical Liberals.[115] His recommendation to concentrate the parading during the day on 2 July differed from Gonçalves Martins's 1858 recommendation to disperse the festivities, but it facilitated authorities' control over the celebrants. In 1860, patriotic battalions still formed the customary nocturnal procession, but the Sociedade Dois de Julho proudly announced that, at the end of the celebrations, the floats would be taken to the newly constructed "decent depository for the symbols of our independence and liberty."[116] Perhaps São Lourenço watched with satisfaction as the allegories were carefully backed into their new depository late in the evening of 4 July 1860.[117] There are no references to a nocturnal procession in later years. In 1861, the *Diário da Bahia* reported that "some people with a martial band" were planning to parade through the city during the evening of 1 July (despite rain, some bands took to the streets in 1863); the allegorical floats did not participate and went straight from the Lapinha pavilion into the 2 July parade.[118] In short, storing the symbols at Lapinha made the nocturnal parade redundant.

The ending of the 1 July procession could be viewed as a reaction to the radical-liberal demonstrations during Dois de Julho celebrations, although it took place after the Exaltados' and Luzias' efforts had waned. Amaral offered no political reasons for the Sociedade Dois de Julho's decision to purchase the building in Lapinha, and Gonçalves Martins alluded only obliquely to radical liberalism in his 1858 letter. His desire to disperse the patriotic "army," however, embodied what James Sanders has referred to as the "primal fear" of a politically engaged *povo*.[119] Later folklorists would attribute the Sociedade's decision to specific violent incidents involving the *caboclos* or the Noite Primeira procession; the incident mentioned by Querino took place in 1864 (see below), while the one described by Varella's informant cannot be documented in other sources. When the Sociedade failed to pay the rent on the coach house before one Dois de Julho, the informant recounted, the landlord attempted to hold the symbols hostage; threatening to kill him, members of the *povo* broke into the depository and removed the symbols.[120]

But who constituted the *povo*, whose parading so troubled the two Conservative statesmen in 1858? Bittencourt's cousins, the city's well-off young men, and the province's "leading men" were not the popular classes. Assier's description of parading "blacks" likely reflected his European racial ideas, not the marchers' self-identification. Yet even the lowest estimate of the number of participants (1849's three to four thousand) amounted to considerably more men than would have constituted the city's middle and upper classes at mid-century. This figure certainly also exceeds the number of people actively involved in Exaltado politics, an indication of Dois de Julho's broadening appeal. Gonçalves Martins's complaint that "thugs and men of colour cor" were winning elections to command patriotic battalions adds a racial dynamic to the concerns about the Noite Primeira. The poet Nepomuceno lamented around this time that even "slave lads [*moleques cativos*] were enlisting" in patriotic battalions, and he mocked a certain Gaspar, a runaway slave, who headed a battalion, dancing and drinking until slave catchers seized him.[121] Nepomuceno's poem was no doubt a satire, but it reflects the degree to which the Noite Primeira had become a popular festival and the extent to which identification with Bahia's independence reached deeply into society. The efforts to end nocturnal parading on Dois de Julho were made at a time when other popular-cultural practices were also coming under concerted attack. At the end of the 1850s, Salvador's city council finally passed an anti-*entrudo* bylaw, and in subsequent years, the police cracked down on the water play and other throwing games that were then an important part of street carnival celebrations. Also during the 1850s and 1860s, periodic campaigns against the Afro-Brazilian religion of Candomblé were launched.[122] To be sure, these efforts fell short as advocates of toleration and those who sought exceptions for their clients undermined the authorities' work. As it happened, though, the construction of the Lapinha pavilion effectively brought an end to the Noite Primeira procession, except for a brief restoration in the mid-1870s.

What the nocturnal procession meant to its participants remains difficult to determine. Was this merely a case of Bahians' penchant for celebration, for which "everything was a pretext," as historian Kátia M. de Queirós Mattoso observes?[123] Or was there more to it? Many historians have recognized the importance of parading as a way for social and occupational groups to publicly display themselves and claim membership in the community or nation.[124] No doubt, such motives drove many members of the patriotic battalions and underlay others' efforts to join the parade. Such participation did not necessarily imply radical liberalism, but to the extent that it constituted a claim to membership in the nation or in the community of Bahians, it shared affinities with radicals' efforts to expand citizenship, in this case through collective claims to public representation. Unsurprisingly, men like Wanderley and Gonçalves Martins saw this as a threat, even if, as is likely, many participants in the Noite Primeira procession were only there to amuse themselves.

## The Great Parade, Official Celebrations, and the Allegories' Return

It is not necessary to dwell in so much detail on the great parade of 2 July, for this procession was not controversial. By the 1850s, it included the army garrison, the National Guard, some patriotic battalions, and members of the *povo*, all of whom marched into the city, leading the symbols. Bittencourt and Varella's informant recalled that the president and other civil and military authorities joined this parade, but I have found no evidence for this in the surviving newspapers. According to Bittencourt, this procession "also sparked great enthusiasm" in 1857, "however more moderate" than that elicited by the Noite Primeira procession, a point on which others concurred.[125] In 1854, 5,000 people participated; in 1858, the army garrison and the National Guard mustered 3,000 men; the following year's military contingent was smaller, with only 1,884 guardsmen and army and police soldiers.[126] Who had the honour of pulling the patriotic symbols over the rough cobblestone streets remains unclear. In 1855, a company of fifty men "dressed in leather uniforms" was expected to perform the task, but there is no indication of who had organized this homage to the leather-clad patriot company from Pedrão that Padre José Maria Brainer had raised for the Exército Pacificador in 1822.[127] Two years later, the triumphal floats' entry was "very moving" because the Caixeiros Nacionais drew them into the city; this was evidently an innovation. In 1859, the Tipógrafos (Typographers) and Liceistas (Students) battalions pulled the floats.[128] After 1860, patriotic battalions regularly joined the 2 July parade. Dapperly dressed in white and sporting green sashes with their battalion name in gold letters, the Caixeiros Nacionais marched on 2 July 1861.[129] In 1862 and 1863, patriotic battalions followed army and guard units in a march past the authorities on the stage or at the Presidential Palace, indications that greater discipline had been imposed on the "popular" celebrants.[130]

At the downtown Terreiro de Jesus, the parade stopped at the temporary stage while the Te Deum took place. In 1859 and 1862, the mass started before the parade arrived, so army and National Guard officers arrived late for the service, an indication that the parade had not been fully incorporated into the other official celebrations.[131] There were complaints that the consular corps, most city councillors, and many high-ranking civil servants had failed to attend in 1864, but this was likely the Conservative *Jornal da Bahia*'s jibe at the Progressista administration.[132] The sermon was, as one correspondent put it, "entirely political" in 1861.[133] In 1863, the *Jornal* claimed that the preacher "pleased [the congregation] with his ideas about harmony and unity" but added that "radical Ligueiros [Progressistas] criticized him for not having lavished praise on the current government."[134] Subsequently, the president unveiled the outdoor portrait of the monarch and led the crowd in cheers. Within nineteenth-century Bahia's civic ritual culture, this was the only regular outdoor public veneration of the imperial image, an indication of the importance of including the *povo* in Dois de Julho celebrations. On other days of national festivity, only members of Bahia's elite and official Salvador paid their respects to the emperor's portrait during the so-called *cortejo*, an indoor ceremony at the Presidential Palace, as described by James Wetherell for 2 December 1852 (Pedro II's birthday).[135]

In the evening, amateur poets entertained the crowds from the illuminated stage, while the São João Theatre put on a gala performance. Accounts of the festival described downtown squares filled with "a very numerous concourse of people of all classes," who appreciated the music and the poetry.[136] Bittencourt later recalled, however, that the "good poets" no longer recited there in 1857 for "the most ignorant part of the *povo* had the bad habit [of] giving *pateadas* [foot stamping to show disapproval], sometimes undeserved." Nevertheless, she and her family spent the evening at the Terreiro de Jesus stage.[137] For two or three days, the symbols remained on display, and at night, the festivities continued in Salvador's main squares. In the 1850s, those symbols stood on the Palace Square in a temporary structure; from 1862 to 1864, they were displayed on Piedade Square.[138] I have found no explanation for this change of locale, which moved them away from the city's political centre (the Presidential Palace, the town council building, and the old cathedral flanked three sides of the Palace Square).

The Dois de Julho festival's final act was the return of the allegorical floats to their depository, either on Maciel de Baixo Street (until 1859) or at Lapinha (thereafter). Like the 1 July parade, this was a nocturnal procession. It may have been more rowdy than the procession to Lapinha, and there were complaints that it drew less distinguished participants than the procession that launched the festival. Writers in *O País* reported the usual political cheers in 1854: "to the NATIONALIZATION OF COMMERCE, to Independence and Liberty, to Dois de Julho, to the memory of ... Nunes Machado, to liberals, to the free press, etc."[139] In 1857, some of those involved "repeated the cry of 'down with the aristocracy'" in front of several houses.[140] One account of 1861's return echoes the enthusiasm with which some had formerly described the Noite Primeira, much of whose route it followed: "Windows and streets were crowded with people, who enthusiastically repeated the patriotic battalions' cheers! On these occasions, the *povo* is a beautiful sight! The harmonious notes of the bands that precede the battalions, the flowers and leaves with which the soldiers are armed, the national colours that flutter gallantly, the lights of a thousand torches, the general enthusiasm, the beauty of the firmament that covers the indescribable scene, all combine to electrify, to transport even those who [normally] look with indifference on these things."[141] The *Diário da Bahia*, however, reported "several conflicts"; one person was injured at the Terreiro de Jesus, while at Lapinha in the early hours of 7 July, "some imprudent [individuals] came to blows."[142] The ending of the 1 July nocturnal parade, it is important to note, did not initially affect this closing parade (after all, the symbols had to be taken back to Lapinha).

In 1863, amid rising partisan political tensions, the return to Lapinha became the flashpoint for Conservative opposition demonstrations. Summarizing the news from Bahia's newspapers, Rio de Janeiro's Historical Liberal *A Atualidade* described a peaceful patriotic celebration disrupted by a patriotic battalion "rudely calling itself the Alabama company," bearing a North American flag (the newspaper did not indicate whether this was the Confederate or the Union standard): "Armed with cudgels, they disrupted almost all of the [other] battalions, so much so that few made it to Lapinha." Several people were injured, and the Alabama battalion vandalized the grille work surrounding one of the city's new water fountains.[143] A Progressista correspondent explained that the *Jornal da Bahia* had accused the government of organizing Alabama to discredit Conservatives, but when the chief of police arrested some of its members a few days later, he discovered that they were in fact "the slaves of some well-known Vermelhos" or Conservatives.[144]

This appears to have been the incident to which Querino attributed the 1 July procession's ending, although he dates it to 1864.[145] Indeed, political tensions resurfaced with a vengeance that year, as opposition

Vermelhos struggled against Progressistas. Both of the *Jornal do Commercio*'s correspondents commented favourably on the numerous allusions to political questions during the *bando*, which they described as better attended and more "animated" than it had been for some years. A company of Zuavos (Zouaves) – identified by one correspondent as Liberals – that had paraded during carnival celebrations earlier in the year joined the *bando*.[146] More controversial was the company of Vermelhos; dressed in red, they bore a flag of the same colour emblazoned with these words:

> We are Conservatives
> A sincere political group
> Whose goal it is to uphold
> God, the Throne, and the Law.

The Conservative correspondent argued that "if the men of the emerging dominant party [*situação política*] can display themselves among the *povo*'s merry-making, those excluded from the *pátria*'s banquet must be allowed to accompany them," but the police did not see it that way and confiscated the banner, much to Progressista observers' satisfaction.[147]

A few days later, President Antônio Joaquim da Silva Gomes (March–October 1864), moved against the custom of returning the floats to Lapinha at night; he ordered that the procession take place at 4 p.m. on a Sunday afternoon.[148] The *Jornal do Commercio*'s correspondents expressed very different views on this initiative. One wholeheartedly supported it, explaining that "the innovation pleased [many] for, in fact, popular festivals during the day are more serious and orderly," echoing the concerns about the 1 July procession.[149] The Conservative correspondent, who had earlier emphasized that Dois de Julho had been celebrated without enthusiasm – the festivities were "merely official," few houses had been illuminated, and many skipped the Te Deum in protest against the government – claimed that the president feared an opposition demonstration during this parade.[150] This decision, however, alienated those who normally supported the government; rumours spread that patriotic battalions would seize the symbols the day before the scheduled return, so the president placed a police guard around them and ordered army cadets to form a loyal patriotic battalion for the return. Only three real patriotic battalions showed up for the ritual, which was dominated by armed forces personnel. In the end, "it was entirely official and completely militarized": there were few cheers and few poems, and people glumly watched the parade from their windows. This correspondent added that many Conservatives actually "applauded the change," not because they were afraid of the nocturnal parade, but because they recognized that Liberals might take advantage of it to attack them. As evidence for this, he cited the *Jornal da Bahia*'s support for the floats' daytime return and the involvement of the patriotic battalion, União Brasileira, commanded by Antônio Olavo da França Guerra, a publisher of Conservative newspapers.[151] Nonetheless, the *Jornal da Bahia* lamented the presence of soldiers armed with swords and lances, likewise judging the procession official and militarized.[152] The last word on this year's Dois de Julho in Rio de Janeiro newspapers came from the correspondent for the Liberal *Correio Mercantil*, who had earlier reported that the festival was taking place "with the greatest of pomp and splendour." In late July, he declared: "I will never fail to challenge what the Vermelho correspondents tell the Corte about this."[153]

It is difficult to elucidate what happened that Sunday afternoon in July 1864. On one level, it was a case of partisan politics, with both Progressistas and Vermelhos seeking to control the festival as well as – more important when it came to news in Rio de Janeiro – the reports about it. But opinions about the change did not divide along clearly partisan lines, and regardless of political affiliations, shared class interests allowed both Conservatives and Liberals to see some virtue in ending a potentially dangerous nocturnal festival, much as men associated with both parties had ended the Noite Primeira procession a few years before.

## Veterans and a Hero

A final development in the mid-century Dois de Julho festivities was the attention paid to veterans of the independence war, which increased as the number of surviving veterans diminished. In the 1850s, veterans formed a patriotic battalion that participated in the Noite

Figure 2.8 | Francisco Moniz Barreto

Source: *Bahia Illustrada*, 1 September 1867.

Primeira procession; poets like Francisco Moniz Barreto regularly hailed these elderly heroes.[154] In 1859, a small group of stalwart veterans formed an honour guard for Emperor Pedro II during his visit to Salvador.[155] I have found no evidence, however, to confirm Querino's assertion that the Viscount of Pirajá (1788–1848) led veterans in the early Noite Primeira processions.[156] Indeed, given Pirajá's views about the festival in 1837–38 (chapter 1), it is hard to imagine him at the head of a patriotic battalion.

On 2 July 1862, the Sociedade Veteranos da Independência (Independence Veterans Society) was founded under the presidency of Joaquim Antônio da Silva Carvalhal, a retired National Guard superior commander and customs officer. The poet Moniz Barreto served as vice-president (see figure 2.8).[157] Much like a lay brotherhood or mutual aid society, the Sociedade offered humanitarian aid to its members and their families, ensured that they would receive decent funerals, and undertook to celebrate masses on important dates: 24 September (Pedro I's death in 1834), 8 November (the Battle of Pirajá in 1822), 6 April (José Bonifácio de Andrada e Silva's death in 1838), and 19 April (the death of José Joaquim de Lima e Silva in 1855). On 25 June, the date on which patriots in Cachoeira proclaimed their allegiance to Pedro I in 1822, the society would have a mass sung for the souls of all the veterans deceased since 2 July 1823. On 7 September and 2 July, the society formed honour guards and participated in the parades. At these functions, Carvalhal unfurled the "legendary flag, discoloured by the sun and rent by enemy bullets," under which the veterans had fought, to cite Amaral's account of its activities.[158] In 1871, a handful "those brave old men" watched the great parade; "the old and tired soldiers of independence" handed the standard to the Acadêmico patriotic battalion, and the "youthful and vigorous soldiers of science" carried it for the rest of the parade.[159]

Little else is known about this society's activities. It struggled to get its statutes officially approved and the requisite documents issued. In 1864, the provincial assembly approved forty lotteries to support the society's charitable work.[160] It sought out veterans who lived outside of Bahia, such as Antônio Pereira Rebouças, whom it named honorary members. In 1870, it even managed to get the Duke of Caxias to join (as a young cadet, he had fought in the independence war in Bahia with the troops from Rio de Janeiro).[161] Anticipating a quick end to the Paraguayan War in early 1868, the society began raising funds to celebrate Brazil's victory (which would not come for another two years).[162] Recognizing that its membership base was inexorably shrinking, the society modified its statutes in 1872 to allow veterans' sons to join as "hereditary members."[163]

While the society's founding reflected the recognition that the generation that had fought in 1822–23 was passing, it likely failed to make much difference in most veterans' lives. To be sure, men like Carvalhal and Moniz Barreto – by then both comfortably if modestly retired civil servants – could use it to revel in their past exploits, but many other veterans were much worse off. On 2 July 1864, José Luiz Bananeira, a septuagenarian veteran, "no longer able to tolerate the misery that had oppressed him for his entire life, poisoned himself because he could no longer live honorably." He refused medical attention and died, leaving what one *Jornal do Commercio* correspondent described as "curious … documents" in which he justified his conduct.[164] Bananeira's tragic story so moved a young Rio de Janeiro journalist, Joaquim Maria Machado de Assis, that he mentioned it in his *crônica* about 7 September 1864. It may also have been the inspiration behind Nepomuceno's critical ode, which concluded with a heroic veteran reduced to begging for food.[165]

Dois de Julho patriots often lauded veterans and regularly cited the commanders and the planters who led the initial mobilization, but only one man achieved the status of "hero," with special celebrations in his honour.[166] In 1848 and 1849, Dois de Julho patriots added a series of demonstrations to recognize Pedro Labatut, commander of the Exército Pacificador, who had retired to Salvador in early 1848.[167] A delegation of patriots went to his house on 2 July, and on the 4th, he was publicly cheered on the stage and recognized at the theatre gala. Similar honours to him took place in 1849 as he and his young daughter, Januária Constança, rode into Salvador with the procession.[168] Upon discovering that they did not need the revenue from the lotteries voted to them by the provincial assembly, festival organizers proposed applying the funds to support Januária. President Gonçalves Martins immediately approved this, for the money would otherwise be "instantly consumed in fireworks or other unproductive expenses," an early indication of his disdain for popular festivals.[169]

Labatut died in early September 1849. In his will, he requested to be interred at Pirajá.[170] It took his executor, José Marcelino dos Santos, four years to raise the necessary funds to acquire the Italian marble urn in which the general's remains were finally laid to rest in the Pirajá parish church, near the site of his greatest victory over Portuguese troops, the 8 November 1822 Battle of Pirajá.[171] The following year, his tomb became the object of a patriotic pilgrimage in late July, first promoted by a teacher, Francisco Álvares dos Santos, and the Minerva Patriotic Battalion, but little is known about the early iterations of this new Dois de Julho ritual.[172] The shrine was an obligatory stop for Pedro II during his 1859 visit to the province.[173]

The newspapers that commented on the 1848–49 surge of interest in the French general offered no explanation of its political significance, although many must have known of his efforts to recruit slaves for the patriot army and his bitter quarrels with Recôncavo planters over this and other issues. In May 1823, before the patriot victory, he had been overthrown by battalion commanders with close ties to the planter class.[174] In this sense, celebrating Labatut was perhaps not a neutral act; it likely had significance for radical liberals. However, like other "successful" heroes, Labatut could be interpreted in different ways. He had turned the ragtag patriot irregulars into a more effective army, so he could be hailed as a great military leader. He settled in Brazil and briefly returned to active service in the early 1830s, so he could be seen as a loyal Brazilian. Unlike Lord Cochrane, the British naval officer who commanded the fleet that was crucial to the blockade of Salvador in 1823, Labatut did not make excessive pecuniary demands on the new empire (moreover, the naval forces had been recruited in Rio de Janeiro, so they included few Bahians, unlike the land forces).[175] Deprived of his command on the eve of the patriot victory, Labatut could be seen as a victim who submitted meekly to his fate; in 1853, a poet urged Bahians to bow before Labatut's grave, for he "was brave in battle" and "humble in peace."[176] Even more convenient for mid-century Bahian patriots, he did not have family or personal ties to Bahia that would have complicated celebrating him. Padre Bernardino judged it a belated recognition of the general's service, and in 1870, *O Alabama* described Labatut as a synthesis of the "warrior virtues of those worthy citizens of the *pátria* who laboured for progress."[177]

The rise and fall of the 1 July parade from the late 1840s to the early 1860s constitutes another cycle of Dois de Julho commemorations, analogous to the 1827–37 phase traced in chapter 1. The proliferation of patriotic battalions highlights the massive level of popular engagement with the commemoration of Bahia's independence. By the 1850s, the festival was moving beyond its origins as primarily a radical-liberal celebration and becoming an important way for Bahians to express their collective identity as Bahians, Brazilians, and patriots, a theme addressed more fully in chapter 4. Most striking about Dois de Julho during the two decades from the mid-1840s to the mid-1860s is the level of popular involvement in the celebrations. The relatively short notices in the correspondents' reports do not offer sufficient evidence to analyze the celebrants' social origins or motives in much detail, but they clearly indicate that something powerful and compelling – and sometimes threatening – took place on Salvador's streets in the first days of July, quite beyond authorities' control. That authorities may have wanted to suppress the nocturnal parade is not surprising, but the active role of the Sociedade de Julho is puzzling, although it indicates that there were very different understandings of the appropriate way to celebrate, even among those most closely associated with the festival.

The ebb and flow of Dois de Julho festivities from 1824 to 1864 followed, in part, the trajectory of national politics, as did most of Brazil's celebrations on days of national festivity, but many elements of the Bahian celebration obeyed their own autonomous logic. The Indian allegories, regardless of their exact form (male or female, active or passive, single or paired), had no counterpart elsewhere in Brazil, nor did the regular, large-scale parades of civilians to commemorate national holidays. The rise and fall of the 1 July nocturnal festival and its contrast to the great parade of 2 July highlight the tensions between Dois de Julho's popular and official elements, which coexisted grudgingly, with neither able to dominate the other. By 1864, the forces of official celebration were on the ascendant, but their victory was far from complete.

## CHAPTER THREE

# "Subdivided into a Thousand Festivals": Late-Imperial Dois de Julho, 1865–89

From the mid-1860s through the 1880s, the Dois de Julho festival's core displayed considerable stability. No great innovations like the rise and fall of the Noite Primeira de Julho procession changed the celebrations, and patriots repeated, year after year, the *bando*, the great parade into the city, the Te Deum and the cheers, the theatre gala, the three or more nights of celebration, and the patriotic symbols' return to Lapinha. Small changes, sometimes appearing only gradually, slowly modified the festival. The great parade became simpler, and after 1875, it turned into a civilian affair dominated by patriotic battalions. The decline of the National Guard, legally confirmed by the elimination of its principal responsibilities in 1873, meant that its members no longer paraded. After a conflict between a patriotic battalion and an army battalion on 2 July 1875, during which two patriots were killed (and several others injured), army units also ceased to participate. By the end of this period, some were perceiving an inexorable decline in the festival, one that they lamented, but this may have referred only to the great parade and the other central celebrations, for the proliferation of neighbourhood celebrations, the so-called Dois de Julho de Bairro, suggests a still-vibrant festival; indeed, the evidence suggests a distinctive late-imperial Dois de Julho. What remained unchanged was Dois de Julho's political importance and the partisan wrangling over the festival. However, it was no longer a radical-liberal festival; instead,

Dois de Julho was the occasion for political parties to pursue their goals in association with the festival's powerful patriotic symbolism.

From the end of 1864 to 1870, the Paraguayan War dominated Bahian and Brazilian politics. The initial mobilization to repel the invasions of Mato Grosso and Rio Grande do Sul tapped an unexpected vein of patriotic enthusiasm, and Bahians flocked to the colours, as did Brazilians everywhere in the country. Victory in that war proved elusive, and as it dragged on, governments resorted to the traditional coercive impressment to supply reinforcements for the forces in Paraguay. In late 1866, they turned to the slave population and instituted a program of paying owners to free slaves on the condition that the men be immediately enlisted. The province contributed some fifteen thousand men to the war effort, including several hundred slaves.[1] For most of the war years, Progressista governments held power nationally and provincially, but the incompatibility of Zacarias de Góes e Vasconcelos (president of the council of ministers, August 1866–July 1868) with the Marquis of Caxias, the army commander closely associated with the Conservatives, finally prompted Emperor Pedro II to call the Saquaremas to power on 16 July 1868. That ministerial change shook the political order. The new government replaced judges, police officials, and other authorities throughout the country in a thorough purge of Progressistas. Historical Liberals and Progressistas came together (the former somewhat hesitantly) to form a new Liberal Party. They boycotted the 1869 elections and devoted their energies to reorganizing their party and to developing a far-reaching reform program; some erstwhile Liberals went further and moved to a republican position in 1870.[2] These events had little direct impact on Dois de Julho, although in 1869, much as in 1849–50, recently ousted Liberals sought to use the festival to score political points against the new administration.

With the advent of peace, Conservative governments (and particularly the long administration of the Viscount of Rio Branco, March 1871 to June 1875) undertook a series of political and institutional reforms, beginning with the difficult passage of a free womb law in September 1871. This measure, long advocated by Pedro II, accelerated slavery's decline, and for a time in the early 1870s, Dois de Julho patriots sought to associate the festival with abolition (see chapter 4). Other reforms, such as the adoption of the metric system, had little direct impact on the festival, but 1873 legislation eliminated the National Guard's obligation to provide men for police detachments and to participate in parades on days of national festivity, while the 1874 draft lottery contributed indirectly to the exclusion of army units from Dois de Julho. Pedro II returned the Liberals to power in early 1878 with a mandate to reform the electoral system, something that the Conservatives had failed to accomplish. In 1881, they instituted direct elections but also mandated literacy as a requirement for voting, which effectively reduced the electorate by about 90 percent. Divisions over whether to take further steps towards abolition marked the end of this period of Liberal rule, but not before the passage of the 1885 sexagenarian law (which freed elderly slaves). This law, however, fell far short of abolitionists' hopes; the Conservative government of the Baron of Cotegipe (João Maurício Wanderley, August 1885–May 1888) implemented it in the narrowest possible way and sought to hold back the rising tide of popular abolitionism. Declining health forced Pedro to seek medical treatment in Europe in 1887, and in early 1888, Princess Isabel removed Cotegipe and appointed João Alfredo Correia de Oliveira to organize a cabinet out of Conservative elements willing to abolish slavery. When parliament convened, legislators quickly passed the 13 May 1888 law that put an end to the institution.[3]

These political events heavily influenced the rhetoric about days of national festivity in Rio de Janeiro.[4] They had less impact on Dois de Julho discourse. Unlike the other days of national festivity (25 March, 7 September, and 2 December), which celebrated, respectively, the constitution, independence, and the emperor's birthday, Dois de Julho did not speak directly to the national institutions that governed Brazil. The limited number of surviving Bahian newspapers makes it difficult to perceive the full range of meanings attributed to Dois de Julho, an issue to which I will return in chapter 4. In the 1870s, Salvador had no neutral newspaper like Rio de Janeiro's *Jornal do Commercio*; the *Diário da Bahia*, founded in 1856, represented the Liberals, joined by the dissident Liberal *O Monitor* (1876–81). The *Jornal da Bahia* (1853–78) and the *Correio da Bahia* (1871–78) both spoke for segments of the Conservative party. The Conservatives' fall in 1878 and the Liberals' rise brought changes; the *Gazeta da Bahia* (1879–90) took over as the Conservatives' organ, while the *Jornal de Notícias*, founded in 1879, attempted to maintain a neutral position. In 1875, the *Diário de Notí-cias* pioneered the "penny press [*imprensa barata*]," which sought to broaden circulation with low prices and more popular content.[5]

The idiosyncratic *O Alabama* (1863–71) is the only surviving example of the critical popular press in Salvador. Its Afro-Brazilian editor advocated slavery's abolition but rejected Candomblé and other manifestations of African culture, as might be expected from an upwardly mobile individual.[6] Isolated issues of other popular periodicals hint at lively political debate. In an 1879 Dois de Julho editorial, *O Santelmo*, a self-described "Democratic Gazette in Favour of the *Povo*," demanded to know why the Liberal cabinet was planning to deprive "the majority of the population" of the "right to vote." "Is the lack of education the *povo*'s fault? Is it only those who know how to read that defend the throne and pay taxes?"[7] The short-lived *Bahia Ilustrada* (1867–70), *O Faisca* (1885–87), and *A Locomotiva* (1888–89) are the only illustrated newspapers from Salvador for which significant runs have survived (*Bahia Ilustrada* for only 1867–68, however).[8] For no year do I have reports on Dois de Julho from Bahian periodicals across the political spectrum (although correspondents' letters and transcriptions from Bahian newspapers in the Rio de Janeiro and Pernambuco press are partial exceptions). As a result, the political significance of many aspects of the festival remains obscure.

This chapter begins with the celebrations' organization. In the early 1870s, the Sociedade Dois de Julho disappeared, and the Direção Geral dos Festejos assumed full responsibility for the celebrations. As in previous decades, organizers counted on the enthusiasm of Salvador's residents, especially those who joined the patriotic battalions or otherwise participated directly in the celebrations. The forms of commemoration changed relatively little during the quarter century from the start of the Paraguayan War to the end of the empire, even as Dois de Julho became a more civilian festival. The proliferation of neighbourhood Dois de Julho celebrations dispersed the festival throughout Salvador and its suburbs and brought it closer to people's immediate communities. The festival and coverage of it in the newspapers remained highly politicized, as opposition and government journalists portrayed the celebrations in ways that advanced their causes; sometimes this competing (and contradictory) coverage makes it almost impossible to determine what happened. The relatively well-documented incidents of 1869, when the new Conservative government sought to forestall Liberal demonstrations during the festival, reveal much about how Bahians conducted politics through Dois de Julho celebrations. The violent incidents of the 1875 festival – themselves not directly related to partisan politics – and the reaction to them by both government and opposition, as well as the extensive national debate about this incident, demonstrate how rhetoric and writing about the celebrations was at least as important as the celebrations themselves.

## Festival Organization

Significant changes occurred in the Dois de Julho celebrations' organization in the early 1870s. The Sociedade Dois de Julho apparently disbanded by 1873, leaving only the Direção Geral dos Festejos to organize the celebrations. As in previous years, organizers struggled to raise funds and to find volunteers willing to continue their work for the next year. Despite these obstacles, they managed to put together a celebration each year from 1865 to 1889, in which the proliferating patriotic battalions and marching bands, both military and civilian, played prominent parts. Alongside the Direção, groups of local organizers put on neighbourhood festivals, and through their work, Dois de Julho spread throughout the city.

During the 1860s, the Sociedade Dois de Julho and the Direção Geral dos Festejos collaborated to organize the celebrations. The Sociedade, however, was increasingly José Álvares do Amaral's vehicle. In 1868, a newspaper reported that the Sociedade's secretary had aided the Direção; three years later, Amaral claimed to have been the "only [person] to run the festival." The following year, the Sociedade received an invitation from the Direção to "take charge of all the celebrations." The Sociedade published the program in its own name, and that is the last mention of it that I have found. The 1873 city almanac contained no listing for the Sociedade.[9] It is not clear who controlled the symbols and their pavilion after the Sociedade's demise, and I have found no discussion of this in the surviving press.

The Direção Geral dos Festejos, whose membership for the following year was announced at the end of each year's celebration, thus became

Table 3.1 | Direção Geral dos Festejos members' social origins, 1865–87

| | Occupation or title listed in announcements of the Direção's composition | | Occupation or title (adjusted with data on merchants from 1873 city almanac) | |
|---|---|---|---|---|
| | Number | % | Number | % |
| Doutor | 116 | 32.6 | 113 | 31.7 |
| Military rank | 52 | 14.6 | 48 | 13.5 |
| Merchant (includes one proprietor and one capitalist) | 6 | 1.7 | 38 | 10.7 |
| Title of nobility | 28 | 7.9 | 24 | 6.7 |
| Desembargador (magistrate) | 16 | 4.5 | 16 | 4.5 |
| Priest | 10 | 2.8 | 10 | 2.8 |
| Engineer | 3 | 0.8 | 3 | 0.8 |
| Other honorific (conselheiro, comendador) | 20 | 5.6 | 17 | 4.8 |
| Pharmacist | 1 | 0.3 | 0 | 0 |
| No information | 104 | 29.1 | 87 | 24.4 |
| Total | 356 | 99.9 | 356 | 99.9 |

Sources: Direção Geral dos Festejos members, 1865, 1868–87; Almanak (1873), 2–4.

the principal festival organizer. There is only one indication of how its members were selected. In 1868, the Baron of Sauípe (João José Leite), a merchant, stepped in to assist the struggling Direção with a significant donation; its members happily named him president for 1869 and accepted all of the individuals whom he proposed as members for that year.[10] I do not know, however, whether the Direção's president named his fellow directors in other years. That Direção members sent resignation letters to the provincial president in 1880 and to the city council in 1886 suggests that these governments had oversight roles, but the annual announcements of the new Direção never alluded to this.[11]

The directors are known for twenty-one of the years between 1865 and 1889, and each year, the Direção included mostly new members. Of the 357 men who served in 1865 and from 1868 to 1887, 286 (80.1 percent) did so only once, 56 (15.7 percent) twice, and 11 (3.1 percent) three times; a mere 4 (1.1 percent) could be persuaded to come back for a fourth time. The limited available information on their social origins (see table 3.1) suggests that little had changed since the 1850s and early 1860s (see table 2.1). The data in the first column of table 3.1 understate the number of merchants, for these men used other titles or honorifics if they had them, and some appear without any title, including Luiz Tarquínio dos Santos, future owner of the Empório Industrial do Norte textile mill. Seventeen men listed as *negociantes nacionais matriculados* (registered Brazilian merchants) in the 1873 city almanac appear among the Direção members without any indication of their occupation, as do another fifteen listed with other titles or honorifics. The second column of table 3.1 thus more accurately represents merchants' involvement in the festival committee (these data are also consistent with table 2.1). Organizers likely sought out merchants because of their financial resources; the fact that twelve of the thirty-three merchants served more than one term (one of them served three times, and two did so four times), almost double the rate at which other members of the Direção returned, indicates that they succumbed to the pressure to contribute to the festival.

I have found no detailed evidence regarding how organizers financed the festival or how much it cost. To judge by bids to construct the stage – the principal structure for which the Direção was responsible – in the mid-1880s that job could be done for 1:700$000 (US$646) to 2:300$000 (US$874).[12] This was, of course, not the only expense for the organizers: the symbols and their wagons had to be repaired and decorated, and stocks of fireworks had to be laid in. In 1886, organizers budgeted 208$800 (US$79) for fireworks and carefully planned their allocation to the festival's components.[13] The provincial government continued to provide an annual subvention of 2:000$000 to the festival organizers, set at that level in the mid-1850s (chapter 2). It also helped by lending portraits for the stage, as can be inferred from criticisms of a president who failed to do so.[14] Festival organizers also welcomed donations, as we have seen with Sauípe's 1868 contribution, and they were expected to contribute themselves. In 1887, the Baron of Santiago (Domingos Américo da Silva), offered 400$000 (US$184) and lamented that his ill health precluded more active participation in the Direção.[15] Business obligations prevented Manoel José do Conde Júnior from taking on the responsibility for organizing 1880's festival, a task that he had earlier accepted. Instead, he offered a donation of 1:000$000 (US$450). The *Jornal do Commercio*'s correspondent judged that this amounted to only a fifth or a sixth of what he personally would have had to spend had he organized a proper celebration.[16]

Mobilizing support and enthusiasm for the festival was another of the Direção's responsibilities. It named fundraising committees, as can be inferred from the fact that several men refused to take on the task in 1888 because they were too busy handling the cargoes of the many ships then in the harbour.[17] In 1881, the Direção named some seventy-five men to fifteen local committees in charge of decorating streets and squares and raising arches.[18] Presumably, their work involved encouraging neighbours to decorate their houses and raising funds or organizing bees (*mutirões*) for the construction of arches; in 1885, the *Diário da Bahia* reported that all the streets on the procession's route were "elegantly decorated, thanks to the efforts of the committees organized for this purpose."[19] One Marcos Aurélio Tude, who in 1870 advertised his skill at constructing "stages and triumphal arches, with good taste and style," no doubt sought to supply this market.[20]

Despite their importance to the festival, the ubiquitous marching bands left few traces in Dois de Julho documentation. Gilberto Freyre observed that brass bands, with their martial music and adaptations of opera tunes, were plentiful in late-imperial society, and Bahia was no exception to this.[21] Several kinds of bands participated in Dois de Julho celebrations. Military and police corporations maintained bands, which provincial presidents could assign to perform at any function, and patriots regularly applied to have them accompany their battalions, while festival organizers requested them to enliven evenings at the stage. Theatre impresarios had them perform during intermissions or in the theatre lobby before galas. In 1877, the commander of arms complained that his musicians were exhausted from rushing from patriotic function to patriotic function during the winter months.[22] Bahia's police band gained considerable popularity during the presidency of Antônio Cândido da Cruz Machado (October 1873–May 1874) because he ordered it to play nightly outdoor concerts; in the 1880s, it performed publicly a few times per week.[23] Civilian philharmonic societies proliferated in late-imperial Bahia, and a music historian has identified the Sociedade Filarmônica Euterpe, founded in 1848, as the first of many in Salvador.[24] Individuals also organized ensembles; thus in 1878, Francisco Amâncio da Silva announced that he had put together a "martial music band" and was offering its services to patriotic battalions.[25]

Strikingly absent from the surviving sources on Dois de Julho are the "barbers' bands" that black men (free, freed, and slave) in that trade maintained.[26] Historians have made note of several such ensembles in the wills of their impresarios, who were some of the wealthiest freedmen in early-nineteenth-century Bahia.[27] A successor to these bands was the Chapada, a barbers' band that, as Querino recalled, mocked other bands during public performances by playing their rivals' music in double time or in a higher octave.[28] Such musical duels sometimes led to fisticuffs. In late 1878, the Chapada clashed with the Sixteenth Infantry's band; officers accused a slave who played trumpet for the barbers of seriously injuring a soldier.[29] A decade earlier, the Chapada had the habit of "insulting and provoking National Guard martial bands" and deliberately playing before them the pieces "that they [the guard bands] play."[30]

The surviving Dois de Julho coverage never mentioned the Chapada, but these black musicians must have crossed paths regularly with military and civilian bands during Dois de Julho celebrations. On 2 July 1875, five bands led patriotic battalions into the city: the police band accompanied the Acadêmicos (students), the navy apprentices' band led Letras e Ciências (Letters and Sciences), and the Quarenta de Voluntários Philharmonic (composed of Paraguayan War veterans who had served in the Fortieth Voluntários da Pátria Battalion) joined the Defensores da Liberdade (Defenders of Liberty); the Artistas Nacionais (National Artisans) and the Caixeiros Nacionais marched, respectively, with the São José and Terpsicore Philharmonics.[31] The army bands presumably marched with their battalions. Most of the information about military bands' performances on Dois de Julho comes from a series of conflicts between the musicians and civilians. In 1877, the Sixteenth Infantry's commander reported that "once again, as so often happens," his musicians were "virulently and heinously insulted and stoned" during the festivities.[32] "Lamentable events" in 1880 began with newspaper articles mocking the Ninth Infantry's band. As it passed other patriotic battalions in the narrow streets north of the Terreiro de Jesus, while accompanying the Artistas Nacionais, this band began to play a march from Carlos Gomes's opera *O Guaraní*. Amid shouts not to play the march, members of the other battalions attacked the army band. In the scuffle, the army musicians drew their swords, but the patriots carried the day, crushing several instruments; one of them effectively silenced the army band by perforating its bass drum with a cane.[33] A few days later, the Sixteenth Infantry's band (disarmed as a precautionary measure) lost several instruments in a brawl, and two of its musicians suffered injuries.[34] The conflicts between military musicians and civilian patriots continued into the 1880s. In 1885, someone threw stones at the Ninth Infantry's band on 30 June as it accompanied Ciências e Artes (Sciences and Arts) and also a patriotic battalion honouring the deceased abolitionist leader, Luiz Gama, on a pre–Dois de Julho outing. Several instruments were damaged, and the band was out of commission for the rest of the festival, but the local subdelegate denied that anything had happened in his district.[35]

Unfortunately, little is known about the patriotic battalions that mobilized hundreds, if not thousands, of men to don white pants and jacket, straw hats, and patriotic insignia, and to accompany the patriotic symbols into Salvador and return them to Lapinha, as well as occasionally parade in the days before or after 2 July. These constituted a festive form of associational life that mobilized Bahians along the lines of several different collective identities. I have identified forty-nine such battalions by name in the sources from 1865 to 1889; a few of them, though, may be the same battalion under a slightly different moniker. Some appeared regularly, like the Acadêmicos, which enlisted students at the medical school. In 1874, they named a nine-person committee to organize their battalion. Ten years later, one student representative from each year constituted the committee. After 1874's Dois de Julho, a student newspaper proudly reported their participation.[36] Other student battalions also appeared regularly, such as Minerva (honouring the Roman goddess of wisdom), organized by a well-respected teacher, Francisco Álvares dos Santos, known as Chico Santos, "a true patriot," who led the first pilgrimages to Pirajá (chapter 2) and turned this battalion into an abolitionist association in the late 1860s (see chapter 4).[37]

Defensores da Liberdade enlisted Paraguayan War veterans, so it was not surprising that the veterans' band paraded with it in 1875. Its leader in 1879 and in the 1880s was Captain Marcolino José Dias, commander of one of the all-black Zuavo companies, who had distinguished himself in the war. He was also closely associated with Liberals – Querino describes him as a sort of local political broker – and he likely gained prominence in Dois de Julho after the party returned to power in 1878.[38] After his death in early 1888, the battalion pledged to honour his memory.[39] The Caixeiros Nacionais also appeared regularly, but they were no longer described as advocates for radical-liberal causes such the nationalizing of retail commerce. They had the means to acquire a richly embroidered banner in Paris for more than 2:000$000 (about US$1,000); so Sílio Boccanera Júnior recalled in 1921 when lamenting this symbol's disappearance.[40] Several artisans' battalions, including that of the Liceu de Artes e Ofícios (a trade school founded in 1872), appear in the records, and in 1877, a store advertised tie clips with "symbols of all of the arts and trades" so that members of these battalions could proudly display their professions.[41] Reflecting the changing nature of labour in Salvador, workers' organizations also began to parade, including the Liga Operária Baiana (Bahian Labour League) and the Liga Fabril (Mechanical [Workers'] League); in 1880, a newspaper published an invitation for the latter to join the parade.[42] Artisans' and workers' Dois de Julho parading had much in common with their counterparts' participation in North American Labour Day parades as they claimed respectability and recognition of their place in society.[43]

Antônio Olavo da França Guerra, whom Querino called an "artist" and a "typographer" but who in fact owned a printing press, never missed a Dois de Julho. Amaral called him a "well-known name in the patriotic festivals, [a] citizen very dedicated to the *pátria*'s days," and Varella's informant recalled him by name.[44] In the 1860s, he led União Brasileira (Brazilian Unity), a battalion open to "all Brazilians," which helped return the symbols to Lapinha.[45] In the 1870s, his vehicle for this was the Defensores de Pirajá (Pirajá's Defenders) battalion. João da Silva Campos described him as a "four-square Conservative [*conservador de quatro costados*]," and these ties were visible in his battalion's

1876 visit to the home of senator and former Minister of War João José Oliveira Junqueira.[46] In 1882, França Guerra turned up at the head of the Defensores do Comércio (Defenders of Commerce) and received fulsome praise from the first and perhaps only issue of a republican newspaper, *O Socialista*, an indication that shared opposition to the Liberal government made for heterogeneous alliances.[47] The Princesa Isabel battalion, which first appeared in 1888, honoured the princess regent who had signed the law ending slavery on 13 May of that year; shoemaker Roque Jacinto presented a wreath to the Count of Eu (Isabel's consort) on this battalion's behalf during his visit to Salvador in June 1889.[48] In 1885, one Laurindo José dos Santos organized a battalion named after Eu; it and three other patriotic battalions managed to borrow horses from the cavalry company for the parade. They treated the animals so roughly that they could not be ridden by soldiers for several days; one abandoned horse only found its way back to the stables at 11 p.m.[49]

The organizing of Dois de Julho celebrations thus mobilized a significant number of people during Bahia's winter months. The president had to weigh the competing demands from patriotic battalions and other celebrants for the services of bands under his control. The Direção Geral dos Festejos had to raise funds, mobilize enthusiasm, and satisfy the inevitable critics of their work. Patriotic battalions' organizers likewise had to convince men to join their battalion. Authorities had to ensure that sufficient police were on hand to keep order. And, of course, as I will discuss further in chapter 4, individuals had to decide how they and their families would celebrate.

## Patterns of Commemoration, 1865–89

In 1877, Michael Mulhall's handbook for visitors to Brazil described "Dos de Julio [*sic*]" as "the most remarkable civic festival in the year."[50] While much of what took place in the lead-up to 2 July (and in subsequent days) resembled the festival of previous decades, the surviving newspaper coverage suggests that there was a distinctive late-imperial Dois de Julho. This festival was more civilian (by the mid-1870s, the army and the National Guard no longer participated in the great parade), less infused with radical-liberal and anti-Portuguese rhetoric, more "popular" (in the sense of relatively more lower-class participation), and increasingly diffuse compared to its predecessors (thanks to the proliferation of neighbourhood celebrations). Like the mid-century festival, however, it was frequently a site for politics.

By this time, Dois de Julho celebrations began on 3 May with the raising of a sort of maypole on the Terreiro de Jesus (officially known as Conde d'Eu Square after 1870) to announce the upcoming festival. In 1867, *O Alabama* referred to it as the "inaugural post [*pau iniciador*]."[51] The ceremony itself was relatively simple. In 1873 and 1876, the Direção requested that the president dispatch military and police bands to play; its members raised the pole and led the crowd in cheers amid the usual cacophony of firecrackers (in 1868, the cheers were to Dois de Julho, to independence veterans, to the army and navy, to the Voluntários da Pátria, and to the Bahian people).[52] According to Rozendo Moniz, 3 May was also the date on which construction of the stage began; Querino suggests that work started soon after this day, while a later folklorist thought that the pole was actually the first upright for the stage.[53] It is not clear when this ceremony first took place. That Mello Moraes Filho did not mention it – he starts his account with the *bando* – may indicate that it was not an important part of the festival that he witnessed as a youth in the 1850s and early 1860s. However, the earliest newspaper reference to it dates from 1854, and an 1858 newspaper already described it as a custom.[54] Varella's informant recalled that this custom lasted only "for a few years."[55] Raising this maypole to launch the annual festival was another connection to Catholic traditions, for throughout Brazil, it was customary to mark the start of saints' festivals with the raising of a "pole [*mastro*]."[56] The date of 3 May linked Dois de Julho to Brazil's discovery in 1500 – a detail that few noted (according to the Gregorian calendar, Pedro Álvares Cabral's fleet sighted land in southern Bahia on that day).[57]

Year after year, the city council issued its traditional proclamation calling on patriots to celebrate the festival in licit and orderly ways. The *bando* took place in the late afternoon of 29 June and retained its carnivalesque character. William Hadfield saw this procession in 1870 and thought that it was the celebration of St. Peter's Day (29 June). He reported "masquerading about the streets" and "windows and balconies ... alive with people."[58] By the 1880s, the procession followed a standard route from Lapinha to the Passeio Público and back to the Terreiro de Jesus.[59] The president assigned army or police bands to accompany the costumed revellers, some of them on foot, some on horseback, and some in coaches. The Direção handed out copies of the proclamation, while poets distributed their work or recited it over the din of fireworks; in 1871, Rozendo Moniz agreed to compose the "*bando* poem," apparently a commissioned text. Other poets would receive this charge in later years.[60]

The costumed participants commented on many issues. In 1866, two of them satirized certain excesses of female fashion; the following year, a man dressed in a Voluntários de Pátria uniform begged for alms in a pointed condemnation of the government's failure to fulfill the promises made to these volunteers.[61] In 1870, a correspondent judged that the formerly tasteful ritual had degenerated into a "carnival of bad taste"; in 1871, one man offended many by dressing up as a veteran with a crippled leg and a hernia-swollen groin, which he ostentatiously displayed to "ladies" watching from windows. In 1872, notwithstanding the rain, the *bando* included "interesting and witty types."[62] Others used the *bando* to promote support for the war effort. In 1866, a model steamer, *Amazonas*, complete with illuminated portholes and the names of battles, served as the centrepiece of a fundraising campaign on behalf of the families of Voluntários da Pátria. This was a sufficiently memorable float that Mello Moraes Filho's mother told him about it. The brainchild of the Ariani brothers, coach-makers with a workshop in Bonfim, the *Amazonas* raised more than 1:000$000 (US$490).[63] With some regularity, newspapers reported that the *bando* had been orderly; in 1880, however, the Ninth Infantry's commander complained that a trombone had been crushed by a streetcar mule and that someone had punctured the bass drum's skin while his battalion's band accompanied the *bando* (apparently the Direção paid for its replacement).[64]

In 1867, *O Alabama* lamented that "popular traditions" like the "night of the 1st, which were the soul of Dois de Julho," had been ended "on the pretext of banal expediency," including the need to keep order, when in fact Bahians always behaved in orderly fashion during the festival.[65] This is one of only a handful of later references to the nocturnal parade that had been abolished as of 1861 after the Lapinha pavilion was constructed. When he was president of the Direção in 1874,

Manoel Pinto de Souza Dantas, one of Bahia's leading Liberal figures, sought to restore this tradition. He announced his intention to do so in April, and during the night of 1–2 July, he led "an immense uncountable number of patriotic battalions, infantry and cavalry," which "conducted to Lapinha the triumphal wagons that would, on the 2nd, carry the precious symbols of our independence." As in the 1850s, patriots drew empty wagons through the city.[66] Querino, who may have participated in this procession, emphasized Dantas's Liberal connections, but he did not mention that this procession took place only once more, in 1875 (see below), nor did Rozendo Moniz.[67]

On 2 July, Salvador's residents awoke to the sound of artillery salutes from the city's forts and from warships in the harbour. These were repeated at noon and at dusk; in 1883, the *Gazeta da Bahia* praised a German corvette that had joined in the salutes as it was leaving the harbour.[68] The procession into the city began at midday, although people started gathering at Lapinha early in the morning. Its participants included National Guard battalions (until 1873), army units when they were available (until 1875), patriotic battalions, and bands, all of which followed the wagons bearing the patriotic symbols – the *caboclos*, a term rarely used in the press – into the city and thereby re-enacted the peaceful occupation of 1823. According to Rozendo Moniz, the marchers tried to arrive at the Terreiro at 2 p.m., the same time that the patriot forces had reached this square on 2 July 1823.[69] Rainy weather, delays in organizing the procession, and slow progress through crowded streets often made it difficult to keep to this schedule. In the square, the floats were pulled up to the stage, which normally had sufficient space to park them. As the rest of the procession's participants reached the Terreiro, the battalions formed up and stood guard during the Te Deum. In 1868, *O Alabama* lamented that the service took so long, for the soldiers were getting hungry.[70] After the mass, the provincial president (or the vice-president when, as often happened, the president was serving in the national legislature) unveiled the emperor's portrait and led the crowd in cheers. The army and guard battalions fired salutes; they and the patriotic battalions then marched past the stage. By this time, it was normally late in the afternoon. In the evening, there was a theatre gala (see chapter 5), while the stage was given over to poetry readings and bands entertained the populace.[71] At this point, explained a correspondent, "the commemorative ritual broke apart and subdivided into a thousand festivals, each more pleasant and surprising [than the other], that continued until the 7th."[72]

Relatively little changed in the public commemoration during these years. The two biggest changes concerned the role of the National Guard and the army battalions. During the war, the guard collapsed under the pressure of providing soldiers to fight against Paraguay, detachments to handle routine garrison duties, and contingents to serve as Salvador's police force. Thus in 1866, one battalion failed to show up for the parade. In 1867, the *Diário do Rio de Janeiro* reported, based on the Conservative *Jornal da Bahia's* coverage, that the guard had mustered only a "small number of men"; by contrast, the *Jornal do Commercio's* Progressista correspondent declared that the guards' parade "was numerous and splendid."[73] By 1871, the guard was completely disorganized; battalions showed up for the 2 July parade with as few as thirty men under the command of captains or lieutenants (no colonels, in fact, showed up).[74] Discipline broke down among the few guardsmen who paraded in 1873: instead of standing guard on the Terreiro, some men from the Fourth Battalion sought out a nearby tavern, while guards from other battalions got into fights.[75] The September 1873 reform eliminated the guard's obligation to participate in such ceremonial.[76] After the war, army battalions were once again stationed in Salvador, and until 1875 (see below), they continued to participate in the great parade, although they may not have cut fine figures. Two days before the 1871 parade, the Fourteenth Infantry Battalion lacked sufficient shoes for its men because the contractor had failed to supply them.[77]

It is difficult to determine whether the elimination of army and National Guard battalions from the 2 July parade reduced its size; after all, guardsmen were now free to join patriotic battalions or to accompany the procession as individuals. No contemporary commented on this, but the ending of guard and army participation meant that the procession now fell more clearly under the control of civilian organizers. The Direção began inviting the commanders of patriotic battalions to meet in June to organize the great parade.[78] Festival programs regularly included detailed orders of march for the patriotic battalions on 2 July and during the symbols' return to Lapinha on 5 July.[79] This organized portion of the great parade contrasted with the "great numbers of the *povo*" that also accompanied the patriotic emblems.[80]

Little controversy attended the Te Deum, although *O Alabama* regularly chided city councillors for failing to attend this function; as part of "a corporation originating from the *povo*," they had an obligation to show up.[81] Querino described the sermon as "always a patriotic oration given by the best preachers of the day."[82] The cheers in which the president or vice-president led the crowd from the stage were still important barometers of the political mood in the 1860s. *O Alabama* judged the response to have been poor in 1866, while the *Jornal do Commercio*'s Progressista correspondent reported that "the *povo* responded with enthusiasm."[83] Journalists expressed much less interest in this during the 1870s and 1880s.

As noted in the previous chapter, in the early 1860s the patriotic symbols were sometimes displayed on Piedade Square. In 1866, Colonel Joaquim Antônio da Silva Carvalhal, president of the Sociedade Veteranos da Independência, then deeply involved in promoting enlistments for the war effort, served as president of the Direção.[84] That year, it was decided to have a temporary pavilion constructed for the triumphal floats on Veteranos Square (formerly Guadalupe Square), just a few blocks from the Palace Square. On 3 July, seven men protested this decision. They claimed to have already spent 450$000 (US$220.50) on the construction of a "shed [*barracão*]" (a temporary structure to house the floats) at Piedade Square, accused Carvalhal of wanting to have them stand in front of his house on that small, muddy square (in fact, "a complete mud hole [*lamaçal*]"), and complained about the armed guardsmen who had accompanied the wagons on 2 July. Protesting that "the celebration is always done at the cost of the *povo*, [so] therefore its [the *povo*'s] will should be done," they called on the president to order the symbols moved to Piedade at once.[85]

In his capacity as police delegate for Salvador's First District, Amaral responded immediately. He first dismissed the petitioners as "some unknown individuals" and declared that it was entirely up to the "festival committee" to decide where to place the triumphal floats (in consultation, however, with him as the Sociedade Dois de Julho's first secretary). Piedade was far from the "festival's centre," and in previous years, the symbols had been vandalized there, despite the organizers' vigilance. Moreover, they were "little visited by families" at Piedade, for "large numbers of Africans, mostly slaves, gathered" there in disorderly and "noisy *batuques*" (dancing and drumming) that "gave the police no little work." He claimed to have suggested the Praça dos Veteranos, for it was "one of the most decent [squares] in this city," thereby exonerating Carvalhal. Amaral learned that at Lapinha on 2 July, "some young fellows, a bit overexcited and imprudent, had decided to raise the alarm and mislead the *povo* into taking the wagons to Piedade, regardless of the consequences," so he arranged for the Caixeiros Nacionais (not the National Guard) to make sure that the floats went to the right place. He condemned these self-proclaimed "spokesmen for the *povo*" who had sought to "besmirch the national festival of Dois de Julho," adding that he had seen no sign of the "imagined shed" that local "businesses [*o comércio*]" had supposedly built at Piedade.[86]

What lay behind this incident is unclear. Amaral's allusion to businesses suggests that Piedade shopkeepers or taverners had hoped to profit from the crowds visiting the *caboclos* (a term not used in the correspondence about this incident). The seven men's claim to speak on behalf of the *povo* suggests popular understandings of the festival, while the efforts to control the symbols' movements highlight their importance, as do Amaral's comments about the theft of items from the wagons, issues to which I will return in the next chapter. In 1867, festival organizers took no chances and placed the emblems on the Terreiro de Jesus; by the 1870s, this was the accepted location for them.[87]

The principal temporary stage stood on the Terreiro's north side in front of the São Domingos church.[88] In 1865, befitting the country's involvement in the Paraguayan War, it featured two towers or castles garrisoned by colourfully dressed companies of Zuavos that would soon embark for the front.[89] *O Alabama* disliked the stage's design in 1868, for it resembled a "funerary monument"; two years later, in 1870, it criticized the design again, though it praised the lavish lighting.[90] The only year for which a detailed description of the Terreiro de Jesus stage survives is 1871, when Amaral commemorated his own work as the festival's self-proclaimed sole organizer in a special illustrated issue of *O Reverbero* (see figure 3.1).[91] He had arranged for the construction of a stage "unlike anything seen for many years." Gothic in style, its façade was painted with "flowers and wreaths of different colours." Portraits

Figure 3.1 | The stage on the Terreiro de Jesus, 1871

*Source: O Reverbero*, 6 August 1871.

of Pedro II, Princess Regent Isabel, and José Joaquim de Lima e Silva (the Exército Pacificador's commander in 1823) hung in the structure's middle section. Artificial tobacco and coffee leaves surrounded Isabel's portrait, and the central "imperial hall" was carpeted, hung with yellow and green silk, and illuminated by a "beautiful" crystal gaslight chandelier. The "patriotic emblems of independence and liberty, represented by the two *caboclos*," stood under the words "Independence" and "Liberty," while the four oval portraits featured Pedro I, Pedro Labatut, the Viscount of Pirajá, and the Baron of Belém (Rodrigo Antônio Falcão Brandão), all men who had played important roles in the struggle for independence. At its extreme right and left, the structure had space for bands. Nine Brazilian flags and twelve banners topped the structure, which was lit by four hundred gas jets.[92]

This stage was illuminated for fully seven nights, from 2 to 8 July. Each night, different authorities unveiled the portraits and led the crowd in cheers: the president and the chief of police, the directors of the Sociedade Veteranos da Independência, the president and members of the city council, the National Guard's superior commander and the commander of the police corps, the commander of arms and chief of the naval station, the directors of the Minerva patriotic battalion, and the Direção dos Festejos.[93] This carefully considered program allowed all of the principal government authorities in Salvador to have

Figure 3.2 | The triumphal arch on the Terreiro de Jesus, 1882

*Source: Gazeta Illustrada,* 9 August 1882.

their moment and also recognized key non-government organizations. Music and poetry entertained the crowds during these seven nights and, according to Amaral, an "incalculable multitude of *povo*" filled the square each night, while "thousands of ladies ... gathered to contemplate the elegant [portrait of] Princess Isabel Regnant." The *povo* also reportedly praised the choice of the four "heroes who contributed so much to Brazil's political emancipation."[94]

Amaral's *O Reverbero* amounts to what historians of early-modern Europe have dubbed "festival books," accounts of public ritual designed to present the message that festival organizers desired and to celebrate their efforts.[95] Thus, it may well have described more what ought to have happened – at least in Amaral's view – than what actually took place. As far as *O Alabama* was concerned, the stage was quite small (if admittedly elegant); the gas company skimped and too quickly left it in the dark, and Amaral himself revealed that he had struggled with limited resources.[96] In addition to the stage, in some years, organizers also constructed a triumphal arch on the Terreiro (figure 3.2).

In 1872, a "colossal statue of the monarch" replaced Pedro II's portrait on the stage. The *Diário da Bahia* reported that this "splendid work" was the handiwork of "two young and distinguished Bahian artists," the sculptor Antonio Machado Peçanha and the painter José Antônio da Cunha Couto.[97] Long after the republic's proclamation, the Liceu de Artes e Ofícios donated this statue to the Instituto Geográfico e Histórico da Bahia, where it is now on display (figure 3.3). The Instituto recorded that Amaral had commissioned this work and had given it to the Liceu.[98] No later description of the stage explicitly mentions this statue, and the one other image of a stage (from 1874) is insufficiently detailed to perceive the effigy's form.[99] Instead, as in 1878's program, the emperor's image was most commonly called an "effigy" (which does not rule out a statue); however, that year, another newspaper's report referred to the effigy as a "portrait."[100]

The week-long festival of 1871 gradually shrank to what Amaral described in 1881 as three days of "illumination and celebration."[101] The allegories' return to Lapinha marked the festival's end. In the 1860s and 1870s, this took place on 8 or 9 July, but by the 1880s the celebrations were ending earlier, on 4, 5, or 6 July. The time of day of the return to Lapinha, controversial back in 1864, varied from 3 p.m. in 1867 to after 9 p.m. in 1877 and to 4 p.m. in 1888 and 1889, suggesting an ongoing tussle between authorities and celebrants over whether to allow this to become a nocturnal procession. Three or four patriotic battalions typically accompanied the symbols, and in 1880 and 1882, the Direção requested that the president give civil servants half a day off and that commercial houses release their employees to participate.[102] In 1889, the *Diário da Bahia* responded to a similar request by stopping its presses on 5 July, which meant that it would not circulate on 6 July.[103]

A large number of people usually joined this procession, and the sounds of bands, fireworks, and poetry accompanied it. In 1871, "everywhere, flowers were thrown on the symbols and on the imposing procession, beautified by the lights in the houses, by the burning torches,

Figure 3.3 | The statue of Emperor Pedro II displayed in 1872

*Source*: IGHBa. Reproduced with permission.

and bathed by the light from the heavenly candelabras"; in this account, Amaral echoed the enthusiastic coverage of the Noite Primeira de Julho during the 1850s.[104] Other assessments were less effusive. In 1872, the *Jornal da Bahia* lamented that "few horsemen, only an understrength patriotic battalion, bands from the police and the Eighteenth Infantry, and a few dozen more people" accompanied the symbols.[105] In 1868, when it appeared that the Progressista cabinet was about to fall, rumour had it that "certain people of rank [*personagens*] were ready to tow the triumphal float for its return" to Lapinha; according to a Progressista correspondent, these Conservative "dreamers about the ministry's fall" would have been a marked departure from the "patriots of little renown" who normally took the triumphal floats back to Lapinha.[106] *O Alabama*, in fact, claimed that the wagons were pulled by what it judged to be "barefoot urchins [*moleques*] and bedraggled Africans."[107]

There are few references to the Pilgrimage to Pirajá, as it eventually became known, but it appears to have been a regular mid-July addendum to the main Dois de Julho celebrations. In the 1860s and early 1870s, the Minerva Patriotic Battalion led this pilgrimage and arranged for the transfer of independence veterans' remains to join Labatut at Pirajá. In 1867, this student battalion, led by Professor Chico Santos, moved Lieutenant General Luiz da França Pinto Garcez's remains from the cemetery to the Santo Antônio dos Militares chapel in preparation for taking them to Pirajá later in July. The following year, they laid Brigadier Manoel Joaquim Pinto Pacca to rest there, and in 1871, they exhumed the remains of Colonel José Jácome de Menezes Dória and Lieutenant Colonel Francisco Lopes Jequiriçá for reinterment in the chapel.[108] In 1879, the pilgrimage was included in the festival program published on 1 July, which noted that those who joined in this "pious effort" would deposit a wreath before Labatut's tomb and hear a mass for the souls of those who had sacrificed themselves in the struggle.[109] An 1885 announcement described those who would go to Pirajá as "horsemen," an indication of the participants' social class; few could afford horses, and the locale was too distant from downtown Salvador to reach easily by foot. An 1889 report distinguished between the "pilgrims" and the "locals," who also heard the mass.[110]

By the 1860s, neither the patriotic emblems' return to Lapinha, nor the pilgrimage to Pirajá, marked the end of Dois de Julho celebrations, for throughout July and August, and sometimes as late as September, neighbourhood celebrations took place in Salvador's suburbs (the latest that I know of took place in mid-September, in 1889).[111] Poorly documented by brief newspaper announcements, requisitions for reinforced policing, and occasional police or newspaper reports, these were "miniature" Dois de Julhos, as Querino and folklorist Antônio Vianna characterized them. Varella's informant recalled that some of them took place with "great pomp."[112] In the mid-1970s, by which time this tradition had long disappeared, folklorist Hildegardes Vianna described them as "miniatures of the official celebrations," dismissing them as "completely ridiculous … in every way"; only a "*povo*" whose members "never understood what was truly the day of our independence and the [Dois de Julho] festival" could appreciate such parades.[113] I have found references to forty-one such celebrations in sixteen different locations in twenty-one of the years between 1854 and 1889 (many more no doubt went undocumented). Their locales ranged from respectable upper- and middle-class neighbourhoods like Itapagipe (which accounts for twelve of the forty-one references), Rio Vermelho, and Vitória (one each) to poor suburbs like Cidade de Palha (today Cidade Nova) and nearby Cruz do Cosme (today Caixa d'Água).

The earliest of these that I know of tended to take place in the first days or weeks of July, often coinciding with the main festival. Thus, in 1854, *O País* complained about the Itapagipe subdelegate's behaviour on 3 July; Marcolino Alves de Souza's henchmen insulted "honorable men" in front of Pedro II's portrait. Not satisfied with the cheer that he received at the stage, he "had the Brazilians' triumphal float taken to his Portuguese distillery, in order to receive doubled cheers before a table, which was decorated with the remains of a wedding feast!" Fearing indigestion, the patriots did not touch the leftovers.[114] In 1857, the celebrations in Penha parish (which included the Itapagipe peninsula) took place on 5 July.[115] Three years later, the three directors of Cruz do Cosme's celebration requested that the president arrange for appropriate honours to the emperor's portrait, which would be displayed on the evenings of 29 to 31 July.[116] The organizers of the 1864 festival at Quitandinha do Capim (in Santo Antônio Além do Carmo parish) requested that the president send a military guard to their stage and that he attend in person to unveil the imperial portrait; he apparently accepted the invitation, for they announced that he would be there on 4 July.[117] There was no central coordination for these neighbourhood festivals, and in 1885, organizers from Itapagipe and Itapuã discovered that they had scheduled their festivals for the same day. Itapuã's organizers delayed their celebrations by two weeks, for their Dois de Julho was a new one and would likely not be able to compete with Itapagipe's well-established celebrations.[118]

Several of these neighbourhood festivals began with the raising of a pole a few weeks before the actual festival and a *bando* the weekend before the celebrations began.[119] The celebrations proper invariably began with a procession during which the "triumphal float," the "*caboclo*'s wagon," or the "symbol of our emancipation" was conducted through the neighbourhood or parish and parked at the stage, which was located on a main square or in some other central location. All of these references are to single allegories, and none – not even the notices of the celebrations in Santo Antônio parish – explicitly state that one of the *caboclos* from Lapinha participated. Rather, it appears that parish festival organizers had their own symbols. In 1864, a soldier recognized "Brotas parish's float"; four years later, the program for that parish's festival indicated that it would be taken to Pitangueiras, where it was stored in the parish church's sacristy.[120] The "depository" for Vitória's "float" was in São Lázaro, while Itapagipe's was customarily in Papagaio (an 1854 complaint about the local justice of the peace indicates that the symbol was already in existence then).[121] In the 1970s, Hildegardes Vianna wondered what became of these "caboclos," but she made no effort to investigate their whereabouts on the grounds that such a search might be "dangerous" and might lead to the relics becoming tourist attractions.[122]

Programs for and descriptions of the neighbourhood symbols' processions note the participation of patriotic battalions and military bands.[123] Some of these patriotic battalions were especially organized for the occasion, such as the Defensores do Ocidente (Defenders of the West); anyone who wished to join this battalion to participate in 1871's Brotas festival was invited to meet at the Campo de Pólvora on 16 July, dressed in white pants, white vest, and black jacket. One Alberto R.F. Silva tried to organize a patriotic battalion by the name of Artistas Nacionais (National Artisans) to take part in "Jacaré's Dois de Julho."[124]

The parish festivals included most of the other elements of Dois de Julho celebrations: nocturnal illumination, music, cheers at the unveiling of imperial portraits, and poetry. In 1865, O Alabama complained about the "flood of verse" that poured from Itapagipe's stage, most of which "caused nausea among the listeners, for every blockhead thinks he is a poet" (and deservedly received "loud foot stamping [pateadas]"). Its writer also commented that "much rum was sucked back [chupou-se muita cachaça], and in some houses there were sambas or the poor man's ball" (at that time, samba referred to any popular celebrations involving dancing, not the twentieth-century musical genre).[125] There are occasional reports of disorderly drunks during these celebrations, along with complaints about open displays of weapons. In 1864, a slave died when someone fired a blunderbuss during the combined Brotas and Vitória celebrations.[126] A few of these celebrations were described as "the children's Dois de Julho," and in 1880, O Monitor criticized Dantas for attempting to make a political speech at one such function.[127] As suggested by their reverent treatment of the emperor's portrait and their requests for military honours, organizers generally strove for respectability. This is also suggested by an Itapagipe restaurateur's advertisement of his "table of select delicacies and fine beverages"; he reminded prospective customers that 27 July 1879 was "Itapagipe's Dois de Julho," a perfect day to "spend delightful time" there.[128]

That a restaurateur could recommend celebrating Dois de Julho in late July at his establishment in Itapagipe indicates how much the festival had evolved in the half century since patriots had first re-enacted the Exército Pacificador's march into Salvador. What had once been a radical-liberal demonstration with significant military involvement had become an increasingly diffuse and popular civilian festival, in the sense of spreading to Salvador's suburbs and in the sense of losing most of its military participants. The parish Dois de Julhos suggest that people were celebrating their local communities as much as Bahia, Bahia's independence, or Brazil. This interpretation is analogous to the observation that the most enthusiastic parading on the Fourth of July in the United States and on Bastille Day in France takes place in small towns, where people celebrate the local community as much as the imagined nation.[129] Nonetheless, the celebrations on 2 July itself retained most of the forms of previous decades, and patriots continued to emphasize Bahia's centrality to Brazilian independence. While Dois de Julho was no longer a radical-liberal festival, it remained a space in which Bahians pursued their political conflicts.

## Festival Politics and Politics in the Festival

Partisan politics invariably shaped the press coverage of Dois de Julho, and political questions regularly arose in the context of Dois de Julho celebrations. That the opposition dismissed celebrations organized by men associated with the government and that both government and opposition used the celebrations to score political points highlights Dois de Julho's importance. Assessments of the enthusiasm with which Bahians celebrated usually amounted to partisan political claims, not objective descriptions. The greater freedom to speak out on political questions during the festival made it a space that encouraged debate, directly or indirectly, about current affairs. Thus, the conflicts and debates that arose on Dois de Julho reveal much about Bahians' concerns and demonstrate how they conducted politics through the festival.

In the second half of the 1860s, the Paraguayan War cast a long shadow over the festivities. Worries about the war's costs and the allies' slow advance into Paraguay undermined the enthusiasm voiced in 1866, and in 1867, *O Alabama* detected an undertone of sadness due to war losses and family members' long absences.[130] That year, the *Jornal da Bahia* judged that there had been "little participation by the *povo*" and "little enthusiasm" and complained that the celebrations had been reduced to official ones – strong words about a festival that drew its legitimacy from popular participation, but not unexpected from an opposition newspaper.[131] The *Correio Mercantil*'s correspondent judged in 1868 that new taxes, continued recruitment, and burdensome National Guard service would undermine enthusiasm for the festival, and on 4 July, he reported that "there was no true happiness, for the times are distressing."[132] The year before, he had gone further, expecting that "a day will come in which these celebrations disappear, such is the indifference and egoism implanted by these terrible times."[133] Victory in the war came in March 1870, but the enthusiastic celebrations of its end apparently did not carry over into Dois de Julho; *O Alabama* attributed this to Bahia's ongoing economic difficulties.[134]

Opposition newspapers frequently used Dois de Julho editorials to lament Brazil's (or Bahia's) lack of progress. In 1867, *Bahia Ilustrada* bemoaned the country's indebtedness and high taxes as well as the interminable carnage in Paraguay; Brazilians seemed unable to value the legacy of liberty left by the patriots of 1823. Three years later, *O Alabama* called for increased immigration, condemned foreigners' domination of commerce, and railed against the many in power who failed to respect citizens' rights. The dissident Liberal *O Monitor* called for extensive political reforms in 1878 to fulfill the hopes of independence-era patriots and had sharp words for the new Liberal cabinet, which, in its estimation, had not moved quickly enough on its reform agenda.[135] In opposition in 1882, the Conservative *Gazeta da Bahia* argued that "these noisy celebrations, in which the *povo* lets loose and exults, are not merely outbursts of a wild enthusiasm." Not only were they a "generous adoration of the *pátria's* traditions," they were also an "eloquent and vigorous protest against today's men, who deprecate and slander this noble land," namely, the provincial government of President Pedro Luiz Pereira de Souza. Three years later, it attributed the lack of enthusiasm for the festival to a long list of political and economic problems, which it blamed on the administration.[136]

Partisan considerations invariably shaped perceptions of enthusiasm. The *Correio Mercantil* of 1867–68 opposed Zacarias's 1866–68 ministry, and its correspondents' comments about 1868's festival were part of its campaign against this government; likewise, the *Jornal da Bahia* was a Conservative organ, while *O Alabama* criticized whomever held power. In 1872, the Liberal *Diário da Bahia* judged that "this festival, which in former times was almost entirely popular, is today reduced solely to official ostentation" – on the part of the Conservative government, its readers would have understood.[137] In the early 1880s, when the Liberals were in power, it was the Conservative *Gazeta da Bahia's* turn to lament that "today indifference has replaced enthusiasm, dejection has killed joy, despair has expelled from [everyone's] heart the hope and the faith that are the magic force that impels nations toward perfectibility and the future."[138] In 1887, with the Conservatives back in office, the *Gazeta* gave qualified praise to the Direção, whose members, unfortunately, had not had sufficient time to organize the celebration.[139]

The coverage of 1889's festival strikingly reveals the competing partisan journalism. The Liberals had just returned to power (7 June 1889), and the Conservative *Gazeta da Bahia* declared bluntly that the celebrations were "very dispirited this year, demonstrating complete decadence." The *Diário do Povo* also wrote about the "population's indifference" and the "societies that did not take part" in the festival, in "complete contrast" to those of previous years. By contrast, the Liberal *Diário da Bahia* wrote effusively about the "great enthusiasm," and the *Diário de Pernambuco*, summarizing the news received from Salvador, noted that the city's newspapers were full of accounts of the celebrations and that the populace had taken part "with much enthusiasm."[140] There is, of course, no way to reconcile such competing assessments, but it is important to recognize that the Dois de Julho festival, in which provincial authorities played an important role, served as something of a plebiscite on the government. For both government and opposition, celebrating Dois de Julho was politics by other means, as was writing about the festival.

Rozendo Moniz pointed out that such politicization normally took place when Conservatives held power; prompted by "false rumours" about Liberal conspiring, the president mobilized additional police and military force that was never needed, thanks to the "peaceful and orderly disposition of the Bahian *povo*."[141] He may well have had 1869's Dois de Julho in mind when he wrote these lines, for that year's festival closely followed this pattern. This was the first Dois de Julho after Pedro's appointment of the 16 July 1868 Conservative cabinet. By mid-1868, a cabinet change was widely expected, and emboldened Conservatives made their presence felt during the festival. The *bando* included many demonstrations against Zacarias's Progressista cabinet; the troops failed to respond to cheers, and President José Bonifácio Nascentes de Azambuja was mocked at the theatre gala.[142] The Conservative *Jornal da Bahia* claimed that the "audience was very large" on 2 July, "more than could have been expected," and contended that this was the *povo*'s protest "against the current government," an assertion that the *Jornal do Commercio*'s Progressista correspondent judged "ridiculous," for the opposite was normally understood to be an indication of dissatisfaction with those in power.[143]

Two weeks later, Pedro called the Conservatives to power and the usual changes in provincial administration followed immediately. Azambuja was dismissed on 18 July; the second vice-president, Antônio Ladislau de Figueiredo Rocha, briefly took over the presidency until the Baron of São Lourenço (Francisco Gonçalves Martins) arrived for his second stint as Bahia's president (August 1868–April 1871). He immediately expanded the purge of Progressista officials launched by Figueiredo Rocha in preparation for the elections.[144] In April 1869, with the elections over (a Conservative sweep, thanks to the Liberal boycott) and Conservatives firmly in local office throughout the province, he temporarily handed the reins of office to the vice-president in order to take his seat for the upcoming senate session.

Conservatives allegedly dominated 1869's Direção; O Alabama identified only one Liberal among its members (the writer likely meant Historical Liberals, for the committee that Sauípe had named included mostly Progressistas).[145] A Liberal correspondent wrote in mid-June that Figueiredo Rocha was expecting a "revolution on the night of 1 July ... plotted by the Liberals" (it appears that he had reiterated prohibitions against the 1 July nocturnal celebrations, which the correspondent judged an illegal order that citizens could disobey).[146] A few days later, O Alabama reported rumours that the police were organizing a patriotic battalion to cheer the government during the celebrations "in reaction to certain degenerate Brazilians, perfidious and disorderly [men] who antagonize and slander a government as good and honorable as this one"; this was how the man who proposed this battalion described the opposition.[147] The Liberal correspondent reported that many costumed police soldiers had infiltrated groups of revellers during the bando.[148] A spy for Chief of Police Antero Cícero de Assis reported that the Sociedade Rossini (a philharmonic society) and an unnamed patriotic battalion had been plotting to steal the "wagons to do a Noite Primeira de Julho" procession. Police searched Lapinha's environs, and São Lourenço summoned Sauípe to the palace to explain the rumours. O Alabama and the Jornal do Commercio's Liberal correspondent condemned these precautions and added that the vice-president had ordered sailors disembarked from a navy ship, distributed munitions to "trustworthy" National Guard battalions, and brought in reliable guardsmen from outside of Salvador.[149] A police spy even tried to infiltrate a private party at a goldsmith's home; he gave himself away when, during toasts, he disagreed with criticisms of "the police's excesses." His cover blown, he blustered like a harpooned whale, tried to arrest the celebrants, and declared that, were it not for "the chief of police's adroitness, the torch of revolution would be lighting everything on fire at this very moment!"[150]

Matters came to a head during the symbols' return to Lapinha. Police and government efforts to create a patriotic battalion bore fruit in the form of the Duque de Caxias Battalion, which honoured the commander who had led the allied forces to Asunción (and whose incompatibility with the Progressista cabinet had prompted the 1868 ministerial change). Liberal accounts declared that the government could only fill this battalion's ranks by dispatching navy apprentices to parade (their dapper step betrayed military training). The Caxias battalion was apparently a direct response to the Argolo Patriotic Battalion, which honoured Alexandre Gomes de Argolo Ferrão (the Viscount of Itaparica), a Bahian field marshal who had distinguished himself in Paraguay but was apparently politically associated with the Liberals.[151] Organized by what a correspondent for Rio de Janeiro's *A Reforma* (the Liberal party organ) called "the flower of [Bahia's] youth," the Argolo battalion had contracted a National Guard band to parade with it. Figueiredo Rocha cancelled this contract, but the Campesina musical society, composed of "young men from the business community," offered to provide the indispensable music for free. Chief of Police Assis personally accompanied the procession to Lapinha to ensure that nothing untoward happened; three members of the Direção commanded, respectively, the division and the two brigades into which the procession was divided.[152]

Liberals declared that "the government looked completely ridiculous" because of the unnecessary police precautions, and added that despite this interference, "the July festivities were never more unenthusiastically celebrated than this year"; furthermore, "the Liberal Party and the men who led it were more acclaimed than ever before."[153] According to *A Reforma*'s correspondent, Figueiredo Rocha's "followers [*apaniaguados*]" declared after the festival that Assis's measures had nipped in the bud "the revolt, planned by the Liberals."[154] The *Jornal do Recife* published an account that completely ignored these conflicts and declared that the festival had ended "in the midst of great joy, enthusiasm, and participation," a report likely taken from a Conservative newspaper. The author of an *apedido* (a paid article) in *O Alabama* later denounced the "many lies" that he had read in the *Jornal do Commercio*.[155] These included the assertion that the Argolo battalion had only mustered 43 men while the Duque de Caxias Battalion numbered 150, among them "some merchants and people of high position" – statements that required "much cynicism" on the part of those who published them, judged *O Alabama*.[156]

In 1870, the Conservative *Jornal da Bahia* praised the peaceful celebrations and lamented that in previous years, "to disguise their fears, Progressista or Liberal governments – it is difficult to categorize them – used to threaten violence and disguise military units as patriotic battalions. The threats were dismissed, the violence never happened, and everyone, soldiers and *povo* alike, marched, because patriotic enthusiasm triumphed and pardoned everything."[157] This account – virtually a mirror image of what Liberals accused Conservatives of doing in 1869 – highlights the difficulty of determining what happened amid the cacophony of accusations and counter-accusations that shaped the press's coverage of Dois de Julho.

### The Frias Villar Incident, 1875

A different sort of politicization marked 1875's Dois de Julho and resulted in a very well-documented festival, despite the lack of any surviving Bahian newspapers for that year. By this time, Conservatives had been in power for seven years, during which they had introduced many of their reforms. Bahia's Liberals, led by Manoel Pinto de Souza Dantas, cultivated ties with members of Salvador's artisan working classes and would, the following year, create the Liga Operária; among their activists was a young painter and student at the Liceu de Artes e Ofícios by the name of Manoel Raimundo Querino.[158] Dantas's 1874 restoration of the Noite Primeira de Julho was no doubt an attempt to link the old tradition and the legacy of mid-century radical liberalism to the new Liberal Party. While this may indicate that Conservative fears about Liberal politicking in 1869 had not been entirely misplaced, I have found no commentary about the Liberal leader's role in 1874. The following year, the Noite Primeira parade was repeated to great enthusiasm, to judge by the Conservative *Jornal da Bahia* and the *Diário de Notícias*; nine or eleven patriotic battalions, "large [and] brilliantly outfitted," accompanied the wagons to Lapinha, where the *caboclos*' statues were mounted (during this procession, the wagons bore the national flag). Amid rousing poetry and speeches, fireworks, and cheers, the patriots reached Lapinha at 2 a.m.[159]

The restored Noite Primeira was, however, completely overshadowed by a violent conflict between an army battalion and a patriotic battalion on 2 July 1875 that led to two civilian deaths and several injuries. The ensuing political crisis revealed deep partisan cleavages nationally and provincially; at the same time, the provincial Liberal leadership's support for Conservative President Venâncio José de Oliveira Lisboa's efforts to maintain order demonstrates these men's shared class interests. Known as the Frias Villar Incident, after the commander of the Eighteenth Infantry Battalion, Lieutenant Colonel Alexandre Augusto de Frias Villar, these events were described by Querino and Rozendo Moniz, both of whom blamed the "soldiery [*soldadesca*]" and their commander, who "ordered [them] to fix bayonets against defenceless people." Querino celebrated Dantas's role in attending the funeral of the first man to die, a typographer, and in calming the crowds that sought vengeance. Both described the army battalion's hasty embarkation and the lynching that Frias Villar narrowly escaped when he was discovered in a closed sedan chair en route to the docks.[160] Later folklorists also mentioned these events; Campos described 1875's Dois de Julho as the last festival "of the old days," and provided some details derived from oral traditions.[161]

No Bahian newspapers for 1875 are available, but Recife and Rio de Janeiro journalists closely followed the incident. By this time, a submarine telegraph cable connected Salvador to the capital, and the first news about the incident reached Rio de Janeiro in the form of terse telegrams published in newspapers the following day, which sometimes conveyed inaccurate information. This "acceleration of the news cycle," to use modern terminology, quickly turned the incident into a national political question. In the second week of July, after copies of

Bahia's newspapers as well as eyewitnesses had arrived in the capital, the two party newspapers, the Conservative *A Nação* and the Liberal *A Reforma*, extensively debated the incident's significance, while the *Jornal do Commercio* presented non-partisan reports and opened its paid columns to partisan accounts.

By the time of this incident, President Lisboa had governed Bahia since June 1874 and Pedro II had just appointed the elderly Duke of Caxias as president of the council of ministers to replace the Viscount of Rio Branco. Two infantry battalions and a cavalry company comprised the provincial garrison. Frias Villar's Eighteenth Infantry had been stationed in the province after the Paraguayan War; unlike the Sixteenth Infantry, which had long-established connections to Bahia, the Eighteenth had no ties to the province.[162] The commander of arms, Brigadier João do Rego Barros Falcão, had long wanted to get rid of Frias Villar because of his "insolence towards his superiors."[163]

Some days after the incident, Frias Villar published a detailed exposition of his conduct in several Bahian newspapers. He explained that, although he had been sick and was expecting a transfer to another battalion, he wanted to lead his men in the Dois de Julho parade. Aware of the potential for disorder, he delayed the payment of salaries due at the start of the month so that the soldiers would not have the means to get drunk during the festival. In the morning, the Eighteenth marched to Lapinha and joined the great parade, but upon arrival in the crowded Conde d'Eu Square (the Terreiro de Jesus), Frias Villar lost control of his men. When he received the order from Barros Falcão to form up his battalion in "closed column" behind the Sixteenth, he discovered that "some of the men were already drunk." From the column's rear, he observed "great confusion and disorder" among the front platoon, so he ordered a cornet to play the orders to stop (he could not shout over the noise) "so that the soldiers not continue to march into the mass of *povo* in front of them." He struggled to reach the column's front, where he learned that a cadet and "a man of the *povo*" had "gotten into a fight." After restoring order, he noticed "new hubbub and disorder" at the column's rear, where "the last platoon and the band" were "completely mixed up with the *povo* because of another fight, resulting from a rock that had hit a musician in the head, leaving him prostrate and covered in blood." He rode into the crowd of disorderly soldiers

to bring them under control; unable to do so completely, he nevertheless managed to get all of his men out of the square and back to their
quarters at Palma Barracks. He forcefully denied that he had ordered
his troops to fix bayonets, and he vigorously defended his honour as
a patriotic Brazilian officer who would never turn his sword against
"peaceful and defenceless citizens who were celebrating a day of such
happy national memories." In a maudlin conclusion, he lamented his
injuries and his arrest pending a court martial, and he pardoned those
who in a "moment of unfortunate insanity, tried to vilify me."[164]

While Frias Villar's statement was no doubt a self-serving account of
the incident, some aspects of it ring true, notably his difficulty keeping
soldiers under discipline and performing basic parade manoeuvres on
the crowded square. The lieutenant colonel was responding to the accounts in Salvador's press that had blamed him for the entire incident.
These had reached Rio de Janeiro by 11 July, and *A Reforma* transcribed
what must have been the Liberal *Diário da Bahia*'s report, while the
*Jornal do Commercio* summarized it (and perhaps also other Bahian
accounts); the *Diário de Pernambuco* transcribed the *Jornal da Bahia*
and the *Diário de Notícias* reports. These note that the incident took
place after the Te Deum (during which the troops had had time to find
drinks), while the battalions were forming up to begin their parade
past the portrait of Pedro II on the stage, which was full of authorities
and "many high-ranking citizens." To the right of the fountain (i.e., between the fountain and the cathedral) stood the patriotic battalion of
the Liceu de Artes e Ofícios. Part of the Eighteenth (presumably what
Frias Villar described as his column's rear) collided with the patriotic
apprentices, who exchanged harsh words with the soldiers and pushed
back to hold their position. During this initial scuffle, according to the
*Diário de Notícias*, Frias Villar repeated the orders to advance and the
soldiers broke the poles that supported the Liceu battalion's standard,
a direct attack on its symbol, which must have prompted the artisans'
reaction. With "condemnable savagery," the soldiers attacked the patriots with bayonets, rifle stocks, and sabres. The patriots defended
themselves valiantly. While neither Frias Villar nor Barros Falcão did
anything, two members of the Direção bravely waded into the crowd
to separate the contending parties; by contrast, the *Jornal da Bahia*
credited the commander of arms, the chief of police, and the police

commander with this. By the time it was over – which took fifteen minutes or half an hour – typographer João Albino de Almeida lay dead (he was also a musician in the Quarenta de Voluntários Philharmonic); an autopsy later showed that the blade had perforated his liver and struck one of his lower vertebrae. Nine more had been injured, including a Portuguese man, Joaquim de Souza Castro, whose life was in danger. Dantas, who served as the Santa Casa de Misericórdia Hospital steward, personally ensured the best medical care for the injured, but doctors could not save Castro, who died on 11 July.[165]

President Lisboa immediately ordered Frias Villar's arrest and confined the Eighteenth to its quarters. According to Campos, angry crowds brandishing rocks and sticks threatened to attack the offending soldiers in Palma Barracks, which was reluctantly protected by the men of the Sixteenth, many of them Bahians who shared the crowd's outrage. The theatre gala went ahead as scheduled, but a poet recited verses about the incident.[166] Barros Falcão, the commander of arms, reported more details: Frias Villar had resisted arrest, arguing (correctly) that the president had no authority to order his arrest (only his military superiors could do so) and protesting that ill health precluded transferring him to a warship. The battalion commander finally agreed to be taken to São Pedro Fort.[167]

The next afternoon, Frias Villar consented to be removed to the safety of a warship but insisted on going in a sedan chair, accompanied only by a brigadier. This operation failed when the *povo* discovered the lieutenant colonel on the steep Conceição Street. In what a Conservative writer described as "an act of cannibalism," they dragged him from the chair and attempted to stone him. Frias Villar and his escort escaped into a mattress store, but the mob broke down the door and the brigadier could not calm them. This bought Frias Villar enough time to hide under a trap door in a neighbouring shop, but he was soon discovered, beaten, and stabbed. A pharmacist, Vasco Teófilo de Oliveira Chaves, and some other citizens finally managed to get him to the nearby·navy hospital. Campos adds the picturesque detail that one of his rescuers told Frias Villar to play dead and loudly shouted to the crowd that they had killed him, which allowed them to get him to safety. Amid "indescribable ... agitation" in downtown Salvador, shopkeepers hastily closed their stores, but nothing untoward happened that night.[168] Rumours that Frias Villar was dead soon reached Barros Falcão, and he hastened to the Eighteenth's barracks to maintain order, before he could confirm that the former commander had survived. "Several times the soldiers mutinied in the barracks," noted Barros Falcão, and one company drove out its captain amid loud boos.

On the morning of 4 July, some three thousand people attended João Albino's funeral at the Campo Santo cemetery. As the mourners returned to the city centre, rumour spread that the soldiers of the Eighteenth were refusing to leave Salvador, or even that they were planning to attack the Presidential Palace, army headquarters, and the populace. Gathering in front of the Presidential Palace, demonstrators demanded arms to protect themselves against the soldiers. At this point, Dantas and other Liberal leaders met with President Lisboa and offered him their support. A Conservative commentator later accused the Liberals of having spent the previous day praising the "*povo* [that] nobly avenged itself." In fact, Dantas and other Liberal leaders had telegraphed the *Jornal do Commercio* that day to report Frias Villar's beating and their "statement ... advising the *povo* to behave prudently and to respect the law." Dantas and Lisboa addressed the crowd from the palace, and the Liberal leader gave his word that the troops would embark. That night, the *Diário da Bahia* offices remained open and Liberals, including a young Rui Barbosa, repeatedly addressed the crowd. From this vantage point (the newspaper's building stood on the Theatre Square's south edge), it was possible to catch glimpses of the troops' embarkation, which took place under the cover of darkness. The *Jornal da Bahia* explained that the nocturnal embarkation was necessary because of the tide.[169] Barros Falcão later reported that he had named an officer from the Sixteenth to serve as acting commander of the Eighteenth and that fully fifty-six of its men were under arrest when they embarked.[170] According to Campos, the soldiers marched barefoot and followed a circuitous route that avoided the downtown. By 10:40 a.m. on 5 July, all three hundred soldiers were on board the coastal steamer *Bahia*, which was set to weigh anchor.[171]

Thus ended three tense days in Salvador. The festival organizers had prudently postponed the triumphal floats' return to Lapinha, originally scheduled for 5 July.[172] On 8 July, the Seventh Infantry Battalion, hastily dispatched from Rio de Janeiro to replace the Eighteenth, arrived in Salvador.[173] The Portuguese victim, who died on 11 July, was buried at government expense. Three patriotic battalions accompanied his funeral procession, as did the Direção, the chief of police, and reportedly eight thousand people. The "festive return of the triumphal floats" to Lapinha took place on 12 July, at 10:30 a.m. – no one was taking chances with a nocturnal procession. The *Jornal da Bahia* noted that "while the time was not ideal because of the burning sun ... the attendance was such that it appeared that there had not been this problem." The Direção, including its president, participated, along with a "numerous multitude" in what the *Jornal da Bahia* characterized as a demonstration of Bahian unity: "It remains a consolation to us that it was not the Bahian *povo* who broke with the traditions of the great day and that all, Brazilians and foreigners alike, applied themselves as much as possible to reducing the fears."[174]

Meanwhile, the Rio de Janeiro press distributed blame and credit. On 10 July, the *Diário Oficial* published the telegrams exchanged between Lisboa and Caxias. Among other things, they revealed Frias Villar's obstreperous character (he had refused to accept the order for his arrest unless it came directly from the president of the council of ministers) as well as authorities' fears of the *povo*. When Lisboa noted that acceding to the *povo*'s demand for Frias Villar's arrest "would aid the authorities," Caxias wired back: "Popular support is not, for now, needed for authorities to do their duty. Prevent gatherings from which can result disturbances to order."[175] *A Reforma* seized on this to criticize Caxias for his lack of faith in the *povo*.[176]

On 13 and 15 July, *A Nação* transcribed lengthy articles from its fellow Conservative newpaper, the *Correio da Bahia*, that criticized the *Diário da Bahia* for its celebration of Liberal leaders' help in keeping order. Instead, argued the *Correio*, most of the credit belonged to President Lisboa, Commander of Arms Barros Falcão, and the chief of police. Even the patriotic battalion Artes e Ofícios (the Liceu's battalion) reportedly cheered Lisboa after returning from the funeral of its deceased member.[177] The author of a paid article in the *Jornal do Commercio*, who described himself as an eyewitness to the events of 2–5 July, concluded that the Liberals who took credit for upholding order were like "the poor fly, sitting on the front of a coach, [and] thinking that he is pulling it."[178] The next day, a Liberal responded to this provocation by pointing out that the *Correio da Bahia* had recognized that Liberals had taken a "dignified and praiseworthy position" during these incidents and that Lisboa had publicly thanked Dantas for his assistance in securing the battalion's embarkation.[179] In 1877, a *cronista* in *O Monitor* praised Dantas's actions in 1875 and claimed that he had in effect assumed the role of president during those tense days.[180]

Behind the partisan wrangling and the tragic death of two Dois de Julho patriots lay another issue that helped change the role of the army garrison in Dois de Julho celebrations. On 1 July 1875, registration for the new draft lottery was supposed to start throughout the country. Violence against the registration boards broke out in many parts of the country, often perpetrated by artisans and other members of the respectable lower and lower-middle classes, who had formerly enjoyed protection from forced recruitment thanks to the patronage networks that they cultivated. Men like the murdered typographer, João Albino, had no desire to be reduced to the status of rank-and-file soldiers, yet this was exactly what the draft lottery might do to them.[181] While in opposition, Liberals had rejected the draft lottery (indeed, they had held a rally against it outside the *Diário da Bahia*'s offices on 1 July 1875) and called for an all-volunteer force. Yet once in power, they did nothing, and in 1880, *O Monitor* recalled Bahian Liberals' anti-draft campaign in the months before 1 July 1875 and condemned the 1878–80 cabinet for having failed to abolish the lottery.[182] This issue no doubt lent an edge to the collision between the artisans and the soldiers. The voluntarism embodied in the patriotic battalions, which echoed the enthusiasm with which Bahians had flocked to the colours during the struggle for independence, contrasted sharply with the impressed status of most of the soldiers in the Eighteenth. Moreover, these men were outsiders to the province, which made their violence all the more offensive.

As Campos noted, after 1875, army battalions no longer joined the 2 July procession into the city.[183] Nevertheless, patriots did not easily forget 1875. Five years later, an angry commander of arms complained about a public display on columns on the Terreiro de Jesus: "Two ridiculous effigies of soldiers with the number 18 on their shakos." Recalling the attempted murder of Frias Villar but not the two men killed by soldiers, he called on the president to have the effigies removed.

"Less prudent" officers had complained of this dishonorable display in front of their men, and he feared this would have "dire consequences."[184] Apparently no such consequences ensued from this incident, but the effigies clearly demonstrated that the army had become an unwelcome presence on Salvador's streets during Dois de Julho and that it served as a useful "other" for Bahian patriots. This marked a major change from the 1840s, when patriots sought the participation of military units in the procession, and reflects the declining status of the army in Bahian society, exacerbated by the traumatic experience of wartime impressment and the threat of a draft lottery.

It was easy to exclude army battalions from the great parade; it was not so easy to dispense with the services of army bands, even as hostility towards the military likely exacerbated the conflicts between military and civilian musicians and the attacks on army bands (discussed earlier in this chapter). Civilian patriots and voluntarist Dois de Julho patriotism could find no room for army personnel, all the more so in the aftermath of 1875's violence. The alleged Liberal revolutionary plot of 1869 and the debate about the Frias Villar incident together reveal that Bahians (and Brazilians) continued to see Dois de Julho through a partisan lens. The passions aroused by both these incidents, as well as the large number of people who protested against the Eighteenth Infantry and Frias Villar, demonstrate Dois de Julho's importance to the Bahian population. The withdrawal of army and National Guard units from the parade turned it into a more popular procession – a *corso*, as Xavier Marques put it, using a term that referred to carnival parades – in which prominent members of society and other social groups sought to display themselves.[185] The popular patriots who joined it rejected the discipline, hierarchy, and forced recruitment associated with the regular army.

The Dois de Julho festival demonstrated considerable continuity in form from the 1860s to the 1880s. In the 1870s, the end of National Guard and army participation in the great parade turned Dois de Julho into a more civilian celebration, but it retained its other principal elements. It also spread widely in Salvador through the neighbourhood festivals, whose adoption of these celebratory forms suggests a local reworking of Bahia's principal civic ritual and of how Bahia's independence was understood. The Sociedade Dois de Julho's disappearance likely simplified the festival's administration by eliminating the need to coordinate between two organizations.

Dois de Julho remained an important space for conducting politics. As many have observed about civic rituals, reports about them were as important as what actually took place on the streets. Authorities and organizers increasingly presented Dois de Julho as a celebration that belonged to *all* Bahians, who had an obligation to honour the generation of heroes that had won independence and founded the Brazilian empire, but patriots took to the streets for many other purposes. As reflected in the politicized newspaper accounts of the time, partisan politics were central to Dois de Julho celebrations; moreover, the presence of abolitionists, artisans, and workers, as well as neighbourhood groups, indicates that many Bahians were determined to claim a place for themselves in the public rituals by marching in patriotic battalions. The passions aroused by the 1875 Frias Villar incident underscore the festival's importance to Bahians. Together, these forms of politicization demonstrated the extent to which Bahians of all classes were engaged citizens, avid followers of the great and petty political issues of the day. To reiterate a point, Dois de Julho celebrations were serious politics, albeit wrapped in a festive and celebratory culture.

Despite the often enthusiastic celebrations of these years and their spread throughout Salvador, some perceived a decline in the Dois de Julho festival that went beyond the opposition's familiar partisan dismissal of government-organized celebrations. Furthermore, a few critics had begun to question the celebrations' traditional forms. Before examining these issues, we turn to Dois de Julho's social history and its theatrical elements.

## CHAPTER FOUR

# "On 2 July Nobody Fights": The Multiple Meanings of a Festival

The Dois de Julho festival began as a radical-liberal demonstration in 1827; then, over the following decades, it turned into a celebration that belonged to all Bahians and that visibly demonstrated membership in the imagined community of Bahia, which was part of the Brazilian nation, to be sure, but distinct from other provinces. Bahians who left the province regularly celebrated Dois de Julho. By the 1850s, the many Bahian students at the Recife law school had turned Dois de Julho into a regular winter festival in the Pernambucan capital.[1] Even as his military career took him to Rio Grande do Sul and Rio de Janeiro after 1839, Ladislau dos Santos Titara continued to commemorate Dois de Julho in verse.[2] Bahian officers serving in the Paraguayan War celebrated with a dinner on 2 July 1866; another Bahian in Entre Rios in 1865 dashed off a Dois de Julho poem in which he expressed his hope to win glorious victories like those of the 1822–23 patriots.[3] The first Bahians at São Paulo's law school celebrated Dois de Julho in 1829 and garnered favourable comment from a local liberal newspaper, whose editors had no difficulty understanding the demonstration's Exaltado meaning.[4] By the late 1860s, however, when the Bahian poet Antônio Frederico de Castro Alves recited his "Ode to Dois de Julho" to São Paulo audiences, he had to preface his performance with an explanation of why Dois de Julho mattered: "The Seventh of September is brother to the Second of July," he told his audience.[5] Brazilians from one end of the empire to the other could easily understand the radical-liberal Dois de Julho of the first decades after independence, regardless of whether they agreed or disagreed with its message. However, it later became more difficult for other Brazilians to understand, much less to accept, Dois de Julho as an essential part of the struggle for Brazil's independence, whose official history had by this time firmly established Emperor Pedro I's actions on 7 September 1822 as the nation-state's founding moment.[6]

This chapter turns away from the chronological narrative of the previous chapters to analyze the multiple meanings attributed to Dois de Julho during the empire, drawing on the well-established theoretical insight that festivals and rituals are polyvalent.[7] Festivals usually exhibit an overarching discourse that expresses a coherent meaning; in practice, though, they signify different things to different people and thus constitute spaces of contestation, in which conflicts over membership in the community, appropriate comportment, and relationships with outsiders shape the patterns of commemoration and people's understanding of rituals. Dois de Julho was no exception to this, and alongside the political questions debated on the day and the partisan politics conducted through the festival, Bahians wrangled over the nature of their society – who were the true Bahians? – over proper behaviour during their festival, and over their relationship to Brazil. We have already touched on some of these themes, but examine them in more depth in this chapter.

For most nineteenth-century Dois de Julho celebrants, the festival necessarily excluded slaves and Africans. Neither citizens nor (in the case of Africans) even potential citizens, they could not be part of the liberal nation envisaged by the Exaltados. African freedmen remained essentially stateless aliens under Brazilian law, and in Bahia they were subject to deportation and poll taxes imposed after the 1835 slave revolt.[8] Their presence also posed a challenge to the provincial elites, who aspired to a civilized and modern Bahia. Unsurprisingly, then, Dois de Julho patriots' rhetoric about winning Brazil's freedom from slavery to Portugal did not apply to slaves. Anti-Portuguese rhetoric and violence was considerably less visible in Dois de Julho sources than folklorists and historians have suggested, even in the early decades of the festival's history. To be sure, the Portuguese served as a rhetorical other for Dois de Julho patriots, but this rhetoric conflated them with despotism and focused primarily on the latter. There are indications of a distinct Afro-Brazilian understanding of the Dois de Julho festival, even as African cultural practices during the festival remained matters for the police to deal with.

When it came to race, liberal Dois de Julho patriots maintained a deafening silence, much as did the 1824 Constitution, although like other Brazilian liberals, they were willing to denounce overt manifestations of racism, appealing implicitly to the charter's articles that mandated equality before the law for all citizens. After the slave trade ended in 1850, the freeing of slaves became a regular feature of Dois de Julho celebrations. While carefully controlled and restricted, these manumissions nevertheless indicated that patriots no longer overlooked the contradiction between celebrating liberty and maintaining slavery. Here too, there are occasional indications that slaves intervened in this process and had their own understanding of Dois de Julho.

Dois de Julho patriots regularly spoke about the importance of order. This meant more than the absence of violence and the preservation of slave property; it also meant upholding norms of public comportment and respecting social hierarchies in a celebration that, for a few days, brought people of all classes onto the streets. This social mixing had its own dangers, and the police had to ensure that the central public spaces of the Dois de Julho celebration were safe for "families" – a code word for respectable members of the middle and upper classes – and were not controlled by the *povo*, as city streets normally were.

As Dois de Julho's radical elements increasingly became a rhetorical legacy, discussions about the day's meaning shifted to place more emphasis on inserting Bahian struggles for independence into the national Brazilian narrative, or official history, which celebrated independence as the product of Pedro I's Grito do Ipiranga on 7 September 1822. Castro Alves and countless other Bahian patriots of all political stripes agreed that Dois de Julho deserved equal billing with Sete de Setembro: they were the twin foundations for the Brazilian nation, of which, it should be emphasized, they envisaged Bahia as an integral part. By the last decades of the empire, when Bahia's economic decline was visible to all, such claims also sought to win symbolic capital for "Cabral's firstborn," as some referred to Bahia in recognition that it had been where the Portuguese first landed in 1500. In these senses, Dois de Julho can be understood as a manifestation of regionalism; it was, however, a distinct form of regionalism, one that clamed centrality for Bahia in Brazil's recent history and that said little about Bahia's cultural distinctiveness.

## Exclusions and Inclusions

Slavery and its legacy – the significant presence of Africans and their culture in Brazil, as well as racial hierarchy – profoundly shaped Bahian society, and the Dois de Julho festival was no exception to this. The wave of African slave revolts that culminated in the Malê Rebellion of January 1835 had no direct impact on Dois de Julho celebrations. Although it was common for slave rebellions to coincide with festivals, only twice did rumour have it that slaves were plotting a revolt for 2 July. In addition to the rumoured "rising of blacks" mentioned by the British consul in 1831 (chapter 1), in 1844, slaves in rural Paripe were reportedly planning to take advantage of the local National Guard's participation in Salvador's parade as a moment to rebel.[9] Early Dois de Julho celebrants paid little attention to slavery; rather, they envisioned a Bahia that was neither African nor Portuguese, and the Indianist symbols exemplified this ideal. Africans and slaves saw things differently, and in various ways they sought to participate in the festival. Journalists and authorities condemned the *batuques* as well as other manifestations of African culture that, in their view, besmirched the festival. They envisaged a society purged of Africanisms in which suitably subordinate slaves could acquire their freedom so long as they respected social hierarchies. When it came to race, however, Dois de Julho patriots generally maintained the discreet silence typical of nineteenth-century Brazilians' flexible approach to racial difference, one that permitted some non-white individuals to rise in society, but in ways that did not challenge the larger social hierarchies.[10]

Dois de Julho patriots regularly deployed the metaphors of slavery and freedom to describe independence and their commitment to liberalism. Domingos Guedes Cabral's *O Guaicuru* proclaimed in 1845 that Bahia was a "land of brave [men] / [A] land that will never again be of slaves."[11] An anonymous poem distributed at the *bando* in 1872 recalled that "the Brave / Broke the heavy irons / Of the humble enslaved people" and that "Holy Liberty / broke the slave's shackles." Following these metaphors for independence and liberty, the poet hailed the fact that, since the 1871 Free Womb Law, "In the land of the Holy Cross / No longer is anyone born a slave."[12] The metaphorical use of slavery and liberty to contrast the colonial regime to independent Brazil, or absolutism to the liberal empire, was never intended to apply to slaves, who were not part of the nation. Thus, a correspondent happily explained that Salvador's police had nothing to do on 2 July 1862, for "no one wants to blemish the great day." Three slaves were the only people arrested, much to the acting chief of police's satisfaction: "Not a single free person was arrested, for there were no disorders, which proves the population's peaceful disposition and good sense."[13] True Bahians, in other words, not slaves, knew how to comport themselves.

Implicit in such declarations was that the Portuguese – the colonial masters – were despots who had enslaved Brazil. In the years immediately after independence, Dois de Julho celebrations made heavy use of anti-Portuguese rhetoric, and radical liberals periodically called for the removal of natives of Portugal from civil and military office. Demands for the outright expulsion of Portuguese nationals regularly surfaced during the unrest of these years.[14] Unsurprisingly, those who had failed to support the struggle for independence or had fought against it were particular targets of nativist ire, as we saw in chapter 1. But as Pedro Octávio Carneiro da Cunha reminded us a long time ago, anti-Portuguese rhetoric was often a political tactic, and nothing would be more erroneous than to reduce post-independence politics to a conflict between Brazilians and Portuguese.[15] While anti-Portuguese rhetoric, especially appeals for the nationalization of retail commerce, regularly appeared during Dois de Julho celebrations and in the radical press, it is striking how rarely the surviving Bahian newspapers and the province's correspondents alluded to actual violence against Portuguese. Nevertheless, in his 1887 account of Dois de Julho celebrations, Alexandre José de Mello Moraes Filho asserted that, "on those days, it was common to have disorder [*fecha-fecha*]," in other words, street violence that obliged shopkeepers to close their establishments, as well as "kill-the-Portuguese-rascals [*mata-marotos*] riots, from which resulted censurable incursions [*correrias*] and frequent murders." Bahian historian José Wanderley de Araújo Pinho claimed that lusophobic patriots threatened to turn each Dois de Julho into a Saint Bartholomew's Day (an allusion to the 1572 massacre of French Huguenots).[16]

The anti-Portuguese violence reported in the newspapers falls far short of this. There were incidents of rock throwing at the Portuguese consul's house in 1855 and 1857 – in the former year, reportedly because he had failed to illuminate his windows. The consul apparently sought satisfaction from the government, but the police could not find the culprits. In 1863, his more circumspect successor made a special point of greeting the procession returning the floats to Lapinha when it passed his home, from which he flew both Brazilian and Portuguese flags.[17] It seems unlikely that the Bahian correspondents who normally stressed that the celebrations had been orderly would have ignored "frequent murders"; comments like those of Mello Moraes Filho may refer to minor incidents magnified in later retelling, while Wanderley Pinho probably reflected the worries of his grandfather, João Maurício Wanderley, in whose biography these remarks appeared. The graphic portrayals of *mata-marotos* riots may be accurate for the periods of armed revolt between 1823 and 1838, but such violence did not normally characterize Dois de Julho celebrations.

Of course, appeals for order may indicate latent worries, but the silence about anti-Portuguese violence and the near-complete absence of anti-Portuguese rhetoric from Dois de Julho by the last decades of the empire suggests that both had largely disappeared from the festival. In 1868, *O Alabama* accused immigrants from the Portuguese islands of mocking Brazil's national anthem during the *bando*, but this anti-Portuguese outburst stands out for its rarity; moreover, the editors recommended that Bahians ignore the provocation.[18] In his 1873 sermon, Romualdo Maria de Seixas Barroso condemned Portuguese exploitation of colonial Brazil but refrained from drawing any connections to contemporary relations between Brazilians and Portuguese.[19] The *Gazeta da Bahia* called for unity between Portuguese and Brazilians on 2 July 1882, for the former "planted among us the seeds of civilization and progress, which bore fruit in the form of liberty," and João Varella's informant recalled that "Brazilians and Portuguese fraternized during the celebrations."[20] Still others held that this marked a major change. The principal character in Xavier Marques's novel set in the 1870s, *O feiticeiro*, Paulo Bôto, was a Brazilian patriot, but his "Brazilianism [*brasileirismo*] ... unfolded in civilized and inoffensive ways." He respected the "liberated *pátria's* symbols," but unlike his father and grandfather, he "did not judge himself obliged to hate and to assault the hard-working Portuguese."[21] *The Anglo-Brazilian Times* reported in 1879 that "the former mode of celebrating [Dois de Julho] by threshing Portuguese [had] of late years gone out of fashion."[22] Such recollections of anti-Portuguese violence in past Dois de Julho celebrations were likely exaggerations, or they were conflations of what took place during revolts with Dois de Julho festivals.

While Brazilians and Portuguese could join in celebrating Dois de Julho, manifestations of Afro-Brazilian culture during the festival (and at other times) remained a cause for concern. In the 1840s, the *Correio Mercantil* led a long campaign against *batuques* and other forms of Afro-Brazilian celebration.[23] People of African descent numerically dominated Salvador's streets and engaged in activities that belied the image that middle- and upper-class patriots sought to project. In addition to the "troops of young people and blacks" who carried flags and torches to the sounds of patriotic slogans and music in 1859's Dois de Julho, Adolphe d'Assier saw "groups of blacks circulating through the streets led by torch[bearers], shouting, gamboling, and gesticulating," actions more redolent of *capoeiras* than of patriotic battalions. They may also have participated in *batuques*, which were apparently common on 2 July.[24] In 1862, for the first time, there were no reports of *batuques* on the Terreiro de Jesus. According to the correspondent, in the past, such celebrations had "lasted until late at night and sometimes until the morning ... but they were a blemish" on the celebrations, which were "marred by too much Africanism and savagery." Still, the campaign against *batuques* was not universally supported, and he questioned the judgment of unspecified individuals who argued that "everyone should have the freedom to amuse himself."[25]

The end of *batuques* in 1862 was not definitive. In 1866, José Álvares do Amaral lamented the disorderly and "deafening *batuques*" on Piedade Square during Dois de Julho celebrations, which made this an inappropriate site to display the triumphal floats.[26] In 1868, *O Alabama* called on the police to, once again, "put an end to the *batuques* on the Terreiro," for besides being inappropriate, they always ended in violent brawls. To its editor's surprise, some masters let their slaves spend the night of 2 July out, even though they returned home the next day "with broken heads [*de cabeça quebrada*]"; "on these days when all are free there is liberty for everything," he lamented.[27] The year before, *Bahia*

Figure 4.1 | The "Little Blacks' *Batuque*," 1867

*Source: Bahia Illustrada, 7 July 1867.*

*Ilustrada* had run a cartoon of the "little blacks' [*pretinhos*] *batuque*" on the Largo de São Francisco, a square adjacent to the Terreiro (see figure 4.1). It included no explanation of the image, which shows a crowded group of dancers, including relatively well-dressed men and women, some without African features. One man is clapping and at least two women are carrying trays of fruit or other foodstuffs on their heads. I have found no other references to *batuques* during Dois de Julho in the surviving primary sources for the rest of the empire, but they no doubt took place. Writing in 1886, Rozendo Moniz described how on Dois de Julho, "to get some relief from their daily labour, the lowest [ínfimas] classes amused themselves in groups and lively *sambas*, to the sound of tambourines, rattles, fiddles, and flutes." At the time, *samba* referred to any sort of celebration involving drumming and dancing, not the musical genre created in the twentieth century. Such activities might resemble *batuques*; in 1877, there were complaints about indecently costumed individuals who held a samba in front of the imperial effigy.[28] Decades later, some would recall these *batuques* as picturesque elements of the festival of bygone days, but at the time, the public presentation of a Bahia without Africanisms was serious business.[29]

What Dois de Julho meant to these Afro-Bahians is not clear. For some slaves, it was clearly a holiday to which they could look forward; for others, like the food sellers in figure 4.1, the day was just another workday, although quite possibly an especially lucrative one and one that could be broken up by recreation. Mello Moraes Filho recalled that household slaves held baskets of flowers for their mistresses to throw on the passing parade, an indication that the day offered no relief to them.[30] In 1865, *O Alabama* ran a dialogue between one of its journalists and an African man who spoke frankly in heavily accented Portuguese (which I will not attempt to reproduce in the translation). The African declared that the "Dois de Julho festival" amounted to the "celebration of liberty ... only in name." Those who worked only got a day off, and slaves toiled publicly on the very streets through which the "wagon of liberty that carries the *caboclo* trampling the serpent" passed. His interlocutor agreed with this analysis of the contrast between "the wooden liberty" and Brazil's "true reality," to which the African added that "the foreigner who sees this festival, who sees the banners in the windows, the flowers on lapels, and the soldiers forming up, this foreigner will get a poor impression of this pitiful place which is completely full of contradiction!"[31]

*O Alabama*'s African also commented on the "barbarism of Xangô" and wondered why, "on the day of Dois de Julho, Bahians put Xangô in the streets; and Xangô passes through Cruz do Pascoal [a small square in Santo Antônio Além do Carmo Parish] with a chain around his neck, in front of the horsemen who lead the wagon of liberty."[32] This passage is difficult to interpret. It may indicate an association of the *caboclo* to Xangô, one of the principal deities in Candomblé, and thus reveal the allegory's significance for practitioners of this Afro-Brazilian religion, but there are several problems with this interpretation. In Candomblé, *caboclo* spirits are today closely connected to the Brazilian land, and no adept would mistake them for the African Xangô.[33] Moreover, the African clearly indicates that the chained "Xangô in the streets" went ahead of the *caboclo* and the mounted escort that preceded the symbol.

I have found no description of this year's parade that casts light on other symbols or allegories that might have formed the basis of the African's remarks. What is clear, however, from both the *batuques* and the remarks about Xangó in the streets, is that Afro-Bahians attributed their own meanings to Dois de Julho and celebrated it in ways distinct from those of Bahia's white elite.

This may also be inferred from *O Alabama*'s 1868 lament that only "barefoot urchins [*moleques*] and bedraggled Africans" were sufficiently devoted to the symbols to take them back to Lapinha, although this may also have been an effort to discredit the Conservatives, who were rumoured to be planning a demonstration that night (chapter 3).[34] The 1866 complaint that, not for the first time, people had pulled "nails" from the symbols while they stood unguarded overnight on Piedade Square points in the same direction, even if it is difficult to interpret (the statues narrowly escaped falling over).[35] Was this merely a case of hardware theft, or did this reflect the desire for talismans closely associated with a powerful symbol? In his argument against displaying the symbols at Piedade that year, Amaral noted that, in the past, people pilfered "certain pieces from the triumphal floats' adornments," including the "busts that decorate the small wagon" and "the gilded stars from the large wagon."[36] These may be the earliest indications of Dois de Julho's Afro-Bahian religious and cultural significance, but the evidence remains opaque. That the Sé parish subdelegate requested four police soldiers to guard the symbols during the nights of 1887's festival suggests that people continued to take things from the *caboclos*.[37]

While foreigners like Assier frequently commented on the race of Dois de Julho celebrants (as they did on the blackness of Bahia's population more generally), Bahians normally maintained a discreet silence about race during the festival, or, like Varella's informant, they emphasized that "no one paid attention to colour or to [political] party when it came to celebrating the *pátria*."[38] In fact, people did pay close attention to party, whereas the few indications of racial tensions during the celebrations all involved someone calling attention to racial difference when Bahians were expected to ignore it. In 1871, *O Alabama* criticized an unnamed "liberal" who had reportedly complained that "on almost every night, a black man appeared on the stage to recite [poetry], lowering the event's standards." The critic should have commented on the poet's "merits" and not on his "skin colour."[39] In 1848, a French resident denounced one of the festival organizers for rudely trying to exclude a freeborn and decently dressed creole woman who was accompanying the family of her godparents and assisting with their youngest child.[40] To thus treat a black woman who apparently conformed to all of the social expectations for godchildren was a particularly egregious violation of racial etiquette.

So was a clumsy request in 1868 that "shop clerks of brown colour" not join the Caixeiros Nacionais for the parade; this attempt to ensure that the corporation was represented only by "white men" drew vigorous criticism from *O Alabama*. Suitably chagrined by the negative reaction, the foreigner apparently responsible for this (one Lupp or Luppe) did not attend the parade, and "the few black men in the retail sector" joined the patriotic battalion.[41] *O Alabama*'s account clearly reveals the limits of anti-racist discourse: the explicitly racist effort to exclude black clerks could easily be condemned, but the newspaper did not comment on the fact that only "a few blacks" were employed in commercial establishments in the first place. The incident prompted some discussion about race and *caixeiros*' social status that led in a very different direction. One commentator remarked that slaves actually had it better than *caixeiros*, for they could not be dismissed on thirty days' notice, and mocked the "cantankerous Luppe" for thinking that *caixeiros* were equivalent to diplomats (until very recently, there were frequent criticisms that the Brazilian foreign service sought to present a white face to the world). "It is only in Bahia that [it can be thought that] *caixeiros* can and should be only white men," he concluded derisively.[42] Without the context of the article to which the writer was responding, this text is difficult to interpret, although the implication is clear: pretentions to whiteness were inappropriate for low-status *caixeiros*.

## Patriots against Slavery

After mid-century, the Dois de Julho patriot leadership sought to do something about the contradiction between celebrating liberty and the presence of slavery on Salvador's streets. Public manumissions during the celebrations began as early as 1851, but these were primarily symbolic gestures, carefully controlled and conducted in ways that would not threaten the social order. Bahian patriots' manumissions on Dois de Julho in the 1850s apparently pioneered these public manifestations of anti-slavery sentiment; even so, Bahia's abolitionist movement of the 1880s lagged behind its counterparts in other provinces.

In 1851, after the slave trade's end, the Sociedade Dois de Julho, along with the Direção Geral dos Festejos, initiated a custom of publicly freeing slaves during the celebrations, usually late in the day on the stage after the public cheers to the imperial portraits. In 1851, six girls gained freedom in this way, followed by eight Brazilian-born children in 1852. In 1855, "some Brazilians of colour who had the misfortune of being born as slaves" likewise received manumission; in 1856, the freed children were all girls. In 1853, the Sociedade Dois de Julho ensured that the (perhaps) appropriately named Antônio Júlio da Boa Sorte (Good Luck), whom its members freed that year, received some basic education, after which he would be sent to the army arsenal's apprentice company to learn a trade.[43] On several of these occasions, the archbishop personally handed out the letters of liberty, confirming Mello Moraes Filho's recollection that Dom Romualdo Antonio de Seixas, who died in 1860, had taken part in this ritual.[44]

Apparently, Dois de Julho manumissions then ceased for a few years. In 1864, a correspondent lamented that the Sociedade Dois de Julho no longer promoted such manifestations "of thoughtful patriotism."[45] There was one manumission that year, but it was apparently a populist gesture on the president's part. He freed an "almost white" child at the start of the allegories' controversial return to Lapinha; the 500$000 (US$270) that it cost to free the child came from a popular subscription, indicating that this was a spontaneous initiative, typical of Brazilians' reaction to "white" slaves, whose existence threatened racial hierarchies.[46] The freeing of slaves in the 1850s and early 1860s does not appear to have had any abolitionist overtones, and I have found no indication that these manumissions were controversial in Bahia; they were apparently limited to Brazilian-born children (usually girls), and their owners were duly compensated. In these respects, the early Dois de Julho manumissions were typical of the Brazilian custom of commemorating important occasions by freeing slaves; that most of the freed were female and children is also typical of manumission prac- tices.[47] Varella's informant well remembered what masters expected of slaves when he recalled that owners only gave freedom to those who "merited" this favour.[48]

The moving story of twenty-five-year-old Veríssimo, the creole slave of Francisco Gonçalves Bastos, resident in Santana Parish, reveals something of Dois de Julho manumissions' significance for slaves. At about 11 a.m. on 2 July 1862, he tried to kill himself by ingesting a mixture of arsenic and laudanum. The subdelegate immediately in- vestigated and learned that Veríssimo had done so "because his plans for freedom, which he hoped to get from the Caixeiros [Nacionais] on 2 July, came to naught."[49] More details soon emerged, and a cor- respondent later transcribed Veríssimo's statement to the police. Recorded in third person, as was all legal testimony, it nevertheless comes as close as anything to a slave's view of Dois de Julho: "Desiring to free himself, he sought to learn how to play cornet, so that by this means he could acquire the necessary funds, that some members of the Caixeiros Nacionais had promised him, [after which] he would be the cornet in their patriotic battalion. Having learned how to play the above-mentioned instrument, he got himself ready for 2 July with his uniform and, on horseback, went in search of the battalion on Com- merce Square and there [illegible] *caixeiros*, became unhappy and [illegible] some paper money, that [illegible] returned home and pre- pared the dose [illegible]."[50]

Despite the lacunae caused by damage to the copy of the news- paper that was microfilmed, Veríssimo's statement underscores several points that the literature on slavery and abolition has made clear. Slaves actively sought manumission. Veríssimo sought out the Caixeiros Nacionais and made a point of learning to play the cornet so that he could earn the peculium that the Caixeiros would match. He obtained a uniform – likely the white pants and jacket, black tie, and straw hat of the Caixeiros (battalion organizers would provide the green sash with its name in gilded letters) – and managed to procure a horse, although one suspects that he "borrowed" the mount from his master or from someone else.[51] The illegible portions of the text make it impossible to know what happened when he sought out the Caixeiros. Had he misunderstood them? Were they playing a cruel joke on him? He did not fit the profile of slaves who received manumission during Dois de Julho celebrations, nor are the Caixeiros mentioned as the sponsors of manumissions during these years. Regardless of what happened, Veríssimo was certainly not the first slave to attempt suicide after the failure of efforts to win freedom.[52]

Dois de Julho manumissions resumed in 1869. The Sociedade Dois de Julho freed eight girls, and the Minerva patriotic battalion freed two more children. While praising these efforts, *O Alabama* lamented:

> They call free, it is true
> The Brazilian nation
> But it has so many children
> Groaning in slavery.

A correspondent added that even some Portuguese had contributed funds to the Sociedade's subscription for freeing children.[53] By this time, abolition was on the political agenda, thanks to Pedro II's 1867 call for parliament to address the "servile question." He kept up the pressure on deputies and senators over the course of 1870–71 and finally put together a cabinet under the Viscount of Rio Branco, who forced the free womb law through a reluctant legislature in September 1871.[54] Many Brazilians celebrated the Paraguayan War's end by freeing slaves, and one civil servant requested that the 6 percent of his salary that he had offered to the war effort now be consigned to an abolitionist society. Some observers suggested that these initiatives amounted to a widespread emancipation movement. After reporting the 1869 foundation of a society in Santo Amaro to celebrate 2 July by freeing slaves, a correspondent concluded: "Everywhere the idea of the servile element's emancipation is making great gains."[55]

The resumption of Dois de Julho manumissions took place in this context, and in 1870, the Direção Geral dos Festejos presented three girls with their manumission papers after the cheers at the stage; these manumissions were paid for with surplus funds raised for the festival. During the return of the allegories to Lapinha, Francisco (Chico) Álvares dos Santos, head of the Minerva patriotic battalion, freed a five-year-old child; the teacher had done this for a number of years.[56] Similar manumissions took place in 1871: the Sociedade Dois de Julho raised funds to free some children, while Chico Santos and the Minerva battalion freed "some captives." Among them was five-year-old Amâncio, owned by the teacher, who insisted that the boy bear the mark of his manumission in his new name: Amâncio Minerva Paraguaçu. During the Brotas parish Dois de Julho celebration, independence veterans freed another child amid loud cheers for the priest who explained the act's significance.[57]

After 1871, there were fewer Dois de Julho manumissions. A major and his wife freed Maria Eugênia "in honour of the memorable day of Dois de Julho, in which Brazil conquered her liberty and independence, and for the good services" that she had performed; this private manumission was not, however, linked to the organized celebrations.[58] Two children were freed in 1876, and according to Manoel Raimundo Querino, "a girl freed in honour of the day" rode on a float immediately after the *caboclo* in 1877's procession, a detail that can be confirmed in the press.[59] The theatre gala on the last night of 1882's Dois de Julho ended with a tableau before which some slaves were freed by the festival committee.[60] The number of Dois de Julho manumissions in the first half of the 1870s, however, is particularly modest when compared to the activities of Salvador's Sociedade Libertadora Sete de Setembro (Seventh of September Liberating Society), which freed about five hundred slaves between 1869 and 1875 and always marked Brazil's independence day with a significant distribution of manumission papers (an average of twenty-three during each of the 7 September celebrations between 1871 and 1874).[61] Until 1872, the provincial government supported the Sociedade Libertadora by allocating the revenue from a surcharge on a tax on slaves to its work (subsequently, the province contributed these monies to the Emancipation Fund established by the 1871 Free Womb Law). Even without this subvention, the Libertadora freed twenty-four slaves on 7 September 1878.[62]

Luiz Anselmo da Fonseca, a contemporary historian of Bahian abolitionism, lamented in 1887 that his province lagged behind the rest of Brazil in its commitment to ending slavery.[63] Fonseca's assessment likely reflected the frustrations of abolitionists, who had hoped for a quick end to slavery, and recent research has shown that, notwithstanding planter resistance, there was significant anti-slavery agitation in the province and that Bahian abolitionists deployed all of the tactics of their counterparts elsewhere in Brazil.[64] Bahia's committed core of anti-slavery activists gradually shifted the rhetoric about slavery and Dois de Julho, so that by the 1880s, the rhetorical contrast between the liberty won at the time of independence and the continuation of slavery could no longer be quietly ignored.[65] A Comissão Abolicionista Dois de Julho (Dois de Julho Abolitionist Commission) was founded in 1884 with the express purpose of finding jobs for freedmen and educating *ingênuos* (children born free under the terms of the 1871 law). This conservative approach to abolition focused on ensuring that former slaves remained reliable workers.[66] The surviving records of Dois de Julho for most of the 1880s do not suggest the same degree of abolitionist activity as on 7 September and 2 December (Pedro II's birthday) in Rio de Janeiro.[67] In an 1886 cartoon, *O Faisca* lamented that the sun still rose over "Brazilian brothers in captivity" on 2 July (see figure 4.2). That year, it also criticized authorities' delays in issuing manumission papers through the Emancipation Fund and suggested that the city council should not have spent money on fireworks when the funds could have been applied to freeing slaves.[68] The following year, the city council was reluctant to accept a financial contribution from an abolitionist society for the celebrations.[69] (These are, incidentally, some of the few indications that the city council had a role in overseeing the festival's organization.) At the Te Deum, Friar Francisco da Natividade Carneiro da Cunha preached for almost two hours (!) and "even demonstrated the incompatibility of tolerating slavery with the duties of Christianity"; this sparked "an electric shock" among his audience. The president then presented some manumission papers; during the rest of the festival, abolitionists freed many more slaves.[70]

When parliament passed the law that ended slavery on 13 May 1888, Bahia, like the rest of Brazil, erupted in a week-long celebration that Aristides Novis, a merchant and sugar planter, described as "complete delirium," a combination of carnival and Dois de Julho, as businesses closed and thousands of newly freed people flocked into Salvador.[71] Based on a handful of sources, historians have long known that at least one of the Dois de Julho symbols joined this celebration, an indication that Bahian popular patriotism and abolitionism had merged.[72] It is difficult to reconstruct how this came about. The first order of business when parliament convened in May was the abolition bill, so

Figure 4.2 | Dois de Julho's dawn still finds Bahians in slavery, 1886

*Source*: *O Faisca*, 4 July 1886.

slavery's end was expected, and Bahia's abolitionists were planning celebrations well before 13 May. On that day, before the news reached Salvador, the *Diário da Bahia* published the program for a "Great Abolitionist Festival," which announced that "in response to the requests received from the enslaved," a "great procession" would go to Lapinha to fetch "the wagon of the gentle *cabocla* who represents the Princess of the Mountains" (an old nickname for Salvador) and take her along the traditional route of the great parade (the use of the term "enslaved" indicates that this program predated the law's promulgation).[73] However, as reported in a telegram received by the *Jornal do Recife*, both "triumphal floats" arrived downtown. The next day, this newspaper's correspondent explained that late in the day on 13 May, an "immense mass of *povo*," led by bands and abolitionist societies, had gone to Lapinha to fetch both of them. Novis also reported that the "*caboclos'* wagons" had been brought from Lapinha.[74]

What likely happened is as follows: Abolitionists initially did not contemplate including either of the symbols of Bahia's independence in the celebrations of slavery's end, but, pressured by Afro-Bahians (including soon-to-be-freed slaves), they agreed to let the passive *cabocla* participate. Albuquerque suggests that the enslaved had asked that both *caboclos* participate but that authorities only permitted the *cabocla* to parade. This reflected their "cautious policy," she argues, as they sought to emphasize the passivity and conciliation exemplified by the unarmed female symbol, but she presents no direct evidence of authorities' intervention (it is not known, moreover, who actually controlled the patriotic symbols at this time).[75] Regardless of what they had planned, authorities and abolitionist leaders were then faced with the fait accompli of both *caboclos* arriving downtown. Unfortunately, I have found nothing in the Recife newspapers (or in the news from Bahia in the Rio de Janeiro press) that indicates who decided that the *caboclo* should return to Lapinha and, more important, how it was ensured that the male symbol did not participate in the rest of the abolition celebrations. For a week, as Albuquerque noted, the *cabocla* appeared in the celebratory processions that circulated through the city.[76] The *Diário de Notícias*'s reports transcribed by the *Diário de Pernambuco* always refer to only "one of the symbols of our political emancipation"; on 20 May it was returned to Lapinha in a procession of "extraordinary proportions, even exceeding the entries of the triumphal floats on 2 July."[77] The *Diário da Bahia* reported that "the legendary *cabocla* that, during the celebrations of our political emancipation, circulates through this part of the city, was conducted in triumph, amid cheers, preceded and followed by an enormous multitude."[78] For Albuquerque, the *caboclos'* importance to the newly freed people "gave abolition the stamp of a popular, even a black, victory."[79] This triumph was, however, subsumed into the larger unified celebrations as described in the *Diário de Notícias*, which focused on the newspapers and the abolitionist societies and said little about popular celebrations except to lament a disorderly "charivari" that blocked a street through which an abolitionist society tried to pass.[80] In these respects, Bahia's abolition celebrations were just like those elsewhere in Brazil. Public rhetoric and newspaper coverage focused mostly on abolitionists and largely ignored the freed.[81]

This was, incidentally, not the first time that one of the allegories had been brought out to celebrate a victory. In March 1868, when news arrived that the Brazilian fleet had finally forced its way past the Paraguayan fortifications at Humaitá, "the triumphal float, symbol of all of Bahia's glories and joys," was taken through the city amid "frenetic cheers of enthusiasm from the *povo*."[82] The correspondent who noted this did not indicate clearly whether this was the *caboclo* or the *cabocla*, but in a cryptic article some months later, *O Alabama* referred to [Francisco] Fausto [da Silva Castro], "the man [involved in] all popular celebrations, who even went to get the *caboclo* from Lapinha at the time of the good news from the war." Another correspondent also mentioned Captain Fausto, a man who would gain some prominence in the next decade as a carnival impresario.[83] No doubt, the *caboclo* was more suited to the celebration of a military victory than the *cabocla*; that said, both these uses of Bahia's independence symbols offer indications of their multiple meanings. I have found no evidence that the allegories were used during the March and April 1870 celebrations of the Paraguayan War's end.

A correspondent expected that 1888's Dois de Julho would be celebrated with more enthusiasm than it had been for many years, thanks to the ending of slavery, to which all had contributed. This would give the celebrations "the stamp of fraternity."[84] The priest who delivered the sermon after the Te Deum connected 2 July and 13 May as dates that marked the "glorious beginning of a new era," and a handbill distributed either in 1888 or 1889 likewise connected independence to abolition (as well as to the victory in the Paraguayan War), all of which "revealed to the world the valour and patriotism of new empire's sons."[85] In mid-July 1888, one newspaper proposed that patriots deposit some relics of the abolitionist movement in Pirajá, alongside Labatut's remains.[86] The *Diário da Bahia* hoped the following year that "the feelings of fraternity are not sacrificed to differences of opinion" after abolition, "a victory won without social unrest" and "an almost bloodless revolution."[87] By this time, struggles over the control of labour were intensifying in the Recôncavo, where former slaves were refusing to subject themselves to labour regimes that smacked of slavery, while planters lamented newly freed workers' inconstancy, not to mention the lack of compensation for lost slave property and insufficient police to drive workers back into the cane fields, all of these problems compounded by a devastating drought.[88]

### Order and Respectability

Describing Dois de Julho in the second half of the nineteenth century, Rozendo Moniz wrote that joy appeared on all visages, "without distinctions of sex, age, race, condition, or class."[89] To be sure, Moniz exaggerated when it came to the lack of differences among Bahians, but Dois de Julho was a festival that involved all members of society, and the rhetoric of unified and orderly celebration dominated the press coverage. Order meant not just an absence of violent incidents and crime, but also the upholding of social conventions and hierarchies at a time when streets and squares were packed with people, including many who would not normally venture out at night.[90]

Year after year, Dois de Julho organizers appealed for the populace to maintain, as they put it in 1884, "peace and tranquility in all the expressions of happiness."[91] The acting chief of police who had needed to arrest only a few Africans in 1862 reported that the celebrations concluded on 5 July "in perfect peace, notwithstanding the enthusiasm." Year after year, Dois de Julho reports echoed this assessment.[92] One correspondent explained in 1868 that this was inherent in Dois de Julho: "When someone tries to provoke a conflict or an altercation starts, voices are heard saying that, on 2 July nobody fights, and such is the magic of these words that the excitement immediately disappears and everything goes back to normal."[93] If there were "some quarrels and disorders [among] the popular [classes], to be expected from the enthusiasm of the day," explained a correspondent in 1887, they were inconsequential.[94] In 1875, the city council called on Bahians to forget partisan differences and to celebrate as united patriots, a call that went unheeded after the conflict between the Eighteenth Infantry and the

Liceu de Artes e Ofícios patriotic battalion; the value placed on order and peaceful celebration, it should be added, made this outbreak of violence especially shocking.[95]

Order was not just the absence of violence, of African *batuques*, or of violations of racial etiquette; it also involved upholding appropriate gender conventions and class hierarchies. Some Dois de Julho gender distinctions, however, transcended race and class. As in so many other societies, men paraded, whether in army, National Guard, or patriotic battalions, while women watched; indeed, women have scarcely been mentioned in this book, except as symbolic figures such as the female Indianist allegory.[96] The early, active version of this allegory was, in fact, mostly written out of Dois de Juho's early history as she gave way to the passive *cabocla*. Similarly, there was no formal role for women in the parades. Assier saw "black women wearing turbans ... signalling to the soldiers whom they recognized" during the parade, adding that most of Bahia's National Guard "soldiers" were black men.[97] Middle- and upper-class women also watched the parades, although from the windowed upper-storey front rooms of their houses, known as *varandas*.[98] In 1887, a correspondent reported that a "brilliant exhibition of ladies in beautiful dress" filled the *varandas* along the parade route. Anna Ribeiro de Góes Bittencourt recalled that women of her class dressed in extravagant yellow and green outfits, which earned them compliments for their patriotism in the 1850s.[99] Clothing and dry goods stores catered to this demand and advertised newly arrived fab- rics and notions "for the great national festival," as the Triunfo store proclaimed in 1872.[100] In 1884, it also advertised hats for men and cashmere suitable for their "colourful costumes," an indication that it was only men who dressed up to participate in the *bando*.[101] In 1890, one store announced that it had six hundred "white straw hats suitable for patriotic battalions" for sale at 1$600 (US$0.74) each.[102] Casa Este- benet advertised its large stock of saddles and other equestrian gear so that riders would make a good impression during the *bando* and the parade.[103]

People flocked to Salvador from elsewhere in the province to par- ticipate in Dois de Julho. An American carpenter working on a Santo Amaro sugar plantation noted in his diary that on 2 July 1853, he was almost alone among the slaves, for the "people has [*sic*] gone to the city and I expect they have a great time there."[104] Many, like Bittencourt's family, sought out relatives who lived on the Noite Primeira procession's route or the 2 July parade route (like her uncle), but the killjoy Amaral, the Sociedade Dois de Julho secretary who had been instrumental in putting an end to the Noite Primeira procession, observed that this was actually an unwelcome burden and cited it as a reason for suppressing the nocturnal parade. Visitors who arrived on 1 July ate all of the food that had been prepared for the next day, forcing the reluctant hosts to purchase more supplies for their unwanted guests.[105] Amaral's complaint is curious, for the evening procession could hardly have been a surprise to Bahians, and Bittencourt offers no indication that her uncle begrudged the visitors; indeed, in "Suzana," she comments that "Bahians' hospitable nature" ensured that it was easy for people to find a place from which to watch the parade. In 1857, she and her uncle's families spent the evening singing and dancing until the procession arrived; they retired after it passed, but some of their neighbours celebrated until dawn.[106] Other memoirists also recalled family gatherings and dinners.[107] If the household was prosperous enough to afford a piano, its members could enjoy music, such as the collection of waltzes titled "A Glória de Pirajá" (Pirajá's Glory), advertised for sale in 1864.[108] At least two piano scores for the Dois de Julho anthem were published in the second half of the nineteenth century, one as the centrefold illustration in *Bahia Ilustrada*.[109] Xavier Marques describes how all members of the fictional Boto family gathered around the piano to sing the anthem as similar sounds echoed from neighbouring houses.[110]

There are also indications of children's celebrations, as we saw in the last chapter's discussion of parish festivals. In 1880, one newspaper referred to "the Sé [parish] children's Dois de Julho," which involved unspecified "group entertainment" for them. Assier saw children towing flower-bedecked cannon in 1859, presumably lightweight models.[111] Twenty-six students at the normal school requested extended holidays from 24 June to 4 July 1875, "desiring to more fully celebrate the glories of the immortal day of Dois de Julho." Because their request contravened the school's regulations, it was turned down. Medical students reportedly began skipping classes in May and stretched their holiday through the "June festivals" and Dois de Julho.[112] Visitors to the Boto household included Alberto Pinto and his daughters, "students uni-formed in white and wearing green and yellow badges."[113]

While there are occasional indications of balls during the festival, such as the one hosted by the Club Comercial in 1887, which drew 2,000 people,[114] members of the middle and upper classes normally spent much time on the streets, which brought them into close contact with the *povo*. "There wasn't a family that did not go to the Terreiro," noted one correspondent in 1861.[115] Writing about 1870's *bando*, William Hadfield referred to "the curious mixture of colour, from the 'irrepressible negro' to the pure white." All were "enjoying the fun," and there was "something wonderful" in the gaiety.[116] As we noted, Bittencourt and her family spent the evening of 2 July 1857 at the downtown stage, where they enjoyed the poetry readings. That Salvador's well-off took to the streets during the festival can also be inferred from news-paper announcements about a lost diamond earring and Ordem da Rosa insignia during the celebrations.[117]

The illuminated ephemeral monuments, the lamps that residents put in their windows, and, starting in the 1860s, the gaslights in the princi-pal squares turned the normally dangerous street into a space that was safe for families. The *Jornal do Commercio*'s correspondent enthusias-tically described the first experiments with gaslight, which produced a "brilliant effect" in 1862: "Never was Dois de Julho so dazzling ... it was illuminated *a giorno*."[118] Fully four thousand gas jets lit up Marques's fictional Terreiro de Jesus on the festival's last night.[119] Likewise, a medical school professor's experiments with battery-powered electric light were enthusiastically welcomed in 1855, and in 1889, the entire stage was illuminated with electric light. A journalist judged this an effective demonstration of why Bahians should patronize the company that was starting to provide electricity to homes.[120]

The emphasis on Dois de Julho's orderly nature implied, of course, that celebrants of all classes respected social hierarchies. Light alone was not enough to ensure that the streets were safe for the middle and upper classes. Police reinforced patrols but could not control every-thing that went on in the Dois de Julho crowds. As we saw in chap-ter 2, Bittencourt recalled that in 1857 there was already much concern about the lack of respect shown to the poets who declaimed from the outdoor stage; complaints about *pateadas* (foot-stamping to show disapproval) and calls for the police to impose respect for the patriotic bards recurred in later years.[121] In 1868, *O Alabama* denounced the pickpockets who had been hard at work during the patriotic symbols' return to Lapinha; police caught one lifting 20$000 (US$6.90) from a foreigner's pocket.[122] At the festival's margins, order was precarious and rank less secure. In 1871, a certain José Roberto allegedly directed "obscene words" at "some ladies" who were returning home from the illuminated Terreiro de Jesus via the Theatre Square.[123] *O Alabama* also criticized the many horsemen who trampled people in the crowds and the police's casual attitude towards "the *povo – a brute mass*" as far as they were concerned. Evidently, they did not try to keep riders out of the Terreiro.[124] Popular annoyance at riders who failed to respect pedestrians may lie behind an incident that Assier witnessed in 1859. An officer hastening to join his battalion fell from his mount amid a group of "free blacks," who laughed at his misfortune and made no effort to help as he struggled to rise. The French traveller saw the incident in racial terms as evidence of Africans' feelings towards Portuguese.[125]

The police worked to keep order in other ways. In 1852, they prohibited a man who planned to construct a temporary *botequim* (food and drink stand) on the Terreiro de Jesus from selling alcohol. That same year, the owner of a tavern was allowed to stay open past the usual curfew hours on the nights of 1 to 4 July, provided that he sell only "juices and not alcoholic spirits."[126] Marques also described booths for games of chance and the sale of sweets.[127] Lieutenant Colonel Frias Villar's problem with drunken soldiers in 1875, however, indicates that liquor was easy to obtain during the celebration, and indeed, many celebrated by drinking. In 1869, a block inspector in Pilar parish, José Tomás de Almeida, normally "dutiful, obedient to his superiors' orders, and of good conduct," drank more wine than he was accustomed to while watching the parade with some friends. This was how the subdelegate (Almeida's immediate superior) tried to mitigate the damning report of the police patrol that, at 9 p.m., knocked on the door of the inspector's house to remind him to illuminate his entry, likely to make him comply with a bylaw that required open doors to be lit at night (an ordinance that sought to prevent suspicious characters from lurking in darkened doorways). Almeida's wife rebuffed the order, after which Almeida, "very drunk, to the point of falling at my feet," insulted the soldier and declared that "the subdelegate could go to shit [*que fosse a trampa*]."[128] Given that the parade had ended six or seven hours earlier, Almeida must have continued drinking for some time. A later folklorist described an incident during the *caboclos'* return to Lapinha in which a normally "well-mannered *caixeiro*," "full of *cachaça*," set fire to a police sergeant's beard with his torch, but managed to escape in the ensuing confusion.[129]

Stores advertised a great variety of fireworks for Dois de Julho and the other June saints' festival days, but pyrotechnics were a constant problem, especially the so-called *buscapés*, crackers, and other types that individuals set off in the streets. Such fireworks startled horses, frightened ladies, and once killed a boy.[130] In 1834, a man died of burns suffered during the festival, likely from fireworks.[131] The police seemed unable to enforce bylaws against these fireworks, and indeed, men who should have upheld the law failed to do so. During the return of the floats in 1868, a National Guard sergeant set off fireworks that ignited a woman's clothing, and in 1870, an errant rocket injured the Guard commander. He arrested the man responsible, only to watch him be released by the São Pedro parish police subdelegate on the grounds that he was a block inspector.[132]

That subdelegates sought to protect their block inspectors from punishment for Dois de Julho excesses such as public intoxication or dangerous fireworks play indicates that there were different understandings of what constituted appropriate conduct and different rules for different celebrants. They also suggest that reports about orderly Dois de Julho celebrations were sometimes more wishful thinking than objective descriptions, but this only underscores the importance of order for those who wrote about the festival.

## Between Brazil and Bahia

Dois de Julho sat uncomfortably alongside Brazil's other days of national festivity. Its origins as a radical-liberal (Exaltado) festival in the 1820s, its celebration of the popular mobilization that had been required to expel the Portuguese from Salvador, and its focus on a single province challenged Brazil's "official" history, which viewed independence as the result of Pedro I's actions and emphasized unity as the empire's greatest achievement. Nevertheless, Bahian patriots stressed that Dois de Julho was about Brazil – that the events that day celebrated had been essential to the winning of independence and the conquest of liberty. Of course, emphasizing the importance of Dois de Julho to Bahia did not preclude pointing out its significance for Brazil. For the radical liberals who dominated early Dois de Julho rhetoric, the connection with Brazil was obvious. They saw themselves as the vanguard of those who would turn the empire into a more liberal regime. As the empire became more firmly established – the nation forged, as Roderick Barman puts it[133] – and as radical-liberal politics diminished after mid-century, Dois de Julho's relationship to Brazil became more complex. Patriots still sought recognition of Dois de Julho as integral to the narrative of national independence, but they now also hoped that this would win their province symbolic capital at a time when its relative decline was increasingly visible.

In this sense, and as many twentieth-century historians have pointed out, Dois de Julho can be viewed as an example of regionalism growing alongside national identity.[134] Dois de Julho, however, differed from twentieth-century regionalist projects that built identity claims around understandings of cultural distinctiveness. Instead, Bahia's patriots saw themselves as Brazilians; more importantly, they claimed that Bahia's independence should be recognized by all Brazilians as crucial to the *nation*'s independence. Theirs was a political claim about the nature of the Brazilian nation-state and their province's place in it.

Bahian journalists across the political spectrum usually agreed on Dois de Julho's importance for Brazil, albeit with some exceptions. In 1843, *O Comércio* published an editorial on Dois de Julho's significance that never once mentioned Brazil.[135] Two years later, *O Guaicuru* avoided mentioning Bahia in its editorial, stressing instead that Dois de Julho was the "day of triumph of our valour and patriotism – the day on which the *pátria*'s independence became a reality"; here, the radical-liberal Domingos Guedes Cabral was implying that Dois de Julho was most important for Brazil. Another article published in that same issue, however, spoke of the day as one that "belongs especially to Bahians," notwithstanding that the events being celebrated had played a major role in securing the "emancipation … of the entire empire of the Holy Cross." In 1846, Cabral described the attack on Manoel

Pessoa da Silva as "the most offensive of all of the insults against the Bahian people's national sentiment."[136] In the 1840s, the *Correio Mercantil* consistently linked Dois de Julho to Brazilian independence; this conservative newspaper once even subordinated Dois de Julho to the Grito do Ipiranga by arguing that Bahians had fought in response to Pedro I's call for a break with Portugal – empirically wrong, for the Bahian struggle had begun well before 7 September 1822 – and it frequently called on Bahians to maintain their loyalty to the monarchy and to the national imperial institutions.[137] In its 1840 proclamation, Salvador's city council stressed that Bahians would celebrate "the anniversary of the day of their political emancipation or, better, that of all of Brazil."[138] Later in the decade, it placed more emphasis on the Bahian aspects of the festival.[139]

Similar patterns appeared in periodicals of the 1850s. The Conservative *Jornal da Bahia* declared in 1857 that Dois de Julho was a "truly national" day and argued that despotism's demise was inevitable in light of the emerging ideas of "civilization" and "progress." A writer in *O País*, an Exaltado newspaper, declared that Pirajá was as important as Ipiranga "because the independence of Brazil could not have been achieved without the liberation of Bahia." The Liberal *Diário da Bahia* editorialized in 1858 about the importance of Pedro I's proclamation of independence and of those "who in 1823 buckled on the sword [and took] to the field of honour to fight for liberty."[140] In 1864, *O Alabama* hailed the day as a "gilded page in the history of the rising empire of the Holy Cross."[141] Likewise, Constantino do Amaral Tavares, the poet and playwright, connected the two "Holy days of July and September / That the *pátria* must never forget / ... / On which despotism felt itself weaken [*abater*]."[142] The allusion to despotism's weakness (but not necessarily death, another meaning for *abater*) underscored the need for liberals to remain vigilant.

Arguments that 2 July 1823 was the "glorious day" on which "Brazil ceased to be a Portuguese colony and became an American nation" highlighted Bahia's primacy in Brazilian independence and sought to win symbolic capital for a province that increasingly lagged behind Rio de Janeiro.[143] *O Alabama*'s editorials sometimes seemed to subordinate Bahians' struggles to national ones; in 1871, for example, it argued that Pedro I's Grito do Ipiranga had echoed from the Amazon to the River

Plate (Brazil's symbolic natural frontiers) and launched Bahia's struggle. But it always returned to emphasizing Bahia's importance: "The entire cause of Brazil would be decided in just one province; Cabral's first-born could no longer tolerate this den of wolves" – a reference to the Portuguese troops in Salvador.[144] In 1867, its editors loudly declared their Bahian pride but also emphasized that they were true Brazilians: despite their relative poverty and subjection to the machinations of "the puppets of Rio de Janeiro," Bahians should not forget that "it was we that fought, and not Rio; it was we who died and not Rio; it was we who slept in the sun and the rain, and not Rio; it was our blood that ran, and not that of Rio; that we are Brazilians, but not Cariocas!"[145]

This tendency to emphasize the contribution of all Bahians to Brazilian independence became increasingly pronounced over the course of the nineteenth century. Editorialists and authors of the *bando* who called on all Bahians to celebrate "the day of your glories" and to pay their respects to the heroes of 1822–23 emphasized that Bahians were "a truly free and independent *povo*, the sons and grandsons of the brave veterans of the *pátria*'s independence," as Antônio Olavo da França Guerra proclaimed in 1876.[146] The 1871 *bando* called on Bahians to honour the "majestic monument that rose from the banks of the Ipiranga to give voice to liberty" and to use Brazil's institutions for "the progressive march of humanity."[147] Ten years later, the *bando* exhorted them to fulfill "one of the most imperious demands on the citizens of a free country," namely, to glorify "the authors of the nation's political existence" and to pay homage to the "heroes who ennoble the *pátria*."[148] Such rhetoric indicated that Dois de Julho had become, at least in these writers' estimation, a festival that belonged to *all* Bahians and that celebrated Brazil's existing institutions.

What Dois de Julho celebrated, then, was Bahians' Brazilian patriotism and their contribution to the empire's independence. The festival did not contradict loyalty to Brazil; rather, it expressed that loyalty by celebrating the patriotic Bahian mobilization of 1822–23. In this sense, the Bahian patriots were far from regionalists, if by this is meant an ideology that contradicts loyalty to the national state. Rather, they were Brazilians – indeed, as far as they were concerned, especially patriotic ones. Thus, Paraguayan War–era recollections of Bahians' struggles for independence amounted to calls for a new generation of patriots to emulate their forebears.[149] Likewise, in 1874, the organizers of the Acadêmico patriotic battalion declared: "This festival does not belong just to Bahia; it belongs to all of Brazil ... The day of 2 July is a day of national festivity."[150] For the dissident Liberal *O Monitor* two years later, 2 July was "a glorious day not just in the annals of Bahia but in those of the *pátria*" – in other words, Brazil – a view that at least one Rio de Janeiro newspaper seconded.[151] This view transcended party lines; thus, the Conservative *Correio da Bahia* likewise stressed the importance of Bahians' struggles for the winning of Brazilian independence, both while Conservatives were in power (1877) and while they were in opposition (1878), a theme that the *Gazeta da Bahia*, the new party organ, reprised for the next three years. In 1881, the *Gazeta* went so far as to declare that 2 July was "the most glorious day for the Empire of Brazil, the anniversary of and the commemoration of our country's independence."[152]

By this time, the imperial regime's critics were constructing a history of independence that downplayed Pedro I's role and emphasized independence's precursors, focusing on the 1789 Inconfidência Mineira and the 1817 republican rebellion in Pernambuco.[153] First articulated by radical liberals after mid-century, this questioning of the imperial regime's "official" history gained republican connotations in the 1870s and 1880s. Thus, while in 1867 *O Alabama* could construct a history of independence that began with the 1789 and 1817 movements, included the Grito do Ipiranga, and that culminated in Bahians' victory on 2 July 1823,[154] a republican poet offered a very different interpretation in 1885. Men like Tiradentes and Padre Roma (executed for their involvement in, respectively, the 1789 and 1817 movements), and Joaquim Nunes Machado (killed during the Praieira Rebellion, the 1848–49 radical-liberal movement in Pernambuco), had fought against despotism while false patriots who "claimed to be liberators" maintained slavery. This was both a condemnation of those who still opposed abolition and a criticism of the imperial regime.[155]

By contrast, Conservatives vigorously defended Brazil's political institutions (especially when they were in power). The *Gazeta da Bahia* acknowledged the precursors of independence but contrasted Brazil's orderly independence – "the sacred fruit ... the result of our ancestors' magnificent efforts" – with that of the empire's Spanish American neighbours, whose headlong rush into independence left "republics in continual agitation, in constant and bloody uproar."[156] According to the 1877 *bando*, independence had sparked the diffusion of "civiliz-ation ... into the land of Cabral," and the 1824 constitution had "se-cured the rights of Brazilian citizens." Bahian patriots had fought for independence in response to Pedro I's Grito do Ipiranga and thereby launched Brazil on "the road of progress" – a heritage to be defended by new generations.[157] In 1880, the *bando* returned to similar themes, stressing the "beneficent influx of the political institutions that govern us" and calling on Bahians to work for their country's progress within that framework.[158]

Dois de Julho presented an interpretation of Brazilian independence that could not be reconciled with the one celebrated on 7 September, and no matter how hard they tried, Bahian patriots failed to con-vince fellow Brazilians that Dois de Julho deserved equal billing with Pedro I's Grito do Ipiranga. Unsurprisingly, the 1828–29 holiday bill failed in parliament. I know of no other attempts to make Dois de Julho a national holiday during the empire, but during the republic, Bahian patriots have frequently (and unsuccessfully) sought to win this status for 2 July. When it came to the relationship with Brazil, the principal themes in Dois de Julho editorials changed little. Just as Dois de Julho patriots of the late 1820s had sought to make the day a national holi-day, so journalists of the late empire stressed Bahia's importance to the struggle for independence. Emphasizing the role of Cabral's first-born in this victory claimed a symbolic importance for Bahia that perhaps offered some consolation to the many who recognized that their prov-ince no longer stood at the forefront of Brazilian affairs. Republican-ism had gained little support in Bahia, and no republican periodicals from the province have survived, so it is impossible to know whether there was a distinctively republican interpretation of Dois de Julho.

For the most part, the newspapers on which this book is based cast their Dois de Julho coverage in political terms. Rarely did they delve into the festival's cultural meanings or its significance for the popular classes, except to condemn inappropriate conduct. A singular exception is found in an 1849 article in *A Marmota*. Próspero Diniz, the editor of this satirical newspaper, called on Bahians to invite Portuguese to join in the celebrations, proposing that patriots find a Portuguese man to serve as the centrepiece for a cultural allegory on the night of 1 July. Seated on a barrel, decorated with *pitanga* (Surinam cherry) leaves, this "Fragoso" would be borne on a litter to Lapinha, where he would be welcomed by a "commission of creole women" and the people, singing a new patriotic anthem that stressed unity. Its refrain underscored the festive aspects of 2 July:

> Let the festival warm up
> Let's have a party,
> The day is great
> Long live unity.

Several of its verses stressed the cultural "Brazilianization" of Portuguese immigrants:

> There are no longer Portuguese
> We are all one people
> They already eat bananas
> They raise themselves on *bobó*
>   [a dish of beans and manioc
>   tempered with African palm
>   (*dendê*) oil]
> …
> They get married here
> They start eating *caruru*
>   [a dish of shrimp, fish, and
>   okra, also tempered with
>   *dendê* oil]
> They eat pepper sauce
> And they venture to dance *lundu*
> …
> There will be *lundu* at Lapinha
> Let the people dance en masse
> It's the day for this, let's have fun
> For life is short, and it will pass.[159]

It is not known whether any Portuguese immigrant willingly subjected himself to this spectacle, but the verses indicate a popular cultural nationalism, one drawing heavily on African-derived cuisine and dance, here appropriated as the symbols of a Brazilian or a Bahian identity, albeit one that excluded Africans ("Fragoso" would be met by creole women, not Africans). The *lundu* – a forerunner of *samba* – flourished in "situations involving racial mixing," according to John Chasteen, but by this time tamer versions of it were widespread in middle- and upper-class circles.[160] Nevertheless, Diniz's account suggests that the Noite Primeira was a crucible of cultural mixture, roughly comparable to Rio de Janeiro's Holy Spirit Festival as analyzed by Martha Abreu.[161] The poem also underscores that, even at a time when Exaltados were vigorously campaigning against President Francisco Gonçalves Martins and resorting to anti-Portuguese rhetoric, others were already dismissing lusophobia.

The cultural nationalism that drew on Bahia's African heritage would, of course, not flourish in public rhetoric until well into the twentieth century, and nothing like Próspero Diniz's remarks appeared in later nineteenth-century accounts of Dois de Julho. Instead, when Bahians remarked on popular culture, it was normally to criticize practices they deemed inappropriate alongside a civic festival that represented the modern, civilized, and orderly Bahia desired by provincial elites and the newspaper-reading public. *Batuques* would not disrupt this Dois de Julho; grateful slaves would receive their liberty from patriots (and return to work); the wealthy would bask in illuminated streets amid a respectful *povo*. And fellow Brazilians would acknowledge Dois de Julho's importance – and, by extension, Bahia's prominence – in the nation. Few of these hopes were realized, and as we will examine more fully in chapter 6, many rejected Dois de Julho's traditions. Before addressing this issue, we turn to the theatre galas and Dois de Julho's representation on stage.

## CHAPTER FIVE

# Dramas "Appropriate for the Public Theatre": Dois de Julho on Stage

As was by then customary, for 2 July 1861, Salvador's Teatro de São João (Saint John's Theatre) announced a "gala spectacle for the anniversary of the entry of the liberating troops." The show would begin after the vice-president's arrival; two actresses and the entire theatre company would sing the "Hino da Independência" (Independence Anthem), and, although not mentioned in the advertisement, the vice-president would lead the audience in cheers. After these civic rituals, the audience would see the "excellent five-act comedy about national customs," *Os estudantes da Bahia* (Bahia's Students), set in 1855–56, written by Luiz Miguel Quadros Júnior, a native of Maranhão and a student at the medical school.[1] On 1 July, however, the Conservatório Dramático da Bahia (Dramatic Conservatory of Bahia), a society of literati charged with both improving Bahian theatre and censoring works to be performed, prohibited the production. The theatre company, which had invested time and money in preparing the play, lobbied the vice-president and the police chief, but both backed the Conservatório. Two of the censors, however, were persuaded to change their minds and allowed the performance to go ahead without the fifth act, "the most immoral of them all." According to the *Diário de Pernambuco*'s correspondent, this would not have harmed the play, for the acts were not linked. After the first four acts, "some individuals in the audience, who it is supposed were deliberately put there, demanded the performance of the fifth act that had been suppressed, and it was scandalously performed, without the police preventing it, as they should have!" "The funniest thing" about the whole affair was that the company subsequently apologized for the fifth act's poor performance, for it had not been properly rehearsed in light of the Conservatório's original decision; instead, the company promised a better performance on 5 July. On 7 July, the Conservatório definitively censored the play as an "offence to Bahian dignity" and prohibited its production in the province.[2]

The *Diário de Pernambuco*'s correspondent wondered about the choice of *Os estudantes da Bahia*, for it was "completely inappropriate for performing on such a great day, which demanded a serious drama, majestic and noble." As he explained, it had been "customary for several years to produce a new drama, written by a Brazilian, and always based on some event of our history." A play that met these criteria was, in fact, performed on 4 July at the small Teatro de São Pedro de Alcântara (Saint Peter of Alcantara Theatre) by the amateur Instituto Dramático (Dramatic Institute): Constantino do Amaral Tavares's *Os tempos da Independência* (The Era of Independence), a "great work" dedicated to the Caixeiros Nacionais. It dealt with an "entirely national [i.e., Brazilian] topic" and began with the 1817 Pernambucan revolt, which it described as "a precursor of our emancipation." It offered a good portrayal of the struggle for independence in Bahia, and in its epilogue, it "very realistically ... reproduces the July celebrations, the entry of the triumphal floats, etc., and concludes with the Dois de Julho anthem and cheers by the *povo*, all of which had a marvellous effect." The correspondent concluded: "This was the drama that was appropriate for the public theatre."[3] His counterpart for Rio de Janeiro's *Jornal do Commercio* did not share this enthusiasm, reporting that Tavares's play (which he had not seen) had not pleased the audience; that the liberal *Diário da Bahia*, to which the playwright had close ties, failed to comment on it reinforced his opinion.[4]

The debate over 1861's Dois de Julho gala highlights several key elements of mid-century Bahian theatre. Since its 1857 founding, the Conservatório had worked to promote the writing and production of Bahian plays and to ensure that on days of national festivity, suitably patriotic works were performed. According to both Rozendo Moniz and Manoel Raimundo Querino, the performance of a drama with a "patriotic" or "national" topic, usually by a Bahian playwright, characterized the Dois de Julho celebrations of bygone days. However, the surviving programs and accounts of theatre galas reveal that this repertoire was concentrated in the 1850s and 1860s. Sílio Boccanera Júnior later described the decade after 1857 as Bahia's great era of historical and national plays; he identified no less than fifteen authors active in this genre but noted that few of their works were published.[5] The provincial government mandated in 1864 that the new dramatic company produce at least four Brazilian plays per year, with those staged on 2 July and 7 September having "a national-historical subject" if possible.[6] Only a small number of these plays have survived; these, and the scattered press commentary on a few other works, reveal how mid-century Bahian playwrights represented recent history. The authors of national-historical plays had to reflect on what constituted national history and on how to present the struggle for independence in Bahia as part of Brazilian history. Like other celebrants, they had to address the legacy of the popular mobilization in the independence war and Dois de Julho's radical-liberal elements. Because Dois de Julho commemorations were also an occasion to debate contemporary political issues, the national-historical plays addressed them implicitly or explicitly.

This chapter begins with a discussion of the context in which Bahians saw these plays – that of the theatre galas held to mark Dois de Julho. The theatre was seen as both a tool for uplifting society and an index of "civilization." This made it an important social and cultural space. I mentioned the galas in previous chapters. They followed a standard form and generally drew large audiences for what amounted to demonstrations of patriotic and political loyalties. This chapter focuses on five plays (four dramas or melodramas and one *elogio dramático* or dramatic laudation) written for Dois de Julho between 1854 and 1864, four of which were staged at this time. In the third section, I review their plots and note that they are but a small sample from the corpus of national-historical works. Finally, I examine key themes in these plays and relate them to the Dois de Julho celebrations. In their silence about race and slavery and in their embrace of *indigenismo*, the playwrights reflected some of the issues examined in previous chapters. The playwrights' radical-liberal sympathies shone through in their appeals to popular sovereignty, their espousal of the Caixeiros Nacionais's demands, their condemnation of eleventh-hour patriots, their favourable portrayals of Pedro Labatut, and their linkage of Bahia's independence struggle to the Pernambucan republican revolt of 1817 and the 1789 Inconfidência Mineira; anti-Portuguese rhetoric, however, was strikingly muted in these plays. In these ways, the playwrights, like so many of the patriotic celebrants on Salvador's streets and squares, constructed a national history of independence that presented the war in Bahia as the true source of Brazil's independence, besides emphasizing the radical-liberal elements in that struggle.

## Theatregoing and Theatre Galas

The theatre galas that were integral to the celebrations on all days of national festivity, not just Dois de Julho, changed little over the course of the imperial regime. They must be understood in the contexts of nineteenth-century theatregoing, the widely held view that the theatre should serve as a school for public morality, the project to foster theatre as a symbol and a measure of Bahia's civilization, and playwrights' efforts to define Dois de Julho. The extensive newspaper commentary on these functions points clearly to the theatre's social and political importance.

Salvador's principal theatre galas took place in the venerable Teatro de São João, opened in 1812. Perched on the edge of the escarpment overlooking the bay on what is today the Praça Castro Alves (see figure 5.1), on the southern edge of Salvador's downtown, the São João was one of the city's most prominent buildings. Benjamin Vicuña Mackenna described it in 1855 as a "notable building" but remarked that it "appears on the verge of falling down ... at the slightest shaking" (the Chilean was apparently unaware that Bahia, unlike his homeland, is not subject to earthquakes); he added that the façade was painted yellow with white trim around the windows. Edward Wilberforce considered it the "grandest" building in Salvador, and many other visitors remarked on its size and prominence.[7] The São João held 340 seats in its pit and 400 spaces in the galleries, along with 60 boxes in three rows; each box held five seats, so the theatre's capacity was 1,040 spectators.[8] Its capacity before renovations in the 1850s may have been a bit less, for in 1840, the *Correio Mercantil* described a full house as 800 people.[9]

Figure 5.1 | The Teatro São João, 6 October 1859

*Source*: AIHGB, Icon. L.36, n.º 9-III.

Who attended performances at the São João remains a difficult question to answer. While ticket prices were low, they were high enough to exclude the vast majority of the city's population. In 1830, floor seats could be had for as little as a *pataca* (320 réis or US$0.15), and places in the highest gallery (the *varanda* [balcony] or *torrinha* [little tower]) went for half that; boxes ranged from 1$000 to 2$000 (US$0.46 to US$0.92). Prices rose over the next decade, and in the 1840s and 1850s, tickets to opera performances in Bahia ranged from 6$000 (just over US$3.00) for the best boxes to 1$000 (just over US$0.50) for seats in the pit; seats in the highest gallery could be had for as little as 640 réis (about US$0.33). In the 1870s, prices for the cheapest places fell to 500 réis (US$.025), but the most expensive boxes went for 12$000 (US$6.00).[10] Prices were typically raised for special events.

Theatregoing was primarily a male activity. Anna Ribeiro de Góes Bittencourt would recall that at the time of her 1857 visit to Salvador, her mother had never been to the theatre; her father, by contrast, "liked theatre a lot" and always went when he was in the capital.[11] Medical and moral opinion generally held that the theatre was bad for women's emotional health.[12] The pit or the floor and the galleries were exclusively male preserves; women attended only in the boxes, safely chaperoned by male family members, which was how Bittencourt attended two shows in 1857. Women reportedly first sat in the pit in 1879 for a gala in honour of composer Antônio Carlos Gomes.[13] According to João da Silva Campos, shop clerks (*caixeiros*), students, and civil servants were assiduous theatregoers; these men formed "theatre parties" (*partidos teatrais*), gangs of rowdies who showered their favourite actresses and prima donnas with "elaborate speeches, poetry, [and] flowers."[14]

The audiences who crammed into the often uncomfortably hot São João thus enacted something of the Bahian social hierarchy. Men and women of means filled the boxes; poorer men sat in the chairs and benches on the floor; the poorest stood in the highest galleries. All of these people mingled as they entered and left the theatre, and President José de Souza Soares de Andréa lamented the ensuing lack of "decency," recommending that separate entrances be built for the *torrinha* and the *varanda* so that the "most respectable people" would not have to rub shoulders with the likes of those who frequented the cheapest places.[15] The chief of police further sought to secure the São João's social exclusivity in 1854 by banning "*pretos* or *pretas*, free or slave," from entering the building unless they were in the service of their masters. The radical-liberal *O Guaicuru* attacked this ambiguously worded clause as an offence against "Brazilians of black colour," but the chief of police's intent was to exclude only Africans (as nouns, *preto* and *preta* generally meant only Africans rather than all blacks).[16] As far as foreigners were concerned, theatre audiences prominently displayed Bahian society's racial diversity. Robert Avé-Lallement, who attend two operas in late 1858, reported that the "select and distinguished" audience would not be out of place in a European theatre, were it not for the many dark-skinned individuals who occupied places from the first-class boxes to the highest galleries.[17]

Avé-Lallement also remarked that he saw "many attractive figures in the boxes," an indication that attending galas in the boxes was a way for members of Bahia's elite to flaunt their wealth and sophistication. Open railings fronted the São João's boxes, so audience members had a full view of the dress and comportment of these elite theatregoers, who in 1840 offered "a truly magnificent view." Ambrosio Ronzi, the *Correio Mercantil*'s theatre columnist, described 1849's Dois de Julho gala as a gathering of "the most select part of Bahian society." James Wetherell added that the "utmost decorum" prevailed in the São João, but that families visited one another's boxes during performances, an indication of the theatre's social function as a meeting place for Bahia's elite.[18]

The much smaller Teatro de São Pedro de Alcântara (1837–79), located on Baixo de São Bento Street (sometimes also known as the Teatrinho da Rua do Baixo), occasionally also held Dois de Julho galas, but usually a day or two later so as not to compete with the São João.[19] Thus, the Instituto Dramático performed Tavares's *Tempos da Independência* on 4 July 1861. Amateur theatre companies like the Instituto were particularly active at the São Pedro in the late 1840s and early 1850s. According to Afonso Ruy, this theatre presented mostly Bahian playwrights' work; because this venue was cheaper to attend, he suggests that its repertoire was more influential among the "popular masses" than that of the more highbrow São João.[20]                         .

Nineteenth-century Bahia's theatrical repertoire has yet to be studied systematically.[21] Wetherell described what he saw at the São João in the mid-1850s as "either bad translations of poor French pieces or stupid Portuguese dramas," but added that the amateur companies produced "very amusing ... Portuguese farces" at the São Pedro. A decade earlier, another visitor judged both the dramatic and operatic performances as "despicable," while William Scully remarked that only third-rate companies made it to Salvador in the 1860s.[22] Bahia's theatre repertoire resembled that of Rio de Janeiro, with historical dramas and melodramas dominating mid-century playbills, along with comedies like *Os estudantes da Bahia*.[23] Classical tragedy and, later, Realism rarely drew significant audiences (despite the efforts of leading literary figures to promote these genres).[24]

The São João was Salvador's public theatre, built by the colonial government and maintained by the provincial government over the entire imperial regime. Provincial presidents appointed managers for the building and contracted with impresarios for plays, operas, and other performances. Little is known about how they did this before the 1840s, but it is clear that no one made money. Managers repeatedly reminded presidents that no theatre in the world functioned without a government subsidy and emphasized theatre's role as "a public school of morality, in the practice of virtue and love of the *pátria*," as Inácio Acioli de Cerqueira e Silva did in early 1837.[25] In 1844, the president lamented that Bahians only frequented the São João on days of national festivity, which certainly had something to do with the quality of the artists that the provincial capital could attract (and which underscored the political and social importance of galas).[26]

In the 1840s, presidents set out to improve the quality of opera and drama and to encourage theatregoing. By 1848, the province had contracts in place with a Companhia Lírica Italiana and a Companhia Dramática Nacional, and the president proudly reported that the São João was "properly organized as is required by the current state of this capital." He urged legislators to fund the building's upkeep and to subsidize the performers who laboured there, for it was a place where "a numerous population seeks the means for honest recreation" and no one could be ignorant of "the importance of theatre as a reliable thermometer to measure nations' level of civilization."[27] Bahian presidents repeatedly used both of these justifications – that theatre could improve the population's civilization, and that its achievements demonstrated Brazil's progress – in their requests for theatre subsidies from the provincial legislature.[28] In these respects, Bahia was part of a broad cultural movement whose proponents saw the theatre as an institution ideally suited to reforming and uplifting society.[29] Not all agreed, and in 1861, a journalist criticized a bill that would have allocated 200:000$000 (US$104,000) over four years to an Italian opera company at a time when provincial coffers were exhausted. The subvention's purpose – "improving customs and moralizing the *povo*" – amounted to making the people "tamer, more patient, more tolerant," and perhaps then more likely to submit to the taxes needed for this expensive luxury, he implied.[30]

Provincial governments found it difficult to achieve their cultural goals. Year after year, presidents lamented that maintenance and repair costs were mounting, that opera and drama companies were flirting with bankruptcy and unable to satisfy the terms of their contracts, and that legislators were reluctant to vote additional subsidies. To be sure, there were some successes in the early 1850s. Under João Maurício Wanderley's administration, the São João was fully renovated, as his successor reported in 1855; a year later, however, the new roof was already leaking.[31] Getting (and keeping) passable opera and dramatic companies was no easy task. Charged with forming a company in Europe, José Antongini spent considerably more than the 10:000$000 (US$5,800) budgeted for 1853, because it was "impossible to get a company, however mediocre," for that sum. His company managed to start performances in the newly renovated São João in September 1854, but two key singers soon quit and he could not replace them, so the company folded.[32] By April 1857, it was common knowledge that José de Vecchy's dramatic troupe, contracted only the year before, was on the verge of bankruptcy and not paying its players and other employees. His company lingered on until at least July, for he commissioned and staged Tavares's *Elogio dramático* (Dramatic Laudation) for that year's Dois de Julho, and in October 1858, its former employees unsuccessfully sought payment from the provincial government.[33] In 1865, another impresario was unable to satisfy his contract's terms.[34]

Presidents lamented that Bahians showed little interest in regularly attending the theatre; as a result, impresarios were frequently driven into bankruptcy. It also meant that the theatre could not work its influence on the population, "softening popular customs, and presenting living examples that should be followed, and dwell in the hearts of all."[35] In frustration, the government changed its policy in the late 1860s: instead of subsidizing theatre companies, it would make the São João available to itinerant troupes and local theatre groups. Government support for opera lingered on into the early 1880s; presidential reports stressed that these drama companies received no subsidy other than use of the building.[36] In Rio de Janeiro, government subsidies secured an annual opera season from the 1840s to the mid-1860s, whereas in Bahia, audiences could only occasionally see performances of what many at the time considered the pinnacle of cultural achievement.[37]

The police carefully monitored the theatre, and not just to prevent the theft of distracted patrons' belongings.[38] They also kept a close watch over theatregoers' comportment, which was tightly regulated for the São João.[39] In 1857, the police arrested two men for trying to smuggle a straw wreath into the theatre – presumably to insult an actor whom they disliked – and a foreigner for stamping his feet in disapproval of a performance. In 1882, the chief of police lamented that he did not have enough police soldiers to assign a few of them to the theatre to control rowdy behaviour among spectators.[40] The police also censored programs. Before 1857, performances required the chief of police's approval; that year, this responsibility was shifted to the Conservatório Dramático. Inácio Acioli squabbled with a moralizing chief of police in 1836–37 over whether *lundu* dances could be performed during intermissions. The chief of police's determination to "combat this stubborn preference for immoral dances" put the theatre manager in a bind, for risqué *lundu* performances were one of the best ways to attract male audiences, even if "families" might be offended.[41] Little is known about how censorship was implemented. In 1845, the manager sent the Dois de Julho program to the chief of police on 28 June, hoping that it would meet with his approval, but this is the only documentary trace of advance censorship for galas that I have found.[42]

Clearly, then, Dois de Julho theatre galas were only a small part of the much larger culture of theatregoing. The São João Theatre was a hotbed of elite and middle-class sociability, a place for people to display style and sophistication, a locale to project Bahia's civilization, and the site of much informal politicking; its social, political, and cultural importance matched its prominent location. For all its pretensions, however, Bahia's public theatre remained a provincial venue that could not keep up with Rio de Janeiro's theatres, which Bahians read about with envy when they received their copies of the national capital's newspapers. Few remarked on Bahians' fascination with foreign artists, but the satirical poet João Nepomuceno da Silva had sharp words for the advantages that foreigners enjoyed:

> Here comes another who knows nothing,
> But as a Frenchman he wants,
> To go sing in the theatre,
> The government says, "Permission granted,"
> And there he goes without fear,
> Instead of singing, howling.[43]

Nepomuceno was a marginal cultural figure; even so, his satires touched nerves and expressed ideas that others would have preferred be left unsaid. Criticism of the reliance on foreigners underlay the Conservatório Dramático's efforts to develop national theatre.

## Dois de Julho Theatre Galas

A review of the Dois de Julho galas' principal elements will help set the context for the national-historical plays of the 1850s and 1860s. Galas were organized separately from the rest of the Dois de Julho celebrations; nevertheless, they were an indispensable part of the day's festivities. Their form changed little over the course of the nineteenth century, and Bahians gathered at the São João year after year to celebrate independence in their province and to display their patriotic identity through cheers, anthems, poetry, and plays.

Galas were not part of the public celebrations organized by the Direção Geral dos Festejos or the Sociedade Dois de Julho, and the detailed programs published by these organizations from the 1850s to the 1880s do not list them.[44] Instead, as early as 1836, contracts with impresarios and theatre managers began to require them to produce galas on days of national festivity, including Dois de Julho. That year, Inácio Acioli undertook to stage two shows per week as well as those required on "days of public national festivity." The 1857 and 1859 opera contracts specified that the lyric season was to open on 2 July and close on 2 December; the 1873 and 1874 seasons were to run from 25 March to 2 December.[45] When there was no theatre or opera company on hand, private groups sometimes took on the task of organizing a gala. On 2 July 1872, the abolitionist Sociedade Libertadora Sete de Setembro (Seventh of September Liberating Society) put on a fundraiser; five years later, the police band raised monies for drought relief in the north.[46] On other occasions, theatre managers scrambled to improvise a gala. Five days before 2 July 1840, the manager was still working to contract a travelling troupe, which had offered to put on "the Dois de Julho show on its own account," presumably hoping to turn a profit. The following year, however, his successor requested funds from the province to cover the extra costs that he and the dramatic company would incur.[47]

Galas were major social and political events, and newspapers regularly noted that the Sao João was full on Dois de Julho (and on other days of national festivity). Sometimes this was meant as an unambiguous political statement: the conservative *Correio Mercantil*'s emphasis on the presence of "a large number of the most highly ranked people," "a brilliant concourse," or "a numerous and glittering gathering" at galas on days of national festivity after the Sabinada Rebellion underscored Bahians' support for the imperial regime.[48] Poor attendance was a matter of serious concern to journalists; so was the authorities' failure to attend. The president's late arrival on 2 July 1870 prompted impatient students to stamp their feet in a noisy demonstration of disapproval.[49]

Dois de Julho galas followed a well-established program. They began when the president or the vice-president arrived. It was he who unveiled the "august effigy of his imperial majesty," or sometimes portraits of Emperor Pedro II and Empress Teresa Cristina, and it was he who led the audience in the "customary cheers." Journalists rarely described the imperial images (portraits or statues) or the customary cheers, likely because these were sufficiently familiar to their readers. On 2 July 1840, the president hailed the emperor, Dois de Julho, and the Exército Pacificador's heroes. A quarter century later, audiences still expected the customary cheers, and in 1864, journalists faulted the president for omitting a cheer to the state religion; he had led cheers to Pedro II, the general legislative assembly, Dois de Julho, and the Bahian people.[50] In 1888, the Dois de Julho cheers were to His Imperial Majesty, the imperial family, the princess regent, the constitution, the Brazilian nation, and the Bahian people.[51] To demonstrate the administration's unpopularity, opposition newspapers claimed there had been poor responses to these cheers; in 1868, this amounted to a "complete fiasco for the president" (who would, in fact, be removed from office shortly after the Conservatives returned to power two weeks later, as we saw in chapter 3).[52] In contrast to the criticisms levelled by Francisco Gonçalves Martins in his 1859 letter (see chapter 2), *Brasil Comercial*'s correspondent claimed that the cheers for Vice-President Manoel Messias de Leão (May–September 1858) demonstrated the contrast between him and his predecessor, João Lins Vieira Cansanção de Sinimbu (August 1856–May 1858). The unpopular Sinimbu had never received "a single cheer" and had resorted to filling the "pit with police officers, urban guards, and soldiers to honour him with applause, just like common comedians, without merit, who spend their salary buying applause and cheers."[53] In 1864, the police purchased eighty seats on the floor for the galas on 2 and 3 July out of their secret budget, presumably to give them to people who would cheer the authorities.[54]

After the cheers, the theatre company or the prima donna (backed by the rest of the opera company) sang the anthem, normally described as either the national anthem or the independence anthem, while the audience respectfully stood.[55] It seems that, as in Rio de Janeiro, the independence anthem was normally performed on 7 September and the national anthem on the other days of national festivity;[56] less clear is which one was performed on 2 July. It is tempting to suggest, as some have done, that the current Dois de Julho anthem, composed by José dos Santos Barreto, whose lyrics' attribution to Ladislau dos Santos Titara remains undocumented (chapter 1), was always performed at Dois de Julho galas, but the evidence for this is weak.[57] Indeed, there are many indications that it was customary to perform the national anthem at Dois de Julho galas, as the chief of police explained to the justice minister in 1846 (which would be consistent with Dois de Julho's emphasis on celebrating the day's importance to Brazil). At that time, Francisco Manoel da Silva's 1831 tune had no official lyrics – the original radical-liberal words had fallen into disuse – so an actor could sing the "national anthem with new stanzas appropriate for the subject" in 1843.[58] To make matters more confusing, later theatre programs and reports appear to use "Hino Nacional" (National Anthem) and "Hino da Independência" (Independence Anthem) interchangeably; the latter probably refers to the anthem composed by Pedro I in 1822, but at least one folklorist would later claim that Barreto had composed the "Independence Anthem or the Dois de Julho Anthem."[59] In 1861, the *Diário de Pernambuco*'s correspondent distinguished clearly between the "Hino da Independência" and the "Hino do Dois de Julho," the latter of which concluded Tavares's *Tempos da Independência*; the stage directions for that play, however, mandated the "Hino Nacional." Tavares directed that his 1857 *Elogio dramático* conclude with "the day's old anthem: *The sun rises on 2 July, etc.*," perhaps an indication that the Dois de Julho anthem was not normally heard on stage at mid-century.[60] In any case, the first theatre program with an explicit mention of the Dois de Julho anthem that I know of dates from 1878.[61] That radical-liberal lyrics were not sung at mid-century seems likely;

emptied of their political meaning, they could be performed in later decades.[62]

Poetry readings followed the anthem. As we saw in chapter 1, Titara regularly declaimed at the São João in the late 1820s and 1830s. Sometimes these readings were scripted and prepared in advance, as in 1843, when the program announced that Francisco Moniz Barreto, then the São João's manager, would recite a Dois de Julho ode between the anthem and the play.[63] This was the appropriate time for poetry, explained President Andréa in 1846, and the chief of police noted that three citizens had recited at that point during that year's gala. However, Manoel Pessoa da Silva surprised them with his declamation against the president between the first and second acts (chapter 1).[64] As Lizir Arcanjo Alves has demonstrated, poetry was a profoundly political art form.[65] There was a boom in radical-liberal verse at mid-century, and Andréa criticized the police for letting poets have full liberty to express themselves.[66] Alves suggests that radical-liberal poets like Francisco Moniz Barreto stayed away from theatre galas during the decade or so after 1848 (when Conservatives returned to power), preferring to declaim before more receptive audiences during the Noite Primeira procession; at least this is what Moniz Barreto claimed in 1858 when he returned to the São João's stage.[67]

Before the opera or the play began, an *elogio dramático* or dramatic laudation was sometimes performed; little beyond the title is known about most of these works. On 2 July 1847, "A Emancipação do Brasil" (Brazil's Emancipation) was performed at the São Pedro de Alcântara; in 1864, a "fine dramatic laudation" by José Antônio da Cunha, the title of which is not recorded, ended with an "anthem sung to liberty." It earned the playwright much applause, and he was called onto the stage to receive the audience's cheers.[68] Only one of these laudations was published – Tavares's 1857 work – and I will analyze it alongside the other national-historical plays in the following sections.

Finally, audiences settled in for the performance of an opera or a play. I know something about what was performed at the São João for only nineteen of the Dois de Julho galas between 1824 and 1870, and three of these references are too vague to be of much help: a "new ... drama" in 1830, a "melodramatic performance" in 1847, and a play whose production "was not good" in 1848.[69] In the decade and a half before the wave of national-historical plays, the São João's audiences saw *Napoleão no Egito* (Napoleon in Egypt, 1840), Jean-Marie-Théodore Baudouin d'Aubigny's *Os dois sargentos* (The Two Sergeants, 1843), and Alexandre Dumas's *Kean* (1849), examples of the "French pieces" that Wetherell considered poorly translated. In June 1841, the São Pedro was criticized for preparing to stage a work titled *A expulsão dos portugueses ou A entrada do Exército Pacificador na capital* (The Expulsion of the Portuguese or the Entry of the Exército Pacificador into the Capital), for it might reopen recently healed wounds and revive old grievances.[70] The São Pedro put on João Batista da Silva Leitão de Almeida Garrett's *Felipa de Vilhena* (Philippa of Vilhena) in 1847 and a new drama titled *Luiz de Camões* in 1848. The latter play was "very well executed," and one writer defended the choice of it for a Dois de Julho gala on the grounds that Camões was not merely a Portuguese author; he was a universal writer whose epics ranked with those of Homer, and thus he could thus be appropriately celebrated in Brazil.[71]

Only a handful of Dois de Julho galas featured opera performances. Gaetano Donizetti's *Lucia di Lammermoor* was on the program in 1868, and possibly there was a performance of Giuseppi Verdi's *I Lombardi alla prima crociata* on that day in 1855. Described as a "showy play," however, this was likely a bowdlerized version of the 1843 opera (by this time, the opera company that had reopened the São João in September 1854 was long defunct). Likewise, the version of *Ernani* performed in 1869 was a "play," Victor Hugo's *Hernani,* and not Verdi's opera based on that play.[72] In the late 1870s and early 1880s, which Boccanera described as years of successful opera seasons, Bahians heard Giuseppi Verdi's *Un Ballo in Maschera* on Dois de Julho in 1879, Carlos Gomes's *Il Guarany* in 1880, and Verdi's *Ernani* in 1882. In the latter year, the week-long Dois de Julho festivities ended with Donizetti's *Lucia.*[73]

After the flurry of national-historical dramas in the late 1850s and 1860s, Dois de Julho programs featured mostly plays (which I have not been able to identify), in addition to operas (1879–82) and a variety show (1871).[74] On the first Dois de Julho after slavery's abolition, Bahians saw a work titled *Fidalgos e operários ou A tomada da Bastilha* (Nobles and Workers or The Taking of the Bastille). This play drew repeated applause, "principally during the scenes contrasting the workers' nobility and the aristocrats' wickedness." It was followed by

Alexandre Fernandes's "brilliant poem" on abolition and by Afonso Olindense's allegory, *A abolição da escravidão no Brasil* (The Abolition of Slavery in Brazil).[75] The recent ending of slavery had brought abolition to the forefront of the celebrations, while the play's radicalism appealed to student theatregoers' diffuse republicanism.

Theatre galas were thus complex social, political, and cultural rituals. Members of Bahia's elite and middle class – the small minority of the city's population who could afford theatre tickets and who owned suitable clothing – displayed their sophistication and demonstrated their political loyalties by attending theatre galas on 2 July and on other days of national festivity. For many, what was actually performed on stage may well have been less important than the galas' social, political, and cultural functions. Dois de Julho galas were closely associated with the imperial regime, and they died with it; with a few exceptions, they did not continue under the republic. But before then, from the mid-1850s to the late 1860s, Bahian playwrights made significant efforts to produce a national-historical repertoire for these galas.

## Bahia's National Historical Plays

National-historical plays were a distinct genre in mid-nineteenth-century Brazil. Most were melodramas (like much of the theatrical repertoire), but they were set in key periods of Brazilian history, and this afforded playwrights the opportunity to provide direct and indirect commentary on Brazilian history and contemporary affairs. This genre formed part of Brazilian Romantics' efforts to create both a national history and a national literature. Most historians of Brazilian theatre suggest that few Romantics put much effort into writing for the stage, and Ivete Susana Kist has recently remarked on the how few dramas were set in Brazil's past; however, these assessments ignore the Bahian playwrights' efforts. Roberto Faria acknowledges that provincial "secondary authors" wrote an "unbelievably large" number of "provincial dramas" in the 1850s but judges few of them worthy of comment.[76] The four plays set during the struggle for independence in the province generally follow the conventions of melodrama, although some may be characterized as Romantic dramas for their lack of a happy ending in which the lovers are united, virtue is rewarded, and villains are punished.[77] I will not be classifying these works by genre, nor will I be situating them in the canon of Brazilian theatre history (from which many of them have been excluded); rather, my interest is in tracing how their authors dealt with the social and political tensions that had shaped the Dois de Julho commemorations over the previous decades. This requires reading these plays as, simultaneously, historical works (accounts of how independence was won) and commentaries on contemporary affairs.

The writers of Bahia's national-historical plays were all members of the Conservatório Dramático da Bahia, founded in August 1857 by Agrário de Souza Menezes. Its principal purposes were to develop local artists and repertoires and to improve the quality of productions, but Agrário, then serving as deputy in the provincial assembly, soon won the Conservatório legislative authority to approve all plays prior to their performance in the province, a measure passed as a rider in the provincial budget.[78] In his speech at the Conservatório's founding meeting, Agrário called on his colleagues to improve Bahia's theatre, for the stage was as important to progress as railways, telegraph lines, commerce, and agricultural development. "A genre of literature that encompasses such powerful elements of civilization should not be left to chance," he continued; moreover, Bahia should not fall behind other provinces or Rio de Janeiro in its literary and cultural development.[79] Literary historian Lizir Arcanjo Alves suggests that Bahian playwrights' efforts to create a Brazilian literature from a provincial perspective constituted a direct challenge to the efforts of Rio de Janeiro–based men of letters to create a national literature that served the interests of the imperial regime.[80]

Dois de Julho was a topic tailor-made for these purposes, and the 2 July 1857 gala exemplified Agrário's goals. It featured works by two Bahians: Antônio Joaquim Rodrigues da Costa's *O Dois de Julho ou O jangadeiro* (2 July or the Boatman), and Constantino do Tavares's *Elogio dramático*. The following year, Agrário de Sousa Menezes's *O dia da Independência* (The Day of Independence) was staged at the São João, and in 1861, Tavares's *Tempos da Independência* was performed at the São Pedro de Alcântara. For Dois de Julho in 1864 or 1865, Francisco Antonio Filgueiras Sobrinho wrote a three-act drama about independence titled *A legenda de um pariá* (The Legend of a Pariah), which for some reason was not performed (it was, however, published in a limited edition in 1923 and staged as part of the Dois de Julho centenary celebrations).[81]

These four plays and the *elogio* are, to my knowledge, the sole survivors of a much larger wave of national-historical plays performed on Dois de Julho. When Boccanera served as the São João's manager (1912–23), he could find no sign of the archive that had reportedly once held hundreds of scripts of all genres.[82] Newspapers alluded to several of these works. For Dois de Julho in 1856, the São João had put on the "interesting original drama" *A queda do tirano Rosas ou O triunfo das armas brasileiras* (The Fall of the Tyrant Rosas or The Triumph of Brazilian Arms), a melodrama about a mother whose son is shot by Juan Manuel de Rosas. Justice is finally done by the Brazilian army, which in the final scene sweeps away the Argentine *caudillo*'s regime.[83] In 1862, amateurs performed a drama titled *A Independência da América* (The Independence of America) on 2 July.[84] Rozendo Moniz Barreto's *Um pequeno grande* (A Great Little Man) was performed to enthusiastic applause on 2 July 1866 "because its author imprinted in it the great achievements of those who fought for the independence of the Empire of the Holy Cross."[85] Agrário's *Matilde* (1854) could be added to this list, for it presaged many of the themes developed in his later works, but this play, written while he was a fifth-year law student in Recife, was never performed on Dois de Julho.[86]

By this time, a national-historical play, or at least a work by a Brazilian author, was expected on Dois de Julho, and *Bahia Ilustrada* lamented in 1867 that a new impresario had staged a foreign translation on 2 July. While well received, such "exotics" would not aid in the development of "a national repertoire and a corpus of theatrical works as is necessary (*comme il faut*)."[87] It is not clear whether the French interjection was a deliberate ironic comment on elite cultural pretensions, but the impresario apparently got the message, and on 7 September, he staged Antônio Frederico de Castro Alves's *Gonzaga ou A Revolução de Minas* (Gonzaga or The Revolution of Minas [Gerais]). On Pedro's birthday in 1868, Bahians saw Domingos Joaquim da Fonseca's *Manuel Beckman*, about a 1684 revolt in Maranhão.[88] Other national-historical plays noted for Bahia's galas included Joaquim Manuel de Macedo's *Amor e Pátria* (Love and Homeland, 4 July 1864); the independence anthem at its conclusion elicited a "frenzy of applause." Costa's *Pedro Primeiro* (Pedro the First), hastily written for 7 September 1864, betrays the influence of Macedo's work.[89] On Brazil's independence day in 1861, Cincinato Pinto da Silva's *Os homens de cera* (The Men of Wax) was produced.[90] Antônio da Cruz Cordeiro's *Prólogo da guerra ou O voluntário da Pátria* (Prologue to the War or The Homeland's Volunteer), performed on 2 July 1865, does not quite belong to the genre of national-historical works; while indubitably patriotic and Brazilian, it is a piece of bombastic Paraguayan War–era propaganda.[91]

The four playwrights whose works on independence in Bahia are the focus of this chapter belonged to a generation of men too young to have fought in the war. Costa (1830–1870), however, in a poem dedicated to his father, proudly noted that he was the son of an independence veteran.[92] He, Tavares (1828–1889), Agrário (1834–1863), and Filgueiras (1842–1878) were all natives of Salvador and had no doubt heard many stories of the independence war as young boys.[93] Although they were too young to have participated in the radical-liberal movements of the 1830s that culminated in the Sabinada Rebellion, they had liberal sympathies. Agrário was closely tied to radical liberals from his student days in Recife; his first published poem declaimed against the National Guard reform that imposed central control over this civilian militia and called for a constituent assembly, then a key radical-liberal demand.[94] Costa, a medical doctor trained in Salvador, encouraged Agrário's literary efforts.[95] Like Agrário, Filgueiras took a law degree in Pernambuco and subsequently pursued a legal career in Salvador; during the Progressista years, he served as a judge.[96] Tavares entered the navy and returned to Salvador in the 1850s, where he worked in the customs house. He too had close ties to Agrário's family, as did the poet Francisco Moniz Barreto.[97] Of them, only Agrário has entered the Brazilian canon, but he is usually considered only a provincial writer.[98]

Before analyzing key themes in these plays, let us briefly review their plots. Costa's *Dois de Julho* begins in 1817, when Pedro Jorge, the *jangadeiro* (boatman) who brings Padre Roma (José Inácio Ribeiro de Abreu e Lima) to Bahia to promote the captaincy's adhesion to Pernambuco's republican revolution, eludes the authorities, who capture the priest. On land, he encounters a fearful *caboclo* fisherman and his daughter, Maria; while trying to convert the fisherman to the cause of liberty, he learns that Maria was the victim of an attempted seduction by a Portuguese *alferes* (infantry second lieutenant), Eduardo da Silva. Despite, or perhaps because of, his growing affection for Maria, Pedro Jorge proposes that the fisherman's patron arrange to have her placed in the Lapa Convent, although she wants to join the revolution that Pedro Jorge is promoting. At this point, soldiers under Eduardo's command arrest Pedro Jorge and the fisherman. The second act takes place in the São Pedro Fort's dungeon on 10 February 1821, the date of Bahia's adhesion to the Portuguese constitutional regime. In narrative dialogue between Pedro Jorge and the jailer, the audience learns that the boatman has spent four years pining for Maria; he receives a letter from her in which she describes the education she has received from the "good and holy Joana Angélica," the convent's abbess, and explains that she has not yet professed, for she still loves him. While the jailer will not let Pedro Jorge escape to visit Maria, he explains the political changes that have taken place in Bahia since November 1820, when news of the constitutionalist revolution in Portugal arrived. After the constitutionalists free the political prisoners, the jailer, the *caboclo* fisherman (held in the same dungeon, unbeknownst to Pedro Jorge), and Pedro Jorge all eagerly join the "revolution for liberty."[99]

The third act takes place on 19 February 1822, the day on which fighting broke out between Portuguese and Bahian troops, resulting in a devastating defeat for the patriots. Narrative dialogue between Pedro Jorge (now a corporal) and the fisherman (now a soldier) outside the Lapa Convent sets the political scene. Pedro Jorge asks the convent's chaplain about Maria, who "despite [having] a calling ... refuses to take her vows," and the fisherman tries to visit his daughter. Eduardo arrives and mocks Pedro Jorge's affection for Maria, and the two men exchange insults. When shooting breaks out in the distance, Pedro Jorge and the fisherman hurry to join their troops, leaving Eduardo and another Portuguese soldier to plot a raid on the convent to kidnap Maria. They kill Joana Angélica – the murder takes place backstage – but Pedro Jorge, the fisherman, and the former jailer (now also a soldier) return just in time to prevent Eduardo from carrying off Maria (who has fainted at the sight of the murder). The fourth act takes place in early June 1823 on the eve of another patriot attack on Salvador's Portuguese defenders. In the opening scenes, Brazilian soldiers lament the lack of food and clothing, as well as the winter cold; they also complain that they must risk their lives, while only officers win glories. Pedro Jorge, now an *alferes*, and the fisherman, now a sergeant, arrive to encourage the troops; all lament the recent deposition of Pedro Labatut from command and speculate about the role of Felisberto Gomes Caldeira in that plot. Pedro Jorge and the fisherman have come to this forward post to receive Maria, who has been shuttling back and forth between the besieged city and the patriot lines as a spy. When she arrives, Pedro Jorge promises that the war will soon end and that she will represent the "symbol of liberty" when the patriots enter the city; he also declares that he will confront Eduardo and take him prisoner in the upcoming battle.[100]

The play concludes at 6 a.m. on 2 July 1823, on Lapinha Square, where two men discuss recent developments: the Portuguese embarkation and the imminent arrival of the Exército Pacificador; the rumour that Pedro Jorge will soon be promoted to captain; and his "intense and personal hatred" for a certain Portuguese *alferes* named Eduardo da Silva, whom he has captured on 3 June and whom he keeps in a special prison. Soon the first patriot troops enter the square to a tumultuous welcome by the populace, and in the climactic scene, "a triumphal float enters, pulled by Lieutenant Pedro Jorge, the fisherman, and the jailer: On the float rides Maria, dressed as a *cabocla*. After the float – an escort of four soldiers, in the midst of which is Alferes Eduardo as a prisoner." Pedro Jorge denounces Eduardo's crimes, strips him of his military insignia, breaks his sword, and forces him to kneel before Maria. To the crowd, he declares that she represents "liberty" while the *alferes* exemplifies "despotism"; Maria takes a garland of coffee leaves from around her neck and places it on Pedro Jorge, declaring, "Liberty crowns love!"[101]

Agrário de Souza Menezes's *O dia da Independência* is the longest and most ambitious of these works.[102] The melodrama involves the rivalry between two half-brothers, Polidoro and Ricardo, both of whom wish to marry Josefa, the illegitimate daughter of a wealthy Portuguese merchant and monopolist in the food trade, D. Manoel, a "hastily made nobleman [*fidalgo feito às pressas*]." Ricardo is D. Manoel's adopted son, and he promises him Josefa's hand, but she loves Polidoro and eventually runs away from her father's house, at which point D. Manoel hatches a complex scheme to reduce Josefa to slavery and to settle much of his fortune on Ricardo. D. Manoel and Ricardo are staunch supporters of the Portuguese government in Salvador; they pay an unscrupulous priest, Friar João, to publish anti-patriot propaganda periodicals and work to cut off communication between the Bahian patriots and Pedro I. When he realizes that the patriots are likely to win, D. Manoel departs for Portugal, but he loses everything in a shipwreck off the Pernambucan coast. Josefa and her two suitors have several dramatic encounters in which Polidoro is portrayed as a noble patriot, in contrast to Ricardo. During the Battle of Pirajá, Polidoro is seriously wounded (perhaps even by Ricardo) and taken prisoner; Josefa thinks that he has died. The final act is set on 2 July 1823 at the Soledade Convent, where Josefa has secluded herself to mourn Polidoro's death. Reduced to begging because of the shipwreck, D. Manoel arrives and confesses his many sins to a veiled Josefa, who recognizes her father and forgives him. Ricardo too arrives and attempts to confess, but Josefa condemns him as "base" and "cowardly" (only at this point does the audience learn that he is Polidoro's half-brother). Polidoro has survived his injuries and enters with the Exército Pacificador. Josefa introduces her father while Ricardo begs Polidoro for the punishment that he deserves, but Polidoro pardons his half-brother and makes a rousing patriotic speech. The play ends to the sounds of the "national anthem."[103]

This already complex melodrama unfolds from 7 September 1822 to 2 July 1823, and Agrário adds an important subplot that provides comic relief. It involves Cornet Luiz Lopes and Maria Quitéria de Jesus, whom he portrays as lovers and inseparable companions. Luiz is a bumbling drunk and (when he can find enough food) a glutton, uncertain of whether he is Portuguese or Brazilian, while Maria is a determined patriot who constantly shores up his commitment to the cause. At the start of the play, they are in São Paulo, where they learn about Polidoro and Josefa, meet Ricardo, and witness Pedro I's Grito do Ipiranga (his declaration of independence). Luiz and Maria then make their way to Bahia. At a rural house belonging to D. Manoel, they meet Josefa; at this point, the audience learns about D. Manoel's plotting against independence. Polidoro arrives, also en route from the south, bearing orders from Pedro I for the patriot troops, but he is arrested. In the next act, Luiz and Maria are temporarily living on Itaparica Island, struggling to subsist from fishing. They aid Josefa in her flight by sheltering her and by misleading a servant of D. Manoel who is searching for her. The setting then switches to a nearby meeting between Labatut and Lord Cochrane; as the two commanders plan strategy and banter about having fought on opposite sides in the Napoleonic Wars, Josefa arrives to plead for Labatut's assistance. She tells of the attempt to reduce her to slavery and of Polidoro's impending execution in Salvador. This prompts Labatut to make a rousing patriotic speech to the assembled people of Itaparica. Shots ring out across the bar from Salvador as the Portuguese execute patriot prisoners, but Polidoro has escaped by swimming towards the island; some of Cochrane's sailors rescue him.

The fourth act takes place soon afterwards at D. Manoel's house in Salvador's lower city. He breaks with Friar João, for he has concluded that the patriots will win, and arranges for Ricardo to inherit his fortune; while he laments losing Josefa, he is determined to reduce her to slavery. When Madeira arrives, D. Manoel explains that he plans to leave for Portugal. Outside, the hungry city populace riots, shouting for the monopolist's head, but he slips out. Polidoro and Josefa enter at the head of the crowd; he delivers an impassioned speech on the populace's behalf and demands the forged documents that will reduce Josefa to slavery. Madeira hands them over, and Polidoro and Josefa lead him to safety through the angry crowd, explaining that the Portuguese commander also loves liberty (he has secured Josefa's freedom) but that he must do his military duty as a loyal servant of his king.

Maria and Luiz return during the fifth act, set at Pirajá on the eve of a battle. In a series of events unlikely to take place in a military outpost, Polidoro and Josefa arrive, arm in arm; he promises to marry her and tells Luiz that he should marry Maria. Ricardo, disguised as a Brazilian soldier, puts in an appearance to reiterate his determination to have Josefa. Friar João enters and declares that he is now a Brazilian patriot (a coward, he disappears before the fighting starts). As the assembled soldiers break out wine to welcome their new recruit, Polidoro reports that the Portuguese have received numerous reinforcements and are planning an attack. The soldiers continue to celebrate, and when the battle begins, Luiz is so drunk that he accidentally plays the orders for a cavalry charge, which so terrifies the Portuguese that they beat a hasty retreat, with Maria brandishing her sword in hot pursuit. Curiously, Maria and Luiz do not appear in the sixth act (which was criticized by the Conservatório for its lack of action), in which the melodrama is resolved.[104]

Tavares's *Tempos da Independência* is full of melodramatic elements but lacks a happy ending.[105] It focuses on a young orphan, Luiz, who arrives in Bahia in 1817 as the ward of Padre Roma. In the play's prologue, set on the eve of the priest's execution, Roma declares that one day Bahia will fight for Brazilian independence, and even the governor, the Count of Arcos, admits that Brazilians have the right to fight for the "liberty" of their "native land." In his tearful farewell to Luiz, Roma tasks him with carrying on the struggle. A few years later, during the February 1822 fighting between Portuguese and Bahian troops, Luiz declares himself a patriot. He is in love with Maria, the niece and ward of a Portuguese soldier, André, and much of the play focuses on the efforts of the Portuguese commander, Madeira, to gain control over the young woman, whom André is willing to give up in return for a reward. Maria, as much a patriot as Luiz, resists the general's blandishments. The villain, Corporal André, moves easily between the lines and continues his scheming to hand over his niece; he almost succeeds when she is captured while undertaking the dangerous mission of carrying patriot proclamations into the besieged city. Luiz, in turn, is the epitome of loyalty, and he warns Labatut of the May 1823 conspiracy against him. There is a happy ending for Luiz and Maria as they are reunited on 2 July 1823, but André avoids returning to Lisbon with the troops. Instead, he resurfaces during the epilogue, a Dois de Julho celebration on the Terreiro de Jesus sometime in the 1850s, during which he falsely presents himself as a veteran of the struggle for independence; Luiz also appears, as an elderly veteran, close to death.[106]

Filgueiras's *Legenda de um pariá* is a darker work, closer to a tragedy, set between 1821 and 1823, but with fewer explicit references to the struggle for independence in Bahia. The pariah of the title is Fábio, the natural son of the corrupt Count of Vilareal, a Portuguese nobleman; he is in love with Dona Paulina, the count's niece. Fábio was raised in the count's household and has spent two years in prison for his involvement in conspiracies four or five years earlier (in other words, at the time of the 1817 Pernambucan rebellion). Early in the play, Fábio denies his paternity, and after his mother dies, Vilareal expels him from the household. Paulina tries to discourage Fábio from joining the patriots, but he declares that he must obey the *pátria*'s call. Fábio falls in with a group of conspirators who include the elderly Gonçalo and his daughter, Maria, as well as another old man, who recounts that at the time of the Inconfidência Mineira, "the Brazilian people had the same ideas that they have today," and who describes Tiradentes's execution. Fábio learns that Felipe, the count's wastrel son, has tried to take advantage of Maria but that Gonçalo is too old to avenge his daughter. In the second act, set during the war, the audience learns that Fábio has risen to the rank of general in the patriot forces but that he still loves Paulina; Maria's husband, Jorge, has been killed, but she has stepped into his place and received the rank of *alferes*. In the final act, titled "A Independência e o futuro" (Independence and the Future), the count, having been imprisoned by the victorious patriots, kills himself after a confrontation between him and Fábio. After it is revealed that Paulina is, in fact, the count's daughter (and that Paulina and Fábio are therefore half-siblings), she poisons herself. Fábio declines to join the patriot troops for their march into Salvador, makes some recommendations about how the victorious patriots should conduct themselves, and declares that he will wander the forests and that the rest of his life will be "a memory between two graves." Like the other plays, this one ends with the victorious patriots entering the stage to the sounds of the "Independence Anthem" and cheers, this time "to the Brazilian *povo*, the Lord D. Pedro I, [and] to Brazil's Independence."[107]

Tavares's *Elogio dramático*, performed on the same night as Costa's *Dois de Julho*, is an allegory in verse about the choices that face Brazil. Despotism has imprisoned Commerce, Letters, and Industry in a cave and explains to Brazil that they, despite their beauty, are his mortal enemies. Brazil asks to speak with them, and Despotism opens the cave to release the "band of assassins." They explain that they cannot flourish under Despotism's regime. Letters describes the suffering of Despotism's many victims, who have included men involved in the Pernambucan revolts of 1817 and 1824 as well as leading figures of the 1789 Inconfidência Mineira. At this point, the spirit of Dois de Julho descends from a cloud, drives away Despotism, and exhorts Brazil to "inaugurate the golden age." The rocks and caves in which Despotism lives crumble as he is consigned to Hell; portraits of Pedro and Teresa Cristina appear, and the choir sings the Dois de Julho anthem.[108]

These plays can be criticized on numerous grounds. The plots are improbable, full of unexpected twists and turns, and the characters are flat, often amounting to little more than caricatures. Indeed, there is good reason why none of them have entered the canon of nineteenth-century Brazilian theatre. But their authors had not set out to write great literature. They were seeking box office success, and melodrama was the most popular theatrical genre; at the same time, they were appealing to patriotic sentiment, which inevitably turned their plays into political works and commentaries on society and culture. Portraying the struggle for independence required them to construct arguments about its causes and consequences.

### Society and Politics on Stage

Several key themes, as well as some notable absences, run through these five plays. At that time, the independence struggle was still part of living memory, but since the 1820s and 1830s, its memory had also been shaped by historical works, most notably by Inácio Acioli de Cerqueira e Silva's *Memórias históricas e políticas da província da Bahia* (Historical and Political Memoirs of the Province of Bahia, 1835–37), but also by Ladislau dos Santos Titara's epic poem, *Paraguaçu* (1835–37), whose footnotes constitute a history of the war,[109] and Bernardino Ferreira Nóbrega's *Memória histórica sobre as vitórias alcançadas pelos itaparicanos no decurso da campanha da Bahia* (Historical Memoir about the Victories Won by the Itaparicans over the Course of the Bahian Campaign, 1827). These playwrights based their works firmly on the historical record but also took numerous liberties with it. It is difficult to determine how much they consulted historical sources, as opposed to oral tradition and living memories of the struggle, but it is easy to identify errors and anachronisms, such as Luiz's reference in *Tempos da Independência* to Prince Regent Pedro as Brazil's "Perpetual Defender" in February 1822 when the future emperor did not take that title until 13 May 1822.[110] Agrário sets the Battle of Pirajá (8 November 1822) after Labatut's meeting with Cochrane at Itaparica, which did not actually take place, for Cochrane had not yet arrived when Labatut went there on 8 May 1823.[111] Nevertheless, one member of the Conservatório judged that *Dia da Independência* did not "offend historical truth even slightly, because [Agrário] dressed in the most vivid and appropriate colours the different characters gathered in his work"; a later commentator remarks that the Romantics did not normally adhere strictly to historical facts.[112] The point, of course, was that national-historical plays should express greater "truths" about the nation's origins and about contemporary society instead of meeting narrow standards of factual accuracy. In this sense, these plays were "political work[s]," as Costa explained while he was writing *Dois de Julho ou O jangadeiro*."[113]

That slaves belonged neither in the Bahian people nor in the Brazilian nation was one of these political "truths," and slavery is scarcely mentioned in these plays. Not one of these authors included a slave character – not even a "good" and "loyal" slave – and there are no allusions to slavery in Costa's work. In Agrário's play, Polidoro condemns Ricardo as a "slave," and of course, D. Manoel seeks to reduce Josefa to slavery, a figurative parallel to Portugal's despotism over Brazil, as Labatut puts it in his appeal to the people of Itaparica. The sole specific allusion to the existence of slavery in *Dia da Independência* is Ricardo's lament during his confession that "not even the slave insurrection, instigated by me, had the effect that I hoped for," but this merely underscores that slaves were a potentially dangerous internal enemy.[114] Tavares went further than his fellow playwrights in his allusions to slavery; with some frequency, his patriotic characters speak figuratively of slavery, as does Padre Roma at the start of *Tempos da Independência*: "I was born free and I will die rather than live as a slave."[115] Most dramatically, in his *Elogio*, Dois de Julho exhorts Brazil: "Purify thy name, which is stained by / The labour of a race that thou hast enslaved."[116] This is an early call for abolition, albeit not one that evinced much concern for the victims of slavery, for it is presented as a necessary precondition for attracting immigrants.

That these playwrights should have largely written slavery out of the patriotic society that they portrayed is no surprise; slaves and black characters more generally were rare in nineteenth-century Brazilian theatre and literature, and efforts to exclude Africans and slaves from the São João Theatre paralleled their exclusion from the nation as envisaged during the festival.[117] While it had been common to free slaves as part of public celebrations in the early 1850s (chapter 4), this gesture did not find its way into mid-century theatre. Slaves' absence, it should be added, meant that there were no on-stage portrayals of the slave/master interactions that were an important part of daily life at the time of independence (and also still at mid-century).

Also striking is the absence of free black characters from these plays. That D. Manoel can contemplate reducing Josefa to slavery in *Dia da Independência* may suggest that she is the daughter of a black or *parda* (mixed-race) woman, but there is no explicit indication of this, and D. Manoel recalls Josefa's mother as a "naïve maiden" whom he has seduced.[118] When describing the contending forces of February 1822 in *Dois de Julho ou O jangadeiro*, Pedro Jorge does not mention the black and *pardo* militia regiments, which figured prominently in the fighting. Prior to the battle scene in *Dia da Independência*, Polidoro briefly takes his leave by saying that he must meet with "the commander of the Henrique Dias [battalion], Gonçalves," the sole indication in these plays that there were black troops among the patriots (Manoel Gonçalves da Silva commanded the black militia battalion during the war).[119]

Costa's *Dois de Julho ou O jangadeiro* is heavily imbued with the rhetoric of *indigenismo*, the Romantic cultural movement that sought the origins of the Brazilian nation in its remote indigenous past, idealized as a heroic epoch analogous to Europe's medieval times.[120] Pedro Jorge exhorts the *caboclo* fisherman to live up to the "blood of the ancient Tupinambas" that runs through his "American veins" and to fight for liberty. He describes Maria's beauty, innocence, and "brown [*morena*] colour of the indigenous people," and he declares to the jailer that even if he had found her "in some Indian hut, dressed like a *cabocla*," he would have thrown himself at her feet in a "frenzy of admiration." All Brazilians, he concludes, should love "the true daughter of the American jungle." Foreshadowing the play's climax, he tells Maria that "Brazilian liberty must truly be represented by a beautiful *cabocla*! I will crown your brow with a lavish feather headdress [*canitar*] ... [and] tie a beautiful feather skirt [*araçóia*] around your waist," which is, of course, how she is dressed as the *cabocla* in the final tableau.[121] In

Tavares's *Elogio*, Brazil is meant to be portrayed as an Indian; Despotism calls him a "despicable *caboclo*," and he dreams of hunting as he sleeps with a bow and arrow at his side.[122] This trope – the male Indian as the allegorical symbol of Brazil – was in fact widespread; the authors of the dramatic laudations performed on days of national festivity in Rio de Janeiro had long deployed it (and it would soon become a cliché in the illustrated press).[123] To portray Brazil as an Indian or to celebrate an Indian woman's beauty, of course, implied downplaying the country's African heritage, as did the use of *caboclos* as Dois de Julho symbols.

Class tensions figure most prominently in Agrário's *Dia da Independência*. To highlight the populace's privations in besieged Salvador, his play includes a food riot in which the crowd shouts, "We want meat! We want [manioc] flour! Death to the monopolist!" D. Manoel has already left for Portugal, and Polidoro can calm the rioters by telling them that the monopolist has departed. Four months before the play's performance on 2 July 1858, Salvador had seen riots over high prices and the poor quality of staples, which also targeted the economic liberal President Sinimbu's efforts to deregulate food markets. This scene was thus a dramatic commentary on recent events.[124] Over the course of the play, it becomes clear that D. Manoel has gained his fortune as the stereotypical gouging merchant who "won a monopoly over basic foodstuffs"; he first secured his position by defrauding his employer while he was still "a poor *caixeiro* who barely earned enough to eat."[125]

Tavares dedicated his play to the Caixeiros Nacionais, as did Agrário. Tavares gives the clerks a prominent role in his play's concluding tableau, while Agrário's Polidoro makes a lengthy speech to Madeira and Ricardo in which he expresses many of the *caixeiros*' traditional demands: "*Caixeiro*, yes I was one. And what did I think then, General Madeira? That the *caixeiro nacional* would never get out of the degrading situation that they imposed on him, without the opportunity to one day become master? The *caixeiro nacional* represents an ideal that is linked to the ideal of independence. It is the commercial class [*comércio*] of this country that dedicates itself to the dogma of liberty. Who can better understand the *povo* that struggles against monopoly and that writhes in hunger?"[126] The *Diário do Rio de Janeiro*'s correspondent reported that the *caixeiros* in the audience "applauded frenetically, grateful for the great honour" of having their program espoused on stage, and they were no doubt behind the laurel wreath presented to Agrário at the play's conclusion.[127]

Polidoro goes further, declaring that as a Brazilian, an artisan, a soldier, and a *caixeiro*, he represents "the enraged *povo* in the streets, that rises from the dust, that gets involved in the war ... I am the *povo*, sometimes flattered by those who seek to make it their instrument, other times sacrificed by those who have already seized power. General, the time of judgment has arrived. It is necessary to understand that authority was not created to be a tool to exterminate the inviolable rights of man. It is necessary to understand that the *povo* does not complain in vain. It is necessary to understand, finally, that its will is the only sovereign."[128] He claims independence for the *povo*, a direct challenge to the view that it derived from the actions of Emperor Pedro I. Of course, popular sovereignty was not so easy to establish, and characters in several of the plays lament continued government corruption, the ways in which officers contrive to win all of the glory while enlisted men endure privations in the trenches, and how only a few of the Exército Pacificador's commanders are true patriots.[129]

Unsurprisingly, eleventh-hour patriots also come in for criticism in these plays. Even before the Portuguese troops have embarked, André has disposed of his cavalry uniform and has begun to "give cheers for [José Joaquim de] Lima [e Silva] and to call for Madeira's death." In the 1850s, he presents himself as a patriot hero and tells a tall tale about almost capturing Madeira at the Battle of Pirajá. When he realizes that he has been recognized, he scurries off, loudly cheering Dois de Julho.[130] Likewise, Agrário's Friar João, an unscrupulous coward, makes himself scarce when the shooting starts, despite having been fêted by the patriots when he joins them.[131]

Notwithstanding the many Portuguese villains and scoundrels in these plays, there are striking limits to the patriots' anti-Portuguese nativism.[132] After D. Manoel decides to cut off the subsidy to Friar João's newspaper, the cleric offers a ten-to-one bet that, even after independence, "the Portuguese will remain the de facto owners of this land." D. Manoel doubts that Brazilians will be so tolerant, but the victorious patriots exhibit remarkable magnanimity towards their erstwhile enemies. As a character in *Dia da Independência* explains, true

Brazilian patriots "are those who do not consider place of birth but rather nobility of character."[133] Josefa pardons her father, and Polidoro refuses to punish Ricardo, declaring that "on Dois de Julho, there is only one word – that of forgiveness."[134] A soldier in Filgueiras's play recalls Fábio's admonition that "no one is foreigner or enemy, except the oppressor: all are brothers, even the defeated."[135] The message is that repentant Portuguese can be accepted into the Brazilian nation. To be sure, there is no pardon for Eduardo in Costa's *Dois de Julho*, but his punishment merely amounts to a public humiliation, even though he is guilty not just of seducing Maria but also of murdering Joana Angélica, the greatest crime committed by any individual character in these plays.[136]

The limited lusophobia in these plays is consistent with the relatively few anti-Portuguese incidents recorded in the press during the mid-century celebrations (chapter 4). One additional such incident, which took place in the newly renovated São João in September 1854, has entered Bahian folklore in ways that exaggerate its lusophobic elements. A new stage curtain featured a painting of Tomé de Sousa's arrival in 1549; in the folklorists' telling, patriots judged the sight of *caboclos* (Indians) bowing before the first Portuguese colonial governor and the Portuguese flag an offence to Bahians, and during the intermission, one hothead slashed the curtain and sparked a riot that required military force to control.[137] Correspondents reported the incident to their readers in Rio de Janeiro and Recife; they and the chief of police made it clear that the curtain itself was undamaged and that the incident took place after the opera had ended, while the audience was leaving. Alferes João José Alves attempted to denounce the offending image, but few paid him any attention. He left the building and joined a small group of "rowdies," "urchins," or "*capoeiras*," who began to throw rocks at the police guard; the police quickly dispersed them and eventually arrested the officer, who, journalists were quick to point out, had been retired for his erratic behaviour. One bystander was hit in the head by a rock, and the *Jornal do Commercio*'s correspondent heard that President Wanderley himself had also been struck. The correspondents also reported that the radical-liberal periodicals *O País*, *O Guaicuru*, and *Marcos Mandinga* had published lengthy articles against the curtain's offending image, which other newspapers, including the *Correio Mercantil*, rebutted.[138]

Wanderley had only just returned from the parliamentary session (he resumed his duties on 19 September); when apprised of the controversy, he resolved not to have the curtain removed, for this would have demonstrated weakness – "and weakness among rulers is their certain death." But he later admitted that, had he known what would happen, he would have gladly sent "Tomé de Souza back to the grave where he rested for three hundred years."[139] Not long after, he commissioned a new (and uncontroversial) curtain with a classical image of dawn.[140] There are strong indications that rivalries among the artists who had bid for the job lay behind the criticisms of the painting.[141] In this case, lusophobia provided a convenient cover for the unsuccessful artists to get rid of a competitor's work.

These playwrights portrayed Portugal's domination over Brazil through gendered metaphors. Madeira's efforts to gain control of Maria in *Tempos da Independência*, D. Manoel's attempted enslavement of Josefa in *Dia da Independência*, and Eduardo's attempt to seduce Maria in *Dois de Julho ou O jangadeiro* all serve as metaphors for Portuguese colonial oppression. The female victims who represent Brazil fight back. Josefa runs away from home, seeks out Labatut, and joins Polidoro at the head of the food rioters. Her nobility of character is all the greater when she pardons her father. The Maria in *Dois de Julho ou O jangadeiro* oscillates between active and passive roles. Early in the play, she declares that she wants to take up arms on behalf of liberty rather than be sent to the convent, but in her letter to Pedro Jorge, she describes herself as entirely devoted to him: "All of this I learned to make myself worthy of your love." During the war, she shuttles between the besiegers and the city, where she spies for the patriots, but she returns to a passive role as an idealized *cabocla* in the concluding tableau.[142]

Tavares's Maria, the object of Madeira's advances, reappears as Alferes Maria Quitéria de Jesus; Agrário and Filgueiras also included her in their plays. The real Maria Quitéria de Jesus (1792–1853) enlisted in the Exército Pacificador in September 1822; disguised as a man, she served with distinction in the Periquitos' Battalion even after her sex was discovered, and was recognized as a cadet. Inácio Acioli briefly mentions her and reproduces the August 1823 decree by which Pedro I rewarded her with an *alferes*'s pension, the grounds for her to claim that rank, which she had not held during the war; Titara also celebrates her in *Paraguaçu*.[143] The other contemporary source on Maria Quitéria is Maria Graham's account of meeting her in Rio de Janeiro, but it appears that only Filgueiras Sobrinho relied on the Englishwoman's 1824 book.[144] Of course, none of the playwrights needed written sources to learn about Maria Quitéria, for she lived in Salvador for the last decade or so of her life, quietly collecting her pension (after the war, she had returned to her hometown in the *sertão*).[145]

The Maria Quitéria in Tavares's *Tempos da Independência* simultaneously provides comic relief and serves as an exemplar of female heroism.[146] Jerônimo, the former shopkeeper and acquaintance of André (Maria's uncle and guardian), now serving as sentinel outside Labatut's headquarters, cannot decide whether to address her as Maricota (her childhood nickname), Mrs. Maricota (given that she has married Luiz), or Mr. Alferes (the correct address for an army officer, but an incorrect way to address a woman).[147] Labatut dispatches her on a mission into Salvador to distribute patriot proclamations and to make contact with certain individuals, but she is captured in an ambush, which gives her a final opportunity to spurn Madeira on 2 July, defiantly dressed in homespun with a dagger in her belt.[148] Filgueiras closely follows Maria Graham's account, noting that Maria Quitéria's father was named Gonçalo (perhaps having difficulty with Maria Quitéria's accent, Graham turned Gonçalo Alves de Almeida into Gonsalves de Almeida), that he received patriot emissaries, and that she volunteered to join the patriot forces, although he presents her as doing so with her husband, Jorge (she was, in fact, single at that time, but she may have married a fellow soldier during the war). When Jorge dies in battle, she dons his uniform.[149]

Agrário took numerous liberties with the historical record in his portrayal of Maria Quitéria. He makes her and Luiz Lopes, another folkloric figure from the independence war, into lovers. According to Inácio Acioli, Lopes was a Portuguese-born bugler who joined the patriots; at the Battle of Pirajá, he misunderstood orders to announce a retreat and played the call for a cavalry charge, which inadvertently turned the tide of the battle, as the terrified Portuguese troops fled back to the safety of their lines. Titara also mentions this episode, and it appears to have been widely known in the 1850s, for Pedro II heard the story during his 1859 visit to the battlefield and Agrário mentioned Luiz Lopes in an 1855 poem.[150] No additional evidence on this incident has come to light, and some scholars dismiss it as a legend, but the best assessment is Antônio Risério's observation that "today we still do not know whether he was incompetent, clumsy, insubordinate, visionary, fanatic, or crazy."[151] Agrário portrays Cornet Lopes as a happy-go-lucky bumbling glutton and drunk who, at the start of the play, does not know whether he is Portuguese or Brazilian. Maria Quitéria, whom the cornet meets in São Paulo on 7 September, is the true patriot in the couple; she declares to Luiz that she went to São Paulo in search of a great man to whom she would swear her oath; she would then go to Bahia "where they will have to struggle most for the cause of independence."[152] She speaks much more than Luiz, and she repeatedly admonishes him to stop complaining about the privations that they must endure as patriots.[153] She brandishes her weapons aggressively and tells D. Manoel's servant: "You don't know what a little Brazilian woman [*brasileirinha*] is when she gets mustard up her nose!" Showing a brace of pistols, she continues: "See these. I'm more likely to go without food than they without bullets."[154] Polidoro calls her "a true Spartan," and in the battle scene, she brandishes a sword as the army advances, while a drunken Luiz stumbles along with his bugle.[155] After Polidoro tells Luiz that he should marry Maria, the bugler laments that he is "a poor devil who will end his days in sorrow, drunk, begging from door to door!" Polidoro's reply that it would be to Brazil's "eternal shame" to forget its independence veterans would have rung hollow for those who knew their history. Inácio Acioli noted that in 1835, "Cornet Lopes today begs for his daily bread; the fact that it is to him that the [Battle of Pirajá's] successful outcome is owed" had already been forgotten.[156]

Maria Quitéria's prominence in these plays contrasts sharply with her absence from the concluding scenes. Luiz and Maria do not even put in a cameo appearance in *Dia da Independência's* final act, nor is there any news of Maria's fate during the epilogue to *Tempos da Independência.* This is, however, consistent with the lack of attention to her during Dois de Julho celebrations. Her return to Salvador did not win her a place in the festival in the way that Pedro Labatut's retirement to Bahia in the late 1840s allowed patriots to make him into a hero in 1848 and 1849. Filgueiras's Maria Quitéria is out of uniform in the last scene, happy that her father has come to fetch her; she agrees to marry the son of a family friend who has long loved her from afar.[157] The real Maria Quitéria's challenge to gender conventions – her mostly conventional postwar life notwithstanding – was apparently too much to accept. In March 1824, *O Independente Constitucional* published a two-page diatribe against her swaggering about Salvador in uniform, while the editor of José Lino Coutinho's *Cora* (a book of instructions for the upbringing of his daughter, published in 1849) argued that she did not deserve mention in Inácio Acioli's book, for nature had designated other roles for women.[158] At mid-century, Maria Quitéria could be represented on stage in obviously fictional and comic ways, but not elsewhere in Dois de Julho celebrations. There is also no indication that she was ever conflated with the *cabocla* in the way that Costa does in *Dois de Julho*; his Maria bears the least direct resemblance to Maria Quitéria, but Maria Graham's observation that her "features, especially her eyes and forehead, have the strongest characteristics of the Indians" suggests that she could easily have served as such a symbol. As the daughter of a rather prosperous rancher – she told Graham that her father owned twenty-six slaves – Maria Quitéria not surprisingly claimed that her parents were Portuguese.[159]

Pedro Labatut also figures prominently in these plays. In *Dia da Independência*, D. Manoel worries about "this terrifying man who seemingly wrenches soldiers from the bowels of the earth," and Friar João turns the general into a special target of his propaganda, while André disparages him as "this French beast" in *Tempos da Independência*.[160] During his meeting with Cochrane, Labatut recounts his career in Napoleon's service, his decision to seek "asylum under the standard of liberty" in the United States, and his service against the "restorationist movement" in Venezuela and New Granada. He declares that "the principle of liberty" guides all of his actions, and after learning about D. Manoel's efforts to enslave Josefa, he rallies the people of Itaparica "against all the tyrants of the world!"[161] After this scene, Labatut disappears from the play; in this way, Agrário avoided having to portray the general's removal from command in May 1823, which he considered a grave injustice, as he explained in the notes to *Matilde*, in which he apologized for some of his characters' anti-Labatut statements.[162]

Led by Colonel Felisberto Gomes Caldeira, battalion commanders closely linked to the planter class and upset at Labatut's high-handed actions (as well as at his efforts to recruit slaves) replaced the French general with Colonel José Joaquim de Lima e Silva, commander of the troops from Rio de Janeiro.[163] Costa suggests that Labatut enjoyed considerable popularity among the ranks. Shortly after his removal, the jailer (now a corporal) laments that Labatut has been robbed of the glory of leading the troops into Salvador, and Pedro Jorge likens his experience to that of Moses, who was only shown the Promised Land.[164] In *Tempos da Independência*, Luiz reports the conspiracy to Labatut; the general remarks that the mere fact of his foreign birth is enough to make it impossible for him to command the patriots, but Luiz stiffens his resolve. As he is being arrested, Labatut declares: "The general of Brazil's independence will always be Labatut, no matter who succeeds him." To the major who arrives to arrest Labatut, Luiz has strong words: "Brazil demands unity from all of her sons so that she can be strong; all of their blood to win her liberty."[165] Both he and Pedro Jorge remark that the conspirators may be writing their own sentences – a specific allusion to Colonel Felisberto, who was murdered by his own troops in October 1824.[166] When Labatut retired to Salvador in 1848, he became a central figure in Dois de Julho celebrations and was subsequently honoured in the annual pilgrimage to Pirajá (chapter 2).

These playwrights were commenting on Bahian and Brazilian society and on some of the prominent figures in the struggle for independence; they were also constructing broader arguments about the origins of Brazil's independence. For them, the events in Bahia were central to Brazilian independence. Nowhere do their characters speak about Bahian independence, autonomy from Rio de Janeiro and Lisbon, or federalism, important issues for the generation of independence and for the radical liberals who invented the Dois de Julho festival. The plays' characters all seek Brazil's independence. By the time these playwrights were writing, the Brazilian nation was firmly established; none of these men had known any other political arrangement. Brazil was their – and their patriotic characters' – *pátria*. They were coming of age just as the imperial regime's political stability was being secured, and their works appeared during the Conciliação or shortly thereafter, when Brazil was no longer in question but when renewed radical-liberal criticisms of the imperial regime were emerging.[167]

Tavares's *Tempos da Independência*, Costa's *Dois de Julho*, and Filgueiras's *Legenda* firmly link the Bahian struggle to the 1817 Pernambucan republican movement.[168] In *Tempos da Independência*, Padre Roma charges the young Luiz with carrying on the struggle and the 1817 movement is a constant presence. Luiz declares to Madeira that "my name is the Bahian *povo*" and that the "martyrs of 1817 rise from their grave to inspire the *povo*." When Labatut is arrested, Luiz looks to the heavens, seeking inspiration from Roma, for the strength to carry on. In his concluding soliloquy set during the celebrations sometime in the 1850s, Luiz declares that he is satisfied to have served his country and looks forward to meeting Roma to report on how he has fulfilled the priest's mission.[169] Luiz is based on Luiz Inácio Ribeiro Roma, the son whom Padre Roma brought to Bahia in 1817; Luiz (and his older brother, José Inácio de Abreu Lima) were forced to witness their father's execution; both made their way to Venezuela, where José Inácio gained the rank of general in Simón Bolivar's patriot forces. Both eventually returned to Brazil but had very different careers there: Luiz was deeply involved in radical-liberal politics in Pernambuco from the late 1820s to 1848, while José Inácio eschewed radical politics in the 1830s; he is today best known for his 1855 book on socialism.[170] Like Tavares's Luiz, Costa's Pedro Jorge continues Padre Roma's work and dreams of the executed priest while in prison; what Filgueiras's Fábio did during the conspiracies of four or five years earlier is not clear in *Legenda*, but he laments: "Oh liberty, for thee I saw my brothers die on the gallows four years ago. For thee I suffered unheard of pains."[171] These favourable portrayals of the 1817 rebellion contrast sharply with Francisco Adolfo Varnhagen's rejection of this movement in his *História geral do Brasil* (General History of Brazil, 1854–57) and with the denial of its importance in other "official" histories of the imperial regime.[172]

The Inconfidência Mineira, the 1789 conspiracy in Minas Gerais, whose scapegoat, Tiradentes, was eventually constructed as a patriotic precursor to Brazilian independence, is but a distant presence in these plays.[173] Padre Roma tells the young Luiz that he should be a hero, willing to sacrifice himself like Tiradentes. In *Legenda*, one of the elderly conspirators speaks at length about Tiradentes and argues that at that time, "the Brazilian people had the same ideas that they have today. Then they had less strength, but were suffering identical oppression."[174] In his *Elogio*, Tavares went even further than simply connecting the 1789 conspiracy and the 1817 rebellion, and added the 1824 Confederação do Equador.[175] Letters explains to Brazil what Despotism has done:

> I will tell you, nevertheless, what he did with their lives
> To pay for the love of the land, in which they were born
> The illustrious Caneca, Padre Roma
> Tiradentes, the poet Claudio,
> Who died in prison; the great Andrada
> Had heavy shackles on his wrists
> And would he who so tortures your brothers
> Be your friend?

Brazil responds that he will "plunge [his] arrows into this tiger."[176] (Friar Caneca was executed for his role in the Confederação do Equador, and the poet Claudio Manoel da Costa committed suicide while imprisoned for his involvement in the Minas Gerais plot. The "great Andrada" is Antônio Carlos Ribeiro de Andrada Machado e Silva, brother of José Bonifácio, imprisoned for his role in the 1817 rebellion.)

In this way, these three playwrights joined in the radical-liberal effort to construct a patriotic history of Brazil that did not attribute the origins of the nation to the actions of Pedro I, who proclaimed independence on 7 September 1822 and granted the constitution on 25 March 1824. This eventually developed into the republican history of independence, which viewed the imperial regime as a detour on the road to republican liberty. In the early 1860s, particularly at the time of the inauguration of the equestrian statue of Pedro I, these issues were widely debated in Rio de Janeiro, most prominently through Teófilo Otoni's pamphlet (in which he explained his refusal to attend the inauguration ceremonies) and the responses to it. The plays suggest that Bahians were discussing these issues well before 1862.[177] They also underscore the extent to which these playwrights were closely tied to the radical-liberal tradition that was so prominent in the early and mid-century Dois de Julho celebrations. And they highlight the political and personal linkages between Bahia and Pernambuco that shaped both the independence struggle in Bahia and Bahian understandings of the struggle's meaning, linkages that have not received sufficient attention.[178] The constant presence of Bahian law students in Pernambuco reinforced these connections; that Bahians had fewer ties to Minas Gerais may explain the lesser role of the Inconfidência Mineira in these plays.

For these men, Dois de Julho celebrated Brazilian independence. The first act of Agrário's *Dia da Independência* firmly links Brazil and Bahia. Maria Quitéria's journey to São Paulo, her encounter with the future Emperor Pedro I, and her prediction about the importance of the struggle for independence in Bahia all underscore the province's centrality to Brazil (Tavares's Padre Roma also makes this prediction about Bahia's role).[179] There are also allusions to the Grito do Ipiranga in *Legenda de um pariá*.[180] Agrário's Pedro I, however, is the liberal prince regent who will "free the small," not the authoritarian emperor whom Exaltados excoriated in 1830–31. Polidoro asserts that only Pedro can raise the cry that will "echo from the Amazon to the Plate," and Pedro declares that henceforth, his motto will be "Independence, Liberty, or Death," not just the "Independence or Death" of the Grito do Ipiranga.[181] Pedro Jorge rallies the troops before the 3 June 1823 attack with cheers to the emperor, to liberty, and to Brazil's independence.[182]

The concluding tableaux likewise firmly connect the Bahian events to those of Brazil. Before the *caboclos*, Luiz leads the populace in cheers to Dois de Julho, the Brazilian constitution, the Bahian people, and their imperial majesties; the curtain falls on *Tempos da Independência* as the "national anthem" is played.[183] Agrário's play ends with Polidoro presenting the assembled patriots with the "gold and green standard" (the Brazilian flag) and leading them in cheers to "the immortal day of 2 July 1823," followed by cheers to Brazil's independence and the "Brazilian people," followed by the "national anthem."[184] *Legenda de um pariá* concludes with the battalion of patriots filling the stage, the "independence anthem," and cheers to the Brazilian people, Pedro I, and "Brazil's Independence."[185] Tavares's *Elogio* culminates in the Dois de Julho anthem, but it is sung before the portraits of Pedro and Teresa Cristina; Dois de Julho tells Brazil he is free.[186] Costa, however, gave no directions for music to accompany the final tableau in which the humiliated Eduardo kneels before the *cabocla*, Maria.[187]

In short, these playwrights argued for the centrality of the Bahian war to Brazilian independence. For them, Brazil was the *pátria* that commanded their characters' loyalty, and what they sought was recognition for Bahia in the national independence story, as well as a more liberal nation-state. Thus, in *Tempos da Independência*'s concluding scene, Luiz understands that reality is far from the ideals of four decades earlier but expresses satisfaction at having done patriotic service in the struggle. He laments the sad fate of forgotten and abandoned "veteran soldiers," but consoles himself: "I had only one desire – the *pátria*'s independence! I am satisfied." For him, the new Brazil – his *pátria* – has not lived up to the hopes of so many characters in these plays for a prosperous, just, and virtuous society, but he can console himself that he has done his duty.[188]

The Bahian playwrights whose national-historical plays have survived were, like many Dois de Julho celebrants, deeply engaged in constructing arguments about the meaning of independence in their home province, about the nature of the Brazilian nation in which they lived, and about their society. These men expressed their liberal, and sometimes radical, ideals on stage. They wrote slavery out of the nation, advocated popular sovereignty, and celebrated popular heroes like Maria Quitéria, Luiz Lopes, and Pedro Labatut; they appealed directly to the Caixeiros' Nacionais and their desire for the nationalization of retail commerce. They were among the first Brazilians to argue that the 1817 Pernambucan Rebellion and even the Inconfidência Mineira were precursors to a radical-liberal independence, which in their view had been won by the people and not solely by Pedro I and his coterie of advisers in Rio de Janeiro. For these playwrights, the real history of Brazil's independence took place in Bahia, culminating on 2 July 1823.

The wave of national-historical plays was short-lived, and by the mid-1860s the playwrights on whom this chapter has focused had dispersed. Agrário died spectacularly in his box at the São João while applauding an August 1863 performance.[189] Costa moved to Rio de Janeiro and died in Macaé in 1870; Tavares also moved to the imperial capital during the Paraguayan War, where he worked in the navy ministry, although he later returned to Salvador. Filgueiras continued his education in Pernambuco, earning a doctorate in law in 1870.[190] *Tempos da Independência*, the only play about independence in Bahia published at that time, was also the only one of these works revived for a later theatre gala, in 1877, as part of the Dois de Julho benefit for drought victims.[191]

National-historical plays continued to be staged on days of national festivity in the later 1860s, but after Rozendo Moniz's *Um pequeno grande* (2 July 1866), none was explicitly about independence in Bahia. The only one of these plays that survives is *Gonzaga ou A Revolução de Minas*, by Antônio Frederico de Castro Alves (1847–71), better known as an abolitionist poet. First performed on 7 September 1867, it is based on the 1789 Inconfidência Mineira, the conspiracy against Portuguese rule in Minas Gerais; in this light, Castro Alves elaborated a theme already present in the earlier Bahian plays. It is a massive work that focuses on the main conspirators and their betrayal to the governor by Silvério. The poet presents the conspirators as Brazilian patriots (not anti-monarchical republicans). Cláudio declares: "Enough with seeing all of Brazilians' aspirations blocked ... When the heart of a Brazilian beats, an iron hand compresses its pulse – the hand of the metropolis."[192] The play ends conventionally but anachronistically to the sounds of the "national anthem," over which Maria, Gonzaga's lover, reads a long poem hailing the conspirators' patriotism.[193] The second theme, dear to Castro Alves's heart, is slavery and abolition, which is scarcely addressed in the earlier plays; he wrote in slave characters, and the plotters are determined abolitionists. Gonzaga looks forward to the day when "under the gigantic American forests, the entire Brazilian family gathers as in the old days ... No more slaves! No more masters!"[194] Slavery is, in fact, the patriots' weakest point, for Silvério's ability to betray the conspiracy depends on his control over Carlota, the slave woman who has grown up without knowing her father, Luiz, Gonzaga's former slave and, at the time of the play, his devoted servant. By holding out the possibility that he will allow Carlota to meet her father, Silvério is able to blackmail her into stealing incriminating documents. When Luiz and Carlota finally meet, the father threatens to kill his daughter for her role in betraying the conspiracy, until he realizes who she is. Silvério sends Carlota away to his plantation to be the "wife" of all of his slave men; she commits suicide and thereby becomes Brazil's first martyr.[195]

Despite a hastily organized production with numerous amateur actors, Castro Alves described *Gonzaga's* opening night as "a triumph greater than anyone else has reportedly obtained in Bahia."[196] Written just after the cohort of national-historical playwrights had dispersed, the play anticipated concerns that would preoccupy intellectuals and literati in the 1870s and 1880s – abolition and the republic. It exemplified a precocious anti-slavery sentiment and joined other early (and increasingly republican) efforts to claim the Inconfidência Mineira as a precursor to independence, efforts to which Tavares contributed with his own *Gonzaga* (1869) – a much less ambitious work than Castro Alves's play – which portrays the conspirators as premature Brazilian patriots (it is not known to have been performed on 2 July in Bahia).[197] Castro Alves's *Gonzaga* was revived for the 1881 Dois de Julho gala.[198]

Much changed in Bahia's theatre scene in the decades after Gonzaga. The province shared in the late-nineteenth-century shift of tastes away from opera towards operetta and musical theatre. Twentieth-century historians lamented Bahian theatre's decadence even as audiences flocked to these new genres and, in the 1890s, to the annual reviews (musicals that commented on the previous year's events).[199] There was money to be made in the new genres, and in 1886, private interests constructed the Politeama Baiano to compete with the São João; the new theatre quickly became Bahia's leading venue.[200] Nonetheless, Boccanera prefaced his 1924 *Teatro na Bahia* (Theatre in Bahia) with a call to restore the theatre's moralizing function.[201] As recent historians of Rio de Janeiro's theatre have demonstrated, such laments have led scholars to overlook the importance of popular genres in late-nineteenth and early-twentieth-century Brazilian culture and society.[202]

However popular, the new genres did not easily lend themselves to civic ritual, and Dois de Julho theatre galas scarcely survived the empire's fall. There are no indications that theatre galas were a regular part of Dois de Julho celebrations after the 1890s, and by the time that Boccanera wrote his few lines about the authors of national-historical plays in the 1910s, these works belonged firmly to a distant past. *Legenda de um pária's* 1923 revival no doubt brought back memories of older ways of commemorating Dois de Julho. Nonetheless, the national-historical plays of the 1850s and 1860s provide insights into how Bahian literati understood their province's place in Brazil. Men like Agrário and his fellow playwrights saw themselves as Brazilians, but they were determined to win recognition for Bahia in the larger story of their country's independence struggle. Like so many other Dois de Julho patriots, their history of independence was a liberal one.

# "Cold as the Stone of Which It Must Be Made": The Monument and Dois de Julho's Bifurcation

On 2 July 1895, a rainy winter day, state government officials and representatives of Salvador's elite inaugurated a large marble and bronze monument to commemorate Dois de Julho (see figure 6.1). It dominated Campo Grande, officially known as Duque de Caxias Square, the centre of a rapidly growing upper-class residential area (see figure 6.2). In raising such a structure, Bahians were participating in a nineteenth-century phenomenon. Historical monuments were widely considered marks of civilization and a necessary means to beautify cities. The "*statuomania* [statue mania]" of France's Third Republic and the proliferation of (mass-produced) Civil War soldier statues in the United States were part of this diffusion of public art into the urban spaces of the Atlantic world. Monuments sought to interpret history in acceptable ways – emancipation in the United States, for example, could be commemorated through statues of Lincoln but not monuments to slaves – but were sometimes the objects of bitter contestation. Successive French regimes removed and replaced the monuments to their predecessors as they imposed their symbols on public space.[1]

Much of the literature on monuments focuses on the complex political and artistic processes that led to their construction. While these are important issues, an equally important test of many a monument came after its construction, as it was inserted into civic commemorations. This was especially the case for the Dois de Julho monument, which its advocates explicitly envisaged as a "lieu de mémoire [memory

Figure 6.1 | The Dois de Julho Monument, 1895

*Source*: Photo by Hendrik Kraay, 2 July 2011.

Figure 6.2 | The Dois de Julho Monument on Campo Grande, 1897
(*Note*: While some have identified this as a photograph of the monument's
2 July 1895 inauguration (among them, Martinez, *2 de Julho*, 119; Kraay,
"'Cold as the Stone,'" 165, and "'Frio como a pedra,'" 52; Baldaia, "Festa,"
87), it actually shows the thanksgiving mass celebrated on 24 November
1897 after the end of the war against Canudos. Levine, *Vale*, 49; Piedade,
*Comitê patriótico*, 275; C. Teixeira, *Cidade*, 166–7.)

*Source*: AIGHBa, pasta 14, reg. 1305. Reproduced with permission.

space]" – an expression coined by Pierre Nora – and as a site that would
fix Bahians' memories of independence now that there were almost
no surviving participants in these struggles.[2] No longer part of living
memory, Bahia's independence had passed into history, and a monument would best attest to the achievements of the men of 1822–23, or
so judged its advocates. At the same time, the monument was part of
an effort by some members of Bahia's elite to do away with the popular
elements of Dois de Julho celebration that they considered objectionable. The mix of carnivalesque elements and civic ritual had become

increasingly embarrassing to them by the 1870s, both because of the extensive popular participation and because the Indianist symbols were less and less acceptable in an age that espoused scientific racism and held that "civilization" emanated from Europe. Constructing a fixed monument and making it the focus of Dois de Julho celebrations would offer a more modern, respectable way to commemorate the patriots' 1823 victory. However, things did not work out the way that the monument's advocates intended. While official commemorations of Bahian independence after 1895 took place around the monument, the popular festival retreated to the other end of the city, to Santo Antônio Além do Carmo Parish, where the *caboclos* remained the focus of commemoration. The monument's advocates could not suppress Dois de Julho popular patriotism.

More broadly, the Dois de Julho monument can be placed in several additional political, social, and cultural contexts. By the end of the imperial regime and the proclamation of the republic, Salvador and the province (state after 1889) of Bahia were in rapid economic and political decline relative to Rio de Janeiro and São Paulo. With its vibrant Afro-Brazilian popular culture and inability to attract even a tiny share of the European immigrants who flooded into the country after 1889, Bahia seemed to be the antithesis of the emerging modern Brazilian society.[3] Nonetheless, state propagandists laboured tirelessly to present a different image. Promotional literature directed at attracting immigrants portrayed Bahia's population as the product of "Portuguese colonization" and the state's customs as "completely European and civilized."[4] José Botelho Benjamin, the author of the 1894 book in which these assertions appeared, added that Bahia was the Brazilian Athens, her educational establishments second to none, and her periodical press highly respected. Her commerce demonstrated "growing activity," despite the difficult regime change and the sudden end of slavery; industry, "already well advanced," would soon "raise itself to a high degree of prosperity and development"; the state already had over 1,100 kilometres of railways, with many more lines projected.[5]

These were the fervent aspirations of Bahia's small and closely interconnected upper class, whose members, as historian Dain Borges has put it, "represented the power of a cosmopolitan capital in a provincial backwater." With their eyes on Europe and Rio de Janeiro, they sought to recast Salvador as a sophisticated showcase capital city. They worried about outsiders' perceptions.[6] In the early twentieth century, state governments intervened extensively in Salvador, widening narrow downtown streets and laying out a broad (but not straight) Sete de Setembro (7 September) Avenue, a pale imitation of the capital's Central Avenue (today Rio Branco Avenue).[7] The Dois de Julho monument can be seen as a precursor to these later urban reforms; certainly, it expressed many of the ideals inscribed on Salvador's urban geography after 1900. Yet the monument included a statue of the *caboclo* atop its pillar, suggesting that the Indian symbol, centre of the popular festival, could not so easily be cast aside, even at a time when *indigenismo* had fallen from favour. Indeed, one historian of Dois de Julho argues that the *caboclo* "took over the city's great noble space," an interpretation that misrepresents the monument advocates' intent.[8] They sought to tame the symbol, freezing it in bronze and fixing it in the monument, and they were adamant about keeping the old symbols away from the new one.

The military coup that led to the republic's proclamation in Rio de Janeiro on 15 November 1889 surprised Bahians. No one in the province had known about the plot, and few Bahians had been involved in the campaign against the monarchy. Military personnel and students at the medical school founded the province's Republican Club in 1888; on 2 July 1889, they began publishing a newspaper, *A República Federal*. When telegrams brought news of the coup late on 15 November, the provincial president called a meeting of the city council and other leading figures, all of whom reaffirmed their loyalty to the monarchy. They sent telegrams to that effect to Rio de Janeiro and prepared a proclamation for publication. The commander of arms, General Hermes Ernesto da Fonseca (brother of the provisional president, Deodoro da Fonseca), also declared his support for the old regime. Late in the day on 16 November, army officers and republicans gathered at São Pedro Fort and proclaimed the republic; violence broke out that night as monarchist members of the lower classes stoned republicans' houses, cheering the monarchy. Hermes changed his mind, as did just about everyone who had participated in the city council meeting on the 16th (five months later, the provisional government would name him governor). On 17 November, the army garrison marched

unopposed into the city centre and instituted the new regime; the following day, Virgílio Clímaco Damásio took office as Bahia's first republican governor.[9]

For the purposes of this chapter, it is not necessary to review the
complex politics of the 1890s, most of which did not directly affect
Dois de Julho celebrations. Contemporary observers provided detailed
narratives of the highly personalist politics of what became known as
Brazil's Old Republic, while late-twentieth-century scholars sought to
discern patterns in the political conflicts that pitted factions named
after their leaders against one another.[10] Several general features shaped
the decade's politics. The state's anemic economic performance meant
that Bahia could not take advantage of the decentralization instituted
by the 1891 constitution. Local political bosses seized power in municipalities, and their alliances with factions of the state oligarchy made
for a highly unstable political order, in which the national government
periodically intervened and in which national political realignments
shifted local politics. Thus, Deodoro's attempted coup in late 1891 led
to a standoff in Bahia between supporters of the pro-Deodoro governor and his opponents, who eventually negotiated his removal from
office.[11] Likewise, the brutal repression of Canudos, a large millenarian
community in northeastern Bahia, was a response to the threat that
this new population centre posed to the local political bosses and their
relationship with state-level political leaders. Moreover, radical republicans in Rio de Janeiro perceived that Canudos was an existential
monarchist threat to the republic.[12] As Borges puts it, it was "a blank
screen upon which urban elites ... projected their fears."[13]

While scholars tend to dismiss republican elections as shams, with
voters herded to the polling stations by local political bosses, Aldrin
Castellucci has recently demonstrated that the new regime roughly
doubled the number of voters from the post-1881 empire and that,
in Salvador, working-class organizations used the electoral system to
good effect. Through alliances with other parties, the Centro Operário
da Bahia (Labour Centre of Bahia) managed to elect city councilors,
members of district juntas (local administration boards), and justices
of the peace. Other Afro-Brazilian working-class candidates made the
alternate lists, from which they occasionally moved into elected office
when incumbents stepped down, as Manoel Raimundo Querino did

for the 1897–99 term. To be sure, such successful candidates – typically from the upper ranks of Salvador's artisans – were a minority of office-holders, but their successes indicate the working classes' active engagement in politics and their efforts to win full citizenship.[14]

As under the empire, the press was highly politicized, although the *Diário de Notícias* and the *Jornal de Notícias* sought to maintain political neutrality in the 1890s. The scattered availability of newspapers for this decade (some of the volumes that I was able to consult in the late 1990s are no longer accessible to researchers) means that coverage of the festival is spottier for this decade than for much of the late empire. Among the 122 periodicals published in Salvador during the 1890s, the city supported five daily newspapers, and in 1893, Francisco Vicente Vianna reported that four of them together published 15,000 copies while the fifth had a "large press run."[15] The *Diário da Bahia*, by then the oldest Bahian paper, was the mouthpiece of Governor Joaquim Manoel Rodrigues Lima (1892–96), while the *Correio de Notícias* spoke for the opposition,in 1895.[16] In 1890, the former Historical Liberal, Cesar Zama, acquired the *Pequeno Jornal*; for a few years, he used it to advocate for reforms. A small weekly, *A Coisa* (1898–1900), is the only example of the critical satirical press to which I have had access.

When it came to Dois de Julho celebrations, early-republican newspapers generally published the same sorts of articles as their late-imperial predecessors: programs, brief reports about the celebrations, editorials about the day's meaning, and *crônicas* in both prose and verse. By this time, however, the provincial correspondence that was such an important source for chapters 2 to 5 had disappeared from the pages of newspapers in Rio de Janeiro and Recife. The *Diário de Pernambuco* and the *Jornal do Recife* published fewer reports about Bahia, whether news summaries or transcriptions from Bahian newspapers, than they had in the 1870s and 1880s. The opening of the Faculdade Livre de Direito da Bahia (Free Law School of Bahia) in 1891 meant that fewer Bahian students attended Recife's law school, and this likely reduced one important constituency for Bahian news in the Pernambucan capital.[17] Also, the Rio de Janeiro dailies of the 1890s published less provincial news than they had in previous decades, and, when they took note of Dois de Julho, it was usually only in perfunctory telegrams from Salvador.

The first Dois de Julho celebrations after the republic's proclamation appeared to follow most of the old imperial forms, but there are indications that state authorities were reluctant to get involved in these festivities because of the potential for opposition demonstrations. Criticisms of the festival had mounted during the last years of the empire, and there was declining interest in the old customs, particularly among the middle and upper classes. These underlay the campaign to erect a monument to Dois de Julho, which dated back to the 1870s but accelerated in 1887–89 and culminated in the 1895 inauguration. Nothing is known about how the monument's design was selected. However, its location was the subject of a decade-long debate that revealed much about Salvador's social geography and the historical significance attributed to the proposed sites. The monument's inauguration expressed the ideals of unity in defence of Bahia's interests and claimed cultural capital for Bahia due to the state's centrality in the struggle for independence. The organizers who hoped to launch a new, "civilized" way of commemorating Bahia's independence nevertheless had to accept the old *caboclos'* participation in the inauguration, and a popular festival concluded that year's Dois de Julho. After 1896, Dois de Julho celebrations split into two, with official festivities surrounding the monument and with popular celebrations in Santo Antônio Além do Carmo parish.

## Dois de Julho in the Early Republic, 1890–94

The republic's proclamation shook Dois de Julho customs, and the new state government doubted the wisdom of supporting the celebrations. It is not clear whether a festival organizing committee had been appointed in 1889, but in mid-June, on the same day the *Pequeno Jornal* condemned government indifference towards the upcoming holiday, Governor Hermes placed the traditional 2:000$000 subsidy (then worth US$920) at the city council's disposal, and councilors took on the task of organizing the festival.[18] Within a few days, they had hired musicians, a "well-known contractor" to build "awnings and band shells," a painter to touch up the "triumphal symbols' wagons," a pyrotechnician, and a priest for the Te Deum.[19] On 29 June, a *bando* announced the upcoming festival, and the following day, the governor decreed a holiday for state employees on 2 July.[20] For the first time since 1875, the procession into the city included two army battalions (who would form one of the brigades); the other brigade consisted of patriotic battalions, students and teachers from the Liceu de Artes e Ofícios, and army and navy apprentices.[21] The three surviving accounts of this Dois de Julho celebration concur that it was poorly attended by an indifferent population. For the Catholic *Leituras Religiosas*, this was no surprise, given the secularizing republic's hostility to the Church; the *Pequeno Jornal*, which still supported the regime change, could only lament that Bahians had failed to demonstrate sufficient patriotism: "An indifferent people will never have a free *pátria*." The two patriotic battalions (Hermes da Fonseca and Siqueira Cavalcante) attracted, respectively, a mere nine and eighteen participants.[22] The *Diário de Notícias* judged these patriotic battalions unworthy of the name and lamented that others had not bothered to show up, but it did claim that the Terreiro de Jesus had been full of "many families and ... a large number of high-ranking people, in addition to groups of *povo*."[23]

Significantly, there are no indications that organizers attempted to display President Deodoro da Fonseca's portrait outdoors, to be unveiled as the emperor's portrait had been, or even that authorities participated in the outdoor celebrations at all. In Valença, local organizers did this and sparked "serious incidents": "The rabble ... tore republican flags and tried to stone the portrait of the provisional government's head, Generalíssimo Deodoro." The following day, after arresting "the most daring troublemakers," authorities replaced his portrait on the stage amid "repeated enthusiastic cheers."[24]

In light of the "enormous expenses for the monument," the 1891 organizing committee resolved to hold only a limited celebration, capped with the inauguration of a new garden on Piedade Square.[25] Because of the last-minute preparations, there was no time to decorate the Terreiro de Jesus and the patriotic symbols were displayed on the Palace Square. Authorities duly inaugurated the Piedade garden, and in the morning proclaimed the new state constitution. In the evening, a theatre gala was held; the program, which included Donizetti's *Lucia di Lammermoor*, began with the Dois de Julho anthem and the "customary cheers" led by Governor José Gonçalves da Silva.[26] On the morning of 3 July, a bold protest stood on the Terreiro de Jesus: "a large pole, at the top of which fluttered a black flag," with a text that read, "Here lie the mortal remains of Dois de Julho, born in 1823 and died in 1891. Disorder and progress."[27] The latter phrase mocked the positivist slogan of "Order and Progress" emblazoned on the new republican flag. I have found no other information about this protest, but many were losing faith in the new regime. By 1892, Cesar Zama's *Pequeno Jornal* was completely disillusioned with the republic, but the *Jornal de Notícias* still sought to associate Dois de Julho with republican virtue. The celebrations of that year and of 1894 (I have not found a description of 1893's festival) closely resembled those of the late empire, although authorities (including the governor) only attended the Te Deum and no efforts were made to conduct public rituals recognizing the state and its representatives.[28]

Other elements of imperial Dois de Julho took place during these poorly documented years, including the symbols' return to Lapinha a few days after Dois de Julho, the pilgrimage to Pirajá, and neighbourhood festivals (two of the latter took place in September 1892).[29] Itapagipe's 1892 celebration began with the raising of an "announcing pole [*poste anunciador*]" on 10 July. The festivities themselves, held on 31 July, were "splendid"; the neighbourhood's "little *cabocla* [*caboclinha*]" wore a "republican cap" during the procession from Bonfim to Madragoa Square, which also included coaches "with richly dressed and coiffured ladies." In contrast to this attempt to assimilate Dois de Julho symbols to the new regime, the well-known Afro-Brazilian critic of the republic, Manoel Benício dos Passos, better known by his nickname Macaco Beleza (Monkey Beauty), "made a speech about deportations and exiles," for which he was much applauded.[30] A few months later, Macaco Beleza "was arrested for making speeches in the street in favour of monarchy. His friends resisted," and only a reinforced police patrol could take him into custody.[31]

These limited sources on early-1890s Dois de Julho suggest that, because of its close association with the imperial regime, republicans found it difficult to celebrate Bahia's independence. Opponents of the new regime, including popular monarchists like Macaco Beleza, the Valença "rabble," and the anonymous 1891 critics, found Dois de Julho a suitable space in which to challenge the new regime, although in this respect they were merely continuing the old tradition of opposition demonstrations in the festival. However, republican governments in the tense 1890s were far less tolerant of opposition, especially when it took monarchist forms. Such republican reticence towards Dois de Julho also derived from older critiques of the festival, which gathered new strength in the 1880s and 1890s.

## Questioning Dois de Julho

In the last decades of the empire, criticism of Dois de Julho customs had mounted in the press, and some observers lamented that the old traditions had entered into a steep decline. These assessments are difficult to evaluate. Some amounted to nostalgia for festivals of bygone days. Others were simply the familiar opposition critique of celebrations controlled by those in power. Still other critics went further and rejected important parts of Dois de Julho civic culture; for them, the construction of a monument was a modern and more appropriate way of recognizing Bahia's independence.

The folklorists, memoirists, *cronistas*, and journalists who wrote about Dois de Julho in the 1880s judged that the festival no longer aroused the enthusiasm of past celebrations, and scholars have echoed this assessment.[32] Alexandre José de Mello Moraes Filho concluded his 1887 description of the mid-century festival that he had known as a youth with the assertion that "this was when this country still had the ideals of the *pátria* and [people] struggled for liberty," implying that Bahians no longer cared about the *pátria* and freedom.[33] Two years earlier, Rozendo Moniz had declared that Dois de Julho was a mere shadow of its former self.[34] The author of an anonymous 1881 *apedido* in the *Diário de Pernambuco* lamented that "such a great celebration has declined so much in recent years."[35] The *Pequeno Jornal*'s poet-*cronista* commented in 1890:

> There was a time in which Dois de Julho
> Was the reason for general celebration
> That mixed the clergy with the nobility and the *povo*
> Amid triumphal anthems.
>
> ...

The scene has changed, the *povo* sleeps
No longer remembering bygone eras,
And the great days that the heroes left us
Today are no more than chimeras.[36]

The *Jornal do Commercio*'s correspondent likewise remarked on the "decadence of public spirit in this province" in 1887.[37]

These writers offered different reasons for these developments. Rozendo Moniz blamed them on politics and on the Brazilian government's lamentable centralization, which his father, Francisco Moniz Barreto, had long criticized.[38] That he and Mello Moraes Filho wrote while Conservatives were in power (August 1885 to June 1889) may mean that their laments were merely traditional opposition critiques (calls for federalism and critiques of Rio de Janeiro had long been Liberal rallying cries), but others cannot be so easily dismissed. The author of the *Diário de Pernambuco*'s *apedido* blamed the decline on "certain individuals, who believe that the *povo* should live in indifference." They "do not cease to shout against the patriotic celebrations, because it seems to them that any popular rejoicing degenerates into anarchy" – a view similar to the critiques of the Noite Primeira procession in the late 1850s (chapter 2).[39] The *Jornal do Commercio* correspondent blamed the disappearance of "the interest that formerly existed among the upper class in the patriotic festivals."[40]

This correspondent added that "the petty [*miúdo*] *povo* … still remembers with some enthusiasm the heroic eras of our history,"[41] but others mocked the popular celebrations. In 1877, *O Monitor* lamented that some "even make fun of the popular demonstrations, laugh at the symbols of liberty, and consider them unsuitable for modern civilization."[42] I have found more defences of Dois de Julho traditions and disapproving comments about the critics than explicit critiques of the popular festival, but in 1891, Júlio Carlos Ferreira, the new state archive's secretary, scorned the old ways of celebrating as suited to "the *povo*'s infantile manner of expressing its feelings."[43] Even as it lamented Dois de Julho's decline, the *Gazeta da Bahia* defended the popular celebrations: "These noisy festivities, in which the ordinary people let loose and jubilate, are not merely outbursts of a wild enthusiasm. They are a noble adoration of the *pátria*'s traditions. They are a sincere homage to the memory of the heroes who gave us independence."[44] Such a defence of Dois de Julho traditions is telling evidence of the criticisms that its customs were facing.

The Indianist symbols emerged as particular targets for critics. The *Jornal do Commercio* correspondent remarked that the rustic allegories amounted to an enigma, "so distant are we from the customs and ostentation of those heroic times."[45] The silence about the symbols in the press coverage of the 1870s and 1880s may indicate a certain embarrassment at representing Bahia and Brazil as Indians.[46] The *caboclo* and the *cabocla* – terms still rarely used in the press – were also called the national symbols, or the symbols of independence (political emancipation) and liberty, while the *caboclo* was often called the "spirit of Brazil." The old term *carros triunfais*, which I have translated as triumphal floats, also appeared regularly.[47] The *Gazeta da Tarde's cronista* wondered whether "it would not be better to leave the *caboclo* couple, which signify nothing of independence and liberty, in their shed, for even our real Indians were enslaved, and they continue in this state in the upper Amazon, working for nothing for rubber tappers and lacking the slightest notion of civilization?"[48] To twenty-first century readers, this is a compelling, if literal, reading of the symbols' meaning, but it did not speak to Dois de Julho patriots. Other Dois de Julho customs also came in for criticism. In 1880, Commander of Arms Hermes thought the *bando* "ridiculous," for newspaper advertisements were a better way to announce upcoming festivals. The army musicians assigned to accompany this ceremony had suffered insults, and he recommended prohibiting it.[49] A few years later, *O Faisca* condemned those "who, stuck in the narrow shell of the egoism, judge it *high time to put an end to patriotic nonsense [patriotadas]*."[50]

In 1896, a *crônica* in the *Diário da Bahia* summarized the changing attitudes towards the festival. After a survey of traditional commemorations, Tupinambá turned to the changes that had taken place:

> Dois de Julho began to be seen not as a legitimate and beautiful manifestation of the people's soul, but as just some patriotic nonsense [*patriotada*], of no importance and with no practical purpose. It got to the point that there were those who were ashamed to go out in patriotic battalions. To pull the *caboclos*

it was now necessary to draft people, because it looked bad for
a man of a certain class to tow those old broken-down wagons,
which should have been locked up for good so that foreigners
did not laugh at our expense, because we were showing off our
savagery and ignorance symbolizing Brazil with the statue of a
*caboclo* who did not even wear pants.

Noting that carnival had recently outstripped Dois de Julho in popularity, Tupinambá blamed this on the shame that some felt at the *caboclo*, "who is not white and only wears feathers. If only he had been
imported from abroad."[51] Tupinambá thus identified the desire for
modernization, Europeanization, and "whitening" on the part of the
city's upper and middle classes as the principal cause of Dois de Julho's
decline. His comments came a year after the inauguration of the Dois
de Julho monument, which featured a four-metre-tall bronze *caboclo*,
cast in Italy, so he also chided the Bahian elite for accepting a foreign
*caboclo* even while rejecting the domestic version.

Tupinambá's comments, and those of the other critics, must be
viewed in the context of an increasingly popular Dois de Julho, as suggested by the identification of the festival with abolition (chapter 4)
and by the proliferation of parish or neighbourhood Dois de Julhos
(chapter 3), which were turning it into something less susceptible to
elite and government control. Thus, when newspapers lamented declining enthusiasm for Dois de Julho, they were speaking of the literate
middle- and upper-class publics for whom journalists wrote, the men
"of a certain class" ashamed to pull the *caboclos* or to march in patriotic
battalions.[52] Among of these developments, as Tupinambá had noted,
was the campaign to erect the Dois de Julho monument. The *Diário
do Povo*, a newspaper that was particularly critical of 1889's celebration (chapter 3), concluded: "It must be agreed that public opinion no
longer tolerates this way of commemorating the memorable day, so let
us immediately promote the great day's perpetual commemoration by
means of a lasting monument that rises before the entire population" –
a view shared by the *Jornal de Notícias*.[53]

Torn between aspirations for "modernity" and "civilization" – seemingly always just out of reach – and a recognition that the old customs
had given Bahia a degree of cultural capital, journalists failed to reach

a consensus about Dois de Julho traditions. While it was easy to criticize the *caboclos*, the old symbols had their defenders – and not just among the *povo*. These men helped ensure the popular festival's survival after the monument's construction.

## The Monument Campaign

Proposals for a Dois de Julho monument had long circulated in Bahia. In 1849, the Sociedade Dois de Julho called a meeting to discuss a monument; nine years later, the *Diário da Bahia* lamented that Bahians' enthusiasm for Dois de Julho "had not been translated into a monument" and called on the Sociedade to lead a campaign for it.[54] That year, three provincial deputies connected to the Society Dois de Julho, José Pedreira França, Pedro Antônio de Oliveira Botelho, and José Martins Alves, sponsored a bill to allocate 10:000$000 (US$5,200) for the erection of a monument to "eternalize the memory of the glorious day of 2 July 1823." Marginal notes on printed copies of the bill indicate that it passed first and second reading by September 1858, but that the budget committee rejected it because the province had more urgent needs.[55] The provincial assembly did, however, vote forty lotteries to the Sociedade for this purpose in 1859.[56] As we saw in chapter 2, the Sociedade put most of its efforts into acquiring the Lapinha coach house to store the *caboclos* in 1859–60. Nothing came of its efforts to raise a monument, and correspondents lamented this in 1862 and 1864: Bahia could not even boast "a humble work of masonry" to commemorate independence, one wrote.[57]

The long-anticipated 30 March 1862 inauguration of the equestrian statue of Emperor Pedro I in Rio de Janeiro made Bahia's lack of progress on a monument particularly galling.[58] Since the 1820s, Bahians had supported the campaigns that led to this monument, but in 1859, they sought to match the capital with their own statue of the first emperor, thereby following the recommendation of the final campaign in Rio de Janeiro, whose leaders urged provinces to raise their own monuments to the empire's founder.[59] The Sociedade Vinte e Quatro de Setembro (24 September Society), dedicated to the memory of Pedro I, who died on that day in 1834, took the lead in this campaign, encouraged by Pedro II's visit to Salvador. At a theatre gala on 7 October 1859, the emperor saw a plaster model for a statue of his father in the act of granting the constitution to Brazil. The handiwork of Camillo Formilli, one of the opera company's singers, it failed to impress Pedro, who judged that the figure bore no resemblance to his father, "nor nobility of posture. It was a hasty effort [É obra de 15 dias]," he sneered in his diary.[60] Pedro wisely kept these opinions to himself, and on 16 November, he participated in a well-attended ceremony to lay the cornerstone for the monument's foundation on Campo Grande. The official orator presented Pedro I as Brazil's liberator and explained that the monument would include "the celebrated names of the brave men who, responding to the redeeming Grito do Ipiranga, died for Independence on our memorable Dois Julho." He added that it would teach the *povo*, "who loves its liberty," about the source of this freedom, an extreme example of the subordination of Dois de Julho to Sete de Setembro that occasionally appeared in Dois de Julho editorials.[61] The society understood its actions as momentous and deposited a copy of the ceremony's register in the Instituto Histórico e Geográfico Brasileiro's archive.[62]

Nothing came of this monument campaign, which likely faltered amid a re-evaluation of Pedro I's significance that quickly made the equestrian statue in Rio de Janeiro obsolete as an expression of dominant views of the first emperor.[63] After the Paraguayan War, efforts to raise a monument to Bahia's independence resumed. In 1872, the provincial president named the Baron of Cotegipe (João Maurício Wanderley) to lead a campaign to raise funds for this purpose. Its "central committee" included some of Bahia's wealthiest men, along with both Liberals like Manoel Pinto de Souza Dantas and Luiz Antônio Barbosa de Almeida, and Conservatives like Cotegipe and Joaquim Elísio Pereira Marinho (the future Baron and Viscount of Guaí).[64] Despite its pedigree, this committee accomplished little, and when a fundraising campaign was finally launched in 1876, it was led by the directors of that year's Dois de Julho celebrations. Sílio Boccanera Júnior suggested that the "unfortunate events" of 1875 – the Frias Villar incident, discussed in chapter 3 – had given additional impetus to the campaign.[65]

The 1876 appeal for donations declared that it was necessary to recognize the "arduous and difficult labours" of those who had ensured the country's "place in the Areopagus of civilized nations." The festival directors traced independence back to the Inconfidência Mineira of 1789 and declared that it was completed "on the memorable day of 2 July" in Bahia. They promised a popular monument: Pedro I and José Bonifácio de Andrada e Silva (whose monument in Rio de Janeiro had been inaugurated in 1872) deserved recognition, but were they greater than "the people, who struggled, sacrificed themselves and triumphed?," asked the directors.[66] In short order, they began raising money. The 1876 stage featured donation boxes, and students put on a theatrical benefit during which they performed Antônio Frederico de Castro Alves's *Gonzaga*.[67] The provincial assembly voted 30:000$000 (US$15,300) in matching funds (fifteen years' worth of the annual contribution of 2:000$000 to Dois de Julho celebrations), on condition that the monument be constructed within three years.[68] The original bill was for only ten years' worth of the annual contributions, and one deputy opposed raising this amount: "a modest and simple monument is enough," he argued, citing the province's straitened finances.[69] Deputy João de Brito defended the increase, for "the utility of monuments has always been recognized, and there is no civilized nation on the globe that does not have them." Monuments were, he continued, history lessons, far more eloquent than the words of historians.[70]

Brito's comments did not address the issue of what history should be commemorated in the monument. Bahia's independence was a historical fact that could not easily be reduced to a single allegorical monument, much less a personal statue. To be sure, the *caboclos* offered well-established symbols, but they were already suspect in the government and elite circles whose support would be necessary for any monument. Moreover, no single individual lent himself to serve as a symbol in the way that Pedro I could be seen as the empire's founder. Not surprisingly, then, the earliest known design for a Dois de Julho monument, dating from 1877, contained nothing distinctively Bahian: it proposed a female allegory atop a column, holding laurels and broken chains in her hands (see figure 6.3).

Where to raise the monument soon became a highly controversial matter. One group proposed the square in front of the theatre, which could be enlarged by expropriating properties adjacent to Capitães Street (today's Rui Barbosa Street).[71] The committee charged with beautifying Campo Grande suggested that the monument be erected there.[72] At the end of 1881's Dois de Julho celebration, the monument's

Figure 6.3 | The earliest known design for a Dois de Julho
monument, 1877

*Source*: AHMS, Fototeca, pasta 77D, foto 582. Arquivo Histórico Municipal
de Salvador / Secretaria Municipal de Cultura e Turismo.

cornerstone was blessed and laid on the Campo dos Mártires (Martyrs' Field, formerly the Campo da Pólvora or Gunpowder Field). The ceremony's official record noted the presence of provincial executive and legislative authorities and reported that the large crowd gave "enthusiastic cheers to the state religion, to His Majesty the Emperor and to the imperial family, to the immortal date of 2 July, to the imperial constitution, to the Bahian people, etc."[73]

It is not known how this site was selected, but many did not accept it; already in 1883, an individual involved with managing lotteries for the monument campaign referred to the projected location as "one of this capital's squares."[74] In 1891, the *Diário de Notícias* recalled its 1883 debate with the *Jornal de Notícias*. The *Diário* defended the choice of the Campo dos Mártires over the Terreiro de Jesus, advocated by the *Jornal*, likely because it was the traditional centre of celebrations.[75] One article in the *Jornal* observed that the Campo da Pólvora had been the traditional location for executing criminals; among them were the men sentenced to death for their involvement in the 1798 Tailors' Conspiracy, as well as Padre Roma, the Pernambucan republican emissary, summarily executed after he was captured in 1817. In recognition of their patriotic martyrdom, the square had been renamed, but as the *Jornal* pointed out, these men had had nothing to do with Bahia's independence (the playwrights discussed in chapter 5 would have disagreed with this assessment).[76] Pernambucan republicans took offence at this slight against their compatriots and published a series of articles that chided Bahians for fighting on behalf of the monarchy in 1822–23 and for forgetting the important support that Pernambucans had lent in the struggle against the Portuguese.[77] Not all Bahians agreed with the monument project. From Feira de Santana, *O Motor* railed against it, "cold as the stone of which it must be made," and declared that its advocates were seeking to suppress the popular festival.[78]

In the mid-1880s, the campaign faltered. Dois de Julho coverage in these years reveals nothing about the monument, but in 1887, the abolitionist writer Luiz Anselmo da Fonseca responded to the appointment of a permanent committee to continue the project by calling on Bahians not to erect a monument as long as slavery persisted in Brazil.[79] Chaired by Augusto Álvares Guimarães, the city council's president and the *Diário da Bahia*'s editor, this committee consisted of forty members.[80] In short order, it ran a design competition, and in April 1889, plaster models of the proposed monument were exhibited in Salvador, to great acclaim from the *Diário do Povo*, which assured its readers that the finished work's price was "comparatively quite modest."[81] The committee welcomed donations from "citizens of all social classes" and received surpluses from the festival's Direção, which closed its books annually.[82] The city council assisted with efforts to track down dormant bank accounts belonging to the long-defunct Sociedades Dois de Julho and Vinte e Quatro de Setembro; the surviving members of the latter had apparently agreed in 1873 that the funds raised for the Pedro I monument should be applied to the Dois de Julho monument, but this transfer had not been carried out.[83] The provincial assembly voted five lotteries and, more important, the substantial sum of 50:000$000 (US$27,000) for the "work of national gratitude." That this monument was intended to replace the old Dois de Julho celebrations is clear from the stipulation in the bill that, once it was inaugurated, the province would no longer subsidize the annual festival.[84] The transcripts of the debates on these bills published in the *Diário da Bahia* do not mention this latter clause, nor do they record that deputies commented on the annual festivities.[85] By August 1889, the monument was contracted for, at a cost of 270,000 francs (US$52,124), to be paid in three instalments.[86]

The inflation of the 1890s and the rapid fall in the mil-réis's value from a peak of US$0.54 in 1889 to US$0.30 in 1891 and to US$0.24 in 1892 wrought havoc with this budget. The committee launched a new fundraising campaign, which raised close to 35:000$000 by November 1891, and it was widely expected that the government would make up the difference (the subscription eventually raised 43:806$788).[87] Nevertheless, there are indications that the committee was desperate. With the third instalment overdue by ninety days, it tried to borrow 30:000$000 from the city council (to be repaid from the subscription's proceeds or from state government contributions).[88] The state's new legislative assembly eventually came through and voted 100:000$000 in its 1892 budget. Deputies further supported the monument with extraordinary allocations of 110:000$000 in 1893, 90:000$000 in 1894, and 12:000$000 in 1895.[89]

Amid this flurry of activity, the monument's location remained an open question. Back in 1889, while the maquettes were still on display,

Figure 6.4 | The cart before the horse

*Source: A Locomotiva, 5 May 1889.*

*A Locomotiva* wondered whether Salvador had a sufficiently clean and tidy square for the monument. It ran a tiny cartoon showing a befuddled bourgeois gentleman gazing at a monument overgrown with weeds and surrounded by grazing livestock (see figure 6.4). Erecting a monument in such a square would be like putting on a jacket and white leather gloves "and going in slippers to pay respects to Their Majesties." Continuing with the metaphor of inappropriate dress, the newspaper recommended more attention to street cleaning, calling on the assembly to purchase "boots so that the old mulatto woman [*mulata velha*, a pejorative nickname for Salvador] shoes herself before she dresses in silks and shows off luxurious adornments."[90]

The *Diário de Notícias* smelled a marketing opportunity; alongside the 1891 fundraising campaign, it sponsored a plebiscite on the monument's location. It invited readers to vote for the Campo dos Mártires, Campo Grande, or the Campo do Barbalho, and to submit justifications for their choices, which it published in a special daily column over the course of July and August. Overwhelmed by the response, the *Diário* restricted voting to residents of Salvador. The result was 16,101 votes for the Campo do Barbalho, 8,251 for the Campo dos Mártires, and 7,840 for Campo Grande.[91] That 32,282 people (both men and women) voted is remarkable, given that only about 9,000 men in the city had the right to vote in the 1890s.[92]

Some praised the plebiscite for stimulating interest in the *pátria*'s history. One participant later recalled that it had been a "lively and interesting debate." Others, however, criticized it.[93] In the *Diário da Bahia*, Eduardo Carigé chided the *Diário de Notícias* for engaging in a cheap publicity stunt and taking advantage of the "*povo*'s electoral mania." He judged that most of those who voted had no right to do so, for they were not registered voters (a correct assessment) and because they had probably not donated to the monument campaigns. The *Diário de Notícias*'s editors retorted that the municipal and state government contributions to the monument campaign were the "indirect product of the *povo*'s sweat," so the people certainly had the right to express their views.[94] The large *chapas* (ballots with multiple votes) – one for Barbalho had 510 names on it, while another for Campo Grande had 714 – indicate organized campaigns to influence the outcome.[95] Women's votes were included on these *chapas*, and Maria Francisca de Paula presented one that included twenty-two women's votes from Itapagipe.[96] As in other elections, there were allegations of fraud. A medical student complained that his name had been included on a *chapa* without his knowledge.[97] The *Diário de Notícias* reported on 1 August that it had received late ballots with about 16,000 votes for Campo Grande and 6,000 for the Campo dos Mártires, including the votes of "highly respectable families." These would not be counted.[98]

Clearly, the plebiscite's results should not be taken as an accurate gauge of public opinion, any more than any other imperial or early republican election reflected the popular will, but the arguments for each of the three locations provide revealing insights into how Bahians thought about the proposed *lieu de mémoire* and the best ways to commemorate Dois de Julho. Although the 1881 cornerstone gave the Campo dos Mártires precedence, this site's advocates had difficulty articulating how the 1817 martyrs were connected to Bahia's independence; their justifications instead cited the benefits that would accrue to the neighbourhood if this square were enlarged and beautified to receive the monument.[99] The advocates of Campo Grande had a long list of reasons for their choice. It was Salvador's largest square, so there would be no need to expropriate properties to expand it or to make it more regular in form; it was already levelled, so there would be no additional costs to prepare the site (this work had been completed in the early 1850s by a crew of liberated Africans under the direction of one Edward Parker, who also oversaw the planting of trees). It was Salvador's most attractive square, surrounded by handsome buildings (mostly elite residences, to be more precise) and well treed. The monument would be visible to those who approached the city by sea, and it was easily accessible by streetcar for foreign and Brazilian visitors. Moreover, an expensive work of art deserved the most aesthetic site, as a group of students argued; another voter put it colloquially: "Those who have fancy furniture [*traste de luxo*] put it in the drawing room." Two remarked that it would conveniently erase the 1859 proposed monument to Pedro I.[100]

Bahia's historians, not yet organized into the Instituto Geográfico e Histórico da Bahia (founded in 1894), came out solidly in favour of the Campo do Barbalho. In lengthy essays, Boccanera, Vianna, and Ferreira argued that historical monuments must be placed on appropriate historical sites. Neither Campo Grande nor the Campo dos Mártires had any historical connection to the events of 1822–23, whereas Barbalho Fort was the first locale in Salvador to fly the new Brazilian flag on 2 July 1823 and, of course, the main patriot force had entered Salvador through Santo Antônio Além do Carmo Parish, where the fort was located. Ferreira cited the oldest contemporary published description of the entry, the 19 August 1823 *Éco da Pátria* article; Boccanera advocated a complementary proposal to turn the fort into a museum.[101] The citizens who voted for Barbalho echoed these arguments, added that the "symbols" were stored in Santo Antônio, and noted that a monument on the Campo do Barbalho would bring "material development" to the parish.[102]

As the advocates of the other sites explained, however, Barbalho had but a weak claim to historical significance. The fort had been in Portuguese hands during the war, and no significant fighting had taken place around it, while the flag raising's meaning remained obscure (it may only have signalled the fort's occupation by patriots).[103] Battlefields like Pirajá had much stronger claims to historical significance, but they were inconveniently distant from the city centre, so no one seriously advocated building the monument there. Partisans for Campo Grande dismissed the historical arguments: "Flipping through dusty old books and claiming rights for Barbalho, Terreiro [de Jesus], [or] Campo dos Mártires did not matter." What was important was to display the monument in a visible and accessible location.[104] The concern with ease of access for foreign visitors – "tourists," as one voter put it – referred to the passengers on transatlantic steamers who spent a few hours on shore to take in the sights while the ships took on mail, passengers, and supplies.[105] One group of advocates for Barbalho pointed out that the projected circular streetcar line would soon make their neighbourhood much more accessible, but for the moment, it was not.[106]

The debate also revealed some of the class tensions in Salvador. One advocate for Campo Grande derided the other locations as "boring and gloomy, [places where] nobody goes, isolated and far from the city centre."[107] Campo Grande was, as Boccanera put it, Salvador's "fashionable south end" (he used the English words sarcastically).[108] A group of advocates for the Campo dos Mártires turned this argument around and retorted that Campo Grande was therefore "too aristocratic" for a monument to liberty.[109] One advocate for Barbalho hoped that the monument would benefit Santo Antônio's residents and would "above all oblige the big-shots [fidalgos] from Vitória [the parish that encompassed Campo Grande] to come to this parish." Another group pointed out that Barbalho was preferable to Campo Grande for the latter was "inhabited by almost a majority of foreigners who have nothing to do with our past glories."[110] One advocate for Campo Grande dismissed all of this as petty neighbourhood rivalries and suggested that, if it were a matter of satisfying everyone, then it would be best to order a large number of small monuments, so that each resident of Salvador could take one home.[111]

While the plebiscite was not binding on the monument committee's members, it placed them in a politically delicate position, for their sympathies lay with Campo Grande. In November, they appointed a committee of five engineers to consider the locations.[112] These experts judged Campo Grande the most suitable site, for it was already a level square (there was enough solid ground at Barbalho and Mártires, but levelling these squares would be costly). It would be much easier to transport the monument's pieces to Campo Grande from the port than it would be to the other locations, which were accessible only by narrow, steep, and winding streets (nonetheless, in 1896, the engineer attributed cost overruns to unexpected difficulties in transporting the monument from the navy yard). Their report quickly turned away from technical considerations. They dismissed the flag-raising at Barbalho as a secondary incident and pointed out that, while a monument to the republic's proclamation might be appropriately located on the Campo dos Mártires, that site had no significance for independence in Bahia. Campo Grande was, moreover, more visible and accessible.[113] In early February, when some of the materials for the monument had already arrived in Salvador, the committee met to decide where they should be taken. Only fifteen members showed up (and Luiz Tarquínio submitted a proxy vote for Campo Grande), so the decision was postponed.[114] I have found no other records of the committee's meetings, but its members eventually settled on Campo Grande, much to Boccanera's annoyance (he was still complaining about the decision in 1904).[115]

This cleared the way for a cornerstone ceremony at the end of the day on 2 July 1892. Blessed by the archbishop, the monument's cornerstone was carried from the cathedral to Campo Grande. Patriotic battalions, army bands, philharmonic societies, the city council, all of the city and state authorities, and a "great mass of the people" were on hand, along with the *caboclos* (described as *carros* or wagons in the newspaper coverage), to celebrate this new beginning. The *Jornal de Notícias* called on all Bahians to join in this "new movement of civilization and, more important, patriotism." Senator Manuel Vitorino Pereira set the tone for the celebrations in a long speech. After invoking the "august religion of the past, pious cult of the most holy traditions," he cryptically and cautiously alluded to some of the issues the monument had raised: "The tenacious resistance that we offer to innovations, the struggle that we sustain between the audacious invasions of progress and our primordial and deep-rooted customs express the effort with which we seek to save the past, which for us merits holy respect for the virtues and nobility of our first citizens." He praised the "patriotic cult and enthusiasm, dedicated to the aboriginal, the Indian in whom we symbolize our origin, constantly resonating in the soul of these commemorative celebrations." He then hailed the monument: "These statues were founded far, very far from us, there in that country where ...

humanity underwent the solemn transfigurations of Michelangelo."[116] The old traditions, in short, were best celebrated in new ways, especially if they incorporated the cultural traditions of Europe. The workers excavating the site unearthed the cornerstone and the commemorative plaque placed there in 1859 for the monument to Pedro I, as well as some silver and gold coins from that time; the artifacts were given to the state archive for safekeeping.[117]

Aloísio de Carvalho, then just beginning his long-running "Cantando e rindo" (Singing and Laughing) *crônica* under the pseudonym of Lulu Parola, predicted major changes in Dois de Julho celebrations:

> The storied Lapinha was overthrown!
>      It no longer has its day!
> Dois de Julho has moved parishes,
>      And is stone and mortar.
> The statue will depose the procession,
> Without any need for intervention
>      By federal forces.
> No one will extract it from Campo Grande ...
> Goodbye! Old *caboclo* and wagons!
> Goodbye stage! Goodbye battalions
> With wreaths on the shoulder and white clothing![118]

His prediction about the demise of traditional Dois de Julho customs was premature, but he cleverly captured the underlying goals of the monument's advocates.

## Inauguration

With the seemingly interminable debate about the monument's location settled, construction could finally begin. The monument was completed and inaugurated in 1895 in a ceremony that projected a transition from old to new. While those who advocated the monument dominated the public discourse about the inauguration, there are indications of underlying tensions between them and the defenders of the old popular traditions, who won some small victories.[119] The inauguration took place in the midst of a deep political crisis prompted by jockeying for who would succeed Governor Manoel Joaquim Rodrigues Lima. Supporters of Luiz Viana (who would succeed Lima in 1896) and José Gonçalves had elected competing state senates, and this *duplicata* led to a legislative standoff that lasted from April to October 1895.[120] Both Vianistas and Gonçalvistas, however, suspended their rivalries to participate in the inauguration.[121]

The inauguration took place on a barren Campo Grande, from which the trees had been cleared to make the monument more visible – a controversial decision that Boccanera considered contrary to the precepts of sensible urbanism – and Bahians got their first good look at the product of two decades' work.[122] Almost 26 metres tall, produced by Carlo Nicoli, Brazilian vice-consul in Carrara, Italy, and a little-known sculptor, it is topped by a 4 metre statue of a *caboclo* in the classic pose of trampling and stabbing the serpent of tyranny.[123] The column bears plaques with the names of twenty-four independence-era heroes; they are, however, too small to be easily read from the ground. Two allegorical figures flank the column: Catarina Álvares Paraguaçu, the Indian woman whose marriage to Diogo Álvares Caramuru served as a symbolic beginning to Portuguese settlement in Bahia, and a robust female allegory of Bahia in the act of proclaiming her independence. Beneath these female allegories, reclining male figures represent Bahia's two principal rivers, the São Francisco and the Paraguaçu. The other two sides of the square base are decorated with victorious eagles rising over war trophies, behind which bronze bas-reliefs commemorate two battles: 25 June 1822 in Cachoeira, and 7 January 1823 in Itaparica. Four other dates are explicitly mentioned, providing a history of Brazil with Bahia at its centre: Brazil's discovery (22 April 1500 in the Julian calendar), Salvador's founding (6 August 1549), the proclamation of independence (7 September 1822), and the patriots' entry into Salvador (2 July 1823). The dates of four other battles are also inscribed on the monument.[124]

Until the records of the design selection surface, we can do little more than speculate on some of the monument's features. Apparently, "one of the committee members" conceived the "work's general outline"; Nicoli then executed it.[125] The bas-reliefs ensured that the monument was as broadly Bahian as possible by including events that were significant to the state's second city, Cachoeira, and to Itaparica

Island (25 June and 7 January were respectively commemorated in these places). The important Battle of Pirajá (8 November 1822) got short shrift (being included with three other lesser battles) but it had never been a significant focus of celebration. The statues represent no independence-era figures – the entire monument is allegorical – and historical actors are only commemorated in the names on the column.

How these twenty-four men were selected is not known, but it must have been a difficult task, for the list is an eclectic one. It includes several of the Recôncavo sugar planters who played key roles in articulating the alliances that led to the recognition of Pedro I's government in Rio de Janeiro and to the siege of Salvador, among them the Viscount of Pirajá (Joaquim Pires de Carvalho e Albuquerque), Rodrigo [Antônio Falcão] Brandão (the Baron of Belém), [Joaquim Inácio] Siqueira Bulcão (the Baron of São Francisco), and [Antônio de] Souza Lima (Itaparica's governor). The Exército Pacificador's two commanders, Pedro Labatut and [José Joaquim de] Lima e Silva, are also recognized. Five of the men had been deputies to the Portuguese Cortes in 1821–23. Manoel Pedro [de Freitas Guimarães], whose removal from command of the garrison in February 1822 sparked the fighting between Portuguese and Bahian troops, is honoured on the monument, as is [José Antônio da] Silva Castro, who organized the Periquitos' battalion later that year. Two officers who died at the Battle of Pirajá are honoured, as is João das Botas, who led the naval defence of Itaparica. Four civilians who played varying roles in the independence struggle, but who were at the time radical liberals, appeared as well: [José] Lino Coutinho, Cipriano [José] Barata de Almeida, [Francisco Gê Acaiaba de] Montezuma, and Antônio Pereira Rebouças. Perhaps surprisingly, the list also includes Cornet Luiz Lopes, whose erroneous playing of the orders for a cavalry charge prompted the key Portuguese retreat during the Battle of Pirajá (chapter 5).

Only one contemporary is known to have commented on the choice of names. Pernambucan historian Francisco Augusto Pereira da Costa described the monument as "beautiful, imposing, [and] majestic," but also "egotistical and unjust," for it did not recognize the assistance that other provinces had lent to Bahia in 1822–23. Lima e Silva was the only Fluminense (native of Rio de Janeiro) acknowledged, and no Pernambucans, not even José de Barros Falcão Lacerda (who commanded the

Pernambucan contingent at the Battle of Pirajá), had their names inscribed on the column. Instead of Falcão, the monument recognized Luiz Lopes, whose story was completely unbelievable, for officers would not have tolerated such a mistake on the battlefield. Pedro I's omission also bothered Pereira da Costa, but he judged this "a nod to the republic," which was not sufficiently generous to recognize the real services to independence of men like the first emperor. The inclusion of Cipriano Barata (who played no role in the fighting in Bahia in 1822–23 and had gone to Pernambuco after leading a walkout of some Brazilian deputies from the Cortes in October 1822) must have been another nod to the republic, but Cipriano was "such a good republican that he accepted a decoration as a dignitary of the Ordem do Cruzeiro [Order of the {Southern} Cross] from Emperor Pedro I."[126] Pereira da Costa's 1900 book, *Pernambuco nas lutas emancipacionistas na Bahia em 1822–1823* (Pernambuco in the Emancipationist Struggles in Bahia in 1822–1823), from which these criticisms are drawn, sought to demonstrate that Pernambucans had played important roles in the struggle against the Portuguese in Salvador.

The *Diário da Bahia*, then the governing party's official newspaper, effusively covered the inauguration, devoting its entire issue to historical documents on the independence war and classic Dois de Julho poetry dating from the 1820s to the 1870s.[127] The inauguration itself began with a carefully organized parade from the Terreiro de Jesus, to which the "allegorical floats with the patriotic emblems" had been brought by a team of municipal firemen.[128] Led by a police cavalry picket, the parade included the Dois de Julho festival committee, the city council, medical and law students with their standards, secondary school students, an artisans' patriotic battalion, a large contingent from the Centro Operário, two Italian mutual aid societies, a float with three elderly independence-war veterans, representatives of industry and of other societies not mentioned by name in the accounts, and at least four bands. Apparently Governor Lima, the acting archbishop, and the Brazilian president's representative awaited the parade at the monument. There, after an outdoor mass, the prelate blessed the monument and a large children's choir sang the Dois de Julho anthem. Orators hailed the monument in prose and verse. The governor unveiled the bronze bas-reliefs and led the crowd in cheers to the republic, "one

and indivisible"; to the president; to Bahia; to Dois de Julho; and
to the Bahian people. All were warmly echoed. Telegrams from the
vice-president, Bahian Manoel Vitorino, and from Senator Damásio
were read out. The president's representative then invited the governor,
the festival committee, the city council, and other "gentlemen" to a
"delectable *lunch*" served in his nearby residence. Magnesium lamps lit
the well-decorated Campo Grande that night, much to the delight of
the "enormous confluence of families and ordinary people [*pessoas do
povo*] who went to appreciate the grandiose memorial."

The *Diário da Bahia*'s Dois de Julho editorial presented an official
interpretation of the monument. It emphasized Bahia's centrality in
Brazilian history as the site of the first Portuguese landing and the
first mass, which made it the "first cell of the current Brazilian society." Repeating the republican interpretation of independence, the
author argued that Pedro I's proclamation had merely consummated
developments already well under way since the 1789 Inconfidência
Mineira. Portuguese resistance meant that "here the passion of Brazilian independence was celebrated." Three-quarters of a century later, it
was high time that "the timber of the generation and the people who
made and consolidated independence be immortalized in permanent
bronze." The editorial called on Bahians to make the monument the
centrepiece of their "patriotic worship," finally hailing it as a republican symbol: "Monument erected in honour of liberty, do not repel,
rather embrace the republican belief, which is a development of the
old codes, repealed or perfected with the influx of the new doctrine
that the apostles of '89 spread throughout the world."[129] In short, the
editorial linked two disparate elements to Dois de Julho: the Church,
which had a leading role in the inauguration, and the republic, whose
connections to Dois de Julho were neither obvious nor fully accepted
in the early 1890s.

In his address, Augusto Álvares Guimarães, the *Diário da Bahia*'s
editor and chair of the monument committee, reiterated that Dois de
Julho was "the most important historical date in Brazilian political life,
not excluding that other eloquent date, on which Pernambucan arms,
two centuries earlier, repelled Dutch domination, and categorically
demonstrated the pride and power of the American people" (this sop
to Pernambuco suggests that he expected criticisms like those articu-

lated by Pereira da Costa). The monument, he continued, should be a "lesson to future generations" so that the people could learn patriotism and "gain from education and work the strength needed so that progress and civilization can penetrate this land."[130]

A few discordant notes marred the inauguration. The opposition *Correio de Notícias* failed to muster as much enthusiasm for the monument as did the *Diário da Bahia*. It remarked that the celebrations, although well attended, "proceeded coldly," and churlishly observed that Gaensly and Lindemann's commemorative poster revealed the "irregular placement of the figures, set out in a poor perspective."[131] Even the *Diário da Bahia* opened its columns to critical commentary. One writer accepted the monument as a "consecration of the past," but, noting the numerous burdens under which the population was suffering, he declared that, were this monument "an affirmation of the present," he would have to proclaim it "a bronze lie inside a cruel marble joke."[132]

Another anonymous author lamented the decline of Dois de Julho's "former pride" under the "attacks on your traditions that have been perpetrated by many of your degenerate sons!"[133] There is another hint that defenders of Dois de Julho traditions were not satisfied with the monument's inauguration. The organizing committee originally contemplated not including the traditional symbols of independence, announcing only on 29 June that "in accordance with the wishes of a growing number of citizens," the triumphal floats would be brought from Lapinha to the Terreiro de Jesus on 1 July. This concession was not satisfactory, and in fact, the *caboclos* were brought to the Terreiro on 2 July (the traditional date for the procession), which meant that the inauguration took place later in the day than originally scheduled.[134] One observer judged that "the *povo* appeared distant and indifferent ... motivated only by curiosity to see the monument." It was, however, "a decent and clean [*aceiada e limpa*] festival," without "*batuques* [or] the noisy, even carnivalesque, demonstrations that the popular masses loved during the three days of celebration, as they were carried away by the most exuberant and uninhibited frenzy with which the rabble [*gentalha*] exhibits and releases its rejoicing." In compensation for this lack of popular enthusiasm, 30,000 people attended, including a "long train of families," code words for members of the respectable middle and upper classes.[135] I have found no indication in the press that the traditional *bando* had taken place, although a later folklorist claimed that it did.[136]

The "patriotic symbols' return" to Lapinha from Campo Grande on 7 July contrasted sharply with the inauguration's official celebrations. Residents of Santo Antônio Além do Carmo parish had prepared "dazzling and noisy diversions," and a group of citizens led by "the bold abolitionist and determined republican," Frederico Lisboa, resolved to dedicate this day to three elderly veterans of the independence war: Francisco Assis Gomes, Inácio Alves Nazaré, and Constantino Nunes Mucugê. Only Nazaré felt well enough to join the parade, and Lisboa called on the *povo* to pull his carriage, noting that "by happy coincidence the old soldiers of liberty were not viscounts nor marquises, but simply three or four men of the *povo*, two of them honorable artisans or goldsmiths and the other a blacksmith." The paraders left an exhausted Nazaré at his downtown residence and continued into Santo Antônio parish. Here the fire brigade, which had up to this point drawn the *caboclos*, turned them over to the "*povo*, who demanded ... to conduct them to Lapinha."[137]

The contrast between this celebration and that of the monument's inauguration five days earlier could not have been greater. Here the people, abolitionists, artisan veterans of the independence war, and the old symbols took centre stage, supplanting authorities and the monument. However, when the *caboclos* left Campo Grande and the Terreiro de Jesus, it would be the last time for many years that they would be seen in those parts of the city.

## The Bifurcated Dois de Julho, 1896–1900

What Dois de Julho celebrations would look like after 1895 remained to be determined. The chair of the 1896 organizing committee was Luiz Tarquínio, whose Empório Industrial do Norte textile mill provided housing, education, and other benefits to its workers in return for their absolute loyalty.[138] He and his committee planned an official civic ritual around the monument, without the old symbols, but a competing popular festival in Santo Antônio Além do Carmo parish, at the other end of the old downtown, kept the old Dois de Julho traditions alive. This set the pattern for the celebrations' bifurcation. Modern scholarship on Dois de Julho has mostly overlooked this split in Bahia's independence commemoration, although Hildegardes Vianna characterized it as a case of the *povo* spurning the monument and its "counterfeit *caboclo*," citing an unnamed contemporary *cronista*.[139]

Heavy rains marred the festival in 1896, and the *Diário da Bahia* reported that the celebrations "ran in an indifferent way"; not even "Joe Public [*Zé povinho*] is interested in his great days anymore," lamented this newspaper's *cronista*. He wondered whether the reserves of patriotism were finally exhausted.[140] The *Diário de Notícias* likewise reported that "almost nothing remains from that ardour, that extraordinary enthusiasm with which the festivities of that glorious and immortal day were celebrated," and its *cronista* lamented this.[141] Such jeremiads were common in these years, but to focus on them would be to miss the nature of the celebrations that actually did take place.

In 1896, they began at noon on 2 July, when the symbols were drawn from their pavilion in Lapinha through Santo Antônio parish to its main square, now known officially as Barão de Triunfo Square. They were accompanied by the local festival's organizing committee, the municipal intendant and his secretary, a police band, a picket of police cavalry, and a small crowd that braved the rain. After leaving the allegories on a stage on the square (see figure 6.5), a "small cortège," including presumably the intendant and some of the parish organizers, hurried to the Terreiro de Jesus, where they attended the Te Deum, along with other officials. A second parade in the late afternoon headed from downtown to Campo Grande, where the Liceu's band braved torrential rains to circle the monument, playing patriotic music.[142] The publication of separate announcements underscored that these were distinct celebrations.[143] Tarquínio's committee proclaimed itself the "committee of the popular celebrations," and the *Diário da Bahia* announced on 2 July that "a popular pilgrimage ... will go to visit the monument," but no one mistook this for a popular festival.[144]

In subsequent years, this pattern of commemoration became firmly established. The afternoon parade from the Terreiro de Jesus to Campo Grande, the "great civic pilgrimage," orderly and carefully organized, included government officials, military and police officers, schoolchildren, and representatives of the press, industry and other associations.

Figure 6.5 | The Dois de Julho stage, Santo Antônio Além do Carmo Parish, early twentieth century (*Note*: A similar image appeared in *Bahia Illustrada*, September 1918, so this photograph likely dates from that year.)

Source: AIGHBa, pasta 6, reg. 0378. Reproduced with permission.

The city government funded this civic ritual, for the state government had stopped subsidizing the Dois de Julho festival (as mandated by the 1889 law that allocated 50:000$000 [US$27,000] to the monument).[145] In 1897, these celebrations were "organized by the municipal government and the press."[146] They usually included fireworks, illumination of the square, and the playing of martial music for two or three evenings. In 1897, the intendant served champagne and ice cream to the wives of the official guests, who watched the fireworks from a viewing stand. Both the *Correio de Notícias* and the *Diário da Bahia* noted the presence of numerous "families," underscoring that this was an elite festival. The *Jornal de Notícias* reported in 1898 that the municipal government "knew how to fulfill its obligations regarding the decoration and illumination" at Campo Grande, but the evening celebrations had moved downscale: instead of fireworks, the city held a large bonfire, "a diversion that so pleases our *povo* that it is an obligatory complement to their festivals." In 1899, journalists roundly condemned the municipality for putting up only some flags around the monument and for failing to illuminate the square, which produced a "poor effect."[147]

The monument itself had a rather limited role in these celebrations. It did not, as the *Diário da Bahia* hoped in 1896, become the focus of a "popular pilgrimage." Nor did it become a sacred symbol like the *caboclos*. One journalist condemned the "treason [*lesa-civismo*]" of those who sat on the steps and even scrambled up the bronze statues to gain a better view of the 1897 celebrations.[148] The use of the monument's image in advertising, however, appears not to have prompted critical comment – a shoe store's ad featuring it appeared regularly in the press of the late 1890s.[149]

Some years, there were still theatre galas to commemorate Dois de Julho. In 1896, the Politeama put on *O Guarani* (The Guarani [Indian]), not Antônio Carlos Gomes's opera but a play based on José de Alencar's novel, and the governor attended. There is no indication of cheers or other elements of late-imperial galas; however, this theatre's 1898 gala included an apotheosis before which the company sang the Dois de Julho anthem and the musicians played the (still wordless) national anthem. The report indicated that the municipal government had sponsored this spectacle (the Politeama was a privately owned theatre, so it had no obligation to stage galas).[150] The São João still belonged to the government, but it had fallen on hard times, and proposals surfaced from time to time to rebuild or replace it. In 1898, it became a movie house (the projection equipment was installed in the old presidential box).[151]

In contrast to the limited 1899 decorations on Campo Grande, Santo Antônio Square was "ostentatiously bedecked with flags" and lit by electricity. For four nights, it would feature band concerts. Judging by the "great influx of people [*gente*]" on the first night, this festival far surpassed that of Campo Grande. Here the old symbols, rather than the monument, were the focus of celebration, which, according to the *Correio de Notícias*, in 1897 followed the "form of the ancient festivals held in this capital." Three years later, this newspaper noted that "although with different origins, two festivals, one complementing the other, were held."[152] In short, all of the traditional popular symbolism and practices of Dois de Julho commemorations had been transferred to Santo Antônio parish, leaving the monument as the object of a primarily state-directed civic ritual – the afternoon parade – which failed to take root in Salvador society. Not everyone judged the two festivals as complementary. In 1898, the *Jornal de Notícias* commented that the Santo Antônio organizers were men "who do not believe in the patriotism of Campo Grande's Italian *caboclo*."[153]

The entire cycle of traditional Dois de Julho activities took place in Santo Antônio (much as in other neighbourhood or parish festivals): the raising of a "maypole" (visible in the foreground of figure 6.5), the *bando* (which in 1899 began at Lapinha and traversed the entire city), the old symbols' parade, their display for several nights at a temporary stage amid a popular festival, and their return to Lapinha.[154] The 1899 *bando* confirms folklorists' recollections that this tradition continued for some time after the monument's inauguration.[155] In 1896 and 1897, the Santo Antônio committee also organized the pilgrimage to Pirajá.[156] Official participation was largely absent from Santo Antônio's festival, which, according to the *Correio de Notícias*, was "entirely popular" in 1897, by which it likely meant to comment both on the participants' social origins and on the fact that these celebrations were not organized by the government.[157]

Of course, the separation between the two festivals was never absolute. In some years, the intendant and municipal officials found time to participate in the Santo Antônio parade and the parish committee invited representatives of the press to join their parade.[158] In 1897, these men joined the Afro-Bahian carnival societies, Embaixada Africana (African Embassy) and Pândegos da África (African Merrymakers), which for their part sent delegations to help take the triumphal floats from Lapinha.[159] Portions of the Santo Antônio parade were sometimes destined for the "civic pilgrimage"; in 1899, for example, an allegorical float, featuring a child representing the state of Bahia, bore a wreath to be laid at the monument. Police lancers, navy apprentices, firemen, and battalions of students, orphans, and workers also occasionally joined the afternoon parade. The eleven patriotic battalions mentioned in these years did not leave Santo Antônio parish. And the symbols remained there.

The images of modernity and progress that we expect to find in the afternoon parade also turned up in Santo Antônio. In 1900, the workers of the Empório Industrial do Norte, accompanied by a band and led by their foreman, marched behind a white banner with the slogans "Peace" and "Labour"; Tarquínio paid for this procession and dispatched his workers to parade.[160] *A Coisa* reported that one of them told a popcorn vendor that he could only buy the snack "surreptitiously because otherwise I'll be fined," an indication of the regimentation the Empório imposed on its employees even outside of the workplace.[161] Schoolchildren were on hand in 1899 to welcome the "patriotic symbols" with the national anthem and the independence anthem; that year, the newspaper also praised the parish's police officials, who had ensured that no "illegal gaming" took place, a sharp contrast to Campo Grande, where journalists had seen people taking and making bets in the numbers game (*jogo do bicho*) during the commemorations.[162] Indeed, one scholar has remarked on the Santo Antônio parade's "rigid and hierarchical structure," an indication that parish organizers sought to create a respectable civic ritual alongside the popular festival.[163] And traditional images sometimes still appeared in the daily newspapers. In 1896, the non-partisan *Diário de Notícias* published on its front page a large engraving of a *caboclo* in the traditional pose of killing a serpent (see figure 6.6).

Thus, in the second half of the 1890s, Santo Antônio Além do Carmo emerged as the centre of popular Dois de Julho celebrations that outshone the city government's efforts to promote Campo Grande and the monument as the premier locale for Bahian independence celebrations. Late-twentieth-century oral tradition attributed Santo Antônio's importance in the festival to the fact that the patriot army had entered Salvador through this parish in 1823, but this simplifies a much more complex process.[164] Locating the symbols' pavilion at Lapinha no doubt helped cement Santo Antônio's identification with Dois de Julho celebrations (they were, in many respects, *that* parish's *caboclos*). João da Silva Campos argued in 1941 that Santo Antônio was the centre of Salvador's "traditionalism" and that Dois de Julho was "the great day of the Papa-Mamões [Papaya-Eaters]," a nickname for its residents. He attributed this cultural role to the parish's mix of rural and urban areas and its relatively homogenous population; relatively few Africans and few "moneyed whites of the elite" had lived there in the nineteenth century.[165]

Figure 6.6 | A *caboclo* on the *Diário de Notícias'* front page, 2 July 1896

*Source: Diario de Noticias,* 1 July 1896.

At least as important, however, were the determined efforts of Santo Antônio notables to preserve the festival rather than join those who rejected it. Little is known about these men, but organizing the festival involved extensive participation, at least judging by the parish committee structure. A central committee appointed block committees to supervise decorations along the parade route.[166] Leaders included

Dr. Tibúrcio Susano de Araújo, "a true patriot" who, according to João Varella, "never missed a national festival"; Querino included this medical doctor among his biographies of prominent black men in Bahian history. Tibúrcio's name headed one of the *chapas* cast for Barbalho in the 1891 plebiscite, and in 1900, he was one of the three men who led the festival organizing committee. Varella adds that he served as justice of the peace.[167] The obituary of Colonel Manoel Lopes Pontes, president of the 1899 parish committee, described him as a "political broker in the district of Santo Antônio." Owner of the Santo Antônio School and a Liberal Party stalwart in the late Empire, he was a National Guard colonel and had served in the state legislature.[168] For such men, organizing a parish festival was an extension of their political activities on behalf of their local community. Pontes's obituary further noted that he was an "oppositionist" in the republic, so perhaps fostering a parish Dois de Julho reflected his opposition to the government and its celebrations at the monument. More broadly, such men reveal the complex cultural politics of a Bahian elite that was not unified in its desire to modernize or civilize Dois de Julho celebrations.

Santo Antônio's festival amounted to a neighbourhood Dois de Julho writ large. A few other such celebrations are noted in the surviving sources, and this tradition would continue for several decades into the twentieth century.[169] Local notables like Dr. Tibúrcio and Colonel Pontes organized these neighbourhood celebrations. The twenty-three directors for Itapagipe's 1892 festival included four deputies, eleven men with military ranks (colonel, major, captain), three merchants, three doctors, one journalist, and one man with the imperial honorific of *conselheiro*.[170] Detailing the directors' occupations or titles was unusual in announcements for neighbourhood festivals; this list underscores that Itapagipe was a respectable middle-class neighbourhood.

Who controlled the symbols during this time remains unclear; residents in the vicinity of Lapinha's square and the Santo Antônio festival's organizers likely had the most say about how they would be used, but others attempted to claim them. This can be inferred from a curious incident that Wlamyra Albuquerque discusses. In 1897, on the day of the pilgrimage to Pirajá, a man claiming to have permission from the festival committee obtained the key to the depository, hitched the *cabocla* to some draft animals, and towed her away for unknown purposes. Annoyed festival committee members complained that the allegories should not be used for any purpose other than "representing, on the correct day, an event of national celebration."[171] In 1895, the president of the new Instituto Geográfico e Histórico da Bahia saw no role for the old allegories and requested that the Instituto be given the "floats" so that they could "continue to attest to future generations the courage, pride, and patriotism of our ancestors," not on the streets but in a museum.[172] Nothing came of this proposal until 1918, when the Instituto finally gained control of the Lapinha pavilion, which it turned into a museum for the *caboclos*.[173]

In the meantime, what to do with the old symbols remained a topic of debate. In 1896, when the *caboclos* took a detour to Mirante, a neighbourhood along the Estrada das Boiadas on the way to Pirajá, during their return to Lapinha, a *cronista* wondered whether they wanted to "go back to the bush, after having lived in civilization for three-quarters of a century."[174] In 1900, *A Coisa* published a dialogue between two men from Santo Antônio, one of whom wanted to do away with all of the partial celebrations of Dois de Julho and concentrate the festival in Campo Grande, so that "the monument is not disdained, as happens every year." As far as the "little *caboclos* [*caboclinhos*]" were concerned, "They're already very old. The best proof of our love that we can give them is to let them rest! There is no shortage of worthy locations." His interlocutor retorted, "Holy Mother of God! How can you celebrate Dois de Julho without the *caboclinhos*? I can't imagine Dois de Julho without them ... Putting away the beloved symbols of our emancipation?! Only in your noggin [*cachola*]! This is no way to end a traditional festival." The journalist gave the last word in this dialogue to the monument's advocate, and it bears quoting at length:

> You and others love the symbols very much, I know that, and, for this reason, someone stole the *cabocla*'s expensive finery! Confess, my friend, that you don't actually love the symbols; you love the wagons that carry them, the little white suit that you put on to go get them from Lapinha! If you cared about them, you would certainly have pity on them and the state in which they find themselves: old, damaged, patched-up, begging, for the love of God, that you don't dishonour them by making them go out

in this condition, for their mission ended, once the event that they symbolized was gloriously perpetuated in the bronze of the monument that Bahians ... raised on Campo Grande to the immortal heroes of '23![175]

The theft of the *cabocla*'s adornments points to, once again, popular – perhaps Afro-Brazilian religious – identification with this symbol, while the comment on patriotic battalions' white uniforms highlights the continued popularity of parading. Even as some felt ashamed to take to the streets, others took their place.

The bifurcated celebrations of the late 1890s make it clear that the monument's advocates did not have their way after 1895. By this time, the festival that since its launch in the 1820s had evolved from a radical-liberal demonstration into a widespread popular festival, could not be so easily suppressed. Too many people remained committed to the annual popular celebrations, and some elected officials, like the intendant and municipal councillors, considered it politically expedient to show their faces in Santo Antônio before heading to Campo Grande on the afternoon of 2 July. They needed the support of local political brokers, who, in turn, could build followings by promoting the annual festival. And, of course, significant sectors of Salvador's lower classes – the *povo* – remained committed to these celebrations, although almost nothing about them appears in the press.

In its reporting on the Dois de Julho celebrations of 1900, the *Correio de Notícias* concluded that "the traditional enthusiasm that stirred the Bahian soul on this glorious day is dead."[176] The *Correio* was far from the only newspaper to proclaim Dois de Julho's death during these years, but such reports were, to say the least, greatly exaggerated, for they often referred only to elite interest in the traditional festival. Similar assessments about the monument are more believable. João Varella's informant remarked in 1910 that "there, isolated, in a square" stood "an old and noble monument ... but forgotten ... [for] the popular spirit still does not understand it."[177] Soon after its inauguration, the monument had been surrounded by a fenced and locked garden that, according to Boccanera, prevented the *povo* from committing "the sacrilege of ruining the *delicate flowers and very rare plants* of the monumental garden"; not even the foreign visitors who hurried to see the "famous monument" could get near it.[178] When state deputies debated allocating funds for the construction of this fence back in 1895, one pointed out that it would keep animals from grazing around the monument and destroying the landscaping, an indication that the 1889 cartoonist had a point (see figure 6.4). In 1896, the assembly voted against this expenditure on the grounds that it was the municipal government's responsibility.[179]

While the Dois de Julho monument's history can readily be fit into interpretations that emphasize late-nineteenth-century Brazilian elites' desire for modernization, Europeanization, progress, and civilization, it also reveals the complexity of this process. As *lieux de mémoire*, monuments aim to freeze historical interpretations in acceptable forms, and as many have argued, once constructed they tend to become natural features of the urban landscape and their interpretations go uncontested, even though their design selection may have been highly controversial.[180] The Dois de Julho monument, by contrast, failed to suppress the *caboclos* and the popular festival, which retreated to the redoubt of Santo Antônio Além do Carmo parish. The monument is what Paulo Knauss would characterize as one of gratitude that "symbolically fixes the alliance between state and society," but this alliance was far from clear during Dois de Julho celebrations as large sectors of society repudiated the state.[181] States may state, to paraphrase a work that was often cited in the 1990s,[182] but people do not always listen. While they may choose to accept the statements embodied in monuments, they may also reject, ignore, or adapt them.

# The "Greatest Symbol of the Bahian *Povo*'s Struggle"

To end this book around 1900, in the aftermath of the Dois de Julho monument's inauguration, is an arbitrary choice, for the conflicts over the festival, whose principal lines were clearly drawn by the late 1890s, lasted well into the twentieth century. The popular festival's critics continued to work against celebrations that they regarded as inappropriate. They won a signal victory in 1918, when the Instituto Geográfico e Histórico da Bahia gained control over the Lapinha pavilion and the *caboclos*. Claiming a mandate from the *povo*, the Instituto renovated the building and turned it into a museum for the old symbols.[1] Those who wished to do so could visit them on 2 July, but for twenty-five years, the triumphal floats did not participate in public Dois de Julho celebrations.

Bahia invested heavily in the centennial of its independence; governments and associations like the Instituto highlighted "modernity" and "civilization," not the old and "backward" traditions of the nineteenth century. While no *caboclos* paraded on 2 July 1923, on 3 July the image of Our Lord of Bonfim was taken in a rare procession through Salvador.[2] Bahians also sharply contrasted Dois de Julho's centennial with that of Sete de Setembro ten months earlier. Braz do Amaral condemned the 1922 centenary organizers' "ardent desire to make Independence into the patriotic property of Rio de Janeiro and São Paulo." Repeating long-standing Bahian rhetoric about Dois de Julho, he called on his fellow Brazilians to recognize that "the culminating event of independence took place here in Bahia," led by the municipal councils ("people worthy of liberty") and the "*povo*'s resistance."[3]

Dois de Julho celebrations in the 1920s and 1930s appear to have been mostly official ones, at least to judge by what contemporaries wrote. Sílio Boccanera Júnior claimed in 1926 that "all the celebrations … converge on the monument, on whose pedestal official elements, associated with the *povo*, institutions, and schools, forming a true *civic procession*, deposit costly wreaths" and listen to speeches.[4] Boccanera's emphasis on the official rituals ignored the continuing tradition of neighbourhood festivals and the pilgrimage to Pirajá. A cursory glance at the newspaper coverage for 1926 reveals reports of celebrations "in various parts of the city" on 2 July (including Santo Antônio Além do Carmo) as well as a neighbourhood festival in Cidade de Palha on 11 July that included a procession with "symbolic floats [*carros emblemáticos*]," presumably that neighbourhood's *caboclos*, as well as another such festival the following week. On 18 July, a pilgrimage to Pirajá took place.[5]

The dramatic rethinking of Bahia's African cultural heritage in the 1930s and 1940s, about which many have written, extended to Dois de Julho. Cultural practices once derided as backward and uncivilized were now embraced as characteristically Bahian, but recognition came with strings attached as governments intervened to shape popular culture and to deploy its manifestations in the interests of promoting tourism and building a unified Bahian identity (*Baianidade*) around certain Afro-Brazilian cultural practices.[6] In 1943, the very same governments and associations that had worked so hard to repress the *caboclos* and the popular festival reinvented the old traditions and created the modern Dois de Julho, with its two-stage parade. Since then, the *caboclos* have been taken from Lapinha to the old downtown in the morning; in the afternoon, they go from there to the monument. That this reworking of the festival took place during the waning years of the Estado Novo dictatorship (1937–45) is a good indication that Dois de Julho was subject to populist efforts to link Getúlio Vargas's regime to Brazilian popular culture. Scott Ickes has observed that the advocates of Afro-Bahian culture who focused on the Nagô (Yoruba) Candomblé traditions tended to look down on Angolan Candomblé traditions, in which the native *caboclo* spirits play a larger role, thereby separating

Dois de Julho from the strains of Afro-Bahian culture that were being celebrated as distinctively Bahian and erasing Dois de Julho's broader Afro-Bahian significance.[7]

According to Fábio Baldaia, a second turning point in twentieth-century Dois de Julho came in 1959, when Salvador's city government took charge of the festival's organization. Over the following decades, the municipality's role in managing the festival increased steadily, especially after the creation of the Fundação Gregório de Matos (Gregório de Matos Foundation; FGM), the municipality's cultural agency, in 1986. Baldaia views this as a process of "rationalization," or the imposition of "greater regulation of public space and of public comportment."[8] Part of Salvador's belated "modernizing transformation," this government intervention in the cultural sphere also mobilized intellectuals and cultural professionals in defence of what they saw as the "correct" traditions. Folklorists and historians like Hildegardes Vianna, Cid Teixeira, and Luiz Henrique Dias Tavares acted to ratify Bahians' collective memory and to reinforce the "sacred character of Bahian patriotism." In 1978, sociologist Thales de Azevedo chaired the festival's organizing committee.[9]

New traditions and attempts to revive old ones characterized the first celebrations after 1959. That year, a relay race to bring a symbolic flame from Cachoeira to Lapinha sought to connect the Recôncavo to Dois de Julho's celebration in Salvador; this practice continues today.[10] Perhaps seeking to replicate the successful 1943 restoration of the *caboclos*' participation, organizers sought to re-create the *bando* in the early 1960s, but this effort failed, despite intellectuals' support. The city also sought to reinvigorate the pilgrimage to Pirajá by providing buses for those who wished to go on this excursion, but there were few takers, and the celebrations at Pirajá increasingly became a local or parish festival.[11] By the end of the 1970s, the municipality had gained effective control over the *caboclos* and the Lapinha pavilion; since then, city employees or professional designers contracted by the FGM have maintained the *caboclos* and prepared them for the parade, although the symbols still nominally belong to the Instituto Geográfico e Histórico da Bahia. The Quebra-Ferro (Iron-Breaker) Battalion that tows the *caboclos* during contemporary parades is comprised of municipal sanitation workers assigned to this task.[12] The FGM has come to see itself as the principal organizer of the Dois de Julho festival; its leadership views the Instituto as a subordinate collaborator. The state government's Instituto do Patrimônio Artístico e Cultural (Institute of Artistic and Cultural Patrimony; IPAC) and its Fundação Pedro Calmon (Pedro Calmon Foundation; FPC) play no direct role in organizing the celebrations; rather, the IPAC focuses on heritage preservation while the FPC focuses on producing educational materials and promoting academic events.[13]

Thus, while the contemporary Dois de Julho celebrations that I have attended (1993, 1996, 2000, 2001, 2002, 2011, and 2017) echo many aspects of the nineteenth-century celebrations, they are very different from those of the period on which this book focuses. It would not be fair to describe them as a mere simulacrum of the old traditions or as a (re)invented tradition in the sense that Hobsbawm and Ranger originally understood the concept, for Dois de Julho retains deep significance to many Bahians. Moreover, as I have shown for the nineteenth-century festival, Dois de Julho changed constantly and was subject to a series of interventions by those who sought to control or restrict the festival, including the state, so its twentieth-century evolution is but another chapter in a long history of change.

Carefully spruced up, the *caboclos* and the old wagons are today towed along the same streets from Lapinha to the Terreiro de Jesus that they traversed in the 1800s. Even more so than in the nineteenth century, they (and especially the *cabocla*) are objects of religious devotion. Certain groups have special rights to participate in the parade, including the Encourados, a group of leather-clad horsemen from the town of Pedrão in Bahia's interior, and the Grupo dos Guaranys from Itaparica Island, who dress as Indians and join the parade (the Guaranys also organize a popular festival on 7 January in Itaparica). Both depend on governments to pay for their travel to Salvador.[14] Governments sometimes pay to bring philharmonic bands from interior towns (where this tradition remains vibrant) to join the parade. It is customary today for both the mayor and the governor to walk the entire parade route; accompanied by entourages of officials, security, and media, they face the cheers or boos of the crowds that line the streets and the people who look on from windows. In the late 1990s, the senator and then political boss of Bahia, Antônio Carlos Magalhães

Figure C.1 | Antônio Carlos Magalhães in the procession, 2 July 1996
(*Note*: Antônio Carlos Magalhães is the man wearing a light-coloured suit
and striped tie in the photograph's centre.)

*Source*: Photo by Hendrik Kraay, 2 July 1996.

(1927–2007), also made a point of joining the parade (see figure C.1),
as he had done for decades.[15] Elaborate decorations, including palm
fronds but also much yellow and green plastic, give the parade route a
festive air, especially in the old city. People wave paper Brazilian and

Bahian flags. Children dress up as Dois de Julho heroes, including Maria Quitéria de Jesus and Joana Angêlica; boys have to make do with soldiers' costumes.[16] The morning parade from Lapinha to downtown is a bit more disorderly and more politicized than the afternoon parade to Campo Grande, which follows Sete de Setembro Avenue, a broader, asphalt-paved street laid out in the 1910s. The *caboclos* today remain on display at Campo Grande for three days, alongside the monument, and are returned to Lapinha in a small but lively evening procession on 5 July.

Some nineteenth-century traditions have disappeared. Today nobody declaims poetry during the celebrations, and nighttime illumination is a normal part of urban life. Neighbourhood Dois de Julho celebrations and the pilgrimage to Pirajá lasted until well after the mid-twentieth century but have since disappeared; a Te Deum is still held in the cathedral, but it has recently been rescheduled to the day before, for the Terreiro de Jesus is too noisy during the day on 2 July.[17] The city employees who form the Quebra-Ferro battalion are the only group that echoes the old patriotic battalions, but many other groups today join the parade.

Dois de Julho remains a highly politicized festival. As in the nineteenth century, it is an occasion for public debate about burning issues in Bahian society, especially during the morning parade, which is where political parties and social movement groups are most prominent. Tensions and violence sometimes erupt. In a widely reported 1994 incident, Antônio Carlos Magalhães (who had just stepped down from the state governorship to run for senator) and Mayor Lídice da Matta quarrelled publicly at Lapinha over whose entourage would take the most prominent place in front of the *caboclos*, a conflict that would have been fully understandable to the members of the nineteenth-century patriotic battalions who came to blows over precedence (or, for that matter, to the many colonial Latin American or early-modern European authorities who squabbled over similar issues).[18] That year, there were also allegations that two hundred state police in mufti had been placed along the route to boo Lídice and other supporters of Luiz Inácio Lula da Silva, then running for president for the second time.[19]

Reflecting the growing diversity of contemporary politics, the so-called new social movements are increasingly prominent during Dois de Julho, although not all are equally welcome. In 2000, the Grupo Gay da Bahia (Gay Group of Bahia) presented a candidate for city council and a small group of its members formed up at Lapinha to join the parade. Before the parade started, thugs roughed up the activists and destroyed their banner, preventing them from parading; *A Tarde* described the incident as a conflict between the Grupo's campaigners and their detractors, but what I saw looked more like an unprovoked attack.[20] That year, the Coordenação Nacional das Entidades Negras (National Coordination [Committee] of Black Organizations) won a court injunction to ensure that members of certain popular groups would not be blocked from joining the parade, as they had been in 1999.[21] Environmentalists disrupted the closing ceremonies at Campo Grande in 2011 by scrambling up the monument and unveiling a banner protesting the Belo Monte dam project. In recent years, animal rights activists have put an end to the Encourados' participation on the grounds that the horses suffer too much on the paved roads. An NGO threatened to sue the Pedrão municipal government in 2011 if the horses paraded (they did, but only for the first half of the parade).[22] Since then, the activists have carried the day, although the Encourados' supporters complain that cowboys on foot or with "symbolic" horses – two of the proposed solutions for their continuing participation – are anachronistic or ridiculous.[23]

Black movement activists have successfully introduced Maria Felipa de Oliveira, a slave woman who reportedly fought against the Portuguese in their attempt to take Itaparica Island in January 1823, as a heroine alongside Maria Quitéria and Joana Angêlica. Historical documentation on Maria Felipa is sparse, although her story is not implausible, and she now regularly appears in didactic materials produced by the FPC and other organizations.[24] The appropriation of Indians as Dois de Julho's symbols has not been the subject of debate, although in the early 1990s, the Associação Nacional de Ação Indigenista (National Association of Indigenist Action) arranged to bring Kiriri Indians to Salvador to participate in the parade as a way of giving the *caboclos* a more clearly indigenous meaning; lack of funding in subsequent years ended this initiative.[25]

Dois de Julho rhetoric today echoes many of the themes that were prominent in the nineteenth century. Speakers and journalists repeat that Dois de Julho is the true date of Brazil's independence. In her speeches at the start of the procession in Lapinha, the late Consuelo Pondé de Sena, long-serving president of the Instituto Geográfico e Histórico da Bahia, repeatedly stressed that Bahia was Brazil's "*terra mater* ... where the political liberation of her people was definitively consolidated," to cite her 2005 address.[26] Governor Rui Costa wrote in the preface to a 2015 textbook on the war for independence in Bahia that Brazil only won its liberty and secured its unity thanks to the Bahians' heroism; the book also quoted a 2010 statement by his predecessor, Jacques Wagner, that "Brazil's independence happened here" in Bahia.[27] Twentieth-century campaigns to make Dois de Julho into a national holiday failed, just as did similar ones in the 1820s.[28] In 1996, Deputy Domingos Leonelli sponsored a bill to designate 2 July the "Day of National Liberation." This was no doubt also intended to call attention to his ultimately unsuccessful campaign for mayor; nevertheless, it indicates Dois de Julho's continuing symbolic power.[29] In 2013, President Dilma Rousseff sanctioned a symbolic law that added 2 July 1823 to "the historical dates on the calendar of national days [*efemérides nacionais*]."[30] The Dois de Julho procession received state designation as intangible cultural heritage in 2006, but efforts to win it national recognition from the Instituto do Patrimônio Histórico e Artístico Nacional (National Institute for Artistic and Historical Patrimony) have apparently not succeeded.[31]

After the premature death of federal deputy Luís Eduardo Magalhães (1955–98), son and political heir apparent to Antônio Carlos Magalhães, the name of Salvador's airport was changed from Aeroporto Internacional Dois de Julho to Aeroporto Internacional Deputado Luís Eduardo Magalhães. This sparked an interminable campaign to change the name back, in recognition of the "greatest symbol of the Bahian *povo*'s struggle for Liberty," as a fan-shaped handbill distributed by a state deputy in 2000 proclaimed; that year, the Campanha Popular pela Restauração do Nome do Aeroporto 2 de Julho (Popular Campaign for the Restoration of the Name Aeroporto 2 de Julho) distributed stickers that declared, "No man replaces a *povo*'s saga."[32] In 2014, federal deputy Alice Portugal, recently elected chair of Chamber of Deputies' cultural committee, declared it her priority to pass a bill dating back to 2002 that would restore the original name. Since early 2015 the bill has remained in committee.[33]

Historians, myself included, are regularly invoked to support arguments about the festival's significance, and historical research on the festival is often viewed as contributing to the celebrations by legitimizing Bahian patriotism and the festival itself. The *Revista do Instituto Geográfico e Histórico da Bahia* published my article on the Frias Villar incident in a section titled "Espaço Aberto Memorial Dois de Julho," rather than among the other research articles, alongside the last speech that President Consuelo delivered at Lapinha (2 July 2014); she died in early 2015.[34] In a 2006 speech in Congress, Deputy Zezéu Ribeiro called for the approval of bills to restore the airport's name and to recognize Dois de Julho as a national day. He cited several historians, including Braz do Amaral (who in 1923 condemned efforts to make the centenary celebrations the property of Rio de Janeiro and São Paulo), Luís Henrique Dias Tavares (who authored a history of the war for independence in Bahia), and Marco Morel (who wrote a biography of Cipriano Barata). Deputy Zezéu also quoted at length from a Portuguese translation of my 1999 article on Dois de Julho, particularly the sections in which I argued that Dois de Julho expressed an alternative nationalism to that of the imperial state and that celebrating the popular origins of Bahian independence challenged the imperial order.[35] My off-the-cuff remarks about Dois de Julho's uniqueness in a 2015 interview immediately turned up in a didactic book on the struggle for independence in Bahia.[36]

Dois de Julho celebrants emphasize their traditions' antiquity. When the trucks contracted to bring the Encourados from Pedrão to Salvador failed to arrive in 2012 and the horsemen missed the parade (perhaps a convenient way to prevent a confrontation between animal rights groups and the cowboys), they and the media lamented that, for the first time in 186 years, they would not be leading the *caboclo* and the *cabocla* into Salvador.[37] They thus dated the start of the Encourados' tradition to 1826, the year in which, according to Manoel Raimundo Querino, the *caboclo* was created to accompany the parade into the city, an indication of how deeply his history of Dois de Julho has penetrated Bahians' popular historical consciousness. Querino's history of the symbols is regularly cited in the media and in other commemorative materials, usually without attribution.[38] In 2005, I published a brief article on Dois de Julho in the popular history magazine *Nossa História*, in which I sketched out the chronology of the early celebrations and implicitly questioned Querino's account of the festival's origins (a very preliminary version of chapter 1). Two irate Bahian readers sent e-mail messages to the magazine editor reaffirming Querino's history of the festival.[39] More recently, journalist Nelson Cadena has published articles based on his research in the Hemeroteca Digital Brasileira that question Querino's history.[40]

Just as in the nineteenth century, Dois de Julho remains a contested celebration and a space for contestation, a festival that means many things to Bahians. In some Angolan Candomblé houses, 2 July is a day for celebrating *caboclo* spirits, and as I have noted, the *caboclos* are the objects of veneration while on the streets. The faithful leave offerings and notes in the wagons or quietly pray before them.[41] In the 1970s and 1980s, Hildegardes Vianna regularly criticized these public manifestations of the *caboclos'* association with Candomblé, and in 2017, evangelical Christian groups tried to surround the symbols to prevent others from approaching them while they stood in front of the city council building.[42]

Contemporary Salvador is a major metropolis of more than three million people, and Dois de Julho celebrations no longer command most of the city's space, nor do they involve a majority of the city's population (Baldaia estimates that the number of participants and observers has remained stable since the 1960s, which means that it has declined significantly in proportional terms).[43] Most *Soteropolitanos* (residents of Salvador) do not parade or watch the parade, nor for that matter do they frequent Candomblé houses. Rather, most Bahians experience Dois de Julho as just a holiday, in much the same way that more North Americans spend 1 or 4 July (depending on which side of the border they live) at a backyard barbecue with family and friends than at a Canada Day or Fourth of July parade or other civic festival. In 2011, Bahia's Pentecostals held a "March for Jesus" from Ondina to Barra on 2 July and claimed that 700,000 people participated, an improbable figure that *A Tarde* nevertheless accepted; there was no indication that the Pentecostals sought to connect their demonstration to Dois de Julho, unlike Bahia's mid-twentieth-century Protestants, who were avid participants in the procession.[44] Salvador's media continue to devote considerable space and time to coverage of Dois de Julho, and the participation of the governor and the mayor is expected. In

2017, this brought the left-wing governor, Rui Costa, into uncomfortable proximity to the right-wing mayor, Antônio Carlos Magalhães Neto (grandson of the late-twentieth-century political boss), at the start of the procession on Lapinha Square. Members of their entourages exchanged sharp words.

Hildegardes Vianna regularly lamented in the second half of the twentieth century that the Bahian *povo* no longer knew its history and that people did not know whether 2 July was a holy day or a civic holiday.[45] The FPC and other organizations' efforts to produce didactic materials for teaching about Dois de Julho and to make them available online may be changing this situation. The nature and content of these materials deserves a careful study, for they appear to reflect a combination of old and new understandings of the festival and of Bahia's place in the Brazilian nation.[46]

Twentieth- and twenty-first-century Dois de Julho's history remains to be written, but it is clear that, like the nineteenth-century festival, Dois de Julho has changed and evolved, subject to Bahia's social, political, and cultural dynamics. To reconstruct nineteenth-century Dois de Julho's history apart from but in dialogue with the folklorists and memoirists who have shaped understandings of the festival is not an effort to tell the "truth" about Dois de Julho's origins and history, although some will no doubt take this book in this way. Rather, I have sought to offer a richer and more complex account of the festival, one that integrates it into nineteenth-century Bahian history. Celebrations are serious business. The engagement of Bahians of all classes in Dois de Julho celebrations, the bitter conflicts over the appropriate forms of celebration, and the voluminous accessible surviving historical sources (themselves but a fraction of what Bahian journalists wrote about the festival) testify to Dois de Julho's importance. My focus on Salvador has required leaving out the many historical and contemporary commemorations of Bahia's independence that have long taken place elsewhere in the state, most notably the celebrations of 25 June in Cachoeira and 7 January in Itaparica.[47]

Festivals like Dois de Julho offer insights into how people defined their society, whom they excluded, whom they included, and how they defined themselves against others. The politics discussed in this book make it clear that many nineteenth-century Bahians were active citizens; they eagerly participated in the radical-liberal-inflected festival of the early decades and thereby claimed citizenship and membership in the nation. Even as the radical-liberal elements of the early celebrations gave way to the more broadly Bahian festival of the decades after 1850, Dois de Julho remained an important space for politics. By the end of the nineteenth century, how Bahians represented themselves on Dois de Julho had become a central preoccupation. Civic festivals have long been political spaces where men and women debate the nature of their society. For these reasons, historians have found the analysis of civic rituals to be a fruitful method for getting at some of the things that mattered to people in the past in their relationship to the state, the nation, and their local community. What makes Dois de Julho unique is its enduring popularity and its unusual nature as a subnational civic ritual that claims to speak for the entire nation. It is far more common for a subnational civic ritual to express a regional identity in opposition to the national state. Catalans do not claim that the *Diada Nacional de Catalunya* (11 September) should be celebrated throughout Spain, nor do Québécois call for their Fête Nationale (Saint-Jean-Baptiste Day, 24 June) to become a Canadian holiday, but Bahians are not separatists.[48] On Dois de Julho, they are Brazilians. Dois de Julho served, and still serves, as a foil to Sete de Setembro and as a challenge to the centralized imperial regime and its republican successors. It offers an alternative vision of independence, one that emphasizes the popular origins of the mobilization against the Portuguese, rather than the actions of Emperor Pedro I or even the leadership of the Recôncavo planter class in 1822–23, but it is undoubtedly Brazilian. Not surprisingly, then, its celebrations have always aroused passions among many Bahians.

# NOTES

## Abbreviations

| | |
|---|---|
| AALPBa | *Anais da Assembleia Legislativa da Província da Bahia* |
| AAPEBa | *Anais do Arquivo Público do Estado da Bahia* |
| ACD | *Anais da Câmara dos Deputados* |
| ACSDEFBa | *Anais da Câmara dos Senhores Deputados do Estado Federal da Bahia* |
| AIGHBa | Arquivo do Instituto Geográfico e Histórico da Bahia |
| AIHGB | Arquivo do Instituto Histórico e Geográfico Brasileiro |
| AHMI | Arquivo Histórico do Museu Imperial |
| AHMS | Arquivo Histórico Municipal de Salvador |
| CFRDJ | Coleção Festejos Relacionados ao 2 de Julho |
| AN | Arquivo Nacional |
| APEBa | Arquivo Público do Estado da Bahia |
| SACP | Seção de Arquivo Colonial e Provincial |
| SR | Seção Republicana |
| SJ | Seção Judiciária |
| IT | Inventários e Testamentos |
| SL | Seção Legislativa |
| APEPe | Arquivo Público do Estado de Pernambuco |
| AS | *Anais do Senado* |
| BN | Biblioteca Nacional |
| Mus. | Divisão de Música |
| SM | Seção de Manuscritos |
| SOR | Seção de Obras Raras |
| CA | Comandante das Armas (Commander of Arms) |
| CLB | *Coleção das Leis do Brasil* |
| CLRBa | *Coleção das Leis e Resoluções da Bahia* |
| CM-S | *Correio Mercantil* (Salvador) |
| CM-R | *Correio Mercantil* (Rio) |
| Corr. | Correspondence from Bahia |
| CP | Chefe de Polícia (Chief of Police) |

| | |
|---|---|
| DP | *Diário de Pernambuco* (Recife) |
| DRJ | *Diário do Rio de Janeiro* |
| HDB | Hemeroteca Digital Brasileira |
| JC | *Jornal do Commercio* (Rio) |
| NARS | National Archives and Records Service (United States) |
| PAEBa | *Publicações do Arquivo do Estado da Bahia* |
| PRO | Public Record Office (Great Britain) |
| FO | Foreign Office |
| RIGHBa | *Revista do Instituto Geográfico e Histórico da Bahia* |
| RIHGB | *Revista do Instituto Histórico e Geográfico Brasileiro* |
| Rio | Rio de Janeiro (City) |

## Author's Note on the Text

1 Exchange rate data are drawn from Duncan, *Public and Private Operations*, 183.

## Introduction

1 Albino José Barbosa de Oliveira to Isabel Augusto da Sousa Queiroz, Rio das Pedras, 8 January 1882, in A.J.B. Oliveira, *Memórias*, 21.
2 Comandante em Chefe do Exército Pacificador da Bahia to Minister of War, 6 July 1823, in *O Reverbero*, 6 August 1871. This report has also been reproduced in I.A.C. Silva, *Memorias*, 4:65–6.
3 *Echo da Patria*, 19 August 1823, transcribed in *AAPEBa* 10 (1923): 86–92 (quote at 88–9). No copies of this periodical are known to have survived; this article has also been reproduced in "Entrada." Two bibliogaphers identify the *Echo*'s editor as José Estanislau Vieira, Torres and Carvalho, *Annaes*, 32.
4 Henry Chamberlain to Lord Canning, Rio, 21 July 1823, PRO/FO 63, vol. 259, fol. 281v.
5 There is no recent comprehensive history of the independence war in Bahia. Still useful are I.A.C. Silva, *Memorias*, vols. 3–4; M.C. Garcia, *Historia*; B.H. Amaral, *Historia da Independencia*; Cavalcanti, "Processo"; L.H.D. Tavares, *Independência*; Morton, "Conservative Revolution"; and Kraay, *Race*, chap. 5. Recent scholarship has emphasized the popular elements in the conflict: J.J. Reis, "Jogo"; Guerra Filho, "Povo" and "Patriotismo"; and Kraay, "Muralhas." New work by Bahian historians is collected in Leal and Sousa, eds., *Capítulos*.
6 Morton, "Conservative Revolution," 260; M.C.P. Almeida, *Batalha*; Bandeira, *Feudo*, 430–5.

7  J.P. Maia, *Marinha*, 66–89; Vale, "Creation," 70–1, 74–5, 81–3, and "Lord Cochrane," 415–28.

8  On Capinam and this image, see "Os pintores e o Dois de Julho," *Diario da Bahia*, 18 June 1943; P.C. Silva, "Notas," 567–8; Querino, *Artistas*, 72–3, and *Bahia*, 318–19; F.B. Barros, "Á margem" (1934), 260; "Dois de Julho," AIHGB, DL, 1591.35.

9  See, for another example, how Pedro Américo de Figueiredo e Melo turned Pedro I's 7 September proclamation of independence into a suitably heroic act in his iconic 1888 painting, Oliveira and Mattos, eds., *Brado*; Sandes, *Invenção*, 69–75.

10  Hobsbawm and Ranger, eds., *Invention*; Anderson, *Imagined Communities*.

11  The literature is vast, and representative works include Biskupski, *Independence Day*; Hazareesingh, *Saint Napoleon*; Unowsky, *Pomp*; Waldstreicher, *In the Midst*; Davis, *Parades*; Travers, *Celebrating*; Ryan, *Civic Wars*, chaps. 2, 6; Hayday and Blake, eds., *Celebrating Canada*; McCrone and MacPherson, eds., *National Days*; Fuller, ed., *National Days*. For Latin American examples, see Salvador, *Efímeras efemérides*; Esposito, *Funerals*; Díaz Arias, *Fiesta*; Beezley and Lorey, eds., *¡Viva Mexico!*; R.H. Duncan, "Political Legitimization" and "Embracing"; Bertoni, "Construir la nacionalidad"; Kraay, *Days*.

12  Mattoso, *Bahia, século XIX*, 205.

13  J. da V.M., "Os dias Santos" (comunicado), *O Noticiador Catholico*, 5 February 1853.

14  On these aspects of ritual, see Kertzer, *Ritual*, 37–9, 72–3, 131–4.

15  "Bahia," *O Farol Paulistano* (São Paulo), 17 May 1831.

16  Albuquerque Jr., *Invention*; Weinstein, *Color*; Blake, *Vigorous Core*; Garfield, *In Search*; Oliven, *Tradition*.

17  I have explored some of these themes in Kraay, "Ritos."

18  Eakin, *Becoming Brazilian*, 45.

19  F.A. Souza, *Eleitorado*; Castellucci, "Trabalhadores" and "Muitos votantes." On the Latin American pattern of large electorates, larger than their counterparts in early nineteenth-century Europe, see Posada-Carbó, ed., *Elections*.

20  Mac Cord, *Artifices*; Jesus, *Visões*; Mac Cord and Batalha, eds., *Organizar*; Morel, *Transformações*; Sanders, *Vanguard*, 15; Alonso, *Flores*; Castilho, *Slave Emancipation*. See also, for comparison, Sabato, *Many*, esp. 49–51; and Forment, *Democracy*. On abolitionist associations, see Alonso, *Flores*, 435–46.

21  This is the major argument of Kraay, *Days*.

22  For examples, see Chambers, *Subjects*; Guardino, *Time of Liberty*.

23 Mallon, *Peasant*; Méndez, *Plebeian Republic*; Thurner, *Two Republics*; Larson, *Trials*.

24 Guardino, *Time*, 15.

25 Wood, *Society*; Sowell, *Early Colombian Labor Movement*; García-Bryce, *Crafting*. Brazil's artisans have yet to find their historian, but see Mac Cord, *Artífices*; L. Reis, *Liberdade*.

26 Warren, *Vagrants*.

27 Andrews, *Afro-Latin America*, 84–115; Lasso, *Myths*; Helg, *Liberty*.

28 Sanders, *Contentious Republicans*; Echeverri, *Indian and Slave Royalism*; Kraay, "Black Kings."

29 For a recent attempt to do so, see Miki, *Frontiers*.

30 J.J. Reis, *Rebelião*; Machado and Castilho, eds., *Tornando-se livre*; W. Fraga, *Crossroads*.

31 For pioneering studies, in addition to the work cited above, see Kittleson, *Practice*. On rebellions, see for an introduction to a vast field Dantas, ed., *Revoltas*.

32 Sanders, *Vanguard*, 52. On this point, see also Centeno's observations about Latin American elites' reluctance to promote nationalism, for fear that an engaged, nationalist citizenry would make excessive demands, *Blood*, 31, 175–8.

33 Pares, *Formation*, 102.

34 Lara, *Fragmentos*, chaps. 1, 4; Mendes, "Festas," 53–7.

35 Harris, *Carnival*, 143.

36 Abreu, *Império*; Kraay, "Barbarous Game"; Reis, "Tambores"; Harding, *Refuge*.

37 For this process in Bahia, see M.C. Santana, *Alma*; Ickes, *African-Brazilian Culture*; Romo, *Brazil's Living Museum*; Mariano, *Invenção*.

38 Schäeffer, *Brasil*, 263.

39 Barickman, *Bahian Counterpoint*, 41; Pang, *Engenho*, 26.

40 A.V. Ribeiro, "Transatlantic Slave Trade," 134, 154.

41 Guerra Filho, "Antilusitanismo," 212–17; Gandon, *Portugueses*.

42 Schwartz, *Sugar Plantations*; Barickman, *Bahian Counterpoint*; Baud and Konings, "Lavoura."

43 R. Graham, *Feeding*; J.R.M. Pinho, *Açambarcadores*, chap. 2; Mattoso, *Bahia: a cidade*. For an 1889 estimate of 4,000 boats and ships in Bahian waters, see D.V. Aguiar, *Descrições*, 305.

44 Barickman, *Bahian Counterpoint*, 42.

45 F.V. Vianna, *Memoria*, 272–6; F.M.G. Calmon, *Vida*, 108–10, 123; W. Mattos, *Panorama*, 97.

46 Pang, *Engenho*; F.M.G. Calmon, *Vida*, 121–2.

47 "Commercial Report" (1 December 1879), NARS, T-331, roll 4.

48  W.F. Oliveira, *Crise*, 54.
49  F.M.G. Calmon, *Vida*, 128–9.
50  F.M.G. Calmon, *Vida*, 107–8, 129–33; W.F. Oliveira, *Crise*, 56–60.
51  Brazil, *Synopse* (1890), 24.
52  Brazil, *Synopse* (1900), 16.
53  J.J. Reis, *Rebelião*, 24.
54  Nascimento, *Dez freguesias*, 95, 141.
55  For analysis of earlier census data, see Kraay, *Race*, 18; J.J. Reis, *Rebelião*, 24; Mattoso, *Bahia, século XIX*, 82–126.
56  Bandeira, *Feudo*, 430; Guerra Filho, "Povo," 115–20; J.S. Campos, "Tradições," 428–31. The indigenous presence was even greater in southern Bahia, *Barickman*, "'Tame Indians.'"
57  Rijckevorsel, *Uit Brazilië*, 1:89. See also Avé-Lallement, *Viagem*, 1:20; Vicuña Mackenna, *Paginas*, 2:301.
58  J.J. Reis, *Rebelião*; Pares, *Formation*; J.J. Reis, *Divining*; Harding, *Refuge*; J.J. Reis, "Revolution."
59  Verger, *Flux*; Candido, "Transatlantic Links."
60  Castillo, "Memory."
61  On slavery in Salvador, see Mattoso, *To Be a Slave*; Andrade, *Mão de obra*; J.J. Reis, *Rebelião*. On the number of occupations, see Andrade, *Mão de obra*, 33–4.
62  Andrade, *Mão de obra*, 36–7, 92.
63  J.J. Reis, *Rebelião*; J.J. Reis, *Divining*; Reis, Gomes, and Carvalho, *Alufá Rufino*; J.J. Reis, "De escravo"; Castellucci Júnior, "De cativos."
64  Andrade, *Mão de obra*, 93.
65  David, *Inimigo*, 129–38.
66  Barickman, "Persistence"; Gonçalves, "Secas," 122–41.
67  L.A. Fonseca, *Escravidão*, 134–5; Graden, *Slavery*; Brito, *Abolição*; R.T.C. Silva, "Caminhos"; Alonso, *Flores*; Castilho, *Slave Emancipation*.
68  Mattoso, *Bahia, século XIX*, 596–8. On worries about vagrants, see W. Fraga Filho, *Mendigos*.
69  Mattoso, *Bahia, século XIX*, 217–19 (quote at 219). See also Borges, *Family*, esp. 37, 69–70.
70  J.J. Reis, *Rebelião*, 400–2; Mattoso, *Bahia, século XIX*, 440, 447.
71  C.N. Sampaio, *50 anos*, 160, 165–82, 203–12, 231–7.
72  D.V. Aguiar, *Descrições*, 303.
73  F.V. Vianna, *Memoria*, 418–19; M.C.B.E. Almeida, "Freguesia," 214–20.
74  Franck, *Working*, 350.
75  On the concept of *melhoramentos*, see Cribelli, *Industrial Forests*.
76  M.G.V. Sampaio, *Navegação*.
77  On the flow of provincial correspondence, see Kraay, "Year."

78  F.M.G. Calmon, *Vida*, 102–3, 128. On the port, see also Cruz, Leal, and Moreno, eds., *Histórias*.

79  D.V. Aguiar, *Descrições*, 304.

80  Wildberger, *Presidentes*, 627.

81  F.V. Vianna, *Memoria*, 160–2; F.M.G. Calmon, *Vida*, 99, 105, 115, 122, 125; R.S. Souza, *Trabalhadores*, 39–74, and *Tudo*, 25–64; Fernandes, *Do mar*, 77–83.

82  C.N. Sampaio, *50 anos*, 108–13, 122–4, 133–4, 155, 183–6, 199–201, 212–17; 256–7; Trinchão, *Parafuso*, 49, 71–9, 85–6, 156–7; Vasconcelos, *Salvador*, 245–321.

83  Belens, *Modernidade*, 117, 173, 186–7.

84  M.J. Ferreira, *Provincia*, 45.

85  These themes have been explored in detail by A.J.M. Silva, *Instituto*, esp. 187–234; Albuquerque, *Algazarra*, 21–51; R.C.N. Leite, *Rainha*.

86  R.C.N. Leite, "Civilização"; Pinheiro, *Europa*, 175–266.

87  Risério, *História*, 379.

88  For surveys of these revolts, see J.J. Reis, *Rebelião*, 44–67; Kraay, *Race*, 142–51; Morton, "Conservative Revolution," chaps. 9, 11; V.M. Oliveira, "Federalistas"; Aras, "Santa federação"; Reis and Kraay, "'Tyrant'"; Kraay, "'As Terrifying'"; P.C. Souza, *Sabinada*; Lopes, *Identidades*; Guerra Filho, "Antilusitanismo."

89  D.O. Araujo, *Tutu*. See also Kraay, *Race*, 162–7, 250–4; and J.W.A. Pinho, "Bahia," 284–311. Pioneering explorations such as M.P. Aguiar's study of the politics of food supply in the late 1870s have remained isolated efforts, *Abastecimento*.

90  D.V. Aguiar, *Descrições*, 306; Mattoso, *Bahia, século XIX*, 288–9; J.M. Carvalho, *Construção / teatro*, 120; J.W.A. Pinho, "Bahia," 302.

91  M.J. Ferreira, *Provincia*, 47; R.C.N. Leite, *Rainha*, 109–76.

92  Kiddy, "Militão"; R. Graham, *Patronage*.

93  Wildberger, *Presidentes*; Bulcão Sobrinho, *Conselho*; R.B. Castro, *Vice-presidentes*, *História*. For a pioneering study of the provincial assembly, see R.S. Santana, "Centralização."

94  Bahia, *Constituição*; F.V. Vianna, *Memoria*, 105–13.

95  Brown, "Vanguard," 62–97; Kraay, *Race*, 162–7, 183–217, 267, "Cotidiano," 240–1.

96  On the National Guard, see Kraay, *Race*, chap. 8; Uricoechea, *Patrimonial Foundations*; J.B. Castro, *Milícia*.

97  Lei, 10 October 1828, *CLB*.

98  On the senado da câmara's role in festivals, see A. Sousa, *Poder*, 116–21; J.S. Campos, *Procissões*, 46–7, 186–9, 197; Mendes, "Festas," 58–80. On the 1809–12 expenditures, see M. Sousa, "Bahia," 109. For late-colonial festival costs in Rio de Janeiro, see Lopez, *Festas*, 82–7.

99   Ruy, *História da Câmara*, 202, 209, 213, 218–21, 301–2.
100  Flory, *Judge*, 71–82, 172–3.
101  Ruy, *História da Câmara*, 333–5; F.V. Vianna, *Memoria*, 113–17.
102  R. Graham, *Patronage*, 107–9, 202.
103  Castellucci, "Muitos votantes," 192–9.
104  R. Graham, *Patronage*, 182–206; F.A. Souza, *Eleitorado*.
105  Castellucci, "Política," 218–19, 223–4, 226.
106  On this point, Castellucci criticizes J.M. Carvalho's view that the Bra-
     zilian population turned away from formal politics during the republic,
     Castellucci, "Política," 206–8; J.M. Carvalho, *Bestializados*, 161–4.
107  Querino, *Bahia*; Querino, *African Contribution*.
108  M. Leal, *Manoel Querino*; J. Calmon, *Vereador Manoel Querino*; Gled-
     hill, *Travessias*, loc. 1457–795, "Manuel Querino e a luta," and "Manuel
     Querino: operários"; L.A.R. Freire, "Manuel Querino"; Burns, "Intro-
     duction," in Querino, *African Contribution*, 1–7, and "Manuel Querino's
     Interpretation." See also C.A. Reis, "Reabilitação"; Afolabi, "Reversing
     Dislocations"; Albuquerque, "Dias."
109  Cooper, "Freedoms," 145.
110  A.J.M. Silva, *Instituto*, 19.
111  M. Leal, *Manuel Querino*, 100–9, 122–5. For Querino's critiques of the
     republic and praise of humble citizens, see *Bahia*, 101, 172–3, 178–9.
112  Querino, *Bahia*, 44–61.
113  Gledhill, *Travessias*, loc. 2160 (obituary); Querino, "Noticia historica,"
     99–100, 101, 102; Moniz, *Moniz Barretto*, 97–8, 101.
114  Querino, "Artistas," 102–3, and *Artistas*, 21.
115  These criticisms are discussed in M. Leal, *Manuel Querino*, 345–6; L.
     Reis, *Liberdade*, 85–6; and Gledhill, *Travessias*, loc. 2316, 2415–29, 3389.
116  F.B. Souza, "Festas." On Souza, see Sacramento Blake, *Diccionario*,
     2:410–11. His role in the Instituto Histórico is noted in *Instituto Histórico
     da Bahia*, M12–M13. On this institute, see A.J.M. Silva, *Instituto*, 99–118.
117  *O Reverbero*, 6 August 1871; J.A. Amaral, *Resumo*, 293–7. Amaral is
     almost certainly the author and editor of this issue. Several passages re-
     appear word for word in his *Resumo*, 300. On Amaral, see Sacramento
     Blake, *Diccionario*, 4:275; and J.T. Barros, "José Alvares do Amaral."
118  J.A. Amaral, *Resumo*, 9; Boccanera Junior, "Bahia," 159.
119  Querino, *Artistas*, 21n2. Querino first presented this criticism of Amaral
     in a 1905 article, "Artistas," 102–3.
120  Sacramento Blake, *Diccionario*, 7:167.
121  Moniz, *Moniz Barretto*, 91–109.
122  "O Dous de Julho, Bahia (Tradicionalismo)," *Gazeta de Noticias* (Rio),
     2 July 1887. Part of the newspaper page in the BN's microfilmed copy is
     torn, but the visible portions of the article match, word for word, sec-

tions of Mello Moraes Filho, *Festas e tradições*, 121–33. In 1888, he first reprinted this article in *Festas populares*, 141–54.

123 Sacramento Blake, *Diccionario*, 1:39; Romero, *Historia*, 2:1405–6; Abreu, "Mello Moraes Filho"; C.B. Ribeiro, "Folclore," 155.

124 Mello Moraes Filho, *Festas e tradições*, 129.

125 Mello Moraes Filho, "2 de Julho," *Diario de Noticias*, 1 July 1896.

126 Marques, *Feiticeiro*, 237–57.

127 J.M.C. Oliveira, *Dois metros e cinco*, 405–10.

128 Bittencourt, "Suzana," 39–54, *Longos serões*, 2:193–7.

129 Varella, *D'outros tempos*, 56–74. This article first appeared as "O 2 de Julho: algumas notas sobre a sua commemoração outr'ora na Bahia," *Diario de Noticias*, 29 June 1920. Varella's birth year is inferred from his assertion that he was a "fully-grown teenager [*rapazola*]" on 4 March 1890, *Da Bahia que eu vi*, 77. His other books are *Da Bahia do Senhor* and *Da Bahia que eu vi*.

130 J.S. Campos, "Cronicas," 295–304.

131 F.B. Barros, "Á margem" (1934), 375–6, 513–14, 557–8.

132 P.C. Silva, "Bahia," 89–99, 546–96.

133 A. Vianna, *Casos*, 103–5; C. Torres, *Vultos*, 106–8.

134 On Hildegardes Vianna, see Boaventura, "Instituto," 186–7. Her main works on Dois de Julho are "Dois de Julho de bairros," "Dois de Julho na Bahia," and "Folclore cívico."

135 C.A. Matos, "Bahia," 11–12, 21; H. Vianna, *Bahia* and *Antigamente era assim*.

136 Varella, *Bahia que eu vi*, 74–5; Gledhill, *Travessias*, loc. 2229.

137 M.A.P. Ribeiro, *Faculdade*, 16, 22, 134; Peard, *Race*, 34.

138 D.V. Aguiar, *Descrições*, 302.

139 R.B. Castro, *Tipografia*, 186; Boccanera, *Bahia historica*, 53, 87, 125; A.J.M. Silva, *Instituto*, 177.

140 For a call to microfilm Bahia's newspaper collection, see J. Calmon, "Prefácio," 19–21. The Biblioteca Virtual Consuelo Pondé is available at http://www.bvconsueloponde.ba.gov.br.

141 On provincial correspondence, see Kraay, "Year."

142 I thank Lizir Arcanjo Alves for calling my attention to many of these sources.

143 D.V. Aguiar, *Descrições*, 310.

144 R.B. Castro, *Tipografia*, 120–1. For one instance of a conviction, see D.A. Silva, "A duras e pesadas penas," 55.

145 J.W.A. Pinho, *Cotegipe*, 246–8; M.M. Molina, *História*, 1:449–56; Kraay, "Year." For recollections of extra-legal coercion, see Querino, *Bahia*, 100–1.

146 Wetherell, *Brazil*, 108.
147 For a forceful statement of this, see Waldstreicher, *In the Midst*, 10.
148 "Repositorio: Descrições de Festejos, Noticias de Jornais," AIGHBa, CX. 18, d. 70.
149 Arquivo Wanderley Pinho, AIHGB, DL 1538.011, 1568.006, 1591.021, 1591.027, 1591.033–035.
150 Albuquerque, *Algazarra*.
151 Kraay, "Between Brazil" and "Entre o Brasil." Those who accept Querino's account include Albuquerque, *Algazarra*, 89–90; J.A.L. Sampaio, "Festa," 155; J.T. Santos, *Dono*, 31–2; Serra, "Triunfo," 58–9; Tiphagne, "Índio," 50.
152 Fortunately, my other publications on Dois de Julho do not contain such errors, and material from them is incorporated into chapters 3, 5, and 6, Kraay, "Política," "Independência," "Frio como a pedra," "Cold as the Stone."
153 A.M. Silva, *Diccionario*, q.v. *pátria*; L.M.S. Pinto, *Diccionario*, q.v. *pátria*; Barman, *Brazil*, 26–30; Lyra, "'Pátria'"; Guerra Filho, "Antilusitanismo," 87–93.
154 A.M. Silva, *Diccionario*, q.v. *povo*; L.M.S. Pinto, *Diccionario*, q.v. *povo*; L.R. Pereira, "Conceito"; Blake, *Vigorous Core*, 27–31; Guerra Filho, "Povo," 52–4; Borges, *Family*, 79–81.

## Chapter One

1 Hobsbawm and Ranger, eds., *Invention*.
2 *Aurora Fluminense* (Rio), 26 November 1830; "Catalogo dos jornaes," 412–18.
3 "Noticias provinciaes: Bahia," *Correio Official* (Rio), 31 March 1840. See also D.O. Araújo, *Tutu*, 195–205.
4 Quoted in D.O. Araújo, *Tutu*, 208.
5 Lei, 9 September 1826, CLB. I have analyzed the development of these days of national festivity in Kraay, *Days*, 32–42.
6 On colonial festivals, see Jancsó and Kantor, eds., *Festa*; Priore, *Festas*; Santiago, *Vila*; B.C.C. Santos, *Corpo*; Tinhorão, *Festas*; Lara, *Fragmentos*; Lopez, *Festas*. On colonial Bahia's festivals, see Schwartz, "Ceremonies"; Campos, *Procissões*; Mendes, "Festas."
7 Watanabe-O'Kelly, "Festival Books."
8 Camara to Pedro I, 20 September 1823, Cartas do Senado, fol. 6v, AHMS.
9 Camara to Pedro, 29 October 1823, Cartas do Senado, fol. 4r–v, AHMS.
10 M.D. Graham, *Journal*, 260; *Relação dos publicos festejos*, 59.
11 Camara to Pedro, 29 October. 1823, Cartas do Senado, fol. 5r–v, AHMS. On the *beija-mão* in Rio, see Kraay, *Days*, 30.

12 Camara to Pedro, 29 October 1823, Cartas do Senado, fol. 5r–v, AHMS.

13 "Bahia," *O Independente Constitucional*, 15 October 1823; F.A.P. Costa, *Pernambuco*, 69.

14 "Chronica dos acontecimentos," 83.

15 Camara to Pedro, 29 October 1823, Cartas do Senado, fol. 5v, AHMS.

16 Barauna, *Oração*, 12, 15.

17 I.A.C. Silva, *Memorias*, 4:96.

18 On the politics of this period in Bahia, see Reis and Kraay, "'Tyrant,'" 402–9; L.H.D. Tavares, *Da sedição*, 187–204. For the national context, see Barman, *Brazil*, 97–129; Cunha, "Fundação," 238–62, 379–404.

19 "Proclamação," *O Independente Constitucional*, 3 May 1824; *O Independente Constitucional*, 8 May 1824. See also L.H.D. Tavares, *Da sedição*, 199–201.

20 J.E. Vieira, *Ao muito augusto senhor*, 3.

21 Kraay, *Days*, 40–1.

22 "Bahia," *O Independente Constitucional*, 13 October 1824; *Grito da Razão*, 14 October 1824; "Dia Doze de Outubro," *Diario: O Independente Constitucional*, 13 October 1825.

23 Governo Provisório to Minister of Empire, 24 January 1824, in Brazil, Arquivo Nacional, *Junta*, 81; *O Grito da Razão*, 14 October 1824.

24 Titara, "Elogio ao Augusto Anniversario do Natalicio e Acclamação de S.M. O Imperador Constitucional do Brasil, recitado no Theatro da Bahia em 12 de Outubro de 1825," in *Obras*, 1:118.

25 "Bahia," *O Independente Constitucional*, 8 September 1824; "Bahia," *Diario: O Independente Constitucional*, 9 September 1825; "Artigos Não Officiaes," *Diario: O Independente Constitucional*, 7 September 1826.

26 President to Pedro, 18 September 1825, AHMI, III-POB-29.06.1825-PI.B.c.

27 Reis and Kraay, "'Tyrant,'" 416–31; L.H.D. Tavares, *Da sedição*, 209–38.

28 "Congratulação aos Brasileiros...," 7 September 1828; "Elogio para o immortal dia 25 de Março de 1829," in Titara, *Obras*, 2:96–9, 143–5 (quote at 2:99).

29 Visconde de Camamú to Francisco Gomes da Silva, 25 October 1829, AHMI, II-POB-07.02.1829-Bar.c.

30 Wildberger, *Presidentes*, 78.

31 "Dia dois de Julho," *O Independente Constitucional*, 5 July 1824; *Grito da Razão*, 6 July 1824.

32 *Diario: O Independente Constitucional*, 4 July 1825; *Grito da Razão*, 9 July 1825, 6 July 1825 (quote).

33 Decreto, 2 July 1825, CLB.

34 *Grito da Razão*, 6 July 1824; "Dia dois de Julho," *O Independente Constitucional*, 5 July 1824.

35 Reis and Kraay, "'Tyrant,'" 411–14; Guerra Filho, "Joio"; Guerra Filho, "Antilusitanismo," 151–211.

36 Note * to "Dia Dois de Julho," *Diario: O Independente Constitucional*, 4 July 1825; "Correspondencias," *Grito da Razão*, 9 July 1825.

37 Camara to Pedro, 26 November 1825, Cartas do Senado, fol. 15r, AHMS.

38 "Bahia," *Diario: O Independente Constitucional*, 3 July 1826. This article was reprinted without attribution in "Bahia," *Diario Fluminense* (Rio), 31 July 1826.

39 Correspondencia, 3 July 1826, *Diario: O Independente Constitucional*, 6 July 1826.

40 "Observações de hum viajante q' passou pela B.ᵃ p.ᵃ hum seo amigo no Rio," AHMI, II-POB-04.09.1827 Hor.c; Kaxangá, *Oração*, 9. Unsure of himself, he incorrectly identified 1827 as the year without a Dois de Julho.

41 Querino, "Noticia historica," 85–6. An anonymous undated late-nineteenth-century manuscript also attributes the symbol to Costa, "Noções sobre a Esculptura na Bahia," BN/SM, II-34, 4, 3, no. 1, fol. 13v–14r.

42 On the attacks on Dois de Julho traditions in the first decades of the twentieth century, see Albuquerque, *Algazarra*, 96–107.

43 Querino, "Artistas," 102–3, *Artistas*, 21.

44 *O Reverbero*, 6 August 1871; J.A. Amaral, *Resumo*, 300.

45 Querino, *Artistas*, 21n2. Querino first published this criticism of Amaral in "Artistas," 102–3.

46 Boccanera Junior, "Bahia," 153–64; Boccanera Junior, *Bahia historica*, 131. Boccanera had particular scorn for Damasceno Vieira, who accepted Amaral's account in his *Memorias*, 2:61n1. To be fair to Vieira, at the time that he was writing, Amaral's history of the caboclos' creation had not yet been challenged by Querino. Later exceptions to the acceptance of Querino include P.C. Silva, "Bahia," 97–8; and F.B. Barros, "Á margem" (1934), 513.

47 See, for examples, J.T. Santos, *Dono*, 31–2; Tiphagne, "Índio," 50, 58–9; H. Vianna, "Dois de Julho na Bahia," 60–2; G.C. Leal, *Salvador*, 196, 198; Franco, *Trancelim*, 91; Kraay, "Between Brazil," 260; Albuquerque, *Algazarra*, 89–90. Martinez first raised questions about Querino's account but did not pursue them, *2 de Julho*, 71.

48 For overviews of Bahia's politics at this time, see Morton, "Conservative Revolution," 286–375; J.J. Reis, *Rebelião*, 44–67; Kraay, *Race*, 142–51. For the national context, see Barman, *Brazil*, 160–88; Needell, *Party*, 30–72; P.P. Castro, "Experiência," 9–60.

49 On Exaltado politics, see Basile, *Ezequiel Corrêa dos Santos* and "Império"; Mello, *Outra independência*; Morel, *Cipriano Barata*; G.S. Ribeiro, *Liberdade*.

50  D.O. Araújo, *Tutu*, 323–7.

51  B.H. Amaral, *Historia da Bahia*, 125.

52  Kraay, *Race*, 154–62.

53  J.J. Reis, "Cor," 296.

54  On federalism, see Dolhnikoff, *Pacto*; Mello, *Outra independência*; Aras, "Santa federação"; V.M. Oliveira, "Federalistas."

55  "Observações...," AHMI, II-POB-04.09.1827 Hor.c.

56  Francisco Joaquim Alvares Branco Moniz Barreto to Pedro I, 1 October 1827, AHMI, II-POB-01.10.1827 Bar.c.

57  On the black militia's role in independence, see Kraay, *Race*, 133–9.

58  Governor of Arms to Vice-President, 30 June 1827, BN/SM, II-33, 19, 2.

59  Merces, *Oração*, 7, 20.

60  President to Camara, 27 June 1828, AHMS/CFRDJ; Titara, *Obras*, 2:68–73.

61  On Corte Imperial, see R.B. Castro, *Tipografía*, 16–17, 63–77. On Neves, see V.M. Oliveira, "Federalistas," 133–4.

62  On *O Bahiano*, see "Catalogo dos jornaes," 418; D.A. Silva, "A duras e pesadas penas," 61–5.

63  On the troop deployments after the Cisplatine War, see Kraay, *Race*, 154, 268–9.

64  *Abelha Pernambucana* (Recife), 7 August 1829; F.G.S. Almeida, *Oração*, 8.

65  Untitled article from *Aurora [Fluminense]* (Rio), n. 221, *O Bahiano*, 1 September 1829.

66  President to Pedro de Araujo Lima, 9 July 1828, BN/SM, I-31, 13, 12.

67  *Aurora Fluminense* (Rio), 6 August 1828. This article was, in turn, reprinted in *O Farol*, 3 October 1828.

68  Petition of José Lino Coutinho, 14 May, ACD (1829), 1:71.

69  Mello, *Rubro veio*.

70  See the debate of 14 July, ACD (1829), 4:106. The chamber noted the senate rejection on 21 July 1830, ACD (1830), 1:451. See also *O Brasileiro Imparcial* (Rio), 24 July 1830.

71  *O Brasileiro Imparcial* (Rio), 3 July 1830.

72  On Maia, see M.B.N. Silva, *Semanário Cívico*; and Sena, *Imprensa*.

73  Resolução, 12 August 1831, CLB. Neither the chamber nor the senate recorded any debate on this resolution, ACD (1831), 1:207; AS (1831), 2:141, 179, 186; ACD (1831), 2:37.

74  Archbishop to Clergy, 26 June 1830, in I.A.C. Silva, *Memorias*, 4:61–3.

75  Santa Cruz, *Memorias*, 69–71 (quote at 71).

76  ACD (1830), 2:623, 635. For another allusion to this issue, see *Nova Luz Brasileira* (Rio), 16 November 1830.

77  "Bahia," *O Brasileiro Imparcial* (Rio), 24 July 1830.

78  *Astrea* (Rio), 7 September 1830.

79  *O Farol Paulistano* (São Paulo), 17 August 1830.

80  *Astrea* (Rio), 7 September 1830.

81  Marescheau to Minister of Foreign Affairs, 23 June 1831, Correspondance Politique du Brésil, vol. 13, Archives du Ministère des Affaires Étrangères (Quai d'Orsay). I thank Marco Morel for sharing this source.

82  *Gazeta da Bahia*, 19 June 1830; *O Bahiano*, 26 June 1830. Both the *Aurora Fluminense* (Rio), 9 August 1830, and *O Farol Paulistano* (São Paulo), 17 August 1830, referred to extensive coverage of the festival by *O Bahiano* and by *O Escudo da Constituição*, but no issues of these Bahian periodicals have survived.

83  "Elogio," Titara, *Obras*, 3:92–3, 93–4, 97. In both of the copies of this volume that I have been able to consult, pages 95–6 are missing.

84  *O Brasileiro Imparcial* (Rio), 24 July 1830. *Chumbeiro* is another pejorative term for Portuguese.

85  *Aurora Fluminense* (Rio), 1 September 1830. See also the issue of 9 August 1830.

86  Morel, *Cipriano Barata*, 257.

87  *Nova Sentinella da Liberdade*, 2 and 3 July 1831. Despite its title, this periodical was not published by Cipriano Barata, for he had been arrested in April and sent to Rio de Janeiro, Marco Morel, *Cipriano Barata*, 260.

88  John Parkinson to John Bidwell, 26 June 1831 (private), PRO/FO 13, vol. 88, fol. 119v. On the peaceful nature of these celebrations, see also Lazaro José Jambeiro to President, Santo Antônio além do Carmo Parish, 3 July 1831, APEBa/SACP, m. 1569; D.O. Araújo, *Tutu*, 258; V.M. Oliveira, "Federalistas," 77.

89  "O grande dia politico da provincia, o jubilozo DOIS de JULHO do Anno de 1823," 12 July 1832, BN/SOR, 102, 6, 52. Francisco Ribeiro Neves, mentioned by Amaral as one of those involved in the creation of the first allegorical float, handled the money raised by this subscription.

90  *Gazeta da Bahia Extraordinaria*, 2 July 1832.

91  Parkinson to Bidwell, 4 July 1834 (private), PRO/FO 13, vol. 113, fol. 210.

92  Titara, *Obras*, 6:68; 7:10, 33–5, 41–5, 62.

93  *O Reverbero*, 6 August 1871; Moreira de Azevedo, "Sociedades," 313; J.A. Amaral, *Resumo*, 369; Wildberger, *Presidentes*, 164; J.W.A. Pinho, *Cotegipe*, 273.

94  Joze Barb.ª Madur.ª e Sz.ª and Primo Jorge dos Santos to Camara, ca. June 1834; Antonio Vieira de Macedo and Luiz Alz. Borges to Camara, 10 June 1835; Joze Francisco de Mello and José Nunes Bahiense to Camara, 28 May 1836; Francisco Joaquim Carv.º, Felix Garcia d'Andr.ᵉ Silveira, and Francisco Nunes Tupiniquin to Camara, 17 May 1837, AHMS/CFRDJ; Lei, 1 October 1828, *CLB*.

95  I.A.C. Silva, *Memorias*, 4:59.

96  Branco, *Ode*, 6.

97  The only surviving and incomplete run (1833–37) of this newspaper, owned by the Biblioteca Pública do Estado da Bahia, has been unavailable to researchers since at least 1999.

98  Campos, "Cronicas," 295–7.

99  Campos, "Cronicas," 298–301. On cucumbis, see Querino, *Bahia*, 69–72.

100 Ramos, *Oração*, 16–17, 24.

101 On Paraguaçu and Caramuru, see Risério, *História*, 57–67; Bandeira, *Feudo*, 33–120; and Amado, "Diogo Álvares."

102 Campos, "Cronicas," 301–3.

103 *O Democrata*, 30 April 1836. On this newspaper, see S.C.P.B. Fonseca, "Federação," 69–79.

104 Chefe, Third Battalion, National Guard, to President, 21 June 1837, APEBa/SACP, m. 3530.

105 Cited in Campos, "Cronicas," 304.

106 "Bahia," *Diario Fluminense* (Rio), 31 July 1826.

107 M.A. Silva, *Restauração*, 53. This same theme appears in Branco, *Ode*, 14–21.

108 I.A.C. Silva, *Memorias*; M.A. Silva, *Restauração*, title page.

109 Agulhon, *Marianne*, 88.

110 Campos, "Cronicas," 299–300; Ramos, *Oração*, 25–6.

111 Mello Moraes Filho, *Festas e tradições*, 126–7.

112 Treece, *Exiles*, 91–3; Belluzzo, *Brasil*, 1:76–85; Athayde, ed., *Bahia*, 161; Lopez, *Festas*, 303–12; Kodama, *Índios*, 54.

113 Earle, *Return*, 50–60.

114 Boccanera Junior, *Télas*, 23–30.

115 Treece, *Exiles*, 160–207; Ricupero, *Romantismo*, 153–78; Haußer, "Civilização"; Risério, *História*, 440; Kodama, *Índios*, 28–30, 60.

116 Bandeira, *Feudo*, 329–31; Edelweiss, *Antroponímia*.

117 Guzmán, *Native*, 40. See also J.P. Oliveira, "Formas," 165–70; Miki, *Frontiers*, 121–5.

118 For a recent discussion of this process in southern Bahia and adjacent provinces, see Miki, *Frontiers*, 137–52.

119 See, for example, Fundação Pedro Calmon, *Florilégio*, 39. L.A. Alves accepts the attribution of the current words to Titara, *2 de Julho*, 90. A century ago, F.B. Barros indicated that the current lyrics' author was unknown, "Á margem" (1918), 171; however, in the expanded later version of this text, he said nothing about the lyrics' authorship, F.B. Barros, "Á margem" (1934), 514. In 1925, F.J.F. Bastos also noted that the authorship

of the Dois de Julho anthem was unknown, *Elementos*, 67–8. Others, however, attributed the words to Titara and the music to Barretto, "Hymnos ao 2 de Julho: suas letras e seus auctores," *Bahia Illustrada* (Rio) 2:9 (August 1918).

120 P. Calmon, "Ladislau dos Santos Titara"; Kraay, *Race*, 180–1.

121 Titara, *Obras*, 2:138–9; 3:60–2. On Barretto, see P.C. Silva, "Notas," 641–2, "Galeria," 68; Querino, *Artistas*, 165–6.

122 C.A. Tavares, *Elogio*, 18. The first verse of the contemporary anthem is also cited in a Recife newspaper's transcription of an allegorical article about Dois de Julho attributed to *Dia Dous de Julho*, apparently a pamphlet or periodical, *O Democrata* (Recife), 5 June 1858.

123 Titara, *Obras*, 2:138. It is not possible to translate this verse in a way that preserves Titara's grammatical structure:

> Nunca mais o Despotismo
> Regerá nossas ações
> Com tiranos não combinam
> Brasileiros corações.

124 Titara, *Obras*, 2:139.

125 Dugrivel, *Des bords*, 384.

126 L.R.N. Santos, "Luminárias," 124.

127 *O Farol Paulistano* (São Paulo), 17 August 1830. In addition to the references to coffee leaves above, see Titara, *Obras*, 6:62, 7:6. On their meaning, see Campos, "Tradições bahianas," 429; Morel, *Cipriano Barata*, 256–7; Kraay, *Days*, 68.

128 Article 5, paragraph 4, Constituição política do Império do Brazil, 25 March 1824, CLB.

129 Reis, *Rebelião*, 47–52; Kraay, *Race*, 110, 114, 116–21, 124, 145, 147–8, 161; Guerra Filho, "Antilusitanismo," 115–211. On anti-Portuguese nativism elsewhere in Brazil, see G.S. Ribeiro, *Liberdade*, 57–106, 243–325; and Mosher, *Political Struggle*, 186–201.

130 This may be a function of the limited sources available to me, for many of those cited in this chapter are unlikely to mention such violence if it took place.

131 Viscount of Pirajá to Regent, 28 June 1838, PAEBa, 4:372–3. The recent discovery of the manumission of João Theodoro by Custódio José de Souza "in remembrance of the Patriotic Day of Dois de Julho" on 1 July 1837 lends credence to Pirajá's lament, APEBa/SJ, Livro de Notas 255, p. 84. The document has been published on www.uranohistoria. blogspot.com.br.

132 On this issue, see Kraay, "'Em outra coisa.'"

133 I thank Lizir Arcanjo Alves for sharing her transcriptions of these articles.

134 P.C. Souza, *Sabinada*; Kraay, "'As Terrifying'"; J.S.C. Lopes, *Identidades*, 58–9, 66–71, 77.

135 On the Regresso, see Needell, *Party*, 55–80; Barman, *Brazil*, 189–216; I.R. Mattos, *Tempo*; Flory, *Judge*, 131–80.

136 Kraay, "'As Terrifying,'" 117–28; D.O. Araujo, *Tutu*, 49–96; Kraay, *Race*, 162–7, 239–40.

137 Kraay, *Days*, 86–111, and "Definindo," 66–73.

138 For national political narratives of this period, see Barman, *Brazil*, 201–35; Needell, *Party*, 80–116; P.P. Castro, "Política," 509–40. On Bahian politics and the limited development of parties, see J.W.A. Pinho, *Cotegipe*, 135, 167–9, 172; D.O. Araújo, *Tutu*, 151, 207.

139 C., Corr., 12 July, DP, 20 July 1846.

140 "A Camara Municipal desta Cidade aos seos honrados Municipes," CM-S, 28 June 1838; Acting Superior Commander to President, 26 June 1838, APEBa/SACP, m. 3534; "Noticias Diversas," CM-S, 3 July 1838.

141 Visconde de Pirajá to Regent, 28 June 1838, PAEBa, 4:372–3; Pirajá, *Elogio*. This is, incidentally, the only documented intervention of Pirajá in the Dois de Julho celebrations, and it contradicts later assertions that he was one of the leading celebrants, A. Costa, "Visconde de Pirajá," 97; Querino, *Bahia*, 52, 171.

142 Annuncios, CM-S, 13 July 1838; "Subscripção para 2 de Julho de 1839," CM-S, 5 March 1839; "Assembléa Provincial," 10 April 1839, CM-S, 30 April 1839.

143 "Noticias Diversas," CM-S, 4 July 1839.

144 Titara, *Obras*, 7:97; "Para o dia Dous de Julho de 1839," CM-S, 6 July 1839; "Ao Dia Dous de Julho – 1839" and "Soneto," in Capirunga, *Poesias*, 1:100–5, 134.

145 Titara, *Obras*, 7:87–8.

146 D.O. Araújo, *Tutu*, 259–60, 262, 268.

147 "Os festejos do Dia Dous de Julho," CM-S, 6 July 1840.

148 "Os festejos do Dia Dous de Julho," CM-S, 6 July 1840; "Noticias provinciaes," DP, 20 July 1840. See the sonnets by A.F.S. Capirunga, Francisco Moniz Barreto, and Manoel Pessoa da Silva published in CM-S, 6 and 10 July 1840.

149 Wildberger, *Presidentes*, 238; Decreto 244, 22 August 1840, CLB.

150 Declaração, CM-S, 26 June 1841.

151 *O Commercio*, 5 July 1843; "Annuncios," *O Commercio*, 27 June 1843.

152 "O Dia Dous de Julho," *O Commercio*, 10 July 1843. See also D.O. Araújo, *Tutu*, 268–9.

153 J.J. Santos, *Relatorio*, 56–7. The original petition is not in the assembly's archives for that year, APEBa/SL.

154 Lei 149, 9 June 1841, CLRBa; Petition of Luiz Maria Álvares Falcão Murici Ramos et al. to Provincial Assembly, ca. February–March 1842, APEBa/SL, livro 981.

155 *O Commercio*, 5 July 1843.

156 C., Corr., 12 July, DP, 20 July 1846; Wildberger, *Presidentes*, 123–43.

157 On Andréa, see Andréa, *Marechal Andréa*; Machado, "Direito," 156–61; Kraay, "Pacificação," 154–5, 162–4, 167. For Bahian criticisms of Andréa, see *O Democrata*, 16 April 1836; and "Mofina," *O Guaycuru*, 12 January 1845.

158 "Noticias provinciaes (Bahia)," *O Social* (Rio), 17 April 1846; Vargas, *Conselheiro Zacarias*, 31; P.P. Castro, "Política," 525.

159 Wildberger, *Presidentes*, 271–85; B.H. Amaral, *Historia da Bahia*, 165–6; Andréa, *Marechal Andréa*, 173–83. On Andréa's quarrels with the provincial assembly, see President to Minister of Empire, 26 June 1846, BN/SM, I-31, 15, 38. On his dispute with the National Guard, see Kraay, *Race*, 248–9; D.O. Araújo, *Tutu*, 166, 170–2. J.W.A. Pinho attributes Andréa's difficulties to his reformist zeal, *Cotegipe*, 239n1.

160 Andréa to Minister of Justice, 9 July 1846, APEBa/SACP, livro 690, fol. 163v.

161 C., Corr., 12 July, DP, 20 July 1846; Andréa to Minister of Justice, 9 July 1846, APEBa/SACP, livro 690, fol. 164v. On the authorization to parade in 1845, see D.O. Araújo, *Tutu*, 270.

162 Letters from "O Artilheiro guarda" and "O Brazileiro," *O Guaycuru*, 28 June 1845.

163 For contemporary accounts of this incident, see "O anniversario de Dous de Julho em 1846 – ultima atrocidade do presidente Andréa – vil cobardia," *O Guaycuru*, 4 July 1846; "Deos Salve a Bahia," *O Guaycuru*, 7 July 1846; CP to President, 3 July 1846; and Corr., 10 July, both in JC, 17 July 1846; C., Corr., 12 July, DP, 20 July 1846; speech of José de Barros Pimentel, 20 July, ACD (1846), 2:262–3; Andréa to Minister of Justice, 9 July 1846, APEBa/SACP, livro 690, fol. 163v–66v; CP to Minister of Justice, 8 July 1846, APEBa/SACP, livro 5696-2, fols. 189v–92r. On Manoel Pessoa da Silva, see Querino, "Noticia biographica," 137–44; Querino, *Bahia*, 331–9. The incident has been widely related by Bahian folklorists and historians, Querino, "Noticia historica," 87–8; Querino, *Bahia*, 332–3; J.A. Amaral, *Resumo*, 296–7; F.B. Barros, "Á margem" (1934), 375–6; L.A. Alves, "Tensos laços," 36–53. The folklorists' accounts are largely consistent with contemporary sources, but none discusses the incident's aftermath, which L.A. Alves analyzes in some detail. Pessoa's poem, "Ao

Glorioso Dous de Julho," appears in *O Guaycuru*, 4 July 1846. For a more favourable view of the marshal, see Andréa, *Marechal Andréa*, 185–8.

164   "Interior, Bahia, 2 de Julho (d'*O Cabalista*)," *O Mercantil* (Rio), 22 July 1846.

165   Speech of Pimentel, 20 July, *ACD* (1846), 2:263.

166   Speech of João Maurício Wanderley, 24 July, *ACD* (1846), 2:313; Speech of D. Manoel do Monte Rodrigues de Araújo, 1 August, *ACD* (1846), 2:384.

167   Speech of Pimentel, 29 July, *ACD* (1846), 2:357, 359.

168   Speech of Antônio Pereira Rebouças, 31 July, *ACD* (1846), 2:368.

169   Speech of João José de Oliveira Junqueira, 1 August, *ACD* (1846), 2:386.

170   L.A. Alves, "Tensos laços," 51–2, 368; L.A. Alves, "Do modo," 250; D.O. Araújo, *Tutu*, 178, 240–1.

171   Querino, "Noticia historica," 86, 88. For an earlier hint of this story, see Querino, *Bahia*, 51.

172   Querino, "Noticia biographica," 139; and *Bahia*, 333.

173   Querino, *Artistas*, 23.

174   *O Reverbero*, 6 August 1871; J.A. Amaral, *Resumo*, 300. This has been accepted by F.B. Barros, "Á margem" (1934), 513; and P.C. Silva, "Bahia," 97.

175   Varella, *D'outros tempos*, 61–2.

176   The historians and other scholars cited above in the note regarding their acceptance of Querino's account of the caboclo's creation also accept his account of the cabocla's creation, with one important exception. Albuquerque dates the cabocla's creation to 1840 and thus combines Querino and Amaral in *Algazarra*, 89–90. For additional examples of Querino's account being accepted, see Verger, *Notícias*, 209; D.O. Araújo, *Tutu*, 282–8.

177   See the issues of *O Guaycuru* for June and July 1846.

178   Martinez, *2 de Julho*, 71–3. For references to a singular allegory, see CM-S, 6 July 1840; *O Commercio*, 5 and 10 July 1843; *O Guaycuru*, 28 June 1845, 9 July 1846; CM-S, 5 July 1847.

179   "Dous de Julho," *O Guaycuru*, 30 June and 2 July 1846; "Dia 2 de Julho," CM-S, 5 July 1847.

180   Debret, *Viagem*, 1:33; Câmara Cascudo, *Dicionário*, 210; Carvalho and Carvalho, "Introdução," 15–17; J.P. Oliveira, "'Wild Indians'," 104; M.A.B. Silva, "Caboclos," 340–1.

181   "O Dous de Julho," *A Tolerancia*, 4 July 1849; Corr., 16 July, *Correio da Tarde* (Rio), 23 July 1849; Speech of Aprigio, in "Bahia. Assemblea Legislativa Provincial, sessão de 12 de julho de 1849," *Correio da Tarde* (Rio), 30 July 1849.

182 Junqueira Freire, *Obra*, 2:88–9. On this poem, see also L.A. Alves, "Tensos laços," 309–26.
183 Mello Moraes Filho, *Festas e tradições*, 127.
184 Querino, *Artistas*, 21; D.O. Araújo, *Tutu*, 283–4; CM-S, 5 July 1847.
185 Many have observed this parallel; see, among others, Baldaia, "Festa," 23–4, 85–6; Kraay, "Between Brazil," 263–4; J.A.L. Sampaio, "Festa," 154.
186 DaMatta, *Carnivals*, chap. 1.
187 Serra, *Rumores*, 159; Serra, "Triunfo," 56–7; Kraay, *Days*, 383.
188 H. Vianna, "'Dois de Julho,'" 61, and "Folclore cívico," 173–5; J.A.L. Sampaio, "Festa," 156; J.J. Reis, "Jogo," 79 (in the accompanying footnote, Reis attributes this argument to Cid Teixeira).
189 L.R.N. Santos, "Entre os festejos," 80–1, and "Luminárias," 130–3.
190 "Relação dos festejos…," *A Ordem* (São João del Rei), 28 September 1842. I thank Adriana Barreto de Souza for calling my attention to this source.
191 Reproduced in, among others, Kraay, *Race*, 38.

## Chapter Two

1 Corr., 8 July, *DP*, 16 July 1861.
2 O Brasileiro, "O aniversario do Dia Dois de Julho no corrente anno," *O Paiz*, 22 July 1854.
3 Wildberger, *Presidentes*, 307–11; "Noticias provinciaes: Bahia," *O Brasil* (Rio), 25 September 1848.
4 J.W.A. Pinho, *Cotegipe*, 181.
5 Barman, *Brazil*, 227–42; Needell, *Party*, 117–66; Iglesias, "Vida," 9–38.
6 Iglesias, "Vida," 38–112; Needell, *Party*, 167–222.
7 "Catálogo dos jornaes," 414–20, 549–51.
8 CP to President, 27 February 1855, APEBa/SACP, m. 2953; Corr., 13 April, JC, 18 April 1855.
9 On Gonçalves Martins's nickname, see *O Farricoco* (Rio), 4 November 1848. On his administration, see J.W.A. Pinho, *Cotegipe*, 181, 183, 238–9; Wildberger, *Presidentes*, 326; Kraay, *Race*, 252–4.
10 "O Dia Nacional da Bahia, o Dia Dous de Julho," CM-S, 18 June 1849.
11 Corr., n.d., CM-R, 1 August 1849.
12 Corr., 16 July, *Correio da Tarde* (Rio), 23 July 1849; Speech of Sr. Aprigio, in "Bahia. Assemblea Legislativa Provincial, sessão de 12 de julho de 1849," *Correio da Tarde* (Rio), 30 July 1849; "Interior, Bahia, As demonstrações oposicionistas," *DRJ*, 26 July 1849 (this article is identified as a transcription from *Mercantil*, perhaps Salvador's *Correio Mercantil*, but I have not been able to find its original source); "O Dous de Julho," *A Tolerancia*, 4 July 1849. According to L.A. Alves, Miguelista was an allusion

to 29 September 1848, the date on which the Conservative cabinet took power; 29 September is the day of Saint Michael the Archangel, "Tensos laços," 57.

13 "O sermão de Fr. Raymundo," *A Marmota*, 7 July 1849; "Carta do Dr. Manoel Jarreta a seo compadre e amigo Pantaleão da Saubara, Beco dos Peccados," *A Marmota*, 14 July 1849.

14 Corr., 12 July, *Correio da Tarde* (Rio), 19 July 1850.

15 "O Dous de Julho como passou," *O Século*, 9 July 1850.

16 "Bahia: O Dous de Julho," CM-R, 18 July 1850 (from CM-S).

17 Marjoribanks, *Travels*, 103, 41.

18 L.A. Alves, "Tensos laços," 218–24.

19 Corr., 25 June, JC, 5 July 1852. Gaspar had recently received a contract to build a new market building in Santa Bárbara to replace the sheds that authorities considered indecent, J.R.M. Pinho, *Açambarcadores*, 158. This was apparently a controversial measure, linked to the larger debate about how to manage the city food supply, personal communication, Richard Graham, 17 April 2012. For the broader context, see R. Graham, *Feeding*.

20 "Uma rusga na Bahia," *Correio da Tarde* (Rio), 23 June 1852.

21 "Os vapores 'Golphinho' e 'Amazonas,'" and "Noticias do Norte," *O Grito Nacional* (Rio), 20 June and 7 July 1852.

22 "Novos boatos aterradores – manifesta provocação do governo," *O Século*, 29 June 1852.

23 "Noticias do norte," *O Grito Nacional* (Rio), 23 July 1852.

24 "Os festejos do memoravel dia DOUS DE JULHO," *O Paiz*, 8 July 1854. In her transcription of this report, Martinez excised all of the radical liberal rhetoric, *2 de Julho*, 79–83, much as J.S. Campos had done with the 1836 *Diario da Bahia* articles (chapter 1).

25 A.R., "Dous de Julho," *O Protesto*, 2 July 1855.

26 Simão, Corr., 2 July, DP, 5 July 1853.

27 "Programa dos Festejos do Dia Dous de Julho Deste Anno," *O Século*, 29 June 1852.

28 Two exceptions that refer to only a singular allegorical float are Corr., 11 July, DRJ, 19 July 1854; and Corr., CM-R, 9 July 1864.

29 F.B. Souza, "Festas," 264. On Souza, see Sacramento Blake, *Diccionario*, 2:410–11. His role in the Instituto Histórico is noted in *Instituto*, M12–M13.

30 C.A. Tavares, *Tempos*, 113, 114.

31 Cited in J.W.A. Pinho, *História*, 535.

32 Mello Moraes Filho, *Festas e tradições*, 128; Pedro Dias d'Ar.º Pinto to President, 27 June 1853, APEBa/SACP, m. 1569.

33 Varella, *D'outros tempos*, 59–60.

34 In addition to the sources cited above, see also "Saudação aos veteranos," *O Paiz*, 6 July 1854; "Bando dos festejos ao glorioso DIA DOUS DE JULHO," *O Paiz*, 28 June 1854.

35 M. Vianna, *"...vou para Bahia,"* 188.

36 Pedro, *Diário*, 7 October 1859.

37 F.V. Vianna, *Memoria*, 348; Boccanera Junior, *Bahia historica*, 201; P.C. Silva, "Bahia," 100; P.C. Silva, "Notas," 576; Salvador, *Monumentos*, 43.

38 "Poesia composta para a noite de 1.º de Julho [de 1854] ... por Dr. Americo Basilio de Souza" (*apedido*), *Diario da Bahia*, 1 July 1858.

39 See, for instance, "Presidencia da Provincia, Expediente do dia 27 de Junho," CM-S, 4 July 1849; Ordem do Dia 18, 30 June, *Diario da Bahia*, 1 July 1858; Superior Commander to President, 28 June 1839 and 1 July 1840, APEBa/SACP, m. 3535 and 3548.

40 Wetherell, *Brazil*, 82.

41 CA to President, 1 July 1861, APEBa/SACP, m. 3399; Petition of Luiz Gonzaga Fernandes to President, 30 June 1863, APEBa/SACP, m. 1569.

42 Corr., 4 July, JC, 8 July 1862; Postscript of 4 July to Corr., 2 July, DRJ, 11 July 1862; Varella, *D'outros tempos*, 62.

43 "O Dia Dous de Julho," CM-S, 7 July 1848.

44 Antonio Dias Coelho et al. to President, 22 April 1864, APEBa/SACP, m. 1575; "Programa dos Festejos do Dia Dous de Julho Deste Anno," *O Século*, 29 June 1852; Commissões Directoras to Camara, 10 May 1853, AHMS/CFRDJ. See also "Programa do Bando, e mais festejos...," *O Guaycuru*, 27 June 1853.

45 Compare the names of the Sociedade Dois de Julho executive elected for 1852 with the list of festival directors printed on the form used to solicit donations, *O Século*, 29 July 1851; José Pedreira França to Secretary of Government, 1 May 1852, APEBa/SACP, m. 1569.

46 Directors' names are listed in Corr., 5 July, CM-R, 11 July 1855; Corr., 17 July, CM-R, 22 July 1857; "Bahia," DP, 13 July 1858; "Demonstrativo da receita e despeza com os festejos ao dia Dous de Julho no anno de 1860," *Diario da Bahia*, 22 June 1861; Corr., 15 July, JC, 21 July 1860; *Diario da Bahia*, 17 July 1861; Corr., 4 July, JC, 8 July 1862; "Bahia" (from *Jornal da Bahia*), DP, 15 July 1863.

47 "Ao distincto e ilustrado corpo eleitoral do 2.º Districto d'esta provincia," 8 July 1881, *A Bahia*, 18 July 1881. He does not appear among the members of Bahia's caucus in *Organizações*, 375.

48 F.V. Bastos, "Quando os intelectuais," 80.

49 *Estatutos*. I thank Matthew Rarey for discovering and transcribing these statutes, long presumed lost at the BN.

50 See the *despachos* on Pedro Antonio Galvão to President, 22 June 1845, 22 June 1846, APEBa/SACP, m. 1575.

51 CM-S, 26 June 1849.

52 Directors to President, c. 1847; Galdino Eustaquio de Figueiredo to President, 1 July 1847, APEBa/SACP, m. 1575. See also Antonio Dias d'Oliveira et al. to CP, 25 June 1845, APEBa/SACP, m. 6178.

53 "Parte Official," *A Marmota*, 9 May and 20 June 1849.

54 Resolução 553, 12 June 1855, CLRBa; Session of 28 June, ACD (1855), 2:276.

55 "O Pavilhão da Lapinha," *O Reverbero*, 6 August 1871; Lei 844, 3 August 1860, CLRBa.

56 *O Commercio*, 5 July 1843; Resoluções 311 and 337, 3 July and 5 August 1848, CLRBa; Corr., 11 July 1849, JC, 23 July 1849; M.J. de Almeida e Couto and Francisco Liberato de Mattos to President, 30 June 1849, AIGHBa, pasta 4, doc. 19; "Bahia," JC, 23 July 1849.

57 See the provincial budgets in CLRBa and the petitions requesting that these funds be released in APEBa/SACP, m. 1569. "A Assemblea Provincial," *O Paiz*, 6 June 1854.

58 "Falla com que o Excellentissimo Sr. Dr. Manoel Jarreta abrio a Assemblea Provincial da Marmota," *A Marmota*, 12 September 1849; "Annuncios," *O Paiz*, 3, 8, 14, and 28 June 1854; José Pedreira to Camara, 1 May 1852; Dr. Malaquias Alvares dos Santos, Leonel Estillita Fran.cº Neto, and Joaquim Ernesto de Souza to Camara, 5 May 1855; [Commissão] to Camara, 14 June 1862, AHMS/CFRDJ.

59 Annuncios, *O Mercantil*, 26 August 1848; "O Banco commercial, e o Dous de Julho," *O Guaycuru*, 1 July 1845.

60 "Demonstrativo da receita e despeza com os festejos do dia Dous de Julho no anno de 1860," *Diario da Bahia*, 22 June 1861.

61 "Programma do Bando, e mais festejos do sempre memoravel dia DOUS DE JULHO...," *O Paiz*, 23 June 1854; "Festejos de Dous de Julho: Programma do Bando, e Mais Festejos...," *Diario da Bahia*, 28 June 1858.

62 Annuncios, *O Mercantil*, 28 June 1848; CM-S, 28 June 1848; *A Marmota*, 23 June 1849.

63 Bittencourt, "Suzana," 40, 41, 47; Annuncios, *O Paiz*, 10 June 1854; Mello Moraes Filho, *Festas e tradições*, 124; Tupinamba, "Cavaquemos," *Diario da Bahia*, 2 July 1896. For later advertising for horses, see *Gazeta da Bahia*, 4 February 1880, 27 June 1886.

64 Corr., 5 July, CM-R, 11 July 1855.

65 Archbishop to Vice-President, 4 July 1854, and "O Dia 2 de Julho," *O Noticiador Catholico*, 8 July 1854; CP to Vice-President, 14 July 1854, APEBa/SACP, m. 2961; *O Noticiador Catholico*, 7 July 1855.

66 *Diario da Bahia*, 1 July 1861; Corr., 8 July, DP, 16 July 1861.

67 Corr., 1 July, *Constitucional* (Rio), 16 July 1862; "Bahia," *DP*, 18 July 1862.

68 Querino, *Bahia*, 44–61. He subsequently incorporated most of this material into "Noticia historica," 92–9.

69 *O Guaycuru*, 28 June 1845.

70 Annuncios, *O Mercantil*, 28 June 1848; CM-S, 28 June 1848; "Programma do Bando, e mais festejos…," *O Paiz*, 23 June 1854; "Festejos de Dous de Julho: Programma…," *Diario da Bahia*, 28 June 1858; Querino, "Noticia historica," 92, and *Bahia*, 51.

71 Annuncios, *A Marmota*, 26 and 27 June 1849.

72 "Dia 2 de Julho," CM-S, 5 July 1847; "Dous de Julho de 1848," CM-S, 5 July 1848; Corr., 16 July, *Correio da Tarde* (Rio), 23 July 1849; "Miscellanea," *A Tolerancia*, 15 July 1849; CM-R, 9 July 1853; "Os festejos do memoravel dia DOUS DE JULHO," *O Paiz*, 8 July 1854; John Morgan to Earl of Clarendon, 16 March 1858, PRO/FO 13, vol. 365, fol. 59v–60r.

73 "O Dia 2 de Julho," *A Marmota*, 4 July 1849; CM-S, 4 July 1849.

74 O Brasileiro, "O anniversario do Dia Dois de Julho no corrente anno," *O Paiz*, 22 July 1854; Corr., 3 July, JC, 10 July 1855. Querino mentioned fifteen battalions by name but does not indicate dates for their participation, *Bahia*, 52, and "Noticia," 92–3.

75 Corr., 2 July, JC, 8 July 1859. On the rivalries, see Bittencourt, *Longos serões*, 2:194.

76 Mello Moraes Filho, *Festas e tradições*, 131; Simão, Corr., 19 July, DP, 22 July 1853; Postscript of 3 July to Corr., 29 June, DP, 7 July 1855.

77 Bittencourt, *Longos serões*, 2:194. See also Mello Moraes Filho, *Festas e tradições*, 124. Tupinamba also recalled "penny straw hats made in the countryside," "Cavaquemos," *Diario da Bahia*, 2 July 1896.

78 P.C. Silva, "Notas," 550–1.

79 Querino, *Bahia*, 52, and "Noticia historica," 93, 99; Mello Moraes Filho, *Festas e tradições*, 124, 128; Rozendo Moniz, *Moniz Barretto*, 96. For a rare newspaper mention of this custom, see "Viva o Dia Dous de Julho de 1822," *Vinte Cinco de Julho*, 15 July 1876.

80 Vicuña Mackenna, *Paginas*, 2:305; Maximilian, *Recollections*, 3:161.

81 On Exaltado symbols, see Kraay, *Days*, 67–8; Morel, *Cipriano Barata*, 256.

82 Corr., 3 July, CM-R, 11 July 1856; Corr., 1 July, CM-R, 9 July 1857; Corr., 7 July, *Brasil Commercial* (Rio), 16 July 1868. The assessment of São Francisco is found in Corr., 7 July, DRJ, 12 July 1858.

83 *O Paiz*, 8 July 1854; "Bahia," DP, 5 July 1858; "Bahia," DP, 1 July 1864.

84 "Annuncios," *O Paiz*, 10 and 14 June 1854.

85 For accounts of these meetings, see "Programma que foi approvado pelos commandantes dos corpos patrióticos…," *O Paiz*, 28 June 1854; "Bahia," DP, 5 July 1858.

86  Corr., 2 July, JC, 8 July 1859.

87  Corr., 5 July, CM-R, 11 July 1855.

88  Assier, *Brésil*, 198–9. Rozendo Moniz also noted foreigners' surprise at the festival, *Moniz Barretto*, 98.

89  "Espelho," *Correio da Tarde* (Rio), 2 July 1857.

90  "Festejos de Dous de Julho: Programma...," *Diario da Bahia*, 28 June 1858; *Jornal da Bahia*, 4 July 1859, in "Repositório: Descrições de Festejos, Notícias de Jornais," AIGHBa, cx. 18, d. 70.

91  "Interior: Bahia, 5 de julho," DP, 19 July 1856; *O Paiz*, 6, 8, 12, and 19 July 1854; Querino, *Bahia*, 49–58, and "Noticia historica," 93–8; Varella, *D'outros tempos*, 60; Bittencourt, "Suzana," 47.

92  Repartição da Policia, CM-S, 5 July 1849; Corr., 11 July, DRJ, 19 July 1854; JC, 17 July 1856; Corr., 2 July, CM-R, 12 July 1858; Corr., 7 July, DRJ, 12 July 1858; "Provincias do Norte," *Correio da Tarde* (Rio), 9 July 1860.

93  Bittencourt, *Longos serões*, 2:194; Corr., 7 July, *Brasil Commercial* (Rio), 16 July 1858.

94  Corr., 3 July, CM-R, 11 July 1856.

95  F.B. Souza, "Festas," 263–4.

96  O Brasileiro, "O anniversario do Dia Dois de Julho no corrente anno," *O Paiz*, 22 July 1854.

97  O Brasileiro, "A festividade do Dia Dois de Julho," *O Paiz*, 14 June 1854.

98  L.A. Alves, "Tensos laços," 80. For one example of each, see "Saudação aos veteranos...," *O Paiz*, 6 July 1854; "Soneto offerecido ao batalhão patriotico da Mocidade," *O Paiz*, 6 July 1854; "Soneto offerecido ao dia Dous de Julho pelo patriotico Batalhão dos Caixeiros," *O Paiz*, 8 July 1854. For examples from 1855, see L.A. Santos, *Ao Dous de Julho*; "Viva a Nacionalisação do Commercio," *O Protesto*, 2 July 1855.

99  Corr., 5 July, CM-R, 11 July 1855 (quote); Corr., 5 July, DP, 9 July 1855; *Diario da Bahia*, 5 July 1858.

100  Gandon, *Portugueses*, 73–5, 90, 93, 119, 172; Borges, *Family*, 33; C. Teixeira, *Bahia*, 53–5.

101  President (Andréa) to Minister of Justice, 9 July 1846, APEBa/SACP, livro 690, fol. 163v.

102  CP to Vice-President, 14 July 1854, APEBa/SACP, m. 2961.

103  Postscript of 3 July to Corr., 29 June, DP, 7 July 1855.

104  A.R., "Dous de Julho," *O Protesto*, 2 July 1855; "O Dia Dois de Julho," *O Cascavel*, 2 July 1852.

105  J.N. Silva, *Satyras*, 118. On Nepomuceno, see Querino, *Bahia*, 321–30.

106  Bahia, President (Sinimbu), *Relatório* (1857): 3.

107  Corr., 7 July, DRJ, 12 July 1858; Corr., 2 July, JC, 8 July 1859.

108  C.A. Tavares, *Tempos*, 106.

109 Corr., 7 July, *Brasil Commercial* (Rio), 15 July 1858.

110 [Francisco] G[onçalves] Martins to [José Antônio] Saraiva, 29 June and 2 July [1858], AIHGB, DL 273.30, fols. 1r–2r. José Wanderley de Araújo Pinho's typewritten transcript of this letter contains a few errors; it is located in AIHGB, DL 1591.033. Neither Wanderley nor Gonçalves Martins had gone to Rio to take their seats in the senate, AS (1858). On Tibério and Messias, see Wildberger, *Presidentes*, 261–9, 337–47.

111 Corr., 7 July, *Brasil Commercial* (Rio), 15 July 1858.

112 "O Pavilhão da Lapinha," *O Reverbero*, 6 August 1871; Varella, *D'outros tempos*, 58. Amaral erred in one or more of the dates, for the acquisition of the building was complete as of 2 July 1860, so the committee must have been named in October 1859, not 1860.

113 "Demonstrativo da receita e despeza com os festejos do dia Dous de Julho no anno de 1860," *Diario da Bahia*, 22 June 1861.

114 On Tibério's politics, see the obituary in Corr., 17 December, DRJ, 22 December 1868.

115 On Amaral, see J.T. Barros, "José Álvares do Amaral," and chapter 3 of this book.

116 "Dous de Julho de 1860" (from *Jornal da Tarde*), DP, 2 July 1860.

117 That year, he did not attend the senate session, AS (1860), so it is possible that he was in Salvador for Dois de Julho.

118 *Diario da Bahia*, 1 July 1861; "Bahia," CM-R, 11 July 1861; Corr., 8 July, DP, 16 July 1861; "Bahia" (from *Jornal da Bahia*), DP, 15 July 1863.

119 Sanders, *Vanguard*, 52. See also Centeno, *Blood*, 31.

120 Querino, *Bahia*, 59, and "Noticia," 99; Varella, *D'outros tempos*, 65–6.

121 "A um sujeito que organizou um batalhão de moleques e dele se fez comandante em um ano de Dous de Julho," J.N. Silva, *Sapeca*, 91.

122 Kraay, "From Entrudo"; J.J. Reis, *Divining*, 1–31.

123 Mattoso, *Bahia, século XIX*, 205.

124 Ryan, "American Parade," and *Civic Wars*, chaps. 2, 6; Davis, *Parades*; Heron and Penfold, *Worker's Festival*, 41–79.

125 Bittencourt, *Longos serões*, 2:195; Bittencourt, "Suzana," fols. 52–3; Varella, *D'outros tempos*, 59; Tupinamba, "Cavaquemos," *Diario da Bahia*, 2 July 1896.

126 Corr., 11 July, DRJ, 19 July 1854; *Diario da Bahia*, 5 July 1858; CA to President, 3 July 1859, APEBa/SACP, m. 3394.

127 Corr., 29 June, DP, 7 July 1855. On Brainer, see Goes, "Veterano," 135–7.

128 Corr., 17 July, CM-R, 22 July 1857; *Jornal da Bahia*, 4 July 1859, in "Repositório," AIGHBa, cx. 18, d. 70.

129 Corr., 8 July, DP, 16 July 1861. On the importance of participating in Dois de Julho for caixeiros, see E.M. Reis, "Três momentos," 78–9.

130 Corr., 4 July, *JC*, 8 July 1862; Corr., 9 July, *JC*, 14 July 1863.

131 *Jornal da* Bahia, 4 July 1859, in "Repositório," AIGHBa, cx. 18, d. 70; Corr., 4 July, *JC*, 8 July 1862.

132 "Bahia" (from *Jornal da Bahia*), *DP*, 15 July 1864.

133 Corr., 8 July, *DP*, 16 July 1861.

134 "Bahia" (from *Jornal da Bahia*), *DP*, 15 July 1863.

135 Wetherell, *Brazil*, 58–60; Kraay, "Definindo," 70–2.

136 "O Dia 2 de Julho," *A Marmota*, 4 July 1849.

137 Bittencourt, *Longos serões*, 2:196. For similar recollections, see Tupinamba, "Cavaquemos," *Diario da Bahia*, 2 July 1896; and Varella, *D'outros tempos*, 62–3.

138 "Os festejos do memoravel dia DOUS DE JULHO," *O Paiz*, 8 July 1854; "Festejos do Dous de Julho: Programma do Bando, e Mais Festejos," *Diario da Bahia*, 28 June 1858; "Bahia" (from *Jornal da Bahia*), *DP*, 18 July 1862, 15 July 1863, 15 July 1864. Mello Moraes Filho also noted this change of location, *Festas e tradições*, 131.

139 "Os festejos do memoravel dia DOUS DE JULHO," *O Paiz*, 8 July 1854; O Brasileiro, "O anniversario do Dia Dous de Julho no corrente anno," *O Paiz*, 22 July 1854.

140 Corr., 14 July, *JC*, 22 July 1857.

141 Corr., 8 July, *DP*, 16 July 1861.

142 *Diario da Bahia*, 8 July 1861; *DRJ*, 19 July 1861.

143 "Noticias diversas," *A Actualidade* (Rio), 13 July 1863.

144 Corr., 15 July, CM-R, 22 July 1863. Curiously, the *Diario da Bahia* reported nothing about this incident. See its report transcribed in Corr., 9 July, *JC*, 14 July 1863.

145 Querino, *Bahia*, 59, and "Noticia," 99. P.C. Silva repeats this story, "Notas," 551.

146 Corr., 28 [*sic*] June and 1 July, *JC*, 5 July 1864.

147 Corr., 1 July, *JC*, 5 July 1864; "Bando," *O Alabama*, 1 July 1864; Corr., 1 July, CM-R, 9 July 1864.

148 Corr., 28 [*sic*] June, *JC*, 5 July 1864.

149 Corr. 2, 15 July, *JC*, 20 July 1864.

150 Corr. 1, 5 July, *JC*, 10 July 1864.

151 Corr. 1, 15 July, *JC*, 20 July 1864. On França Guerra's politics, see Campos, "Cronicas," 351.

152 "Bahia" (from *Jornal da Bahia*), *DP*, 16 July 1864.

153 Corr., 1 July, CM-R, 9 July 1864; Corr., 5 July, CM-R, 10 July 1864; Corr., 29 July, CM-R, 3 August 1864.

154 "Os festejos do memorável dia DOUS DE JULHO," *O Paiz*, 8 July 1854; Barreto, *Canto* and *Veteranos*; Doria, *Enlevos*, 131–2.

155 B.X.P. Souza, *Memorias*, 90–2; Querino, *Bahia*, 228–31.

156 Querino, *Bahia*, 52.

157 *Almanak* (1863), 295; Corr., 4 July, *JC*, 8 July 1862; Postscript of 4 July to Corr., 2 July, *DRJ*, 11 July 1862. On Carvalhal, see Kraay, "Companheiros," 145–7.

158 Society activities are described in J.A. Amaral, *Resumo*, 294–5. On the flag, see also "Bahia," *DP*, 19 July 1862.

159 "O festim da independência no presente anno," *O Reverbero*, 6 August 1871.

160 Petitions of Sociedade Veteranos da Independencia to President, ca. 1863, APEBa/SACP, m. 3802; and ca. 1864 and 1866, APEBa/SACP, m. 1575. "Estatutos da Sociedade Veteranos da Independencia," APEBa/ SACP, m. 3802; Lei 920, 14 April 1864, *CLRBa*.

161 Antônio Pereira Rebouças, Diploma de sócio correspondente, Sociedade Veteranos da Independência, 8 November 1865, BN/SM, I-3, 24, 58; "Diploma de Título de Sócio, Marechal Duque de Caxias," 1 October 1870, AIHGB, DA 3.1.21; A.B. Souza, *Duque de Caxias*, 125–38.

162 "Sociedade Veteranos," *O Alabama*, 27 March 1868; Postscript of 4 April to Corr., 1 April, *JC*, 10 April 1868.

163 Ata, Sociedade Veteranos da Independência, 13 December 1872 (copy), APEBa/SACP, m. 1575.

164 Corr., 5 July, *JC*, 10 July 1864; "Ao acaso" (folhetim), *DRJ*, 11 September 1864. See also Silva Junior, *Bravo*.

165 J.N. Silva, *Satyras*, 82–3. Other poets also lamented veterans' penury, Agrário de Souza Menezes, "Pirajá," in J.S. Menezes, *Agrário de Menezes*, 85; A.S. Menezes, *Mathilde*, 91, 142n; "O soldado," in Mendonça, *Poesias*, 118–21.

166 On heroes and the politics surrounding their commemoration, see Brunk and Fallow, eds., *Heroes*; and L. Johnson, ed., *Death*; Enders, *Vultos*, 175–234, 303–28; A.B. Fraga, *Heróis*.

167 "Dous de Julho de 1848," *CM-S*, 5 July 1848; "O Dia Dous de Julho," *CM-S*, 7 July 1848; "O Dia 2 de Julho," *A Marmota*, 4 July 1849; Ruy, *Dossier*, 221–3.

168 *A Tolerancia*, 4 July 1849, in Ruy, *Dossier*, 233n1A.

169 Domingos José Glz. Ponce de Leão to President, 8 July 1849, AIGHBa, pasta 4, doc. 19; Bahia, President, *Relatório* (1849): 49. Parliament eventually approved a pension to her, *ACD* (1850), 2:316.

170 Will of Pedro Labatut, 18 June 1848, *RIGHBa* 54 (1928): 198.

171 "O aniversario da morte do General Labatut," *O Guaycuru*, 16 September 1850; "Parte Official," *A Verdadeira Marmota*, 28 February 1852; José Marcellino dos Santos to President, 8 August 1853, APEBa/SACP, m.

3804; "Ao povo Bahiano," *O Guerreiro* (Rio), 27 July 1853; "Conclusão," *O Reverbero*, 6 August 1871; Campos, "Cronicas bahianas," 336–7. See also the notices in *O Noticiador Catholico*, 6 and 13 September 1851, 30 October and 20 November 1852, 3 September 1853.

172 Ruy, *Dossier*, 229; Querino, "Noticia," 102; Teixeira, *Bahia*, 59–61. The pilgrimage is rarely mentioned in the press, but see Corr., 21 July, *JC*, 25 July 1862.

173 Pedro, *Diário*, 9 October 1859.

174 Kraay, *Race*, 122, 127–9.

175 Vale, *Audacious Admiral Cochrane*, 139–40, 148–9, 153–6, 158, 163–4, 170–1.

176 Mendonça, *Poesias*, 162.

177 F.B. Souza, "Festas," 261; *O Alabama*, 2 July 1870.

## Chapter Three

1 On Bahia's manpower contribution to the war effort, see "Mappa da força com que cada uma das Provincias do Imperio concorreu para a Guerra do Paraguay," in Brazil, Ministério da Guerra, *Relatório* (1872). On the war and Bahia's mobilization, see Doratioto, *Maldita guerra*; Kraay, "Companheiros" and "Slavery."

2 Nabuco, *Estadista*, 658–69; Barman, *Citizen Emperor*, 193–9; Needell, *Party*, 239–49; Iglesias, "Vida," 103–12; Holanda, "Do Império," 7–10, 105–16; J.M. Carvalho, "*Clamar*", 19–32.

3 Reform and its limits are key themes in E.V. Costa, "1870–1889." On the political history of abolition see Needell, *Party*, 272–314, and "Brazilian Abolitionism"; Conrad, *Destruction*; Alonso, *Flores*. Electoral reform is analyzed by R. Graham, *Patronage*, 182–206. A general political survey is Holanda, "Do Império."

4 Kraay, *Days*, chaps. 8–9.

5 P. Calmon, *História da literatura*, 125–6; K.M.C. Silva, *O Diário*, 64, 153; Torres and Carvalho, *Annaes*, 70–62, 112, 115–16, 127; Carvalho Filho, "Jornalismo," 80, 82, 87; Bizarria, "Manuel Lopes da Silva Cardoso," 63–78.

6 Graden, *From Slavery*, 78–80, 125–8.

7 "2 de Julho," *O Santelmo*, 2 July 1879.

8 Torres and Carvalho, *Annaes*, 90, 126. This catalogue and "Catalogo dos jornaes" list other illustrated newspapers. On *Bahia Illustrada*, see also Querino, *Bahia*, 320.

9 "Bahia," *DP*, 2 July 1868; "O festim da independencia no presente anno," *O Reverbero*, 6 August 1871, note *; "Bahia" (from *Diario da Bahia*), *DP*, 2 July 1872; *Almanak* (1873).

10  *O Alabama*, 5 June 1868; Corr. 1, 7 July, JC, 21 July 1868.

11  M.<sup>el</sup> José do Conde J.<sup>or</sup> to President, ca. March 1880, APEBa/SACP, m. 1569; B.S. Thiago to Camara, 5 May 1887, AHMS/CFRDJ.

12  Julio Xavier dos Anjos, "Proposta," 12 June 1885; Pedro Augusto da S.ª and José Augusto Trigueiro Lima to Directores, 12 June 1885; Jovino Simplicio Ribeiro, "Proposta," 15 June 1886, AHMS/CFRDJ.

13  For a bid for repairing and decorating the wagons for 450$000 (US$171), see Melchiades José Garcia to Camara and Directores dos Festejos, 12 June 1885, AHMS/CFRDJ. The fireworks plan is Francisco Idilaco Bastos, "Relação e distribuição dos fogos para os festejos do dia 2 de Julho...," 19 June 1886, AHMS/CFRDJ.

14  First Secretary (Amaral), Sociedade Dois de Julho, to President, 2 June 1868, APEBa/SACP, m. 1569; Apedido, *O Alabama*, 25 August 1869.

15  B.S. Thiago to Camara, 5 May 1887, AHMS/CFRDJ. For a similar donation, see Fernando A[ntunes] da Luz to Camara, 12 June 1886, AHMS/CFRDJ.

16  M.<sup>el</sup> José do Conde J.<sup>or</sup> to President, ca. March 1880, APEBa/SACP, m. 1569; Corr., 27 June, JC, 16 July 1880.

17  Antonio [illegible] Oliveira et al. to Secretary of Direção dos Festejos do dia 2 de Julho, 30 June 1888, AHMS/CFRDJ.

18  "Dous de Julho," *Gazeta da Bahia*, 22 June 1881; "Dois de Julho," *O Monitor*, 22 June 1881.

19  "Bahia" (from *Diario da Bahia*), DP, 8 July 1885.

20  "Atenção," *O Alabama*, 29 March 1870. His immediate interest, of course, was to secure commissions for the celebrations of the Paraguayan War's end.

21  Freyre, *Order*, 70–1.

22  CA to Adjutant General, 18 July 1877 (copy), and to President, 31 August 1877, APEBa/SACP, m. 3446. For a patriotic battalion's request for a band, see Leocadio Ozorio da Fonseca et al. to Direcção dos Festejos de Dous de Julho, 17 May 1885, AHMS/CFRDJ; for a request to play in the theatre's salon, see Manager to President, 29 June 1847, APEBa/SACP, m. 4073.

23  Campos, *Musica*, 5, 6–9; Diniz, "Glória," 127–9; Campos, "Tradições," 526–9; Querino, *Bahia*, 289; Marques, *Feiticeiro*, 77–80.

24  Schwebel, *Bandas*, 11.

25  "Banda de Musica," *O Monitor*, 15 June 1878; for another such announcement, see "À commissão dos festejos de Dois de Julho," *O Monitor*, 26 June 1880.

26  M. Alves, "Música"; Querino, *Bahia*, 164.

27  J.J. Reis, *Death*, 76, 79; Mattoso, *To Be a Slave*, 213–20; Kraay, "Urban Slavery," 281–7.

28 Querino, *Bahia*, 290. One contemporary recalled that the Chapadista replaced barbers' ensembles at the Rio Vermelho *jangadeiros'* festival, A. Garcia, "Festa," 283.

29 CA to President, 8 January 1879, APEBa/SACP, m. 3442.

30 Superior Commander to CP, 27 March 1869, APEBa/SACP, m. 6458.

31 "Bahia" (from *Diario da Bahia*), *Jornal do Recife*, 10 July 1876.

32 Lt. Col. Commander, Sixteenth Infantry, to CA, 7 July 1877, APEBa/SACP, m. 3446.

33 CA to President, 3 July 1880; 2nd Lt. Adjutant to Maj. *Fiscal*, Ninth Infantry, 3 July 1880 (copy), APEBa/SACP, m. 3441; "Festejos do Dous de Julho," *Gazeta da Bahia*, 4 July 1880.

34 CA to President, 6 July 1880, APEBa/SACP, m. 3463.

35 CA to President, 1 July 1885, APEBa/SACP, m. 3447; Subdelegado, São Pedro, to CP, 3 July 1885; CP to President, 6 July 1885, APEBa/SACP, m. 2976.

36 *Instituto Academico*, 1 July 1874; "Festejos do Dous de Julho," *Gazeta da Bahia*, 14 June 1882; "Revista Noticiaria," *Instituto Academico*, 16 July 1874.

37 "Sociedade Veteranos," *O Alabama*, 5 June 1869. On Santos's nickname, see Varella, *D'outros tempos*, 61.

38 "Bahia" (from *Diario da Bahia*), DP, 10 July 1879; Lt. Col. Commander to CA, 6 July 1880, APEBa/SACP, m. 3441; Varella, *D'outros tempos*, 61; Varella, *Da Bahia que eu vi*, 13–17; Kraay, "Companheiros," 142–4, 146, 152, 156, 158; Querino, *Bahia*, 177.

39 João Felippe de Santiago to Directores dos Festejos do 2 de Julho, 1 June 1888, AHMS/CFRDJ.

40 *O Alabama*, 4 July 1865; Bahia (from *Jornal da Bahia*), DP, 10 July 1870; Boccanera Junior, *Bahia historica*, 294.

41 "Para os Batalhões de Artes e Officios," *Correio da Bahia*, 19 June 1877.

42 *Diario de Noticias*, 11 June 1880.

43 Heron and Penfold, *Workers' Festival*, 41–79; Davis, *Parades*, 113–53.

44 Querino, *Bahia*, 59; "O festim da independencia no presente anno," *O Reverbero*, 6 August 1871; Varella, *D'outros tempos*, 61.

45 "Aviso Patriotico," *O Alabama*, 8 July 1865; "Annuncio: Regimento – União Brasileira," *O Alabama*, 6 July 1867; "Annuncios," *O Alabama*, 4 July 1868.

46 "Annuncios," *O Alabama*, 28 May 1870; "Allocução dirigida ao batalhão patriotico – Defensores de Pirajá – pelo seu comandante Antonio Olavo da França Guerra," *O Alabama*, 9 July 1870; Campos, "Cronicas," 351; Antonio Olavo da França Guerra, "A levada dos carros triumphaes à Lapinha," *Vinte Cinco de Junho*, 15 July 1876.

47 "Os festejos do 2 de Julho," *O Socialista*, 21 July 1882.

48 CA to President, 26 June 1888, APEBa/SACP, m. 3464; "Dous de Julho," *Diario do Povo*, 3 July 1889; Querino, *Bahia*, 223. Roque Jacinto's occupation is mentioned in Albuquerque, *Jogo*, 171.

49 "Batalhão Conde d'Eu," *Gazeta da Tarde*, 25 May 1885; CA to Dr. Augusto Ferreira França, 4 July 1885, AHMS/CFRDJ.

50 Mulhall, *Handbook*, 136.

51 *O Alabama*, 3 May 1866, 7 May 1867.

52 President of Direcção dos Festejos do dia 2 de Julho to President, 28 April 1873, APEBa/SACP, m. 1569; José Luiz d'Almeida Couto to President, 28 April 1876, APEBa/SACP, m. 1569; *O Alabama*, 5 May 1868; "Emblema," *Correio da Bahia*, 12 June 1877.

53 Moniz, *Moniz Barretto*, 93–4; Querino, "Noticia historica," 88; Varella, *Da Bahia do Senhor*, 96.

54 Mello Moraes Filho, *Festas e tradições*, 124; "Annuncios," *O Paiz*, 2 May 1854; "Collocação do distico annunciador dos festejos do sempre memoravel Dous de Julho," *Diario da Bahia*, 28 April 1858; Folhetim, *Diario da Bahia*, 11 May 1858. In his manuscript notes on the festival's history, José Wanderley de Araújo Pinho mentioned a 19 May 1846 "notice [*dístico anunciador*]" for the upcoming festival on the Terreiro de Jesus, but he did not record the source, "Festa de Dois de Julho," AIHGB, DL 1591.33, fol. 4.

55 Varella, *D'outros tempos*, 58.

56 Câmara Cascudo, *Dicionário*, 563–4; H. Vianna, *Folclore brasileiro*, 59.

57 Tupinamba, "Cavaquemos," *Diario da Bahia*, 2 July 1896.

58 Hadfield, *Brazil*, 22.

59 "Programma dos festejos do 2 de Julho," *O Monitor*, 28 June 1881; "Bando," *Gazeta da Bahia*, 29 June 1882; "Programma do bando annunciador dos festejos de 2 de julho d'este anno," *Gazeta da Bahia*, 28 June 1885; Querino, "Noticia historica," 90.

60 "Programma dos festejos do immorredouro – Dous de Julho – neste anno," *O Reverbero*, 6 August 1871; Corr., 29 June, JC, 9 July 1871; "Bando de Dois de Julho," *Diario da Bahia*, 1 July 1886, in "Repositório: Descrições de Festejos, Notícias de Jornais," AIGHBa, cx. 18, d. 70. Querino published a poem by Antonio Alves de Carvalhal, read during the 1882 bando, "Noticia historica," 91–2, and *Bahia*, 49–51. Another example of a poem "written for the purpose of inviting the Bahian populace to celebrate 2 July with splendor" is Rabello, "Bando," *Obras*, 200–3.

61 "Bahia. – S. Salvador, 30 de Junho de 1866," DRJ, 5 July 1866; *O Alabama*, 2 July 1867.

62 Corr., 12 July, DRJ, 18 July 1870; *O Alabama*, 2 July 1871; "Bahia" (from *Jornal da Bahia*), DP, 5 July 1872.

63 Mello Moraes Filho, *Festas e tradições*, 126; Corr., 30 June, DRJ, 5 July 1866; Corr., 30 June, JC, 7 July 1866; *O Alabama*, 5 July 1866; "Bahia" (from *Jornal da Bahia*), DP, 9 July 1866; Corrs. 1 and 2, 11 July 1866, JC, 18 July 1866.

64 "Bahia," *Jornal do Recife*, 13 July 1880; *Diario da Bahia*, 1 July 1881, in "Repositório," AIGHBa, cx. 18, d. 70; Lt. Col. Commander, Ninth Infantry, to CA, 28 and 30 June 1880, APEBa/SACP, m. 3441.

65 *O Alabama*, 6 July 1867.

66 "Festejos do Dous de Julho," *Correio da Bahia*, 24 April 1874 (NARS, M-121, roll. 43); Corr., 6 July, JC, 21 July 1874; "Bahia" (from *Correio da Bahia*), DP, 7 July 1874; "Bahia" (from *Correio da Bahia*), *Jornal do Recife*, 7 July 1874.

67 Querino, *Bahia*, 59, "Noticia historica," 99; Moniz, *Moniz Barretto*, 96. In 1877, a *cronista* praised Dantas for his role in restoring the "famous festival" in 1874, "Chronica," *O Monitor*, 8 July 1877.

68 "O festim da independencia no presente anno," *O Reverbero*, 6 August 1871; "Festejos do 2 de Julho," *Gazeta da Bahia*, 4 July 1883.

69 Moniz, *Moniz Barretto*, 97. Marques also notes the 2 p.m. arrival, *Feiticeiro*, 239.

70 *O Alabama*, 4 July 1868.

71 For standard accounts, see "Interior: Noticias, Bahia," DRJ, 16 July 1867; *O Alabama*, 9 July 1870; "Interior: Noticias do Norte, Bahia: 10 de Julho," *Jornal da Tarde* (Rio), 13 July 1870; Corr., 12 July, JC, 23 July 1871; "Noticias do Norte" (from *Jornal da Bahia*), DRJ, 16 July 1871; Corr., 6 July, JC, 21 July 1874; "Noticiario" (from *Correio da Bahia*), DRJ, 10 July 1874; *Gazeta de Noticias* (Rio), 11 July 1876; "Dous de Julho," *Gazeta da Bahia*, 4 July 1886; Corr., 9 July, JC, 19 July 1887.

72 Corr., 14 July, JC, 18 July 1867.

73 *O Alabama*, 5 July 1866; "Interior: Noticias, Bahia" (from *Jornal da Bahia*), DRJ, 16 July 1867; Corr., 14 July, JC, 18 July 1867.

74 *O Alabama*, 6 July 1871; Bahia, President, *Relatório*, 17 October 1871.

75 "Bahia" (from *Jornal da Bahia*), DP, 7 July 1873.

76 J.B. Castro, "Guarda Nacional," 298.

77 CA to President, 30 June 1871, APEBa/SACP, m. 3453.

78 "Convite," *Correio da Bahia*, 21 June 1877; "Festejos do Dous de Julho" (*apedido*), *Correio da Bahia*, 22 June 1878; "Dois de Julho," *O Monitor*, 22 June 1881.

79 "Bahia," *Jornal do Recife*, 2 July 1869; "Bahia," *Jornal do Recife*, 30 June 1877; "Bahia" (from *Diario da Bahia*), DP, 10 July 1879; "Direcção dos festejos do 2 de julho," *Gazeta da Bahia*, 28 June 1881; "Bahia," DP, 8 July 1882.

80 "Festejos do 2 de Julho," *Gazeta da Bahia*, 4 July 1883.

81 "Festejos officiaes," *O Alabama*, 6 July 1867; "Interior: Noticias, Bahia" (from *Jornal da Bahia*, 2 July), DRJ, 16 July 1867. See also *O Alabama*, 4 July 1868; "La vae verso," *O Alabama*, 6 July 1871.

82 Querino, "Noticia historica," 101–2.

83 *O Alabama*, 5 July 1866; Corr., 14 July, JC, 18 July 1867. Mello Moraes Filho also noted the cheers' importance, *Festas e tradições*, 131.

84 On Carvalhal, see Kraay, "Companheiros," 145–7.

85 Petition of Marcellino Fernandes Japiassú et al. to President, 3 July 1866, APEBa/SACP, m. 2962.

86 Delegado, 1º Distrito (Amaral), to CP, 3 July 1866, APEBa/SACP, m. 2962.

87 *O Alabama*, 5 July 1866, 6 July 1867, 9 July 1870.

88 Mello Moraes Filho, *Festas e tradições*, 131; Marques, *Feiticeiro*, 249.

89 Corr., 5 July, JC, 11 July 1865.

90 *O Alabama*, 4 July 1868, 9 July 1870.

91 "O festim da independencia no presente anno," *O Reverbero*, 6 August 1871, note *.

92 "O palacete," *O Reverbero*, 6 August 1871.

93 "Programma," *O Reverbero*, 6 August 1871.

94 "O festim da independencia no presente anno" and "O palacete," *O Reverbero*, 6 August 1871.

95 Watanabe-O'Kelly, "Festival Books."

96 *O Alabama*, 6 July 1871; "Programma," *O Reverbero*, 6 August 1871.

97 "Bahia" (from *Diario da Bahia*), DP, 2 July 1872.

98 "Offertas," RIGHBa 4.12 (June 1897): 295.

99 "Palanque dos festejos do dia 2 de Julho de 1874," foto 5023, MFN 21364, AIGHBa. This image also appeared in *Estado da Bahia*, 16 June 1943.

100 "Festejos do 2 de Julho," *Correio da Bahia*, 28 June 1878; "Dous de Julho," *O Monitor*, 4 July 1878.

101 J.A. Amaral, *Resumo*, 293.

102 "Provincial News: Bahia," *The Anglo-Brazilian Times* (Rio), 24 July 1865; *O Alabama*, 11 July 1865; Corr., 8 July, CM-R, 23 July 1866; *O Alabama*, 10 July 1867; Corr., 10 July, CM-R, 24 July 1868; "Bahia," DP, 2 July 1868 and 2 July 1869; *O Alabama*, 8 July 1871; "La vae verso," *O Alabama*, 13 July 1871; "O festim da independencia no presente anno," *O Reverbero*, 6 August 1871; "Bahia" (from *Diario da Bahia*), DP, 13 July 1872; "Dous de Julho," *O Monitor*, 10 July 1877; "Revista do Interior," DRJ, 17 July 1877; "Bahia," *Jornal do Recife*, 16 July 1877; "Bahia" (from *Diario da Bahia*, 11 July 1878), DP, 11 July 1878; "Festejos de 2 de Julho," *Gazeta da Bahia*, 4 July 1880; "Festejos do Dous de Julho," *Gazeta da Bahia*, 7 July 1880;

"Festejos do Dois de Julho," *Diario da Bahia*, 7 July 1881, in "Repositório," AIGHBa, cx. 18, d. 70; "Levada dos Carros," *Gazeta da Bahia*, 4 July 1882; "Provincias do Norte: Bahia," *Gazeta de Noticias* (Rio), 14 July 1883; "Festejos do Dous de Julho," *Gazeta da Bahia*, 8 July 1886; "Programa dos Festejos do Dois de Julho," *Diario da Bahia*, 4 July 1888, in "Repositório," AIGHBa, cx. 18, d. 70; "Bahia," DP, 10 July 1888; "Programma dos festejos do Dous de Julho," *Diario da Bahia*, 4 July 1889.

103   "Diario da Bahia," *Diario da Bahia*, 5 July 1889.

104   "O festim da independencia no presente anno," *O Reverbero*, 6 August 1871.

105   "Bahia" (from *Jornal da Bahia*), DP, 13 July 1872.

106   Corr., 17 July, JC, 28 July 1868.

107   *O Alabama*, 9 July 1868.

108   "Romaria," *O Alabama*, 19 July 1865; "Interior: Noticias do Norte," CM-R, 16 July 1867; "Interior: Noticias, Bahia," DRJ, 16 July 1867; Corr., 10 July, CM-R, 24 July 1868; "Bahia," *Jornal do Recife*, 15 July 1868; "Bahia," *Jornal do Recife*, 13 July 1871; "Conclusão," *O Reverbero*, 6 August 1871.

109   "Programa dos festejos do dia 2 de Julho," *Gazeta da Bahia*, 1 July 1879; "Romaria a Pirajá," *Gazeta da Bahia*, 11 July 1880.

110   "Romaria a Pirajá," *Gazeta da Bahia*, 11 July 1885; "Romaria patriotica," *Diario da Bahia*, 16 July 1889.

111   *Reporter*, 14 September 1889.

112   Querino, "Noticia historica," 105; A. Vianna, *Casos*, 105; Varella, *D'outros tempos*, 66.

113   H. Vianna, "Dois de Julho de bairros," 275–7.

114   O Itapagipense, "O Dois de Julho da Penha" (comunicado), *O Paiz*, 12 July 1854.

115   CP to President, 11 July 1857, APEBa/SACP, m. 2962.

116   Directores to President, 28 July 1860, APEBa/SACP, m. 1569. H. Vianna cites this document, "Dois de Julho de Bairros," 277.

117   Guilherme José Pereira Caldas to President, 25 June 1864, APEBa/SACP, m. 1569; *O Alabama*, 1 July 1864. Two years later, the Brotas organizers also invited the president to attend, Commissão to President, 5 and 12 July 1866, APEBa/SACP, m. 1569.

118   "Dois de Julho de Itapoã," *Gazeta da Bahia*, 17 July 1885; "Dois de Julho de Itapoan," *Gazeta da Bahia*, 18 July 1885.

119   For the raising of poles, see *O Alabama*, 15 May 1869 (Brotas); *O Alabama*, 4 June 1870 (rua dos Artistas, Santo Antônio além do Carmo); "Dous de Julho da Penha," *O Monitor*, 22 July 1876; "Dous de Julho dos meninos da parochia de Nossa Senhora dos Mares," *Gazeta da Bahia*, 11 July 1880; "Dous de julho de Itapagype," *Gazeta da Bahia*, 8 July 1886.

For *bandos anunciadores*, see "Bando," *O Monitor*, 16 July 1876 (Brotas); "Bando," *Correio da Bahia*, 20 July 1878 (Tororó); "Bando," *O Monitor*, 21 July 1878 (Itapagipe); "Bando," *O Monitor*, 23 July 1881 (Itapagipe); "Dous de Julho de Itapoã," *Gazeta da Bahia*, 15 July 1885.

120 Furriel André Lúcio de Meirelles, "Parte," 11 July 1864 (copy), APEBa/SACP, m. 2993; "Programma dos festejos do dia 2 de julho de Brotas," *Diario da Bahia*, 8 July 1868.

121 "Dous de Julho," *O Monitor*, 10 August 1876; "Programma dos festejos do 2 de Julho de Itapagipe," *O Monitor*, 30 July 1881.

122 H. Vianna, "Dois de Julho de Bairros," 283.

123 For a few examples, see "Dous de Julho de Brotas," *O Alabama*, 7 July 1868; "Programa dos festejos do dia 2 de julho de Brotas," *Diario da Bahia*, 8 July 1868; *O Alabama*, 12 July 1870 (Brotas); *O Alabama*, 23 July 1870 (Santo Antônio); *O Alabama*, 27 July 1870 (Itapagipe); "Programma do 2 de Julho de Itapagipe," *Gazeta da Bahia*, 29 July 1886.

124 "Batalhão patriotico Defensores do Occidente," *O Alabama*, 15 July 1871; "2 de Julho do Jacaré" (*apedido*), *Correio da Bahia*, 26 July 1878; "Batalhão patriótico Artistas Nacionaes" (*apedido*), *Correio da Bahia*, 27 July 1878.

125 *O Alabama*, 19 July 1865.

126 Subdelegado, Penha, to CP, 26 July 1864, APEBa/SACP, m. 6236; *O Alabama*, 12 July 1870; Delegado to President, 13 July 1864, APEBa/SACP, m. 2993.

127 "Bando," *Gazeta da Bahia*, 16 July 1881; "Correspondencia Particular," *Diario de Noticias*, 7 July 1880; "A lei da conscrição," *O Monitor*, 26 August 1880.

128 *O Sentinella do Povo*, 26 July 1879.

129 Geisler, "Calendar Conundrum," 19; White, "National Days," 58–9, 70.

130 *O Alabama*, 30 June 1866; "Carta do compadre da cidade ao compadre da roça," *O Alabama*, 2 August 1866; Corr., 6 July, *JC*, 18 July 1866; *O Alabama*, 6 July 1867.

131 "Bahia" (from *Jornal da Bahia*), *DP*, 8 July 1867.

132 Corr., 28 June, *CM-R*, 4 July 1868; Postscript, 4 July, to Corr., 1 July, *CM-R*, 13 July 1868.

133 Corr., 30 June, *CM-R*, 7 July 1867.

134 *O Alabama*, 9 July 1870. See also Corr., 10 July, *JC*, 17 July 1870.

135 *Bahia Illustrada*, 30 June 1867; "O dia Dous de Julho de 1823," *O Alabama*, 2 July 1870; "O dia Dous de Julho," *O Monitor*, 2 July 1878.

136 "Dous de Julho," *Gazeta da Bahia*, 2 July 1882; "Dous de Julho," *Gazeta da Bahia*, 2 July 1885.

137 Three newspapers quoted this passage from the *Diario da Bahia*: "Provincia da Bahia," *A Republica* (Rio), 14 July 1872; "Revista das Provincias:

Bahia," *Correio do Brazil* (Rio), 14 July 1872; "Bahia," *Jornal do Recife*,
9 July 1872.

138  "O dia 2 de Julho," *Gazeta da Bahia*, 1 July 1883. See also "Festejos do
     Dous de Julho," *Gazeta da Bahia*, 4 July 1880; and "Festejos do Dous de
     Julho," *Gazeta da Bahia*, 4 July 1884.

139  "Bahia" (from *Gazeta da Bahia*, 5 July), *DP*, 15 July 1887.

140  "Bahia" (from *Gazeta da Bahia*), *DP*, 16 July 1889; "Dous de Julho," *Diario
     do Povo*, 3 July 1889; "Festejos do dia 2 de julho," *Diario da Bahia*, 7 July
     1889; "Bahia," *DP*, 5 and 9 July 1889.

141  Moniz, *Moniz Barretto*, 94.

142  Corr., 1 July, CM-R, 13 July 1868; *O Alabama*, 4 July 1868.

143  Corr. 1, 7 July, *JC*, 21 July 1868.

144  On 1868's politics, see Kraay, "Year."

145  *O Alabama*, 7 July 1869.

146  Corr., 17 June, *JC*, 1 July 1869.

147  *O Alabama*, 23 June 1869.

148  Corr., 14 July, *JC*, 27 July 1869.

149  *O Alabama*, 2 July 1869; Corr., 14 July, *JC*, 27 July 1869.

150  *O Alabama*, 14 July 1869.

151  *O Alabama* laid out the politics behind the two battalions' creation in
     early June, when they were first mooted, *O Alabama*, 5 June 1869; it
     published the invitation to join the Caxias battalion on 2 July 1869. On
     Argolo, see Lago, *Generais*, 11–18.

152  Corr., 14 July, *A Reforma* (Rio), 20 July 1869; Postcript of 16 July to Corr.,
     14 July, *JC*, 27 July 1869; *O Alabama*, 7 July and 25 August 1869; "Bahia,"
     *DP*, 2 July 1869.

153  Postscript of 16 July to Corr., 14 July, *JC*, 27 July 1869; Corr., 14 July,
     *A Reforma* (Rio), 20 July 1869.

154  Corr., 14 July, *A Reforma* (Rio), 20 July 1869.

155  "Bahia," *Jornal do Recife*, 15 July 1869; Apedido, *O Alabama*, 25 August
     1869. This may be a reference to Corr., 22 July, *JC*, 6 August 1869.

156  *O Alabama*, 18 August 1869. I have not been able to locate the articles or
     correspondence to which *O Alabama* referred.

157  "Interior: Bahia" (from *Jornal da Bahia*, 4 and 9 July), *DRJ*, 14 July 1870.

158  M.G.A. Leal, *Manuel Querino*, 203–57.

159  "Bahia," *DP*, 4 July 1875; "Uma reminiscencia historica: o 2 de Julho em
     1875" (from *Diario de Noticias*, 1 July 1875), *A Manhã*, 2 July 1920; "Bahia"
     (from *Jornal da Bahia*, 4 July), *DP*, 10 July 1875; "Bahia" (from *Diario de
     Noticias*), *Jornal do Recife*, 10 July 1875.

160  Moniz, *Moniz Barretto*, 80; Querino, "Noticia historica," 104–5 (Querino
     misdates the incident to 1873).

161 Barros, "Á margem" (1934), 377–8; Campos, "Tradições," 458–62 (quote at 458).

162 On the garrison's composition, see Kraay, "Cotidiano," 241.

163 CA to President, 5 June 1875 (*reservado*), APEBa/SACP, m. 3434. Barros Falcão's dim view of Frias Villas is also clear from his official report on the incident, published two decades later in "3 de julho de 1875," *Diario de Noticias*, 3 July 1896.

164 Alexandre Augusto de Frias Villar, "Ao publico desta capital e desta provincia," *A Nação* (Rio), 13 July 1875.

165 *JC*, 11 July 1875; "Transcrição: Os tumultos da Bahia," *A Reforma* (Rio), 11 July 1875; "Bahia" (from *Jornal da Bahia*, 4 July), DP, 10 July 1875; "Bahia" (from *Diario de Noticias*), *Jornal do Recife*, 10 July 1875. Castro's death was reported in "Provincia da Bahia" (Gazetilha), *JC*, 18 July 1875.

166 Campos, "Tradições," 459–60. The poet may have been Aureliano Lisboa, whose sonnet Querino transcribed, "Noticia historica," 104–5.

167 "3 de julho de 1875," *Diario de Noticias*, 3 July 1896.

168 *JC*, 11 July 1875; "Transcripção: Os tumultos da Bahia," *A Reforma* (Rio), 11 July 1875; Campos, "Tradições," 461; "3 de julho de 1875," *Diario de Noticias*, 3 July 1896. The assessment of this as an act of cannibalism appeared in P.R., "Acontecimentos da Bahia" (*apedido*), *JC*, 15 July 1875.

169 "Imprensa das provincias: Os acontecimentos da Bahia (*Diario da Bahia*)," *A Reforma* (Rio), 14 July 1875; "3 de julho de 1875," *Diario de Noticias*, 3 July 1896; "Bahia" (from *Jornal da Bahia*, 4 July), DP, 10 July 1875. Campos provides the number of mourners but incorrectly dates the funeral to the 3rd, "Tradições," 460. The Conservative criticism appears in P.R., "Acontecimentos da Bahia" (*apedido*), *JC*, 15 July 1875. The Liberal leaders' telegram was published under the title "Especial para o *Jornal do Commercio*," 3 July, *JC*, 4 July 1875. A telegram that wrongly announced Frias Villar's death also reported an improbable 30,000 people at João Albino's funeral. See "Telegramas," 5 July, *JC*, 6 July 1875; and the correction regarding Frias Villar, "Bahia" (Gazetilha), *JC*, 7 July 1875. For the *Diario da Bahia*'s location, see Dourado, "Praça," 215.

170 "3 de julho de 1875," *Diario de Noticias*, 3 July 1896.

171 Campos, "Tradições," 462; telegram received by Companhia Brazileira de Navegação a Vapor, 10:40 am, 5 July 1875, *JC*, 6 July 1875.

172 *JC*, 11 July 1875.

173 "Tropa" (Gazetilha), *JC*, 5 July 1875; "Telegramas," *JC*, 10 July 1875.

174 "Bahia" (from *Jornal da Bahia*, 14 July), DP, 19 July 1875. The date of the return is not clear from this article.

175 See the telegrams dated 3 July, published in "Acontecimentos da Bahia," *DRJ*, 11 July 1875.

176 "O apoio do povo," *A Reforma* (Rio), 13 July 1875.

177 "Imprensa das provincias: Acontecimentos da Bahia," *A Nação* (Rio), 13 July 1875; "Imprensa das provincias: Conservadores e liberaes" (from *Correio da Bahia*), *A Nação* (Rio), 15 July 1875. This latter article also appeared in *JC*, 15 July 1875.

178 P.R., "Acontecimentos da Bahia" (*apedido*), *JC*, 15 July 1875.

179 "Acontecimentos da Bahia," *JC*, 16 July 1875.

180 "Chronica," *O Monitor*, 8 July 1877.

181 Beattie, *Tribute*, 64–98; Kraay, "Reconsidering," 23–30; K.M.C. Silva, *O Diário*, 34.

182 "A lei da conscripção," *O Monitor*, 26 August 1880.

183 Campos, "Tradições," 462. In his brief remarks on post-1865 Dois de Julho celebrations, Querino failed to perceive this change. He accurately transcribed the patriotic battalions' 1877 parading order and route but, perhaps thinking about earlier festivals, he added National Guard and army battalions. Compare Querino, "Noticia historica," 100–1; and the program and report in "Dous de Julho," *Correio da Bahia*, 26 June 1877; "Dous de Julho," *Correio da Bahia*, 4 July 1877. Campos first pointed out this error, "Cronicas," 347.

184 CA to President, 3 July 1880, APEBa/SACP, m. 3441. For another later recollection of this incident, see "2 de Julho," *O Santelmo*, 2 July 1879.

185 Marques, *Feiticeiro*, 241.

## Chapter Four

1 See the regular coverage of the students' celebrations in DP and *Jornal do Recife.*

2 Titara, *Obras*, 7:175–6, 224–6, 243–5; 8:251–3.

3 Bello, "Diário," 144; Amando Gentil, "Saudação ao Dois de Julho," acampamento em Entre Rios, 2 July 1865, AIHGB, DL 242.002.

4 *O Observador Constitucional* (São Paulo), 8 July 1831.

5 Marques, *Vida*, 128.

6 On Sete de Setembro, see Kraay, *Days.*

7 Kertzer, *Ritual*, 69–75.

8 J.J. Reis, *Rebelião*, chaps. 15–16.

9 CP to President, 27 June 1844, APEBa/SACP, m. 2952; CP to Delegado, 3° Distrito, 27 June 1844, APEBa/SACP, m. 5693, fol. 206v–7r. See also D.O. Araújo, *Tutu*, 124. For slave conspiracies reported at the time of festivals, see J.J. Reis, *Rebelião*, 71, 102, 125, 244–5, 421–42.

10 R. Graham, "Free African Brazilians," 42–7.

11 *O Guaycuru*, 1 July 1845. For another example, see José Pedro Xavier Pinheiro, "Ao memoravel dia Dous de Julho: Canto Triunfal," *O Commercio*, 10 July 1843.

12 "Bahia" (from *Jornal da Bahia*), DP, 5 July 1872.

13 Corr., 4 July, JC, 8 July 1862; Acting CP to President, 3 July 1862, APEBa/SACP, m. 3139–26. For another example, see CP to President, 4 July 1859, APEBa/SACP, m. 3139–18.

14 The most thorough analysis of these manifestations is Guerra Filho, "Antilusitanismo."

15 P.O.C. Cunha, "Fundação," 382–91.

16 Mello Moraes Filho, *Festas e tradições*, 125; J.W.A. Pinho, *Cotegipe*, 190.

17 Carta da Bahia, 21 July, CM, 28 July 1855; CP to Presdent, 11 July 1857, APEBa/SACP, m. 2962; L.A. Alves, "Tensos laços," 125–6; J.W.A. Pinho, *História*, 536.

18 *O Alabama*, 2 July 1868.

19 Barroso, *Oração*, 12.

20 "Dous de Julho," *Gazeta da Bahia*, 2 July 1882; Varella, *D'outros tempos*, 66.

21 Marques, *Feiticeiro*, 84.

22 "Provincial," *The Anglo-Brazilian Times* (Rio), 15 July 1879.

23 J.J. Reis, "Tambores," and *Divining*, chap. 1; J.T. Santos, "Divertimentos."

24 Assier, *Brésil*, 199.

25 Corr., 4 July, JC, 8 July 1862.

26 Delegado (José Álvares do Amaral) to CP, 3 July 1866, APEBa/SACP, m. 2962.

27 *O Alabama*, 7 July 1868.

28 Moniz, *Moniz Barretto*, 102; J.T. Santos, *Dono*, 39.

29 Varella, *D'outros tempos*, 64–6; "Antigamente era assim...," *Diario da Bahia*, 10 June 1943.

30 Mello Moraes Filho, *Festas e tradições*, 126.

31 *O Alabama*, 4 July 1865.

32 *O Alabama*, 4 July 1865.

33 On caboclos in Candomblé, see J.T. Santos, *Dono*; Pares, *Formation*, 242, 396–9.

34 *O Alabama*, 9 July 1868.

35 *O Alabama*, 7 July 1866.

36 Delegado (Amaral) to CP, 3 July 1866, APEBa/SACP, m. 2962.

37 Subdelegado, Sé Parish, to CP, 3 July 1887, APEBa/SACP, m. 6252.

38 Varella, *D'outros tempos*, 57.

39 "A pedido," *O Alabama*, 15 July 1871.

40 Um Francez, na Bahia, "Correspondencia," CM-S, 5 July 1848. The writer did not indicate where this incident took place.

41 "Leiam! Leiam!" *O Alabama*, 4 July 1868; "A pedido," *O Alabama*, 7 July 1868.

42 "Resposta ao dialogo do caturra Luppe e C...," *Diario da Bahia*, 8 July 1868. On diplomats' whiteness, see Dávila, *Hotel Trópico*, 3–4 and passim. On caixeiros' status in a slightly later period as a group of mostly white men who nevertheless felt socially disadvantaged, see M.A.S. Santos, *Casa*, chap. 5.

43 *O Noticiador Catholico*, 12 July 1851; "Programa dos Festejos do Dia Dous de Julho Deste Anno," *O Seculo*, 29 June 1852; *O Noticiador Catholico*, 10 July 1852; Corr., 3 July 1855, JC, 10 July 1855; Corr., 3 July, CM, 11 July 1856; Sociedade Dois de Julho to President, Salvador, 28 August 1853, APEBa/SACP, maço 1575.

44 Mello Moraes Filho, *Festas e tradições*, 131.

45 Corr. 1, 15 July, JC, 20 July 1864.

46 Corrs. 1 and 2, 15 July, JC, 20 July 1864. On these manumissions, see Kraay, "White Slaves."

47 Mattoso, *To Be a Slave*, 164–5.

48 Varella, *D'outros tempos*, 65.

49 Acting CP to President, 4 July 1862, APEBa/SACP, m. 3139–26.

50 Corr., 21 July, DRJ, 27 July 1862. The correspondent first reported this incident in the 4 July postscript to Corr., 2 July, DRJ, 11 July 1862. Correspondents for the JC, the DP, the CM, and *Constitucional* (Rio) did not mention this incident in their letters. The BN's microfilm, digitized for the Hemeroteca Digital Brasileira, was photographed from the Real Gabinete Português de Leitura's copy of the DRJ, which, by 2017, had deteriorated to the point of being unavailable to researchers. To my knowledge, there are no other collections of the DRJ.

51 The description of the Caixeiros' uniform is from the stage directions to C.A. Tavares, *Tempos*, 114.

52 J. Ferreira, "Por hoje," 215.

53 "Interior," DRJ, 18 July 1869; "Bahia," *Jornal do Recife*, 8 July 1869; "Provincial," *The Anglo-Brazilian Times* (Rio), 23 July 1869; *O Alabama*, 7 July 1869; Corr., 22 July, JC, 6 August 1869.

54 Conrad, *Destruction*, 90–105; Pena, *Pajens*; Needell, *Party*, 272–314.

55 Petition of Jorge Luis Schwind Alv.ª to Presdent, 17 September 1869, APEBa/SACP, m. 3673; Corr., 1 August, JC, 24 August 1869. On this early phase of abolitionism, see Castilho, *Slave Emancipation*, chap. 1.

56 "Interior: Noticias do Norte, Bahia, 10 de Julho," *Jornal da Tarde* (Rio), 13 July 1870; "Bahia" (from *Diario da Bahia*), *Jornal do Recife*, 10–11 July 1870; "Interior: Bahia" (from *Jornal da Bahia*), DRJ, 14 July 1870; *O Ala-*

*bama*, 9 July 1870. The 1870s manumissions are also noted by J.T. Santos, *Dono*, 40; L.A. Fonseca described Chico Santos (who died in 1871) as a pioneering abolitionist, *Escravidão*, 256–9. Bittencourt anachronistically mentions Chico Santos's involvement in manumissions in her novel, set in 1861, "Suzana," 53.

57 "Interior: noticias do Norte," *Jornal da Tarde* (Rio), 4 July 1871; *O Rever-bero*, 6 August 1871; "Bahia," *Jornal do Recife*, 13 July 1871; *O Alabama*, 15 July 1871.

58 "Provincia da Bahia" (Gazetilha), *Jornal do Recife*, 8 July 1874.

59 "Norte do Imperio," DRJ, 11 July 1876; "Bahia" (from *Diario da Bahia*, 4 July), *Jornal do Recife*, 10 July 1876; "Bahia," *Jornal do Recife*, 10 July 1877; Querino, "Noticia historica," 100.

60 "Festejos do Dous de Julho," *Gazeta da Bahia*, 9 July 1882.

61 L.A. Fonseca, *Escravidão*, 245. Statistics on the 1871–74 manumissions are compiled from the "Chronica nacional," *Folhinha Laemmert* (Rio), 1873–76.

62 "Sociedade Libertadora Sete de Setembro," *Correio da Bahia*, 10 September 1878; "Sociedade Libertadora 'Sete de Setembro,'" *O Monitor*, 11 September 1878. R.T.C. Silva, "Sociedade Libertadora Sete de Setembro," 302–3, 306–8.

63 L.A. Fonseca, *Escravidão*, 134–5.

64 Brito, *Abolição*, 62, 94, 95–116; Graden, *From Slavery*, 159–96; R.T.C. Silva, "Caminhos," 222–98.

65 For examples, see "Dois de Julho" and Tic, "Zun Zun" (folhetim), *Gazeta da Tarde*, 1 July 1885; Amélia Rodrigues, "Ainda não" (originally published in 1887), in *Mulheres*, ed. L.A. Alves, 167.

66 *Diario de Noticias*, 3 July 1884. Graden stresses the conservative orientation of Bahia's abolitionist societies, *From Slavery*, 146–7. See also Conceição, "Educar."

67 Kraay, *Days*, 330–9.

68 *O Faisca*, 27 June, 4 and 11 July 1886.

69 Corr., 24 June, JC, 24 June 1887.

70 Corr., 9 July 1887, JC, 19 July 1887.

71 Aristides Novis to Barão de Cotegipe, 16 May 1888, AIHGB, lata 918, doc. 23.

72 Albuquerque, *Jogo*, 127–30; and *Algazarra*, 89–92. See also Brito, *Abolição*, 18, 265n1.

73 *Diario da Bahia*, 13 May 1888, in K.M.C. Silva, *O Diário*, 118–19. She incorrectly describes this program as an editorial.

74 Telegrama, 12:30 pm, *Jornal do Recife*, 17 May 1888; Corr., 14 May, *Jornal do Recife*, 18 May 1888; Novis to Cotegipe, 16 May 1888, AIHGB, lata 918, doc. 23.

75 Albuquerque, *Jogo*, 129.

76 Albuquerque, *Algazarra*, 92–3.

77 "Festividades: a grande festa nacional da Bahia" (from *Diario de Noticias*, 14 May), *DP*, 23 May 1888; "Festividades: festas da abolição na Bahia" (from *Diario de Noticias*, 22 May), *DP*, 29 May 1888.

78 *Diario da Bahia*, 15 May 1888, cited in Brito, *Abolição*, 18.

79 Albuquerque, *Jogo*, 129.

80 "Festividades: a grande festa nacional na Bahia" (from *Diario de Noticias*, 16 May), *DP*, 25 May 1888.

81 Among others, see E. Silva, "Sobre versos"; and R.F. Moraes, "Abolição."

82 Corr. 2, 17 March, *JC*, 24 March 1868.

83 *O Alabama*, 8 August 1868; Corr. 1, 17 March, *JC*, 24 March 1868. On Captain Fausto, see Kraay, "From Entrudo."

84 Corr., 1 July, *JC*, 11 July 1888. See also "Dous de Julho," *Correio da Manhã*, 3 July 1888.

85 Querino, "Noticia historica," 101n7; untitled handbill, AIGHBa, pasta 44, doc. 5-K. A similar theme appeared in "Dous de Julho de 1888," *O Domingo*, 15 July 1888.

86 "Dous de Julho de 1888," *O Domingo*, 15 July 1888.

87 "Dous de Julho," *Diario da Bahia*, 2 July 1889.

88 W. Fraga, *Crossroads*, 139–60; Mata, "Treze de Maio," chap. 1; Medrado, *Terra*, 66–8.

89 R. Moniz, *Moniz Barretto*, 93.

90 The following discussion draws in a general way on DaMatta's argument about the house and the street, the former representing patriarchal order and the latter dangerous disorder, *Casa*.

91 "Festejos do Dous de Julho," *Gazeta da Bahia*, 1 July 1884. For other examples, see "Programa dos Festejos do Dia Dous de Julho Deste Anno," *O Seculo*, 29 June 1852; "Programa do Bando, e mais festejos," *O Guaycuru*, 27 June 1853; "Festejos de Dous de Julho: programma…," *Diario da Bahia*, 28 June 1858; "Programma dos festejos do immorredouro – Dous de Julho – neste anno," *O Reverbero*, 6 August 1871; "Bahia," *DP*, 2 July 1872.

92 Acting CP to President, 7 July 1862, APEBa/SACP, m. 3139–26; "Bahia," *DP*, 11 July 1874; "Bahia" (from *Jornal da Bahia*, 4 July), *DP*, 10 July 1876; "Bahia" (from *Diario da Bahia*), *DP*, 10 July 1879; "Bahia" (from *Diario da Bahia*, 4 July), *DP*, 10 July 1883; "Dous de Julho," *Gazeta da Bahia*, 4 July 1886.

93 Corr., 13 July, *DRJ*, 18 July 1868. For similar assertions, see Corr., 14 July, *JC*, 18 July 1867; and Corr., 6 July, *JC*, 21 July 1874; C.A. Tavares, *Tempos*, 106.

94  Corr., 9 July, *JC*, 19 July 1887. For a similar assessment, see "Bahia" (from *Diario da Bahia*), *DP*, 8 July 1885.

95  "Edital," 1875, quoted in Querino, "Noticia historica," 90, and *Bahia*, 48.

96  For the United States, see Ryan, *Civic Wars*, 67, 244–51.

97  Assier, *Brésil*, 198.

98  Wetherell, *Brazil*, 19–20.

99  Corr., 9 July, *JC*, 19 July 1887; Bittencourt, *Longos serões*, 2:195; Bittencourt, "Suzana," 39. These customs were also noted by Mello Moraes Filho, *Festas e tradições*, 126; Marques, *Feiticeiro*, 239–40; Moniz, *Moniz Barretto*, 97; Varella, *D'outros tempos*, 58; Maria Joaquina Pires Bulcão da Cruz Rios, interviewed in "Antigamente era assim …," *Diario da Bahia*, 10 June 1943.

100  See the advertising in *Diario da Bahia*, 18 June 1865 (APEBa/SJ/IT 07/ 2957/07); *Correio da Bahia*, 14 June 1872; *O Monitor*, 11 May 1878; *Gazeta da Bahia*, 13 June 1883.

101  *Gazeta da Bahia*, 22 June 1884.

102  *Pequeno Jornal*, 28 June 1890. Other advertisements that mentioned straw hats appeared in *Correio da Bahia*, 14 June 1878; and *Pequeno Jornal*, 21 June 1892.

103  *Gazeta da Bahia*, 26 June 1883, 22 June 1884.

104  Simão, Corr., 2 July, *DP*, 5 July 1853; Corr., 14 July, *JC*, 18 July 1867; Tupinamba, "Cavaquemos," *Diario da Bahia*, 2 July 1896; Dunham, "Journal," 119 (quote).

105  Bittencourt, *Longos serões*, 2:195; "O Pavilhão da Lapinha," *O Reverbero*, 6 August 1871.

106  Bittencourt, *Longos serões*, 2:193–5; Bittencourt, "Suzana," 40 (quote), 41–6. See also R. Moniz, *Moniz Barretto*, 102; Querino, *Bahia*, 58, and "Noticia historica," 97; and "Bahia" (from *Jornal da Bahia*, 4 July), *DP*, 10 July 1875.

107  R. Moniz, *Moniz Barretto*, 92; Mello Moraes Filho, *Festas e tradições*, 131; Varella, *D'outros tempos*, 65; Rios, interviewed in "Antigamente era assim…," *Diario da Bahia*, 10 June 1943.

108  *O Alabama*, 29 June 1864.

109  "Hymno Patriotico Dous de Julho," BN/Mus., A-I-74ms; "Hymno 2 de Julho," BN/Mus., M784.7, B-I-14a (from an unidentified issue of *Bahia Illustrada*).

110  Marques, *Feiticeiro*, 243–5.

111  "A lei da conscripção," *O Monitor*, 26 August 1880; Assier, *Brésil*, 198.

112  Petition of Alumnos do Externado Normal to President, 19 June 1875, APEBa/SACP, m. 1569; M.A.P. Ribeiro, *Faculdade*, 80.

113  Marques, *Feiticeiro*, 237.

114 Corr., 9 July, *JC*, 19 July 1887.

115 Corr., 8 July, *DP*, 16 July 1861.

116 Hadfield, *Brazil*, 22.

117 *O Espectador*, 7 July 1845; CM-S, 7 July 1848.

118 Corr., 4 July, *JC*, 8 July 1862.

119 Marques, *Feiticeiro*, 249.

120 Ribeiro, *Faculdade*, 138–9; Ruy, *História da Câmara*, 294; "Festejos do 2 de Julho," *Jornal de Noticias*, 3 July 1889, in "Repositório: Descrições de Festejos, Notícias de Jornais," *AIGHBa*, cx. 18, d. 70.

121 *Bahia Illustrada*, 11 July 1867; *O Alabama*, 9 July 1870, 6 July 1871.

122 For increased patrols, see Acting Subdelegado, Sé Parish, to CP, 28 June 1861, APEBa/SACP, m. 6234. On the pickpockets, see *O Alabama*, 7 July 1868.

123 *O Alabama*, 8 July 1871.

124 *O Alabama*, 4 and 9 July 1868 (quote), 9 July 1870, 6 July 1871.

125 Assier, *Brésil*, 199.

126 See the rulings on petitions of Francisco Ignacio do Nacim.to and Joaquim Joze da Costa to CP, ca. June 1852, APEBa/SACP, m. 6403.

127 Marques, *Feiticeiro*, 238.

128 Subdelegado, Pilar, to CP, 9 July 1869; Antonio Alves Joaquim, Parte, 2 July 1869, APEBa/SACP, m. 6240; Postura 74, in Salvador, *Posturas*, 18.

129 A. Vianna, *Casos*, 104–5.

130 *O Alabama*, 13 June 1868 (advertising), 9 July 1870, 6 July 1871. See also *O Alabama*, 7 July 1869.

131 Petition of Saturnino Vieira de Moura Carvalho to Camara, ca. 1841, AHMS/CFRDJ.

132 *O Alabama*, 9 July 1868; Corr., 10 July, *JC*, 17 July 1870.

133 Barman, *Brazil*, 217–42.

134 See the summary of this point in Eakin, *Becoming*, 17–18, 87–9. Key works on twentieth-century regionalism include Albuquerque Jr., *Invention*; Weinstein, *Color*; Blake, *Vigorous Core*; Oliven, *Tradition Matters*; Garfield, *In Search*.

135 "O Dia Dous de Julho," *O Commercio*, 3 July 1843.

136 "Dous de Julho!" and "O Dia Dous de Julho" (communicado), *O Guaycuru*, 1 July 1845; "O anniversario de Dous de Julho em 1846," *O Guaycuru*, 4 July 1846.

137 "Bahia, 2 de Julho," CM-S, 3 July 1840; Redacção, CM-S, 1 July 1847; "O Dia Nacional da Bahia, o Dia Dous de Julho," CM-S, 18 June 1849.

138 Editais, CM-S, 30 June 1840, 26 June 1841.

139 Edital, *O Guaycuru*, 6 June 1846; Camara to President, 16 June 1847, 7 June 1848, APEBa/SACP, m. 1400.

140 "O dia 2 de julho" (transcribed from *Jornal da Bahia*), DP, 11 July 1857; "O Dous de Julho de 1823 e um dos seus bravos em 1854" (comunicado), *O Paiz*, 15 July 1854; untitled editorial, *Diario da Bahia*, 1 July 1858.

141 "O Dous de Julho," *O Alabama*, 1 July 1864.

142 C.A. Tavares, "Ao dia Dous de Julho," in *Minhas poesias*, 74. For much the same interpretation, see "Ao grande 2 de Julho," *Correio da Tarde* (Rio), 2 July 1859.

143 *O Alabama*, 2 July 1869. For a similar statement, see "O 2 de Julho de 1823," *O Alabama*, 2 July 1870. For the early twentieth century, this broader theme is analyzed by R.C.N. Leite, *Rainha*.

144 *O Alabama*, 2 July 1871. Similar themes appeared in the 1875 bando and the 1873 sermon, "Edital," in Querino, "Noticia historica," 89, and *Bahia*, 47–8; R.M.S. Barroso, *Oração*, 16–17.

145 *O Alabama*, 2 July 1867.

146 Edital, 23 June, *Diario da Bahia*, 27 June 1868; "Viva o Dia Dous de Julho de 1823!" *Vinte Cinco de Junho*, 15 July 1876.

147 Edital, 28 June, DP, 2 July 1871.

148 Edital, 28 June, *Jornal do Recife*, 9 July 1881. Similar themes appeared in "Dois de Julho," *Diario de Noticias*, 1 July 1884.

149 *O Alabama*, 1 July 1865, 2 July 1868. See also the 1867 bando, published in Corr., 30 June, JC, 6 July 1867; "Bahia," DP, 1 July 1869.

150 "O Directorio do Batalhão Patriotico Academico aos seus collegas," *Instituto Acadêmico*, 1 July 1874.

151 "Dous de Julho," *O Monitor*, 2 July 1876; "Dous de Julho," *O Futuro* (Rio), 2 July 1881.

152 *Correio da Bahia*, 4 July 1877, 2 July 1878; "Dous de Julho," *Gazeta da Bahia*, 2 July 1879; "A Bahia e o 2 de Julho," *Gazeta da Bahia*, 2 July 1880; "Dous de Julho," *Gazeta da Bahia*, 2 July 1881 (quote).

153 I examine this issue in Kraay, *Days*, 294–7. On these movements, see Maxwell, *Conflicts*; Furtado, *Manto*; G.L. Leite, *Pernambuco 1817*; Mosher, *Political Struggle*, 9–40; E.C. Mello, *Outra Independência*, 25–63.

154 "Dous de Julho," *O Alabama*, 2 July 1867. See also *O Alabama*, 2 July 1870, in which the years since independence are described as "the time of liberty, about which Tiradentes dreamed so much." For a similar approach, see the 1881 bando, "Dous de Julho," *Gazeta da Bahia*, 1 July 1881.

155 Reynaldo Casimiro, "Dous de Julho de 1885," *Almanach Litterario e de Indicações*, 20 January 1889.

156 "Dous de Julho," *Gazeta da Bahia*, 2 July 1879.

157 "Camara municipal," *Correio da Bahia*, 23 June 1877.

158 "Festejos do Dous de Julho," *Gazeta da Bahia*, 27 June 1880.

159 *A Marmota*, 30 June 1849.

160  Chasteen, "Prehistory," 35–6. On *lundu*'s popularity, see Bittencourt, *Longos serões*, 2:52.
161  Abreu, *Império*, 103–6.

## Chapter Five

1  *Diario da Bahia*, 1 July 1861.
2  Corr., 8 July, DP, 16 July 1861; *Diario da Bahia*, 8 July 1861.
3  Corr., 8 July, DP, 16 July 1861. The *Diario da Bahia* noted the upcoming production of this play on 1 July 1861.
4  Corr., 15 July, JC, 19 July 1861.
5  Moniz, *Moniz Barretto*, 101; Querino, "Noticia historica," 102; Boccanera Júnior, *Teatro na Bahia*, 164–5.
6  Bahia, President, *Relatório* (1864), *Anexo* 3.
7  Vicuña Mackenna, *Paginas*, 2:305; Wilberforce, *Brazil*, 86. For contemporary images of the brightly coloured theatre, see Athayde, ed., *Bahia*, 47–8, 63. For other contemporary descriptions, see Maximilian, *Recollections*, 3:121; Champagnac and Olivier, *Brasil*, 20; Mulhall, *Handbook*, 122; Naeher, *Excursões*, 102.
8  Boccanera Júnior, *Teatro na Bahia*, 60; Affonso Ruy, *História do teatro*, 85–6.
9  "Os Festejos do Dia Dous de Julho," CM-S, 6 July 1840.
10  Ruy, *História do teatro*, 41n24; Boccanera Júnior, *Teatro na Bahia*, 151. The original source for the 1840s prices is an undated document, "Condições para o fim de conseguir-se no Theatro de S. João as representações das Companhias Nacional e de Cantores Italianos," APEBa/SACP, m. 4072.
11  Bittencourt, *Longos serões*, 2:192
12  A.D. Reis, *Cora*, 92–3, 126, 171.
13  Boccanera Júnior, *Teatro na Bahia*, 123; Ruy, *História do teatro*, 37; Neves, *De La Traviata*, 72–3, 195.
14  Campos, "Cronica," 323–4 (quote at 324). On theatre parties, see Neves, *De La Traviata*, 177–90; Boccanera Júnior, *Teatro na Bahia*, 154–5, 178–9; J.S. Menezes, *Agrário*, 147–55. For an account of one such party's disruptive activities, see "Triumpho dramatico na noite de 2 de dezembro," *O Alabama*, Salvador, 15 December 1864; for a literary portrayal, see Marques, *Familia*, 132–5.
15  On the heat, see Bittencourt, *Longos serões*, 2:192; on social mixing, see Bahia, President, *Relatório* (1846), 35.
16  Corr., 6 October, CM-R, 12 October 1854. See also L.A. Alves, "Tensos laços," 129; Neves, *De La Traviata*, 68–9.

17 Avé-Lallement, *Viagem*, 1:147. See also Spix and Martius, *Viagem*, 2:292.

18 Avé-Lallement, *Viagem*, 1:147; "Os Festejos do Dia Dous de Julho," CM-S, 6 July 1840; A[mbrosio] Ronzi, "Chronica theatral" (folhetim), CM-S, 7 July 1849. See also "O Dia 2 de Julho," *A Marmota*, 4 July 1849; Wetherell, *Brazil*, 71-2.

19 For a description of the São Pedro, see Pedro, *Diário*, 10 October 1859.

20 J.G. Sousa, *Teatro*, 1:279-80; Ruy, *História do teatro*, 45 (quote), 88; Querino, "Theatros," 128; Boccanera Júnior, *Teatro na Bahia*, 60-1.

21 The best introduction is Neves, *De La Traviata*.

22 Wetherell, *Brazil*, 71; Johnson, *Journals*, 254; Scully, *Brazil*, 351.

23 Kist, "Tragédia," 75-7.

24 On Realism, see S.C.M. Souza, *Noites*.

25 M.S. de Mello to President, 8 May 1826 (typescript); Ignacio Accioli de Cerqueira e Silva to President, 18 February 1837, APEBa/SACP, m. 4072.

26 Bahia, President, *Relatório* (1844): 18.

27 Bahia, President, *Relatório* (1848): 40-1.

28 Bahia, President, *Relatório* (1861): 95; (1 September 1861): 30; (1870): 28.

29 Souza, *Noites*, 25-6, 67-73, 231, 269; F.V. Bastos, "Quando os intelectuais," 25-36, 42.

30 *O Cosmopolita*, 3 November 1861, quoted in Passos, *Agrário de Menezes*, 103.

31 Bahia, President, *Relatório* (1855): 49; J.W.A. Pinho, *Cotegipe*, 265; Francisco Justiniano da C.ª Rebello to President, 19 November 1856, APEBa/SACP, m. 4073.

32 Bahia, President, *Relatório* (1854): 39 (quote); (1855): 49; Querino, "Theatros," 122.

33 Corr., 15 April, JC, 21 April 1857; Bahia, President, *Relatório* (1857): 126; C.A. Tavares, *Elogio*, 3; *Pareceres* 131 (ca. October 1858) and 248 (19 November 1858), APEBa/SL, livro 147, fols. 316r, 368r-v.

34 Bahia, President, *Relatório* (1865): 17.

35 Bahia, President, *Relatório* (1 September 1861): 30-1 (quote at 31); (1870): 28.

36 Bahia, President, *Relatório* (1869): 51-2; (1871): 53; (1874): 234; (1876): 151; (1879): 16-17; (1880): 17; (1882): 62; (1886): 34. On itinerant opera companies, see Moseley, *Notes*, 77; C. Teixeira, *Bahia*, 181-3.

37 On the cultural value attributed to opera, see Aguilar, "National Opera," 83-94. On opera in Rio, see V.B. Freire, *Rio de Janeiro*; Giron, *Minoridade*.

38 On thefts, see Delegado Inspector do Theatro to CP, 3 May 1844, APEBa/SACP, m. 2952; A.D. Reis, *Cora*, 50; CP to President, 18 April 1855, APEBa/SACP, m. 3139-15.

39 While there are numerous allusions to these theatre regulations, such as the debate about whether *pretos* or *pretas* could enter the building, no copy of them is known to exist.

40 CP to President, 9 June 1882, APEBa/SACP, m. 2972; Parte geral, Corpo de Polícia, 30 November 1857, APEBa/SACP, m. 3011–1.

41 CP to Administrador do Theatro Publico (Inácio Acioli), 22 October 1836 (copy); Administrador (Inácio Acioli) to CP, 30 September 1837 (copy); Administrador (Inácio Acioli) to President, 4 October 1837, APEBa/SACP, m. 4072. This issue has been analyzed by Neves, *De La Traviata*, 123–54; Boccanera Júnior, *Teatro na Bahia*, 152–3; and F.V. Bastos, "Quando os intelectuais," 11–12.

42 Domingos Alves Pinto to CP, 28 June 1845, APEBa, m. 6403.

43 J.N. Silva, *Satyras*, 10.

44 For examples, see "Festejos do Dous de Julho: Programma," *Diario da Bahia*, 28 June 1858; "Programma do Dous de Julho," *Diario da Bahia*, 27 June 1861; *Diario da Bahia*, 29 June 1868; "Dous de Julho," *Diario de Noticias*, 1 July 1886.

45 "Condições com que o Sñr. Ignacio Accioli de Cerqueira e Silva deve receber a administração do Theatro de S. João...," 9 July 1836, APEBa/SACP, m. 4072; Boccanera Júnior, *Teatro na Bahia*, 158; Bahia, President, *Relatórios* (1857), *Anexo*; (1859), *Anexos*; (1872): 21.

46 "Bahia," *DP*, 9 July 1872; "Dous de Julho," *Correio da Bahia*, 4 July 1877.

47 Angelo da Costa Ferreira to President, 27 June 1840; Joaquim José de Araújo to President, 23 June 1841, APEBa/SACP, m. 4072.

48 CM-S, 9 April 1839, 16 September 1841, 4 December 1841.

49 "O Dous de Julho vae a expirar," *O Alabama*, 9 July 1870.

50 "Os Festejos do Dia Dous de Julho," CM-S, 6 July 1840; Corr., 3 July, JC, 10 July 1855; Corr., 5 July, JC, 10 July 1864.

51 "Bahia," *DP*, 10 July 1888.

52 Postscript of 4 July to Corr., 1 July, CM-R, 13 July 1868 (quote).

53 Corr., 7 July, *Brasil Commercial* (Rio), 15 July 1858.

54 "Conta do que despendeo o Thesoureiro d'esta Repartição...," 5 October 1864, APEBa/SACP, m. 2978.

55 F.B. Souza, "Festas," 265.

56 Kraay, *Days*, 212–13.

57 L.A. Alves, "Tensos Laços," 38.

58 CP to Minister of Justice, 8 July 1846, APEBa/SACP, livro 5696–2, fol. 190r–v; "Theatro de S. João," *O Commercio*, 30 June 1843. On Brazil's anthems, see Lira, *História*.

59 Compare the programs and reports on the 1861 and 1882 galas: "Theatro de S. João," *Diario da Bahia*, 1 July 1861; *Diario da Bahia*, 4 July 1861;

"Bahia," CM-R, 11 July 1861; "Theatro S. João," *Gazeta da Bahia*, 2 July 1882; "Festejos do Dous de Julho," *Gazeta da Bahia*, 4 July 1882. The folklorist is P.C. Silva, "Galeria," 68. See also F.B. Souza, "Festas," 265.

60 Corr., 8 July, DP, 16 July 1861; C.A. Tavares, *Tempos*, 117; C.A. Tavares, *Elogio*, 18.

61 "Theatro S. João," *Correio da Bahia*, 2 July 1878.

62 "Theatro S. João," *Gazeta da Bahia*, 1 July 1879, 1 July 1880, 2 July 1882, 2 July 1886; *Diario de Noticias*, 3 July 1886.

63 "Theatro de S. João," *O Commercio*, 30 June 1843.

64 President (Andréa) to Minister of Justice, 9 July 1846, APEBa/SACP, livro 690, fol. 164r–v; CP to Minister of Justice, 8 July 1846, APEBa/SACP, m. 5696–2, fol. 190v.

65 Alves, "Tensos laços."

66 President (Andréa) to Minister of Justice, 9 July 1846, APEBa/SACP, livro 690, fol. 164r–v.

67 L.A. Alves, "Tensos laços," 79–80.

68 "Dia 2 de Julho," CM-S, 5 July 1847; Corr., 5 July, JC, 10 July 1864; "Bahia," DP, 15 July 1864.

69 *Astrea* (Rio), 7 September 1830; "Dia 2 de Julho," CM-S, 5 July 1847; "O Dia Dous de Julho," CM-S, 7 July 1848.

70 Letter from O Moderador, CM-S, 23 June 1841. I do not know whether this play was performed.

71 "Dia 2 de Julho," CM-S, 5 July 1847; "O Dia Dous de Julho," CM-S, 7 July 1848; Letter from O Bahiano, *O Mercantil*, 1 July 1848.

72 *Diario da Bahia*, 29 June 1868; Corr., 3 July, JC, 10 July 1855; "Bahia" (from *Diario da Bahia*), *Jornal do Recife*, 8 July 1869.

73 Boccanera Júnior, *Teatro na Bahia*, 180; "Theatro S. João," *Gazeta da Bahia*, 1 July 1879, 1 July 1880, 2 July 1882; "Festejos do Dous de Julho," *Gazeta da Bahia*, 9 July 1882. See also Neves, *De La Traviata*, 198–9.

74 *Raphael* (DP, 9 July 1872); *A virgem do mosteiro* (*Gazeta de Notícias* [Rio], 11 July 1876); *O colar de ouro* (*Correio da Bahia*, 2 July 1878); *Periquito* ("Bahia," DP, 8 July 1885); Manoel Joaquim Pinheiro Chaves's *A morgadinha de Val-Flor* (*Gazeta da Bahia*, 2 July 1886); "Bahia," *Jornal do Recife*, 13 July 1871.

75 "Bahia," DP, 10 July 1888; "Noticiario," *Correio da Manhã*, 3 July 1888.

76 Kist, "Tragedia," 84, 90, 91; J.G. Sousa, *Teatro*, 1:169–87; Faria, *Idéias*, 19–83 (quotes at 63); Enders, *Vultos*, 113–24, 141–9.

77 Kist, "Tragédia," 77–9, 92–4; Azevedo, "O Drama," 95; Faria, *Idéias*, 27–9, 43–9.

78 Paragraph 14, Lei 662, 31 December 1857, CLRBa; Boccanera Júnior, *Teatro na Bahia*, 159–60; Ruy, *História do teatro*, 69–74; Ruy, "Conservatório

Dramático," 183–8; J.S. Menezes, *Agrário*, 273–80; L.A. Alves, "Tensos laços," 299–303; F.V. Bastos, "Quando os intelectuais," 43–55.

79 A.S. Menezes, *Discurso*, 4–5, 17 (quote), 18–19.

80 L.A. Alves, "Tensos laços," 9–25, and, on playwrights, 308–9.

81 Boccanera Junior, *Theatro nacional*, 403–4; Boccanera Júnior, *Teatro na Bahia*, 172. Filgueiras gives the date of this play as 1865 in "Biographia," 261–2.

82 Boccanera Júnior, *Teatro na Bahia*, 113; Passos, *Agrário*, 74n1.

83 Corr., 3 July, CM-R, 11 July 1856. For a summary of the plot, see the advertisement in *Periodico dos Pobres* (Rio), 5 September 1854.

84 Corr., 4 July, *JC*, 8 July 1862.

85 Corr., 11 July, *DRJ*, 19 July 1866.

86 A.S. Menezes, *Mathilde*. On this play's reception in Bahia, see F.V. Bastos, "Quando os intelectuais," 85.

87 "Theatro de S. João," *Bahia Illustrada*, 7 July 1867. On the play's reception, see Corr., 14 July, *JC*, 18 July 1867.

88 *O Alabama*, 4 December 1868. On Fonseca and this play, see Boccanera Junior, *Theatro nacional*, 316–17.

89 Corr., 5 July, *JC*, 10 July 1864; Macedo, "Amor"; A.J.R. Costa, *Pedro*.

90 Boccanera Júnior, *Theatro nacional*, 398.

91 Cordeiro, *Prólogo*. This play was performed (and praised by the press) in Bahia, Pernambuco, and the author's native Paraíba, Sacramento Blake, *Diccionario*, 1:145.

92 A.J.R. Costa, *Cantos*, 5–21.

93 Biographical information on them is found in Sacramento Blake, *Diccionario*, 1:20–2; 1:205–6; 2:135–7; 2:394–5; Boccanera Junior, *Theatro nacional*, 103–17, 391–3, 395–6, 402–4.

94 J.S. Menezes, *Agrário*, 24–6, 68–74, 304; Passos, *Agrário de Menezes*, 30–2, 96, 100; F.V. Bastos, "Quando os intelectuais," 64–101.

95 A.S. Menezes, preface to *Calabar*, x.

96 Filgueiras, "Biographia," 260–2.

97 J.S. Menezes, *Agrário*, 15, 137–8.

98 For a criticism of this assessment, see Passos, *Agrário*, 119.

99 A.J.R. Costa, "Dous de Julho," 25r, 33v–34r.

100 A.J.R. Costa, "Dous de Julho," 41r, 59r.

101 A.J.R. Costa, "Dous de Julho," 68v, 75v, 76v.

102 The Biblioteca Nacional acquired this play in 1884, J.G. Sousa, *Teatro*, 2:351. For a time in the twentieth century, the manuscript was lost, but it has since been found; recent theatre historians have therefore not looked for it and repeat assertions that the play has disappeared: Passos, *Agrário*, 124n2; Kist, "Tragédia," 105; L.A. Alves, "Tensos laços," 304. J.S. Menezes also did not have access to this play, *Agrário de Menezes*, 78, 170.

103 A.S. Menezes, "Dia," passim (quotes at 76v, 97r, 103v).
104 "Conservatorio dramatico. Sessão de 23 de maio de 1858," *Jornal da Bahia*, 25 May 1858.
105 Kist, "Tragédia," 111–12.
106 C.A. Tavares, *Tempos*, passim (quote at 24).
107 Filgueiras Filho, *Legenda*, 24, 35, 57, 75.
108 C.A. Tavares, *Elogio*, 9, 16.
109 For an analysis of Titara's footnotes, see J.W.A. Pinho, "Guerra."
110 C.A. Tavares, *Tempos*, 49.
111 I.A.C. Silva, *Memorias*, 4:440–2; Nobrega, *Facsimile*, 165.
112 Parecer, João Alves Portela, quoted by L.A. Alves, "Tensos laços," 304; Passos, *Agrário*, 153–4.
113 A.J.R. Costa to Franklin Doria, Natiba, 23 March 1856, quoted in L.A. Alves, "Tensos laços," 337.
114 A.S. Menezes, "Dia," 31r, 48r, 98r.
115 C.A. Tavares, *Tempos*, 12; see also 14, 44, 48, 50; and C.A. Tavares, *Elogio*, 11.
116 C.A. Tavares, *Elogio*, 16.
117 Kist, "Tragédia," 104; Sayers, *Negro*, 137–64; Brookshaw, *Race*, 21–4. An exception to this tendency is A.S. Menezes's *Mathilde*, in which Jorge is not just a loyal slave, but also the mouthpiece for anti-slavery messages, 43–9, 133–5n13.
118 A.S. Menezes, "Dia," 55r.
119 A.J.R. Costa, "Dous de Julho," 38v; A.S. Menezes, "Dia," 73r. References to the black troops' involvement appear in I.A.C. Silva, *Memorias*, 3:398, 4:55–6; and Titara's *Paraguaçu*, *Obras*, 4:47, 65; 5:92, 238. On Gonçalves, see Kraay, *Race*, 103, 135–6, 138, 224.
120 Treece, *Exiles*; Ricupero, *Romantismo*, 153–78. A.J.R. Costa considered making the protagonist into an Indian, to Doria, Natiba, 23 March 1856, in L.A. Alves, "Tensos laços," 337.
121 A.J.R. Costa, "Dous de Julho," 13r–14r (quote 13r), 30r–1r (quotes at 30v, 31r), 60r, 75v.
122 C.A. Tavares, *Elogio*, 5, 6.
123 Kraay, *Days*, 237–8.
124 A.S. Menezes, "Dia," 62r–4v (quote at 63v); Reis and Aguilar, "'Carne'"; M.P. Aguiar, *Abastecimento*, 61–73. For the context of food market regulations, see R. Graham, *Feeding*; J.R.M. Pinho, *Açambarcadores*.
125 A.S. Menezes, "Dia," 23v, 55r.
126 A.S. Menezes, "Dia," 65r–v.
127 Corr., 7 July, *DRJ*, 12 July 1858; M.C. Garcia, "Discurso," 57.
128 A.S. Menezes, "Dia," 65v–66r.

129 Filgueiras Sobrinho, *Legenda*, 18–20; A.J.R. Costa, "Dous de Julho," 49r–51v; A.S. Menezes, "Dia," 69r–v.

130 C.A. Tavares, *Tempos*, 88, 107–9.

131 A.S. Menezes, "Dia," 76v–80v, 83v.

132 Contemporaries noted this for A.S. Menezes's "Dia," L.A. Alves, "Tensos laços," 305.

133 A.S. Menezes, "Dia," 14r.

134 A.S. Menezes, "Dia," 52r, 102v.

135 Filgueiras Sobrinho, *Legenda*, 60.

136 A.J.R. Costa, "Dous de Julho," 75v–76v.

137 Boccanera Júnior, *Teatro na Bahia*, 103–4; Querino, *Artistas*, 63–65n1; B.H. Amaral, *Historia da Bahia*, 193–4; F.B. Barros, "Á margem" (1934), 376–7; J.A. Amaral sets the riot in the theatre, *Resumo*, 390.

138 CP to President, 25 September 1854, APEBa/SACP, m. 4073; Corr., 26 September, JC, 2 October 1854; Corr., 3 October, CM-R, 12 October 1854; Corr., 15 October, DP, 21 October 1854. For one of the rebuttals, see "Abertura do Theatro de San [*sic*] João" (from CM-S), DP, 9 October 1854. No copies of the radical-liberal periodicals have survived, but L.A. Alves located two of their articles in a Pernambucan periodical, "Tensos laços," 131–2.

139 J.W.A. Pinho, *Cotegipe*, 273.

140 Boccanera Júnior, *Teatro na Bahia*, 104. That Cotegipe commissioned the new curtain is noted in Administrador to President, 27 March 1856, APEBa/SACP, m. 4073.

141 L.A. Alves, "Tensos laços," 130.

142 A.J.R. Costa, "Dous de Julho," 17r, 25r, 56v, 75v–76v.

143 I.A.C. Silva, *Memorias*, 3:400n67; Titara, *Obras*, 5:159–60, 160n2.

144 M. Graham, *Journal*, 292–3.

145 Reis Júnior, *Maria Quitéria*. She sometimes had difficulties collecting her pension, Thesoureiro Geral das Tropas to President, Salvador, 10 November 1829, APEB/SACP, m. 3221; and Petition of Maria Quiteria de Jezus to President, 28 January 1846, APEB/SACP, m. 3766.

146 Agrário's portrayal of Maria Quitéria contrasts sharply with his characters' misogynistic outbursts in *Mathilde* and the note in which he explains that women are incapable of understanding the concept of *pátria*, A.S. Menezes, *Mathilde*, 35, 89, 134.

147 C.A. Tavares, *Tempos*, 60, 63, 65.

148 C.A. Tavares, *Tempos*, 68–9, 80, 93–5.

149 Filgueiras Sobrinho, *Legenda*, 27–30, 48–51. On the possible marriage, see Reis Júnior, *Maria Quitéria*, 48.

150 I.A.C. Silva, *Memorias*, 3:399; Titara, *Obras*, 4:77–8, 78n1; Pedro, *Diário*, 9 October 1859; J.S. Menezes, *Agrário*, 83–4.

151 Deniers include L.H.D. Tavares, *Independência*, 123–4; J.C.B. Silva, "Folclore," no pagination. Those who accept the story include Bandeira, *Feudo*, 431–5; B.H. Amaral, *História da Independência*, 273; and M.C.P. Almeida, *Batalha*, 33–5. Risério's assessment is in *História*, 325.

152 A.S. Menezes, "Dia," 2v–4v (quote at 4v).

153 A.S. Menezes, "Dia," 18r, 68r.

154 A.S. Menezes, "Dia," 17r.

155 A.S. Menezes, "Dia," 72v, 85v.

156 A.S. Menezes, "Dia," 72v; I.A.C. Silva, *Memorias*, 3:399.

157 Filgueiras Sobrinho, *Legenda*, 68–9.

158 Letter from Uma Bahiana, *O Independente Constitucional*, 6 March 1824; Reis, *Cora*, 73, 191.

159 M. Graham, *Journal*, 292–3 (quote at 292).

160 A.S. Menezes, "Dia," 26r, 25r, 50r; C.A. Tavares, *Tempos*, 66.

161 A.S. Menezes, "Dia," 43v–44v, 48r.

162 A.S. Menezes, *Mathilde*, 136–7.

163 Kraay, *Race*, 122; Ruy, *Dossier*, 105–50.

164 A.J.R. Costa, "Dous de Julho," 54v–55r.

165 C.A. Tavares, *Tempos*, 74–81 (quotes at 81, 79–80).

166 C.A. Tavares, *Tempos*, 77; A.J.R. Costa, "Dous de Julho," 56r. On Felisberto's murder, see Reis and Kraay, "'Tyrant,'" 418–19; L.H.D. Tavares, *Da sedição*, 210–12.

167 This point is emphasized by Barman, *Brazil*, 217–42.

168 On the 1817 movement, see G.L. Leite, *Pernambuco 1817*; Mosher, *Political Struggle*, 9–40; Mello, *Outra independência*, 25–63.

169 C.A. Tavares, *Tempos*, 18–19, 49, 50, 81, 110.

170 F.A.P. Costa, *Dicionário*, 549–70, 626–9; Chacon, *História*, 145–87.

171 A.J.R. Costa, "Dous de Julho," 12r, 22r; Filgueiras Sobrinho, *Legenda*, 11.

172 Varnhagen, *História*, 2:392. See also Guimarães, "Entre a monarquia," 152–61.

173 On the Inconfidência Mineira, see Maxwell, *Conflicts*; Furtado, *Manto*. On the construction of Tiradentes as a national hero, see Milliet, *Tiradentes*; J.M. Carvalho, *Formação*, 55–73; Kraay, *Days*, 172–3, 296–69, 368, 370; Enders, *Vultos*, 212–15.

174 C.A. Tavares, *Tempos*, 18; Filgueiras Sobrinho, *Legenda*, 22.

175 On the Confederação do Equador, see G.L. Leite, *Pernambuco 1824*; Mosher, *Political Struggle*, 64–77; Mello, *Outra independência*, 163–237.

176 C.A. Tavares, *Elogio*, 14–15.

177 I analyze these issues in Kraay, *Days*, 140–2, 166–75.

178 The only detailed study that I know of is F.A.P. Costa, *Pernambuco*, but see also Aras, "Bahia."

179 A.S. Menezes, "Dia," 4v; C.A. Tavares, *Tempos*, 19.

180 Filgueiras Sobrinho, *Legenda*, 52–3.

181 A.S. Menezes, "Dia," 12r, 14v, 15v.

182 A.J.R. Costa, "Dous de Julho," 64v.

183 C.A. Tavares, *Tempos*, 113–14, 116–17. The final anthem played on 4 July 1861 may have been the Hino ao Dois de Julho.

184 A.S. Menezes, "Dia," 102v–3r.

185 Filgueiras Sobrinho, *Legenda*, 75.

186 C.A. Tavares, *Elogio*, 18.

187 A.J.R. Costa, "Dous de Julho," 75v–76v.

188 C.A. Tavares, *Tempos*, 110; L.A. Alves, "Constantino do Amaral Tavares," xi. For examples of hopes for Brazil, see Filgueiras Sobrinho, *Legenda*, 75; A.S. Menezes, "Dia," 33v; C.A. Tavares, *Elogio*, 11–12.

189 A Passos, *Agrário*, 167; J.S. Menezes, *Agrário*, 296–8.

190 Sacramento Blake, *Diccionario*, 1:205–6; 2:135, 394.

191 "Dous de Julho," *Correio da Bahia*, 4 July 1877.

192 Castro Alves, "Gonzaga," 585.

193 Castro Alves, "Gonzaga," 659–61.

194 Castro Alves, "Gonzaga," 590.

195 Castro Alves, "Gonzaga," 632–3, 638–9.

196 Castro Alves to Augusto Álvares Guimarães, [no date] September 1867, in *Obra completa*, ed. Gomes, 746. On the play's reception, see also Ruy, *História do teatro*, 57–8; Boccanera Júnior, *Teatro na Bahia*, 121. See also Kist, "Tragédia," 104, 113–15; J.G. Sousa, *Teatro*, 1:177–8; Faria, *Idéias*, 67–74; A.C. Silva, *Castro Alves*, 67–70. My reading of *Gonzaga* differs significantly from that of Castilho, "Performing," 396–9.

197 C.A. Tavares, *Gonzaga*, 46–50.

198 "Bahia," *Gazeta de Noticias* (Rio), 12 July 1881; "Noticias do Sul do Império: Bahia," DP, 9 July 1881.

199 Ruy, *História do teatro*, 46–51; Boccanera Júnior, *Teatro na Bahia*, 182–96; Querino, "Theatros," 117–18; Passos, *Agrário*, 59–61. On *revistas*, see Sussekind, *Revistas*.

200 J.G. Sousa, *Teatro*, 280; Boccanera Júnior, *Teatro na Bahia*, 63–5.

201 Boccanera Júnior, *Teatro na Bahia*, 17–49.

202 Among others, see Marzano, *Cidade*; Mencarelli, *Cena aberta*.

## Chapter Six

1 The literature on monuments is vast; useful studies include Savage, *Standing Soldiers*; Driskel, *As Befits a Legend*; Bogart, *Public Sculpture*; Agulhon, "'Statuomanie'"; Cohen, "Symbols"; Michalski, *Public Monuments*. On Brazil, see the articles in Paulo Knauss, ed., *Cidade*; Coelho, *No coração*; Kraay, *Days*, 146–77.

2 Nora, "Between Memory."

3 These themes are examined in, among others, Borges, "Salvador's 1890s"; Levine, "Singular Brazilian City"; Butler, *Freedoms*, 129–209; R.C.N. Leite, *Rainha*, 197–335.

4 Benjamim, *Breve noticia*, 30.

5 Benjamim, *Breve noticia*, 27–8, 37 (quote), 69 (quote), 71–4. See the analysis of these themes in R.C.N. Leite, *Rainha*, 337–98.

6 Borges, *Family*, 30, 31, 61 (quote), 63.

7 R.C.N. Leite, "Civilização"; Pinheiro, *Europa*, 175–266; Ferreira Filho, "Desafricanizar."

8 Martinez, *2 de Julho*, 112.

9 Carvalho Neto, "Proclamação," 91–101; Ruy, *História da Câmara*, 323–32; B.H. Amaral, *Historia da Bahia*, 319–44; B.H. Amaral, "Memoria historica sobre a proclamação"; Bulcão Sobrinho, "Pregoeiro" and "Proclamação."

10 An example of the former is Aragão, *Bahia*; for examples of the latter, see C.N. Sampaio, *Partidos*, chaps. 1–2; C.N. Sampaio, *Poder*; Pang, *Bahia* chap. 2; Carvalho Júnior, *Barão*, 185–216, 241–96.

11 B.H. Amaral, "Memoria historica sobre os acontecimentos."

12 Levine, *Vale*; Carvalho Júnior, *Barão*, 241–96.

13 Borges, "Salvador's 1890s," 48.

14 Castellucci, "Política," 207–26. See also his "Classe."

15 "Catalogo dos jornaes," 567–72; F.V. Vianna, *Memoria*, 399–401.

16 Torres and Carvalho classify the *Correio de Notícias* as the Partido Federalista's newspaper after 1894, *Annaes*, 145.

17 On the Faculdade Livre de Direito, see F.V. Vianna, *Memoria*, 254.

18 *Pequeno Jornal*, 18 June 1890; Governor to Intendente and Conselho Municipal, 18 June 1890, AHMS/CFRDJ; "Dous de Julho," *Pequeno Jornal*, 20 June 1890.

19 "Dous de Julho," *Pequeno Jornal*, 26 June 1890.

20 "Festejos do Dous de Julho," *Pequeno Jornal*, 28 June 1890; "2 de Julho," *Pequeno Jornal*, 30 June 1890.

21 "Dois de Julho," *Jornal de Noticias*, 1 July 1890.

22 *Leituras Religiosas*, 6 July 1890; "2 de julho," *Pequeno Jornal*, 3 July 1890; "Porque tanta indifferença?" *Pequeno Jornal*, 3 July 1890 (quote).

23 "Estado da Bahia" (from *Diario de Noticias*, 3 July), DP, 8 July 1890.

24 "Graves acontecimentos," *Pequeno Jornal*, 5 July 1890; "Grande desacato" (from *Diario de Noticias*, 7 July), DP, 16 July 1890.

25 "Bahia," *Jornal do Recife*, 1 July 1891; "Estado da Bahia," DP, 1 July 1891.

26 "Festejos do Immortal 2 de Julho," *Pequeno Jornal*, 1 July 1891; "Programma dos festejos do imortal dia 2 de Julho promovidas pela commissão popular" and "Dois de Julho," *Diario de Noticias*, 1 July 1891; "Dois

de Julho," "Jardim da Piedade," and "Espectaculo de Grande Gala," *Diario de Noticias*, 3 July 1891.

27 "Dois de Julho," *Diario de Noticias*, 3 July 1891.

28 "Revista diaria," *Pequeno Jornal*, 1 July 1892; "O Dia da Patria," *Jornal de Noticias*, 1 July 1892; "Festejos do 2 de Julho," *Pequeno Jornal*, 4 July 1892; and "Os Festejos do 2 de julho," *Jornal de Noticias*, 4 July 1892; "Dois de Julho," *Diario da Bahia*, 4 July 1894, in "Repositório: Descrições de Festejos, Notícias de Jornais," AIGHBa, cx. 18, d. 70.

29 "Estado da Bahia" (from *Diario de Noticias*, 7 July), DP, 16 July 1890; "2 de Julho," *Diario de Noticias*, 6 July 1891; "Os festejos do 2 de julho," *Jornal de Noticias*, 6 July 1892; Antonio de Freitas Tantu to Conselho Municipal, 8 July 1893, AHMS/CFRDJ; "Bahia," *Jornal do Recife*, 13 July 1894. For a reference to the pilgrimage, see "Romaria," *Jornal de Noticias*, 15 July 1892. For neighbourhood festivals, see "2 de Julho de Castro Neves," *Diario de Noticias*, 30 July 1891; "Dous de Julho," *Pequeno Jornal*, 23 July 1891 (Garcia); Abaixo-Assinado of Pedro Macario da Motta, *Jornal de Noticias*, 2 September 1892 (Jacaré); *Jornal de Noticias*, 13 September 1892 (Cruz do Cosme).

30 "Festas de 2 de julho em Itapagipe," "Commemorações do dia 2 de julho em Itapagipe," and "Dois de Julho em Itapagipe," *Jornal de Noticias*, 9 and 11 July and 1 August 1892.

31 "Provincial Notes," *The Rio News*, 13 September 1892. On Macaco Beleza, see Varella, *Da Bahia que eu vi*, 173–6; W. Fraga, *Crossroads*, 241–2; Albuquerque, *Jogo*, 155; H. Vianna, *Proclamação*, 4–5, 13, 18n13.

32 J.T. Santos, *Dono*, 36; H. Vianna, "'Dois de Julho' na Bahia," 64–5.

33 Mello Moraes Filho, *Festas e tradições*, 133.

34 Moniz, *Moniz Barretto*, 94n*.

35 "Dous de Julho" (*apedido*), DP, 2 July 1881.

36 *Pequeno Jornal*, 1 July 1890.

37 CP, 9 July, JC, 19 July 1887.

38 Moniz, *Moniz Barretto*, 94n*, 102–3, 105 (quote).

39 "Dous de Julho" (*apedido*), DP, 2 July 1881.

40 CP, 9 July, JC, 19 July 1887.

41 CP, 9 July, JC, 19 July 1887.

42 *O Monitor*, 1 July 1877.

43 Julio Carlos Ferreira, "Dous de Julho," *Diario da Bahia*, 2 July 1891. Ferreira's occupation is noted in F.V. Vianna, *Memoria*, title page.

44 "Dous de Julho," *Gazeta da Bahia*, 2 July 1882.

45 CP, 9 July 1887, JC, 19 July 1887.

46 For a different interpretation of the Indian symbol's decline as a representation of Brazil, but one that does not take into account popular

understandings, see Beattie, "Illustrating." Albuquerque emphasizes popular identification with the *caboclos*, *Jogo*, 169–71; and *Algazarra*, 89–110.

47  J.A. Amaral, *Resumo*, 293; Moniz, *Moniz Barretto*, 94; "Bahia," DP, 13 July 1871, 11 July 1878, 8 July 1885; "Dous de Julho," *Gazeta da Bahia*, 2 July 1884; "Bahia" (from *Jornal da Bahia*, 4 July), DP, 10 July 1876; "Bahia" (from *Correio da Bahia*), DP, 7 July 1874; "Bahia" (from *Diario da Bahia*), DP, 1 July 1879; "Bahia" (from *Jornal da Bahia*), DP, 10 July 1870; "Bahia" (from *Diario da Bahia*), DP, 10 July 1877.

48  Tic, "Zun Zun," *Gazeta da Tarde*, 1 July 1885.

49  CA to President, 3 July 1880, APEBa/SACP, m. 3441.

50  "De relance," *O Faisca*, 4 July 1886. Italics in original.

51  Tupinamba, "Cavaquemos," *Diario da Bahia*, 2 July 1896. In 1887, *O Faisca* likewise asserted that "carnival killed Dois Julho," "Carnavalia," *O Faisca*, 26 February 1887.

52  Tupinamba, "Cavaquemos," *Diario da Bahia*, 2 July 1896. On elite avoidance of participation in popular street festivals, see Borges, *Family*, 64.

53  "Dous de Julho," *Diario do Povo*, 3 July 1889; "Festejos do 2 de Julho," *Jornal de Noticias*, 3 July 1889, in "Repositório," AIGHBa, cx. 18, d. 70.

54  Annuncios, *O Século*, 18 October 1849; *Diario da Bahia*, 28 June 1858.

55  Projecto 248 (1858) and Parecer 27, Commissão 1ª da Fazenda, APEBa/SL, livro 872.

56  Lei 786, 8 July 1859, CLRBa.

57  Corr., 21 July, JC, 25 July 1862; Corr., 5 July, JC, 10 July 1864 (quote).

58  On this monument, see Kraay, *Days*, 146–77.

59  *Diario: O Independente Constitucional*, 11 November 1825; CM-S, 7 September 1838; Kraay, *Days*, 152.

60  Pedro, *Diário*, 7 October 1859; B.X.P. Souza, *Memorias*, 39.

61  B.X.P. Souza, *Memorias*, 171, 178–9.

62  Manuel Maria do Amaral and Constantino do Amaral Tavares to Instituto Histórico e Geográfico Brasileiro, ca. September 1860, AIHGB, lata 565, pasta 10. The *ata* itself has, unfortunately, been lost.

63  Kraay, *Days*, 166–77, 316–26.

64  Acta, 31 October 1871, AHMB/CFRDJ.

65  Boccanera Júnior, *Bahia cívica*, 4. See also Albuquerque, *Algazarra*, 96–7.

66  "Monumento ao 2 de Julho," *O Monitor*, 7 June 1876. On José Bonifácio de Andrada e Silva's monument, see Kraay, *Days*, 303–8.

67  "Monumento ao Dous de Julho," *O Monitor*, 1 July 1876; Petition of Acadêmicos to President, 22 June 1876, APEBa/SACP, m. 1569; "Programma da festa," *O Monitor*, 16 July 1876.

68  Resolução, 10 July 1876, CLRBa.

69 Speech of Porto, 25 May, *AALPBa* (1876), 1:131.

70 Speech of João de Brito, 25 May, *AALPBa* (1876), 1:129.

71 *Diario da Bahia*, 27 October 1878, quoted in K.M.C. Silva, *O Diario*, 138–9.

72 M. Adriano to Antonio Pereira Rebouças, 13 February 1879, BN/SM, I-3, 23, 4.

73 "Acta da collocação da primeira pedra," 5 July 1881, *O Monitor*, 13 July 1881; *Gazeta da Bahia*, 13 July 1881. The manuscript *ata* is in AIGHBa, livro 4.

74 Francolino Augusto de [illegible] to Câmara, 20 July 1883, AHMS/CFRDJ.

75 "Plebiscito: Monumento ao 2 de Julho de 1823," *Diario de Noticias*, 4 July 1891.

76 F.A.P. Costa, *Pernambuco*, 81–2.

77 F.A.P. Costa, *Pernambuco*, 315–24.

78 "Memoravel Dous de Julho," *O Motor*, 30 June 1877.

79 L.A. Fonseca, *Escravidão*, 240.

80 "Monumento ao Dous de Julho," *Pequeno Jornal*, 25 June 1891.

81 "Monumento ao Dois de Julho," *Diario do Povo*, 10 April 1889.

82 "Dous de Julho," *Diario da Bahia*, 2 July 1889; Antonio Bernardo Mendes to Câmara, 18 July 1887, AHMI/CFRDJ.

83 "Camara Municipal, Expediente do dia 20 de fevereiro de 1889," *Diario da Bahia*, 28 March 1889; "Sociedade Dous de Julho," *Diario da Bahia*, 2 March 1889.

84 Leis 2650, 14 May 1889; and 2667, 10 June 1889, CLRBa.

85 Sessions of 5, 8, and 9 April, and 3 May, "Assembléa Provincial," *Diario da Bahia*, 13, 18, 21, and 24 April, and 4 June 1889.

86 Commissão do Monumento... to President, 17 August 1889, APEBa/ SACP, m. 1569.

87 "Monumento ao 2 de Julho," *Pequeno Jornal*, 14 November 1891. On the expectation of a government contribution, see "Bahia," *Jornal do Recife*, 1 July 1891; "Estado da Bahia," *DP*, 1 July 1891. On exchange rates, see J.S. Duncan, *Public and Private Operations*, 183. On the subscription's total, see "O Monumento," *RIGHBa* 2.5 (1895): 238n[*].

88 Commissão Executiva do Monumento ao Dois de Julho to Intendencia, 30 September 1891, AHMI/CFRDJ.

89 Lei 8, 11 January 1892; Lei 35, 4 July 1893; Resolução 58, 25 July 1894; Lei 139, 17 May 1895, CLRBa. On the 1894 allocation, see also *ACSDEFBa* (1894): 3:130, 198; 4:18, 22, 67, 92, 180.

90 *A Locomotiva*, 3 May 1889.

91 "Plebiscito," *Diario de Noticias*, 23 July and 4 August 1891.

92 For the 1890 and 1896 elections, 9,414 and 8,530 voters respectively were registered; in 1892, 9,660 men voted, Castellucci, "Política," 222.

93 "A proposito do plebiscito," *Diario de Noticias*, 7 August 1891; Boccanera Júnior, *Bahia cívica*, 12.

94 "Tem graça!" *Diario de Noticias*, 4 August 1891. I only have the *Diario de Noticias*' response to Carigé (the IGHBa's volume of the *Diario da Bahia* was in no condition to be consulted in 2011).

95 "Plebiscito," *Diario de Noticias*, 27 and 29 July 1891.

96 "Plebiscito," *Diario de Noticias*, 24 July 1891.

97 "A proposito do plebiscito," *Diario de Noticias*, 5 August 1891.

98 "Plebiscito," *Diario de Noticias*, 1 August 1891.

99 Votes of Fr. Rocha et al. and Manoel Velho; Fulgencio Coelho; Aurlino de Sá Amorim et al.; Paulino José Nunes et al., "Plebiscito," *Diario de Noticias*, 17, 20, 23 July, and 1 August 1891.

100 Votes of Jeronymo Leopoldo Nunes et al.; Antonio Rodrigues Cezimbra et al.; Niceu Dantas Nunes et al.; A. Costa Junior; Euclides Ribeiro de Salles et al.; Arthenio Candido A. Silva (quote); Francisco Jorge Rabello et al.; Mocidade Academica; L.A. Vianna et al., *Diario de Noticias*, 9, 10, 11, 18, 20, and 29 July 1891; Manoel Pinto da Fonseca, "A proposito do plebiscito," *Diario de Noticias*, 6 August 1891. On Campo Grande's history, see Boccanera Junior, "Pagina," 112–15.

101 Silio Boccanera Junior, "A propósito do plebiscito (conclusão)," *Diario de Noticias*, 1 [*sic* = 3] July 1892; Julio Carlos Ferreira, "Dous de Julho," *Diario da Bahia*, 2 July 1891; F.V. Vianna, "A proposito do plebiscito," *Diario de Noticias*, 8 and 10 August 1891. The *Echo da Patria*'s report is also cited in "A proposito do plebiscite," *Diario de Noticias*, 13 August 1891. See also F.V. Vianna, *Memoria*, 416, 647.

102 Votes of Julio de Calasans, Felicissima Bernardina da Gloria Barborino, Carlos Martins Bastos et al., Francisco Pinto de Castro et al., "Plebiscito," *Diario de Noticias*, 10, 11, and 27 July 1891 (quote).

103 Barroso de Souza, "A proposito do plebiscito," *Diario de Noticias*, 18 and 19 August 1891.

104 Vote of Jeronymo Leopoldo Nunes et al., "Plebiscito," *Diario de Noticias*, 9 July 1891.

105 Votes of A. Costa Junior (quote), Antonio de Araujo Seixas et al., and Fulgencio Coelho, "Plebiscito," *Diario de Noticias*, 11, 20, and 21 July 1891.

106 Vote of Florentino José de Lemos et al., "Plebiscito," *Diario de Noticias*, 17 July 1891.

107 Vote of A. Costa Junior, "Plebiscito," *Diario de Noticias*, 11 July 1891.

108 Boccanera Junior, "A proposito do plebiscito," *Diario de Noticias*, 1 [*sic* = 3] July 1891.

109  Vote of Paulino José Nunes et al., "Plebiscito," *Diario de Noticias*, 1 August 1891.
110  Votes of Luiza da França Pessoa da Silva and Quirino da Rocha Amorim et al, "Plebiscito," *Diario de Noticias*, 22 and 18 July 1891.
111  Vote of Antonio Rodrigues Cezimbra, "Plebiscito," *Diario de Noticias*, 10 July 1891.
112  "Monumento 2 de Julho," *Pequeno Jornal*, 13 November 1891.
113  Jacome Martins Baggi et al. to Commissão Executiva do Monumento ao 2 de Julho, 21 November 1891, APEBa/SR, cx. 2294, doc. 2898; Parecer 14, 8 May, ACSDEFBa (1896): 2:22.
114  "Ata da 1ª Sessão da Commissão do Monumento ao Dois de Julho," 4 February 1892, APEBa/SR, cx. 2294, doc. 2898.
115  Boccanera Junior, "Pagina," 111, 117–19. For another complaint, see "O 2 de Julho," *Diário da Bahia*, 2 July 1910.
116  "O Monumento," *Jornal de Noticias*, 6 July 1892; "Festejos do 2 de Julho," *Pequeno Jornal*, 6 July 1892; "O Munumento [*sic*]," *Jornal de Noticias*, 5 July 1892; Speech of Manoel Victorino Pereira, *Jornal de Noticias*, 6 July 1892.
117  "Monumento a Pedro I," *Jornal de Noticias*, 8 July 1892; "Estado da Bahia," *DP*, 16 July 1892.
118  Lulu Parola, "Cantando e Rindo – 155," *Jornal de Noticias*, 7 July 1892, cited in L.A. Alves, ed., *2 de Julho*, 139–40. "Cantando e Rindo" ran for 6,708 days, A. Carvalho, "Imprensa," 53.
119  Parenthetically, it should be noted that, while monument committee members joined the Instituto Geográfico e Histórico da Bahia, the new institute had no role in planning the inauguration, contrary to recent scholars' assertions, A.J.M. Silva, *Instituto*, 240; R.C.N. Leite, "Memória," 66.
120  Aragão, *Bahia*, 97–112; C.N. Sampaio, *Partidos*, 69–74.
121  "Discurso do Dr. Augusto França," 3 July 1895, RIGHBa 2.5 (1895): 238.
122  Boccanera Junior, "Pagina," 115. A character in a 1905 novel set in 1889 also complains (anachronistically) about the trees' imminent removal, J.M.C. Oliveira, *Dois metros*, 86.
123  On Nicoli, see Bénézit, *Dictionnaire*, 10:205.
124  There are numerous published descriptions of the monument, all based on a text originally produced by Alexandre Freire Maia Bittencourt, the engineer who oversaw the monument's installation (this text was circulated as a pamphlet at the inauguration), "Descripção do Monumento," *Jornal de Noticias*, 3 July 1895; "Monumento ao Dous de Julho," *Diario da Bahia*, 2 July 1895; "O monumento," RIGHBa 2.5 (1895): 231–41; F.V. Vianna, *Memoria*, 344–7; Boccanera Junior, *Bahia historica*, 236–42n36;

P.C. Silva, "Bahia," 89–96; P.C. Silva, "Notas," 568–75; J.B. Mattos, *Monumentos*, 167–72.

125 "Bahia," *DP*, 11 July 1895.

126 F.A.P. Costa, *Pernambuco*, 86 (quote), 84, 34–5, 148 (quote). On Cipriano's decoration, see Morel, *Cipriano Barata*, 160, and Morel, ed., Sentinela, 63–4.

127 *Diario da Bahia*, 2 July 1895.

128 The following account is based on "Festejos do 2 de Julho," *Correio de Noticias*, 3 July 1895; "Noticiario," *Diario da Bahia*, 4 July 1895; "Inauguração do Monumento," *RIGHBa* 2.5 (1895): 218–22. The *DP* also published a report on the inauguration without indicating its source, "Bahia," *DP*, 11 July 1895.

129 *Diario da Bahia*, 2 July 1895.

130 Augusto A. Guimarães, "Discurso," *RIGHBa* 2.5 (1895): 227–9.

131 "Festejos do 2 de Julho," *Correio de Noticias*, 4 July 1895; "Photo-gravura," *Correio de Noticias*, 3 July 1895. The *Diario de Noticias* of 3 July also made this point, *RIGHBa* 2.5 (1895): 237. The print is held by the Museu Tempostal, Coleção Antônio Marcelino.

132 R[aimundo] Bizarria, "Outr'ora e hoje," *Diario da Bahia*, 2 July 1895.

133 A., "A maior data," *Diario da Bahia*, 2 July 1895.

134 "Noticiario," *Diario da Bahia*, 29 June 1895. For the original schedule, see "Programma dos festejos do dia Dous de Julho," *Diario da Bahia*, 29 June 1895.

135 Giulio, "Cousas da Rua," *Sirius*, 10 July 1895.

136 Varella, *Da Bahia do Senhor*, 96–7.

137 "2 de Julho," *Correio de Noticias*, 6 July 1895; "Festejos de 2 de Julho," *Correio de Noticias*, 8 July 1895; "Volta dos emblemas patrioticos," *Diario da Bahia*, 9 July 1895.

138 *Diario da Bahia*, 4 July 1895. On Tarquínio, see Varella, *Da Bahia que eu vi*, 5–12; Dumêt, *Semeador*; Borges, "Salvador's 1890s," 51–2.

139 H. Vianna, "Dois de Julho na Bahia," 65. Martinez alludes to this bifurcation in passing, *2 de Julho*, 124; while Albuquerque glosses over the monument and the changes in the festival, *Algazarra*.

140 "2 de Julho," *Diario da Bahia*, 4 July 1896; Rabelais Neto, "Aos Domingos," *Diario da Bahia*, 5 July 1896.

141 "2 de Julho," *Diario de Noticias*, 3 July 1896; A. Belly, "Devaneios: 2 de Julho em dois periodos," *Diario de Noticias*, 4 July 1896. See also "2 de Julho," *O Paiz* (Rio), 2 July 1896.

142 "2 de Julho," *Diario da Bahia*, 4 July 1896; "2 de Julho," *Diario de Noticias*, 3 July 1896.

143 "Festejos ao 2 de Julho," *Diario da Bahia*, 1 July 1896; "Dous de Julho: Freguesia de Santo Antonio," *Diario da Bahia*, 2 July 1896.

144 "Festejos populares," *Diario de Noticias*, 1 July 1896; "Dous de Julho," *Diario da Bahia*, 2 July 1896.

145 Leis 2667, 10 June 1889; 111, 13 August 1895; 153, 17 August 1896; 211, 19 August 1897, *CLRBa*. Dois de Julho subventions of 2:000$000 reappeared in the budget for 1899 and were last allocated for 1904, Leis 283, 6 September 1898; 526, 30 November 1903, *CLRBa*.

146 "Festejos do 2 de Julho," *Diario da Bahia*, 4 July 1897.

147 "2 de Julho," *Cidade do Salvador*, 1 July 1897; "2 de Julho," *Correio de Noticias*, 5 July 1897; "Dois de Julho," *Diario da Bahia*, 1 July 1897; "Festejos de Dois de Julho," *Diario da Bahia*, 6 July 1897; "Dois de Julho," *Correio de Noticias*, 4 July 1898, in "Repositório," AIGHBa, cx 18, d. 70; "2 de Julho," *Jornal de Noticias*, 3 July 1899.

148 "Dous de Julho," *Diario da Bahia*, 2 July 1896; Paul Kine, "Cavaquemos," *Diario da Bahia*, 4 July 1897.

149 See, for example, *Revista Popular*, September 1897.

150 "Polyanthea Bahiano," *Diario da Bahia*, 2 July 1896; "2 Julho," *Diario de Noticias*, 3 July 1896; "Bahia," *Diario de Pernambuco*, 21 July 1898.

151 Boccanera Júnior, *Teatro na Bahia*, 126–7; Neves, *De La Traviata*, 42, 56, 90, 209; Dourado, "Praça," 211, 214.

152 "2 de Julho," *Jornal de Noticias*, 3 July 1899; "2 de Julho," *Correio de Noticias*, 5 July 1897; "Dois de Julho," *Correio de Noticias*, 4 July 1900. On these elements, see also Albuquerque, *Algazarra*, 69–72.

153 "Revista dos Jornais," *Diario da Bahia*, 5 July 1898 (summarizing *Jornal de Noticias*, 1 July 1898), quoted in J.T. Santos, *Dono*, 34. I have not had access to these newspapers for 1898.

154 "Dous de Julho," *Correio de Noticias*, 4 May 1900 (the "bandeira anunciadora"); "2 de Julho," *Correio de Noticias*, 30 June 1897; "Festas," *Jornal de Noticias*, 27 June 1899 (the *bando*); "2 de Julho," *Jornal de Noticias*, 27 June 1900 (the stage's construction); "2 de Julho," *Diario de Noticias*, 6 July 1896 (the return to Lapinha).

155 Varella, *Da Bahia do Senhor*, 96–7; Campos, "Cronicas," 295.

156 "2 de Julho: Romaria" and "Romaria a Pirajá," *Diario de Noticias*, 6 and 7 July 1896. That there was a pilgrimage in 1897 can be inferred from an incident discussed by Albuquerque, *Algazarra*, 67–8.

157 "2 de Julho," *Correio de Noticias*, 3 July 1897.

158 "Dois de Julho," *Correio de Noticias*, 4 July 1898, in "Repositório," AIGHBa, cx. 18, d. 70; "2 de Julho," *Jornal de Noticias*, 3 July 1900; Commissão dos Festejos to *Diario da Bahia*, 18 June 1897, *Diario da Bahia*, 23 June 1897; "2 de Julho," *Cidade do Salvador*, 27 June 1898; "2 de Julho," *Jornal de Noticias*, 21 June 1900.

159 "Festejos de 2 de Julho," *Diario da Bahia*, 4 July 1897. Unaware of this article, Albuquerque argues that African carnival societies did not participate in this festival, *Algazarra*, 76. On these African carnival societies, see Butler, *Freedoms*, 177–86.

160 "2 de Julho," *Jornal de Noticias*, 3 July 1900; Albuquerque, *Algazarra*, 63–4. Calmon Sobrinho wrote that Tarquínio did this in 1896, but he appears to have confused Tarquínio's role as president of the organizing committee of that year with the 1900 workers' march, "Homenagem," 228.

161 Tia Tatá, "Pipocas," *A Coisa*, 8 July 1900.

162 "2 de Julho," *Jornal de Noticias*, 4 July 1899; "Festas: 2 de Julho," *Jornal de Noticias*, 6 July 1899.

163 J.T. Santos, *Dono*, 37.

164 Interview with Raimundo de Almeida Gouveia, 17 November 1998, in U.C. Araújo, ed., *Salvador*, 1:48.

165 Campos, *Procissões*, 258–61.

166 See, for examples, "Dous de Julho," *Diario da Bahia*, 28 June 1896; "2 de Julho," *Correio de Noticias*, 26 June 1897.

167 Varella, *Da Bahia do Senhor*, 21–2; Querino, "Homens," 356; Vote of Dr. Tiburcio Susano de Araujo et al., "Plebiscito," *Diario de Noticias*, 23 July 1891; "2 de Julho," *A Bahia*, 3 July 1900.

168 "Necrologia," *Jornal de Noticias*, 7 July 1899.

169 "2 de Julho," *Correio de Noticias*, 1 September 1896; Petition of Fausto Pereira dos Santos et al. to Intendente, 2 August 1897, AHMS/CFRDJ; Albuquerque, *Algazarra*, 79–83; H. Vianna, "Dois de Julho de bairros."

170 "2 de Julho de Itapagipe," *Pequeno Jornal*, 28 June 1892.

171 Albuquerque, *Algazarra*, 102–3. Lulu Parola also made fun of this incident, "A retirada do carro da cabocla, do seu antigo barracão," *Jornal de Noticias*, 23 July 1897.

172 Tranquilino L. Torres to A[ugusto] Guimarães, 19 June 1895, AIGHBa, Arquivo Augusto Guimarães.

173 Boccanera Júnior, *Bahia histórica*, 129.

174 "2 de Julho," *Diario de Noticias*, 6 July 1896; A. Belly, "Devaneios," *Diario de Noticias*, 7 July 1896.

175 Jayme Borreaux, "Linhas alegres," *A Coisa*, 1 July 1900.

176 "Dois de Julho," *Correio de Noticias*, 4 July 1900.

177 Varella, *D'outros tempos*, 67.

178 Boccanera, "Pagina," 115–16.

179 Speech of Rodrigues Brandão, 26 July, ACSDEFBa (1895), 4:203. The measure's defeat apparently resulted from the negative recommendation from the finance committee, ACSDEFBa (1896), 3:64.

180 Savage, *Standing Soldiers*, 7–8; Knauss, "Imagens," 299.

181  Knauss, "Introdução," in *Cidade vaidosa*, ed. Knauss, 9.
182  Corrigan and Sayer, *Great Arch*, 3.

## Conclusion

1  Albuquerque, *Algazarra*, 101–3.
2  Albuquerque, *Algazarra*, 105–7; F.B. Barros noted that this was only the second time that such a procession had taken place, "Á margem" (1934), 557–8.
3  B.H. Amaral, *Ação*, 9, 17. Amaral also emphasized these themes in his other books published that year, *Historia da Bahia*, 24–5n1; and *Historia da Independencia*, 335–6, 463–4. These arguments had long been expressed by the Instituto, R.C.N. Leite, "Memória e identidade," 67–9, 72, and *Rainha*, 59–82; M.A.S. Sousa, "História," 188–9. On the centennial celebrations, see also Albuquerque, *Algazarra*, 116–22; and Galo Ledezma, "Religiosidade."
4  Boccanera Junior, *Bahia civica*, 3.
5  "A nossa maior data: o 2 de Julho vae ser commemorado em Santo Antonio," *A Tarde*, 26 June 1926; "Dous de Julho," *O Imparcial*, 4 July 1926; "2 de Julho infantil da Cidade de Palha," *Diario de Noticias*, 10 July 1926; "A Avenida Soares vae festejar agora o 2 de Julho," *A Tarde*, 17 July 1926; "A romaria a Pirajá," *O Imparcial*, 31 July 1926; "Romaria a Pirajá," *O Jornal*, 31 July 1926.
6  Ickes, *African-Brazilian Culture*; Romo, *Race*; M.C. Santana, *Alma*; Mariano, *Invenção*.
7  Very little has been written on this reinvention, but see H. Vianna, "'Dois de Julho' na Bahia," 65–6; Martinez, *2 de Julho*, 143; Baldaia, "Festa," 94–6; Ickes, "Santos," 29–39.
8  Baldaia, "Festa," 26.
9  Baldaia, "Festa," 109–11.
10  Baldaia, "Festa," 102–4; Martinez, *2 de Julho*, 145.
11  Baldaia, "Festa," 104–7, 124–6.
12  Baldaia, "Festa," 117–21, 97 (on the Quebra-Ferro Battalion).
13  Baldaia, "Festa," 191–205.
14  On these groups, see Baldaia, "Festa," 166; "'Abre-te campo formoso,'" and "Construção."
15  See the 1968 photograph in Baldaia, "Festa," 134.
16  See, for example, the front-page photograph, *A Tarde*, 3 July 2011. See also Baldaia, "Festa," 208–11.
17  Baldaia does not indicate when the piligrimage last took place and does not discuss the neighbourhood celebrations, "Festa."

18  Serra, "Triunfo," 61n11; Baldaia, "Festa," 147. On colonial precedents, see Mendes, "Festas," 81–110; Schwartz, "Ceremonies," 19–22; Cañeque, *King's Living Image*, 119–55.

19  "Grupo é mobilizado para vaiar Lula em Salvador" and "PT vai ao TRE contra governo da Bahia," *Folha de S. Paulo*, 3 and 4 July 1994, www1.folha.uol.com.br.

20  "Uso politico não tira o brilho da festa," *A Tarde*, 3 July 2000.

21  "Habeas-corpus no 2 de Julho," *A Tarde*, 1 July 2000.

22  "Prefeito de Pedrão afirma que Encourados vão participar do desfile no 2 de Julho" and "Encourados estão prontos para desfilar no cortejo de hoje," *A Tarde*, 30 June and 2 July 2011.

23  Baldaia, "Festa," 166–8.

24  E.K.V. Farias, *Maria Felipa de Oliveira*; Fundação Pedro Calmon, *2 de Julho*, 58; Pestana, *Dois de Julho*, 17; Carvalho Júnior and Porto Filho, *2 de Julho*, 109.

25  Tiphagne, "Índio," 51–2; J.A.L. Sampaio, "Festa," 153.

26  Consuelo Pondé de Sena, "No 2 de Julho de 2005," *RIGHBa* 100 (2005): 279–81.

27  Carvalho Júnior and Porto Filho, *2 de Julho*, 5, 121.

28  For efforts to make Dois de Julho into a national holiday, see *Bahia Illustrada* (Rio) 4.32 (July 1920); Boccanera Junior, *Bahia cívica*, 31; Albuquerque, *Algazarra*, 115.

29  *Bahia Hoje*, 28 June 1996; Leonelli, *2 de Julho*; "Você sabia que em 2 de Julho nós, os baianos, travamos e ganhamos uma verdadeira guerra de Libertação Nacional," campaign flyer distributed on behalf of Domingos Leonelli, 2 July 1996, author's collection.

30  Biaggio Talento, "Tempo Presente," *A Tarde*, 3 July 2011; Lei 12.819, 5 June 2013, *CLB*.

31  "Iphan divulga o resultado da pré-seleção do Edital de Patrimônio Imaterial 2009" (which includes "Tradições Populares no Cortejo do Dois de Julho") and "Região Nordeste – bens registrados nos Estados," portal.iphan.gov.br.

32  "Aeroporto é 2 de Julho," handbill distributed on behalf of State Deputy Moema Gramacho, 2 July 2000, author's collection; Domingos Leonelli, "2 de Julho alegria e tristeza," *A Tarde*, 2 July 1998.

33  "Alice: renomear Aeroporto 2 de Julho é 'Prioridade,'" 19 February 2014, www.brasil247.com. The progress of the bill, PL 6106/2002, can be followed on http://www.camara.gov.br.

34  Kraay, "Política"; Consuelo Pondé de Sena, "No Dois de Julho de 2014," *RIGHBa* 109 (2014): 281–3.

35 Speech of Zezéu Ribeiro, 4 July, *Diário da Câmara dos Deputados* (2006): 33, 780. Deputy Zezéu's (or his aides') reading list included B.H. Amaral, *Ação* and *História da Bahia*; L.H.D. Tavares, *Independência*; Morel, *Cipriano Barata*; Kraay, "Entre o Brasil."

36 Carvalho Júnior and Porto Filho, *2 de Julho*, 138. The interview was published in *Bahia com História* 1 (July 2015), http://bahiacomhistoria.ba.gov.br.

37 "Problema com transporte quebra tradição dos 'Encourados de Pedrão,'" 2 July 2012, http://g1.globo.com/bahia.

38 For other examples, see "2 de Julho," a 2012 DVD intended for use by schoolteachers; "Cabocla só foi incorporada ao desfile a partir de 1846," *A Tarde*, 1 July 2011; "Recursos são liberados para decoração dos carros," *A Tarde*, 12 June 2012; "Governo do Estado da Bahia: Festa do 2 de Julho, Dia da Independência do Brasil na Bahia, 2000," flyer produced by Congregações Mariana de Salvador for distribution on 2 July 2000, author's collection.

39 Kraay, "Independência baiana"; email messages, 15 and 25 July 2005, author's collection.

40 Nelson Cadena, "O 2 de Julho não nasceu do povo" and "2 de Julho começou em Itaparica," *Correio da Bahia*, 26 June 2015 and 1 July 2016, www.correio24horas.com.

41 J.A.L. Sampaio, "Festa de Dois de Julho," 156–7; Serra, "Triunfo," 62–5, 70–3; J.T. Santos, *Dono*, 45–9. Based on his research in the 1980s and early 1990s, Santos suggests that the *caboclo* was more venerated than the *cabocla*, but my impression from observing the symbols while on display is that more people gather around the *cabocla*.

42 H. Vianna, "'Dois de Julho' na Bahia," 61, 67–9; "Folclore cívico," 178; "Comemorações do 2 de Julho," *Diário Oficial*, 2 July 1982. On criticism of this veneration, see Baldaia, "Festa," 174.

43 Baldaia, "Festa," 63–4.

44 "Marcha para Jesus reúne milhares de pessoas na Barra," *A Tarde*, 3 July 2011; Baldaia, "Festa," 127–8.

45 H. Vianna, "Entre verdes e amarelos," *A Tarde*, 1 July 1996.

46 In addition to the materials cited above, see Albuquerque, *ABC*.

47 The Cachoeira festival has yet to find its historian. On Itaparica's celebrations, see Baldaia, "'Abre-te campo formoso'" and "Construção."

48 Molina A. de Cienfuegos and Martínez Barcena, "National Days," 254–5; Foster, "Canadian Days," 41; Gagnon, "'Adieu le mouton.'"

# BIBLIOGRAPHY

## Archives and Libraries

Acervo de Memória e Documentação Clemente Mariani, Universidade Federal do Recôncavo da Bahia
Arquivo do Instituto Geográfico e Histórico da Bahia (AIGHBa)
Arquivo do Instituto Histórico e Geográfico Brasileiro (AIHGB)
Arquivo Histórico do Museu Imperial (AHMI)
Arquivo Histórico Municipal de Salvador (AHMS)
    Coleção Festejos Relacionados ao 2 de Julho (CFRDJ)
Arquivo Nacional (AN)
Arquivo Público do Estado da Bahia (APEBa)
    Seção de Arquivo Colonial e Provincial (SACP)
    Seção Republicana (SR)
    Seção Judiciária (SJ)
        Inventários e Testamentos (IT)
    Seção Legislativa (SL)
Arquivo Público do Estado de Pernambuco (APEPe)
Biblioteca Nacional (BN)
    Divisão de Música (Mus.)
    Hemeroteca Digital Brasileira (HDB)
    Seção de Cartografia
    Seção de Manuscritos (SM)
    Seção de Obras Gerais
    Seção de Obras Raras (SOR)
    Seção de Periódicos
Biblioteca Pública do Estado da Bahia (BPEBa)
    Centro de Memória da Bahia
    Hemeroteca
Fundação Casa de Rui Barbosa
Museu Tempostal
    Coleção Antônio Marcelino
National Archives and Records Service (NARS)

Microcopy M-121 ("Despatches from United States Ministers to Brazil, 1809–1906")

Microcopy T-331 ("Despatches from United States Consuls in Bahia, 1850–1906")

Microcopy T-432 ("Despatches from U.S. Consuls in St. Salvador, Brazil, 1808–1849")

Oliveira Lima Library, Catholic University of America

Public Record Office (PRO)

Foreign Office (FO) 13 ("General Correspondence before 1906: Brazil" [microfilm])

Foreign Office (FO) 63 ("General Correspondence before 1906: Portugal")

## Newspapers

Most of the newspapers cited in this book are now available electronically from the Hemeroteca Digital Brasileira (HDB), maintained by Brazil's Biblioteca Nacional (memoria.bn.br). Prior to the HDB's launch in 2012, most of the BN's holdings of Bahian periodicals were microfilmed and catalogued in its *Catálogo de periódicos brasileiros microfilmados*, 57–71. In addition to these periodicals, I also consulted the following newspapers at other libraries and archives:

*O Alabama*, 1864–71 (AIGHBa)

*Bahia Illustrada*, 1867–68 (AIHGB)

*O Brazil*, 1883 (AN)

*Cidade do Salvador*, 1898–99 (BPEBa)

*A Coisa*, 1898–1900 (BPEBa)

*Correio da Manhã*, 1888 (APEPe)

*Correio de Noticias*, 1895–97 (BPEBa)

*Diario: O Independente Constitucional*, 1825–26 (BN/SOR)

*Diario da Bahia*, 1858, 1861, 1868, 1891 (AIGHBa); 1895–97 (BPEBa)

*Diario de Noticias*, 1886, 1891, 1896 (AIGHBa)

*Estado da Bahia*, 1896 (APEBa)

*Gazeta da Bahia*, 1832 (BPEBa)

*Gazeta da Tarde*, 1885 (APEPe)

*Gazeta Illustrada*, 1882 (APEPe)

*O Guaycuru*, 1853 (BPEBa)

*O Independente Constitucional*, 1823–24 (BN/SOR)

*Jornal da Tarde*, 1853 (BPEBa)

*Jornal de Noticias*, 1892 (AIGHBa and BPEBa), 1898 (AIGHBa), 1899–1900 (AIGHBa, APEBa, and BPEBa)

*O Santelmo*, 1879 (APEPe)
*O Seculo*, 1852 (APEPe)
*Sirius*, 1895 (Fundação Casa de Rui Barbosa)
*Tolerancia*, 1849 (APEBa)

I also searched for reports about Dois de Julho and provincial correspondence in the following periodicals from outside of Bahia; unless otherwise indicated, all are currently available in the HDB:

*A Actualidade* (Rio), 1859–64
*The Anglo-Brazilian Times* (Rio), 1865–84
*Astrea* (Rio), 1826–32
*Aurora Fluminense* (Rio), 1827–35
*O Brasil* (Rio), 1840–52
*O Brasileiro Imparcial* (Rio), 1830
*Brazil Commercial* (Rio), 1858
*Constitucional* (Rio), 1862–64
*Correio da Tarde* (Rio), 1855–62
*Correio Mercantil* (Rio), 1848–68
*Correio Official* (Rio), 1833–41
*O Democrata* (Recife), 1858 (APEPe)
*Diario de Noticias* (Rio), 1885–95
*Diario de Pernambuco* (Recife), 1826–1900
*Diario do Rio de Janeiro*, 1821–78
*Diario Fluminense* (Rio), 1823–33
*Echo Pernambucano* (Recife), 1851–56 (APEPe)
*O Farol Paulistano* (1930)
*O Farricoco* (Rio), 1848–49 (AN)
*Folhinha Laemmert* (Rio), 1830–89 (AIHGB)
*O Futuro* (Rio), 1881
*Gazeta da Tarde* (Rio), 1880–1900
*Gazeta de Noticias* (Rio), 1875–1900
*O Grito Nacional* (Rio), 1848–58
*O Guerreiro* (Rio), 1853
*Jornal da Tarde* (Rio), 1869–72
*Jornal do Brazil* (Rio), 1891–1900
*Jornal do Commercio* (Rio), 1827–1900
*Jornal do Recife*, 1859–1900
*O Mercantil* (Rio), 1844–47
*A Nação* (Rio), 1872–76
*Nova Luz Brasileira* (Rio), 1829–31

*O Paiz* (Rio), 1884–1900
*Periodico dos Pobres* (Rio), 1850–56
*A Reforma* (Rio), 1869–79
*A Republica* (Rio), 1870–74
*O Social* (Rio), 1845–46

## Published Sources

*2 de Julho: a Independência do Brasil na Bahia*. DVD. Salvador: CIPÓ-Comunicação Interativa, n.d. [ca. 2012].

Abreu, Martha. *O império do divino: festas religiosas e cultura popular no Rio de Janeiro, 1830–1900*. Rio: Nova Fronteira; São Paulo: FAPESP, 1999.

– "Mello Moraes Filho: festas, tradições populares e identidade nacional." In *A história contada: capítulos de história social de literatura no Brasil*, ed. Sidney Chalhoub and Leonardo Affonso de M. Pereira, 171–93. Rio: Nova Fronteira, 1998.

Afolabi, Niyi. "Reversing Dislocations: African Contributions to Brazil in the Words of Manuel Querino, 1890–1920." *History Compass* 11.4 (2013): 259–67.

Aguiar, Durval Vieira de. *Descrições práticas da província da Bahia...*, 2nd ed. Rio: Livraria Editora Cátedra, (1888) 1979.

Aguiar, [Manoel] Pinto de. *Abastecimento: crises, motins e intervenção*. Rio: Philobiblion, 1985.

Aguilar, Gonzalo. "The National Opera: A Migrant Genre of Imperial Expansion." *Journal of Latin American Cultural Studies* 12.1 (2003): 83–94.

Agulhon, Maurice. *Marianne into Battle: Republican Imagery and Symbolism in France, 1789–1880*, trans. Janet Lloyd. Cambridge: Cambridge University Press, 1981.

– "La 'statuomanie' et l'histoire." *Ethnologie Française* 8 (1978): 145–72.

Albuquerque, Wlamyra R. de. *ABC do Dois de Julho*. Salvador: Fundação Gregório de Matos, 2006.

– *Algazarra nas ruas: comemorações da Independência na Bahia (1889–1923)*. Campinas: Editora da UNICAMP, 1999.

– "Os dias de julho para ler com Querino." In *Manuel Querino – seus artigos na Revista do Instituto Geográfico e Histórico da Bahia*, ed. Jaime Nascimento and Hugo Gama, 29–40. Salvador: IGHBa, 2009.

– "A festa do Dois de Julho: as comemorações públicas da Independência nacional." In *2 de Julho: a Bahia na Independência nacional*, ed. Fundação Pedro Calmon, 38–48. Salvador: Fundação Pedro Calmon, n.d. [2010].

– *O jogo da dissimulação: Abolição e cidadania negra no Brasil*. São Paulo: Companhia das Letras, 2009.

Albuquerque Jr., Durval Muniz de. *The Invention of the Brazilian Northeast*, trans. Jerry D. Metz. Durham: Duke University Press, 2014.

*Almanak administrativo, commercial e industrial da provincia da Bahia para o anno de 1873...* Salvador: Typ. de Oliveira Mendes & C., 1872.

*Almanak administrativo, mercantil e industrial da Bahia...* Salvador: Typ. de Camillo de Lellis Masson, 1854–63.

Almeida, Francisco Gomes dos Santos e. *Oração gratuloria recitada na Se Catedral no dia dous de Julho...* Salvador: Typ. Imp.ᵃˡ e Nacional, 1829.

Almeida, Maria do Carmo Baltar Esmaty de. "A freguesia da Vitória, da Colônia à República." In *A urbanização de Salvador em três tempos: Colônia, Império e República*, 2 vols., ed. Jaime Nascimento and Hugo Nascimento, 1:211–27. Salvador: IGHBa, 2011.

Almeida, Miguel Calmon du Pin e. *A batalha de Pirajá (8 de novembro de 1822)*. Rio: Imprensa Nacional, 1923.

Alonso, Angela. *Flores, votos e balas: o movimento abolicionista brasileiro (1868–88)*. São Paulo: Companhia das Letras, 2015.

Alves, Lizir Arcanjo. "Constantino do Amaral Tavares e o drama histórico na Bahia." In Constantino do Amaral Tavares, *Os tempos da Independencia: drama historico*, facsimile ed., v–xiii. Salvador: IGHBa, 2000.

– "Do modo de ser poeta baiano ... e seus obstáculos." *Estudos Linguísticos e Literários* 23.4 (June–December 1999): 249–63.

– "Os tensos laços da nação: conflitos político-literários no Segundo Reinado." PhD diss., Universidade Federal da Bahia, 2000.

– ed. *O 2 de Julho na Bahia: antologia poética*. Salvador: Fundação Pedro Calmon and Quarteto Editora, 2010.

– ed. *Mulheres escritoras na Bahia: as poetisas, 1822–1918*. Salvador: Étera, 1999.

Alves, Marieta. "Música de barbeiros." *Revista Brasileira de Folclore* 7.17 (1967): 5–14.

Amado, Janaína. "Diogo Álvares, o Caramuru e a fundação mítica do Brasil." *Estudos Históricos* 14.25 (2000): 3–40.

Amaral, Braz H[ermenegildo] do. *Ação da Bahia na obra da Independência nacional*, 2nd ed. Salvador: EdUFBa, (1923) 2005.

– *Historia da Bahia do Imperio à Republica*. Salvador: Imprensa Official da Bahia, 1923.

– *História da Independência na Bahia*, 2nd ed. Salvador: Prefeitura do Município de Salvador, (1923) 1957.

– "Memoria historica sobre a proclamação da Republica na Bahia." RIGHBa 30 (1904): 3–60.

– "Memoria historica sobre os acontecimentos de 24 de Novembro de 1891 na Bahia." RIGHBa 29 (1903): 3–68.

Amaral, José Alvares do. *Resumo chronologico e noticioso da provincia da Bahia desde o seu descobrimento em 1.500*, 2nd ed., ed. J[osé] Teixeira Barros. Salvador: Imp. Official do Estado, (1881) 1922.

Anderson, Benedict. *Imagined Communities: Reflections on the Origin and Spread of Nationalism.* London: Verso, 1996.

Andrade, Maria José de Souza. *A mão de obra escrava em Salvador, 1811–1860.* São Paulo: Corrupio, 1988.

Andréa, José. *O Marechal Andréa nos relevos da história do Brasil.* Rio: Biblioteca do Exército Editora, 1977.

Andrews, George Reid. *Afro-Latin America, 1800–2000.* New York: Oxford University Press, 2004.

Aragão, Antonio Ferrão Moniz de. *A Bahia e seus governadores na República,* facsimile ed. Salvador: Fundação Pedro Calmon and UEFS Editora, (1923) 2010.

Aras, Lina Maria Brandão de. "Bahia e Pernambuco em suas relações regionais na primeira metade do século XIX." *Clio* (Recife) 20 (2002): 7–18.

– "A santa federação imperial: Bahia, 1831–1833." PhD diss., Universidade de São Paulo, 1995.

Araújo, Dilton Oliveira de. *O tutu da Bahia: transição conservadora e formação da nação, 1838–1850.* Salvador: EdUFBa, 2009.

Araújo, Ubiratan Castro de, ed. *Salvador era assim: memórias da cidade,* 2 vols. Salvador: IGHBa, 1999–2001.

Assier, Adolphe d'. *Le Brésil contemporain: races, moeurs, institutions, paysages.* Paris: Durand et Lauriel, 1867.

Athayde, Sylvia Menezes de, ed. *A Bahia na época de D. João: a chegada da Corte portuguesa, 1808.* Salvador: Museu de Arte da Bahia; Solisluna Design e Editora, 2008.

Augel, Moema Parente. *Visitantes estrangeiros na Bahia oitocentista.* São Paulo: Cultrix, 1980.

Avé-Lallemant, Robert. *Viagem pelo Norte do Brasil no ano de 1859,* trans. Eduardo de Lima Castro. 2 vols. Rio: Instituto Nacional do Livro, 1961.

Azevedo, Elizabeth Ribeiro. "O Drama." In *História do teatro brasileiro,* vol. 1: *Das origens ao teatro profissional da primeira metade do século XX,* ed. João Roberto Faria, 94–119. São Paulo: Perspectiva and Edições SESCSP, 2012.

– "Introdução: o drama histórico e a construção da nacionalidade." In *Antologia do teatro romântico,* ed. Elizabeth Ribeiro Azevedo, ix–xxii. São Paulo: Martins Fontes, 2006.

Bahia. *Annaes da Assembléa Legislativa Provincial da Bahia.* Salvador: 1873–86.

– *Annaes da Câmara dos Senhores Deputados do Estado Federado da Bahia.* Salvador: Typographia do "Correio de Noticias," 1894–96.

– *Collecção das leis e resoluções da Provincia da Bahia.* Salvador: 1862–89.

– *Constituição do Estado da Bahia: promulgada em 2 de julho de 1891.* Salvador: Typographia do "Diario da Bahia," 1891.

– *Leis e resoluções do Estado da Bahia.* Salvador: 1891–1900.

- President. *Relatório*. Salvador: 1839–89.
- Secretaria da Educação e Cultura, ed. *Aspectos do 2 de Julho*. Salvador: Secretaria da Educação e Cultura, 1973.
- Secretaria da Cultura e Turismo. *Dicionário de autores baianos*. Salvador: Fundo de Cultura da Bahia, Governo da Bahia, Secretaria da Fazenda [e] Secretaria da Cultura e Turismo 2006.

Baldaia, Fábio Peixoto Bastos. "'Abre-te campo formoso': uma análise dos festejos da Independênica de Itaparica – BA através da trajetória do Grupo dos Guaranys." In *Festas na Baía de Todos os Santos: visibilizando diversidades, territórios, sociabilidades*, ed. Fátima Tavares and Francesca Bassi, 81–104. Salvador: EdUFBa, 2015.
- "A construção de uma brasilidade: um estudo histórico sobre os festejos da Independência do Brasil em Itaparica." MA thesis, Universidade Federal da Bahia, 2011.
- "A festa, o drama e a trama: cultura e poder nas comemorações da Independência da Bahia (1959–2017)." PhD diss., Universidade Federal da Bahia, 2018.

Bandeira, Luiz Alberto Moniz. *O feudo: a Casa da Torre de Garcia d'Ávila, da conquista dos sertões à Independência do Brasil*. Rio: Civilização Brasileira, 2000.

Barauna, Francisco. *Oração gratulatoria pronunciada no convento de N. Senhora do Desterro, aos 14 de Outubro do presente anno...* Salvador: Typographia Nacional, 1823.

Barickman, B[ert] J. *A Bahian Counterpoint: Sugar, Tobacco, Cassava, and Slavery in the Recôncavo, 1780–1860*. Stanford: Stanford University Press, 1998.
- "Persistence and Decline: Slave Labour and Sugar Production in the Bahian Recôncavo, 1850–1888." *Journal of Latin American Studies* 28.3 (October 1996): 581–633.
- "'Tame Indians,' 'Wild Heathens,' and Settlers in Southern Bahia in the Late Eighteenth and Early Nineteenth Centuries." *The Americas* 51.3 (January 1995): 325–68.

Barman, Roderick J. *Brazil: The Forging of a Nation, 1798–1852*. Stanford: Stanford University Press, 1988.
- *Citizen Emperor: Pedro II and the Making of Brazil, 1825–1891*. Stanford: Stanford University Press, 1999.

Barreto, Francisco Moniz. *Canto dos veteranos ao alvorecer do Dia Dous de Julho de 1855...* Salvador: Typ. de Camillo de Lellis Masson & C., 1855.
- *Os veteranos: canto recitado nas fileiras do batalhão dos veteranos da Independencia ao alvorecer do dia dous de julho de 1856...* Salvador: Typ. de Camillo de Lellis Masson & C., 1856.

Barros, F[rancisco] Borges de. "Á margem da historia da Bahia." *AAPEBa* 3 (1918): 1–179.

- "Á margem da historia da Bahia." *AAPEBa* 23 (1934): 3–584.

Barros, J[osé] Teixeira. "Folklore brasileiro (contribuição regional)." *RIGHBa* 51 (1925): 109–47.

- "José Alvares do Amaral." In José Alvares do Amaral, *Resumo chronologico e noticioso da provincia da Bahia desde o seu descobrimento em 1.500*, 2nd ed., ed. J[osé] Teixeira Barros, 3–6. Salvador: Imp. Official do Estado, 1922.

Barroso, Romualdo Maria de Seixas. *Oração gratulatoria recitada no Dia Dous de Julho de 1873 na Cathedral da Bahia...* Salvador: Typographia do Diario, 1877.

Basile, Marcello Otávio Neri de Campos. *Ezequiel Corrêa dos Santos: um jacobino na Corte imperial.* Rio: Editora FGV, 2001.

- "O Império em construção: projetos de Brasil e ação política na Corte regencial." PhD diss., Universidade Federal do Rio de Janeiro, 2004.

Bastos, Fernanda Villela. "Quando os intelectuais 'roubam a cena': o Conservatório Dramático da Bahia e sua missão 'civilizatória' (1855–1875)." MA thesis, Universidade Federal da Bahia, 2014.

Bastos, Filinto Justiniano F. *Elementos de instrução e educação civicas de direito publico e de direito constitucional brasileiro*, 2nd ed. Salvador: Joaquim Ribeiro & Co., (1916) 1925.

Baud, Michiel, and Kees Konings. "A lavoura dos pobres: Tobacco Farming and the Development of Commercial Agriculture in Bahia, 1870–1930." *Journal of Latin American Studies* 31.2 (1999): 287–329.

Beattie, Peter M. "Illustrating Race and Nation in the Paraguayan War Era: Exploring the Decline of the Tupi Guarani Warrior in the Embodiment of Brazil." In *Military Struggle and Identity Formation in Latin America: Race, Nation, and Community during the Liberal Period*, ed. Nicola Foote and René D. Harder Horst, 174–203. Gainesville: University Press of Florida, 2010.

- *The Tribute of Blood: Army, Honor, Race, and Nation in Brazil, 1864–1945.* Durham: Duke University Press, 2001.

Beezley, William H., and David E. Lorey, eds. ¡*Viva Mexico!* ¡*Viva La Independencia! Celebrations of September 16.* Wilmington: Scholarly Resources, 2001.

Belens, Adroaldo. *Modernidade sem rostos: Salvador e a telefonia (1881–1924).* Simões Filho: Kalanga, 2010.

Bello, Joaquim Cavalcanti d'Albuquerque. "Diário do Tenente-Coronel Albuquerque Bello: notas extraídas do caderno de lembranças do autor sobre sua passagem na Guerra do Paraguai," ed. Ricardo Salles and Vera Arraes. *Documentos Históricos* 92 (2011): 37–227.

Belluzzo, Ana Maria de Moraes. *O Brasil dos viajantes*, 2nd ed., 3 vols. in 1. São Paulo: Metalivros; Rio: Objetiva, 1999.

Bénézit, Emmanuel. *Dictionnaire critique et documentaire des peintres, sculpteurs, dessinateurs et graveurs de tous les temps*, rev. ed., 14 vols. Paris: Grund, 1999.

Bertoni, Lilia Ana. "Construir la nacionalidad: héroes, estatuas y fiestas patrias, 1887–1891." *Boletin del Instituto de Historia Argentina y Americana – Dr. E. Ravignani*, 3rd ser. 5 (First Semester 1992): 77–110.

Biskupski, M.B.B. *Independence Day: Myth, Symbol, and the Creation of Modern Poland*. Oxford: Oxford University Press, 2012.

Bittencourt, Anna Ribeiro de Góes. *Longos serões do campo*, 2 vols., ed. Maria Clara Mariani Bittencourt. Rio: Nova Fronteira, 1992.

– "Suzana." Typescript. Acervo de Memória e Documentação Clemente Mariani, Universidade Federal do Recôncavo da Bahia.

Bizarria, Raimundo. "Manuel Lopes da Silva Cardoso." In *Apontamentos para a história da imprensa da Bahia*, 2nd ed., ed. Luis Guilherme Pontes Tavares, 63–78. Salvador: Academia de Letras da Bahia, (2003) 2008.

Blake, Stanley E. *The Vigorous Core of Our Nationality: Race and Regional Identity in Northeastern Brazil*. Pittsburgh: University of Pittsburgh Press, 2011.

Boaventura, Edivaldo. "Instituto Geográfico e Histórico da Bahia – 2006." *RIGHBa* 102 (2007): 185–7.

Boccanera Junior, Silio. *Bahia civica e religiosa, subsidios para a historia*. Salvador: A Nova Graphica, 1926.

– *Bahia epigraphica e iconographica (resenha historica)*. Salvador: Typ. da Revista Renascença, 1928.

– "A Bahia e seus historiadores (sem comentarios)." *RIGHBa* 45 (1919): 153–64.

– *Bahia historica: reminiscencia do passado, registo do presente*. Salvador: Typ. Bahiana de C. Melchiades, 1921.

– "Pagina de historia: o Campo Grande da Bahia – sua origem – divida de honra." *RIGHBa* 30 (1904): 111–19.

– *O teatro na Bahia: da Colônia à República*, facsimile ed. Salvador: EdUFBa, (1924) 2008.

– *As télas historicas do paço municipal da Bahia: biographias*. Salvador: Livraria e Typographia do Commercio, 1922.

– *Theatro nacional: autôres e actôres dramaticos, bahianos, em especial, biographias*. Salvador: Imprensa Official do Estado, 1923.

Bogart, Michele. *Public Sculpture and the Civic Ideal in New York City, 1890–1930*. Chicago: University of Chicago Press, 1989.

Borges, Dain. *The Family in Bahia, Brazil, 1870–1945*. Stanford: Stanford University Press, 1992.

- "Salvador's 1890s: Paternalism and Its Discontents." *Luso-Brazilian Review* 30.2 (Winter 1993): 47–57.
Botelho, Benjamim José. *Breve noticia sobre o Estado da Bahia...* Salvador: Typ. e Encadernação do "Diario da Bahia," 1894.
Branco, Manoel Alves. *Ode ao Dia Dous de Julho.* Salvador: Imprensa Economica, 1879.
Brazil. *Anais da Câmara dos Deputados.* Rio: 1826–89.
- *Anais do Senado.* Rio: 1826–89.
- *Coleção das Leis do Brasil.* Rio: 1822–89.
- Arquivo Nacional. *A Junta Governativa da Bahia e a Independência.* Rio: Arquivo Nacional, 1973.
- Biblioteca Nacional. *Catálogo da Exposição de História do Brasil,* 3 vols., facsimile ed. Brasília: Editora da Universidade de Brasília, (1881) 1981.
- Directoria Geral de Estatisticas. *Recenseamento da população do Brazil a que se procedeu no dia 1 de agosto de 1871,* 21 vols. Rio: Leuzinger & Filhos, 1873–76.
- Fundação Biblioteca Nacional. *Catálogo de periódicos brasileiros microfilmados.* Rio: Biblioteca Nacional, 1994.
- Ministério da Guerra, *Relatório,* 1827–89.
- Ministerio da Industria, Viação e Obras Publicas. Directoria Geral de Estatistica. *Synopse do Recenseamento de 31 de Dezembro de 1890.* Rio: Officina da Estatistica, 1898.
- *Synopse do Recenseamento de 31 de Dezembro de 1900.* Rio: Typographia da Estatistica, 1905.
Brito, Jailton Lima. *A Abolição na Bahia, 1870–1888.* Salvador: Centro de Estudos Baianos, 2003.
Brookshaw, David. *Race and Color in Brazilian Literature.* Metuchen: Scarecrow Press, 1986.
Brown, Alexandra K. "'On the Vanguard of Civilization': Slavery, the Police, and Conflicts between Public and Private Power in Salvador da Bahia, Brazil, 1835–1888." PhD diss., University of Texas at Austin, 1998.
Brunk, Samuel, and Ben Fallow, eds. *Heroes and Hero Cults in Latin America.* Austin: University of Texas Press, 2006.
Bulcão Sobrinho, Antônio de Araújo de Aragão. "Chefes de polícia da Bahia no Império." *RIHGB* 253 (October–December 1961): 12–33.
- *O Conselho Geral da Província, 1828 a 1834.* Salvador: Tip. Manú Editora, 1957.
- "O pregoeiro da República: Virgílio Clímaco Damásio." *RIHGB* 264 (July–September 1964): 373–81.
- "A proclamação da República na Bahia." *RIHGB* 257 (October–December 1962): 6–15.

- "Relembrando o velho senado baiano." *RIHGB* 218 (January–March 1953): 138–203.
- "Representantes da Bahia na Câmara Federal da Primeira República." *RIGHB* 263 (April–June 1964): 55–86.
- "Titulares bahianos." *Revista do Instituto Genealógico da Bahia* 2 (1946): 26–40; 3 (1948): 55–8.

Burns, E. Bradford. "Manuel Querino's Interpretation of the African Contribution to Brazil." *Journal of Negro History* 59.1 (January 1974): 78–86.

Butler, Kim D. *Freedoms Given, Freedoms Won: Afro-Brazilians in Post-Abolition São Paulo and Salvador.* New Brunswick: Rutgers University Press, 1998.

Calmon, Francisco Marques de Góes. *Vida econômica-financeira da Bahia: elementos para a história de 1808 a 1899*, 2nd ed. Salvador: Fundação de Pesquisas and CPE, (1923) 1978.

Calmon, Jorge. "Prefácio à 1ª edição: a imprensa exige sua história." In *Apontamentos para a história da imprensa da Bahia*, 2nd ed., ed. Luis Guilherme Pontes Tavares, 19–21. Salvador: Academia de Letras da Bahia, (2003) 2008.
- *O vereador Manoel Querino.* Salvador: Câmara Municipal de Salvador, 1995.

Calmon, Pedro. *História da literatura baiana.* Salvador: Prefeitura Municipal de Salvador, 1949.
- "Ladislau dos Santos Titara." *RIGHBa* 86 (1976–77): 159–83.

Calmon Sobrinho, Miguel. "Homenagem a Luiz Tarquínio no centenário do seu nascimento, em 22 de julho de 1944." *RIGHBa* 72 (1945): 221–31.

Câmara Cascudo, Luís da. *Dicionário do folclore brasileiro*, 9th ed. Rio: Ediouro, n.d.

Campos, J[oão] da Silva. "Cronicas bahianas do seculo XIX." *AAPEBa* 25 (1937): 295–365.
- *A musica da policia da Bahia.* Salvador: Imprensa Oficial do Estado, 1933.
- *Procissões tradicionais da Bahia*, 2nd ed. Salvador: Conselho Estadual de Cultura, (1941) 2005.
- "Tradições bahianas." *RIGHBa* 56 (1930): 353–557.

Candido, Mariana P. "Transatlantic Links: The Benguela-Bahia Connections, 1700–1850." In *Paths of the Atlantic Slave Trade: Interactions, Identities, and Images*, ed. Ana Lucia Araújo, 239–72. Amherst: Cambria Press, 2011.

Cañeque, Alejandro. *The King's Living Image: The Culture and Politics of Viceregal Power in Colonial Mexico.* London: Routledge, 2004.

Capirunga, Antonio Ferreira Santos. *Poesias*, vol. 1. Salvador: Typ. de M.A. da S. Serva, 1843.

Carvalho, Aloysio de. "A imprensa na Bahia em 100 anos." In *Apontamentos para a história da imprensa da Bahia*, 2nd ed., ed. Luis Guilherme Pontes Tavares, 41–61. Salvador: Academia de Letras da Bahia, (2003) 2008.

Carvalho, José Murilo de. *Os bestializados: o Rio de Janeiro e a República que não foi*, 3rd ed. São Paulo: Companhia das Letras, 1999.

- *"Clamar e agitar sempre": os radicais da década de 1860*. Rio: Topbooks, 2018.

- *A construção da ordem: a elite política imperial / Teatro de sombras: a política imperial*, rev. ed. Rio: Relume-Dumará, 1996.

- *A formação das almas: o imaginário da República no Brasil*. São Paulo: Companhia das Letras, 1990.

Carvalho, Maria Rosário de, and Ana Magda Carvalho. "Introdução." In *Índios e caboclos: a história recontada*, ed. idem and idem. Salvador: EduFBa, 2012.

Carvalho Filho, Aloísio de. "Jornalismo na Bahia, 1875–1960." In *Apontamentos para a história da imprensa da Bahia*, 2nd ed., ed. Luis Guilherme Pontes Tavares, 79–100. Salvador: Academia de Letras da Bahia, (2003) 2008.

Carvalho Júnior, Álvaro Pinto Dantas de. *O Barão de Jeremoabo e a política do seu tempo: trajetória de um líder conservador na Bahia*. Salvador: Secretaria de Cultura e Turismo, 2006.

Carvalho Júnior, Álvaro Pinto Dantas de, and Ubaldo Marques Porto Filho. *2 de Julho: independência da Bahia e do Brasil*, 2nd ed. Salvador: Casa de Cultura Carolina Taboada, (2015) 2016.

Carvalho Neto, Joviniano S. de. "Proclamação da República na Bahia no olhar de um cientista político." *RIGHBa* 106 (2011): 87–114.

Castellucci, Aldrin A.S. "Classe e cor na formação do Centro Operário da Bahia." *Afro-Ásia* 41 (2010): 85–132.

- "Muitos votantes e poucos eleitores: a difícil conquista da cidadania operária no Brasil Império (Salvador, 1850–1881)." *Varia História* 30.52 (January–April 2014): 183–206.

- "Política e cidadania operária em Salvador (1890–1919)." *Revista de História* 162 (2010): 205–41.

- "Os trabalhadores e a política no Brasil império: o problema da cidadania operária em uma sociedade escravista (Salvador, 1850–1881)." In *Barganhas e querelas da escravidão: tráfico, alforria e liberdade (séculos XVIII e XIX)*, ed. Lisa Earl Castillo, Wlamyra Albuquerque, and Gabriela dos Reis Sampaio, 281–314. Salvador: EduFBa, 2014.

Castellucci Júnior, Wellington. "De cativos a baleeiros: uma amizade indissolúvel entre dois africanos no outro lado do Atlântico (Itaparica, 1816–1866)." *Topoi* 15.29 (July–December 2014): 444–72.

Castilho, Celso Thomas. "Performing Abolitionism, Enacting Citizenship: The Social Construction of Political Rights in 1880s Recife, Brazil." *Hispanic American Historical Review* 93.3 (August 2013): 377–409.

- *Slave Emancipation and Transformations in Brazilian Political Citizenship*. Pittsburgh: University of Pittsburgh Press, 2016.

Castillo, Lisa Earl. "Between Memory, Myth, and History: The Transatlantic Voyagers of the Casa Branca Temple." In *Paths of the Atlantic Slave Trade: Interactions, Identities, and Images*, ed. Ana Lucia Araújo, 208–38. Amherst: Cambria Press, 2011.

Castro, Jeanne Berrance de. "A Guarda Nacional." In *História geral da civilização brasileira*, tomo 2: *O Brasil monárquico*. 5 vols., ed. Sérgio Buarque de Holanda, 2:274–98. São Paulo: Difel, 1966–71.

– *A milícia ciadadã: a Guarda Nacional de 1831 a 1850*. São Paulo: Companhia Editora Nacional, 1977.

Castro, Paulo Pereira. "A 'experiência republicana,' 1831–1840." In *História geral da civilização brasileira*, tomo 2: *O Brasil monárquico*, 5 vols., ed. Sérgio Buarque de Holanda, 2:9–67. São Paulo: Difel, 1966–71.

– "Política e administração de 1840 a 1848." In *História geral da civilização brasileira*, tomo 2: *O Brasil monárquico*, 5 vols., ed. Sérgio Buarque de Holanda, 2:509–40. São Paulo: Difel, 1966–71.

Castro, Renato Berbert de. *História do Conselho Geral da Província da Bahia, 1824/1834*. Salvador: Assembléia Legislativa do Estado da Bahia, 1984.

– *A Tipografia Imperial e Nacional da Bahia: Cachoeira, 1823 – Salvador, 1831*. São Paulo: Ática, 1984.

– *Os vice-presidentes da província da Bahia*. Salvador: Fundação Cultural do Estado da Bahia, 1978.

Castro Alves, Antônio Frederico. "Gonzaga ou A Revolução de Minas." In *Obra completa*, ed. Eugênio Gomes, 579–661. Rio: Nova Aguilar, 1986.

"Catálogo da Coleção Antônio P. Rebouças." *Anais da Biblioteca Nacional* 88 (1968): 109–203.

"Catálogo de documentos sôbre a Bahia existentes na Biblioteca Nacional." *Anais da Biblioteca Nacional* 68 (1949): 1–431.

"Catalogo dos jornaes bahianos," RIGHBa 21 (1899): 409–20; 22 (1899): 549–79.

Cavalcanti, Zélia. "O processo de Independência na Bahia." In *1822: dimensões*, ed. Carlos Guilherme Mota, 231–50. São Paulo: Perspectiva, 1972.

Centeno, Miguel Angel. *Blood and Debt: War and the Nation-State in Latin America*. University Park: Pennsylvania State University Press, 2002.

Chacon, Vamireh. *História das idéias socialistas no Brasil*. Rio: Civilização Brasileira, 1965.

Chambers, Sarah. *From Subjects to Citizens: Honor, Gender, and Politics in Arequipa, Peru, 1780–1854*. University Park: Pennsylvania State University Press, 1999.

Champagnac, J.-B.-J., and Olivier. *O Brasil: segundo Champagnac e Olivier*. Rio: Associação Atlética do Brasil, 1957.

Chasteen, John Charles. "The Prehistory of Samba: Carnival Dancing in Rio de Janeiro, 1840–1917." *Journal of Latin American Studies* 28.1 (February 1996): 29–47.

"Chronica dos acontecimentos da Bahia, 1809–1828." *AAPEBa* 26 (1938): 49–95.

Coelho, Geraldo Mártires. *No coração do povo: o monumento à República em Belém, 1891–1897.* Belém: Editora Paka-Tatu, 2002.

Cohen, William. "Symbols of Power: Statues in Nineteenth-Century Provincial France." *Comparative Studies in Society and History* 31.3 (July 1989): 491–513.

Conceição, Miguel Luiz da. "Educar para bem servir: entre a Abolição e a República: as elites baianas e a educação de escravos e libertos." In *Política, instituições e personagens da Bahia (1850–1930),* ed. Jeferson Bacelar and Cláudio Pereira, Salvador: EdUFBa and CEAO, 2013.

Conrad, Robert. *The Destruction of Brazilian Slavery, 1850–1888.* Berkeley: University of California Press, 1972.

Cooper, Elizabeth. "Freedoms Betwixt and Between: Work, Revelry, and Race in the Urban Post-Emancipation Atlantic World: Salvador da Bahia and Havana, 1808–1930." PhD diss., University of Chicago, 2007.

Cordeiro, Antonio da Cruz. *Prologo da guerra ou O voluntario da patria.* Rio: Typ. do Imperial Instituto Artistico, 1865.

Corrigan, Philip, and Derek Sayer. *The Great Arch: English State Formation as Cultural Revolution.* Oxford: Blackwell, 1985.

Costa, Afonso. "O Visconde de Pirajá no centenário de sua morte." *RIGHBa* 75 (1948–49): 95–9.

Costa, Antonio Joaquim Rodrigues da. *Cantos patrioticos ao dia Dois de Julho.* Salvador: Typ. de Camillo Lellis Masson, 1854.

– "Dous de Julho ou O jangadeiro." BN/SM I-08, 27, 009. Manuscript.

– *Pedro Primeiro,* 2nd ed. Rio: Typ. Americana, 1869.

Costa, Emilia Viotti da. "1870–1889." In *Brazil: Empire and Republic, 1822–1930,* ed. Leslie Bethell, 161–213. Cambridge: Cambridge University Press, 1989.

– *The Brazilian Empire: Myths and Histories.* Chicago: University of Chicago Press, 1985.

Costa, F[rancisco] A[ugusto] Pereira da. *Dicionário biográfico de pernambucanos célebres,* facsimile ed. Recife: Fundação de Cultura Cidade do Recife, (1882) 1982.

– *Pernambuco nas luctas emancipacionistas da Bahia em 1822–23.* Recife: Typ. do "Jornal do Recife," 1900.

Cribelli, Teresa. *Industrial Forests and Mechanical Marvels: Modernization in Nineteenth-Century Brazil.* Cambridge: Cambridge University Press, 2016.

Cruz, Maria Cecília Velasco e, Maria das Graças Andrade Leal, and José Ricardo Pinto Moreno, eds. *Histórias e espaços portuários: Salvador e outros portos*. Salvador: EduFBa, 2016.

Cunha, Pedro Octávio Carneiro da. "A fundação de um império liberal." In *História geral da civilização brasileira*, tomo 2: *O Brasil monárquico*, 5 vols., ed. Sérgio Buarque de Holanda, 1:135–78, 238–62, 379–404. São Paulo: Difel, 1966–71.

DaMatta, Roberto. *Carnivals, Rogues, and Heroes: An Interpretation of the Brazilian Dilemma*, trans. John Drury. Notre Dame: University of Notre Dame Press, 1991.

– *A casa e a rua: espaço, cidadania, mulher e morte no Brasil*. São Paulo: Brasiliense, 1985.

Dantas, Mônica Duarte, ed. *Revoltas, motins, revoluções: homens livres pobres e libertos no Brasil do século XIX*. São Paulo: Alameda, 2011.

David, Onildo Reis. *O inimigo invisível: epidemia na Bahia no século XIX*. Salvador: SarahLetras and EduFBa, 1996.

Dávila, Jerry. *Hotel Trópico: Brazil and the Challenge of African Decolonization, 1950–1980*. Durham: Duke University Press, 2010.

Davis, Susan G. *Parades and Power: Street Theater in Nineteenth-Century Philadelphia*. Philadelphia: Temple University Press, 1986.

Debret, Jean-Baptiste. *Viagem pitoresca e histórica ao Brasil*, 3 vols. in 2, trans. Sergio Milliet. São Paulo: Livraria Martins Editora and Editora da Universidade de São Paulo, 1972.

Díaz Arias, David. *La fiesta de la independencia en Costa Rica, 1821–1921*. San José: Editorial Universidad de Costa Rica, 2007.

Diniz, Fernando. "Uma glória da banda da Polícia Militar da Bahia: Maestra [*sic*] Antonio do Espírito Santo." *RIGHBa* 85 (1972–75): 125–30.

Dolhnikoff, Miriam. *O pacto imperial: origens do federalismo no Brasil*. São Paulo: Globo, 2005.

Doratioto, Francisco. *Maldita guerra: nova história da Guerra do Paraguai*. São Paulo: Companhia das Letras, 2002.

Dorea, Luiz Eduardo. *Histórias de Salvador nos nomes das suas ruas*. Salvador: EduFBa, 2006.

Dória, Franklin Américo de Menezes. *Enlevos*. Recife: Typograhia Universal, 1859.

Dourado, Odete. "A Praça Castro Alves: do lamento dos 'cantos' à mundaneidade deslavada: Salvador, 1850–1930." In *A urbanização de Salvador em três tempos: Colônia, Império e República*, 2 vols., ed. Jaime Nascimento and Hugo Gama, 2:199–238. Salvador: IGHBa, 2011.

Driskel, Michael Paul. *As Befits a Legend: Building a Tomb for Napoleon, 1840–1861*. Kent: Kent State University Press, 1995.

Dugrivel, [C.M.]A. *Des bords de la Saône à la Baie de San Salvador, ou Promenade sentimentale en France et au Brésil*. Paris: Ledoyen, 1843.

Dumêt, Eliana Bittencourt. *O semeador de idéias: o pensamento, a vida e a obra de Luiz Tarquínio, um empresário de idéias revolucionárias, em pleno século XIX*. São Paulo: Editora Gente, 1999.

Duncan, Julian Smith. *Public and Private Operations of Railways in Brazil*. New York: Columbia University Press, 1932.

Duncan, Robert H. "Embracing a Suitable Past: Independence Celebrations under Mexico's Second Empire, 1864–66." *Journal of Latin American Studies* 30.2 (May 1998): 249–77.

– "Political Legitimization and Maximilian's Second Empire in Mexico, 1864–1867." *Mexican Studies* 12.1 (Winter 1996): 27–66.

Dunham, George F. "Journal of George Dunham, 1853." Woodson Research Center, Rice University, Americas Collection, ms. 518. Manuscript.

Eakin, Marshall C. *Becoming Brazilian: Race and National Identity in Twentieth-Century Brazil*. Cambridge: Cambridge University Press, 2017.

Earle, Rebecca. *The Return of the Native: Indians and Myth-Making in Spanish America, 1810–1930*. Durham: Duke University Press, 2007.

Echeverrí, Marcela. *Indian and Slave Royalists in the Age of Revolution: Reform, Revolution, and Royalism in the Northern Andes, 1780–1825*. Cambridge: Cambridge University Press, 2016.

Edelweiss, Frederico G. *A antroponímia patriótica da Independência*. Salvador: Centro de Estudos Baianos, 1982.

Enders, Armelle. *Os vultos da nação: fábrica de heróis e formação dos brasileiros*. Rio: FGV Editora, 2014.

"Entrada do Exército Pacificador na Bahia." *Revista de Cultura da Bahia* 17 (1998): 125–33.

"Enumeração dos 'Documentos' existentes no Archivo do Instituto Geographico e Historico da Bahia, em Dezembro de 1928." *RIGHBa* 55 (1929): 585–746.

Esposito, Matthew D. *Funerals, Festivals, and Cultural Politics in Porfirian Mexico*. Albuquerque: University of New Mexico Press, 2010.

*Estatutos da Sociedade Dous de Julho*. Salvador: Typ. de José da Costa Villaça, 1845.

Faria, João Roberto. *Idéias teatrais: o século 19 no Brasil*. São Paulo: Perspectiva, 2001.

Farias, Eny Kleyde Vasconcelos. *Maria Felipa de Oliveira: heroina da Independência da Bahia*. Salvador: Quarteto Editora, 2010.

Fernandes, Etelvina Rebouças. *Do mar da Bahia ao rio do Sertão: Bahia and San Francisco Railway*. Salvador: Secretaria da Cultura e Turismo, 2006.

Ferreira, Jackson. "'Por hoje se acaba a lida': suicídio escravo na Bahia (1850–1888)." *Afro-Ásia* 31 (2004): 197–234.

Ferreira, Manoel Jesuino. *A provincia da Bahia: apontamentos.* Rio: Imp. Nacional, 1875.

Ferreira Filho, Alberto Heráclio. "Desafricanizar as ruas: elites letradas, mulheres pobres e cultura popular em Salvador (1890–1937)." *Afro-Ásia* 21–2 (1998–99): 239–56.

Filgueiras, Luiz Antonio. "Biographia do Dr. Francisco Antonio Filgueiras Sobrinho." *RIGHBa* 46 (1920): 259–71.

Filgueiras Sobrinho, Francisco Antonio. *A legenda de um pariá.* Salvador: Imp. Off. do Estado, 1923.

Flexor, Maria Helena Ochi. *Abreviaturas manuscritas dos séculos XVI ao XIX,* 3rd ed. Rio: Arquivo Nacional, 2008.

Flory, Thomas. *Judge and Jury in Imperial Brazil, 1808–1871: Social Control and Political Stability in the New State.* Austin: University of Texas Press, 1981.

Fonseca, Luiz Anselmo da. *A escravidão, o clero e o abolicionismo,* facsimile ed. Recife: Fundação Joaquim Nabuco and Editora Massangana, (1887) 1988.

Fonseca, Silvia C.P. de Brito. "Federação e república na imprensa baiana (1831–1836)." In *Entre a Monarquia e a República: imprensa, pensamento político e historiografia (1822–1889),* ed. Silvia C.P. de Brito Fonseca and Monica Leite Lessa, 61–81. Rio: EdUERJ, 2008.

Forment, Carlos A. *Democracy in Latin America, 1760–1900,* vol. 1: *Civic Selfhood and Public Life in Mexico and Peru.* Chicago: University of Chicago Press, 2003.

Foster, Derek. "Canadian Days, Non-Canadian Ways." In *National Days, National Ways: Historical, Political, and Religious Celebrations around the World,* ed. Linda Fuller, 41–58. Westport: Praeger, 2004.

Fraga, André Barbosa. *Os heróis da pátria: política cultural e história do Brasil no Governo Vargas.* Curitiba: Editora Prismas, 2015.

Fraga, Walter. *Crossroads of Freedom: Slaves and Freed People in Bahia, Brazil, 1870–1910,* trans. Mary Ann Mahony. Durham: Duke University Press, 2016.

– *Mendigos, moleques e vadios na Bahia do século XIX.* São Paulo: Hucitec; Salvador: EdUFBa, 1996.

Franck, Harry A[lverson]. *Working North from Patagonia: Being the Narrative of a Journey Earned on the Way, through Southern and Eastern South America.* Garden City: Garden City Publishing Company, 1921.

Franco, Tasso. *O trancelim da baiana: crônicas.* Rio: Relume-Dumará, 2002.

Freire, Luiz Alberto Ribeiro. "Manuel Querino, o 'Vasari' brasileiro." In *Personalidades negras: trajetórias e estratégias políticas,* ed. Jaime Nascimento and Hugo Gama, 107–38. Salvador: Quarteto, 2012.

Freire, Vanda Bellard. *Rio de Janeiro, século XIX: cidade da ópera.* Rio: Garamond, 2013.

Freyre, Gilberto. *Order and Progress: Brazil from Monarchy to Republic,* trans. Rod W. Horton. Berkeley: University of California Press, 1986.

Fuller, Linda, ed. *National Days, National Ways: Historical, Political and Religious Celebrations around the World.* Westport: Praeger, 2004.

Fundação Pedro Calmon. *2 de Julho: a Bahia na Independência nacional.* Salvador: Fundação Pedro Calmon, n.d. [ca. 2010].

– *Florilégio do Dois de Julho: Castro Alves.* Salvador: Fundação Pedro Calmon, 2012.

Furtado, João Pinto. *O manto de Penélope: história, mito e memória da Inconfidência Mineira de 1788–89.* São Paulo: Companhia das Letras, 2002.

Gagnon, Marc-André. "'Adieu le mouton, salut les Québecois!' The Lévesque Government and Saint-Jean-Baptiste Day/Fête Nationale Celebrations, 1976–1984." In *Celebrating Canada,* vol. 1: *Holidays, National Days, and the Crafting of Identities,* ed. Matthew Hayday and Raymond Blake, 356–79. Toronto: University of Toronto Press, 2016.

Galo Ledezma, Gerson. "Religiosidade cívica na Bahia: comemorando o primeiro centenário da Independência a 2 de julho de 1923. Entre a memória nacional e a memória regional." *Revista Esboços* 16.21 (2009): 69–87.

Gandon, Tânia Risério d'Almeida. *Portugueses na Bahia da segunda metade do séc. XIX: emigração e comércio,* 2nd ed. Salvador: Ed. UNEB, (1985) 2010.

Garcia, Antonio. "A festa dos jangadeiros (usanças bahianas)." *RIGHBa* 48 (1923): 283–86.

Garcia, Manoel Correia. "Discurso necrologico … Dr. Agrario de Souza Menezes." *Periodico do Instituto Historico da Bahia* 4 (January 1864): 57.

– *Historia da Independencia da Bahia.* Salvador: Typ. e Encadernação – Empreza Editora, 1900.

García-Bryce, Iñigo. *Crafting the Republic: Lima's Artisans and Nation-Building in Peru, 1821–1879.* Albuquerque: University of New Mexico Press, 2004.

Garfield, Seth. *In Search of the Amazon: Brazil, the United States, and the Nature of a Region.* Durham: Duke University Press, 2013.

Geisler, Michael. "The Calendar Conundrum: National Days as Unstable Signifiers." In *National Days: Constructing and Mobilising National Identity,* ed. David McCrone and Gayle McPherson, 10–25. Houndmills: Palgrave Macmillan, 2009.

Giron, Luis Antonio. *Minoridade crítica: a ópera e o teatro nos folhetins da Corte.* São Paulo: EdUSP, 2004.

Gledhill, Sabrina. "Manuel Querino: operários e negros diante da desilusão republicana." In *Política, instituições e personagens da Bahia (1850–1930),* ed. Jefferson Bacelar and Cláudio Pereira, 125–43. Salvador: EdUFBa, 2013.

– "Manuel Querino e a luta contra o 'racismo científico.'" In *Personalidades negras: trajetórias e estratégias políticas,* ed. Jaime Nascimento and Hugo Gama, 17–54. Salvador: Quarteto, 2012.

– *Travessias no Atlântico negro: reflexões sobre Booker T. Washington e Manuel R. Querino.* e-book. n.c.: Editora Fumilayo Publishing, 2018.

Goes, Innocencio. "Um veterano da Independencia: Padre Fr. José Maria Brayner (o padre dos couros)." *RIGHBa* 30 (1904): 135–41.

Gonçalves, Graciela Rodrigues. "As secas na Bahia do século XIX (sociedade e política)." MA thesis, Universidade Federal da Bahia, 2000.

Gondim, Eunice Ribeiro. *Pseudônimos e rúbricas de autores brasileiros*. Rio: Estado de Guanabara, Secretaria de Estado da Educação e Cultura, Biblioteca Estadual, 1961.

Graden, Dale T. *From Slavery to Freedom in Brazil: Bahia, 1835–1900*. Albuquerque: University of New Mexico Press, 2006.

Graham, Maria Dundas. *Journal of a Voyage to Brazil and Residence There during Part of the Years 1821, 1822, 1823*. London: Longman, Hurst, Rees, Orme, Brown, and Green, 1824.

Graham, Richard. *Feeding the City: From Street Market to Liberal Reform in Salvador, Brazil, 1780–1860*. Austin: University of Texas Press, 2010.

– "Free African Brazilians and the State in Slavery Times." In *Racial Politics in Contemporary Brazil*, ed. Michael Hanchard, 30–58. Durham: Duke University Press, 1999.

– *Patronage and Politics in Nineteenth-Century Brazil*. Stanford: Stanford University Press, 1990.

Guardino, Peter. *The Time of Liberty: Popular Political Culture in Oaxaca, 1750–1850*. Durham: Duke University Press, 2005.

Guerra Filho, Sérgio Armando Diniz. "O antilusitanismo na Bahia (1822–1831)." PhD diss., Universidade Federal da Bahia, 2015.

– "O joio e o trigo: debates antilusitanos e as (in)definições nacionais na Bahia de 1831." In *Sociedade e relações de poder na Bahia: séculos XVII–XX*, ed. Dilton Oliveira de Araújo and Maria José Rapassi Mascarenhas, 113–32. Salvador: EdUFBa, 2014.

– "Patriotismo na Guerra da Bahia: tensões e configurações na ordem paternalista." In *Capítulos de história da Bahia: Independência*, ed. Maria das Graças Andrade Leal and Avanete Pereira Sousa, 285–301. Salvador: Assembléia Legislativa da Bahia and EdUNEB, 2017.

– "O povo e a guerra: participação das camadas populares nas lutas pela Independência da Bahia." MA thesis, Universidade Federal da Bahia, 2004.

Guimarães, Lúcia Maria Paschoal. "Entre a Monarquia e a República: a Revolução Pernambucana de 1817 e suas representações no Instituto Histórico e Geográfico Brasileiro." In *Entre a Monarquia e a República: imprensa, pensamento político e historiografia (1822–1889)*, ed. Maria Leite Lessa and Silvia Carla Pereira de Brito Fonseca, 152–61. Rio: EdUERJ, 2008.

Guzmán, Tracy Devine. *Native and National in Brazil: Indigeneity after Independence*. Chapel Hill: University of North Carolina Press, 2013.

Hadfield, William. *Brazil and the River Plate, 1870–76*. Sutton: W.R. Church, 1877.

Harding, Rachel. *A Refuge in Thunder: Candomblé and the Alternative Spaces of Blackness.* Bloomington: Indiana University Press, 2000.

Harris, Max. *Carnival and Other Christian Festivals: Folk Theology and Folk Performance.* Austin: University of Texas Press, 2003.

Haußer, Christian. "Civilização e nação: o índio na historiografia brasileira oitocentista." *Jahrbuch für Geschichte Lateinamerikas* 44 (2007): 235–57.

Hayday, Matthew, and Raymond Blake, eds. *Celebrating Canada,* vol. 1: *Holidays, National Days, and the Crafting of Identities.* Toronto: University of Toronto Press, 2016.

Hazareesingh, Sudhir. *The Saint-Napoleon: Celebrations of Sovereignty in Nineteenth-Century France.* Cambridge: Cambridge University Press, 2004.

Helg, Aline. *Liberty and Equality in Caribbean Colombia, 1770–1835.* Chapel Hill: University of North Carolina Press, 2004.

Heron, Craig, and Steve Penfold. *The Worker's Festival: A History of Labour Day.* Toronto: University of Toronto Press, 2005.

Hobsbawm, Eric J., and Terence Ranger, eds. *The Invention of Tradition.* Cambridge: Cambridge University Press, 1988.

Holanda, Sérgio Buarque de. "Do Império à República." In *História geral da civilização brasileira,* tomo 2: *O Brasil monárquico,* 5 vols., ed. Sérgio Buarque de Holanda, 5:7–435. São Paulo: Difel, 1966–71.

Ickes, Scott. *African-Brazilian Culture and Regional Identity in Bahia, Brazil.* Gainesville: University Press of Florida, 2013.

– "Santos e Caboclos – Religious and Civic Ritual Performance and Discourse in Salvador, Bahia, 1940–1955." Paper presented to the Congress of the Latin American Studies Association, San Francisco, 23–26 May 2012.

Iglesias, Francisco. "Vida política, 1848–1866." In *História geral da civilização brasileira,* tomo 2: *O Brasil monárquico,* 5 vols., ed. Sérgio Buarque de Holanda, 3:9–112. São Paulo: Difel, 1966–71.

"Inauguração do Monumento." *RIGHBa* 2.5 (1895): 217–22.

Instituto Geográfico e Histórico da Bahia. *Índice: Revista do Instituto Geográfico e Histórico da Bahia,* 2 vols. Salvador: Secretaria de Cultura e Turismo do Estado da Bahia, 1999–2000.

Instituto Histórico da Bahia. *O Instituto Histórico da Bahia e seu periódico (1856–1877),* facsimile ed. Salvador: Fundação Cultural do Estado da Bahia, 2001.

Jancsó, István, and Iris Kantor, eds. *Festa: cultura e sociabilidade na América portuguesa,* 2 vols. São Paulo: Hucitec, 2001.

Jesus, Ronaldo P. de. *Visões da monarquia: escravos, operários e abolicionismo na Corte.* Belo Horizonte: Argumentum, 2009.

Johnson, Daniel Noble. *The Journals of … (1822–1853), United States Navy,* ed. Mendel L. Peterson. Washington: Smithsonian Institution, 1959.

Johnson, Lyman L., ed., *Death, Dismemberment, and Memory: Body Politics in Latin America*. Albuquerque: University of New Mexico Press, 2004.

Junqueira Freire, José Joaquim. *Obra poética de...*, 2 vols., ed. Janaina Amado Mayer. Salvador: Editora Janaina, 1970.

Kaxangá, João da Virgem Maria. *Oração d'acção de graças pela feliz restituição à Patria dos seus denodados filhos marciaes, no dia de 31 de julho de 1831 celebrada na Igreja dos religiosos Franciscanos...* Salvador: Viuva Serva e Filhos, 1831.

Kertzer, David I. *Ritual, Politics, and Power*. New Haven: Yale University Press, 1988.

Kiddy, Elizabeth W. "Militão and the Guerreiros: Local Feuds, Long Memories, and Brazil's Struggle to Control the São Francisco River." *The Americas* 70.1 (2013): 9–32.

Kist, Ivete Susana. "A tragédia e o melodrama." In *História do teatro brasileiro*, vol. 1: *Das origens ao teatro profissional da primeira metade do século XX*, ed. João Roberto Faria, 75–94. São Paulo: Perspectiva and Edições SESCSP, 2012.

Kittleson, Roger A. *The Practice of Politics in Postcolonial Brazil: Porto Alegre, 1845–1895*. Pittsburgh: University of Pittsburgh Press, 2005.

Knauss, Paulo. "Imagens da cidade: monumentos e esculturas no Rio de Janeiro." In *Entre Europa e África: a invenção do carioca*, ed. Antonio Herculano Lopes, 289–300. Rio: Topbooks and Edições Casa Rui Barbosa, 2000.

Knauss, Paulo, ed. *Cidade vaidosa: imagens urbanas do Rio de Janeiro*. Rio: Sette Letras, 1999.

Kodama, Kaori. *Os índios e o Império do Brasil: a etnografia do IHGB entre as décadas de 1840 e 1860*. São Paulo: EdUSP, 2009.

Kraay, Hendrik. "'As Terrifying as Unexpected': The Bahian Sabinada, 1837–38," *Hispanic American Historical Review* 72.4 (November 1992): 501–27.

– "The 'Barbarous Game': Entrudo and Its Critics in Rio de Janeiro, 1810s–1850s." *Hispanic American Historical Review* 95.3 (August 2015): 427–58.

– "Between Brazil and Bahia: Celebrations of Dois de Julho in Nineteenth-Century Salvador." *Journal of Latin American Studies* 31.2 (May 1999): 255–86.

– "Black Kings, Cabanos, and the Guarda Negra: Reflections on Popular Royalism in Nineteenth-Century Brazil." *Varia História* 35.67 (January–April 2019): 141–75.

– "'Cold as the Stone of Which It Must Be Made': *Caboclos*, Monuments and the Memory of Independence in Bahia, Brazil, 1870s–1900." In *Images of Power: Iconography, Culture, and the State in Latin America*, ed. Jens Anderman and William Rowe, 165–94. London: Berghahn Books, 2005.

– "Os companheiros de Dom Obá: os zuavos baianos e outras companhias negras na Guerra do Paraguai." *Afro-Ásia* 46 (2012): 121–61.

- "O cotidiano dos soldados na guarnição da Bahia, 1850–1889." In *Nova História Militar Brasileira*, ed. Celso Castro, Vitor Izecksohn, and Hendrik Kraay, 237–68. Rio: Editora da Fundação Getúlio Vargas and Editora Bom Texto, 2004.
- *Days of National Festivity in Rio de Janeiro, Brazil, 1823–1889*. Stanford: Stanford University Press, 2013.
- "Definindo a nação e o Estado: rituais cívicos na Bahia pós-Independência (1823–1850)." *Topoi* 3 (September 2001): 63–90.
- "'Em outra coisa não falavam os pardos, cabras e crioulos': o 'recrutamento' de escravos na guerra da independência no Brasil, 1822–1823." *Revista Brasileira de História* 22.43 (2002): 109–26.
- "Entre o Brasil e a Bahia: as comemorações do Dois de Julho em Salvador, século XIX," *Afro-Asia* (Salvador) 23 (2000): 49–87.
- "'Frio como a pedra de que se há de compor': caboclos e monumentos na comemoração da independência na Bahia, 1870–1900." *Tempo* 7.14 (January–June 2003): 51–81.
- "From Entrudo to Carnaval in Salvador, Bahia, Brazil." Paper presented to the Canadian Association for Latin American and Caribbean Studies Conference, Calgary, 1–3 June 2016.
- "Independência baiana." *Nossa História* 2.21 (July 2005): 60–3.
- "Muralhas da Independência e liberdade do Brasil: a participação popular nas lutas políticas (Bahia, 1820–1825)." In *A Independência brasileira: novas dimensões*, ed. Jurandir Malerba, 303–41. Rio: Editora da Fundação Getúlio Vargas, 2006.
- "Pacificação e política, 1835–1846." In *Pacificação: o que é e a quem se destina*, ed. Angela Moreira, Adriana Barreto de Souza, Maud Chirio, and Luis Edmundo de Souza Moraes, 151–74. São Paulo: Alameda, 2017.
- "Política partidária e festa popular: o 'Incidente Frias Villar' e o Dois de Julho de 1875." *RIGHBa* 109 (2014): 285–303.
- *Race, State, and Armed Forces in Independence-Era Brazil: Bahia, 1790s–1840s*. Stanford: Stanford University Press, 2001.
- "Reconsidering Recruitment in Imperial Brazil." *The Americas* 55.1 (July 1998): 1–33.
- "Ritos políticos e politização popular no Brasil imperial." *Almanack* 9 (April 2015): 30–40.
- "Slavery, Citizenship and Military Service in Brazil's Mobilization for the Paraguayan War." *Slavery and Abolition* 18.3 (December 1997): 228–56.
- "Urban Slavery in Salvador, Bahia, Brazil: The Wills of Captain Joaquim Félix de Santana, Colonel Manoel Pereira da Silva, and Rosa Maria da Conceição (1809, 1814, 1843)." In *Colonial Lives: Documents on Latin American History (1550–1850)*, ed. Richard Boyer and Geoffrey Spurling, 279–83. New York: Oxford University Press, 2000.

– "White Slaves in Nineteenth-Century Brazil." Paper presented to the Canadian Association for Latin American and Caribbean Studies Conference, Montreal, 17 May 2018.

– "A Year of Provincial Correspondence to the Corte: Bahia, 1868." Paper presented to the American Historical Association Conference, Denver, 6 January 2017.

Lago, Laurênio. *Os generais do Exército brasileiro de 1860 a 1889: traços biográficos*. Rio: Imprensa Nacional, 1942.

Lara, Silvia Hunold. *Fragmentos setecentistas: escravidão, cultura e poder na América portuguesa*. São Paulo: Companhia das Letras, 2007.

Larson, Brooke. *Trials of Nation-Making: Liberalism, Race, and Ethnicity in the Andes, 1810–1910*. New York: Cambridge University Press, 2003.

Lasso, Marixa. *Myths of Harmony: Race and Republicanism during the Age of Revolution: Colombia, 1795–1831*. Pittsburgh: University of Pittsburgh Press, 2007.

Leal, Geraldo da Costa. *Salvador: dos contos, cantos e encantos*. Salvador: Gráfica Santa Helena, 2000.

Leal, Maria das Graças de Andrade. *Manuel Querino: entre letras e lutas*. São Paulo: Annablume, 2010.

Leal, Maria das Graças de Andrade, and Avanete Pereira Souza, eds. *Capítulos de história da Bahia: Independência*. Salvador: Assembléia Legislativa da Bahia and EdUNEB, 2017.

Leite, Glacyra Lazzari. *Pernambuco 1817*. Recife: Fundação Joaquim Nabuco and Editora Massangana, 1988.

– *Pernambuco 1824*. Recife: Fundação Joaquim Nabuco and Editora Massangana, 1989.

Leite, Rinaldo Cesar Nascimento. "A civilização imperfeita: tópicos em torno da remodelação urbana de Salvador e outras cenas em torno da civilidade, 1912–1916." *Estudos Ibero-Americanos* 24.1 (June 1998): 95–129.

– "Memória e identidade no Instituto Geográfico e Histórico da Bahia (1894–1923): origens da Casa da Bahia e celebração do 2 de Julho." *Patrimônio e Memória* 7.1 (June 2011): 54–77.

– *A rainha destronada: discursos das elites sobre as grandezas e infortúnios da Bahia nas primeiras décadas republicanas*. Feira de Santana: UEFS Editora, 2012.

Leonelli, Domingos, et al. *2 de Julho: a verdadeira Independência do Brasil!* Brasília: Publicação do Gabinete do Deputado Federal Domingos Leonelli, ca. 1997.

Levine, Robert M. "The Singular Brazilian City of Salvador." *Luso-Brazilian Review* 30.2 (Winter 1993): 59–69.

– *Vale of Tears: Revisiting the Canudos Massacre in Northeastern Brazil, 1893–1897*. Berkeley: University of California Press, 1992.

Lira, Mariza. *História do Hino Nacional Brasileiro*. Rio: Biblioteca do Exército Editora, 1954.

Lopes, Juliana Serzedello Crespim. *Identidades políticas e raciais na Sabinada (Bahia, 1837–1838)*. São Paulo: Alameda, 2013.

Lopez, Emílio Carlos Rodrigues. *Festas públicas, memória e representação: um estudo sobre manifestações políticas na Corte do Rio de Janeiro, 1808–1822*. São Paulo: Humanitas, 2004.

Lyra, Maria de Lourdes Viana. "'Pátria do cidadão': a concepção de pátria/ nação em Frei Caneca." *Revista Brasileira de História* 18.36 (1998): 395–420.

Mac Cord, Marcelo. *Artífices da cidadania: mutualismo, educação e trabalho no Recife oitocentista*. Campinas: Editora UNICAMP, 2012.

Mac Cord, Marcelo, and Claudio H.M. Batalha, eds. *Organizar e proteger: trabalhadores, associações e mutualismo no Brasil (séculos XIX e XX)*. Campinas: Editora da UNICAMP, 2014.

Macedo, Joaquim Manuel de. "Amor e pátria." In *Teatro completo*, 3 vols., 1: 149–72. Rio: MEC, Fundação Nacional de Arte, Serviço Nacional de Teatro, 1979.

Machado, André Roberto de A. "O direito e o arbítrio em tempos de guerra: os debates no parlamento em torno das garantias constitucionais durante a repressão à Cabanagem (1835–40)." In *Dimensões políticas do Império do Brasil*, ed. Lúcia Maria Bastos P. Neves and Tânia Maria Bessone, 135–61. Rio: Contra Capa, 2012.

Machado, Maria Helena P.T., and Celso Thomas Castilho, eds. *Tornando-se livre: agentes históricos e lutas sociais no processo de Abolição*. São Paulo: EdUSP, 2015.

Maia, [João do] Prado. *A Marinha de Guerra do Brasil na Colônia e no Império: tentativa de reconstituição histórica*. 2nd ed. Rio: Cátedra, (1965) 1975.

Mallon, Florencia E. *Peasant and Nation: The Making of Postcolonial Mexico and Peru*. Berkeley: University of California Press, 1995.

Mariano, Agnes. *A invenção da baianidade*. São Paulo: Annablume, 2009.

Marjoribanks, Alexander. *Travels in North and South America*, 5th ed. London: Simpkin, Marshall and Company, 1854.

Marques, [Francisco] Xavier [Ferreira]. *Uma familia bahiana*, 2nd ed. Salvador: Imprensa Popular, 1888.

– *O feiticeiro*. Rio: Leite Ribeiro, (1897) 1922.

– *Vida de Castro Alves*. Rio: Annuario do Brasil, 1924.

Martinez, Socorro Targino. *2 de Julho: a festa é história*. Salvador: Prefeitura Municipal do Salvador, Secretaria Municipal de Educação e Cultura, Fundação Gregório de Mattos, 2000.

Martins, Ana Cecília, et al. *Iconografia baiana do século XIX na Biblioteca Nacional*. Rio: Edições Biblioteca Nacional, 2005.

Marzano, Andrea. *Cidade em cena: o ator Vasques, o teatro e o Rio de Janeiro, 1839–1892*. Rio: FAPERJ and Folha Seca, 2008.

Mata, Iacy Maia. "Os Treze de Maio: ex-senhores, política e libertos na Bahia pós-abolição (1888–1889)." MA thesis, Universidade Federal da Bahia, 2002.

Matos, Consuelo Almeida. "A Bahia de Hildegardes Vianna: um estudo sobre a representação de mulheres negras." MA thesis, Universidade do Estado da Bahia, 2008.

Mattos, Ilmar Rohloff de. *O tempo saquarema*. São Paulo: Hucitec, 1987.

Mattos, João Baptista de. *Os monumentos nacionais: Estado da Bahia*. Rio: Imp. do Exército, 1956.

Mattos, Waldemar. *Panorama econômico da Bahia, 1808–1960*, 2nd ed. Salvador: Assembléia Legislativa do Estado da Bahia, (1961) 2011.

Mattoso, Kátia M. de Queiroz. *Bahia: a cidade de Salvador e seu mercado no século XIX*. São Paulo: Hucitec, 1978.

– *Bahia, século XIX: uma província no Império*. Rio: Nova Fronteira, 1992.

– *To Be a Slave in Brazil, 1550–1888*, trans. Arthur Goldhammer. New Brunswick: Rutgers University Press, 1986.

Maximilian, Emperor of Mexico. *Recollections of My Life*, 3 vols. London: R. Bentley, 1868.

Maxwell, Kenneth R. *Conflicts and Conspiracies: Brazil and Portugal, 1750–1808*. Cambridge: Cambridge University Press, 1973.

McCrone, David, and Gayle McPherson, eds. *National Days: Constructing and Mobilising National Identity*. Houndmills: Palgrave Macmillan, 2009.

Medrado, Joana. *Terra de vaqueiros: relações de trabalho e cultura política no sertão da Bahia, 1880–1900*. Campinas: Editora da UNICAMP, 2012.

Mello, Evaldo Cabral de. *A outra independência: o federalismo pernambucano de 1817 a 1824*. São Paulo: Ed. 34, 2004.

– *Rubro veio: o imaginário da restauração pernambucana*, 2nd ed. Rio: Topbooks, (1986) 1997.

Mello Moraes, [Alexandre José de]. *Praças, ruas e ladeiras da cidade do Salvador*. Salvador: Prefeitura Municipal da Cidade do Salvador, 1959.

Mello Moraes Filho, [Alexandre José de]. *Festas e tradições populares do Brasil*, 3rd ed. Rio: F. Briguiet, (1895) 1946.

– *Festas populares do Brasil: tradicionalismo*. Rio: B.L. Garnier, 1888.

Mencarelli, Fernando Antônio. *Cena aberta: a absolvição de um bilontra e o teatro de revista de Arthur Azevedo*. Campinas: Editora da UNICAMP, 1999.

Mendes, Ediana Ferreira. "Festas e procissões reais na Bahia colonial, séculos XVII e XVIII." MA thesis, Universidade Federal da Bahia, 2011.

Méndez, Cecilia. *The Plebeian Republic: The Huanta Rebellion and the Making of the Peruvian State, 1820–1850*. Durham: Duke University Press, 2005.

Mendonça, Antonio Augusto de. *Poesias de..., natural da Bahia*. Salvador: Typographia Constitucional de França Guerra, 1864.

Menezes, Agrario de Souza. *Calabar*. Salvador: Typ. do Bazar, 1888.

– "O dia da Independencia." BN/SM 23, 1, 18. Manuscript.

– *Discurso proferido na installação do Conservatorio Dramatico da Bahia*. Salvador: Typ. A.O. de França Guerra, 1857.

– *Mathilde*. Recife: Typographia Universal, 1854.

Menezes, Jayme de Sá. *Agrário de Menezes: um liberal do Império*, 2nd ed. Rio: Cátedra; Brasília: INL, (1968) 1983.

Merces, Joaquim das. *Oração gratulatoria que pronunciou na Sé da Bahia, metropolitana do Brazil, a Dous de Julho...* Salvador: Typ. Imp. e N.ᵃˡ, 1828.

Michalski, Sergiusz. *Public Monuments: Art in Political Bondage*. London: Reaktion Books, 1998.

Miki, Yuko. *Frontiers of Citizenship: A Black and Indigenous History of Postcolonial Brazil*. Cambridge: Cambridge University Press, 2018.

Milliet, Maria Alice. *Tiradentes: o corpo do herói*. São Paulo: Martins Fontes, 2001.

Molina A. de Cienfuegos, Ignacio, and Jorge Martínez Bárcena. "National Days throughout the History and the Geography of Spain." In *National Days, National Ways: Historical, Political, and Religious Celebrations around the World*, ed. Linda Fuller, 241–60. Westport: Praeger, 2004.

Molina, Matías M. *História dos jornais no Brasil*, vol. 1: *Da era colonial à Regência (1500–1840)*. São Paulo: Companhia das Letras, 2015.

Moniz, Rozendo. *Moniz Barretto: o repentista*. Rio: B.L. Garnier, 1886.

"O monumento." RIGHBA 2.5 (1895): 231–41.

Moraes, Renata Figueiredo. "A Abolição no Brasil além do parlamento: as festas de maio de 1888." In *Tornando-se livre: agentes históricos e lutas sociais no processo de Abolição*, ed. Maria Helena P.T. Machado and Celso Thomas Castilho, 315–34. São Paulo: EdUSP, 2015.

Moreira de Azevedo, Manoel Duarte. "Sociedades fundadas no Brasil desde os tempos coloniaes até o começo do actual reinado." RIHGB 48.2 (1885): 265–322.

Morel, Marco. *Cipriano Barata na sentinela da liberdade*. Salvador: Academia de Letras da Bahia and Assembléia Legislativa do Estado da Bahia, 2001.

– *As transformações dos espaços públicos: imprensa, atores políticos e sociabilidades na cidade imperial*. São Paulo: Hucitec, 2005.

Morel, Marco, ed. Sentinela da Liberdade *e outros escritos (1821–1835)*. São Paulo: EdUSP, 2009.

Morton, F.W.O. "The Conservative Revolution of Independence: Economy, Society and Politics in Bahia, 1790–1840." DPhil thesis, Oxford University, 1974.

Moseley, Henry Nottidge. *Notes by a Naturalist on the "Challenger."* London: John Murray, 1892.

Mosher, Jeffrey C. *Political Struggle, Ideology, and State Building: Pernambuco and the Construction of Brazil, 1817–1850.* Lincoln: University of Nebraska Press, 2008.

Mulhall, M[ichael] G[eorge]. *Handbook of Brazil.* Buenos Aires: n.p., 1877.

Muniz, Antonio da Virgem Maria. *Oração gratulatoria que, no solemne tedeum, celebrado em o dia 2 de julho de 1843, recitou na Cathedral da provincia da Bahia.* Salvador: Typ. Galdino José Bizerra e Comp.ᵃ, 1843.

Nabuco, Joaquim. *Um estadista do Império.* Rio: Nova Aguilar, (1897) 1975.

Naeher, Julius. *Excursões na província da Bahia: a terra e a gente da província brasileira da Bahia*, trans. Osvaldo Augusto Teixeira. Salvador: CIAN, 2011.

Nascimento, Ana Amélia Vieira do. *Dez freguesias da cidade do Salvador: aspectos sociais e urbanos do século XIX.* Salvador: Fundação Cultural do Estado da Bahia, 1986.

Needell, Jeffrey D. "Brazilian Abolitionism, Its Historiography, and the Uses of Political History." *Journal of Latin American Studies* 42.2 (May 2010): 231–61.

– *The Party of Order: The Conservatives, the State, and Slavery in the Brazilian Monarchy, 1831–1871.* Stanford: Stanford University Press, 2006.

Neves, Maria Helena Franca. *De La Traviata ao maxixe (variações estéticas da prática do Teatro São João).* Salvador: Secretaria da Cultura e Turismo, Fundação Cultural do Estado, Empresa Gráfica da Bahia, 2000.

Nobrega, Bernardino Ferreira. *Fac-simile da primeira e unica edição da Memoria historica sobre as victorias alcançadas pelos itaparicanos no decurso [da] campanha da Bahia*, ed. Pirajá da Silva. Salvador: Typ. Social, (1827) 1923.

Nora, Pierre. "Between Memory and History: *Les Lieux de Mémoire*," trans. Marc Roudebush. *Representations* 26 (Spring 1989): 7–25.

Oliveira, Albino José Barbosa de. *Memórias de um magistrado do Império*, ed. Américo Jacobina Lacombe. São Paulo: Nacional, 1943.

Oliveira, Cecília Helena de Salles, and Cláudia Valladão de Mattos, eds. *O brado do Ipiranga.* São Paulo: EdUSP and Museu Paulista da Universidade de São Paulo, 1999.

Oliveira, J[osé] M[anuel] Cardoso de. *Dois metros e cinco: aventuras de Marcos Parreira (costumes brasileiros)*, 3rd ed. Rio: F. Briguiet & C:a, (1905) 1936.

Oliveira, João Pacheco de. "Las formas del olvido: la muerte del indio, el indianismo y la formación de Brasil (siglo XIX)." *Desacatos* 54 (May–August 2017): 160–81.

– "'Wild Indians,' Tutelary Roles, and the Moving Frontier in Amazonia: Images of Indians in the Birth of Brazil." In *Manifest Destinies and Indigenous Peoples*, ed. David Maybury-Lewis, Theodore Macdonald, and Biorn Maybury-Lewis, 85–117. Cambridge: Harvard University Press, 2009.

Oliveira, Vinícios Mascarenhas de. "Federalistas na Bahia: trajetórias, ideias, sociedades e movimentos (1831–1838)." MA thesis, Universidade Federal da Bahia, 2012.

Oliveira, Waldir Freitas. *A crise da economia açucareira do Recôncavo na segunda metade do século XIX.* Salvador: Centro de Estudos Baianos, 1999.

Oliven, Ruben George. *Tradition Matters: Modern Gaúcho Identity in Brazil.* New York: Columbia University Press, 1996.

*Organizações e programas ministeriais: regime parlamentar no Império,* 2nd ed. Rio: Departamento de Imprensa Nacional, (1889) 1962.

Paiva, Tancredo de Barros. *Achêgas de um diccionario de pseudonymos, iniciais, abreviaturas e obras anonymas de auctores brasileiros e de estrangeiros, sobre o Brasil ou no mesmo impressas.* Rio: J. Leite, 1929.

Palma, Alcides Passos, ed. *História da Polícia Civil da Bahia.* Salvador: Governo do Estado da Bahia, 1979.

Pang, Eul-Soo. *Bahia in the First Brazilian Republic: Coronelismo and Oligarchies, 1889–1934.* Gainesville: University Press of Florida, 1979.

– *O Engenho Central do Bom Jardim na economia baiana: alguns aspectos de sua história, 1875–1891.* Rio: Arquivo Nacional and Instituto Histórico e Geográfico Brasileiro, 1979.

Pares, Luis Nicolau. *The Formation of Candomblé: Vodun History and Ritual in Brazil,* trans. Richard Vernon. Chapel Hill: University of North Carolina Press, 2013.

Passos, Alexandre. *Agrário de Menezes e o romantismo.* Rio: Pongetti, 1956.

Peard, Julyan G. *Race, Place, and Medicine: The Idea of the Tropics in Nineteenth-Century Brazil.* Durham: Duke University Press, 2000.

Pedro II. *Diário do imperador, 1840–1891.* CD-ROM. Petrópolis: Museu Imperial, [1999].

Pena, Eduardo Spiller. *Pajens da casa imperial: jurisconsultos, escravidão e a lei de 1871.* Campinas: Editora da UNICAMP, 2001.

Pereira, Luisa Rauter. "O conceito político de povo no período da Independência: história e tempo no debate político (1820–1823)." *Revista Brasileira de História* 33.66 (2013): 31–47.

Pestana, Maurício. *Dois de Julho: a Bahia na Independência do Brasil.* Salvador: Fundação Pedro Calmon, 2013.

Piedade, [Antonio Olavo] Lélis. *Histórico e relatório do Comitê Patriótico da Bahia (1897–1901), coordenado por Lélis Piedade,* 2nd ed., ed. Antonio Olavo. Salvador: Portfolium Editora, (1901) 2002.

Pinheiro, Eloisa Petti. *Europa, França e Bahia: difusão e adaptação de modelos urbanos (Paris, Rio e Salvador),* 2nd ed. Salvador: EdUFBa, (2002) 2011.

Pinho, José Ricardo Moreno. *Açambarcadores e famélicos: fome, carestia e conflitos em Salvador, 1858–1878.* Salvador: Selo Editorial Castro Alves, 2016.

Pinho, [José] Wanderley [de Araújo]. "A Bahia – 1808–1856." In *História geral da civilização brasileira*, tomo 2: *O Brasil monárquico*, 5 vols., ed. Sérgio Buarque de Holanda, 2:242–311. São Paulo: Difel, 1966–71.

– *Cotegipe e seu tempo: primeira phase, 1815–1867*. São Paulo: Ed. Nacional, 1937.

– "A Guerra da Independência: crônica de toda a campanha." *RIHGB* 278 (1968): 35–86.

– *História de um engenho do Recôncavo, Matoim–Novo Caboto–Freguesia, 1552–1944*, 2nd ed. São Paulo: Companhia Editora Nacional, (1946) 1982.

Pinto, Luiz Maria da Silva. *Diccionario da lingua brasileira*. Ouro Preto: Typ. da Silva, 1832.

Pirajá, Joaquim Pires de Carvalho e Albuquerque, Visconde de. *Elogio offerecido a S.M.I. o senhor D. Pedro 2º, pelo fiel criado...* Salvador: Typ. de Serva e Cia, 1838.

Posada-Carbó, Eduardo, ed. *Elections before Democracy: The History of Elections in Europe and Latin America*. London: Macmillan, 1996.

Priore, Mary del. *Festas e utopias no Brasil colonial*. São Paulo: Brasiliense, 1994.

*Publicações do Arquivo do Estado da Bahia: a Revolução de 7 de Novembro de 1837 (Sabinada)*, 5 vols. Salvador: Escola Typographica Salesiana, 1937–48.

Querino, Manuel [Raimundo]. *The African Contribution to Brazilian Civilization*, trans. E. Bradford Burns. Tempe: Arizona State University Center for Latin American Studies, 1978.

– "Os artistas bahianos." *RIGHBa* 31 (1905): 93–115.

– *Artistas bahianos (indicações biographicas)*, 2nd ed. Salvador: Officinas da Empreza "A Bahia," (1909) 1911.

– *A Bahia de outrora*, 3rd ed. Salvador: Progresso, (1916) 1955.

– "Os homens de côr preta na Historia." *RIGHBa* 48 (1923): 353–63.

– "Noticia biographica de Manuel Pessoa da Silva." *RIGHBa* 36 (1910): 137–44.

– "Noticia historica sobre o 2 de Julho de 1823 e sua commemoração na Bahia." *RIGHBa* 48 (1923): 77–105.

– "Theatros da Bahia." *RIGHBa* 35 (1909): 117–33.

Rabello, Laurindo José da Silva. *Obras poeticas...*, ed. J. Norberto de Souzasylva. Rio: B.L. Garnier; Paris: E. Belhatte, 1876.

Ramos, João Pereira. *Oração gratuloria, que, recitou na Sé Cathedral d'esta cidade, que por occasião do Te Deum celebrado em que o sempre e jubiloso anniversario da gloriosa entrada, que do reconcavo fez para a capital o Exercito Pacificador...* Salvador: Typ. do Diario de G.J. Bizerra e Comp., 1836.

Reis, Adriana Dantas. *Cora: lições de comportamento feminino na Bahia do século XIX*. Salvador: Centro de Estudos Baianos, 2000.

Reis, Antonio Simões dos. *Pseudonimos brasileiros: pequenos verbetes para um dicionario*, 2 vols. Rio: Z. Valverde, 1941.

Reis, Carlos Antonio. "A reabilitação do negro e do mestiço na história do Brasil: Manuel Querino e seu projeto de identidade nacional." In *Personalidades negras: trajetórias e estratégias políticas*, ed. Jaime Nascimento and Hugo Gama, 55–106. Salvador: Quarteto, 2012.

Reis, Eliane Maia dos. "Três momentos de mutualismo em Salvador, 1850–1887." MA thesis, Universidade Federal da Bahia, 2016.

Reis, João José. "Cor, classe, ocupação, etc.: o perfil social (às vezes pessoal) dos rebeldes baianos (1823–1833)." In *Escravidão e suas sombras*, ed. João José Reis and Elciene Azevedo, 279–314. Salvador: EdUFBa, 2012.

– "De escravo a rico liberto: a trajetória do africano Manoel Joaquim Ricardo na Bahia oitocentista." *Revista de História* 174 (January–June 2016): 15–68.

– *Death Is a Festival: Funeral Rites and Rebellion in Nineteenth-Century Brazil*, trans. H. Sabrina Gledhill. Chapel Hill: University of North Carolina Press, 2003.

– *Divining Slavery and Freedom: The Story of Domingos Sodré, an African Priest in Nineteenth-Century Brazil*, trans. H. Sabrina Gledhill. Cambridge: Cambridge University Press, 2015.

– "O jogo duro do Dois de Julho: o 'partido negro' na Independência da Bahia." In João José Reis and Eduardo Silva, *Negociação e conflito: a resistência negra no Brasil escravista*, 79–98. São Paulo: Companhia das Letras, 1989.

– *Rebelião escrava no Brasil: a história do levante dos Malês em 1835*, rev. and expanded ed. São Paulo: Companhia das Letras, 2003.

– "The 'Revolution of the *Ganhadores*': Urban Labour, Ethnicity and the African Strike of 1857 in Bahia, Brazil." *Journal of Latin American Studies* 29.2 (May 1997): 355–93.

– "Tambores e temores: a festa negra na Bahia na primeira metade do século XIX." In *Carnavais e outras f(r)estas: ensaios de história social da cultura*, ed. Maria Clementina Pereira da Cunha, 101–55. Campinas: Editora da UNICAMP, 2002.

Reis, João José, Flávio Gomes dos Santos, and Marcus J.M. de Carvalho. *O alufá Rufino: tráfico, escravidão e liberdade no Atlântico negro (c. 1822–c. 1853)*. São Paulo: Companhia das Letras, 2010.

Reis, João José, and Hendrik Kraay. "'The Tyrant is Dead': The Revolt of the Periquitos, Bahia, 1824." *Hispanic American Historical Review* 89.3 (August 2009): 399–434.

Reis, João José, and Márcia Gabriela D. de Aguilar. "'Carne sem osso e farinha sem caroço': o motim de 1858 contra a carestia na Bahia." *Revista de História* (July–December 1996): 133–59.

Reis, Lysie. *A liberdade que veio do ofício: práticas sociais e cultura dos artífices da Bahia do século XIX*. Salvador: EdUFBa, 2012.

Reis Júnior, [Manoel] Pereira. *Maria Quitéria*. Rio: Imprensa Nacional, 1953.

*Relação dos publicos festejos que tiverão lugar do 1. de abril até 9. pelo feliz regresso de SS. MM. II. e A.I. voltando da Bahia à Corte Imperial*. Rio: Na Imperial Typographia de Plancher, 1826.

Ribeiro, Alexandre Vieira. "The Transatlantic Slave Trade to Bahia, 1582–1851." In *Extending the Frontiers: Essays on the New Transatlantic Slave Trade Database*, ed. David Eltis and David Richardson, 130–54. New Haven: Yale University Press, 2008.

Ribeiro, Cristina Betioli. "Folclore e nacionalidade na literatura brasileira do século XIX." *Tempo* 10.20 (January 2006): 143–58.

Ribeiro, Gladys Sabina. *A liberdade em construção: identidade nacional e conflitos antilusitanos no Primeiro Reinado*. Rio: Relume-Dumará, 2002.

Ribeiro, Marcos Augusto Pessoa. *A Faculdade de Medicina da Bahia na visão de seus memorialistas*. Salvador: EduUFBa, 1997.

Ribeyrolles, Charles. *Brasil pittoresco; história-descripções-viagens-instituições-colonisação, por ... acompanhado de um Album de vistas, panoramas, paisagens, costumes, etc. por Victor Frond*, 4 vols. Rio: Typ. Nacional, 1859–61.

Ricupero, Bernardo. *O romantismo e a idéia de nação no Brasil (1830–1870)*. São Paulo: Martins Fontes, 2004.

Rijckevorsel, Elie Van. *Uit Brazilië*, 2 vols. Rotterdam: Elsevier, 1886.

Risério, Antonio. *Uma história da cidade da Bahia*. Rio: Versal Editores, 2004.

Romero, Sylvio. *Historia da literatura brazileira*, 2 vols. Rio: B.L. Garnier, 1888.

Romo, Anadelia A. *Brazil's Living Museum: Race, Reform, and Tradition in Bahia*. Chapel Hill: University of North Carolina Press, 2010.

Ruy [de Souza], Affonso. "O Conservatório Dramático da Bahia: esplendor e decadência – 1857–1884." *Revista da Academia de Letras da Bahia* 19–20 (1961): 183–90.

– *Dossier do Marechal Pedro Labatut*. Rio: Biblioteca do Exército, 1960.

– *História da Câmara Municipal da cidade do Salvador*, 2nd ed. Salvador: Câmara Municipal de Salvador, (1953) 1996.

– *História do teatro na Bahia: séculos XVI–XX*. Salvador: Progresso, 1959.

Ryan, Mary P. "The American Parade: Representations of the Nineteenth-Century Social Order." In *The New Cultural History*, ed. Lynn Hunt, 131–53. Berkeley: University of California Press, 1989.

– *Civic Wars: Democracy and Public Life in the American City during the Nineteenth Century*. Berkeley: University of California Press, 1997.

Sabato, Hilda. *The Many and the Few: Political Participation in Republican Buenos Aires*. Stanford: Stanford University Press, 2001.

Sacramento Blake, Augusto Victorino Alves do. *Diccionario bibliographico brazileiro*, 7 vols. Rio: Typ. Nacional, 1883–1902.

Salvador. *Posturas da Camara Municipal da Cidade de S. Salvador, capital da Provincia da Bahia*. Salvador: Typ. de Manoel Agostinho Cruz Mello, 1860.

- Prefeitura Municipal. *Os monumentos e a Independência*. Salvador: Prefeitura Municipal de Salvador, 1973.

Salvador, José María. *Efímeras efemérides: fiestas cívicas y arte efímero en la Venezuela de los siglos XVII–XIX*. Caracas: Universidad Católica Andrés Bello, 2001.

Sampaio, Consuelo Novais. *50 anos de urbanização: Salvador da Bahia no século XIX*. Rio: Versal, 2005.

- *Os partidos políticos da Bahia na Primeira República: uma política de acomodação*, 2nd ed. Salvador: EdUFBa, (1978) 1998.

- *O poder legislativo da Bahia: Primeira República (1889–1930)*. Salvador: Assembléia Legislativa and UFBa, 1985.

Sampaio, José Augusto Laranjeiras. "A festa de Dois de Julho em Salvador e o 'lugar' do índio." *Cultura* 1.1 (1988): 153–9. .

Sampaio, Marcos Guedes Vaz. *Navegação a vapor na Bahia oitocentista (1839–1894)*. Salvador: EdUFBa, 2014.

Sanders, James. *Contentious Republicans: Popular Politics, Race, and Class in Nineteenth-Century Colombia*. Durham: Duke University Press, 2004.

- *The Vanguard of the Atlantic World: Creating Modernity, Nation, and Democracy in Nineteenth-Century Latin America*. Durham: Duke University Press, 2014.

Sandes, Noé Freire. *A invenção da nação: entre a Monarquia e a República*. Goiânia: UFG and AGEPEL, 2000.

Santa Cruz, Romualdo Antonio de Seixas, Marquês de. *Memorias do ..., arcebispo da Bahia*. Rio: Typ. Nacional, 1861.

Santana, Mariely Cabral de. *Alma e festa de uma cidade: devoção e construção na colina do Bonfim*. Salvador: EdUFBa, 2009.

Santana, Rosane S. "Centralização, descentralização e unidade nacional, 1835–1841: o papel da elite política baiana." MA thesis, Universidade Federal da Bahia, 2002.

Santiago, Camila Fernandes Guimarães. *A vila em ricas festas: celebrações promovidas pela câmara de Vila Rica, 1711–1744*. Belo Horizonte: C/Arte, FACE-FUMEC, 2003.

Santos, Beatriz Catão Cruz. *O Corpo de Deus na América: a festa de Corpus Christi nas cidades da América portuguesa, século XVIII*. São Paulo: Annablume, 2005.

Santos, Jocélio Teles dos. "Divertimentos estrondosos: batuques e sambas no século XIX." In *Ritmos em trânsito: sócio-antropologia da música baiana*, ed. Livio Sansone and Jocélio Teles dos Santos, 17–38. São Paulo: Dynamis, 1998.

- *O dono da terra: o caboclo nos candomblés da Bahia*. Salvador: SarahLetras, 1995.

Santos, José Joaquim. *Relatório dos trabalhos da Assemblea Legislativa Provincial da Bahia na sessão de 1841.* Salvador: Typ. de Epifanio J. Pedroza, 1841.

Santos, Lídia Rafaela Nascimento dos. "Entre os festejos e as disputas políticas: as comemorações do Sete de Setembro de 1829 no Recife." *Clio* 33.2 (2015): 74–99.

– "Luminárias, músicas e 'sentimentos patrióticos': festas e política no Recife (1817–1848)." PhD diss., Universidade Federal Fluminense, 2018.

Santos, Luiz Alvares dos. *Ao dous de julho de 1855: harmonia patriotica composta e offerecida aos Ill.*^mos *Snr.*^s *da Commissão dos Festejos Publicos.* Salvador: Typ. de Camillo de Lellis Masson e C., 1855.

Santos, Mário Augusto da Silva. *Casa e balcão: os caixeiros de Salvador (1890–1930).* Salvador: EdUFBa, 2009.

Savage, Kirk. *Standing Soldiers, Kneeling Slaves: Race, War, and Monument in Nineteenth-Century America.* Princeton: Princeton University Press, 1997.

Sayers, Raymond S. *The Negro in Brazilian Literature.* New York: Hispanic Institute in the United States, 1956.

Schäeffer, Georg Anton von. *O Brasil como império independente: analisado sob os aspectos histórico, mercantilístico e político,* trans. Arthur Blásio Rambo. Santa Maria: EdUFSM, (1824) 2007.

Schwartz, Stuart B. "Ceremonies of Public Authority in a Colonial Capital: The King's Processions and the Hierarchies of Power in Seventeenth-Century Salvador." *Anais de História de Além-Mar* 5 (2004): 7–26.

– *Sugar Plantations in the Formation of Brazilian Society: Bahia, 1550–1835.* Cambridge: Cambridge University Press, 1985.

Schwebel, Horst Karl. *Bandas filarmônicas e mestres da Bahia.* Salvador: Centro de Estudos Baianos, 1987.

Scully, William. *Brazil: Its Provinces and Chief Cities; the Manners & Customs of the People ...* London: Murray & Co., 1866.

Sena, Consuelo Pondé de. *A imprensa reacionária na Independência:* Sentinella Bahiense. Salvador: Centro de Estudos Baianos, 1983.

Serra, Ordep. *Rumores de festas – o sagrado e o profano na Bahia.* Salvador: EdUFBa, 2000.

– "Triunfo dos caboclos." In *Índios e caboclos: a história recontada,* ed. Maria Rosário de Carvalho and Ana Magda Carvalho, 55–77. Salvador: EdUFBa, 2012.

Silva, Alberto da Costa e. *Castro Alves.* São Paulo: Companhia das Letras, 2006.

Silva, Aldo José Morais. *Instituto Geográfico e Histórico da Bahia: origens e estratégias de consolidação institucional.* Feira de Santana: UEFS Editora, 2012.

Silva, Antonio de Moraes. *Diccionario da lingua portugueza...* Lisbon: Typographia Lacerdina, (1789) 1823.

Silva, Daniel Afonso. "A duras e pesadas penas: imprensa, identidade e nacionalidade no Brasil imperial." *Topoi* 10.19 (July–December 2009): 55–69.

Silva, Eduardo. "Sobre versos, bandeiras e flores." In *Panfletos abolicionistas: o 13 de maio em versos*, ed. Renato Pinto Venâncio, 16–40. Belo Horizonte: Arquivo Público Mineiro, 2007.

Silva, Ignacio Accioli Cerqueira e. *Memorias historicas e politicas da provincia da Bahia*, 6 vols., ed. Braz do Amaral. Salvador: Imprensa Official do Estado, (1835–36) 1919–40.

Silva, J[oão] Nepomuceno da. *A sapeca: satyras de ..., natural da Bahia*. Recife: Typ. do Jornal do Recife, 1861.

– *Satyras*. Rio: Typographia de Domingos Luiz dos Santos, 1864.

Silva, José Calasans Brandão da. "O folclore da Independência." In *Aspectos do 2 de Julho*, no pagination. Salvador: Secretaria de Educação e Cultura, 1973.

Silva, Kátia Maria de Carvalho. *O Diário da Bahia e o século XIX*. Rio: Tempo Brasileiro, 1979.

Silva, Manoel Antonio da. *A restauração da Bahia em 1625 ou A expulsão dos holandeses*. Salvador: Typ. da Aurora de Serva e Comp., 1837.

Silva, Marcio Antonio Both da. "Caboclos." *História Unisinos* 18.2 (May–August 2014): 338–51.

Silva, Maria Beatriz Nizza da. Semanário Cívico: *Bahia, 1821–1823*. Salvador: EdUFBa, 2008.

Silva, Pedro Celestino da. "A Bahia e seus monumentos: memoria apresentada ao Instituto pelo Prof..." *RIGHBa* 59 (1933): 75–377.

– "Galeria cachoeirana." *RIGHBa* 68 (1942): 1–90.

– "Notas epigraphicas e iconographicas dos feitos heroicos da campanha da independencia pelo Prof..." *AAPEBa* 27 (1941): 531–644.

Silva, Ricardo Tadeu Caires. "Caminhos e descaminhos da Abolição: escravos, senhores e direitos nas últimas décadas da escravidão (Bahia, 1850–1888)." PhD diss., Universidade Federal do Paraná, 2007.

– "A Sociedade Libertadora Sete de Setembro e o encaminhamento da questão servil na província da Bahia (1869–1878)." In *Tornando-se livre: agentes históricos e lutas sociais no processo da Abolição*, ed. Maria Helena P.T. Machado and Celso Thomas Castilho, 293–314. São Paulo: EdUSP, 2015.

Silva Junior, Manuel Francisco da. *O bravo do Pirajá: poesia à memoria do infeliz veterano da independencia, o suicida da Bahia José Luiz Bananeira*. Rio: Typ. da Crença, 1864.

Sousa, Avanete Pereira. *Poder político e vida cotidiana: a Câmara Municipal da Cidade de Salvador no século XVIII*. Vitória da Conquista: Edições UNEB, 2013.

Sousa, J. Galante de. *O teatro no Brasil*, 2 vols. Rio: MEC/INL, 1960.

Sousa, Maria Aparecida Silva. "Bahia: de capitania a província, 1808–1823." PhD diss., Universidade de São Paulo, 2008.

– "História, memória e historiografia: abordagens sobre a Independência na *Revista do Instituto Geográfico e Histórico da Bahia* (1894–1923)." *Politéia* 5.1 (2005): 177–95.

Souza, Adriana Barreto de. *Duque de Caxias: o homem por trás do monumento*. Rio: Civilização Brasileira, 2008.

Souza, Antonio Loureiro de. *Baianos ilustres, 1564–1925*, 2nd ed. Salvador: Secretaria de Educação e Cultura, (1949) 1973.

S[ouza], [Bernardo Xavier] P[into] de. *Memorias da viagem de Suas Magestades Imperiaes à provincia da Bahia*. Rio: Typographia Industria Nacional de Cotrim & Campos, 1867.

Souza, Felipe A. *O eleitorado imperial em reforma*. Recife: Massangana, 2014.

Souza, Francisco Bernadino de. "Festas populares: o dia Dous de Julho na Bahia." *Revista Popular* 4.13 (1862): 261–5.

Souza, Paulo Cesar. *A Sabinada: a revolta separatista da Bahia (1837)*. São Paulo: Brasiliense, 1987.

Souza, Robério S. *Trabalhadores dos trilhos: imigrantes e nacionais livres, libertos e escravos na construção da primeira ferrovia baiana (1858–1863)*. Campinas: Ed. UNICAMP, 2015.

– *Tudo pelo trabalho livre! Trabalhadores e conflitos no pós-abolição (Bahia, 1892–1909)*. Salvador: EdUFBa, 2011.

Souza, Silvia Cristina Martins de. *As noites do Ginásio: teatro e tensões culturais na Corte (1823–1868)*. Campinas: Editora da UNICAMP, 2002.

Sowell, David. *The Early Colombian Labor Movement: Artisans and Politics in Bogotá, 1832–1919*. Philadephia: Temple University Press, 1992.

Spix, Johann Baptiste von, and Karl Friedrich Philipp von Martius. *Viagem pelo Brasil*, 4 vols., trans. Lucia Furquim Lahmeyer. Rio: Imprensa Nacional, 1938.

Sussekind, Flora. *As revistas do ano e a invenção do Rio de Janeiro*. Rio: Nova Fronteira and Fundação Casa de Rui Barbosa, 1986.

Tavares, Constantino do Amaral. *Elogio dramatico composto para ser representado no Theatro de S. João da Bahia, no dia dous de julho de 1857...* Salvador: Typ. de França Guerra, 1857.

– *Gonzaga: drama histórico em 3 actos*. Rio: Tip. de F.A. de Souza, 1869.

– *Minhas poesias*. Salvador: Typ. de Camillo de Lellis Masson & C., 1856.

– *Os tempos da Independencia: drama historico*, facsimile ed. Salvador: IGHBa, (1861) 2000.

Tavares, Luís Guilherme Pontes, ed. *Apontamentos para a história da imprensa na Bahia*, 2nd ed. Salvador: Academia de Letras da Bahia, (2003) 2008.

Tavares, Luís Henrique Dias. *Da sedição de 1798 à revolta de 1824 na Bahia.* Salvador: EdUFBa; São Paulo: EdUNESP, 2003.

– *A Independência do Brasil na Bahia,* 2nd ed. Rio: Civilização Brasileira, 1982.

Teixeira [Cavalcante], Cid [José]. *Bahia em tempo de província.* Salvador: Fundação Cultural do Estado da Bahia, 1985.

– *Cidade Alta,* ed. Fernando Oberlaender. Salvador: EPP Publicações e Publicidade, 2017.

Thurner, Mark. *From Two Republics to One Divided: Contradictions of Postcolonial Nationmaking in Andean Peru.* Durham: Duke University Press, 1997.

Tinhorão, José Ramos. *As festas no Brasil colonial.* São Paulo: Editorial 34, 2000.

Tiphagne, Nicolas. "O índio e Salvador: uma construção histórica." In *Índios e caboclos: a.história recontada,* ed. Maria Rosário de Carvalho and Ana Magda Carvalho, 31–54. Salvador: EdUFBa, 2012.

Titara, Ladislau dos Santos. *Obras poeticas,* 8 vols. Salvador: [various publishers], 1827–39; Rio Grande: Typ. de Berlink, 1851–52.

Torres, Carlos. *Vultos, fatos e coisas da Bahia.* Salvador: Imprensa Oficial da Bahia, 1950.

Torres, João Nepomuceno. *A giria brazileira: colleção de annexins, adagios, rifões e locuções populares.* Salvador: Typographia e Encadernação do *Diario da Bahia,* 1899.

Torres, João N[epomuceno], and Alfredo de Carvalho. *Annaes da imprensa da Bahia.* Salvador: Typ. Bahianna de Cincinnato Melchiades, 1911.

Travers, Len. *Celebrating the Fourth: Independence Day and the Rites of Nationalism in the Early Republic.* Amherst: University of Massachussetts Press, 1997.

Treece, David. *Exiles, Allies, Rebels: Brazil's Indianist Movement, Indigenist Politics, and the Imperial Nation-State.* Westport: Greenwood, 2000.

Trinchão, Gláucia Maria Costa. *O Parafuso: do meio de transporte a cartão-postal.* Salvador: EdUFBa, 2010.

Unowsky, Daniel L. *The Pomp and Politics of Patriotism: Imperial Celebrations in Habsburg Austria, 1846–1916.* West Lafayette: Purdue University Press, 2007.

Uricoechea, Fernando. *The Patrimonial Foundations of the Brazilian Bureaucratic State.* Berkeley: University of California Press, 1980.

Vale, Brian. *The Audacious Admiral Cochrane: The True Life of a Naval Legend.* London: Conway Maritime Press, 2004.

– "The Creation of the Brazilian Navy, 1822–1823." *Mariner's Mirror* 57 (1972): 63–88.

– "Lord Cochrane in Brazil: 1. The Naval War of Independence." *Mariner's Mirror* 57 (1972): 415–42.

Valverde, Angélica. "Catalogação e fichamento dos documentos existentes no arquivo do IGHB." *RIGHBa* 86 (1976–77): 487–576.

Varella, João. *Da Bahia do Senhor do Bomfim (factos, vultos e typos populares de tempos idos)*. Salvador: n.p., 1936.

– *Da Bahia que eu vi: factos, vultos e typos populares*. Salvador: n.p., 1935.

– *D'outros tempos*. Salvador: Typ. de S. Joaquim, 1921.

Vargas, Tulio. *O conselheiro Zacarias (1815–1977)*, 2nd ed. Curitiba: Juruá, (1977) 2007.

Varnhagen, Francisco Adolpho de. *Historia geral do Brazil, isto é do descobrimento, colonização, legislação e desenvolvimento deste Estado, hoje imperio independente, escripta em presença de muitos documentos autenticos recolhidos nos archivos do Brazil, de Portugal, da Hespanha e da Hollanda*, 2 vols. Rio: E. & H. Laemmert, 1854–57.

Vasconcelos, Pedro de Almeida. *Salvador: transformações e permanências (1549–1999)*, 2nd ed. Salvador: EdUFBa, 2017.

Verger, Pierre. *Flux et reflux de la traite des nègres entre le Golfe de Bénin et Bahia de Todos os Santos*. Paris: Mouton, 1968.

– *Notícias da Bahia – 1850*. Salvador: Corrupio, 1981.

Vianna, Antônio. *Casos e coisas da Bahia*. Salvador: Typ. Beneditina, 1950.

Vianna, Francisco Vicente. *Memoria sobre o Estado da Bahia*. Salvador: Typographia e Encadernação do "Diario da Bahia," 1893.

Vianna, Hildegardes. *Antigamente era assim*. Rio: Record, 1994.

– *A Bahia já foi assim (crônica de costumes)*, 2nd ed. São Paulo: Edições GRD, (1973) 1979.

– "Dois de Julho de Bairros." *RIGHBa* 86 (1976–77): 275–85.

– "Dois de Julho na Bahia: uma festa cívica-folclórica." *Revista Brasileira de Folclore* 13.40 (September–December 1974): 59–71.

– *Folclore brasileiro: Bahia*. Rio: Ministério de Educação e Cultura, 1981.

– "Folclore cívico na Bahia." In *Ciclo de conferências sobre o sesquicentenário na Bahia em 1973*, 167–78. Salvador: Universidade Católica do Salvador, 1977.

– *A proclamação da República na Bahia: aspectos folclóricos*. Salvador: Centro de Estudos Baianos, 1955.

Vianna, Marisa. *"...vou pra Bahia": Cidade do Salvador em cartões postais (1898–1930)*. Salvador: Bompreço, 2004.

Vicuña MacKenna, Benjamin. *Paginas de mi diario durante tres años de viaje, 1853–1854–1855*, 2 vols. Santiago: Universidad de Chile, [1936].

Vieira, Damasceno. *Memorias historicas brasileiras (1500–1837)*, 2 vols. Salvador: Officinas dos Dois Mundos, 1903.

Vieira, José Estanisláo. *Ao muito augusto senhor D. Pedro de Alcantara, primeiro imperador do Brazil*. Salvador: Typographia Nacional, [1824].

Waldstreicher, David. *In the Midst of Perpetual Fêtes: The Making of American Nationalism, 1776–1820*. Chapel Hill: University of North Carolina Press, 1997.

Warren, Richard A. *Vagrants and Citizens: Politics and the Masses in Mexico City from Colony to Republic*. Wilmington: Scholarly Resources, 2001.

Watanabe-O'Kelly, Helen. "Festival Books in Europe from Renaissance to Rococo." *The Seventeenth Century* 3.2 (1988): 181–201.

Weinstein, Barbara. *The Color of Modernity: São Paulo and the Making of Race and Nation in Brazil*. Durham: Duke University Press, 2015.

Wetherell, James. *Brazil: Stray Notes from Bahia ...*, ed. William Hadfield. Liverpool: Webb and Hunt, 1860.

White, Richard. "National Days and the National Past in Australia." *Australian Cultural History* 22 (January 2003): 55–72.

Wilberforce, Edward. *Brazil Viewed through a Naval Glass: With Notes on Slavery and the Slave Trade*. London: Longman, Brown, Green, and Longmans, 1856.

Wildberger, Arnold. *Os presidentes da Provincia da Bahia*. Salvador: Tipografia Beneditina, 1942.

Wood, James A. *The Society of Equality: Popular Republicanism and Democracy in Santiago de Chile, 1818–1851*. Albuquerque: University of New Mexico Press, 2011.

# INDEX

7 September, 40, 45–6, 129, 212, 269

abolition: in Bahia, 17, 182, 183–6; independence, linked to, 186–7; Pedro II, role in, 181

abolitionism, 10, 12, 17, 129, 179; and Dois de Julho, 40, 182–3, 214–15, 226, 256

Académico patriotic battalion, 107, 123, 135, 136, 196

Africa, trade with, 14, 17

Africans, 11, 18, 21, 40, 46; cultural life, 16–17; freedmen, stateless, 169; percentage in population, 15–16

Afro-Bahian culture, 31; *Baianidade*, 286; barbers' bands, 135; *batuques*, 144, 171, 174–6, 199; carnival societies, 278; *cucumbi*, 65. *See also* Candomblé

Afro-Bahians: and Dois de Julho, 85, 169–70, 176–8, 283

Alabama patriotic battalion, 119

*Alabama, O*, 130, 194–5

Albuquerque, Joaquim Pires de Carvalho e, 71, 270

Alencar, José de, 277

Almeida, Cipriano José Barata de, 56, 270, 271

Almeida, Francisco Gomes dos Santos e, 59

Almeida, João Albino de, 162, 163

Almeida, José Manoel de, 58

Almeida, Manoel Joaquim de, 54

Almeida, Tomás Xavier Garcia de, 72

Álvares, Catarina. *See* Paraguaçu, Catarina Álvares

Álvares, Diogo. *See* Caramuru, Diogo Álvares

Alves, José Martins, 257

Amaral, José Álvares do, 39, 92; Dois de Julho, writings on, 32, 54–5, 59, 174; Lapinha coach house proposal, 113–14; Sociedade de Dois de Julho, 100–1, 131

*Amor e Pátria*, 217–18

Andréa, Francisco José de Souza Soares de, 76–7, 82, 101, 105–6, 111; *caboclos*, controversy over, 39, 79–80, 83, 92, 93–4; theatre gala incident, 77–9; theatre galas, commentary on, 205, 213

Angélica, Joana, 219, 230

anthems, 68–70, 212–13

anti-Portuguese nativism, 23–4, 40–1; National Guard, 65–6; plays, muted in, 203, 229–30; radical liberals, 44, 56, 70–1, 90; rhetoric, 53, 62, 138, 169, 199; stage curtain incident, 230–1; violence, 49, 57, 71, 169, 172–4

Araújo, Tibúrcio Susano de, 281

Argolo patriotic battalion, 157–8

army, 22, 26–7, 40, 73; Bahian attitudes toward, 165–6; bands, 101,

135–6, 140, 166, 255; Dois de Julho, exclusion from, 127, 129, 138, 142, 166; Dois de Julho, participation in, 77, 98–9, 105–6, 141; draft lottery, 129, 165, 166; great parade, 116–17, 142; proclamation of the republic, 247–8. *See also* Exército Pacificador; Frias Villar Incident; Jesus, Maria Quitéria de

Arquivo Histórico Municipal de Salvador, 37

Arquivo Público do Estado da Bahia, 35, 37

Artistas Nacionais patriotic battalion, 135, 136

Associação Nacional de Ação Indigenista, 291

associational life, 10. *See also* Direção Geral dos Festejos; patriotic battalions; Sociedade Dois de Julho

*Aurora Fluminense*, 59

Avenida Sete de Setembro, 30–1

Azambuja, José Bonifácio Nascentes de, 155, 156

Bahia: Afro-Brazilian cultural heritage, 286; Brazil, relationship to, 9, 40; Brazilian Athens, 24, 246; economic decline of, 14, 170, 246; exports, 14–15; independence and identity, 9, 235, 238–9, 242; international trade, 13–15; military and police, 26–7; national politics, role in, 24; politics after 1891 constitution, 25–6, 248–9; officials, key government, 26; propaganda for, 246–7; province, creation as, 25; state, creation as, 25; *terra mater* of Brazil, 292

Bahia Gas Company, 22–3

*Baianidade*, 286

*bando anunciador*, 47, 64–5, 104–5, 255; costume and dress, 75–6, 139–40, 188, 190; restoration in 1960s, 287; rhetoric, 195, 197

bands, 131, 134–5, 138. *See also* army: bands

Barão de Triunfo Square. *See* Santo Antônio Square

Barauna, Francisco, 48–9, 51–2

Barbalho Fort, 4, 19, 265

Barbosa, Rui, 163

Barbuda, José Egídio Gordilho de, 51, 59–60

Barreto, Francisco Joaquim Álvares Branco Moniz, 58

Barreto, Francisco Moniz, 32–3, 122, 123, 218, 254; poetry reading, 51, 93, 213

Barreto, José dos Santos, 69, 212

Barreto, Rozendo Moniz, 32–3, 217; Dois de Julho, writings on, 175, 187, 201, 253–4

Barros, Francisco Borges de, 34

Barros, José Teixeira de, 34

Belém, Baron of. *See* Brandão, Rodrigo [Antônio Falcão]

Bittencourt, Ana Ribeiro de Góes, 33, 107, 118, 188–9, 204–5

Boccanera Júnior, Sílio, 32, 217, 241, 265

Bonfim Church, 21

Botas, João das, 270

Botelho, Pedro Antônio de Oliveira, 257

Brainer, José Maria, 117

Brandão, Rodrigo [Antônio Falcão], 145, 270

Brazil: founding date alternatives, 45–6; patriotic history, construction of, 237–8

Brazilian independence tree. *See* croton leaves, as decoration and symbol

Bulcão, [Joaquim Inácio] Siqueira, 270

Bulcão, José de Araújo Aragão, 108

*cabocla*, 31; misgendered, 39, 67, 83, 94; origin stories, 80–1, 91–3; passive symbol, transformed into, 39, 67, 188; Piedade Square fountain, 94

*caboclo* (acculturated Indian), 16

*caboclo* (symbol). See *caboclos*

*caboclos*: abolition celebrations, used in, 183–6; allegorical floats, 53–4, 63, 66–7, 255; allegorical floats, return of, 118–19, 120–1, 147–9; America as symbol, 59, 61, 65, 67, 92; appearance, 80–1; *carro da bagagem*, 93; disposition, debate over, 281–3; Indian statues, 39, 102; Indianist allegory, 53, 59, 188; Indianist symbols, 45, 82–3, 171, 246; Indianist symbols, appropriation of, 67–8, 291; Indianist symbols, criticism of, 42, 54, 255–6; *indigenismo*, 227–8; Lapinha coach house, 39–40, 102–3, 114–15; meanings, as symbols, 92–7; in neighbourhood festivals, 151, 252; objects of religious devotion, 288; origin stories, 53–5, 79–81, 82–3, 91–3; secular saints, resemblance to, 82; theft from, 170, 283; victory celebration, used in, 186. *See also* monument to Dois de Julho: *caboclo* statue

Cabral, Domingos Guedes, 45, 65, 77, 171, 193

Caçapava, Baron of. *See* Andréa, Francisco José de Souza Soares de

Cachoeira, 57, 122, 269, 287

Caixeiros Nacionais patriotic battalion, 106, 201, 228–9; anti-racist discourse, 178; commerce, nationalization of, 106, 110, 239; parading, 117, 135, 137, 144; Veríssimo manumission incident, 180–1

Caldeira, Felisberto Gomes, 235; *O Dois de Julho ou O jangadeiro*, mentioned in plot of, 220

Camamu, Viscount of. *See* Barbuda, José Egídio Gordilho de

*câmaras municipais*, 27

Campo da Pólvora. *See* Campo dos Mártires

Campo do Barbalho, 263, 264, 265, 266–7

Campo dos Mártires, 263, 264, 265, 266–7

Campo Grande, 20, 41, 42; monument, site for, 263, 264–5, 266–7

Campos, João da Silva, 34, 64

Candomblé, 12, 17, 30, 116, 130; and Dois de Julho, 176–7, 286–7, 294

Canudos, 248

Capinam, Bento José Rufino, 6, 8, 16

Caramuru, Diogo Álvares, 65, 269

*carros triunfais*. See *caboclos*: allegorical floats

Carvalhal, Joaquim Antônio da Silva, 122–3, 143–4

Carvalho, Aloísio de, 268

Castro, Joaquim de Souza, 162, 164

Castro, José Antônio da Silva, 270

Castro Alves, Antônio Frederico de, 168, 170, 217, 240–1, 259

Caxias, Duke of. *See* Lima e Silva, Luís Alves de

Caxias, Marquis of. *See* Lima e Silva, Luís Alves de

Centro Operário da Bahia, 248, 271

Chapada barbers' band, 135

cheers: claques, 78, 212; manumission during, 179, 181–2; Noite Primeira de Julho, 108; official civic rituals, during, 47–8, 51, 118, 145–6; partisan politics, tool of, 143, 211–12; partisan reporting on, 75, 76, 88, 89, 118–19; plays, appearance in, 224, 229, 238; political mood, barometers of, 143, 150, 155, 211, 288; subjects for, 118–19, 139, 211, 261, 271–2; theatre galas, during, 50, 52, 200, 211

Ciências e Artes patriotic battalion, 136

citizenship, 9–12; 1881 electoral reform, 11, 28, 129; elections, 10, 27–8; terms, in 1824 Brazilian constitution, 70

civic rituals, 6–7, 8, 10; acclamation of Pedro I, 46–9, 50; Brazil's founding, dates proposed for, 45–6; monarchy, creation of ties to, 51; official festivities, Brazilian empire's, 44, 46; in political conflict, 51

class, 4, 187, 188; monument location, tensions over, 266; national historical plays, tensions in, 228; and social order, 18–19, 121, 159, 190; theatre audience composition, 205–6, 215

Cochrane, Thomas, 10th Earl of Dundonald, 4, 125; as play character, 222, 225–6, 234

coffee leaves, 53, 62, 145, 220; worn as patriotic symbol, 61, 65, 70, 107

Comissão Abolicionista Dois de Julho, 183

Companhia Dramática Nacional, 207

Companhia Lírica Italiana, 207

Conciliação, 86, 91, 110, 112

Conde d'Eu, Praça. *See* Terreiro de Jesus

Confederação do Equador, 50, 237

Conselho Geral da Província, 25

Conservatives: Dois de Julho, partisanship during, 156–8; majority, of Pedro II, 73. *See also* party politics

Conservatório Dramático da Bahia, 200–1, 209, 216, 223, 226

constitution, Bahian (1891), 25, 26, 248, 251

constitution, Brazilian (1824), 27, 49, 57, 170, 197; 25 March, swearing of oath on, 46; Brazilian citizenship, terms of, 70–1; Coordenação Nacional das Entidades Negras, 291

Corte Imperial, Francisco José, 54, 59

*Cortejo*, 118

Costa, Antônio Joaquim Rodrigues da, 216, 218, 226, 238–9

Costa, Manoel Inácio da, 53, 81

Costa, Rui, 292, 295

Cotegipe, Baron of. *See* Wanderley, João Mauricio

Coutinho, José Lino, 56, 60, 61, 234, 270

Couto, José Antônio da Cunha, 147

*cronistas*, 35

croton leaves, as decoration and symbol, 53, 70, 107–8

*cucumbi*, 65

Cunha, Francisco da Natividade Carneiro da, 183, 213

d'Assier, Adolphe, 108–9

Dantas, Manoel Pinto de Souza, 140–1, 152, 158–9, 258; Frias Villar incident, 159, 162, 163, 165

Defensores da Liberdade patriotic battalion, 135, 137

Defensores de Pirajá patriotic battalion, 137

Defensores do Comércio patriotic battalion, 138

Defensores do Ocidente patriotic battalion, 151

*dia da Independência, O,* 216, 226; class tensions in, 228; and free black characters, 227; Labatut, Pedro (Pierre), as character, 222, 234; Maria Quitéria de Jesus, as character, 221–3, 233–4; plot, 220–3; slavery, mention of, 226–7; tableau, concluding, 238. *See also* Jesus, Maria Quitéria de; Menezes, Agrário de Souza; national historical plays; theatre galas

Dias, Marcolino José, 137

Direção Geral dos Festejos, 39, 104, 138, 145, 262; festival leadership, 140, 142, 147, 155, 157; festival organization, 114, 130, 131, 133–4, 139; Frias Villar incident, in the, 161, 164; manumissions, 179, 181; membership, 99–101, 103, 131–3, 143, 156

Dois de Julho: Bahian identity, importance to, 8, 9, 66, 84, 125; Brazilian independence, central to, 41, 66, 153, 194–6, 235; carnivalesque aspects of, 5, 44, 64, 81–2, 139; carnivalesque aspects, disapproval of, 105, 245–6, 273; celebrations, bifurcation of, 274–7, 283; celebrations, family, 189–90; celebrations, first occurrences, 51–3; celebrations, modern, 288–90, 294–6; celebrations, sources for information, 37–8; as civic ritual, 5, 7, 8, 167, 296; as civilian festival, 40, 56, 152; costume and dress, 64–5, 188; as day of national festivity in Bahia, 39, 44, 196; dispensed holy day, 60–1; festival, criticism of, 112–13, 253–7; festival, distinct nature of, 7–8, 55–6; festival, duration of, 147; festival of the free, 18; festival, organization by Salvador, 287–8; festival, political, 8–9, 25, 63, 290–1; festival, popular, 5, 9, 12, 39, 56; fictional accounts, 33; historian-folklorist accounts, 32, 33–5; inaugural post, 139; invention of (*see* Radical Liberals); memoirs of, 32–3; national holiday, campaign to create as, 8, 59–60, 197; nationalism, popular cultural, 197–9; official history, 43, 53–5; order and norms, 170, 187–8, 190–2; participation of diverse sectors of society, 84–5; political importance, 8, 127–8; political space, 25, 153, 167, 296; as politics by other means, 87–9, 154–5; popular engagement, 124–5; Portuguese, satire on, 197–9; in republic, 250–3; rhetoric, modern, 291–4; ritualizing, 81–2; social movements, 290–1; travellers' accounts, 35, 90; urban spaces, connection to, 19–21; women, role in, 188. *See also* anthems; *bando anunciador; cabocla; caboclos;* Candomblé; fireworks; horses; national historical plays;

newspapers and periodicals; parades and parading; police; salutes; Te Deum; Terreiro de Jesus; theatre galas

Dois de Julho de Bairro. *See* neighbourhood festivals

*Dois de Julho ou O jangadeiro, O,* 216; free black characters, absence of, 227; *indigenismo*, 227–8; plot, 218–20; slavery, absence of, 226–7; tableau, concluding, 238. *See also* Costa, Antônio Joaquim Rodrigues da; national historical plays; theatre galas

*Dois metros e cinco: aventuras de Marcos Parreira (costumes brasileiros)*, 33

Doria, José Jácome de Menezes, 149

Duque de Caxias patriotic battalion, 157

Eighteenth Infantry Battalion, 149; in Frias Villar incident, 159, 160, 162, 163–4, 165–6

elections. *See* citizenship: elections

*elogio dramático* (term for dramatic laudation), 213

*Elogio dramático* (title of work), 69–70, 208, 212, 226, 237; *indigenismo*, 228; plot, 224–5; slavery, mentions of, 226–7; tableau, concluding, 238. *See also* national historical plays; Tavares, Constantino do Amaral

*Emancipação do Brasil, A,* 213

Emancipation Fund, 182, 183

Embaixada Africana, 278

Encourados, 288, 291, 293

*entrudo*, 116

Estrada das Boiadas, 14, 282

*estudantes da Bahia, Os,* 200–1

Eu, Count of, 19, 138

Exaltados. *See* Radical Liberals

Exército Pacificador, 3–5, 6, 38, 64–5; 1823 entry, re-enacted, 113; Maria Quitéria de Jesus, 231; members as play character(s), 220, 221; Pedrão, company from, 117; slaves who served, freed, 71. *See also* Labatut, Pedro (Pierre); Lima e Silva, José Joaquim de

*expulsão dos portugueses ou a entrada do Exército Pacificador na capital, A,* 214

Falcão, João do Rego Barros, 160, 161–2, 163, 164

federalist revolts, 23–4, 57

Ferrão, Alexandre Gomes de Argolo, 157

festival books, 8, 146

fireworks: expenditures, complaints about, 183, 124; in Dois de Julho celebrations, 108, 133, 192, 276

Fonseca, Deodoro da, 247, 248, 251

Fonseca, Domingos Joaquim da, 217

Fonseca, Hermes Ernesto da, 247, 250, 255

Fourteenth Infantry Battalion, 142

Fourth Infantry Battalion, 142

França, José Pedreira, 99, 257

Free Womb Law, 128, 172, 181, 182. *See also* abolition; abolitionism

Frias Villar Incident, 158–66; *povo* in, 160, 162, 163, 164

Fundação Gregório de Matos, 287

Garcez, Luiz da França Pinto, 108, 149

gaslights, 22–3, 190

Gomes, Antônio Joaquim da Silva, 120

*Gonzaga ou A Revolução de Minas*, 217, 240–1, 259
Grupo dos Guaranys, 288
Grupo Gay da Bahia, 291
Guadalupe Square. *See* Veteranos Square
*Guarani, O* (play), 277
Guerra, Antônio Olavo da França, 121, 137–8, 195
Guimarães, Manoel Pedro de Freitas, 270
Gunpowder Field. *See* Campo dos Mártires

Hermes da Fonseca patriotic battalion, 251
Historical Liberals. *See* Radical Liberals
Históricos. *See* Radical Liberals
*homens de cera, Os*, 218
horses: Dois de Julho celebrations, 64, 104–5, 138, 149, 191; parading, twentieth and twenty-first centuries, 288, 291

*Idade de Ouro do Brasil*, 46
*Imprensa barata*, 130
Inconfidência Mineira, 41, 196, 236–7, 239, 241
independence: history, construction of, 196–7. *See also* Inconfidência Mineira; Pernambuco: 1817 rebellion, as precursor to independence
Independence flower. *See* croton leaves, as decoration and symbol
independence war: mobilization, patriotic, 4; Salvador, end of siege, 3–5. *See also* Sociedade Veteranos da Independência
*Independência da América, A*, 217

Indians: depiction of, 6; in patriot forces, 16. *See also cabocla*; *caboclos*
*indigenismo*, 67–8, 227–8, 247
Instituto Dramático, 201, 206
Instituto Geográfico e Histórico da Bahia, 30, 34, 147, 265; *caboclos*, control of, 282, 285, 287
Instituto Histórico da Bahia, 32, 86
Instituto Histórico e Geográfico Brasileiro, 37, 258
Interim Council of Government, 5
Isabel, Princess, 129, 146
Itapagipe Peninsula, 21
Itaparica, Viscount of. *See* Ferrão, Alexandre Gomes de Argolo
Itaparica Island, 269–70, 288, 291

Jequiriça, Francisco Lopes, 149
Jesus, Maria Quitéria de, 41, 234; as play character, 221–3, 231–4, 238
Jorge, Pedro (play character), 218–20, 227, 235, 236, 238
Junqueira, João José Oliveira, 79, 138

Kaxangá, João da Virgem Maria, 51

Labatut, Pedro (Pierre), 4, 5; hero, honoured as, 124–5, 145, 149, 186, 270; national historical plays, as inspiration for, 203, 225–6; as play character, 222, 223, 232, 234–5, 236. *See also* Pirajá: pilgrimage to
Lacerda, José de Barros Falcão, 270–1
Ladeira da Montanha, 23
Lapinha, 19, 58, 105, 278, 279
Lapinha pavilion. *See* Amaral, José Álvares do: Lapinha coach house proposal; *caboclos*: Lapinha coach

house; Noite Primeira de Julho: Lapinha coach house

Lapinha pavilion. *See* Amaral, José Álvares do: Lapinha coach house proposal; *caboclos*: Lapinha coach house; Noite Primeira de Julho: Lapinha coach house

Leão, Manuel Messias de, 113, 211

*legenda de um pariá, A*: Maria Quitéria de Jesus, as play character, 232; plot, 223–4; tableau, concluding, 238. *See also* national historical plays; Sobrinho, Francisco Antonio Filgueiras

Legião da Imprensa patriotic battalion, 107

Leite, João José, 132

Leonelli, Domingos, 292

Letras e Ciências patriotic battalion, 135

Liberal Party. *See* Radical Liberals

Liberal Quinquennium, 76, 85

Liberals. *See* Radical Liberals

Liceistas patriotic battalion. *See* Liceu de Artes e Ofícios: patriotic battalion

Liceu de Artes e Ofícios, 29, 147, 158; patriotic battalion, 137, 161, 187–8, 251

Liga Fabril, 137

Liga Operária Baiana, 29, 137, 158

Liga Progressista. *See* Progressistas

Lima, Álvaro Tibério Moncorvo, 89

Lima, Antônio de Souza, 270

Lima, Joaquim Manoel Rodrigues, 249, 269

Lima, José Inácio de Abreu, 236

Lima, José Inácio Ribeiro de Abreu e. *See* Roma, Padre

Lima e Silva, José Joaquim de, 3, 5, 122, 235; monument to Dois de Julho, 270; portrait, 145

Lima e Silva, Luís Alves de (Baron, Marquis, and Duke of Caxias), 123, 128, 160, 164

Lisboa, Venâncio José de Oliveira, 159, 160, 162, 163, 164–5

Lopes, Luiz, 232–3, 270, 271; as play character, 221–3, 232–3

Luiz (play character based on Luiz Inácio Ribeiro Roma), 223, 225, 235, 236, 238–9

*lundu*, 198, 199, 209

lusophobia. *See* anti-Portuguese nativism

Luzias. *See* Radical Liberals

Macaco Beleza (Monkey Beauty). *See* Passos, Manoel Benício dos

Macedo, Joaquim Manuel de, 217, 218

Machado, Antônio Cândido da Cruz, 134

Machado, Joaquim Nunes, 88, 118, 196

Maciel de Baixo Street coach house, 81, 88, 102, 113–14

Magalhães, Antônio Carlos, 288–9, 290

Maia, Joaquim José da Silva, 60, 61, 63, 72

*Manuel Beckman*, 217

manumissions, 18, 71; Dois de Julho commemoration, 40, 170, 178–80, 181–2, 183; Sociedade Libertadora Sete de Setembro, 182. *See also* Caixeiros Nacionais patriotic battalion: Veríssimo manumission incident

Marques, Francisco Xavier Ferreira, 33; *corso*, use of term, 166; *O feiticeiro*, attitude toward Portuguese, 173–4; *O feiticeiro*, festival descriptions in, 189, 190, 191

Marques, Xavier. *See* Marques, Francisco Xavier Ferreira

Martins, Francisco Gonçalves: and Dois de Julho, 39, 112–13, 114–15, 116, 124; presidency, 23, 85, 156; Radical Liberal opposition to, 85–6, 87–8

*Matilde*, 217, 235

*maxambombas*, 21

*melhoramentos* (improvements), 22–3, 216

Mello Moraes Filho, Alexandre José de, 33; Dois de Julho, criticism of, 253–4; Dois de Julho, recollections of, 140, 172–3, 176, 179; festival appearance, 104; festival apparel, commentary and disputation on, 107; maypole, omission of, 139; *caboclos*, history of, 39, 67, 81, 92, 93

*Memória histórica sobre as vitórias alcançadas pelos itaparicanos no decurso da campanha da Bahia*, 225

*Memórias históricas e políticas da província da Bahia*, 66, 225

Menezes, Agrário de Souza, 101, 216, 218, 239; Caixeiros Nacionais, 228, 229; as historian, 225–6, 232, 234–5; play themes, 217, 238. See also *dia da Independência, O*; *Matilde*

Mercês, Joaquim das, 58

military and police participation. *See* army; militia; National Guard; parades and parading; *individual infantry battalions*

militia, 26–7, 58, 59, 61, 227

Minerva patriotic battalion, 124, 136, 149, 181, 182

Montezuma, Francisco Gê Acaiaba de, 270

monument to Dois de Julho: as allegory, 270; appearance, 269–70; *caboclo* statue, 247; campaign for, 257, 258–9, 261–2; cornerstone ceremony, 258, 259–61, 267–8; criticism of, 261, 273; dates commemorated, 269–70; design of, 259, 261–2; and elite aspirations, 246–7; fence, 283–4; fundraising, 258–9, 262; inauguration, 41–2, 268–9, 271–7, 273–4; interpretation, 272, 284; limited role in celebrations, 277, 278; location of, 259, 260, 262–6; as memory space, 243, 245; names commemorated, 270–1; and popular patriotism, 245–6; as republican symbol, 272

monument to Pedro I, 257, 258, 265, 268

monuments, 243, 284

National Guard: anti-Portuguese controversy, 65–6; bands, 101, 135, 157; *caboclos*, accompaniment of, 64, 77, 98–9, 117, 141; creation of, 26–7; parading, 73, 75, 142; parading, end of, 40, 127, 138, 166; race of members, 188; reform of, 73, 129, 142, 218

national historical plays: anti-Portuguese nativism, limits to, 203, 229–30; in Bahia, 201–2, 215, 216–18; censorship, 200–1, 209; criteria for, 201; as distinct genre, 215; free black characters, omission of, 227; historical accuracy of, 225–6; patriots, depiction of, 229; playwrights, depiction of independence by, 41, 202–3, 235–6; as political works, 202, 225, 226; Portuguese,

gendered metaphors for, 231; titles
with no surviving script, 217–18.
*See also names of individual
playwrights and plays*
nations, construction of, 6–7, 10–11
neighbourhood festivals, 40, 131,
150–2, 166–7, 252; twentieth-
century, 286, 290. *See also* Santo
Antônio Além do Carmo Parish
Neves, Francisco Ribeiro, 54, 59
newspapers and periodicals, 10, 22,
30, 35; Dois de Julho accounts, 31,
35, 249; partisan politics, coverage
of, 87–9, 90, 153–8, 167; as source
material, 35–6, 37, 44–5. *See also*
press freedom
Nicoli, Carlo, 269. *See also*
monument to Dois de Julho
Ninth Infantry Battalion, 135–6, 140
Nóbrega, Bernardino Ferreira, 48,
59, 61, 225
Noite Primeira de Julho, 31; end
of, 114–15, 116, 120–1, 140–1;
Lapinha coach house, 113–15, 116;
nocturnal parading, 39, 104–6,
108–10; participants, significance
to, 111–12, 116; poetry recitations,
109; politics and rhetoric, 110–11,
112–13; race and Conservative
concerns, 115–16; restoration of,
140–1, 158–9. *See also* Dantas,
Manoel Pinto de Souza; patriotic
battalions

Old Republic, 248
Oliveira, João Alfredo Correia de,
129
Oliveira, João José Barbosa de, 101
Oliveira, João Manuel Cardoso de, 33
Oliveira, Maria Felipa de, 291

Pacca, Manoel Joaquim Pinto, 149
Palace Square, 19, 48, 63, 118, 251
Pândegos da África, 278
parades and parading: bifurcated
celebrations, during, 274–5, 278–9;
great parade, 116–17, 126, 127, 166;
militia participation, 58, 59, 61;
parade route, 19; Santo Antônio
parade, 278–9; two-stage parade,
64–5, 286. *See also* Noite Primeira
de Julho: nocturnal parading
*Paraguaçu* (poem), 68, 225, 232, 233
Paraguaçu, Catarina Álvares, 65, 67,
79, 269
Paraguayan War, 128, 135, 144, 153–4,
181
Parola, Lulu. *See* Carvalho, Aloísio
de
Party of Order. *See* Saquaremas
party politics, 24–5, 40; Ato
Adicional (Additional Act), 57,
72, 73; majority of Pedro II, 72, 73,
75; Regresso, 72; during return to
Lapinha, 119
Passos, Manoel Benício dos, 252
*pátria*, 38, 66; as exemplar, 125;
and independence, 4, 51, 52, 193,
195–6; indifference to, fear of, 251,
253; Labatut, Pedro (Pierre), in
plays, 235–6, 239; in poetry, 50, 62,
111–12, 194; rhetoric about, 60, 154,
177, 207, 254–5
patriotic battalions, 106–7, 109–10,
117, 125, 282–3; controvery,
partisan, 120–1, 158; costume and
dress, 106, 107–8, 117, 136, 188;
defined, 39; membership, 113,
115–16, 136–8, 151; Noite Primeira
de Julho, 87, 104, 109, 114. *See also
names of individual battalions*

Pedro I, 4; abdication, 44, 57, 60; acclamation, 46–8; anthem, composer of, 212; anthems, subject of, 70; as authoritarian, 71; civic rituals, 46–7, 49–51, 52–3, 60; Dois de Julho monument, omission from, 271; founding of Brazil, stories of, 52–3, 56; Grito do Ipiranga, 45, 50; Indian symbols, portrayed with, 82–3; and independence, 169, 192, 194–5, 196, 197; as liberal champion, 70; in plays, 237, 238–9; portrait, 47–8, 50, 51, 62, 145. *See also* monument to Pedro I

Pedro II, 62, 94, 122, 124, 160; and abolition, 129, 181; effigy, 65, 147; Liga Progressista, 86; Luzias, pardon for, 73; portrait, 110, 118, 144–5, 150, 211; proclamation of majority and coronation, 73, 75; Sabinada, amnesty for, 72–3; statue, 147

*Pedro Primeiro*, 218

Pelourinho, 19, 64

*pequeno grande, Um*, 217, 240

periodicals. *See* newspapers and periodicals

Periquitos' Rebellion, 23, 50

Pernambuco: 1817 rebellion, as precursor to independence, 41, 60, 196, 203, 236; 1817 rebellion, portrayed in theatre, 201, 202–3, 224, 238–9; Dois de Julho monument, 261, 270–1, 272–3; Praieira rebellion, 85, 88, 196

philharmonic societies, 134

Piedade Square, 20, 106, 118, 143–4, 174; fountain, 94; garden, 251

Pinho, José Wanderley de Araújo, 37, 172

Pirajá, 3, 194, 265, 282, 287; battle of, 4, 53, 122, 270, 271; patriots, interment of, 124, 149, 186; pilgrimage to, 124, 136–7, 149, 235, 286–7; pilgrimage to, twentieth century, 286, 287, 290

Pirajá, Viscount of. *See* Albuquerque, Joaquim Pires de Carvalho e

poetry, 109, 118, 140, 152, 190–1; as political expression, 91, 111, 213; in publications, 35, 45, 75, 271; theatre galas, performances in, 48, 59, 141, 213

police, 27, 73; bands, 134, 135, 139–40, 149; Duque de Caxias patriotic battalion, 157; censorship, 200–1, 209, 213; Dois de Julho, 75, 78, 88, 89, 105; *entrudo* crackdown, 116; political partisanship, 156–7, 212, 290; public order, enforcers of, 170, 172, 173, 174, 190–2; sources for information, 37; theatre comportment, enforcers of, 205, 208–9, 230

Politeama Baiano, 241, 277

political parties. *See* Conservatives; Progressistas; Radical Liberals; Saquaremas

Pontes, Manoel Lopes, 281

portrait of the monarch, public veneration of, 47–8, 118, 179; on days of national festivity, 46, 49–50; in national historical plays, 225, 238; in neighbourhood celebrations, 150, 152; Isabel, Princess, depiction of, 145, 146; program, official, 211; provincial government, participation in, 133, 141; radical rhetoric about, 110; statue of Pedro II, 147; Teresa

Cristina, Empress, depiction of, 211, 225, 238; in Terreiro Square, 141, 144–5; violence during, 161. *See also* Frias Villar Incident

portraits of patriots and officials: public display of, 144–5, violence toward, 251

Portuguese, 13, 16, 71, 197–9; role in commerce, 13, 106–7, 110. *See also* anti-Portuguese nativism

*povo*, 38; *caboclos*, significance to, 96, 115, 184–5, 256–7; class mingling, 190, 191, 199; composition of, 11, 115–16, 274, 283; Dois de Julho, as festival for, 82, 88, 89, 109–10, 118; Dois de Julho participation, 116–17, 118, 119, 146; Dois de Julho participation, criticisms of, 111, 144, 150, 254; families, contrasted to, 170, 251, 272, 273–4, 276; fear of, 8, 115, 155, 158, 283–4; floats, location controversy, 143–4; history, knowledge of, 150, 295; independence struggle, role in, 195, 285–6, 292; monument to Dois de Julho, reaction to, 273, 275; in plays, 41, 93, 224, 228–9, 236; political engagement of, 11–12, 130, 253–4, 264; political mood, barometers of, 88, 143, 153, 154, 155–6; race of, 115, 191; improving, in need of, 207, 258. *See also* Frias Villar Incident

Praieira Rebellion, 85, 88, 196

Presidential Palace, in Dois de Julho celebrations, 65, 81, 117, 118

press freedom, 10, 36; abuse of, 36, 44–5, 87, 91

Princesa Isabel patriotic battalion, 138

Princess of the Mountains, 184–5

Progressistas, 86, 118, 119–20, 121, 128. *See also* Radical Liberals

*Prólogo da guerra ou O voluntário da Pátria*, 218

public rituals. *See* civic rituals

Puritanos. *See* Saquaremas

Quadros Júnior, Luiz Miguel, 200

Quarenta de Voluntários Philharmonic, 135, 162. *See also* bands

Quebra-Ferro Battalion, 287, 290

*queda do tirano Rosas ou O triunfo das armas brasileiras, A*, 217

Queimado, Companhia do, 22, 94

Querino, Manoel Raimundo, 28–30, 293; Dois de Julho, writings on, 31–2, 53–5, 79–80, 105, 109; official history, source of, 43, 92, 293–4; scholarship on, 30–2; source for Mello Moraes Filho, Alexandre José de, 33

Quinze de Novembro, Praça. *See* Terreiro de Jesus

race: Africans and slaves, not defined as Bahians, 40; anti-racist discourse, 178; black patriots, exclusion from Capinam lithograph, 6; census data, 15–16; Dois de Julho festival, tensions, 169–70, 177–8; free blacks, omission from national historical plays, 227; militia, black and mulatto, 26, 58, 61, 227; patriotic battalions, concerns about, 115–16; and political expression, 16; theatre audience composition, 205. *See also* Afro-Bahian culture; slavery; slaves

Radical Liberals: Dois de Julho, claim to own, 87–8; Dois de Julho, invention of, 9, 24, 44–5, 58, 81–2; Dois de Julho, partisan actions during, 110, 156–8; Dois de Julho festival, as political expression, 25, 45, 90–1; Dois de Julho, as political tool, 39, 44; Historical Liberals, 86, 101, 114, 128, 156; ideals, Afro-Brazilian support of, 24; ideology, 56; Liberal Quinquennium, 76, 85; party, characteristics of, 56–7; patriotic history, construction of, 237–8; patriots' march, re-enacted, 53. *See also* anti-Portuguese nativism; party politics
railways, 22
Raimundo, Friar, 88, 89
Rebouças, Antônio Pereira, 56, 59, 78–9, 123, 270
Recôncavo, 4, 13–14, 22, 187, 287
regionalism, 9, 170–1, 193–6, 291–2, 296; and *pátria*, 66
Regresso, 72
republic, proclamation of, 247–8
*Reverbero, O*, 32, 144, 146
Rio Branco, Viscount of, 128, 160, 181
Rio Vermelho, 4, 21, 150
Rocha, Antônio Ladislau de, 156
Rocha, Manoel da, 114
Roma, Luiz Inácio Ribeiro, 236
Roma, Padre, 196, 218, 236, 261; as play character, 223, 226, 236–7, 238
Rousseff, Dilma, 292

Sabinada Rebellion, 27, 39, 45, 72–3
Sabino, Bento, 54
salutes, 98
Salvador: Africa, connection to, 16–17; city council, 27; class structure, 18–19, 21; as commercial centre, 13–14; as cultural centre, 86–7; decline, 86, 246; modernization, 21, 22–3; population, 15–16, 18; propaganda for, 246–7; siege, end of, 3–5; trade, 13–14
Santiago, Baron of. *See* Silva, Domingos Américo da
Santo Antônio Além do Carmo Parish, 42, 265; popular celebration, centre of, 246, 274–5, 277–81, 284, 286
Santo Antônio dos Militares chapel, 149
Santo Antônio Fort, 19
Santo Antônio Square, 275, 277–8
Santos, Francisco (Chico) Álvares dos, 124, 136, 149, 181–2
Santos, Laurindo José dos, 138
Santos, Luiz Tarquínio dos, 133
São Francisco, 1st Baron of. *See* Bulcão, [Joaquim Inácio] Siqueira
São Francisco, 2nd Baron of. *See* Bulcão, José de Araújo Aragão
São José Philharmonic, 135
São Lourenço, Baron and Viscount of. *See* Martins, Francisco Gonçalves
São Pedro Fort, 120, 247
Saquaremas, 72–3, 85–6, 87–90, 128. *See also* Conservatives
Sauípe, Baron of. *See* Leite, João José
Seixas, Romualdo Antonio de, 179
Sena, Consuelo Pondé de, 292
*senados da câmara.* See câmaras municipais
Serra, João Duarte Lisboa, 85
*Sertão*, 22
Seventh Infantry Battalion, 163–4

Sexagenarian Law, 129. *See also* abolition; abolitionism

Silva, Antônio Carlos Ribeiro de Andrada Machado e, 237

Silva, Domingos Américo da, 133

Silva, Francisco Amâncio da, 135

Silva, Francisco Manoel da, 212

Silva, Inácio Acioli de Cerqueira e, 64, 66, 207, 225

Silva, João Nepomuceno da, 111, 209

Silva, José Bonifácio de Andrada e, 122, 237, 259

Silva, José Gonçalves da, 251

Silva, Manoel Gonçalves da, 227

Silva, Manoel Pessoa da, 77–9, 193–4, 213

Silva, Manuel Antonio da, 66

Silva, Pedro Celestino da, 34, 107

Sinimbu, João Lins Vieira Cansanção de, 112, 211–12, 228

Siqueira Cavalcante patriotic battalion, 251

Sixteenth Infantry Battalion, 135–6, 160

slave resistance, 11

slave revolts, 18, 171

slave trade, 13, 16–17

slaveownership, 17

slavery, 17–18; and Dois de Julho, 18; end, celebration of, 183–6; and liberty, metaphor of, 171–2, 176–7; in national historical plays, 226–7. *See also* race; slaves

slaves: daily life in Salvador, 17, 21; Independence War, participation in, 4; place in the nation for, 18, 226–7; Salvador population, percentage of, 15–16, 17. *See also* abolition; abolitionism; Africans; manumission; slavery

*sobrados*, 21

Sobrinho, Francisco Antonio Filgueiras, 216–17, 218, 232

Sociedade Dois de Julho, 39, 63–4, 72; end of, 130, 131, 167; fundraising and activities, 88, 99, 101, 102–3, 210; members, 99–101, 103–4; monument campaign, 257, 262; nocturnal processions, suppression of, 85, 115, 125–6, 189. *See also caboclos*: Lapinha coach house; manumissions

Sociedade Filarmônica Euterpe, 135

Sociedade Libertadora Sete de Setembro, 182, 210

Sociedade Rossini, 156

Sociedade Veteranos da Independência patriotic battalion, 122, 143

Sociedade Vinte e Quatro de Setembro, 257

Soledade Convent, 3

Souza, Francisco Bernardino de, 32, 92

Souza, Marcolino Alves de, 150

Souza, Pedro Luiz Pereira de, 154

steam navigation, 22

streetcars, 21

sugar, 14–15, 17

sugar cane, as decoration, 53

Tarquínio, Luiz, 267, 274, 275, 279

Tavares, Constantino do Amaral, 218, 239–40, 241; anthems in scripts, 212, 238; poetry, 194; slavery, allusions to, 226

Te Deum, 52, 61, 73–4, 143; non-attendance as protest, 120; Pedro I, for acclamation of, 47, 48–9; as platform for abolitionism, 183, 186; as platform for political speech, 51–2, 58–9, 65, 88, 117–18;

as platform for warnings, 48–9; in the twenty-first century, 290

Teatrinho da Rua do Baixo. *See* Teatro de São Pedro de Alcântara

Teatro de São João, 19, 203, 206–8, 210, 277; audience composition, 204–6, 209, 215; programming, 200, 206, 213–14, 216–17; stage curtain incident, 230–1

Teatro de São Pedro de Alcântara, 201, 206

Teixera [Cavalcante], Cid [José], 34

telegraph, 22, 159, 164

telephones, 23

*tempos da Independência, Os,* 93, 112, 201, 206, 228; plot, 223–4, 231, 232, 236; slavery, mentions of, 226–7; tableau, concluding, 238. *See also* national historical plays; Tavares, Constantino do Amaral

Teresa Cristina, Empress, 211, 225, 238

Terpsicore Philharmonic, 135. *See also* bands

Terreiro de Jesus, 19, 47, 53, 99; stage, 144–5; stage program, 145–7; triumphal arch, 147

theatre: audience, gender of, 204–5; bankruptcies, 207–8; censorship, 200–1, 209; play as political allegory, 66–7; plays, Bahian, 41, 201–2, 206; policing of, 208–9; *povo,* representation of, 229; repertoire in Bahia, 206, 209, 213–15; role in society, 202, 203, 207, 208, 209; subsidies, 206–8. *See also* cheers; national historical plays; Teatro de São João; theatre galas

theatre galas, 41, 210–11, 241, 277; Andréa incident, 77–9; anthems, 212–13; cheers, 211–12; *elogio dramático,* 213; newspaper reports, 210–11; opera, 208, 210, 214, 241; plays, appropriate topics for, 201–2; poetry readings, 213; program, customary, 211–13, 214; as ritual, 41, 215; stage curtain incident, 230–1. *See also* national historical plays; theatre

Tipógrafos patriotic battalion, 117

Tiradentes, 196, 236–7

Titara, Ladislau dos Santos: anthem, Dois de Julho, 68–70, 212; *Paraguaçu,* 225, 232, 233; poetry, 59, 62, 63, 168; theatre gala recitations, 50, 74, 213

tobacco leaves, as decoration, 53, 70, 107, 145

Torres, Carlos, 34

tradition, invention of, 6, 43

União Brasileira patriotic battalion, 107, 121, 137

Varella, João, 33–4

Vasconcelos, Bernardo Pereira de, 60

Vasconcelos, José Joaquim Pinheiro de, 75, 76

Vasconcelos, Zacarias de Góes e, 128

Veiga, Evaristo Ferreira da, 59, 60

Vermelhos, 86, 119–20, 121. *See also* Conservatives

Veteranos Square, 143

Vianna, Antônio, 34, 150

Vianna, Francisco Vicente, 249, 265

Vianna, Hildegardes, 34, 150, 275, 287; *caboclos,* writings on, 151, 294

Vieira, José Estanislau, 48, 49

Villar, Alexandre Augusto de Frias, 159–4, 165

Wagner, Jacques, 292
Wanderley, João Maurício, 87, 89, 94, 207, 258; abolition, 129; Andréa theatre gala incident, 78; Noite Primeira de Julho, 112–13, 116; stage curtain incident, 230–1
women: in Dois de Julho, 188; in monument campaign, 263–4; as theatre audience, 204–5

Xangô, 176–7

Zama, Cesar, 249, 252
Zuavos, 120, 137, 144